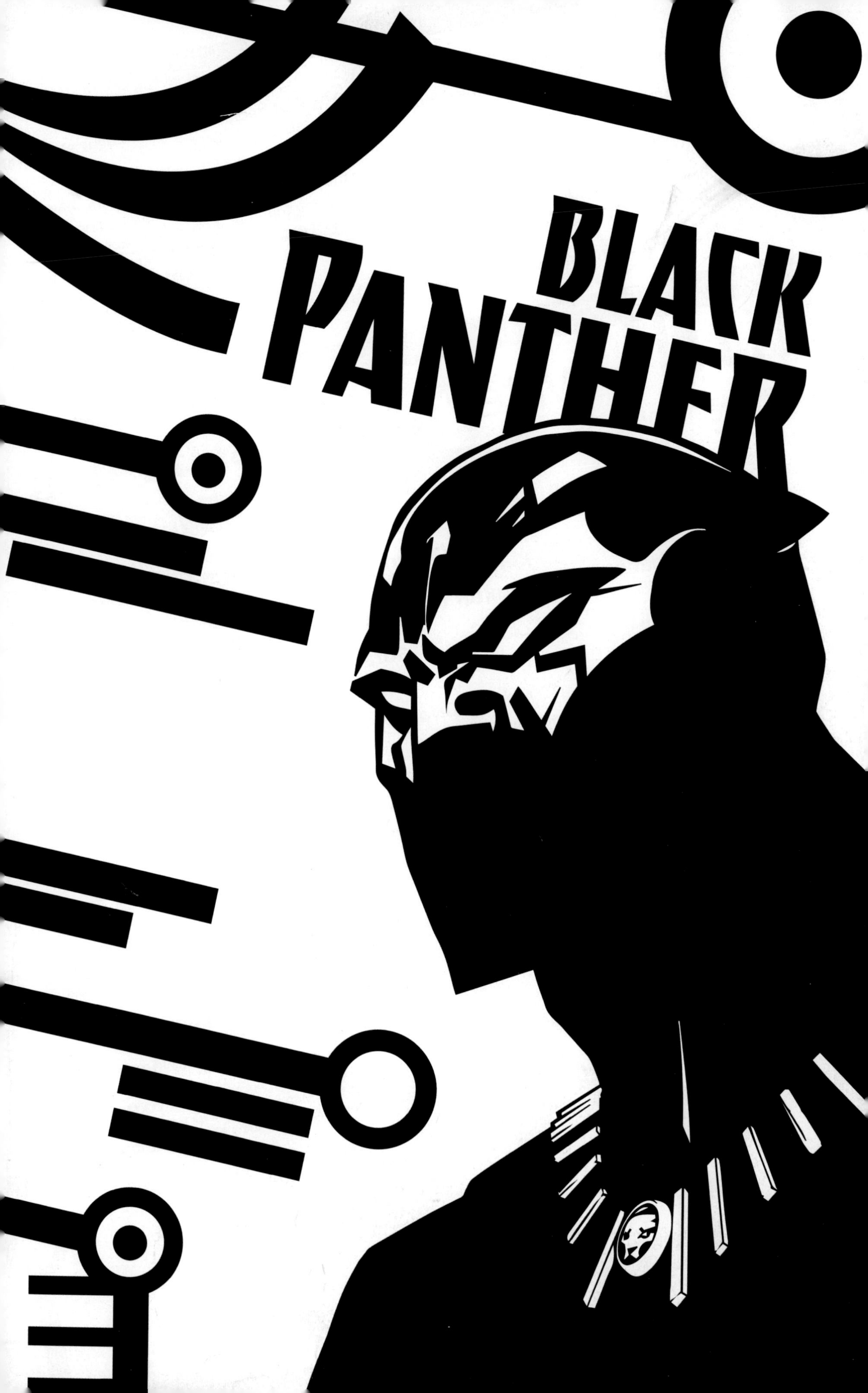
BLACK
PANTHER

In the aftermath of a rebellion that set change against tradition, the nation against its king and even the living against the dead...Wakanda must now rebuild.

The forces of rebellion have quieted with the arrest of **Tetu**, one of the rebel leaders, while the other, **Zenzi**, remains at large. The royal family and the people of Wakanda are attempting to move forward together. T'Challa began this process by calling together a council of representatives from each region to write a new constitution and enact a new government. In discussions with his mother **Ramonda** and sister **Shuri**, T'Challa has expressed both trepidation and hope for this new era in Wakandan history.

But as T'Challa moves forward, he keeps one eye on his past...

Writer/**Ta-Nehisi Coates**

#13-15

Pencilers/**Wilfredo Torres**
with **Jacen Burrows** (#14)
& **Adam Gorham** (#15)

Inkers/**Wilfredo Torres** (#13, #18),
Terry Pallot (#14-15),
Jacen Burrows (#14)
& **Adam Gorham** (#15)

Color Artists/**Laura Martin**
with **Andrew Crossley** (#13)

Cover Art/**Brian Stelfreeze**
with **Laura Martin** (#13)

#16-17

Pencilers/**Chris Sprouse**

Inkers/**Walden Wong** (#16),
Karl Story (#16-17)
& **Dexter Vines** (#16-17)

Color Artists/**Laura Martin**
with **Andrew Crossley** (#16-17)

Cover Art/**Brian Stelfreeze**
with **Laura Martin** (#16)

#18

Pencilers/**Wilfredo Torres**
& **Chris Sprouse**

Inkers/**Wilfredo Torres**
& **Karl Story**

Color Artist/**Laura Martin**

Cover Art/**Brian Stelfreeze**
with **Laura Martin**

Letterer/**VC's Joe Sabino**

Logo Design/**Rian Hughes**

Assistant Editors/**Chris Robinson**
& **Charles Beacham**

Associate Editor/**Sarah Brunstad**

Editor/**Wil Moss**

COLLECTION EDITOR/**JENNIFER GRÜNWALD**
ASSISTANT EDITOR/**CAITLIN O'CONNELL**
ASSOCIATE MANAGING EDITOR/**KATERI WOODY**
EDITOR, SPECIAL PROJECTS/**MARK D. BEAZLEY**
VP PRODUCTION & SPECIAL PROJECTS/**JEFF YOUNGQUIST**
SVP PRINT, SALES & MARKETING/**DAVID GABRIEL**
BOOK DESIGNERS/**JAY BOWEN** & **MANNY MEDEROS**

EDITOR IN CHIEF/**C.B. CEBULSKI**
CHIEF CREATIVE OFFICER/**JOE QUESADA**
PRESIDENT/**DAN BUCKLEY**
EXECUTIVE PRODUCER/**ALAN FINE**

BLACK PANTHER CREATED BY **STAN LEE** & **JACK KIRBY**

BLACK PANTHER

AVENGERS OF THE NEW WORLD

#166-167

Penciler/**Leonard Kirk**

Inkers/**Marc Deering**
with **Leonard Kirk** (#166)

Color Artists/**Laura Martin**
with **Matt Milla** (#167)

Cover Art/**Brian Stelfreeze**
with **Laura Martin** (#167)

#168

Penciler/**Chris Sprouse**

Inkers/**Karl Story**
with **Walden Wong**

Color Artists/**Matt Milla**
with **Chris Sotomayor**

Cover Art/**Brian Stelfreeze**

#169-172

Penciler/**Leonard Kirk**

Inkers/**Leonard Kirk**
with **Marc Deering** (#172)
& **Walden Wong** (#172)

Color Artists/**Laura Martin**
with **Matt Milla** (#172)

Cover Art/**Brian Stelfreeze**
& **Laura Martin** (#169, #171),
Phil Noto (#170) and
Chris Sprouse, Karl Story
& **Matt Milla** (#172)

BLACK PANTHER VOL. 2: AVENGERS OF THE NEW WORLD. Contains material originally published in magazine form as BLACK PANTHER #13-18 and #166-172. First printing 2018. ISBN 978-1-302-90895-9. Published by MARVEL WORLDWIDE, INC., a subsidiary of MARVEL ENTERTAINMENT, LLC. OFFICE OF PUBLICATION: 135 West 50th Street, New York, NY 10020. Copyright © 2018 MARVEL. No similarity between any of the names, characters, persons, and/or institutions in this magazine with those of any living or dead person or institution is intended, and any such similarity which may exist is purely coincidental. **Printed in China.** DAN BUCKLEY, President, Marvel Entertainment; JOHN NEE, Publisher; JOE QUESADA, Chief Creative Officer; TOM BREVOORT, SVP of Publishing; DAVID BOGART, SVP of Business Affairs & Operations, Publishing & Partnership; DAVID GABRIEL, SVP of Sales & Marketing, Publishing; JEFF YOUNGQUIST, VP of Production & Special Projects; DAN CARR, Executive Director of Publishing Technology; ALEX MORALES, Director of Publishing Operations; DAN EDINGTON, Managing Editor; SUSAN CRESPI, Production Manager; STAN LEE, Chairman Emeritus. For information regarding advertising in Marvel Comics or on Marvel.com, please contact Vit DeBellis, Custom Solutions & Integrated Advertising Manager, at vdebellis@marvel.com. For Marvel subscription inquiries, please call 888-511-5480. **Manufactured between 6/22/2018 and 9/3/2018 by R.R. DONNELLEY ASIA PRINTING SOLUTIONS, CHINA.**

10 9 8 7 6 5 4 3 2 1

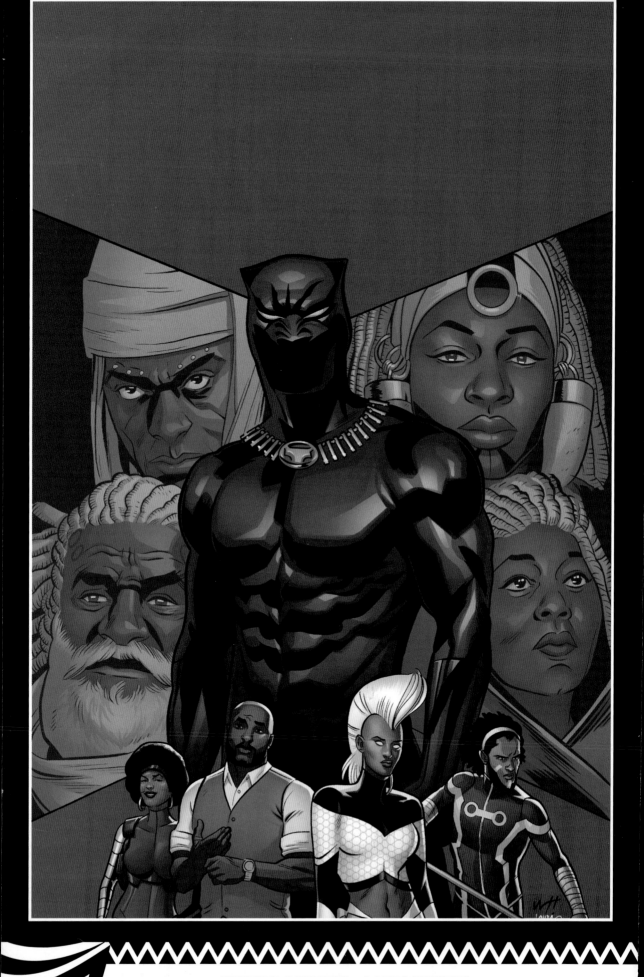

#13 VARIANT BY **WILFREDO TORRES** & **LAURA MARTIN**

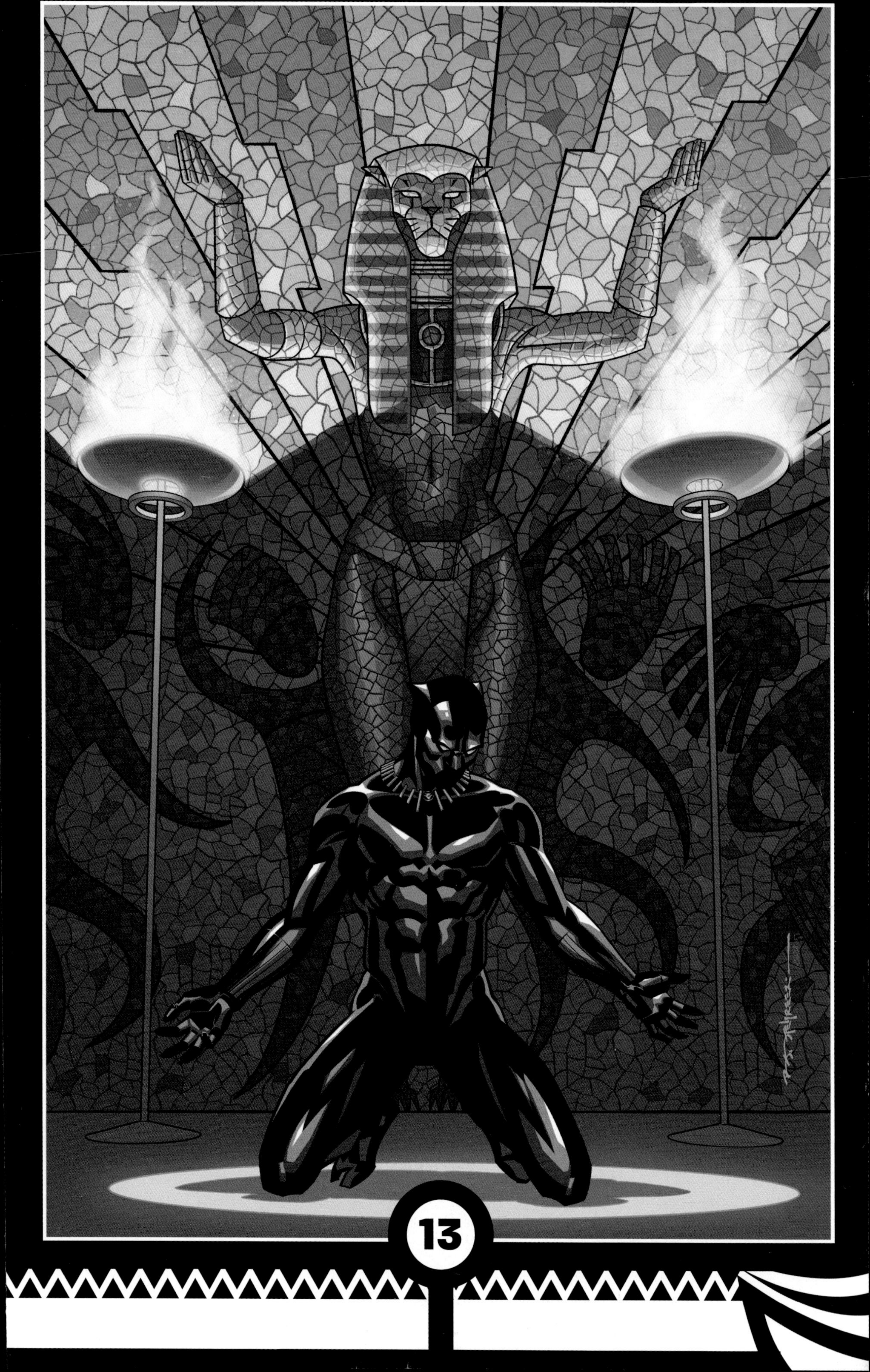
13

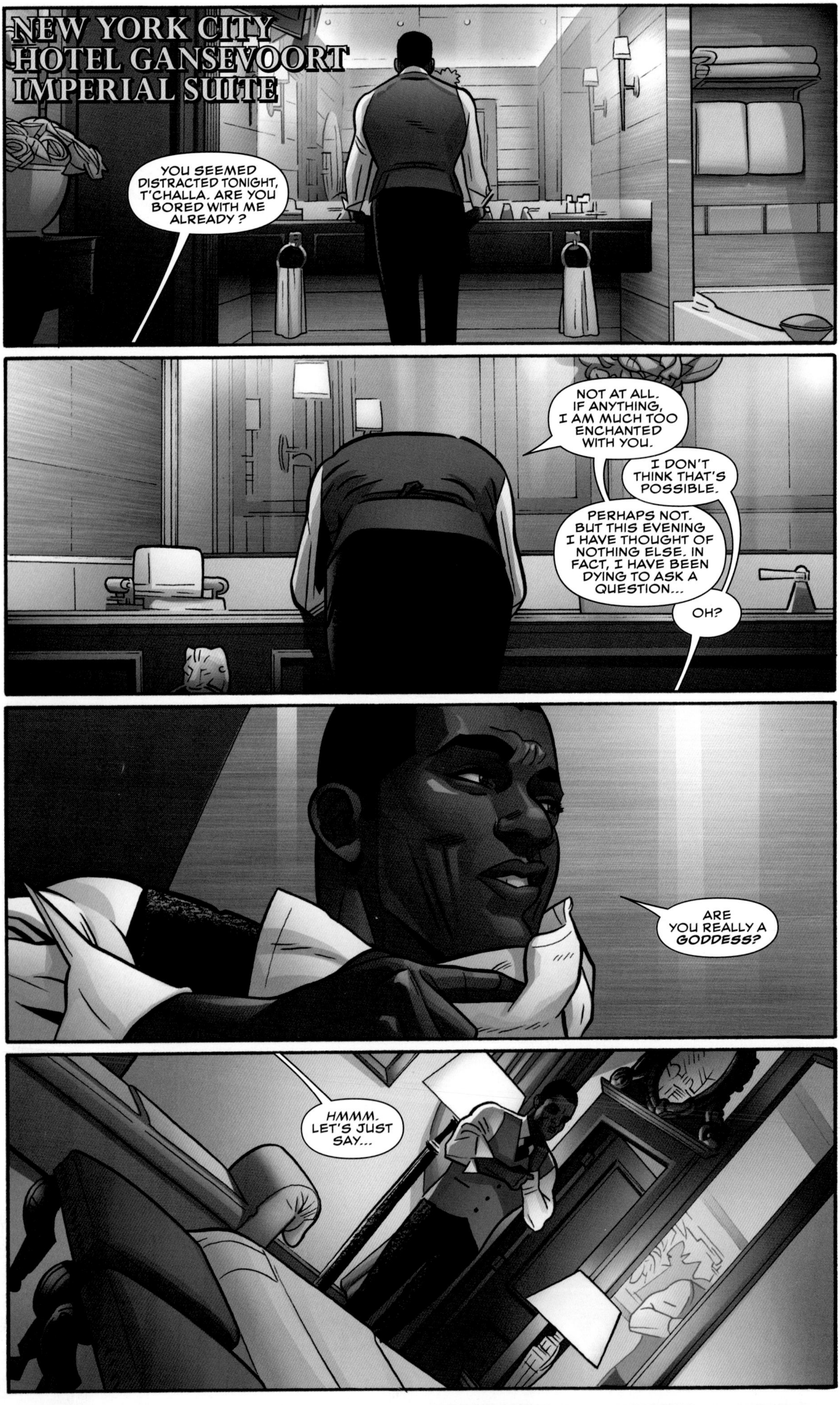
NEW YORK CITY
HOTEL GANSEVOORT
IMPERIAL SUITE
YOU SEEMED DISTRACTED TONIGHT, T'CHALLA. ARE YOU BORED WITH ME ALREADY?
NOT AT ALL. IF ANYTHING, I AM MUCH TOO ENCHANTED WITH YOU.
I DON'T THINK THAT'S POSSIBLE.
PERHAPS NOT. BUT THIS EVENING I HAVE THOUGHT OF NOTHING ELSE. IN FACT, I HAVE BEEN DYING TO ASK A QUESTION...
OH?
ARE YOU REALLY A *GODDESS?*
HMMM. LET'S JUST SAY...

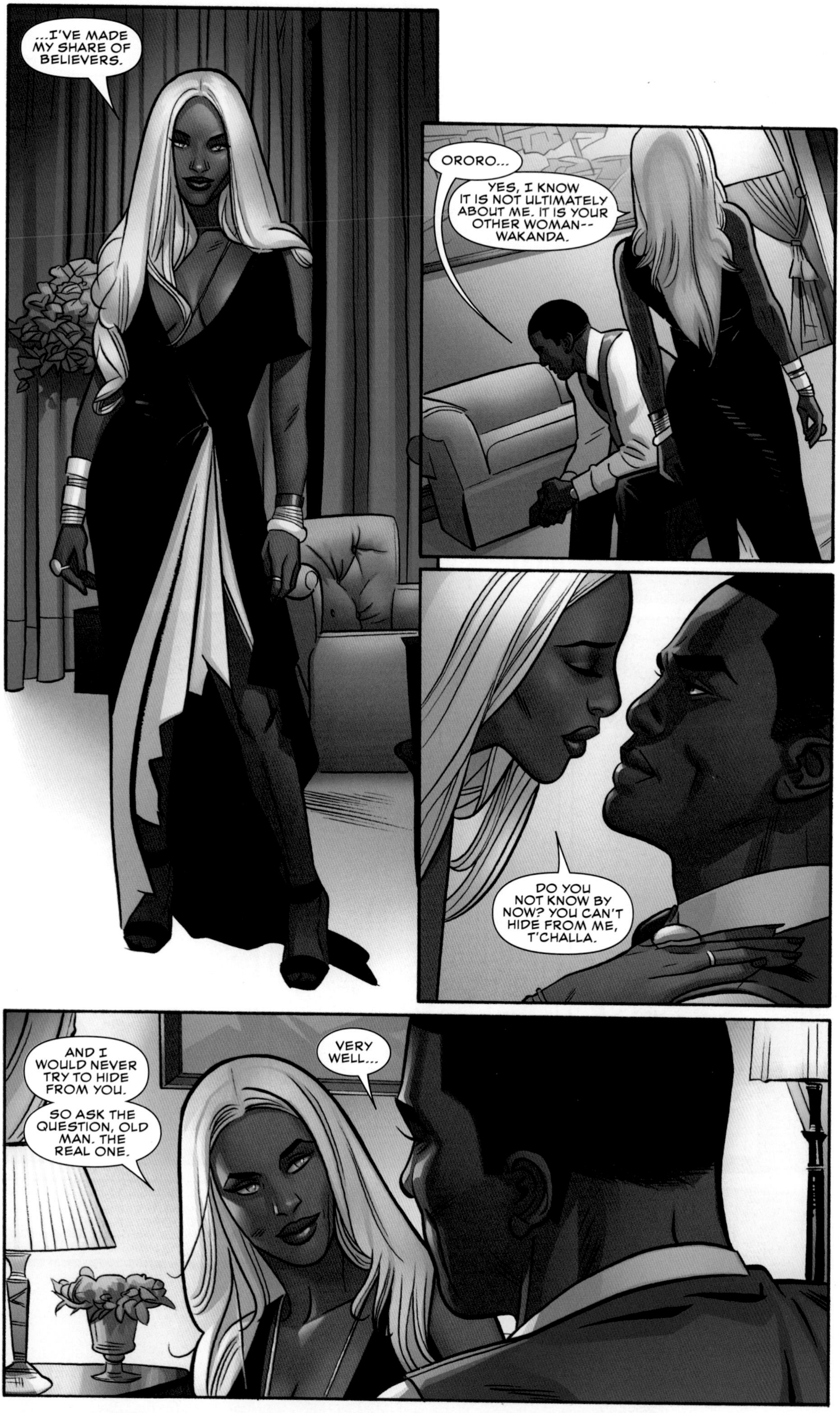
...I'VE MADE MY SHARE OF BELIEVERS.
ORORO...
YES, I KNOW IT IS NOT ULTIMATELY ABOUT ME. IT IS YOUR OTHER WOMAN--WAKANDA.
DO YOU NOT KNOW BY NOW? YOU CAN'T HIDE FROM ME, T'CHALLA.
AND I WOULD NEVER TRY TO HIDE FROM YOU.
SO ASK THE QUESTION, OLD MAN. THE REAL ONE.
VERY WELL...

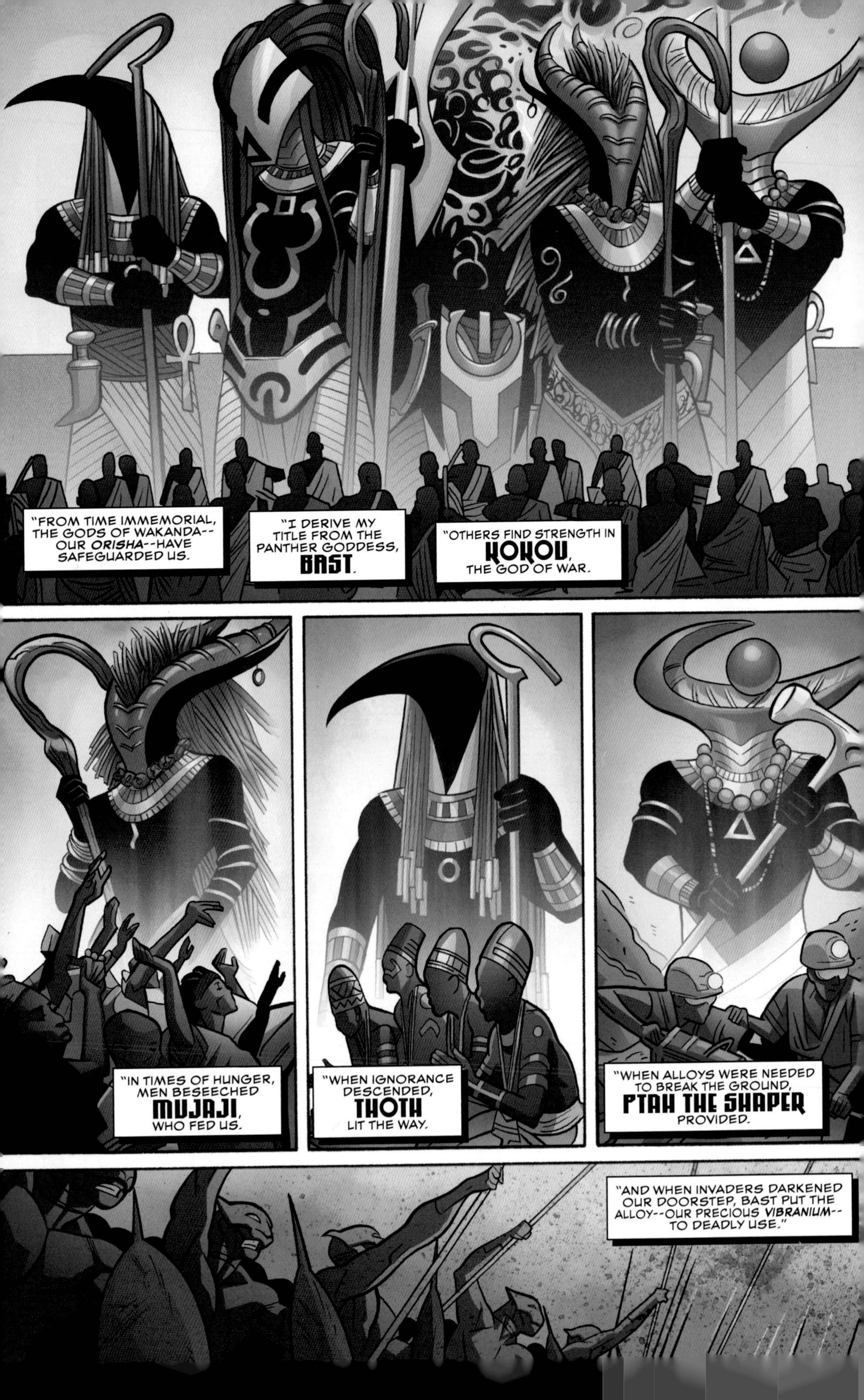
"FROM TIME IMMEMORIAL, THE GODS OF WAKANDA--OUR *ORISHA*--HAVE SAFEGUARDED US.
"I DERIVE MY TITLE FROM THE PANTHER GODDESS, **BAST**.
"OTHERS FIND STRENGTH IN **KOKOU**, THE GOD OF WAR.
"IN TIMES OF HUNGER, MEN BESEECHED **MUJAJI**, WHO FED US.
"WHEN IGNORANCE DESCENDED, **THOTH** LIT THE WAY.
"WHEN ALLOYS WERE NEEDED TO BREAK THE GROUND, **PTAH THE SHAPER** PROVIDED.
"AND WHEN INVADERS DARKENED OUR DOORSTEP, BAST PUT THE ALLOY--OUR PRECIOUS *VIBRANIUM*--TO DEADLY USE."

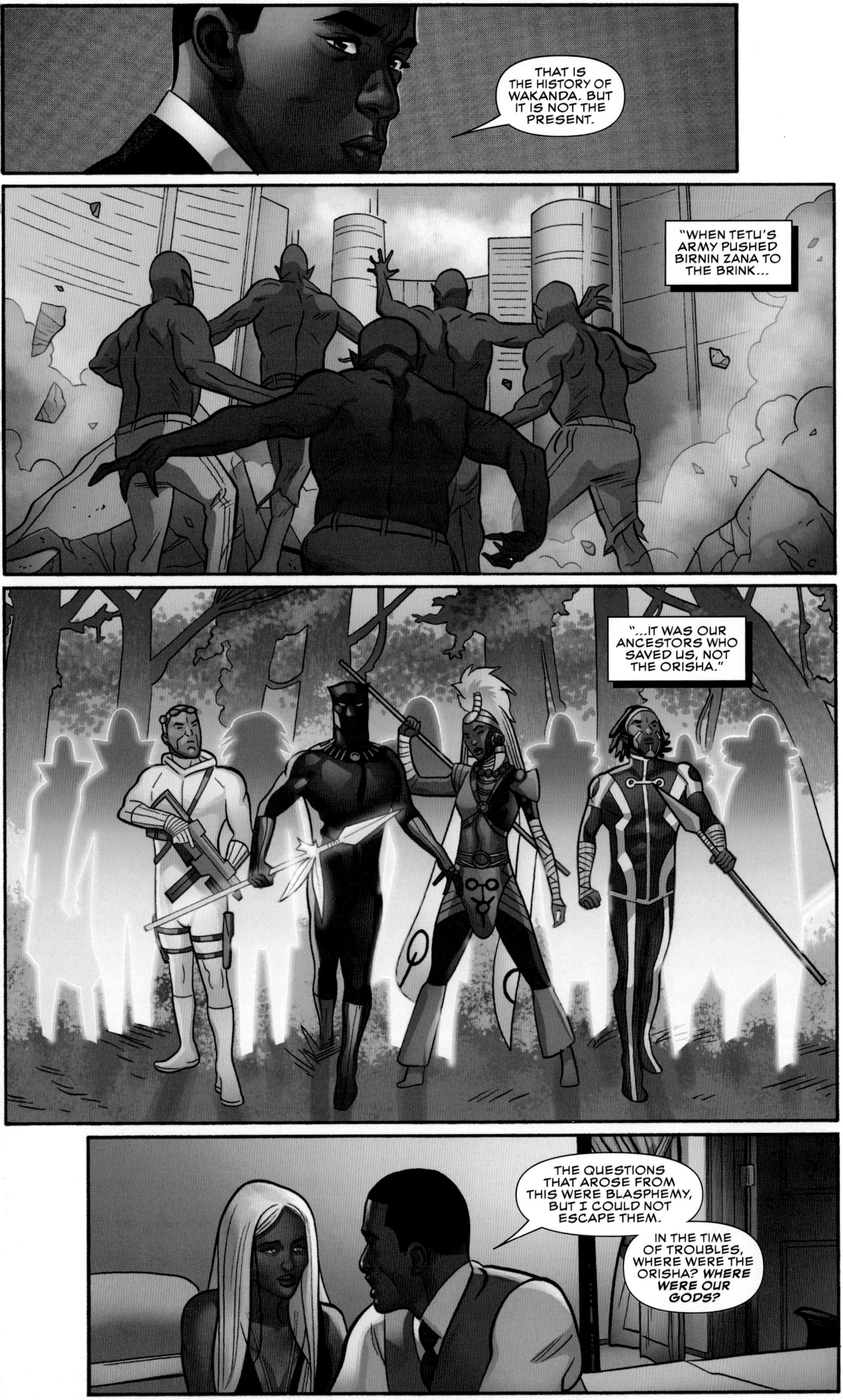
THAT IS THE HISTORY OF WAKANDA. BUT IT IS NOT THE PRESENT.
"WHEN TETU'S ARMY PUSHED BIRNIN ZANA TO THE BRINK...
"...IT WAS OUR ANCESTORS WHO SAVED US, NOT THE ORISHA."
THE QUESTIONS THAT AROSE FROM THIS WERE BLASPHEMY, BUT I COULD NOT ESCAPE THEM.
IN THE TIME OF TROUBLES, WHERE WERE THE ORISHA? *WHERE WERE OUR GODS?*

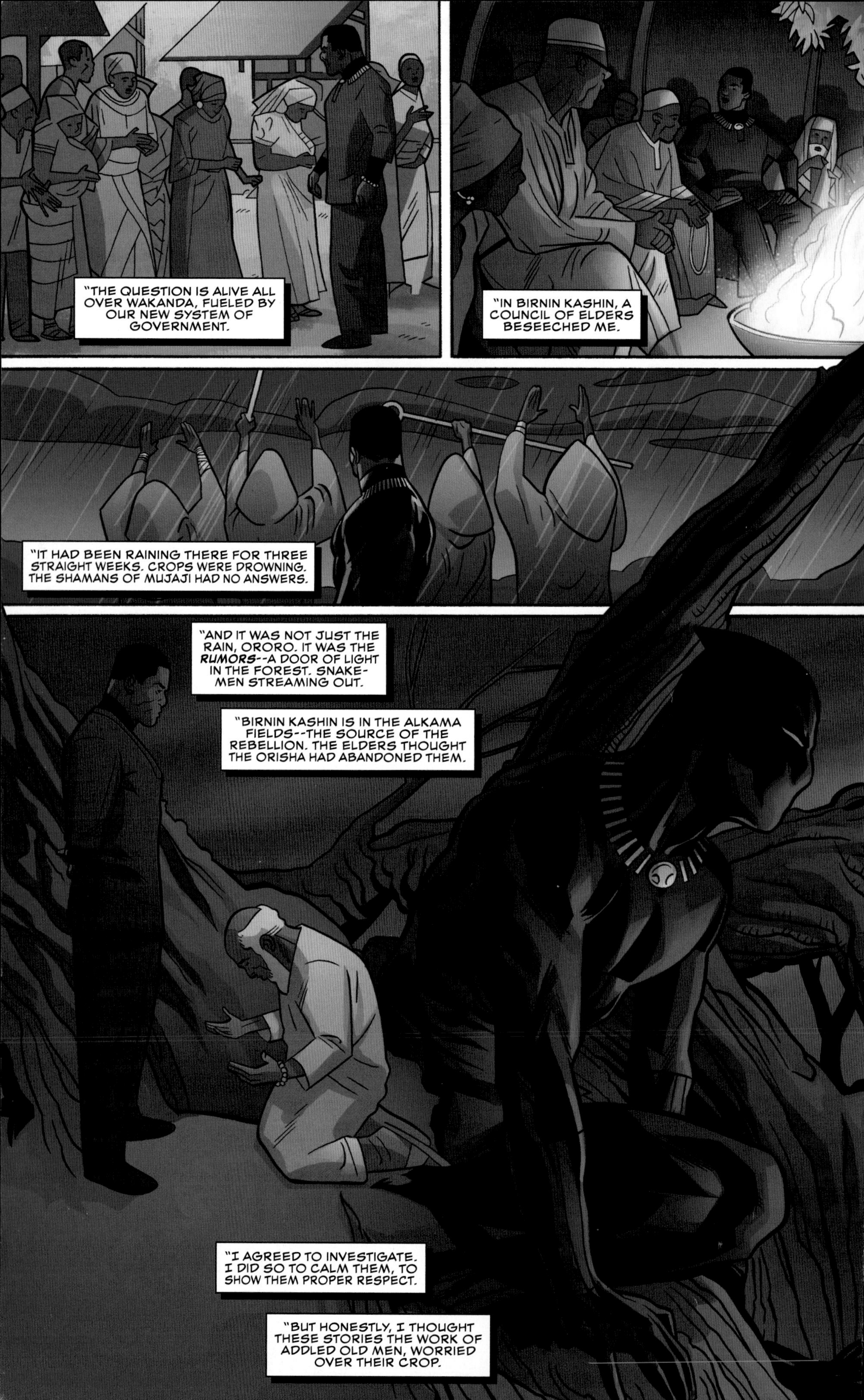
"THE QUESTION IS ALIVE ALL OVER WAKANDA, FUELED BY OUR NEW SYSTEM OF GOVERNMENT.
"IN BIRNIN KASHIN, A COUNCIL OF ELDERS BESEECHED ME.
"IT HAD BEEN RAINING THERE FOR THREE STRAIGHT WEEKS. CROPS WERE DROWNING. THE SHAMANS OF MUJAJI HAD NO ANSWERS.
"AND IT WAS NOT JUST THE RAIN, ORORO. IT WAS THE RUMORS--A DOOR OF LIGHT IN THE FOREST. SNAKE-MEN STREAMING OUT.
"BIRNIN KASHIN IS IN THE ALKAMA FIELDS--THE SOURCE OF THE REBELLION. THE ELDERS THOUGHT THE ORISHA HAD ABANDONED THEM.
"I AGREED TO INVESTIGATE. I DID SO TO CALM THEM, TO SHOW THEM PROPER RESPECT.
"BUT HONESTLY, I THOUGHT THESE STORIES THE WORK OF ADDLED OLD MEN, WORRIED OVER THEIR CROP.

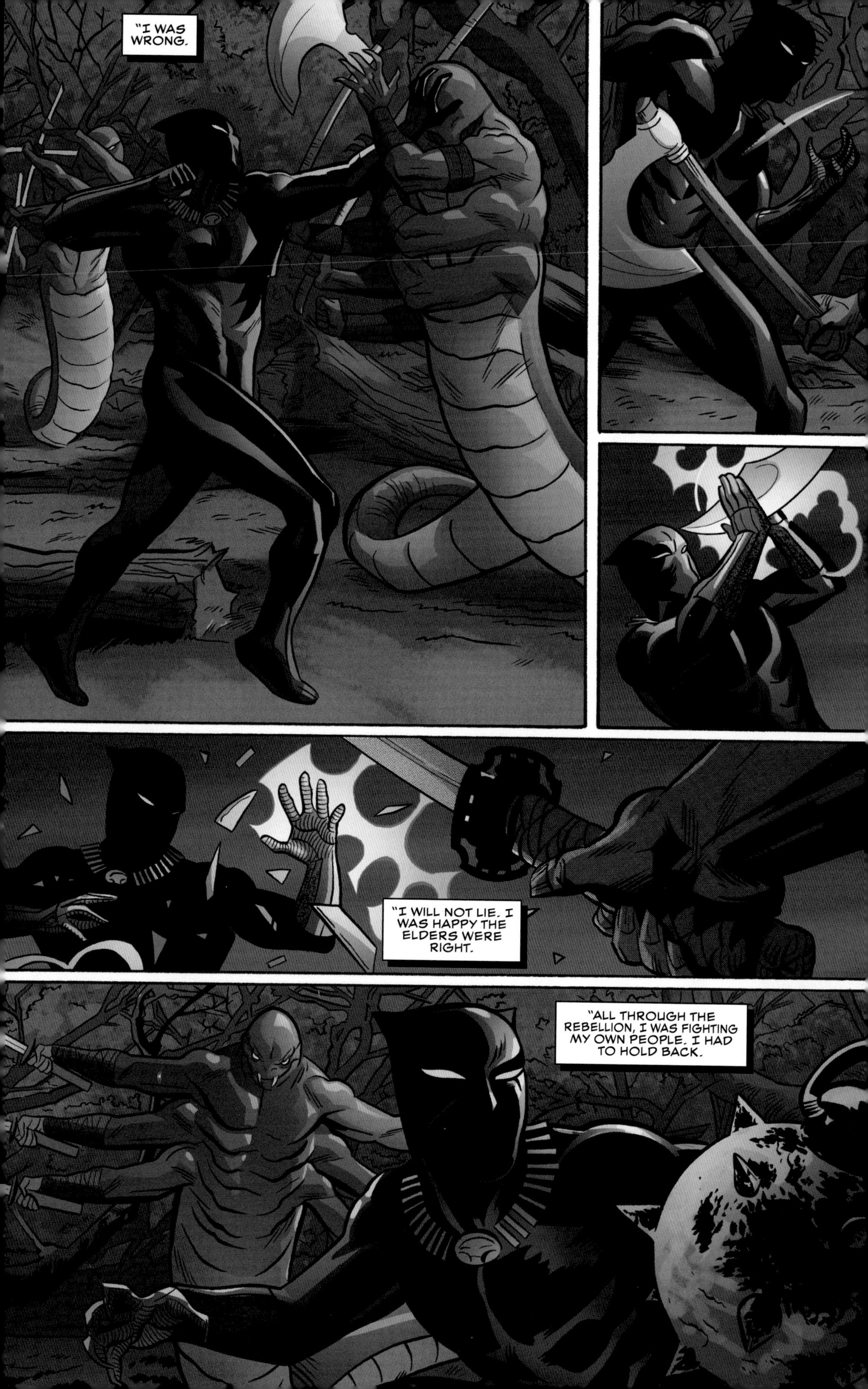
"I WAS WRONG.
"I WILL NOT LIE. I WAS HAPPY THE ELDERS WERE RIGHT.
"ALL THROUGH THE REBELLION, I WAS FIGHTING MY OWN PEOPLE. I HAD TO HOLD BACK.

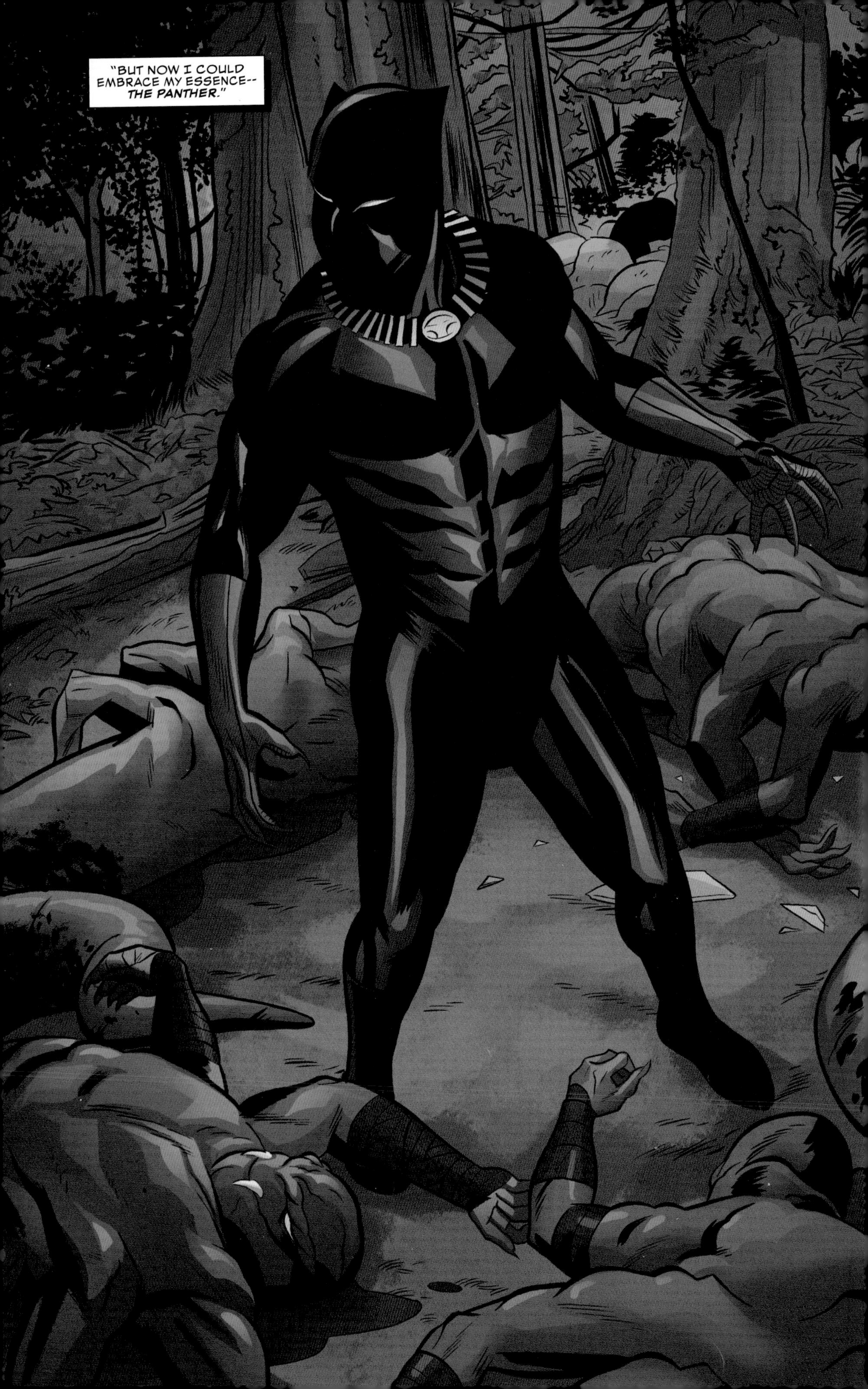
"BUT NOW I COULD EMBRACE MY ESSENCE-- *THE PANTHER.*"

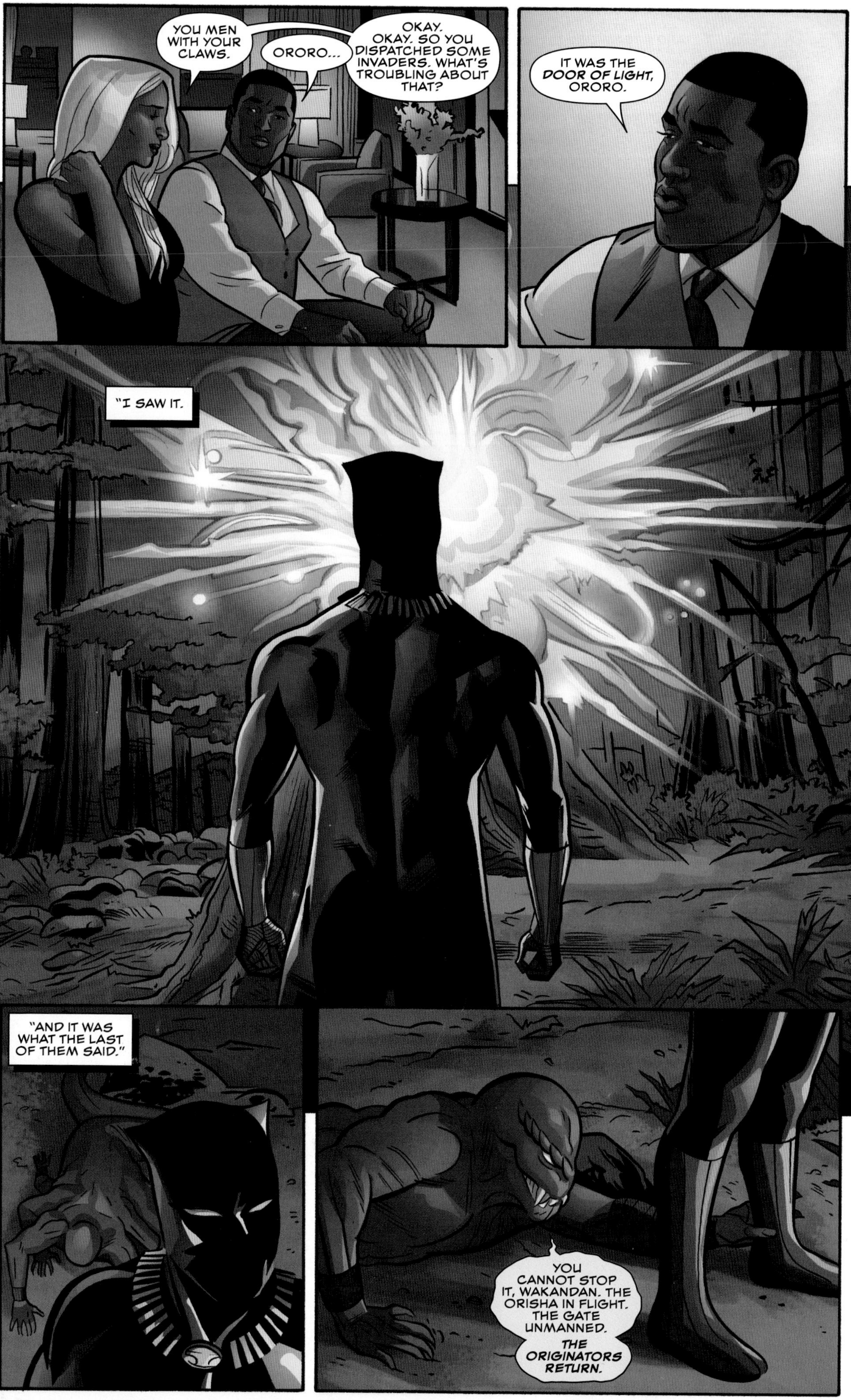

YOU MEN WITH YOUR CLAWS.
ORORO...
OKAY. OKAY. SO YOU DISPATCHED SOME INVADERS. WHAT'S TROUBLING ABOUT THAT?
IT WAS THE *DOOR OF LIGHT,* ORORO.
"I SAW IT.
"AND IT WAS WHAT THE LAST OF THEM SAID."
YOU CANNOT STOP IT, WAKANDAN. THE ORISHA IN FLIGHT. THE GATE UNMANNED. *THE ORIGINATORS RETURN.*

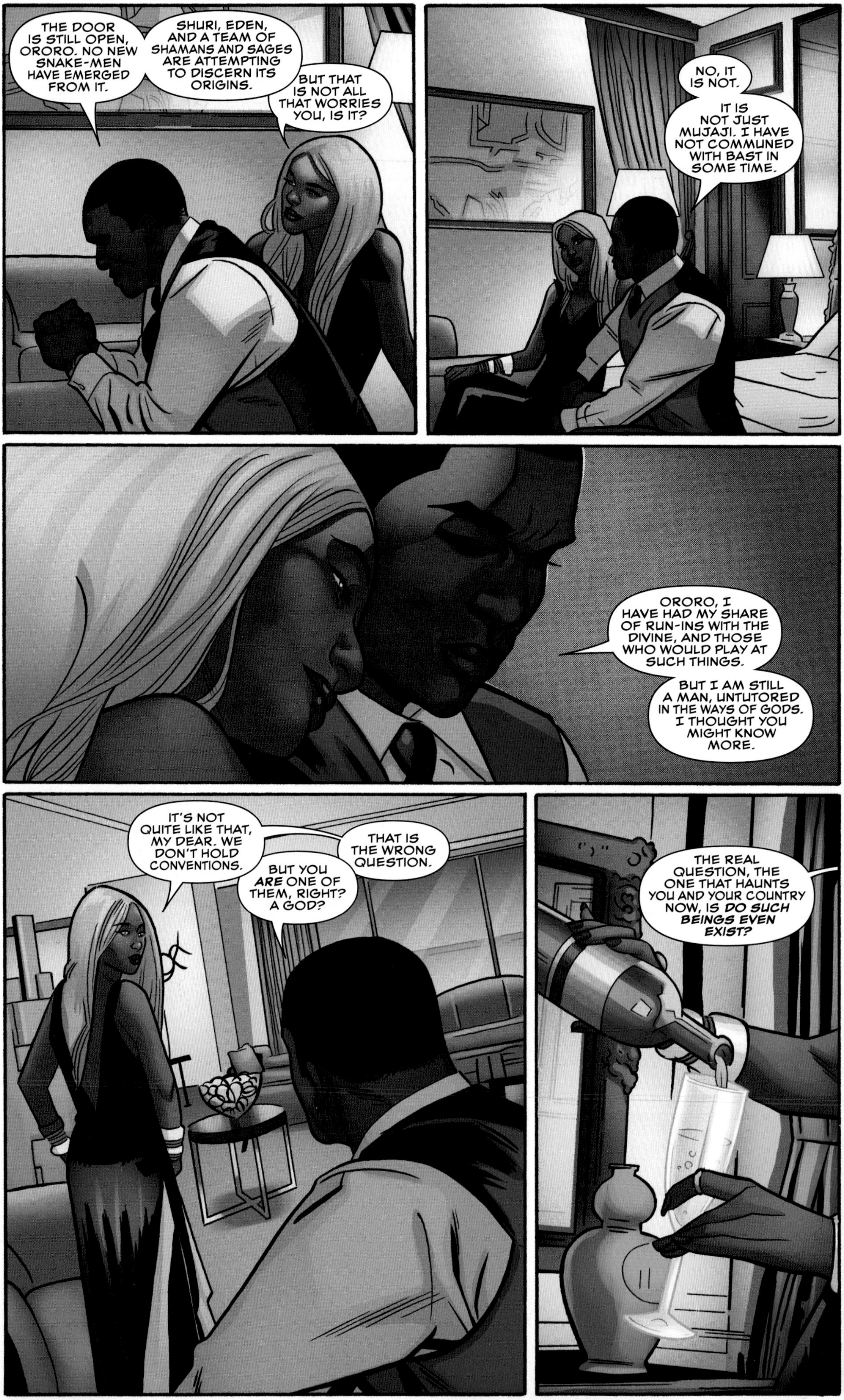
THE DOOR IS STILL OPEN, ORORO. NO NEW SNAKE-MEN HAVE EMERGED FROM IT.
SHURI, EDEN, AND A TEAM OF SHAMANS AND SAGES ARE ATTEMPTING TO DISCERN ITS ORIGINS.
BUT THAT IS NOT ALL THAT WORRIES YOU, IS IT?
NO, IT IS NOT.
IT IS NOT JUST MUJAJI. I HAVE NOT COMMUNED WITH BAST IN SOME TIME.
ORORO, I HAVE HAD MY SHARE OF RUN-INS WITH THE DIVINE, AND THOSE WHO WOULD PLAY AT SUCH THINGS.
BUT I AM STILL A MAN, UNTUTORED IN THE WAYS OF GODS. I THOUGHT YOU MIGHT KNOW MORE.
IT'S NOT QUITE LIKE THAT, MY DEAR. WE DON'T HOLD CONVENTIONS.
BUT YOU ***ARE*** ONE OF THEM, RIGHT? A GOD?
THAT IS THE WRONG QUESTION.
THE REAL QUESTION, THE ONE THAT HAUNTS YOU AND YOUR COUNTRY NOW, IS ***DO SUCH BEINGS EVEN EXIST?***

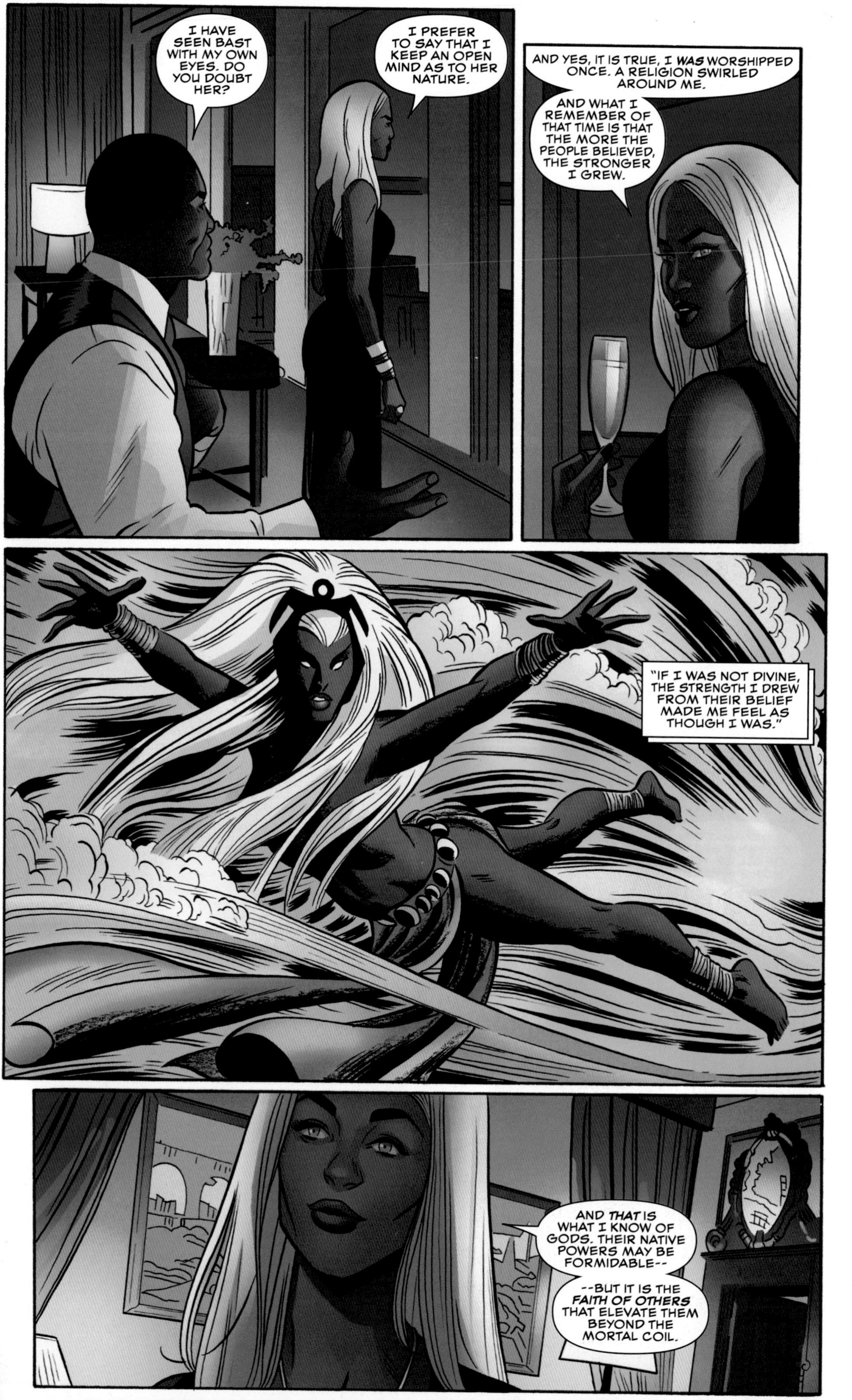

I HAVE SEEN BAST WITH MY OWN EYES. DO YOU DOUBT HER?
I PREFER TO SAY THAT I KEEP AN OPEN MIND AS TO HER NATURE.
AND YES, IT IS TRUE, I *WAS* WORSHIPPED ONCE. A RELIGION SWIRLED AROUND ME.
AND WHAT I REMEMBER OF THAT TIME IS THAT THE MORE THE PEOPLE BELIEVED, THE STRONGER I GREW.
"IF I WAS NOT DIVINE, THE STRENGTH I DREW FROM THEIR BELIEF MADE ME FEEL AS THOUGH I WAS."
AND *THAT* IS WHAT I KNOW OF GODS. THEIR NATIVE POWERS MAY BE FORMIDABLE--
--BUT IT IS THE ***FAITH OF OTHERS*** THAT ELEVATE THEM BEYOND THE MORTAL COIL.

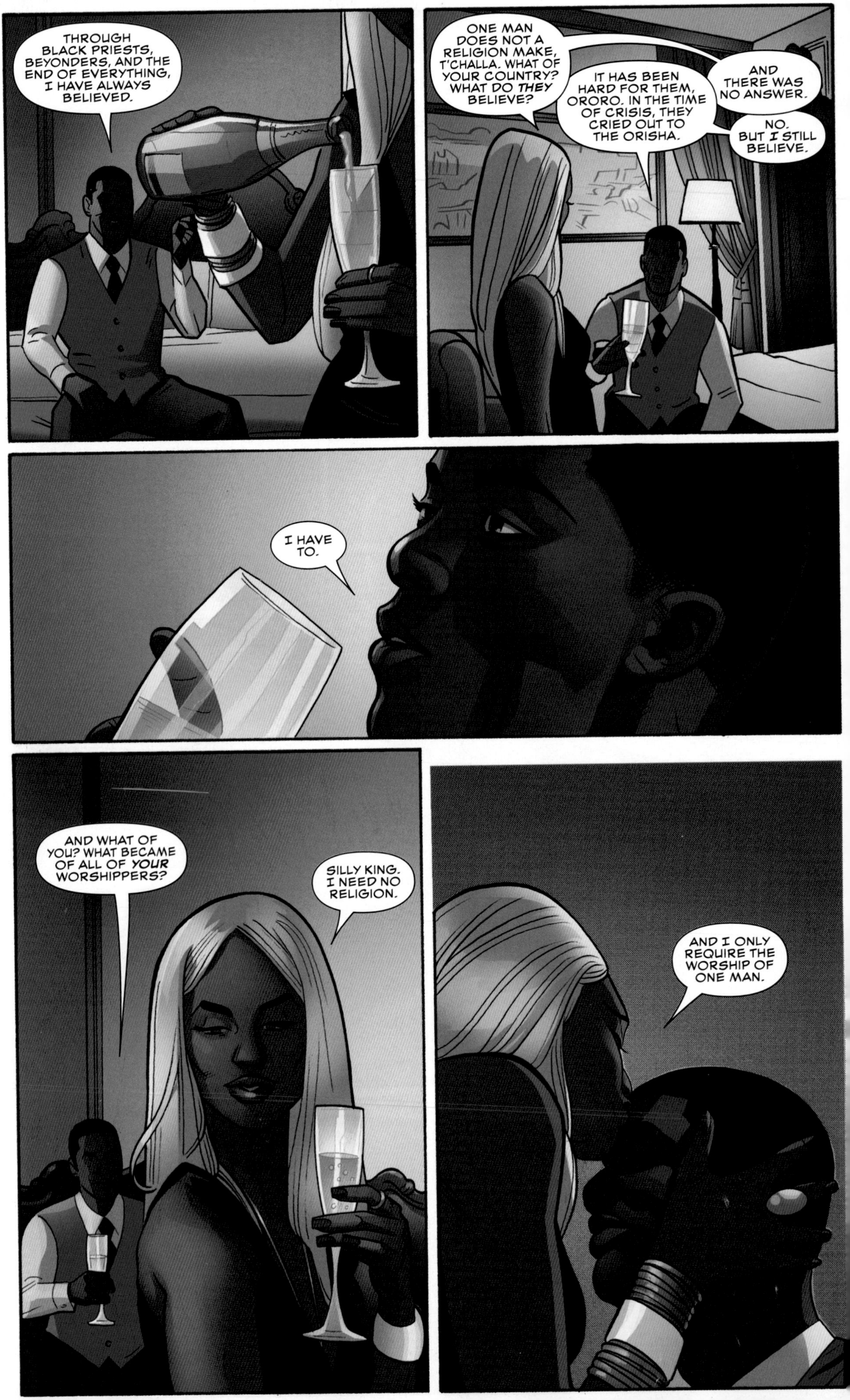
THROUGH BLACK PRIESTS, BEYONDERS, AND THE END OF EVERYTHING, I HAVE ALWAYS BELIEVED.
ONE MAN DOES NOT A RELIGION MAKE, T'CHALLA. WHAT OF YOUR COUNTRY? WHAT DO *THEY* BELIEVE?
IT HAS BEEN HARD FOR THEM, ORORO. IN THE TIME OF CRISIS, THEY CRIED OUT TO THE ORISHA.
AND THERE WAS NO ANSWER.
NO. BUT *I* STILL BELIEVE.
I HAVE TO.
AND WHAT OF YOU? WHAT BECAME OF ALL OF *YOUR* WORSHIPPERS?
SILLY KING. I NEED NO RELIGION.
AND I ONLY REQUIRE THE WORSHIP OF ONE MAN.

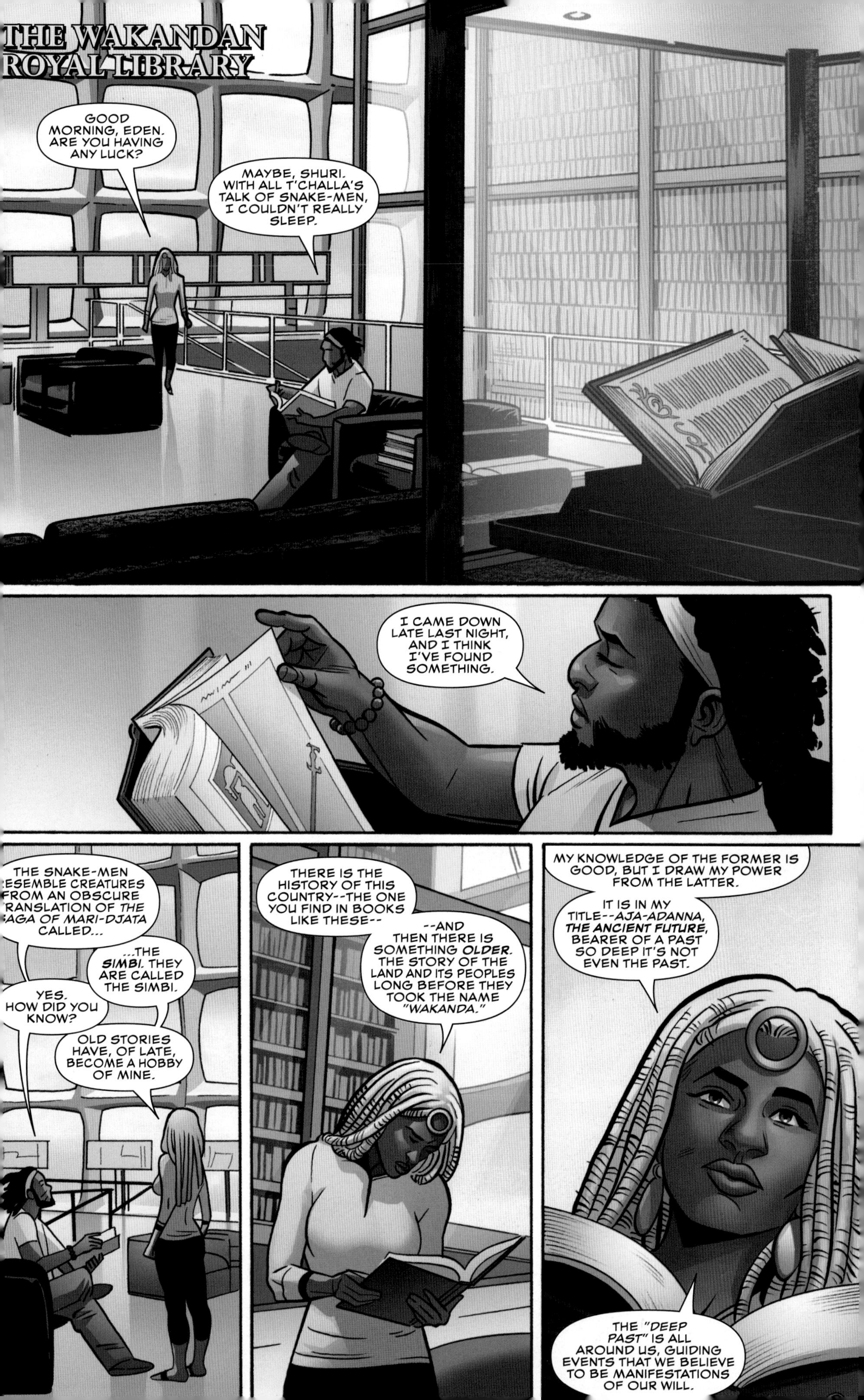
THE WAKANDAN ROYAL LIBRARY
GOOD MORNING, EDEN. ARE YOU HAVING ANY LUCK?
MAYBE, SHURI. WITH ALL T'CHALLA'S TALK OF SNAKE-MEN, I COULDN'T REALLY SLEEP.
I CAME DOWN LATE LAST NIGHT, AND I THINK I'VE FOUND SOMETHING.
THE SNAKE-MEN RESEMBLE CREATURES FROM AN OBSCURE TRANSLATION OF THE SAGA OF MARI-DJATA CALLED...
...THE SIMBI. THEY ARE CALLED THE SIMBI.
YES. HOW DID YOU KNOW?
OLD STORIES HAVE, OF LATE, BECOME A HOBBY OF MINE.
THERE IS THE HISTORY OF THIS COUNTRY--THE ONE YOU FIND IN BOOKS LIKE THESE--
--AND THEN THERE IS SOMETHING OLDER. THE STORY OF THE LAND AND ITS PEOPLES LONG BEFORE THEY TOOK THE NAME "WAKANDA."
MY KNOWLEDGE OF THE FORMER IS GOOD, BUT I DRAW MY POWER FROM THE LATTER.
IT IS IN MY TITLE--AJA-ADANNA, THE ANCIENT FUTURE, BEARER OF A PAST SO DEEP IT'S NOT EVEN THE PAST.
THE "DEEP PAST" IS ALL AROUND US, GUIDING EVENTS THAT WE BELIEVE TO BE MANIFESTATIONS OF OUR WILL.

THE SIMBI. THEY ARE OF THAT DEEP PAST?

YES.

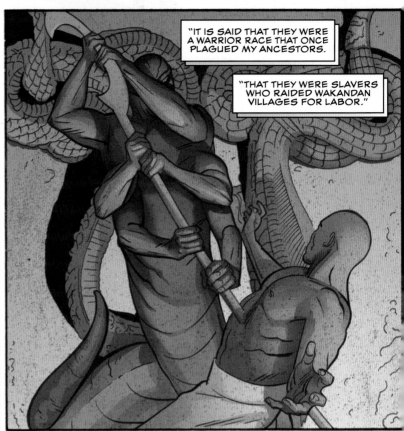

"IT IS SAID THAT THEY WERE A WARRIOR RACE THAT ONCE PLAGUED MY ANCESTORS."

"THAT THEY WERE SLAVERS WHO RAIDED WAKANDAN VILLAGES FOR LABOR."

IS IT TRUE THAT IT WAS MARI-DJATA WHO VANQUISHED THEM?

I DO NOT KNOW. TALES OF THE SIMBI DISAPPEAR BEFORE MARI-DJATA'S RULE EVEN BEGAN.

BUT MY MASTERY OF THE DEEP PAST IS NOT TOTAL. MY VOYAGE THROUGH THE DJALIA WAS CUT SHORT.

I HAVE TRIED NOT TO HOLD THAT AGAINST YOU.

I--I'M SORRY.

IT WAS A JOKE, EDEN. THE AJA-ADANNA IS ALLOWED TO JOKE.

RIGHT...OF COURSE.

ANYWAY, VOYAGES ARE MY SPECIALTY. I'VE EXAMINED THE DOOR IN THE WOODS. IT REJECTS ME AS EASILY AS--

PARDON ME, EDEN... GO AHEAD, T'CHALLA.

IT HAS HAPPENED AGAIN. I NEED YOU BOTH HERE. AND I NEED YOU READY.

THE DOOR?

YES. BUT A DIFFERENT ONE.

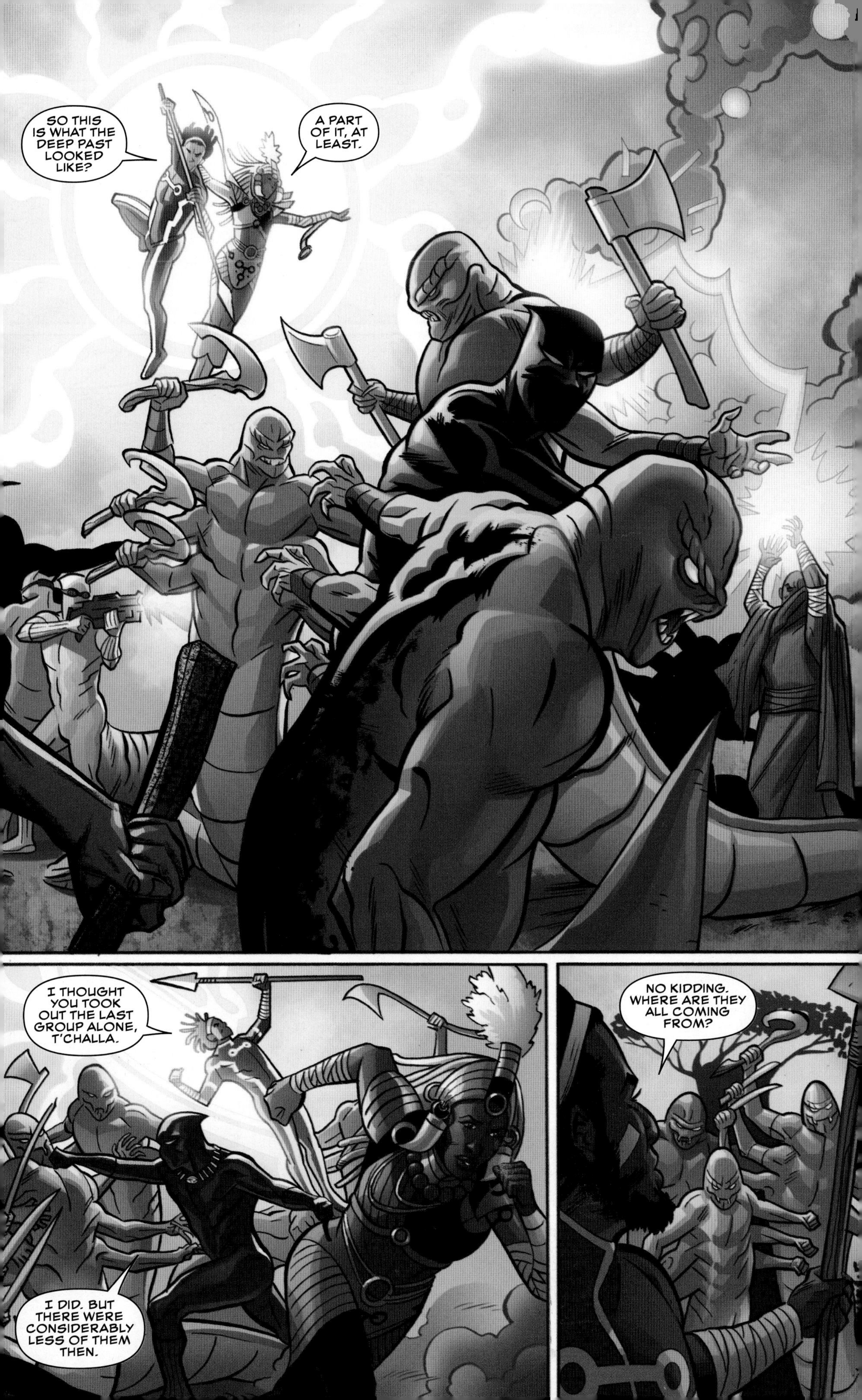
SO THIS IS WHAT THE DEEP PAST LOOKED LIKE?
A PART OF IT, AT LEAST.
I THOUGHT YOU TOOK OUT THE LAST GROUP ALONE, T'CHALLA.
I DID. BUT THERE WERE CONSIDERABLY LESS OF THEM THEN.
NO KIDDING. WHERE ARE THEY ALL COMING FROM?

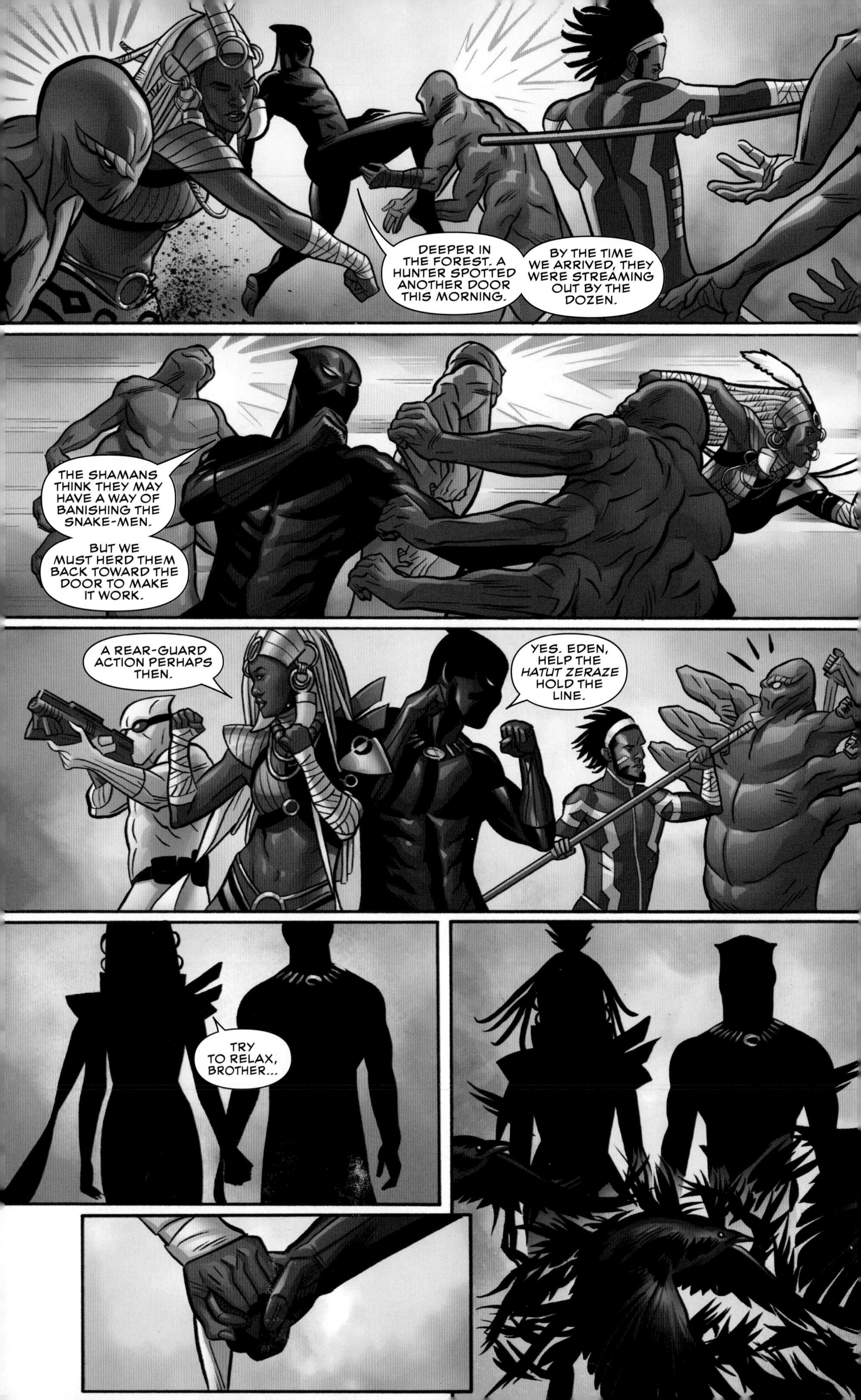
DEEPER IN THE FOREST. A HUNTER SPOTTED ANOTHER DOOR THIS MORNING.
BY THE TIME WE ARRIVED, THEY WERE STREAMING OUT BY THE DOZEN.
THE SHAMANS THINK THEY MAY HAVE A WAY OF BANISHING THE SNAKE-MEN.
BUT WE MUST HERD THEM BACK TOWARD THE DOOR TO MAKE IT WORK.
A REAR-GUARD ACTION PERHAPS THEN.
YES. EDEN, HELP THE *HATUT ZERAZE* HOLD THE LINE.
TRY TO RELAX, BROTHER...

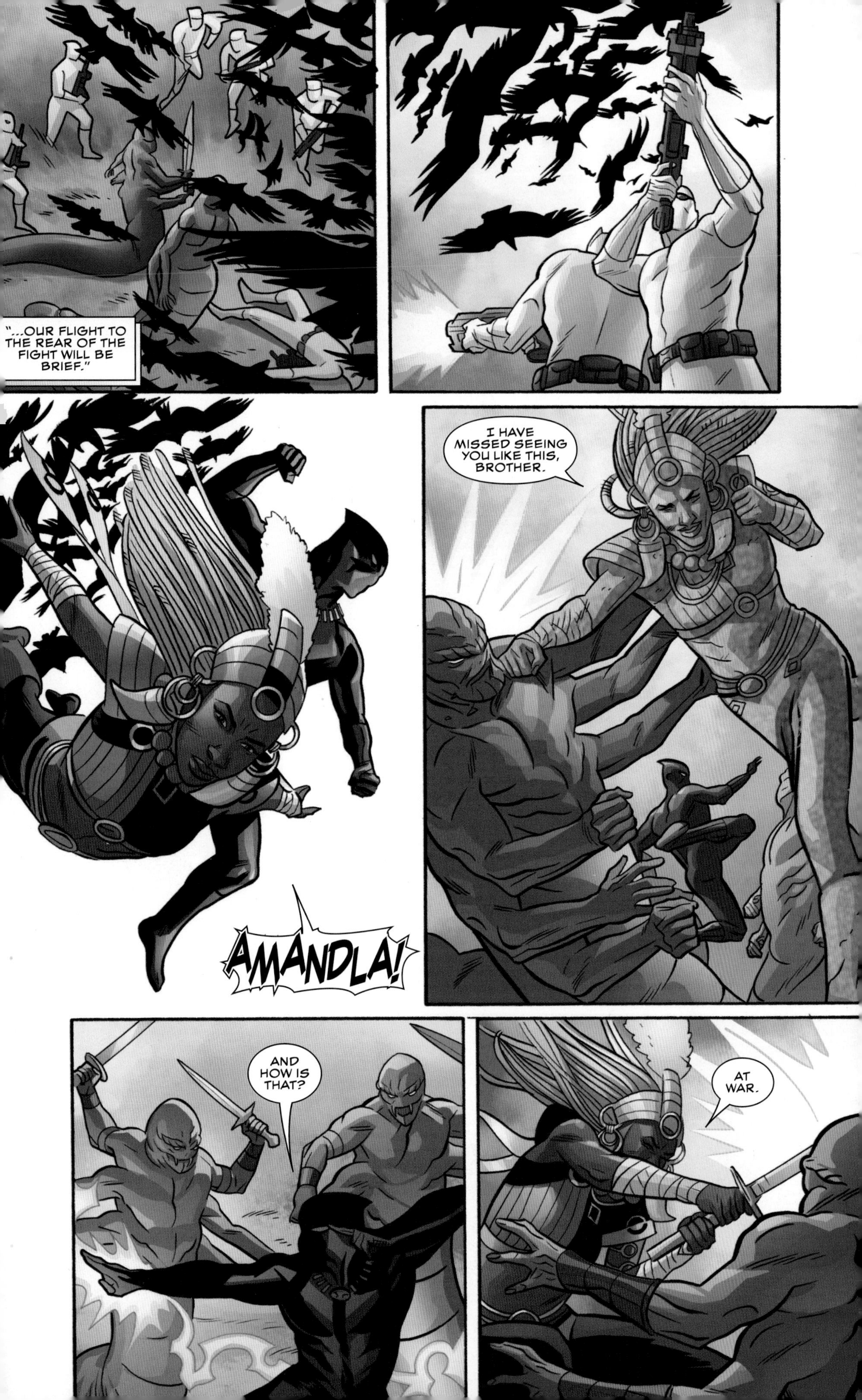
"...OUR FLIGHT TO THE REAR OF THE FIGHT WILL BE BRIEF."
I HAVE MISSED SEEING YOU LIKE THIS, BROTHER.
AMANDLA!
AND HOW IS THAT?
AT WAR.

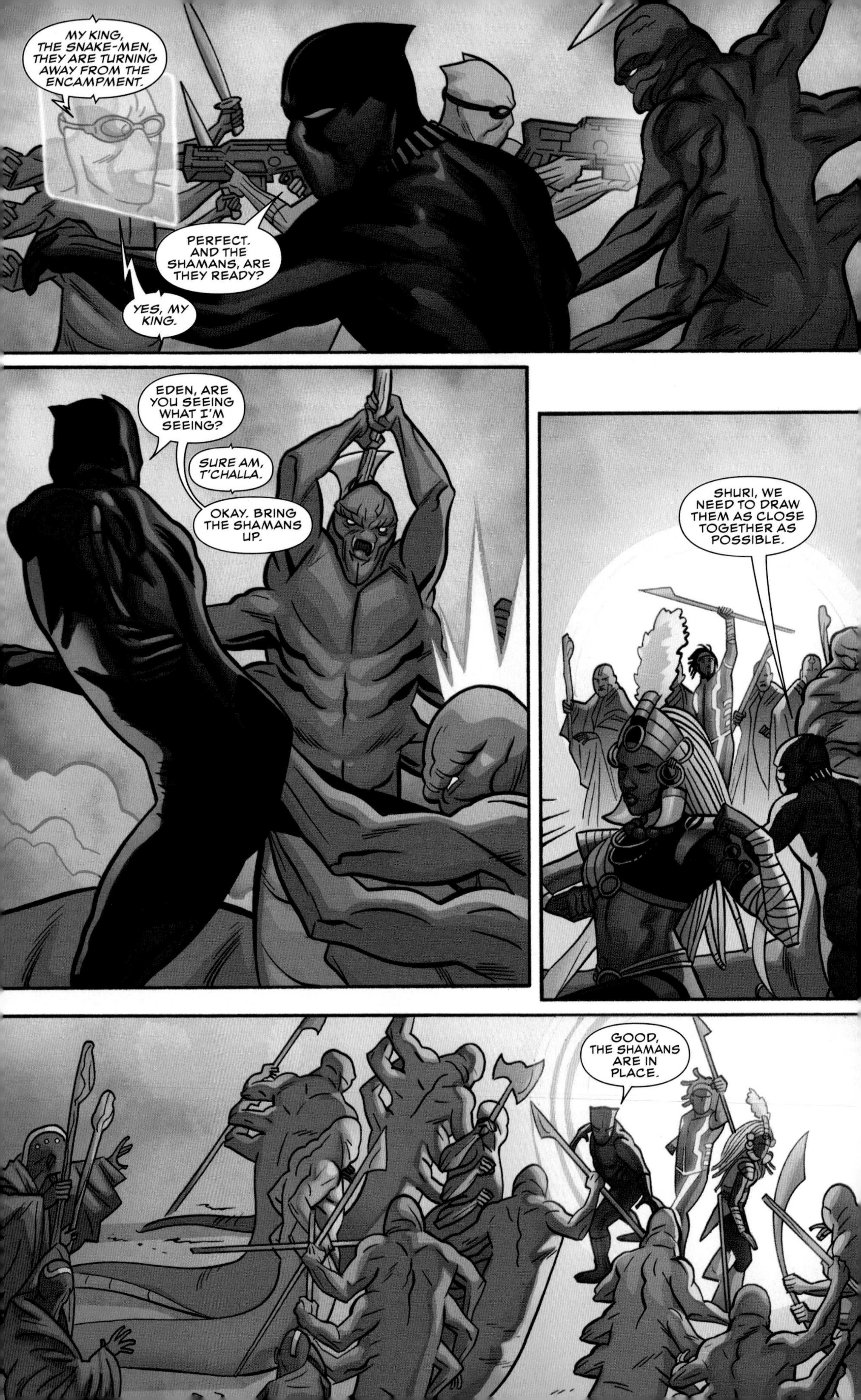
MY KING, THE SNAKE-MEN, THEY ARE TURNING AWAY FROM THE ENCAMPMENT.
PERFECT. AND THE SHAMANS, ARE THEY READY?
YES, MY KING.
EDEN, ARE YOU SEEING WHAT I'M SEEING?
SURE AM, T'CHALLA.
OKAY. BRING THE SHAMANS UP.
SHURI, WE NEED TO DRAW THEM AS CLOSE TOGETHER AS POSSIBLE.
GOOD, THE SHAMANS ARE IN PLACE.

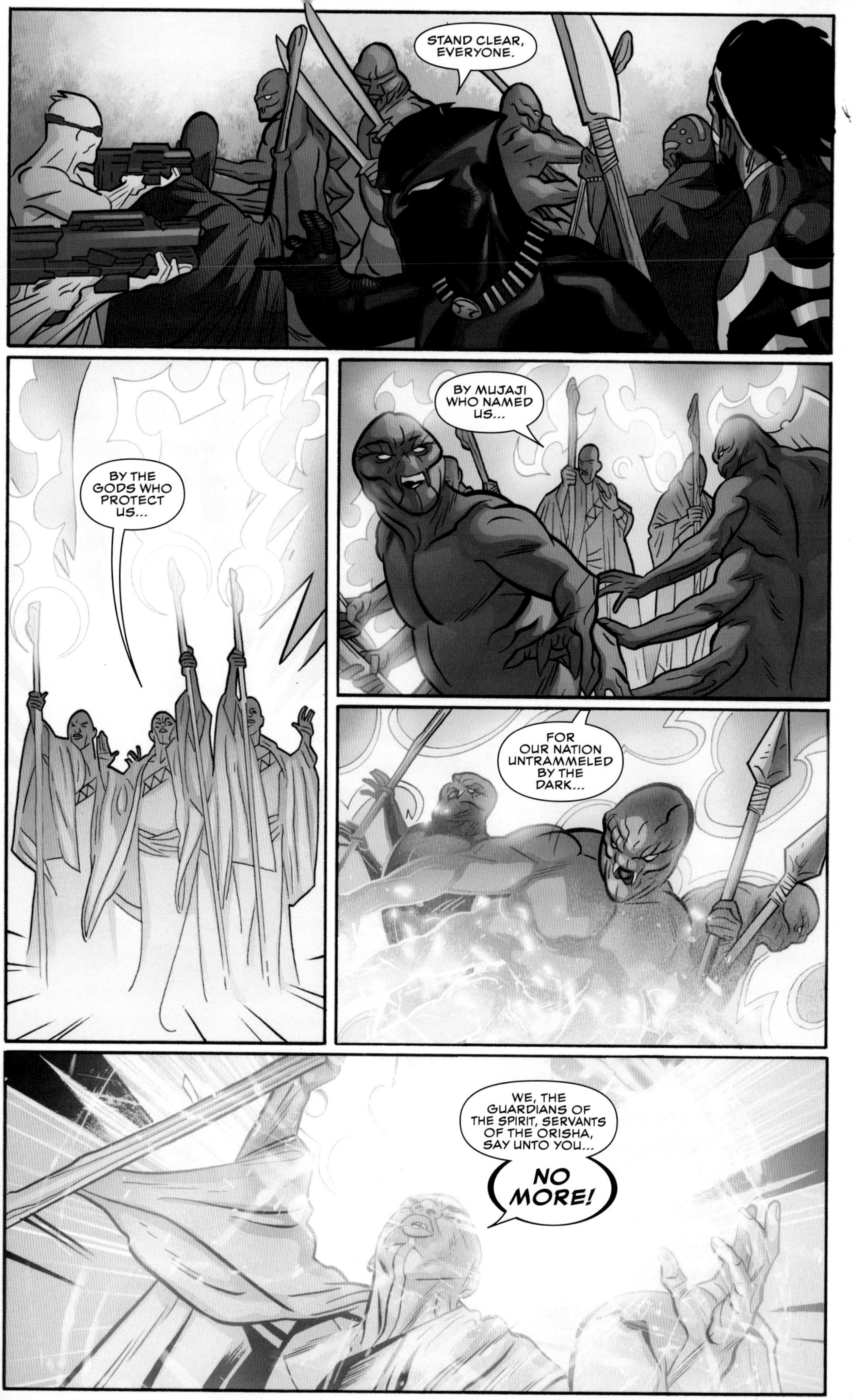
STAND CLEAR, EVERYONE.
BY THE GODS WHO PROTECT US...
BY MUJAJI WHO NAMED US...
FOR OUR NATION UNTRAMMELED BY THE DARK...
WE, THE GUARDIANS OF THE SPIRIT, SERVANTS OF THE ORISHA, SAY UNTO YOU...
NO MORE!

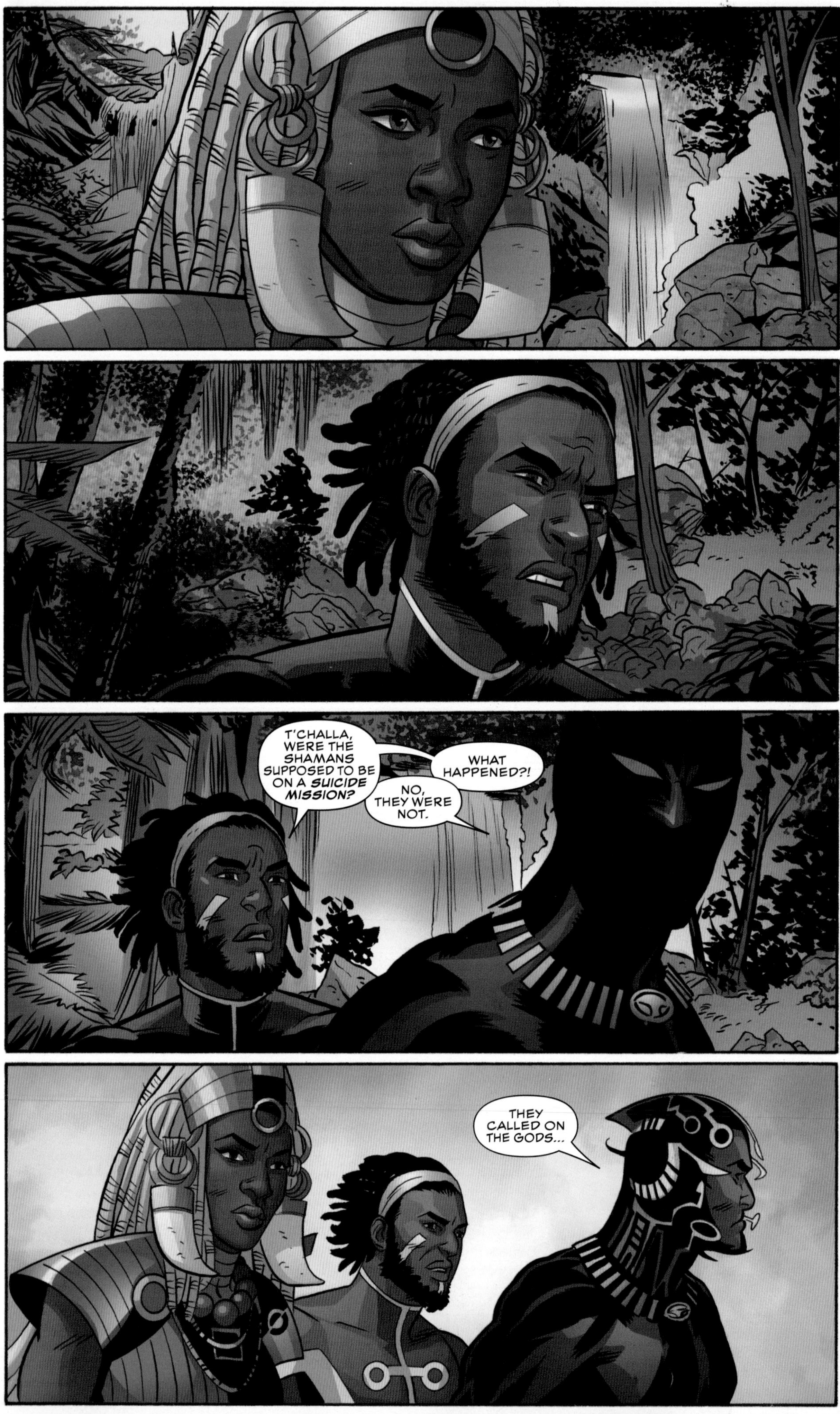

T'CHALLA, WERE THE SHAMANS SUPPOSED TO BE ON A SUICIDE MISSION?
WHAT HAPPENED?!
NO, THEY WERE NOT.
THEY CALLED ON THE GODS...

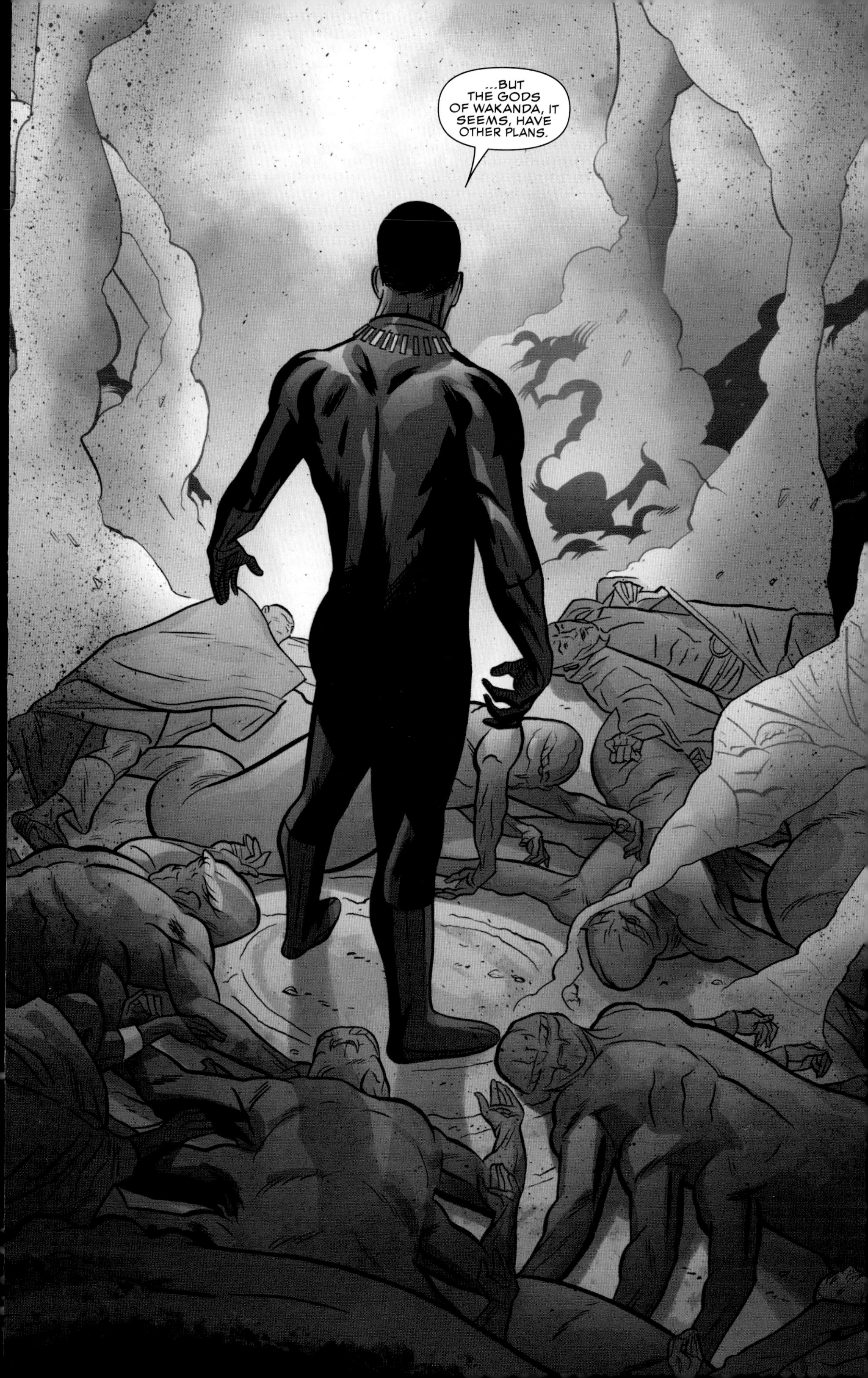
...BUT THE GODS OF WAKANDA, IT SEEMS, HAVE OTHER PLANS.

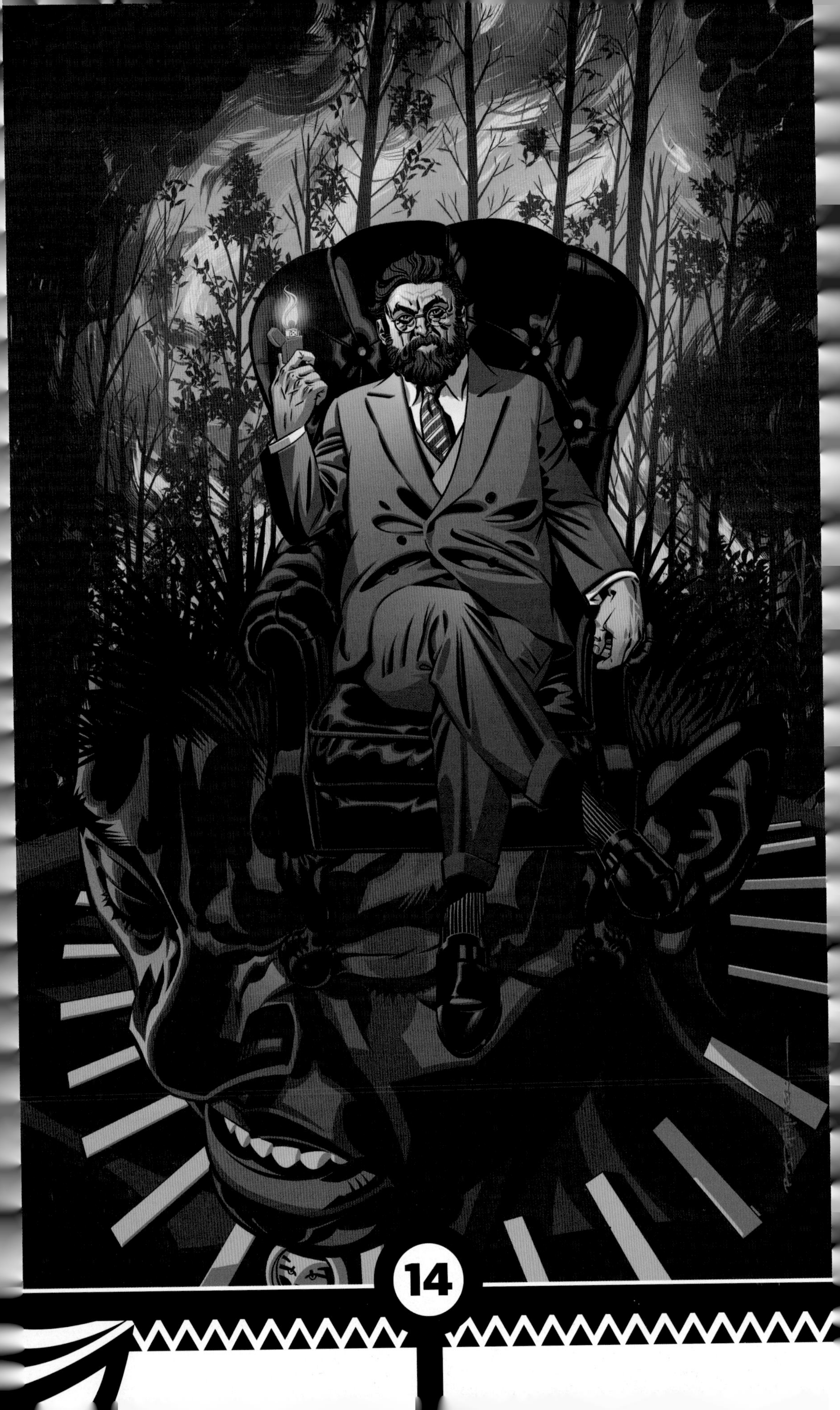
14

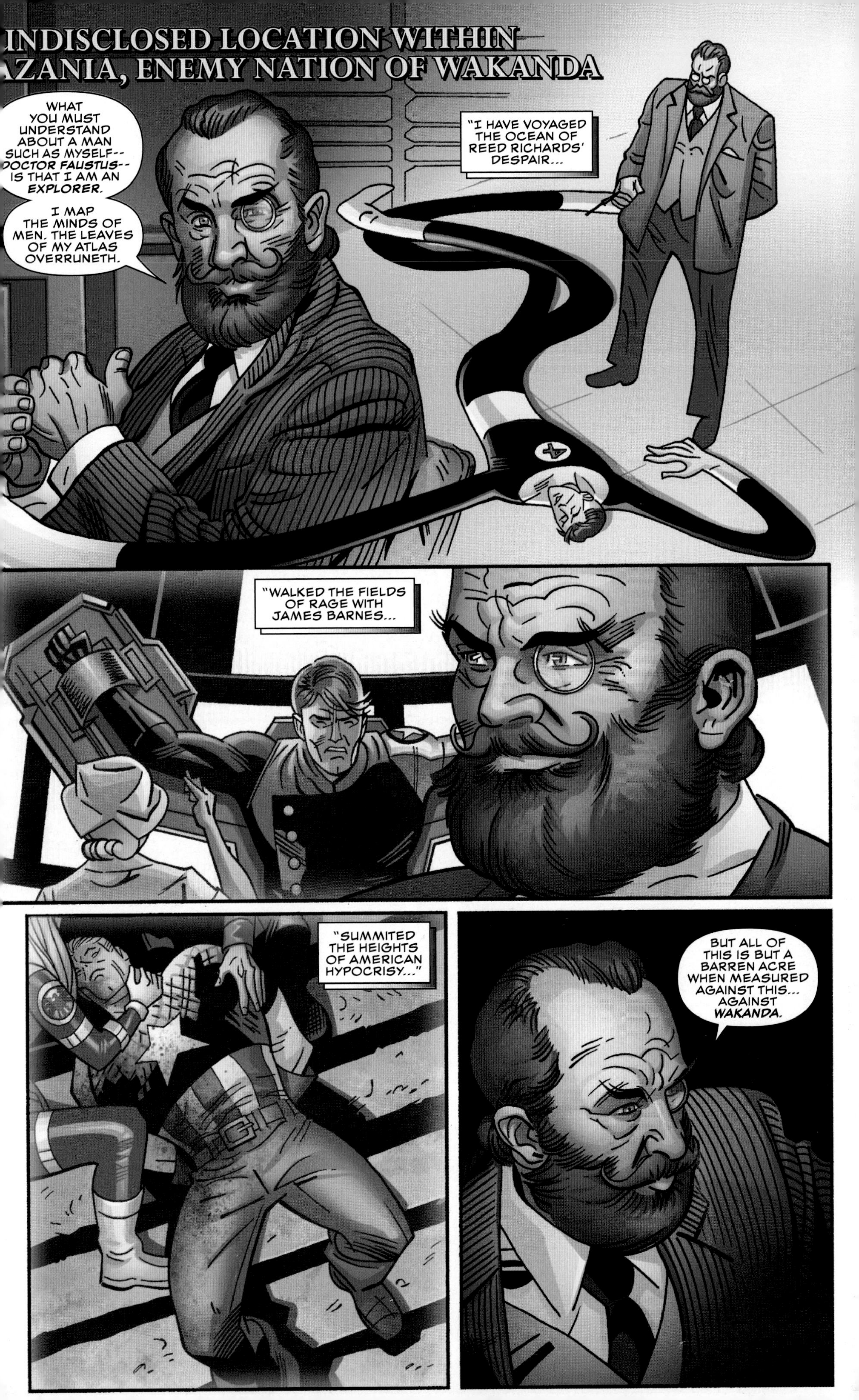
INDISCLOSED LOCATION WITHIN
AZANIA, ENEMY NATION OF WAKANDA
WHAT YOU MUST UNDERSTAND ABOUT A MAN SUCH AS MYSELF-- DOCTOR FAUSTUS-- IS THAT I AM AN EXPLORER.
I MAP THE MINDS OF MEN. THE LEAVES OF MY ATLAS OVERRUNETH.
"I HAVE VOYAGED THE OCEAN OF REED RICHARDS' DESPAIR...
"WALKED THE FIELDS OF RAGE WITH JAMES BARNES...
"SUMMITED THE HEIGHTS OF AMERICAN HYPOCRISY..."
BUT ALL OF THIS IS BUT A BARREN ACRE WHEN MEASURED AGAINST THIS... AGAINST WAKANDA.

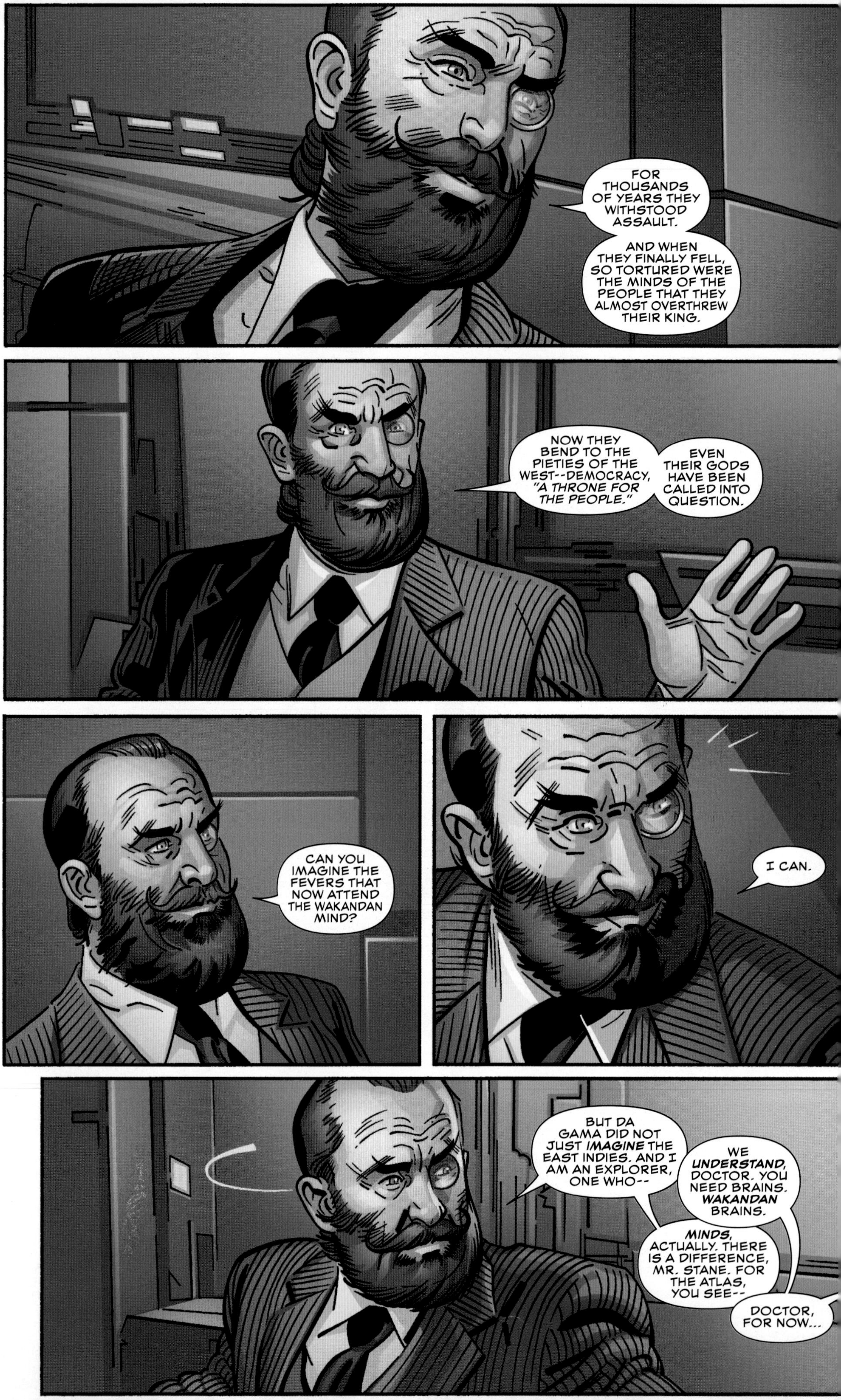

FOR THOUSANDS OF YEARS THEY WITHSTOOD ASSAULT.
AND WHEN THEY FINALLY FELL, SO TORTURED WERE THE MINDS OF THE PEOPLE THAT THEY ALMOST OVERTHREW THEIR KING.
NOW THEY BEND TO THE PIETIES OF THE WEST--DEMOCRACY, *"A THRONE FOR THE PEOPLE."*
EVEN THEIR GODS HAVE BEEN CALLED INTO QUESTION.
CAN YOU IMAGINE THE FEVERS THAT NOW ATTEND THE WAKANDAN MIND?
I CAN.
BUT DA GAMA DID NOT JUST ***IMAGINE*** THE EAST INDIES. AND I AM AN EXPLORER, ONE WHO--
WE ***UNDERSTAND,*** DOCTOR. YOU NEED BRAINS. ***WAKANDAN*** BRAINS.
MINDS, ACTUALLY. THERE IS A DIFFERENCE, MR. STANE. FOR THE ATLAS, YOU SEE--
DOCTOR, FOR NOW...

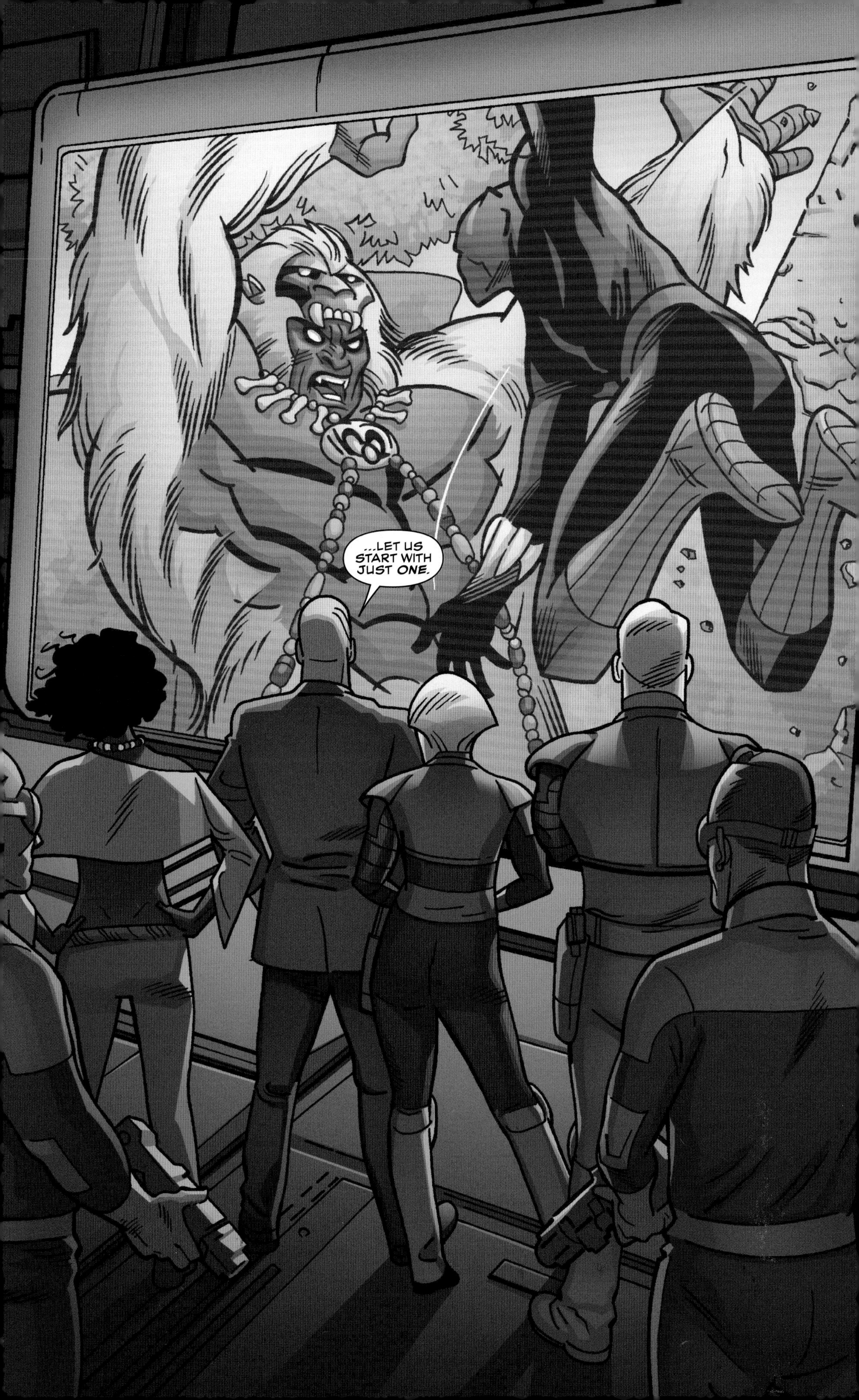
...LET US START WITH JUST ONE.

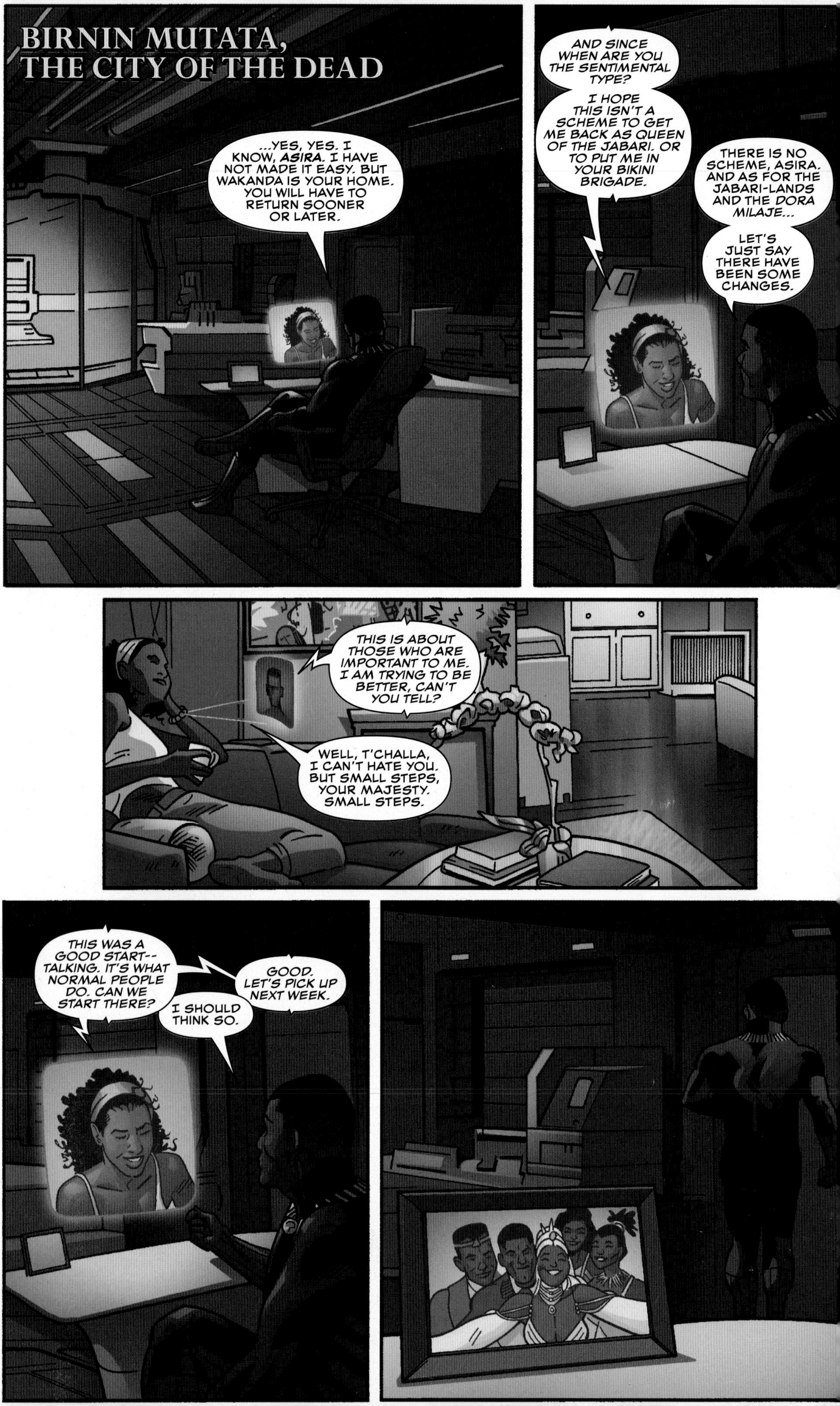
BIRNIN MUTATA, THE CITY OF THE DEAD
...YES, YES. I KNOW, ASIRA. I HAVE NOT MADE IT EASY. BUT WAKANDA IS YOUR HOME. YOU WILL HAVE TO RETURN SOONER OR LATER.
AND SINCE WHEN ARE YOU THE SENTIMENTAL TYPE?
I HOPE THIS ISN'T A SCHEME TO GET ME BACK AS QUEEN OF THE JABARI. OR TO PUT ME IN YOUR BIKINI BRIGADE.
THERE IS NO SCHEME, ASIRA. AND AS FOR THE JABARI-LANDS AND THE DORA MILAJE...
LET'S JUST SAY THERE HAVE BEEN SOME CHANGES.
THIS IS ABOUT THOSE WHO ARE IMPORTANT TO ME. I AM TRYING TO BE BETTER, CAN'T YOU TELL?
WELL, T'CHALLA, I CAN'T HATE YOU. BUT SMALL STEPS, YOUR MAJESTY. SMALL STEPS.
THIS WAS A GOOD START-- TALKING. IT'S WHAT NORMAL PEOPLE DO. CAN WE START THERE?
I SHOULD THINK SO.
GOOD. LET'S PICK UP NEXT WEEK.

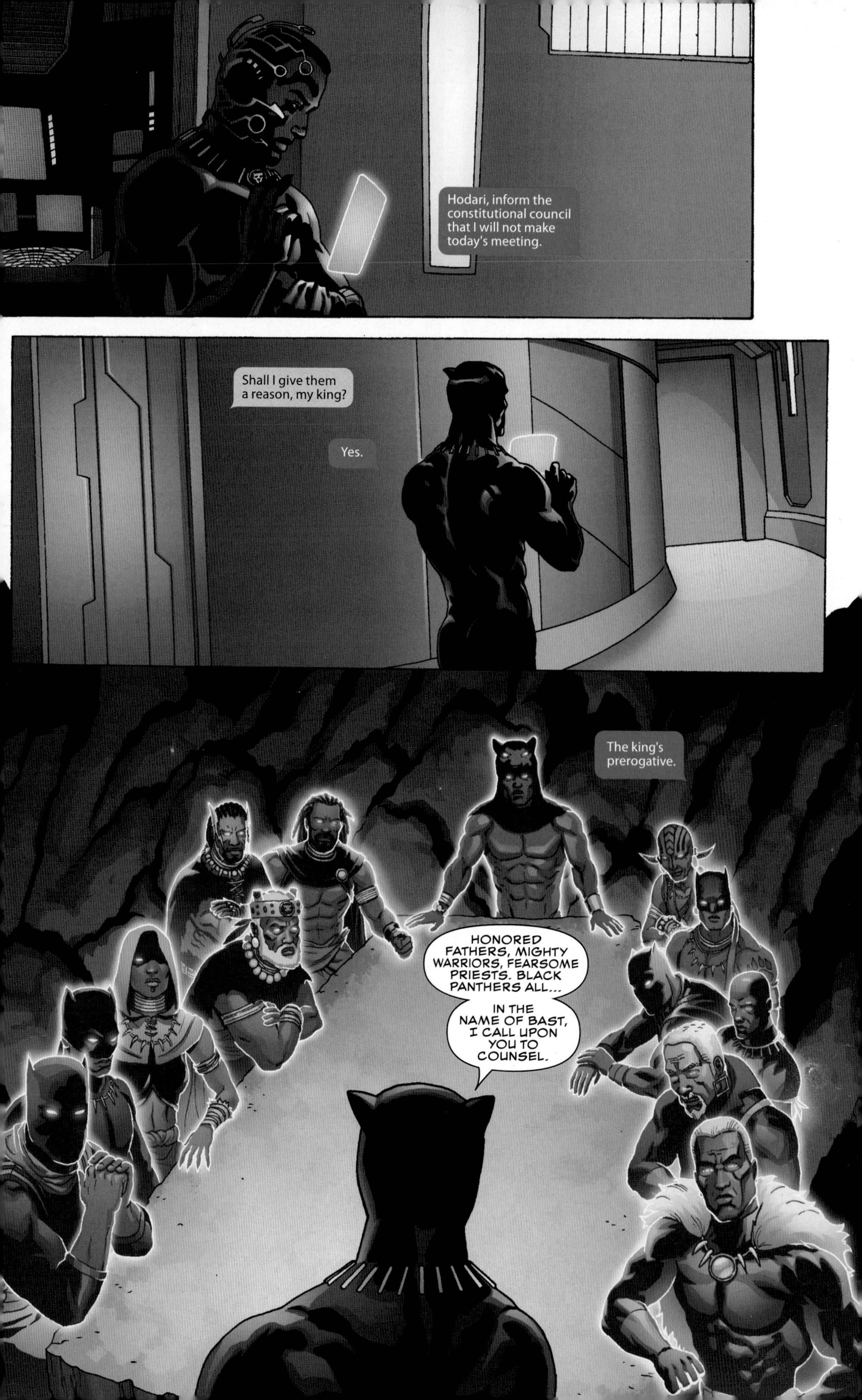
Hodari, inform the constitutional council that I will not make today's meeting.
Shall I give them a reason, my king?
Yes.
The king's prerogative.
HONORED FATHERS, MIGHTY WARRIORS, FEARSOME PRIESTS. BLACK PANTHERS ALL...
IN THE NAME OF BAST, I CALL UPON YOU TO COUNSEL.

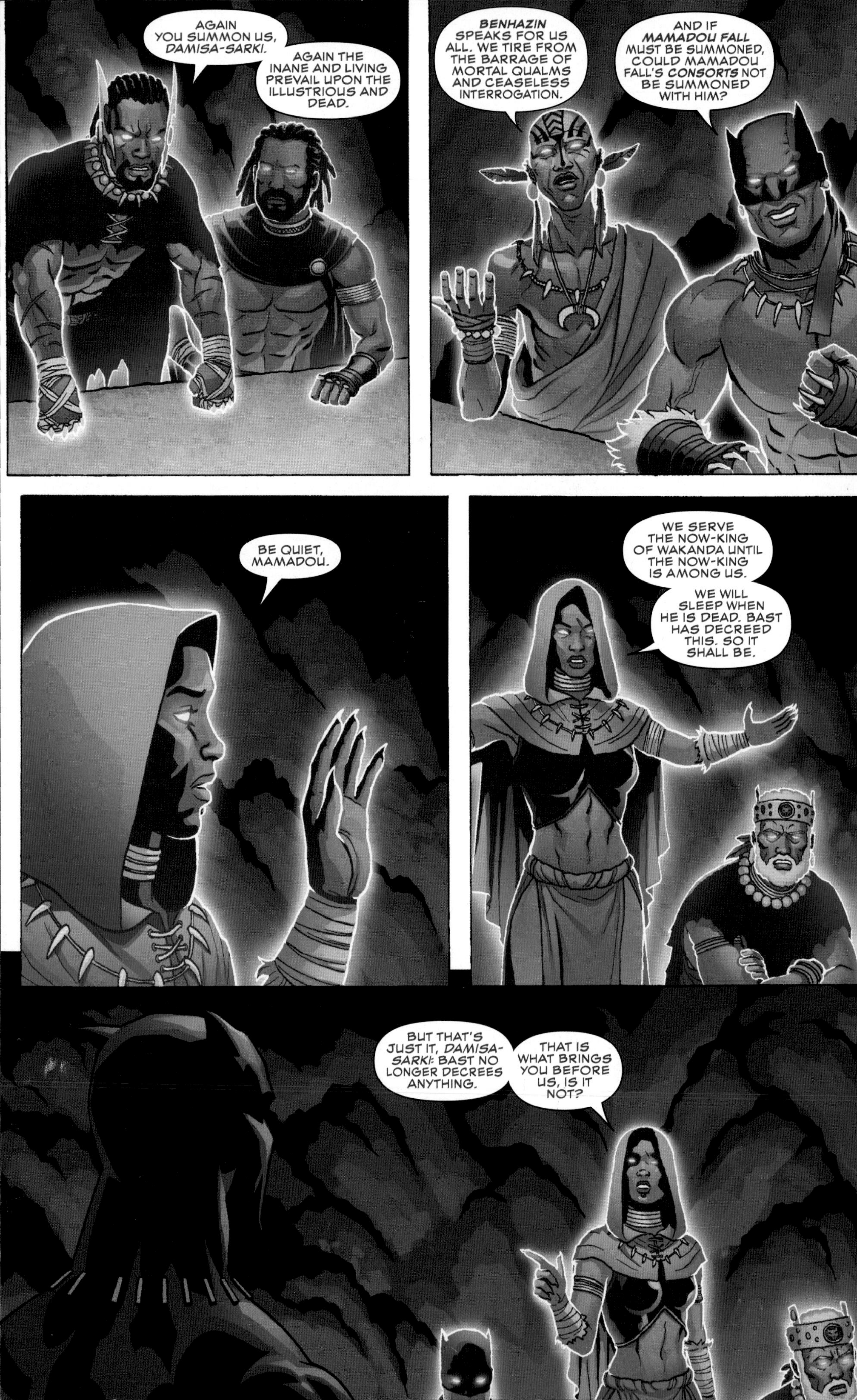
AGAIN YOU SUMMON US, *DAMISA-SARKI.*
AGAIN THE INANE AND LIVING PREVAIL UPON THE ILLUSTRIOUS AND DEAD.
BENHAZIN SPEAKS FOR US ALL. WE TIRE FROM THE BARRAGE OF MORTAL QUALMS AND CEASELESS INTERROGATION.
AND IF ***MAMADOU FALL*** MUST BE SUMMONED, COULD MAMADOU FALL'S ***CONSORTS*** NOT BE SUMMONED WITH HIM?
BE QUIET, MAMADOU.
WE SERVE THE NOW-KING OF WAKANDA UNTIL THE NOW-KING IS AMONG US.
WE WILL SLEEP WHEN HE IS DEAD. BAST HAS DECREED THIS. SO IT SHALL BE.
BUT THAT'S JUST IT, *DAMISA-SARKI:* BAST NO LONGER DECREES ANYTHING.
THAT IS WHAT BRINGS YOU BEFORE US, IS IT NOT?

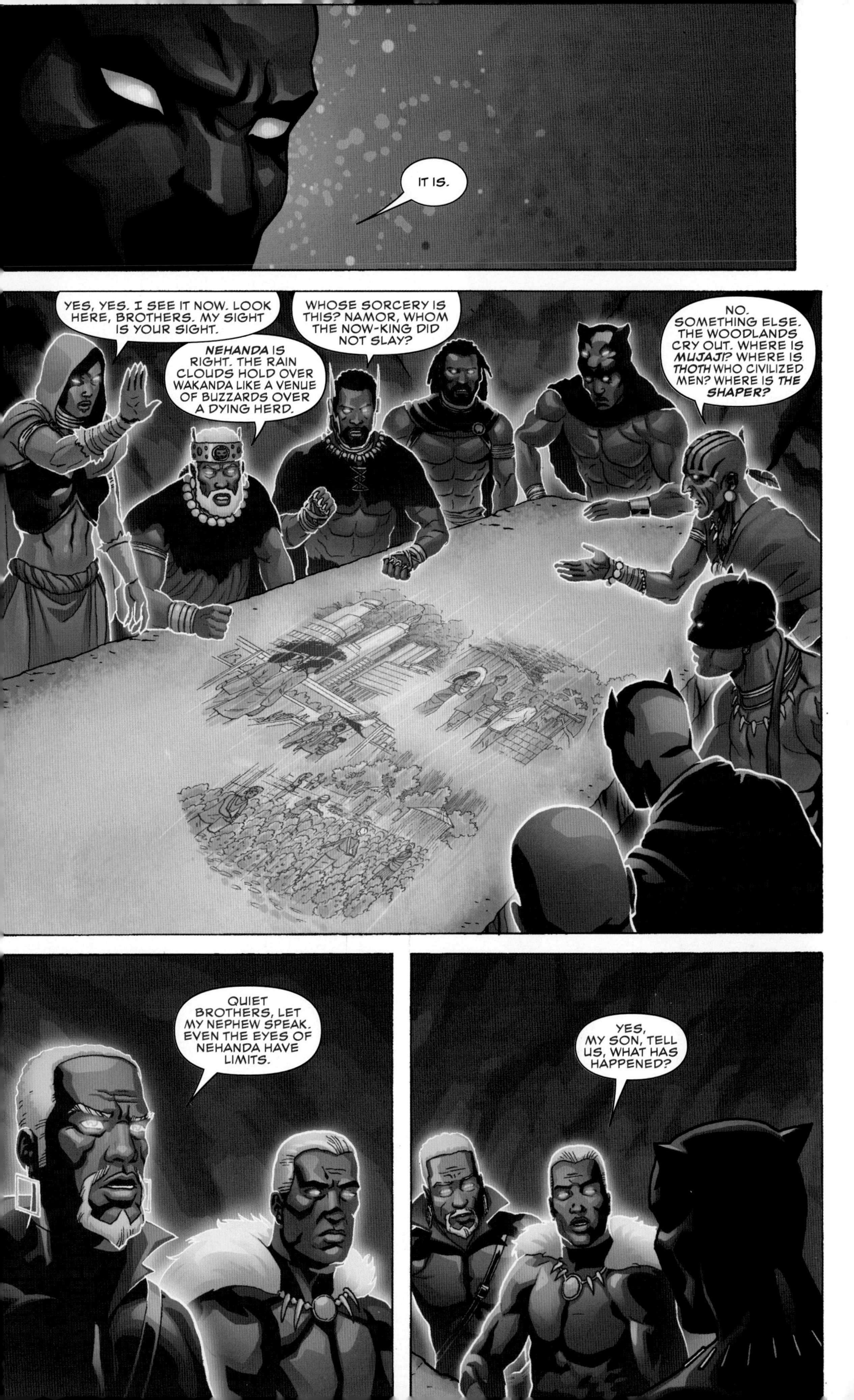
IT IS.
YES, YES. I SEE IT NOW. LOOK HERE, BROTHERS. MY SIGHT IS YOUR SIGHT.
NEHANDA IS RIGHT. THE RAIN CLOUDS HOLD OVER WAKANDA LIKE A VENUE OF BUZZARDS OVER A DYING HERD.
WHOSE SORCERY IS THIS? NAMOR, WHOM THE NOW-KING DID NOT SLAY?
NO. SOMETHING ELSE. THE WOODLANDS CRY OUT. WHERE IS MUJAJI? WHERE IS THOTH WHO CIVILIZED MEN? WHERE IS THE SHAPER?
QUIET BROTHERS, LET MY NEPHEW SPEAK. EVEN THE EYES OF NEHANDA HAVE LIMITS.
YES, MY SON, TELL US, WHAT HAS HAPPENED?

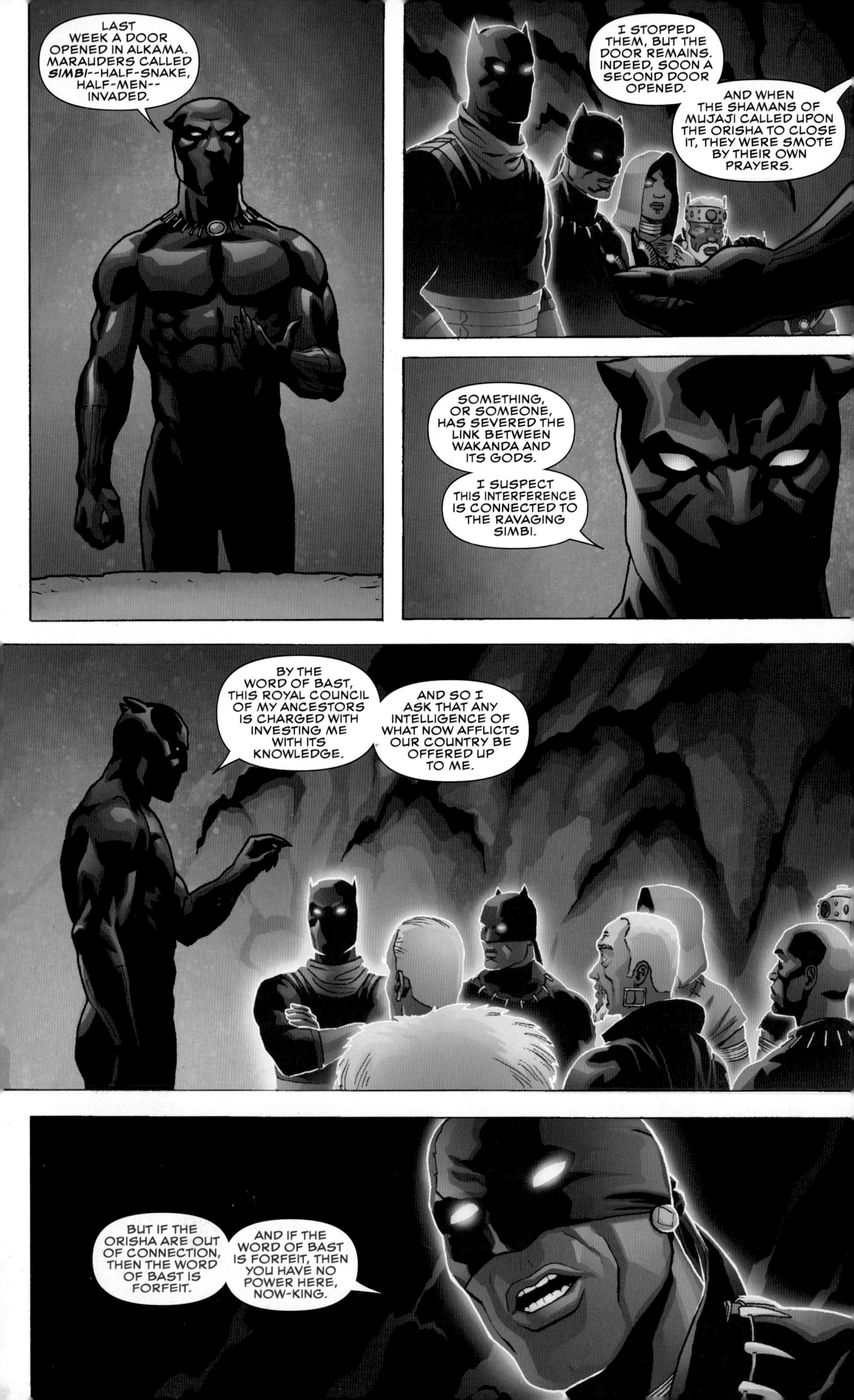
LAST WEEK A DOOR OPENED IN ALKAMA. MARAUDERS CALLED SIMBI--HALF-SNAKE, HALF-MEN--INVADED.
I STOPPED THEM, BUT THE DOOR REMAINS. INDEED, SOON A SECOND DOOR OPENED.
AND WHEN THE SHAMANS OF MUJAJI CALLED UPON THE ORISHA TO CLOSE IT, THEY WERE SMOTE BY THEIR OWN PRAYERS.
SOMETHING, OR SOMEONE, HAS SEVERED THE LINK BETWEEN WAKANDA AND ITS GODS.
I SUSPECT THIS INTERFERENCE IS CONNECTED TO THE RAVAGING SIMBI.
BY THE WORD OF BAST, THIS ROYAL COUNCIL OF MY ANCESTORS IS CHARGED WITH INVESTING ME WITH ITS KNOWLEDGE.
AND SO I ASK THAT ANY INTELLIGENCE OF WHAT NOW AFFLICTS OUR COUNTRY BE OFFERED UP TO ME.
BUT IF THE ORISHA ARE OUT OF CONNECTION, THEN THE WORD OF BAST IS FORFEIT.
AND IF THE WORD OF BAST IS FORFEIT, THEN YOU HAVE NO POWER HERE, NOW-KING.

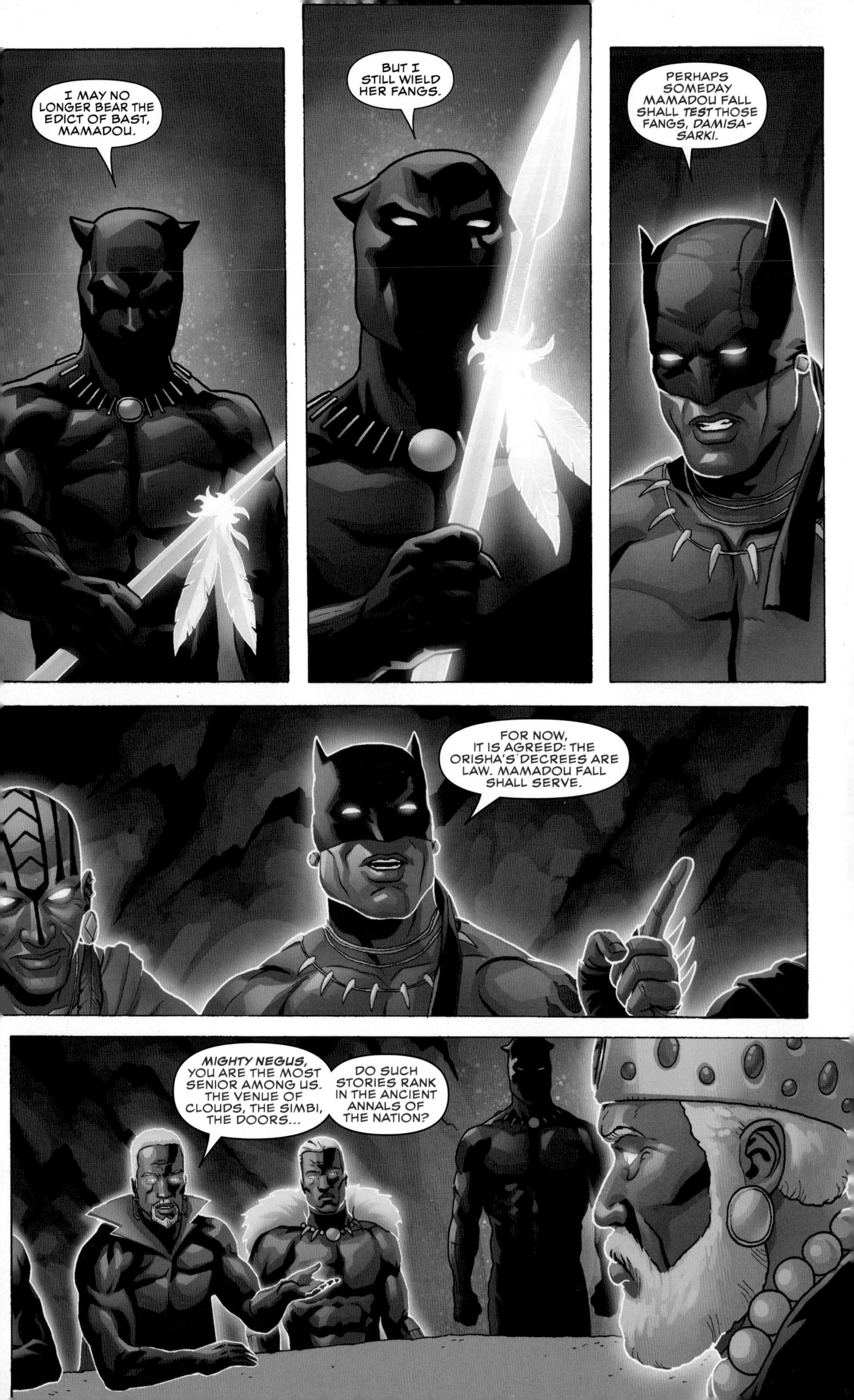
I MAY NO LONGER BEAR THE EDICT OF BAST, MAMADOU.
BUT I STILL WIELD HER FANGS.
PERHAPS SOMEDAY MAMADOU FALL SHALL *TEST* THOSE FANGS, *DAMISA-SARKI.*
FOR NOW, IT IS AGREED: THE ORISHA'S DECREES ARE LAW. MAMADOU FALL SHALL SERVE.
MIGHTY NEGUS, YOU ARE THE MOST SENIOR AMONG US. THE VENUE OF CLOUDS, THE SIMBI, THE DOORS...
DO SUCH STORIES RANK IN THE ANCIENT ANNALS OF THE NATION?

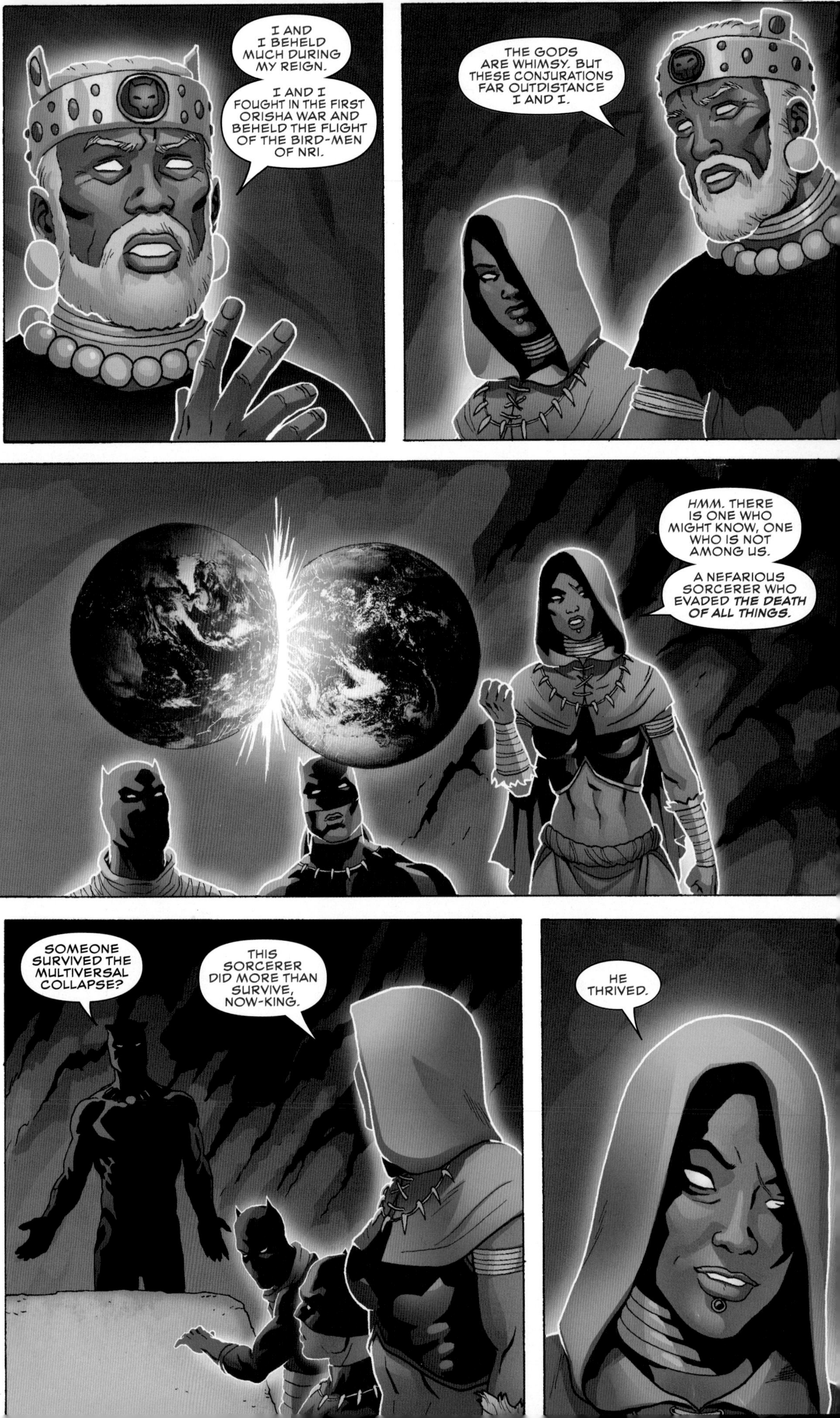
I AND I BEHELD MUCH DURING MY REIGN.
I AND I FOUGHT IN THE FIRST ORISHA WAR AND BEHELD THE FLIGHT OF THE BIRD-MEN OF NRI.
THE GODS ARE WHIMSY. BUT THESE CONJURATIONS FAR OUTDISTANCE I AND I.
HMM. THERE IS ONE WHO MIGHT KNOW, ONE WHO IS NOT AMONG US.
A NEFARIOUS SORCERER WHO EVADED THE DEATH OF ALL THINGS.
SOMEONE SURVIVED THE MULTIVERSAL COLLAPSE?
THIS SORCERER DID MORE THAN SURVIVE, NOW-KING.
HE THRIVED.

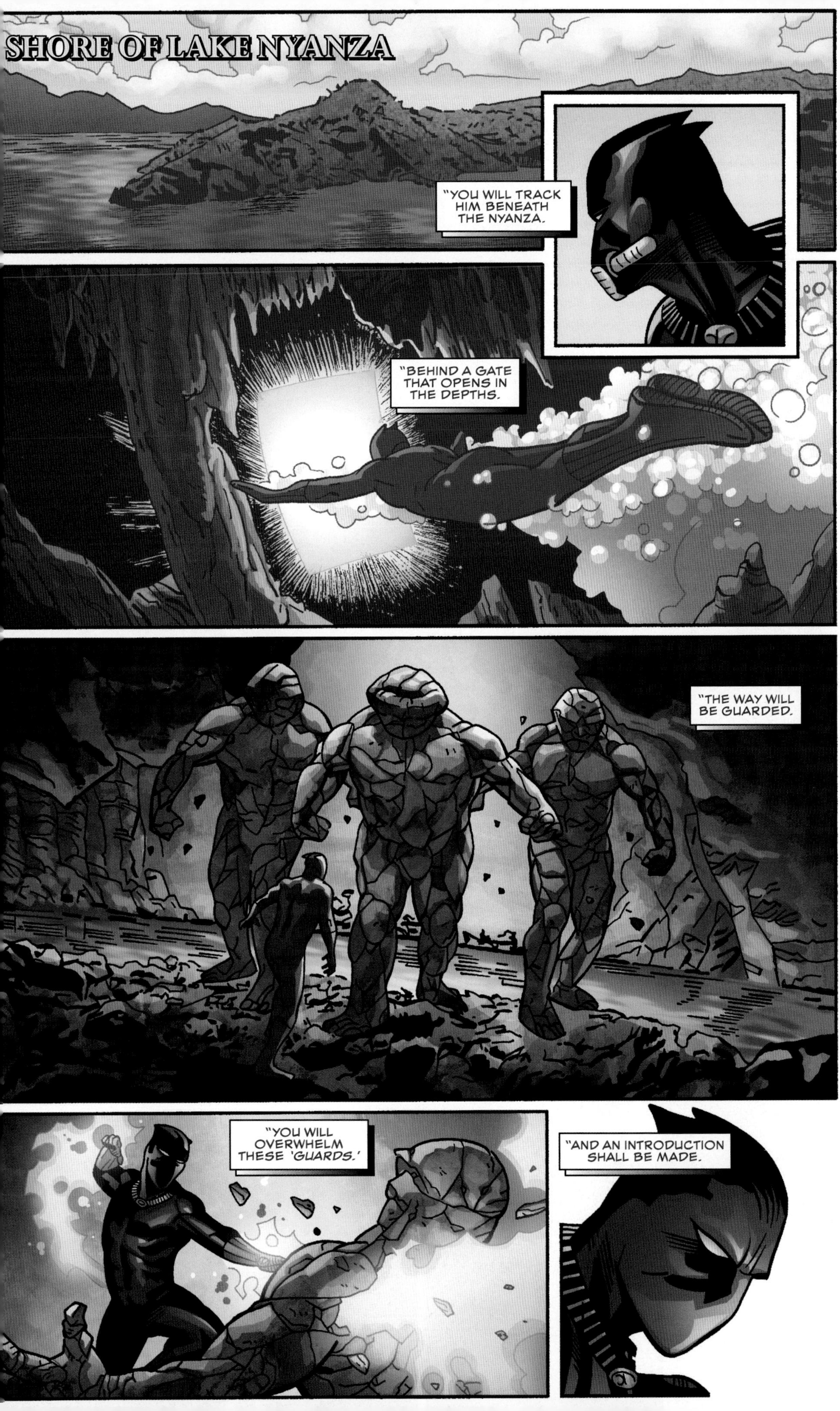
SHORE OF LAKE NYANZA
"YOU WILL TRACK HIM BENEATH THE NYANZA.
"BEHIND A GATE THAT OPENS IN THE DEPTHS.
"THE WAY WILL BE GUARDED.
"YOU WILL OVERWHELM THESE 'GUARDS.'
"AND AN INTRODUCTION SHALL BE MADE.

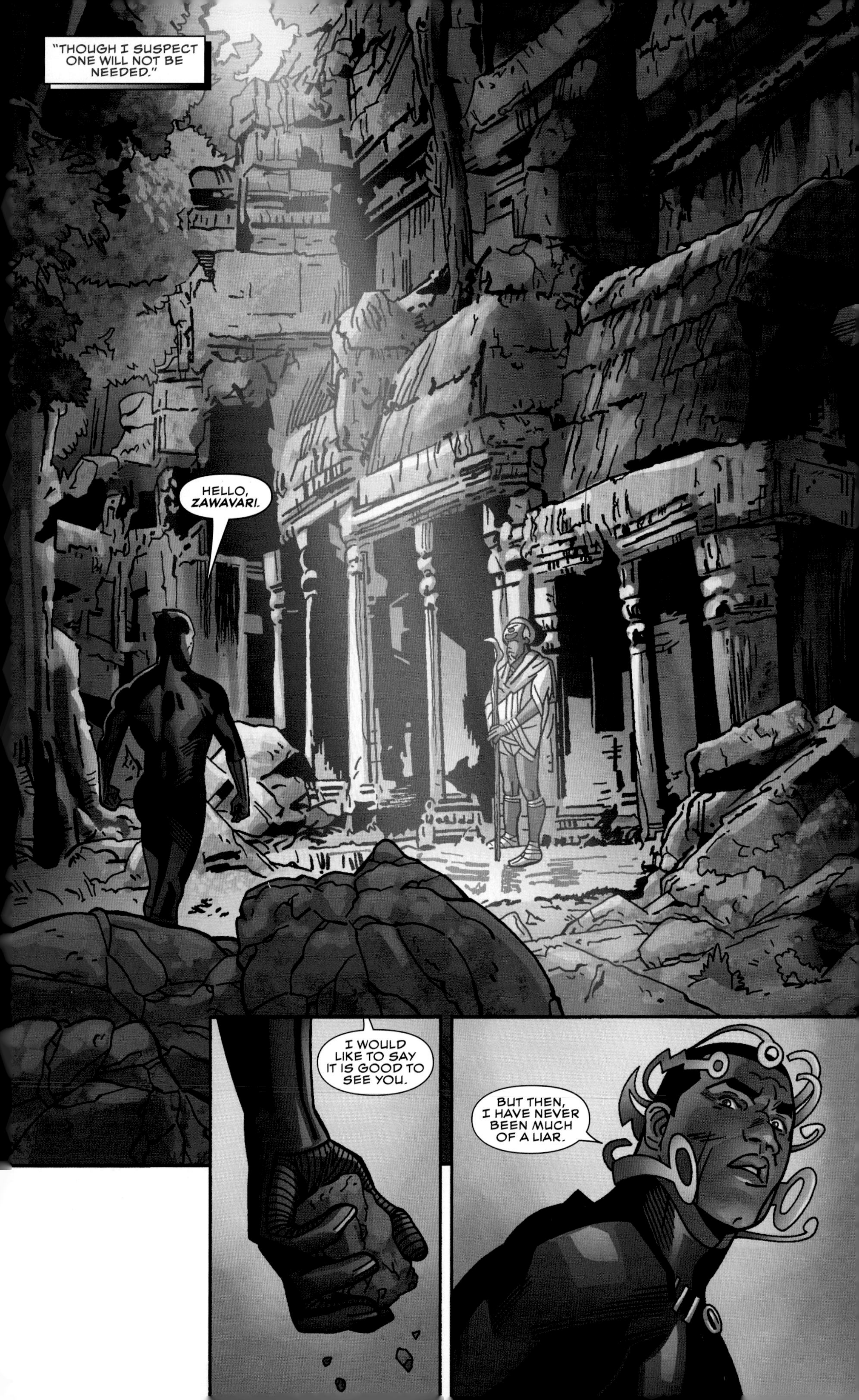
"THOUGH I SUSPECT ONE WILL NOT BE NEEDED."
HELLO, ZAWAVARI.
I WOULD LIKE TO SAY IT IS GOOD TO SEE YOU.
BUT THEN, I HAVE NEVER BEEN MUCH OF A LIAR.

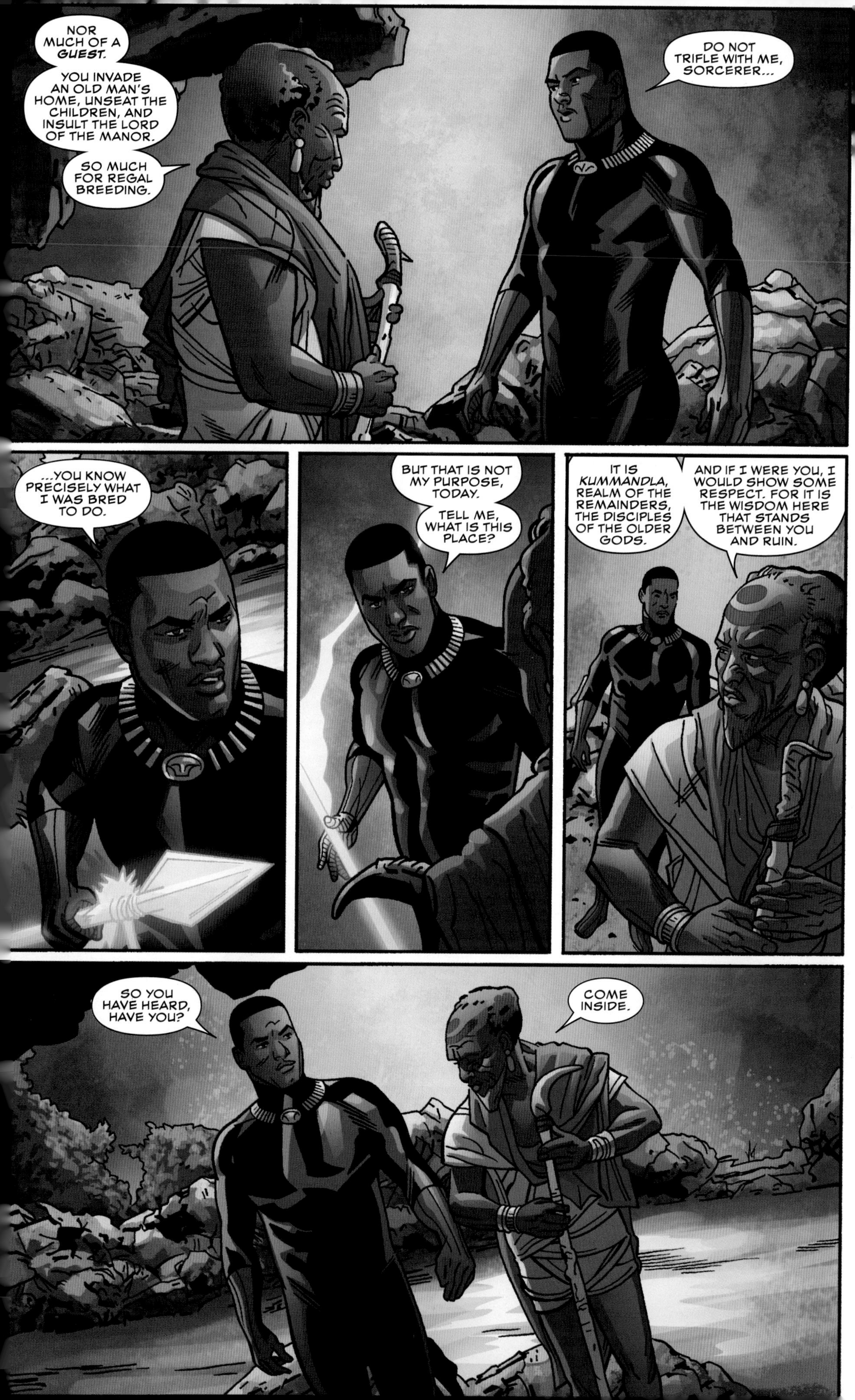
NOR MUCH OF A *GUEST.*
YOU INVADE AN OLD MAN'S HOME, UNSEAT THE CHILDREN, AND INSULT THE LORD OF THE MANOR.
SO MUCH FOR REGAL BREEDING.
DO NOT TRIFLE WITH ME, SORCERER...
...YOU KNOW PRECISELY WHAT I WAS BRED TO DO.
BUT THAT IS NOT MY PURPOSE, TODAY.
TELL ME, WHAT IS THIS PLACE?
IT IS *KUMMANDLA,* REALM OF THE REMAINDERS, THE DISCIPLES OF THE OLDER GODS.
AND IF I WERE YOU, I WOULD SHOW SOME RESPECT. FOR IT IS THE WISDOM HERE THAT STANDS BETWEEN YOU AND RUIN.
SO YOU HAVE HEARD, HAVE YOU?
COME INSIDE.

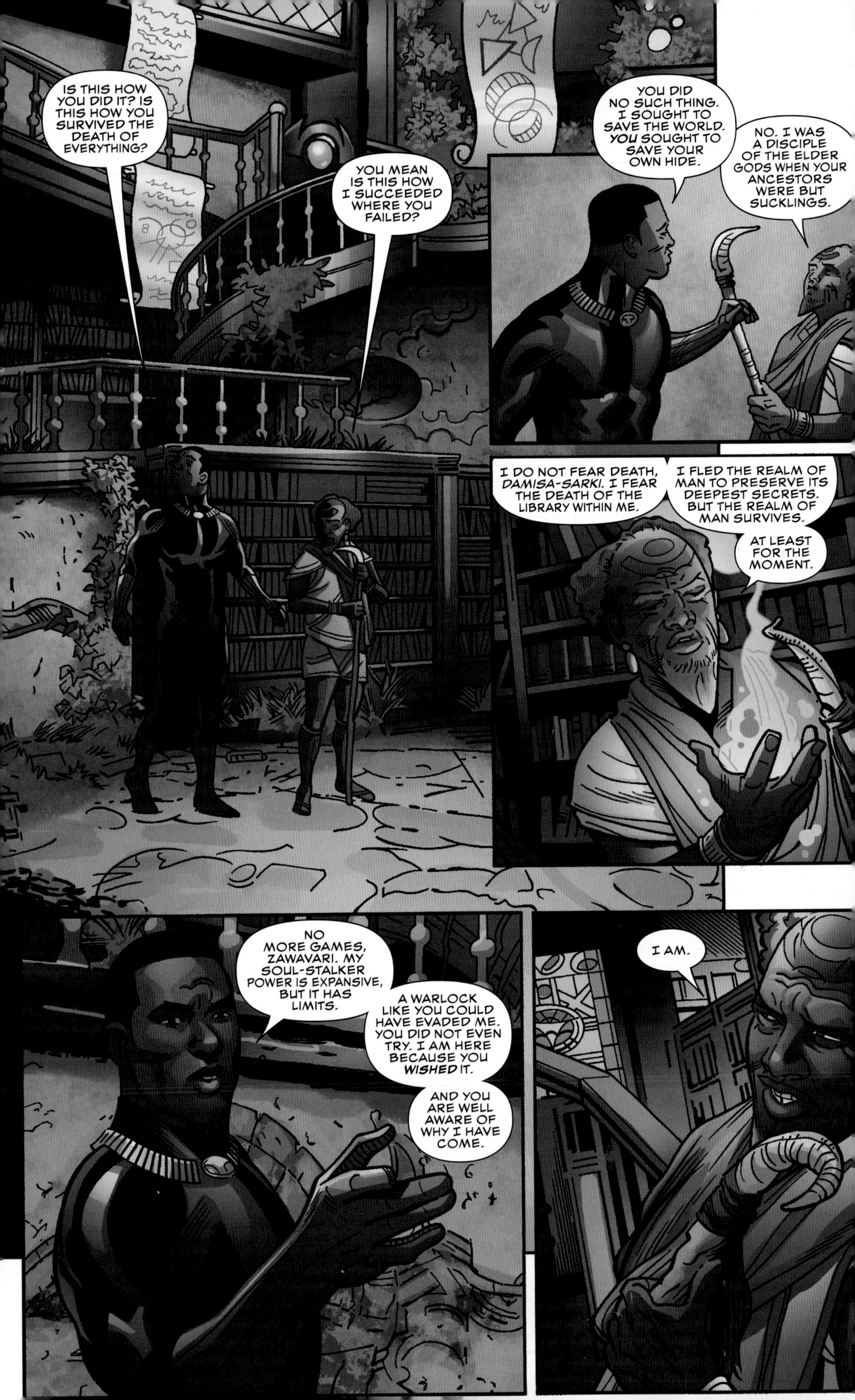
IS THIS HOW YOU DID IT? IS THIS HOW YOU SURVIVED THE DEATH OF EVERYTHING?
YOU MEAN IS THIS HOW I SUCCEEDED WHERE YOU FAILED?
YOU DID NO SUCH THING. I SOUGHT TO SAVE THE WORLD. YOU SOUGHT TO SAVE YOUR OWN HIDE.
NO. I WAS A DISCIPLE OF THE ELDER GODS WHEN YOUR ANCESTORS WERE BUT SUCKLINGS.
I DO NOT FEAR DEATH, DAMISA-SARKI. I FEAR THE DEATH OF THE LIBRARY WITHIN ME.
I FLED THE REALM OF MAN TO PRESERVE ITS DEEPEST SECRETS. BUT THE REALM OF MAN SURVIVES.
AT LEAST FOR THE MOMENT.
NO MORE GAMES, ZAWAVARI. MY SOUL-STALKER POWER IS EXPANSIVE, BUT IT HAS LIMITS.
A WARLOCK LIKE YOU COULD HAVE EVADED ME. YOU DID NOT EVEN TRY. I AM HERE BECAUSE YOU WISHED IT.
AND YOU ARE WELL AWARE OF WHY I HAVE COME.
I AM.

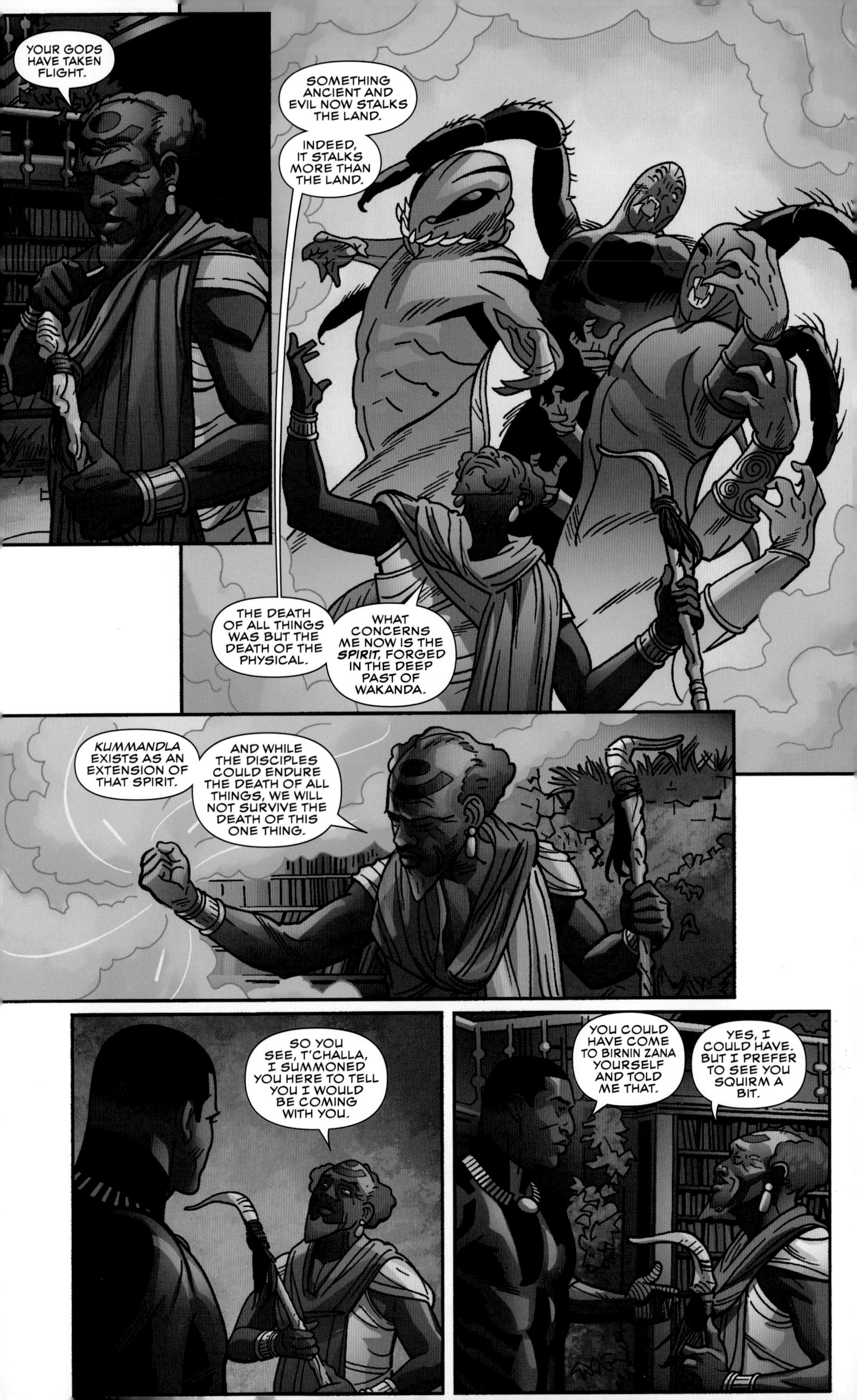
YOUR GODS HAVE TAKEN FLIGHT.
SOMETHING ANCIENT AND EVIL NOW STALKS THE LAND.
INDEED, IT STALKS MORE THAN THE LAND.
THE DEATH OF ALL THINGS WAS BUT THE DEATH OF THE PHYSICAL.
WHAT CONCERNS ME NOW IS THE *SPIRIT*, FORGED IN THE DEEP PAST OF WAKANDA.
KUMMANDLA EXISTS AS AN EXTENSION OF THAT SPIRIT.
AND WHILE THE DISCIPLES COULD ENDURE THE DEATH OF ALL THINGS, WE WILL NOT SURVIVE THE DEATH OF THIS ONE THING.
SO YOU SEE, T'CHALLA, I SUMMONED YOU HERE TO TELL YOU I WOULD BE COMING WITH YOU.
YOU COULD HAVE COME TO BIRNIN ZANA YOURSELF AND TOLD ME THAT.
YES, I COULD HAVE. BUT I PREFER TO SEE YOU SQUIRM A BIT.

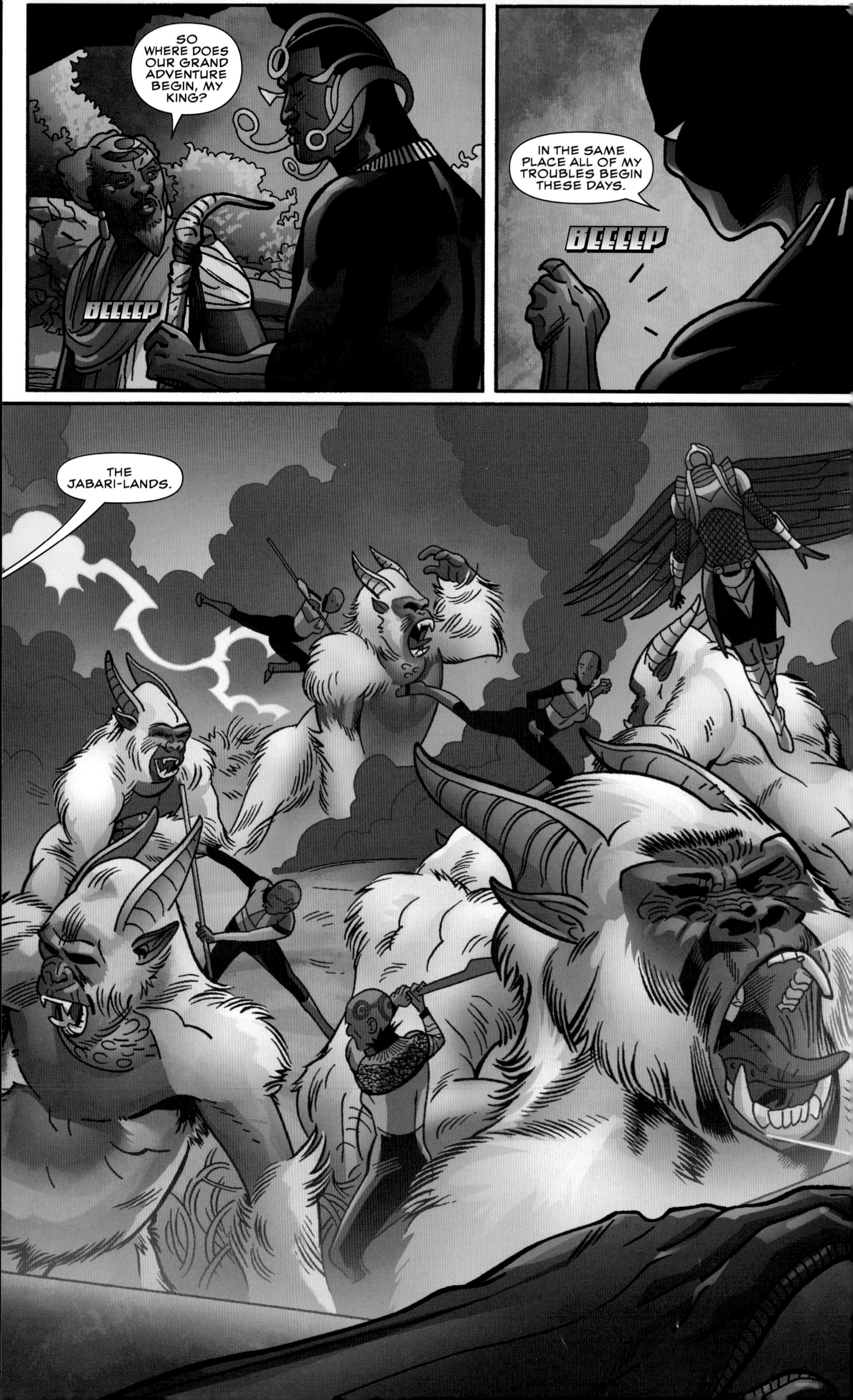
SO WHERE DOES OUR GRAND ADVENTURE BEGIN, MY KING?
BEEEEP
IN THE SAME PLACE ALL OF MY TROUBLES BEGIN THESE DAYS.
BEEEEP
THE JABARI-LANDS.

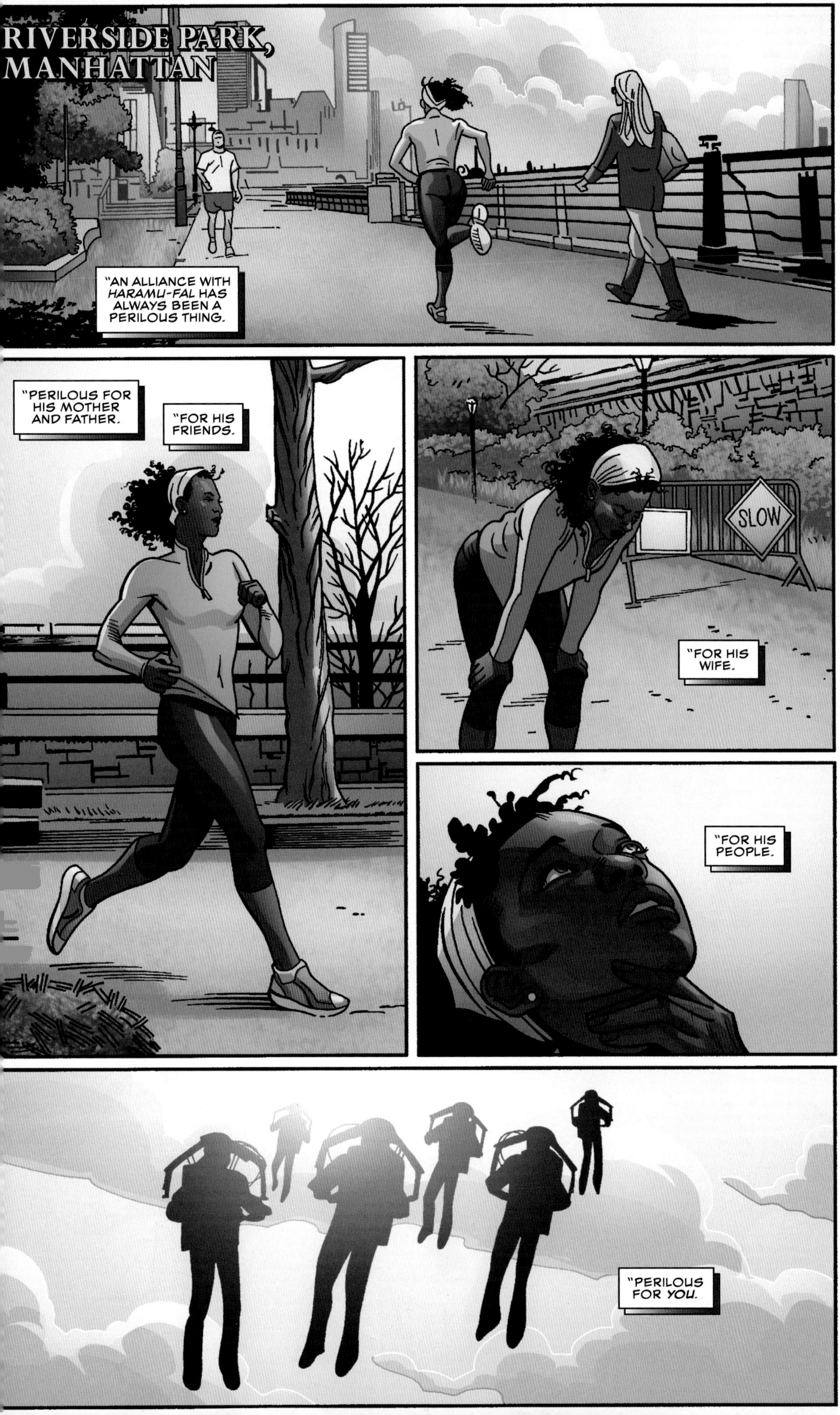
RIVERSIDE PARK, MANHATTAN
"AN ALLIANCE WITH HARAMU-FAL HAS ALWAYS BEEN A PERILOUS THING.
"PERILOUS FOR HIS MOTHER AND FATHER.
"FOR HIS FRIENDS.
SLOW
"FOR HIS WIFE.
"FOR HIS PEOPLE.
"PERILOUS FOR *YOU*.

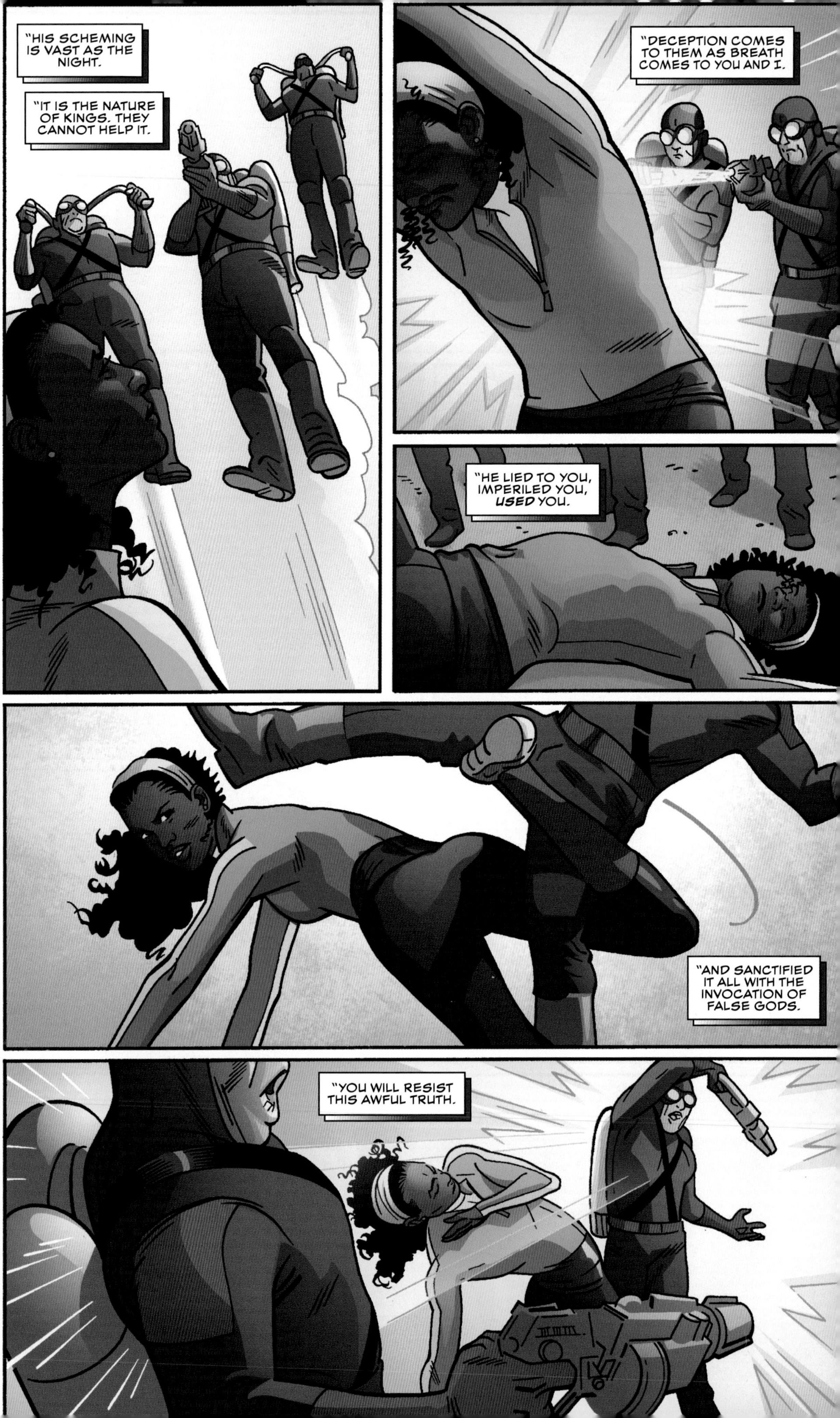
"HIS SCHEMING IS VAST AS THE NIGHT.
"IT IS THE NATURE OF KINGS. THEY CANNOT HELP IT.
"DECEPTION COMES TO THEM AS BREATH COMES TO YOU AND I.
"HE LIED TO YOU, IMPERILED YOU, *USED* YOU.
"AND SANCTIFIED IT ALL WITH THE INVOCATION OF FALSE GODS.
"YOU WILL RESIST THIS AWFUL TRUTH.

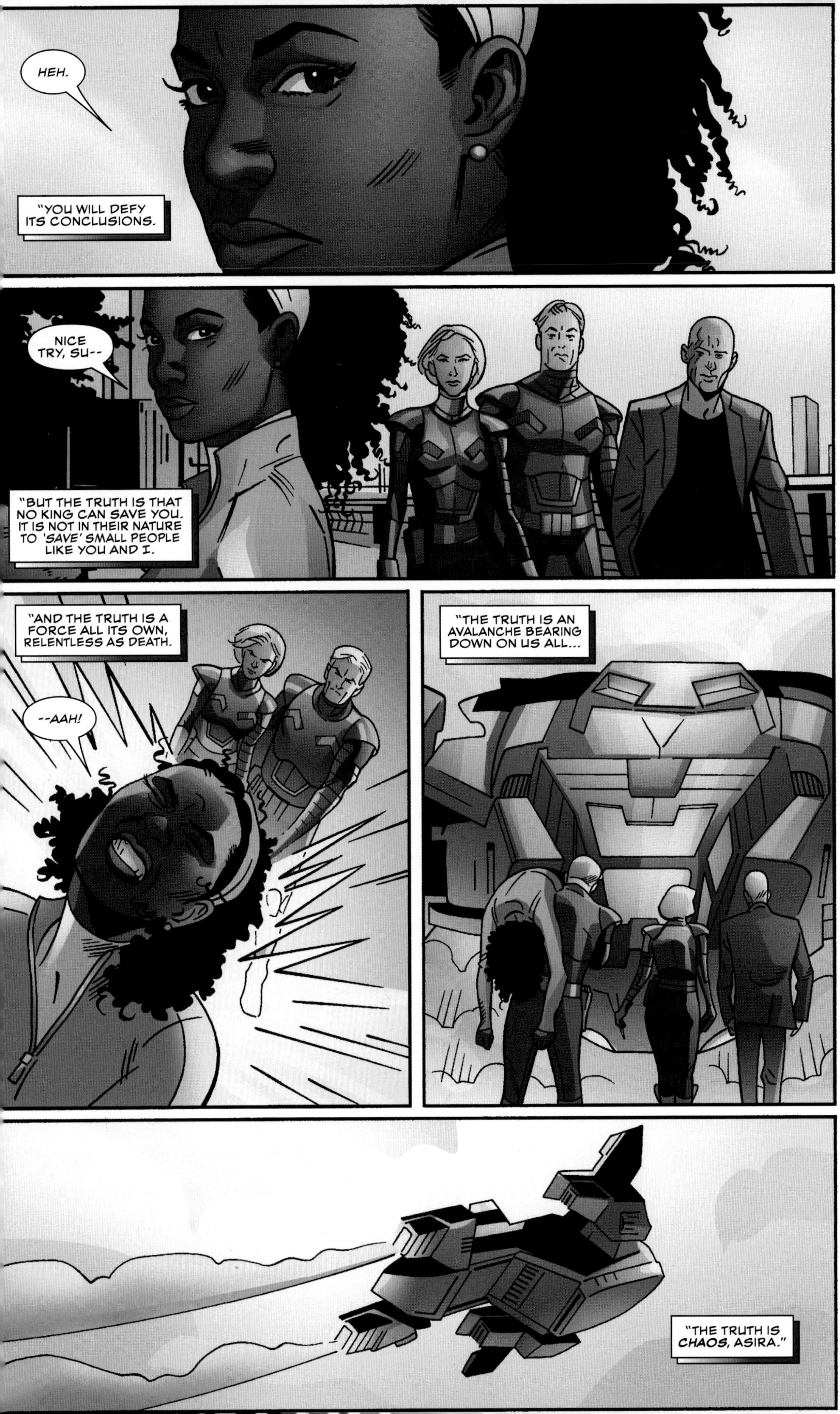
HEH.
"YOU WILL DEFY ITS CONCLUSIONS.
NICE TRY, SU--
"BUT THE TRUTH IS THAT NO KING CAN SAVE YOU. IT IS NOT IN THEIR NATURE TO 'SAVE' SMALL PEOPLE LIKE YOU AND I.
"AND THE TRUTH IS A FORCE ALL ITS OWN, RELENTLESS AS DEATH.
--AAH!
"THE TRUTH IS AN AVALANCHE BEARING DOWN ON US ALL...
"THE TRUTH IS CHAOS, ASIRA."

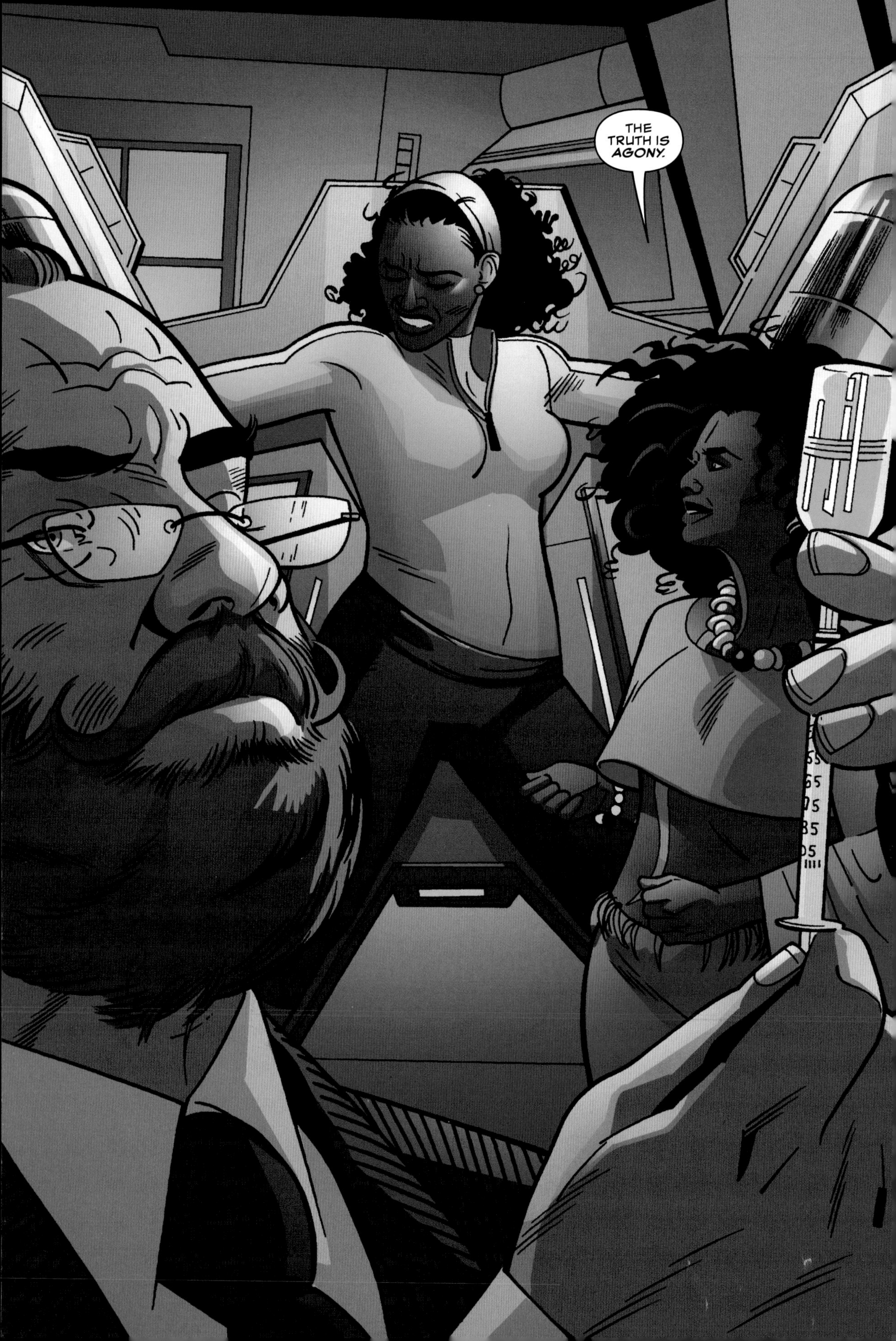
THE TRUTH IS AGONY.

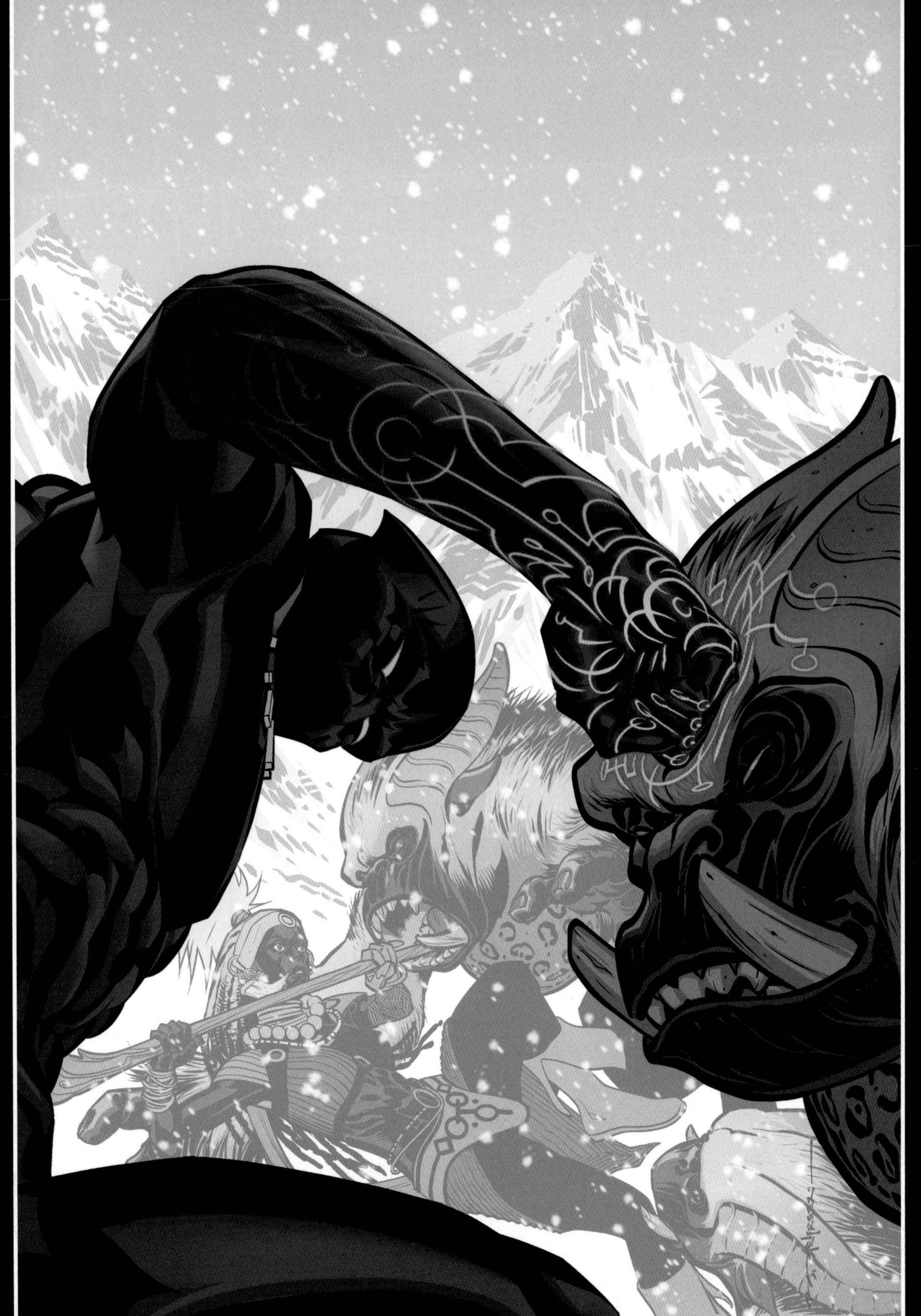

15

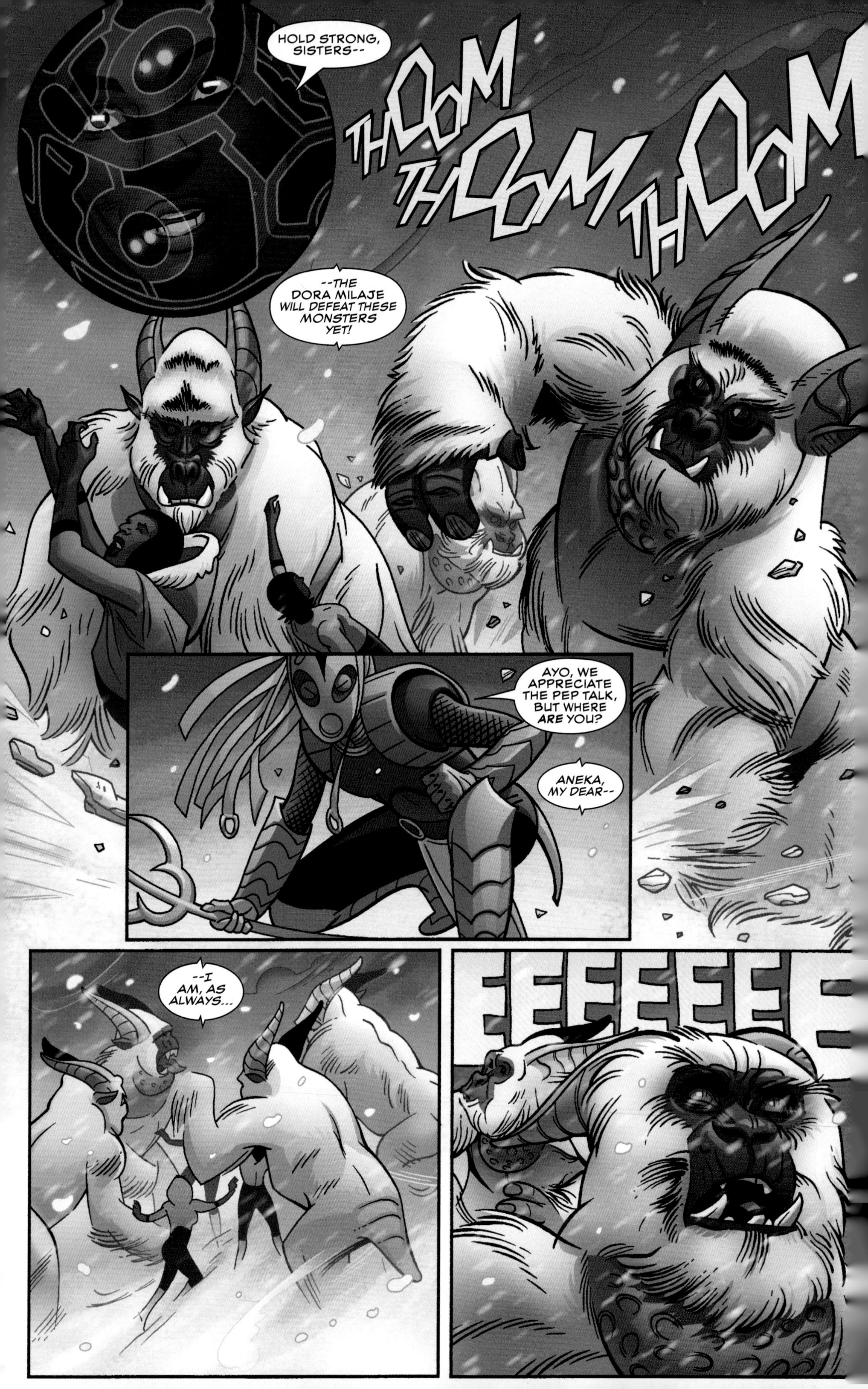
HOLD STRONG, SISTERS--
THOOM THOOM THOOM
--THE DORA MILAJE WILL DEFEAT THESE MONSTERS YET!
AYO, WE APPRECIATE THE PEP TALK, BUT WHERE ARE YOU?
ANEKA, MY DEAR--
--I AM, AS ALWAYS...
EEEEEEE

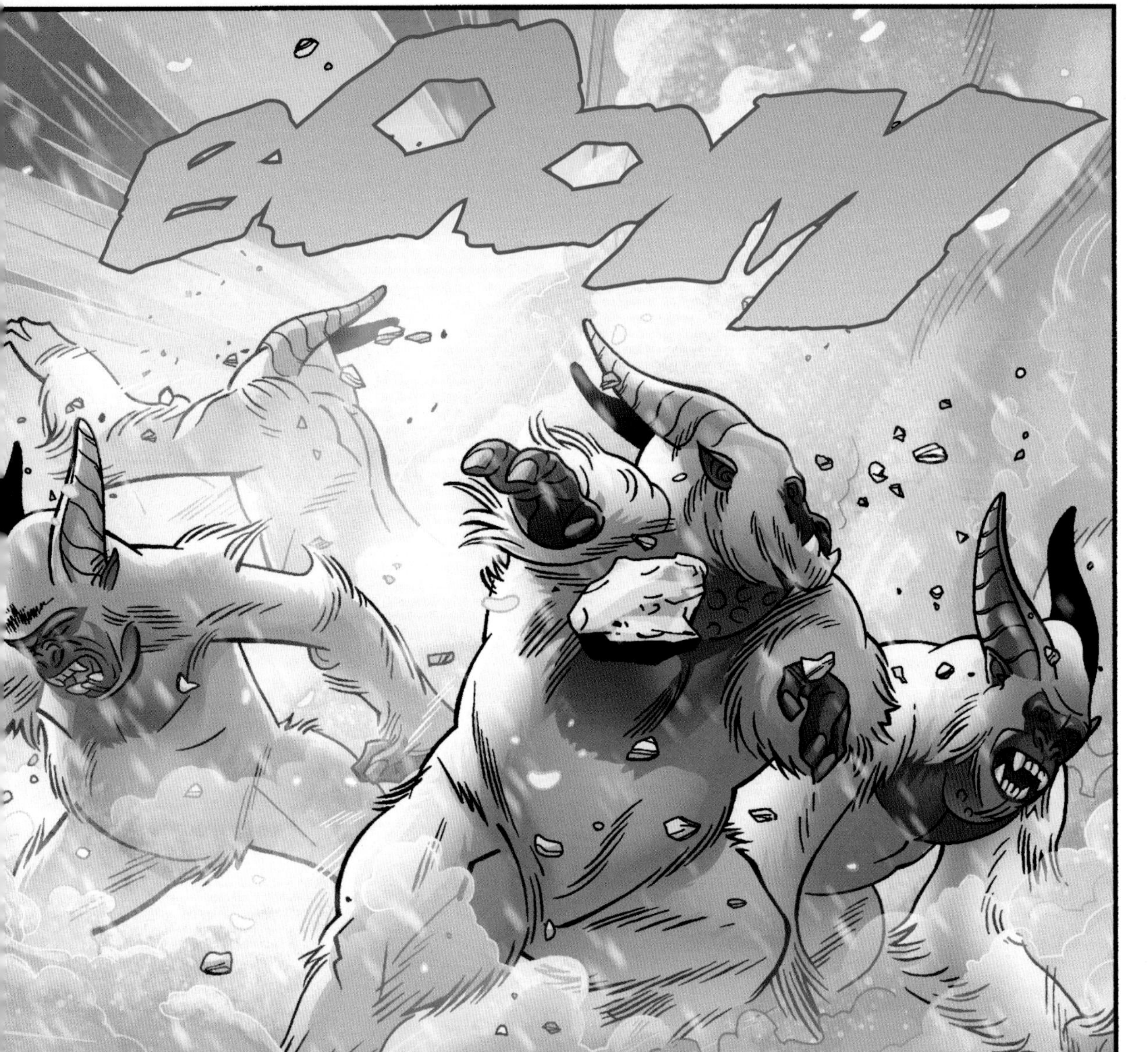
BOOM

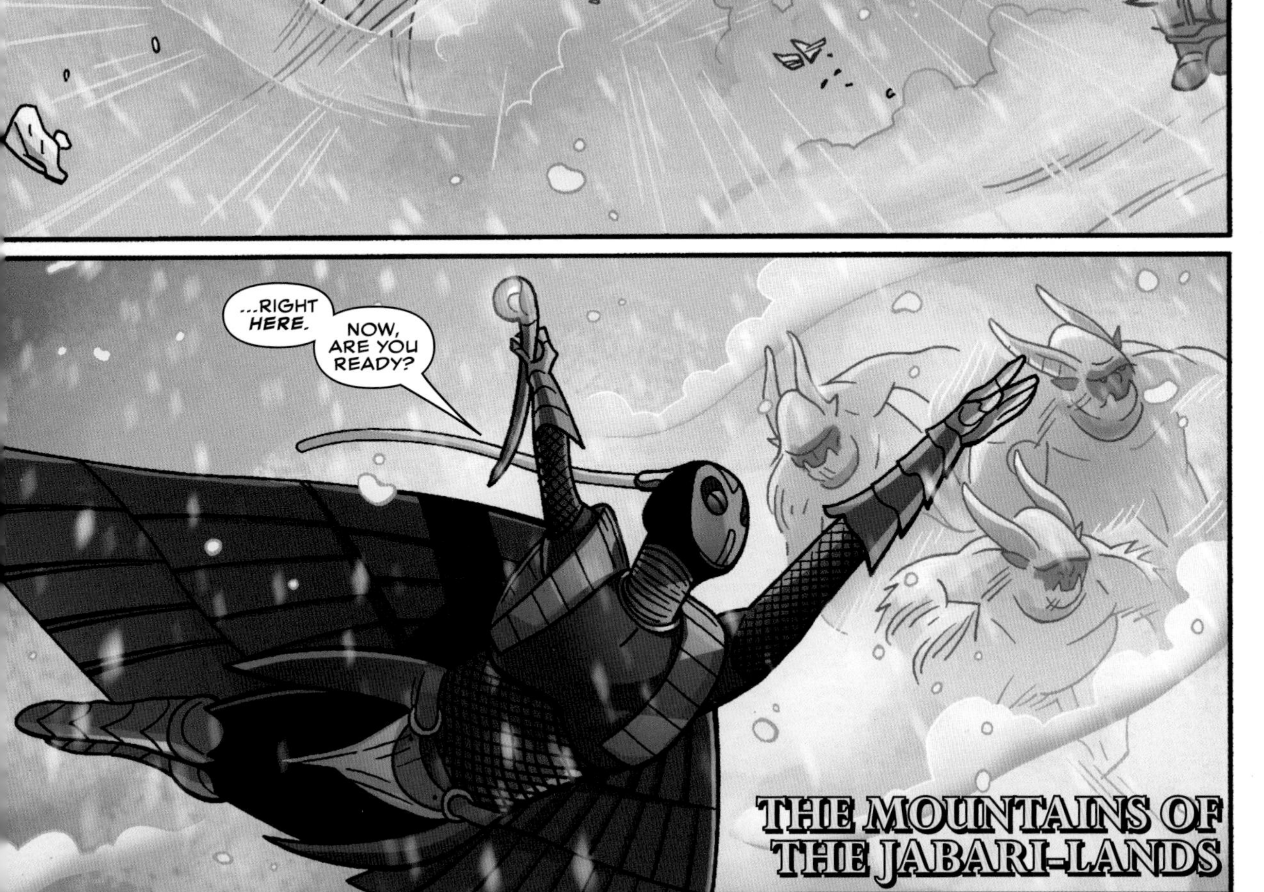
...RIGHT HERE.
NOW, ARE YOU READY?
THE MOUNTAINS OF THE JABARI-LANDS

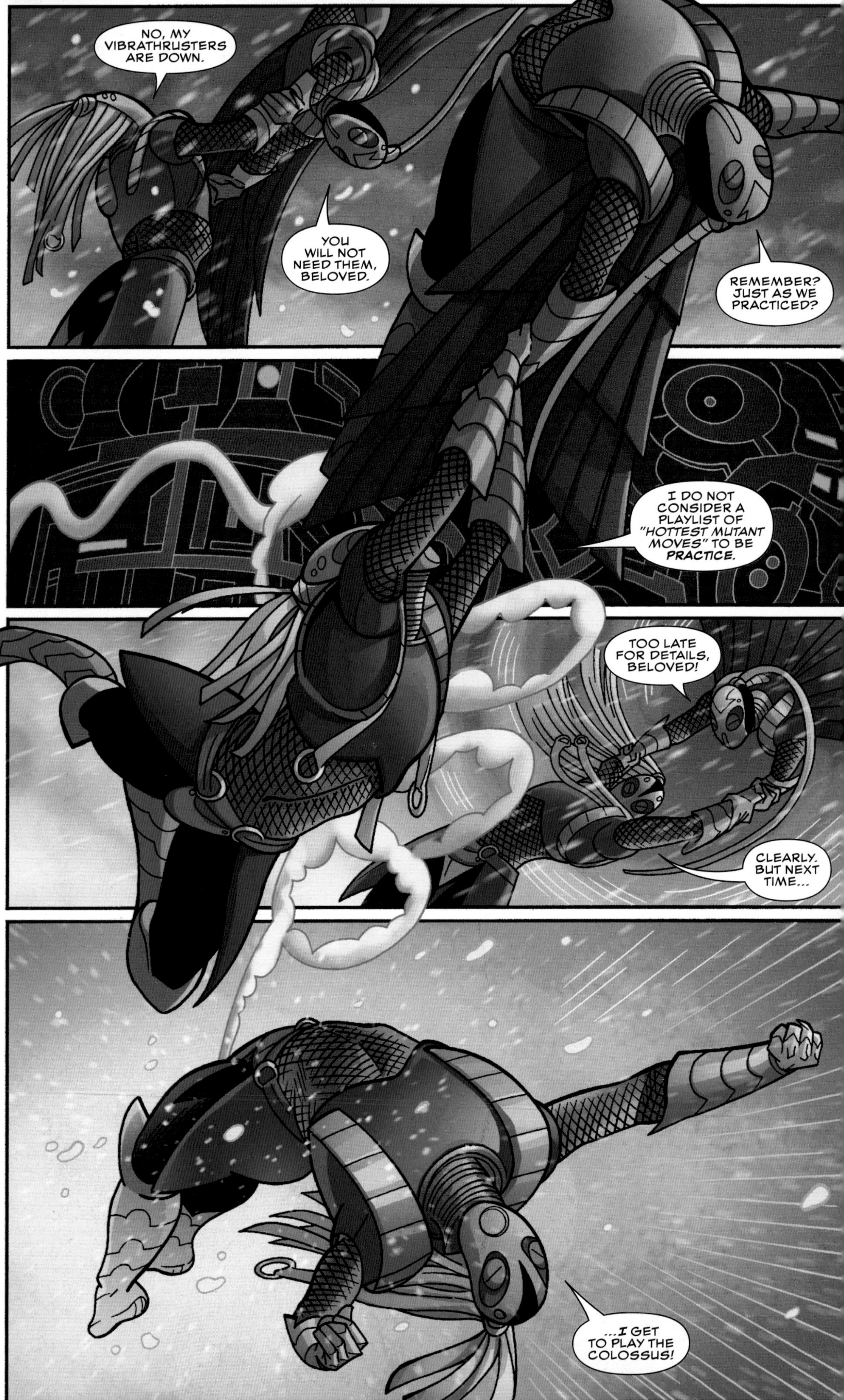
NO, MY VIBRATHRUSTERS ARE DOWN.
YOU WILL NOT NEED THEM, BELOVED.
REMEMBER? JUST AS WE PRACTICED?
I DO NOT CONSIDER A PLAYLIST OF "HOTTEST MUTANT MOVES" TO BE PRACTICE.
TOO LATE FOR DETAILS, BELOVED!
CLEARLY. BUT NEXT TIME...
...I GET TO PLAY THE COLOSSUS!

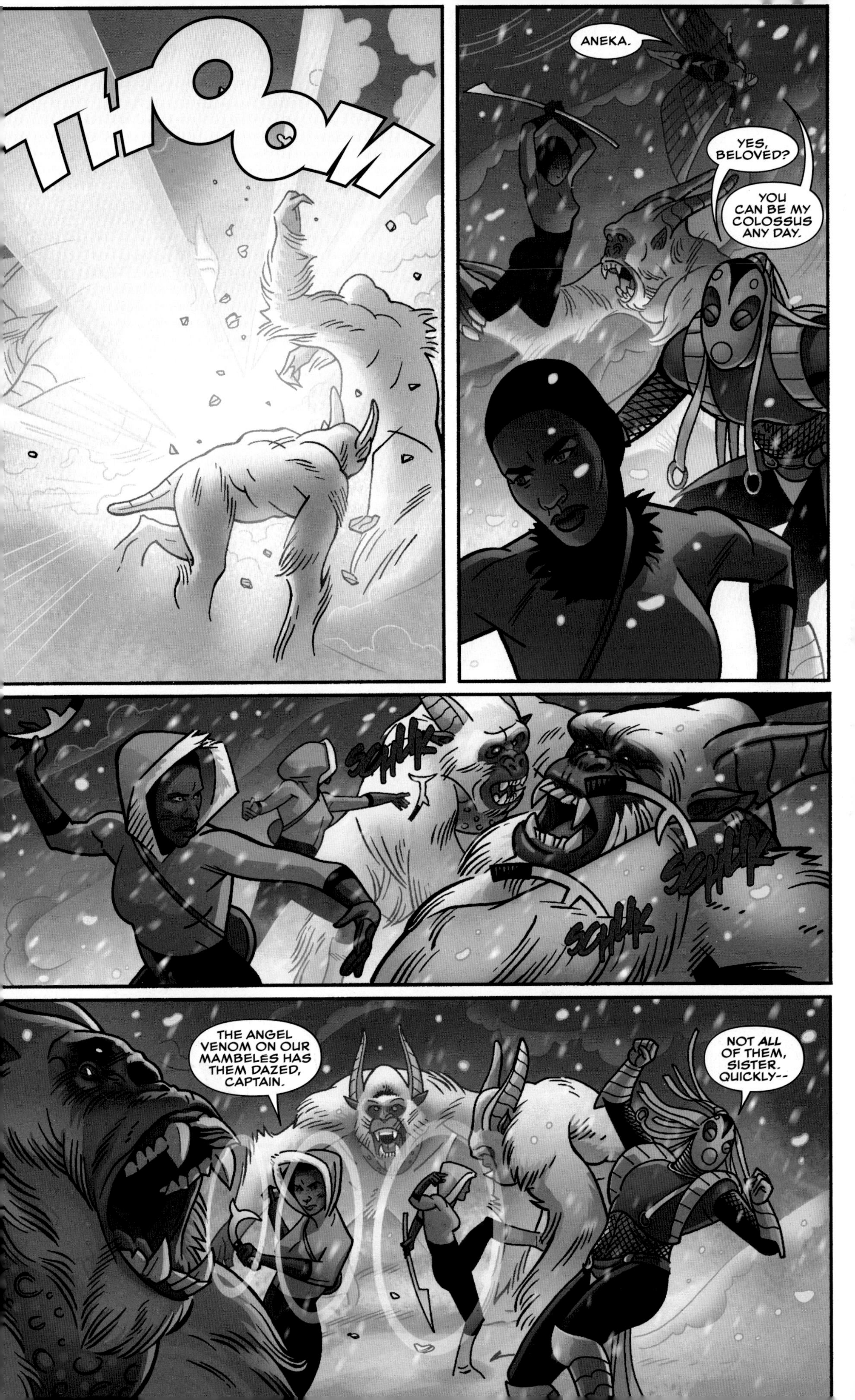
THOOM
ANEKA.
YES, BELOVED?
YOU CAN BE MY COLOSSUS ANY DAY.
SCHUK
SCHUK
SCHUK
THE ANGEL VENOM ON OUR MAMBELES HAS THEM DAZED, CAPTAIN.
NOT ALL OF THEM, SISTER. QUICKLY--

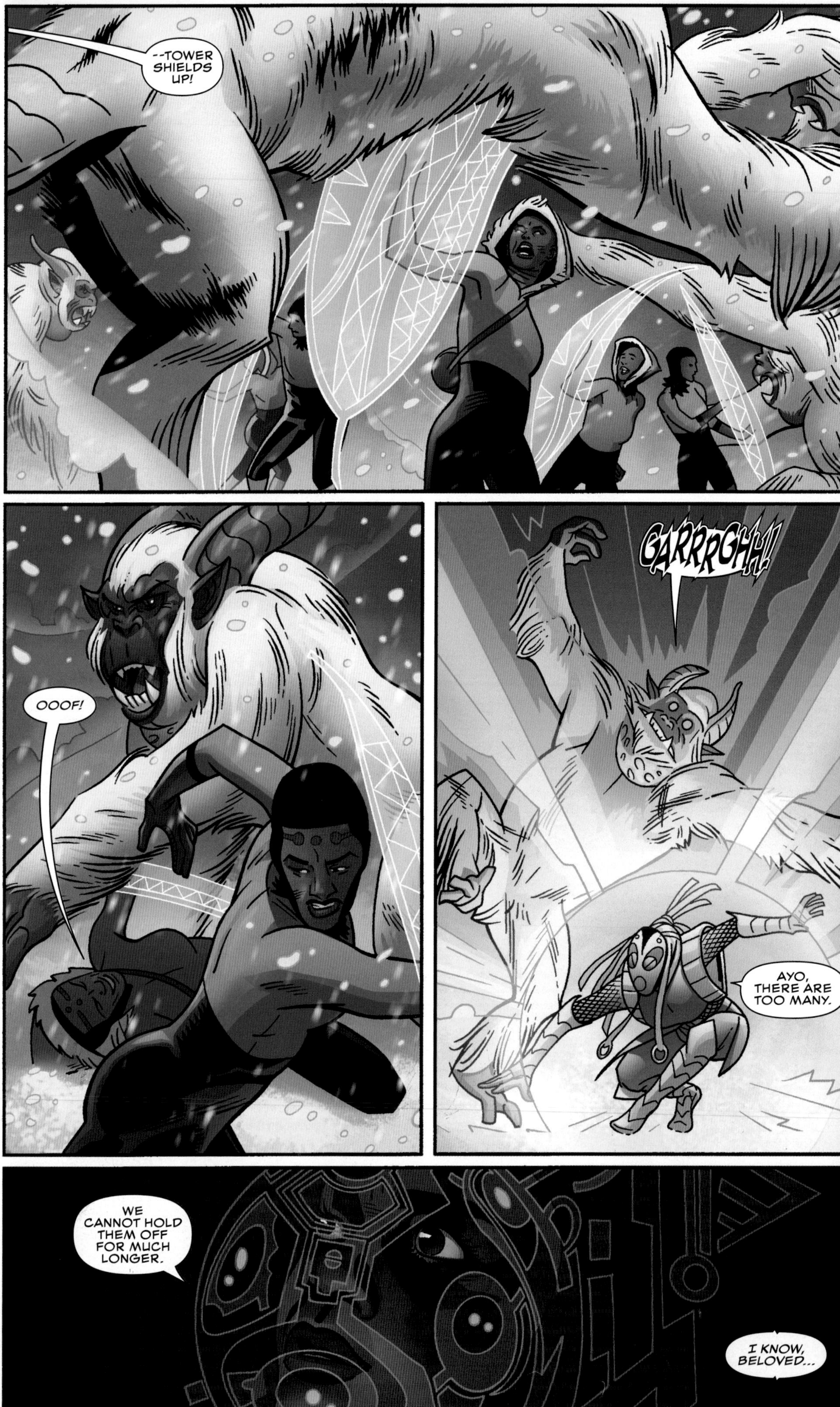
--TOWER SHIELDS UP!
OOOF!
GARRRGHH!!
AYO, THERE ARE TOO MANY.
WE CANNOT HOLD THEM OFF FOR MUCH LONGER.
I KNOW, BELOVED...

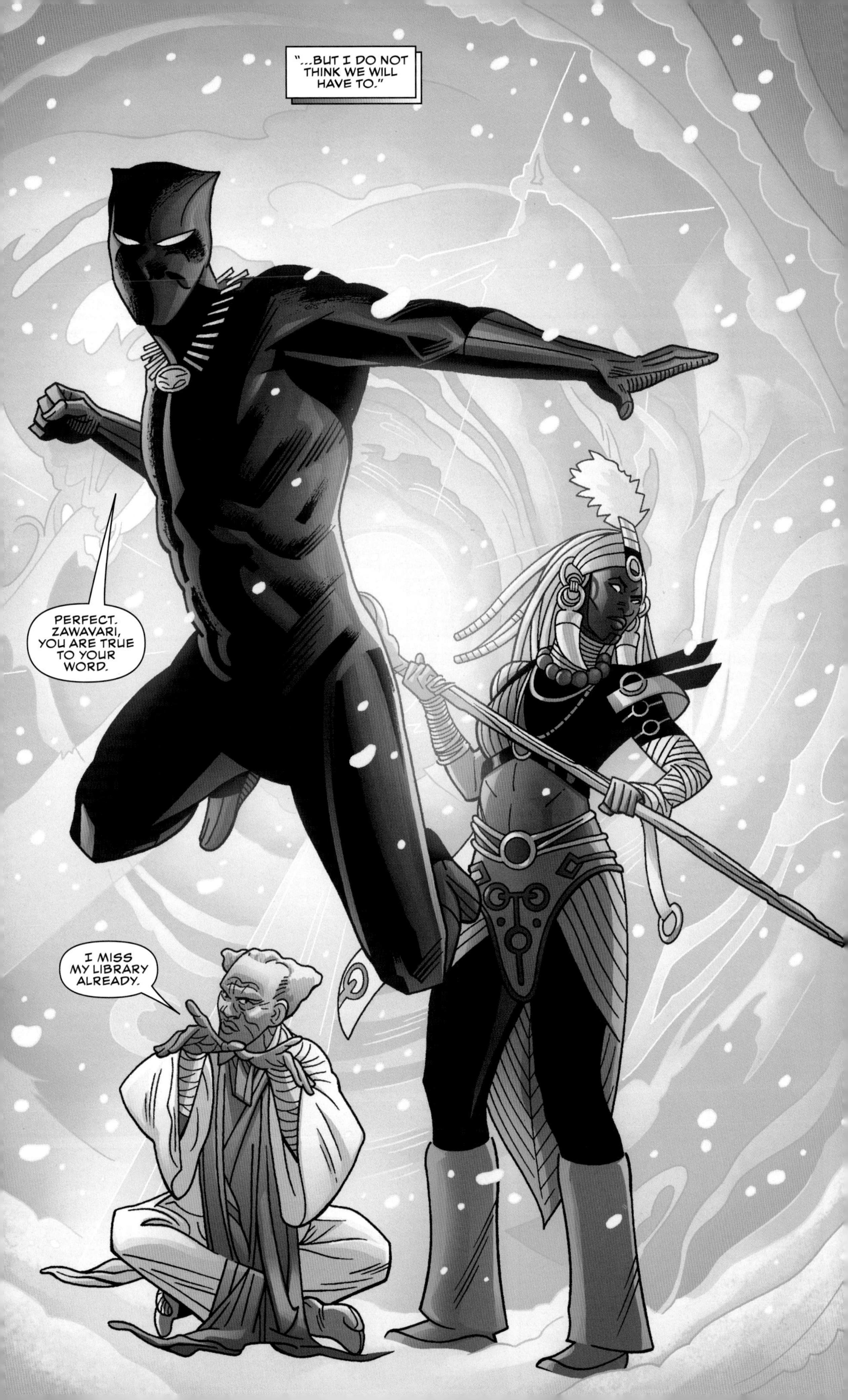
"...BUT I DO NOT THINK WE WILL HAVE TO."
PERFECT. ZAWAVARI, YOU ARE TRUE TO YOUR WORD.
I MISS MY LIBRARY ALREADY.

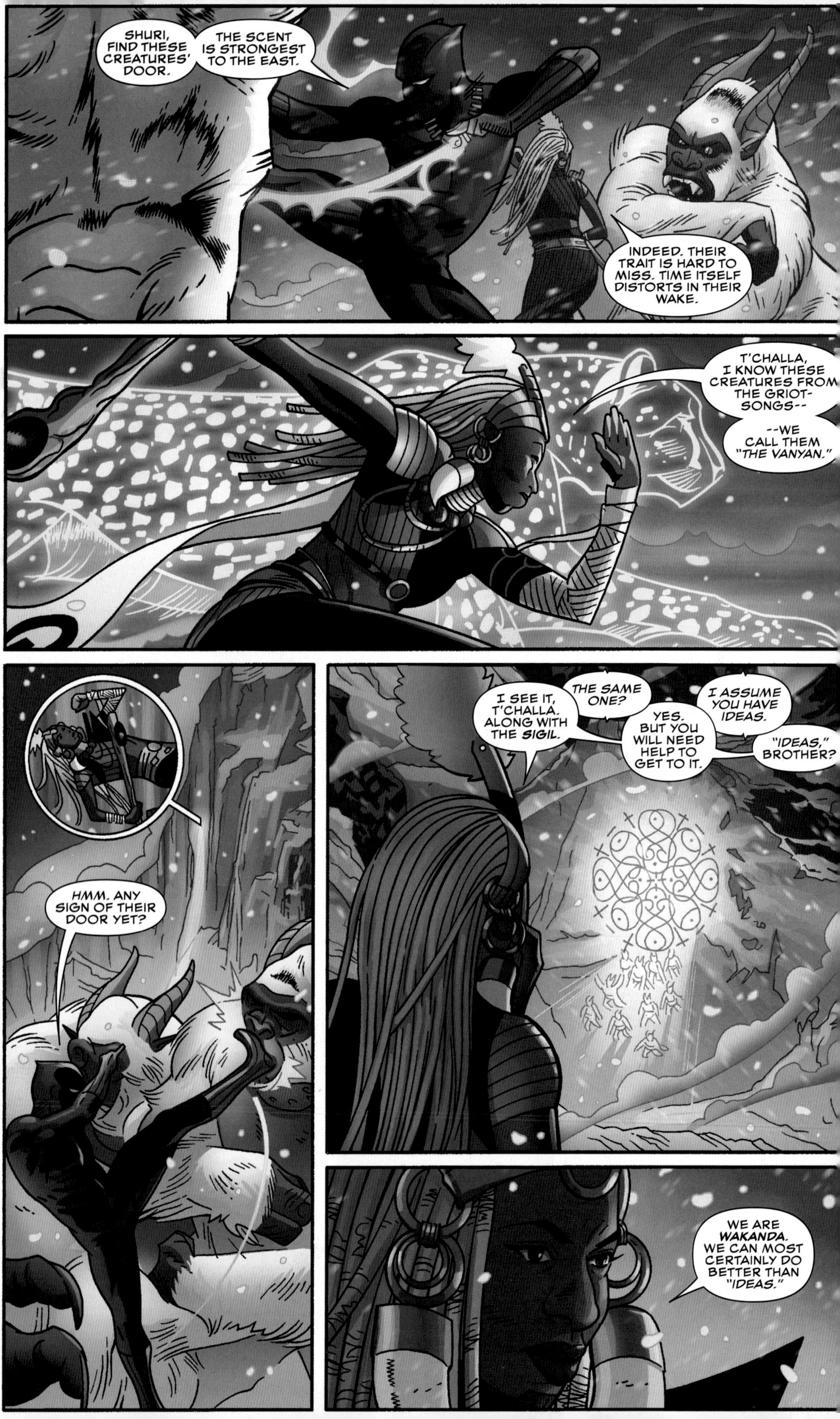
SHURI, FIND THESE CREATURES' DOOR.
THE SCENT IS STRONGEST TO THE EAST.
INDEED. THEIR TRAIT IS HARD TO MISS. TIME ITSELF DISTORTS IN THEIR WAKE.
T'CHALLA, I KNOW THESE CREATURES FROM THE GRIOT-SONGS--
--WE CALL THEM "THE VANYAN."
HMM. ANY SIGN OF THEIR DOOR YET?
I SEE IT, T'CHALLA. ALONG WITH THE SIGIL.
THE SAME ONE?
YES. BUT YOU WILL NEED HELP TO GET TO IT.
I ASSUME YOU HAVE IDEAS.
"IDEAS," BROTHER?
WE ARE WAKANDA. WE CAN MOST CERTAINLY DO BETTER THAN "IDEAS."

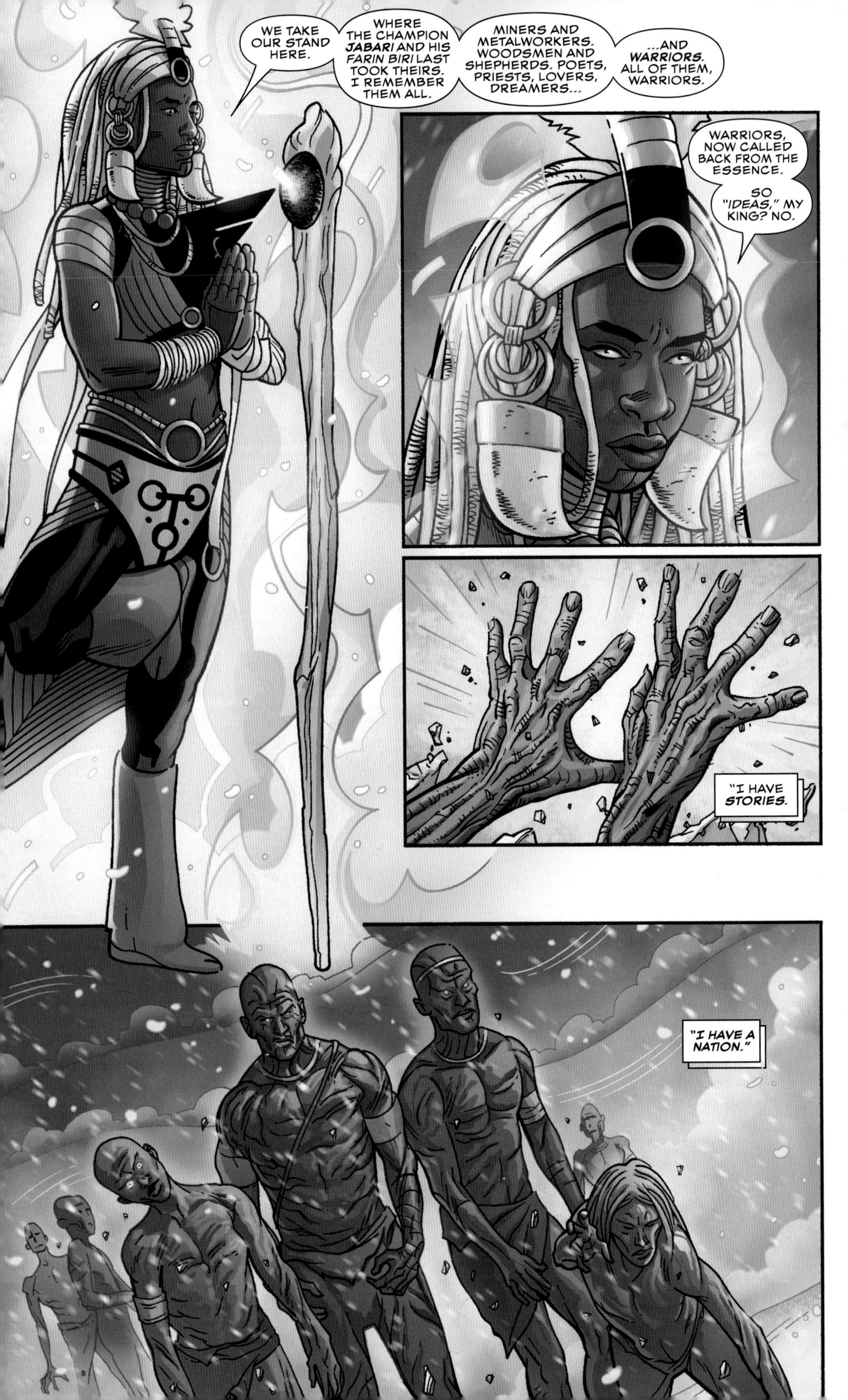
WE TAKE OUR STAND HERE.
WHERE THE CHAMPION JABARI AND HIS FARIN BIRI LAST TOOK THEIRS. I REMEMBER THEM ALL.
MINERS AND METALWORKERS. WOODSMEN AND SHEPHERDS. POETS, PRIESTS, LOVERS, DREAMERS...
...AND WARRIORS. ALL OF THEM, WARRIORS.
WARRIORS, NOW CALLED BACK FROM THE ESSENCE.
SO "IDEAS," MY KING? NO.
"I HAVE STORIES.
"I HAVE A NATION."

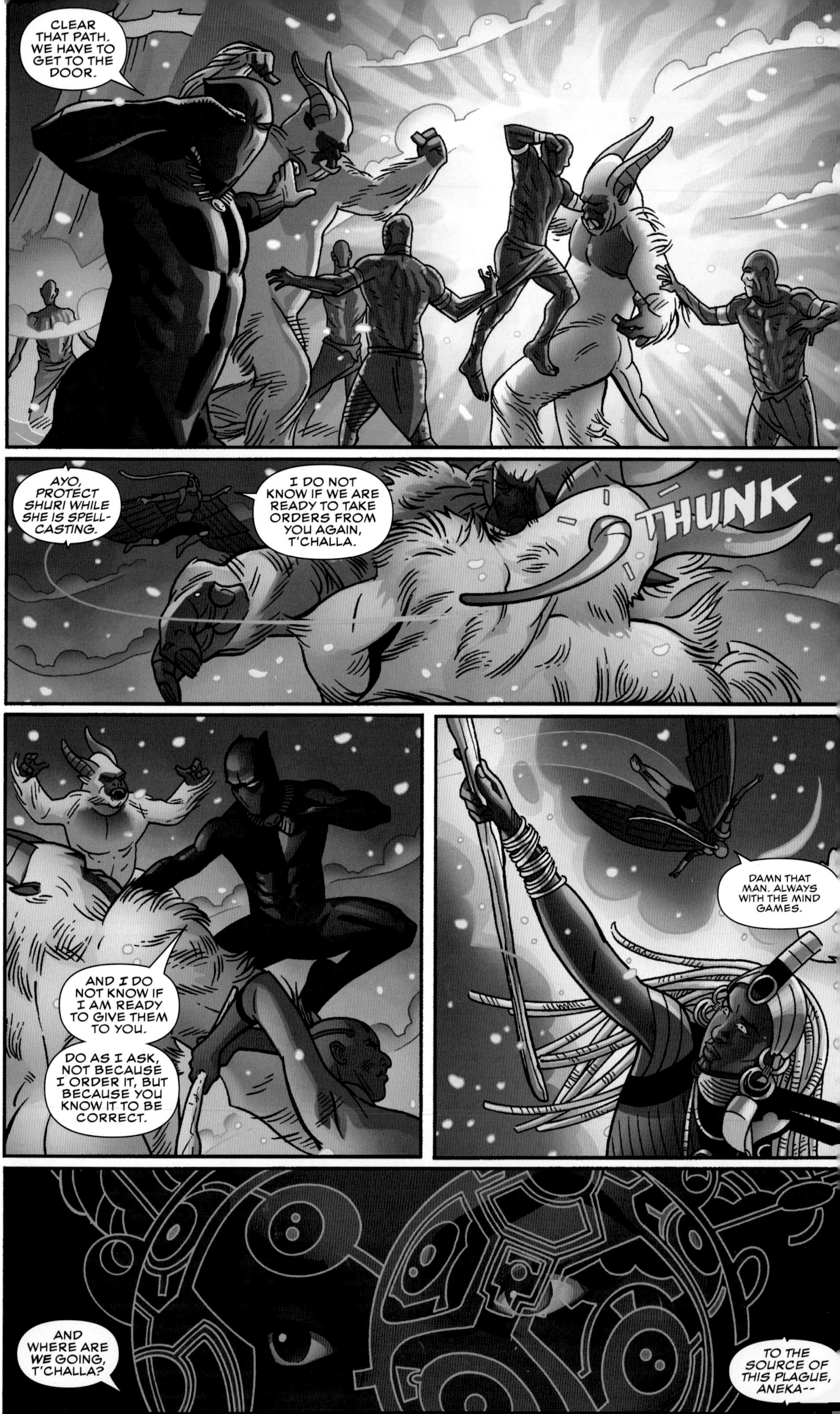
CLEAR THAT PATH. WE HAVE TO GET TO THE DOOR.
AYO, PROTECT SHURI WHILE SHE IS SPELL-CASTING.
I DO NOT KNOW IF WE ARE READY TO TAKE ORDERS FROM YOU AGAIN, T'CHALLA.
THUNK
AND I DO NOT KNOW IF I AM READY TO GIVE THEM TO YOU.
DO AS I ASK, NOT BECAUSE I ORDER IT, BUT BECAUSE YOU KNOW IT TO BE CORRECT.
DAMN THAT MAN. ALWAYS WITH THE MIND GAMES.
AND WHERE ARE WE GOING, T'CHALLA?
TO THE SOURCE OF THIS PLAGUE, ANEKA--

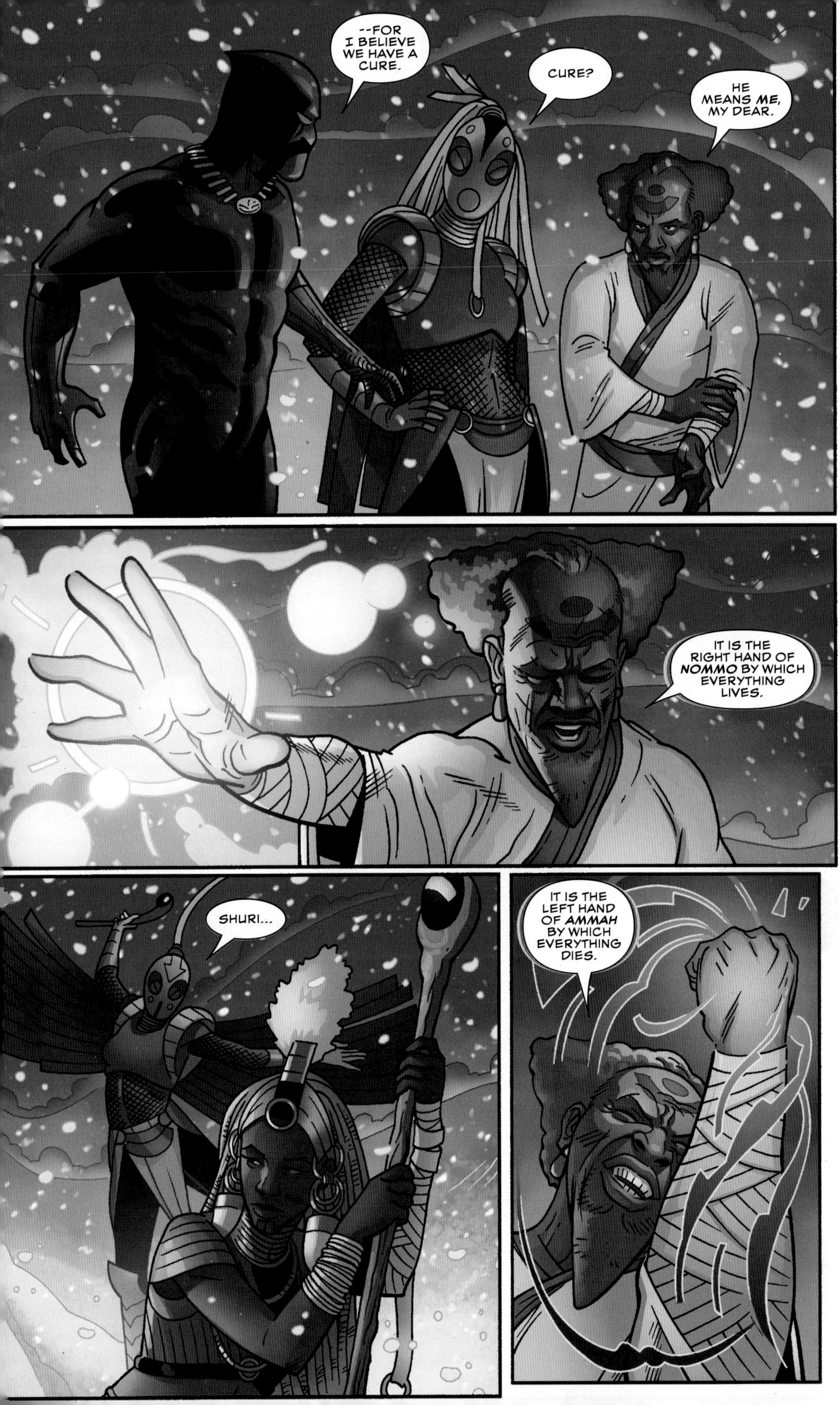
--FOR I BELIEVE WE HAVE A CURE.
CURE?
HE MEANS ME, MY DEAR.
IT IS THE RIGHT HAND OF NOMMO BY WHICH EVERYTHING LIVES.
SHURI...
IT IS THE LEFT HAND OF AMMAH BY WHICH EVERYTHING DIES.

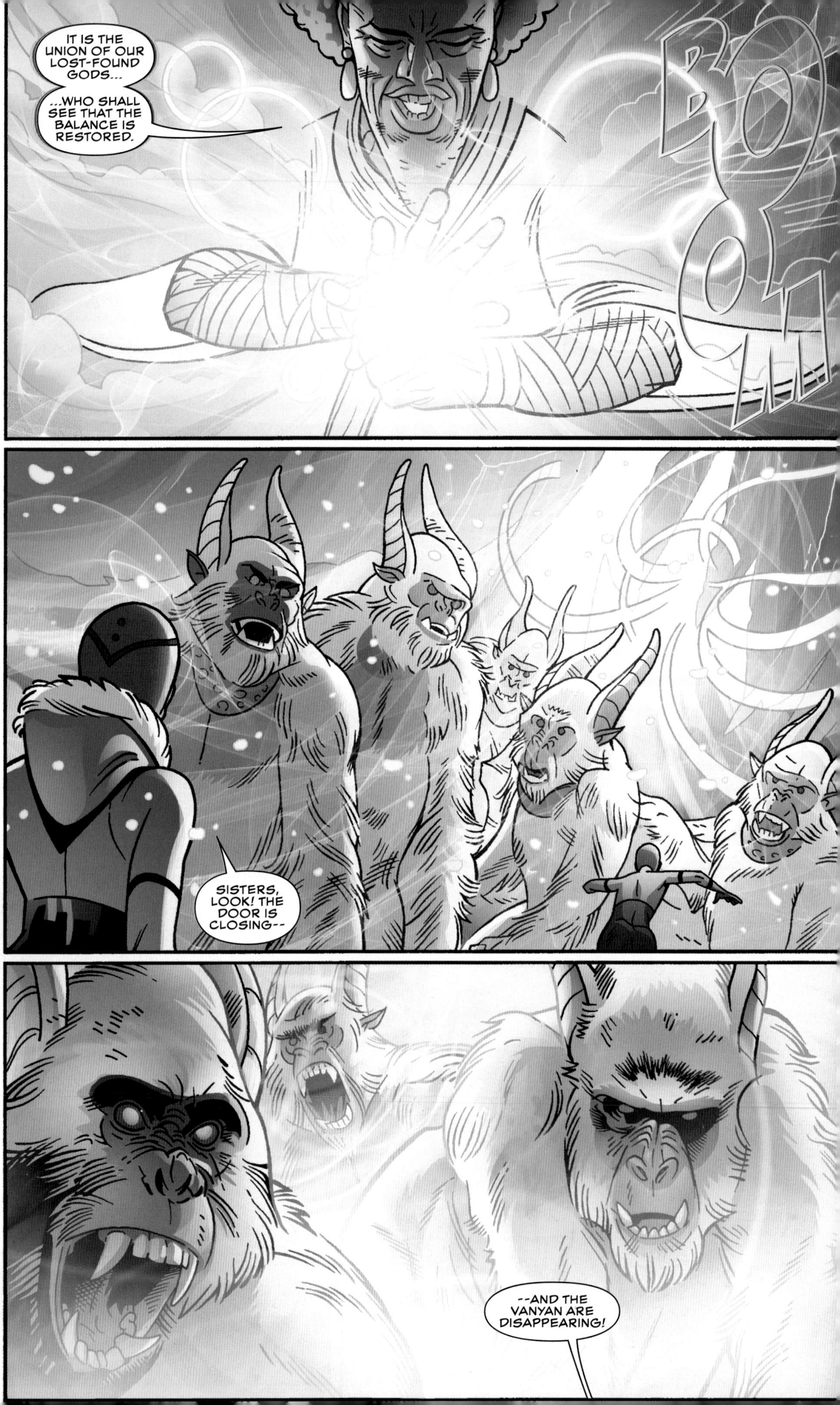
IT IS THE UNION OF OUR LOST-FOUND GODS...
...WHO SHALL SEE THAT THE BALANCE IS RESTORED.
BOOM
SISTERS, LOOK! THE DOOR IS CLOSING--
--AND THE VANYAN ARE DISAPPEARING!

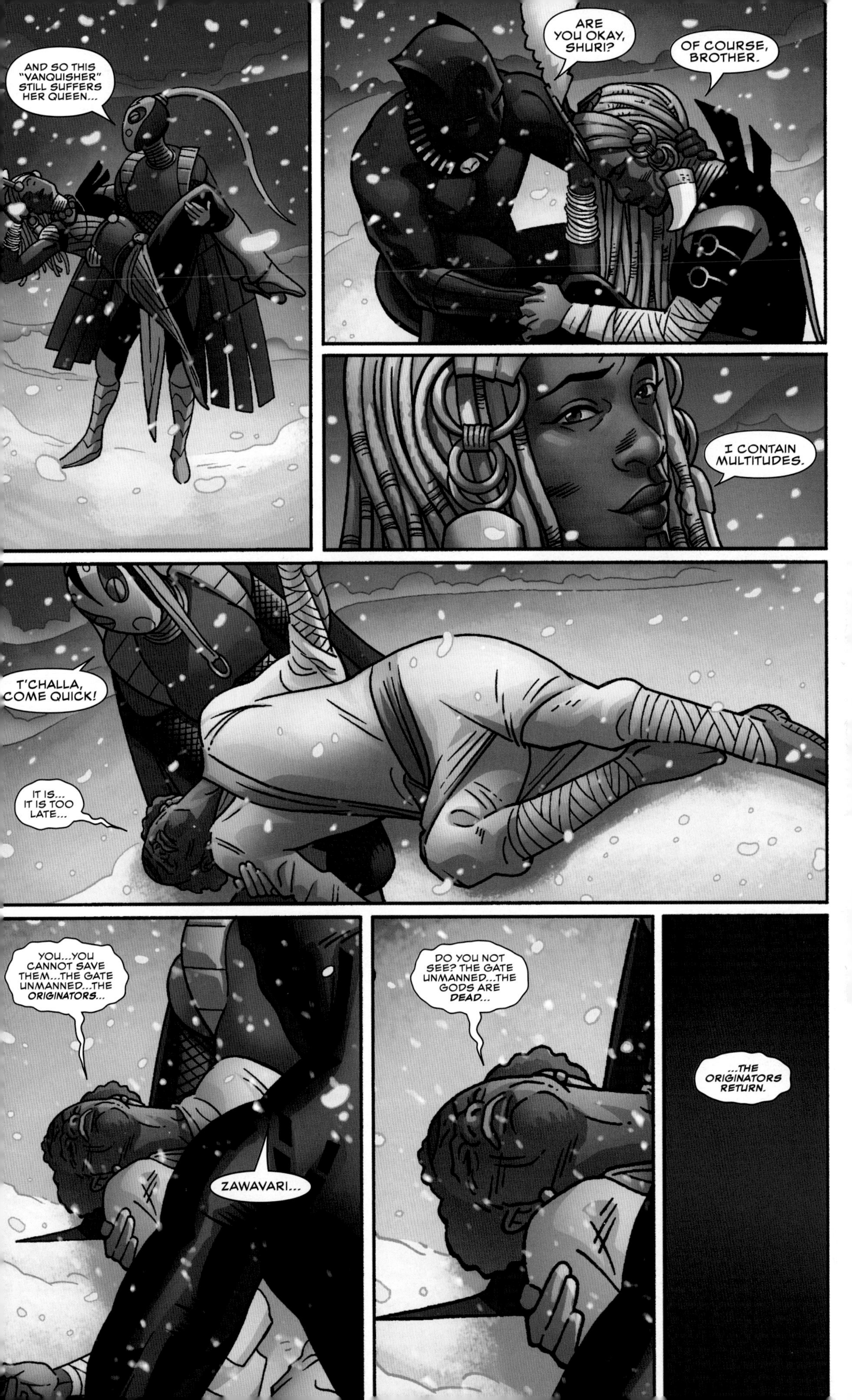
AND SO THIS "VANQUISHER" STILL SUFFERS HER QUEEN...
ARE YOU OKAY, SHURI?
OF COURSE, BROTHER.
I CONTAIN MULTITUDES.
T'CHALLA, COME QUICK!
IT IS... IT IS TOO LATE...
YOU...YOU CANNOT SAVE THEM...THE GATE UNMANNED...THE *ORIGINATORS*...
ZAWAVARI...
DO YOU NOT SEE? THE GATE UNMANNED...THE GODS ARE *DEAD*...
...THE *ORIGINATORS* RETURN.

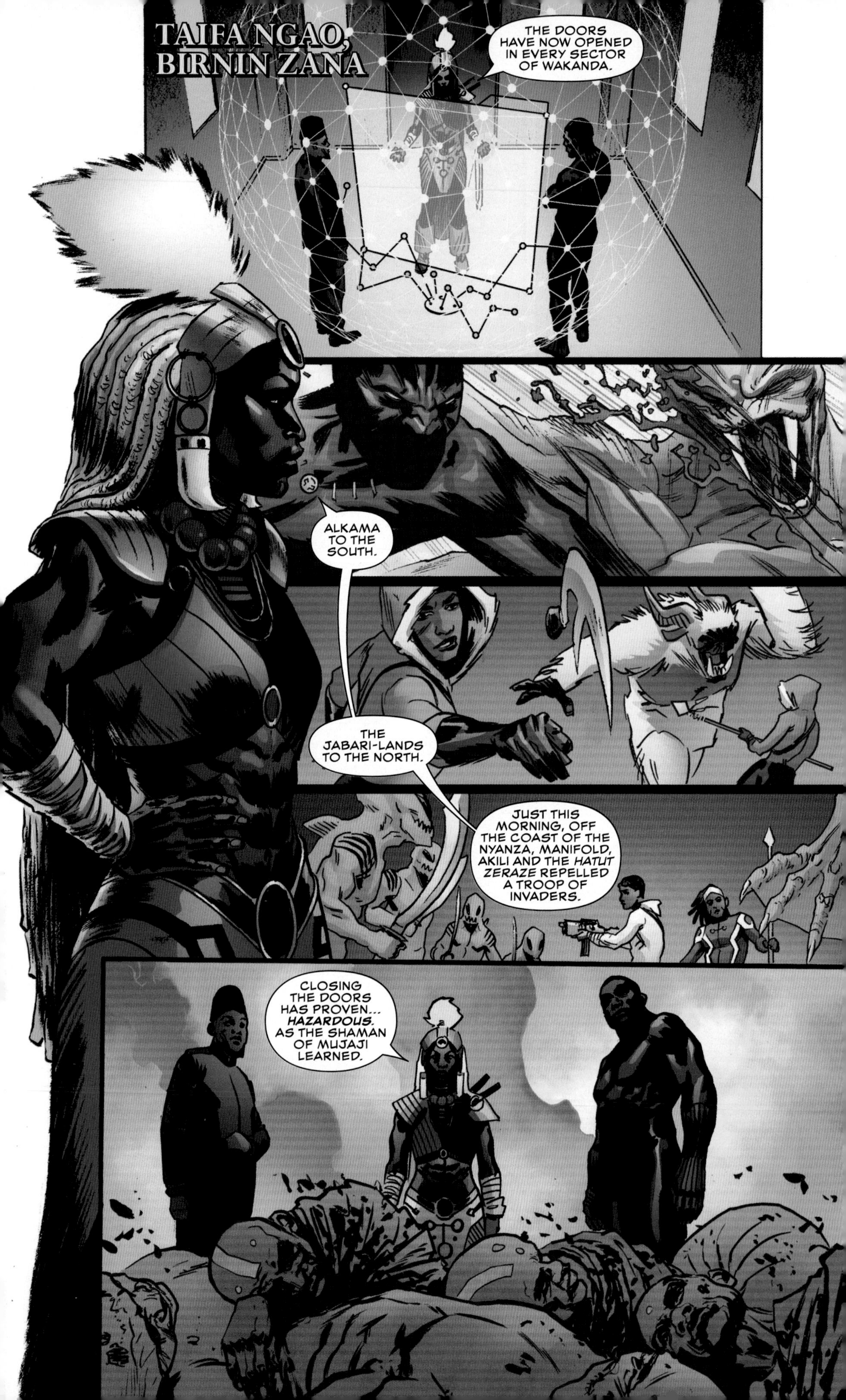

TAIFA NGAO, BIRNIN ZANA
THE DOORS HAVE NOW OPENED IN EVERY SECTOR OF WAKANDA.
ALKAMA TO THE SOUTH.
THE JABARI-LANDS TO THE NORTH.
JUST THIS MORNING, OFF THE COAST OF THE NYANZA, MANIFOLD, AKILI AND THE *HATUT ZERAZE* REPELLED A TROOP OF INVADERS.
CLOSING THE DOORS HAS PROVEN... ***HAZARDOUS.*** AS THE SHAMAN OF MUJAJI LEARNED.

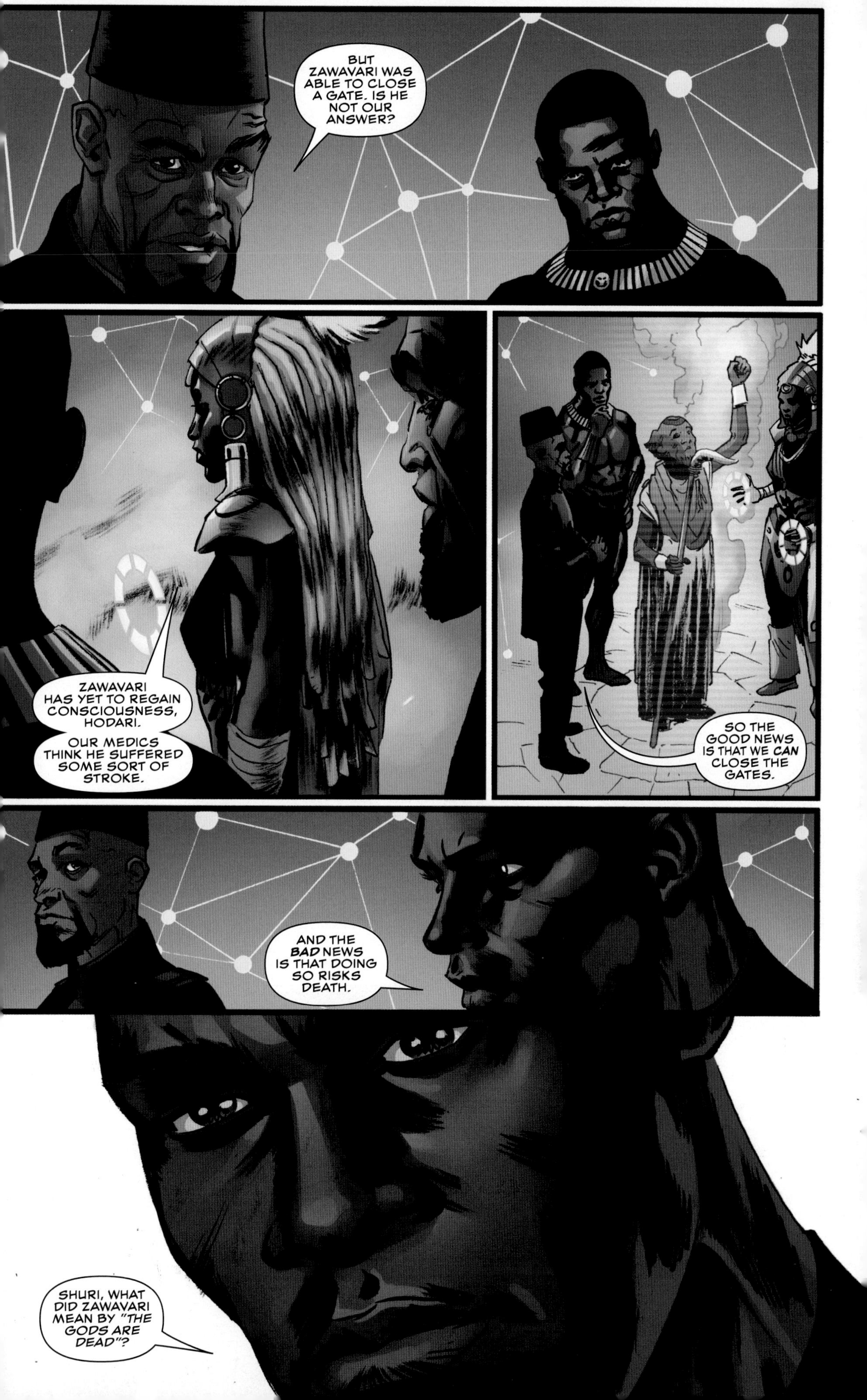
BUT ZAWAVARI WAS ABLE TO CLOSE A GATE. IS HE NOT OUR ANSWER?
ZAWAVARI HAS YET TO REGAIN CONSCIOUSNESS, HODARI.
OUR MEDICS THINK HE SUFFERED SOME SORT OF STROKE.
SO THE GOOD NEWS IS THAT WE *CAN* CLOSE THE GATES.
AND THE *BAD* NEWS IS THAT DOING SO RISKS DEATH.
SHURI, WHAT DID ZAWAVARI MEAN BY *"THE GODS ARE DEAD"*?

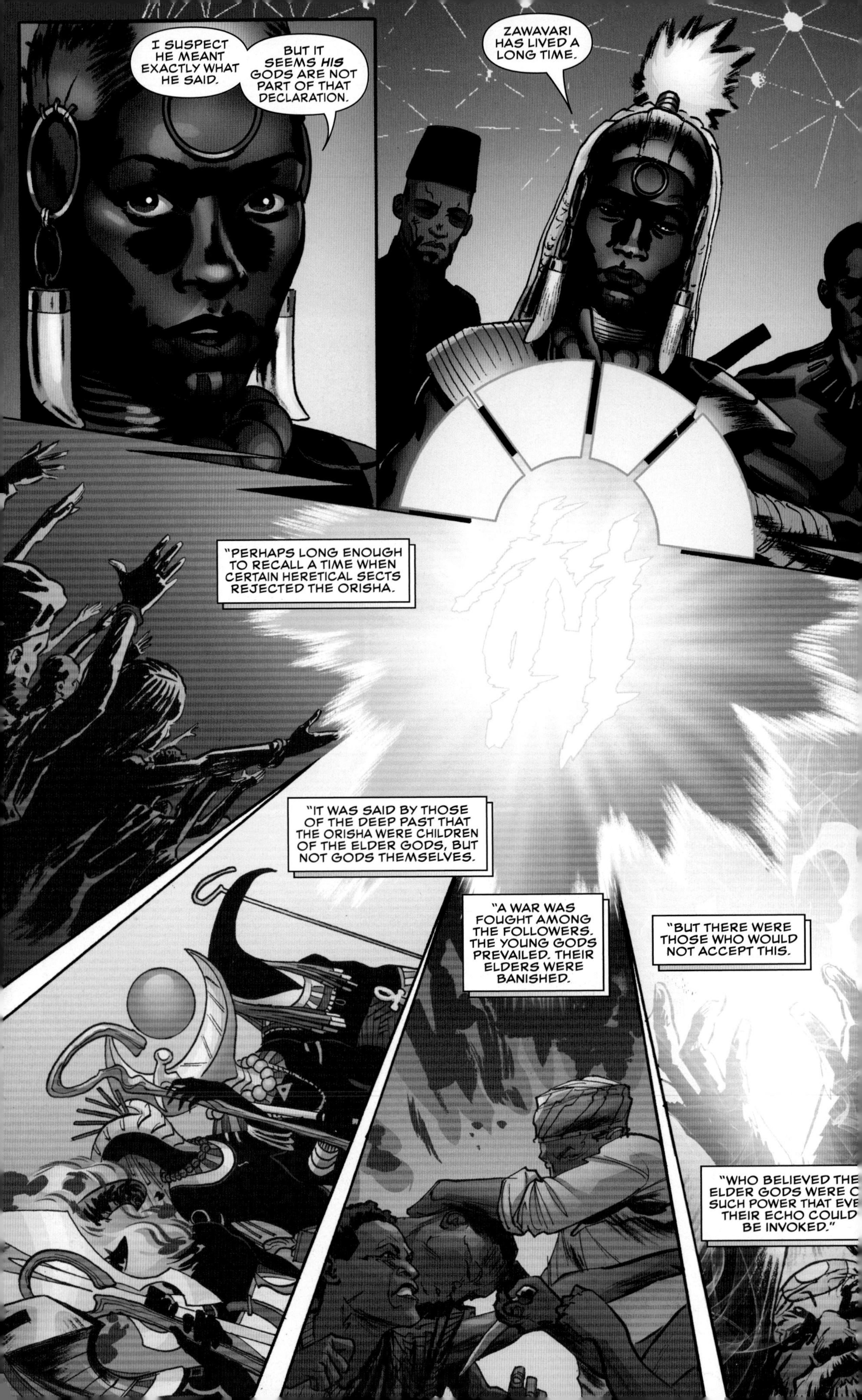

I SUSPECT HE MEANT EXACTLY WHAT HE SAID.
BUT IT SEEMS HIS GODS ARE NOT PART OF THAT DECLARATION.
ZAWAVARI HAS LIVED A LONG TIME.
"PERHAPS LONG ENOUGH TO RECALL A TIME WHEN CERTAIN HERETICAL SECTS REJECTED THE ORISHA.
"IT WAS SAID BY THOSE OF THE DEEP PAST THAT THE ORISHA WERE CHILDREN OF THE ELDER GODS, BUT NOT GODS THEMSELVES.
"A WAR WAS FOUGHT AMONG THE FOLLOWERS. THE YOUNG GODS PREVAILED. THEIR ELDERS WERE BANISHED.
"BUT THERE WERE THOSE WHO WOULD NOT ACCEPT THIS.
"WHO BELIEVED THE ELDER GODS WERE O SUCH POWER THAT EVE THEIR ECHO COULD BE INVOKED."

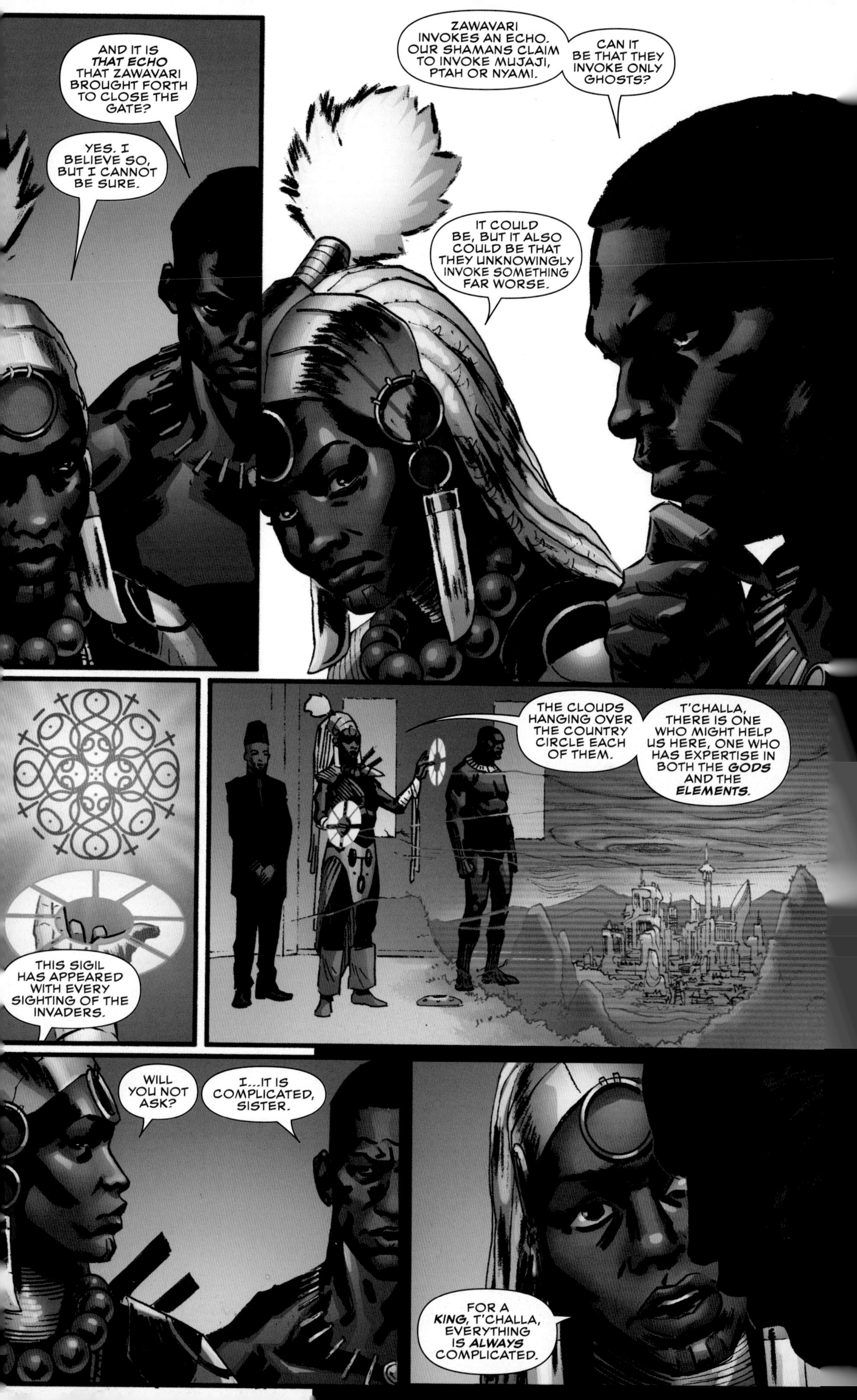
AND IT IS *THAT ECHO* THAT ZAWAVARI BROUGHT FORTH TO CLOSE THE GATE?
YES. I BELIEVE SO, BUT I CANNOT BE SURE.
ZAWAVARI INVOKES AN ECHO. OUR SHAMANS CLAIM TO INVOKE MUJAJI, PTAH OR NYAMI.
CAN IT BE THAT THEY INVOKE ONLY GHOSTS?
IT COULD BE, BUT IT ALSO COULD BE THAT THEY UNKNOWINGLY INVOKE SOMETHING FAR WORSE.
THIS SIGIL HAS APPEARED WITH EVERY SIGHTING OF THE INVADERS.
THE CLOUDS HANGING OVER THE COUNTRY CIRCLE EACH OF THEM.
T'CHALLA, THERE IS ONE WHO MIGHT HELP US HERE, ONE WHO HAS EXPERTISE IN BOTH THE *GODS* AND THE *ELEMENTS*.
WILL YOU NOT ASK?
I...IT IS COMPLICATED, SISTER.
FOR A *KING*, T'CHALLA, EVERYTHING IS *ALWAYS* COMPLICATED.

THIS WAS SUPPOSED TO BE FUN.

NO ROYAL DUTIES.

THE VILLAGE OF KANANNA-MDOGO

NO AFFAIRS OF STATE.

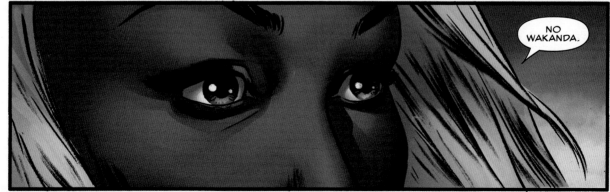

NO WAKANDA.

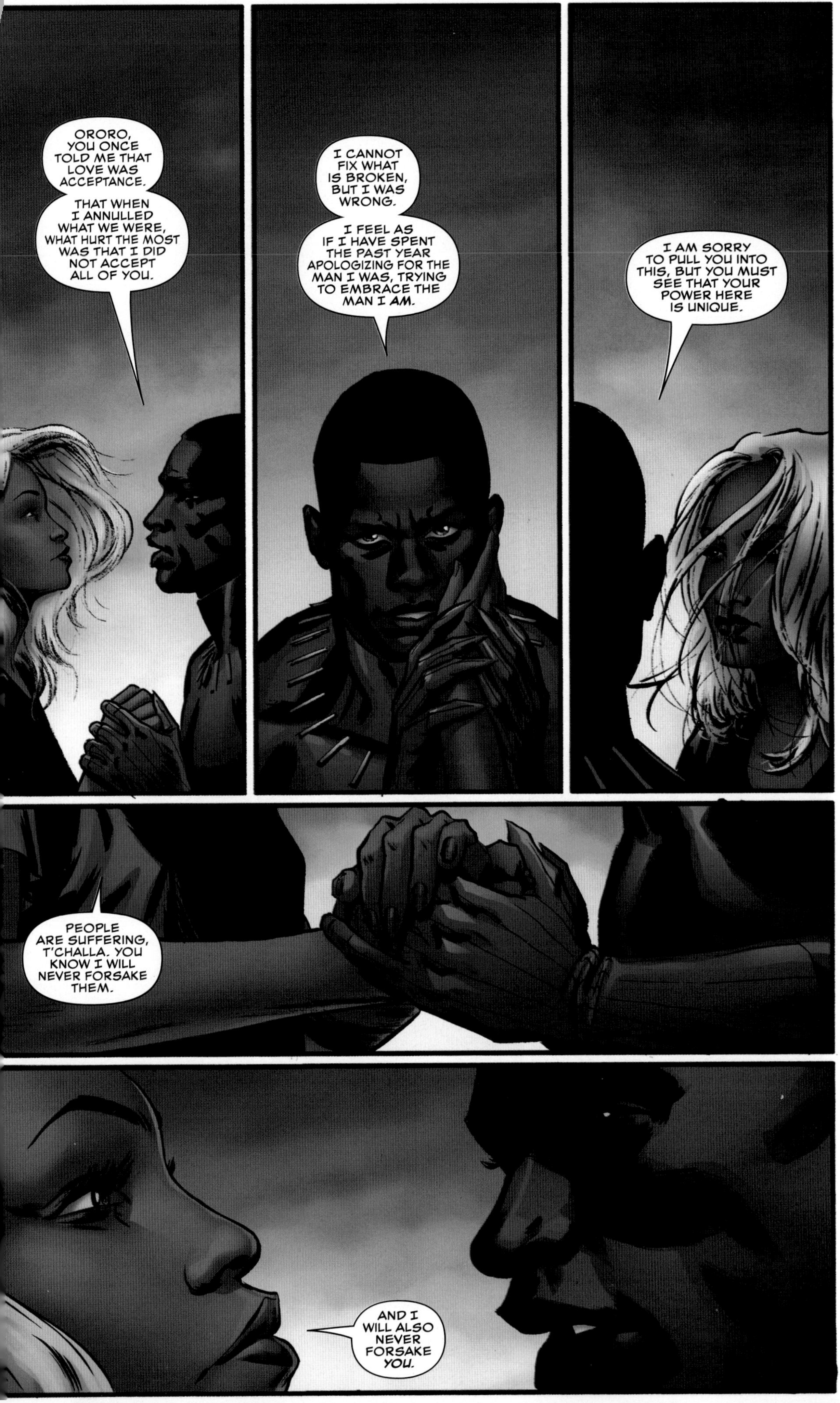

ORORO, YOU ONCE TOLD ME THAT LOVE WAS ACCEPTANCE.
THAT WHEN I ANNULLED WHAT WE WERE, WHAT HURT THE MOST WAS THAT I DID NOT ACCEPT ALL OF YOU.
I CANNOT FIX WHAT IS BROKEN, BUT I WAS WRONG.
I FEEL AS IF I HAVE SPENT THE PAST YEAR APOLOGIZING FOR THE MAN I WAS, TRYING TO EMBRACE THE MAN I *AM.*
I AM SORRY TO PULL YOU INTO THIS, BUT YOU MUST SEE THAT YOUR POWER HERE IS UNIQUE.
PEOPLE ARE SUFFERING, T'CHALLA. YOU KNOW I WILL NEVER FORSAKE THEM.
AND I WILL ALSO NEVER FORSAKE *YOU.*

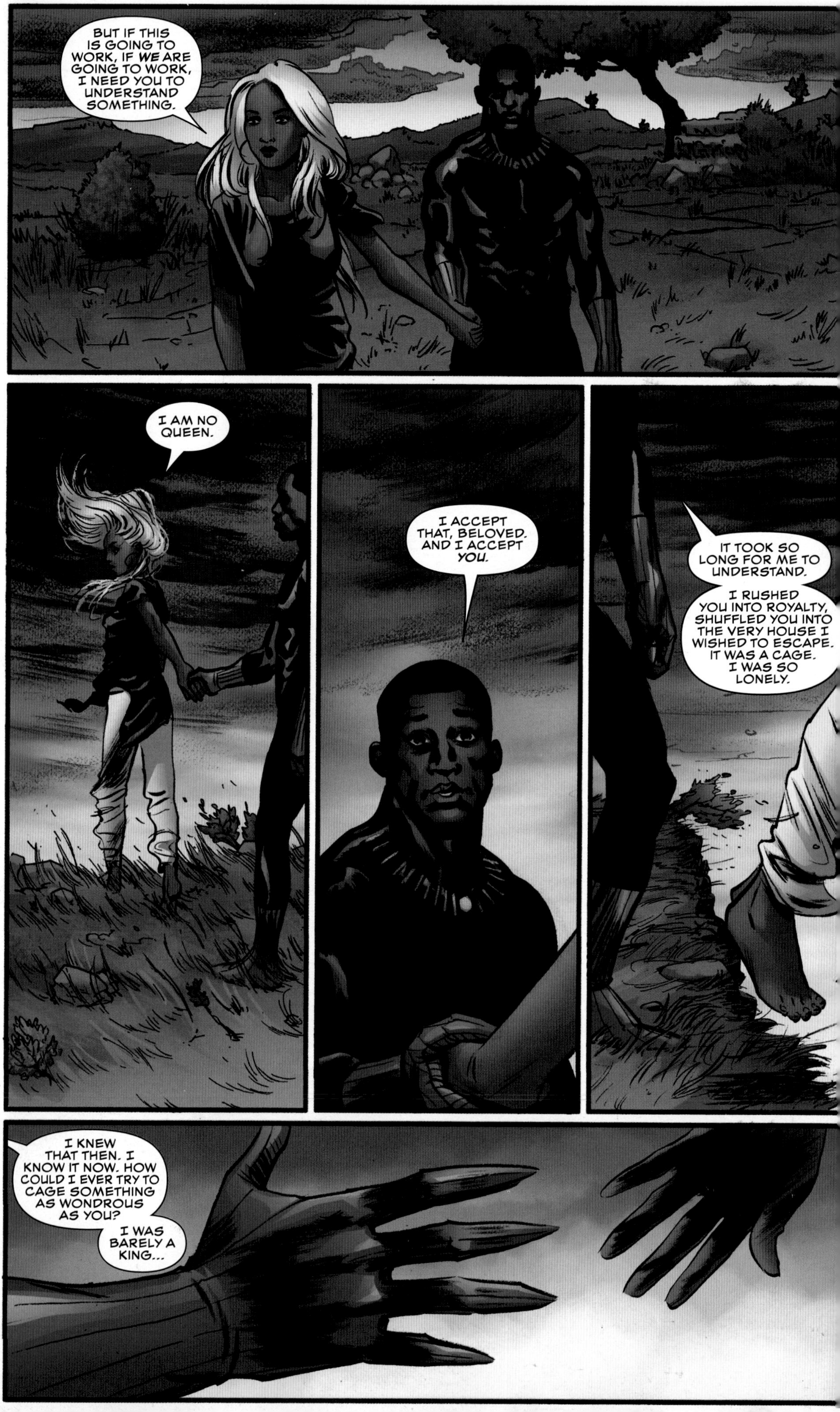
BUT IF THIS IS GOING TO WORK, IF *WE* ARE GOING TO WORK, I NEED YOU TO UNDERSTAND SOMETHING.
I AM NO QUEEN.
I ACCEPT THAT, BELOVED. AND I ACCEPT *YOU.*
IT TOOK SO LONG FOR ME TO UNDERSTAND.
I RUSHED YOU INTO ROYALTY, SHUFFLED YOU INTO THE VERY HOUSE I WISHED TO ESCAPE. IT WAS A CAGE. I WAS SO LONELY.
I KNEW THAT THEN. I KNOW IT NOW. HOW COULD I EVER TRY TO CAGE SOMETHING AS WONDROUS AS YOU?
I WAS BARELY A KING...

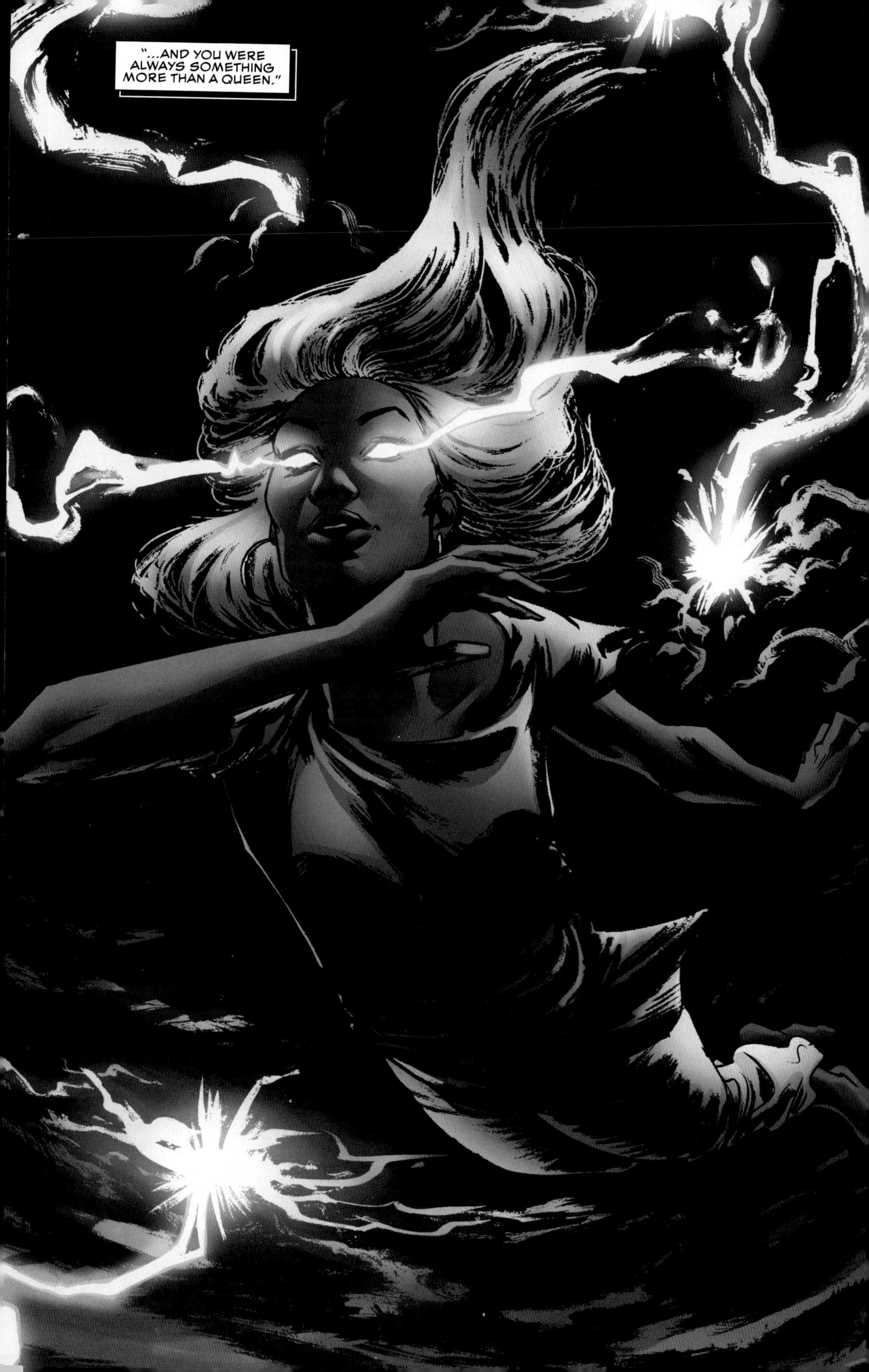
"...AND YOU WERE ALWAYS SOMETHING MORE THAN A QUEEN."

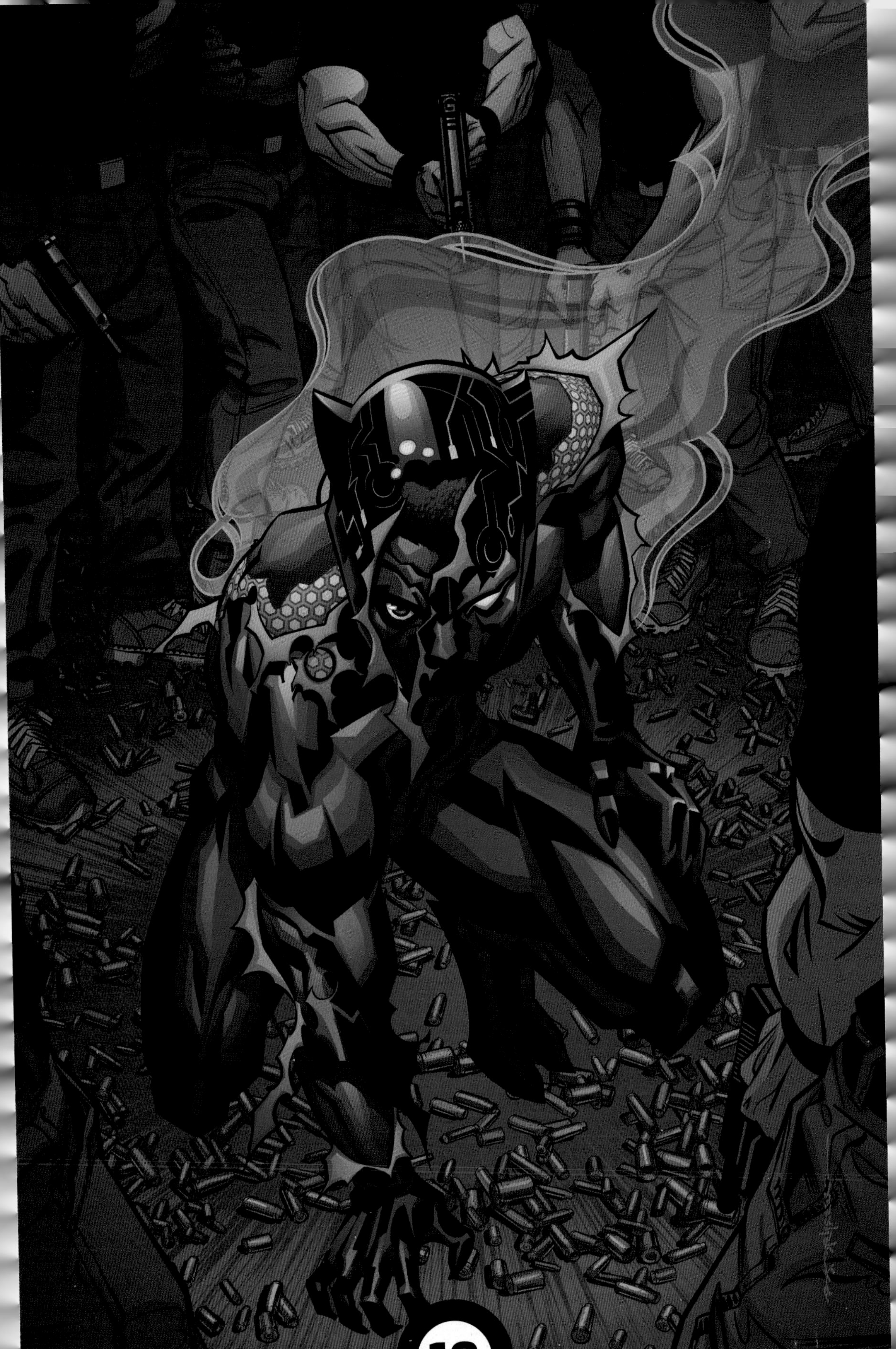

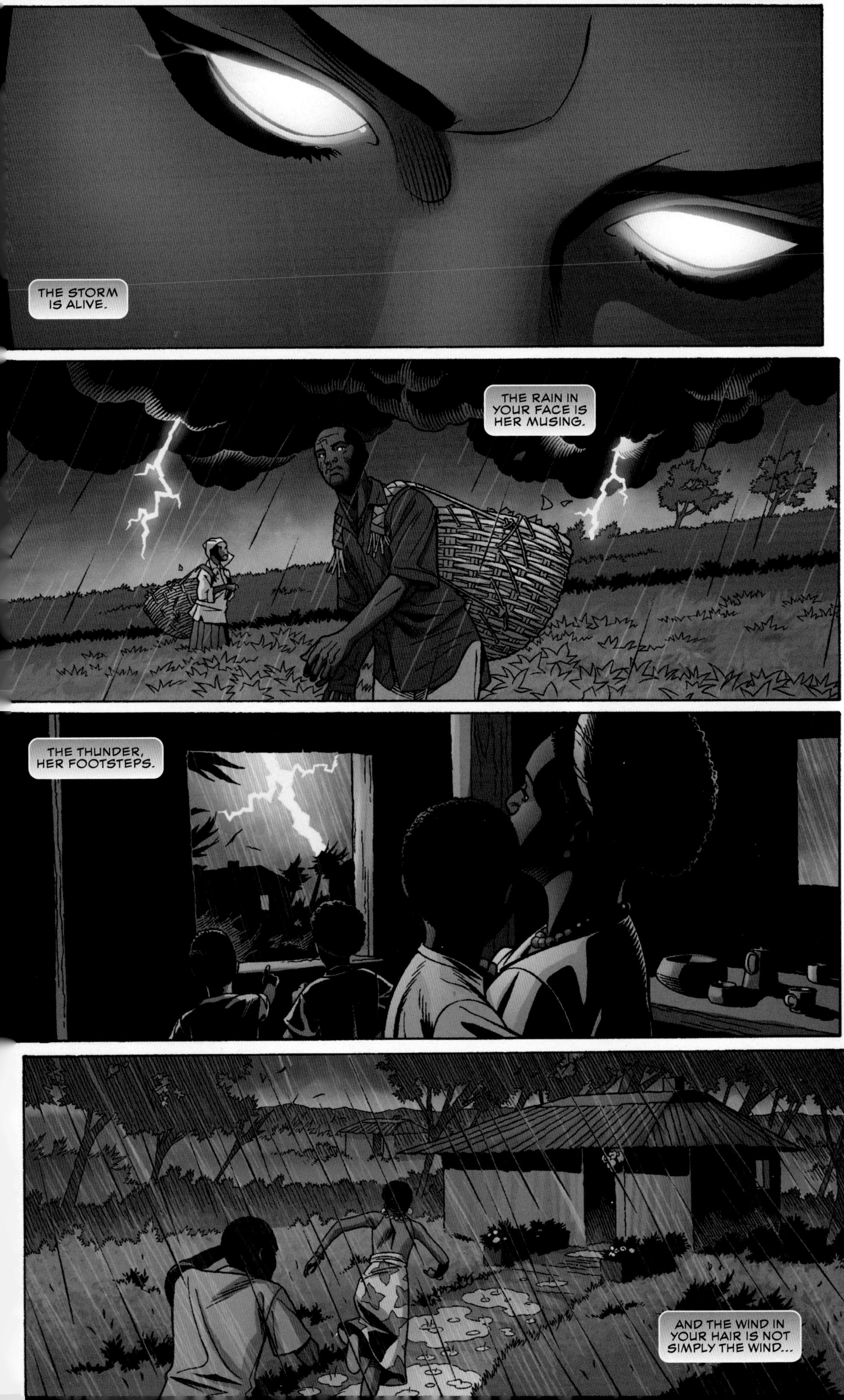
THE STORM IS ALIVE.
THE RAIN IN YOUR FACE IS HER MUSING.
THE THUNDER, HER FOOTSTEPS.
AND THE WIND IN YOUR HAIR IS NOT SIMPLY THE WIND...

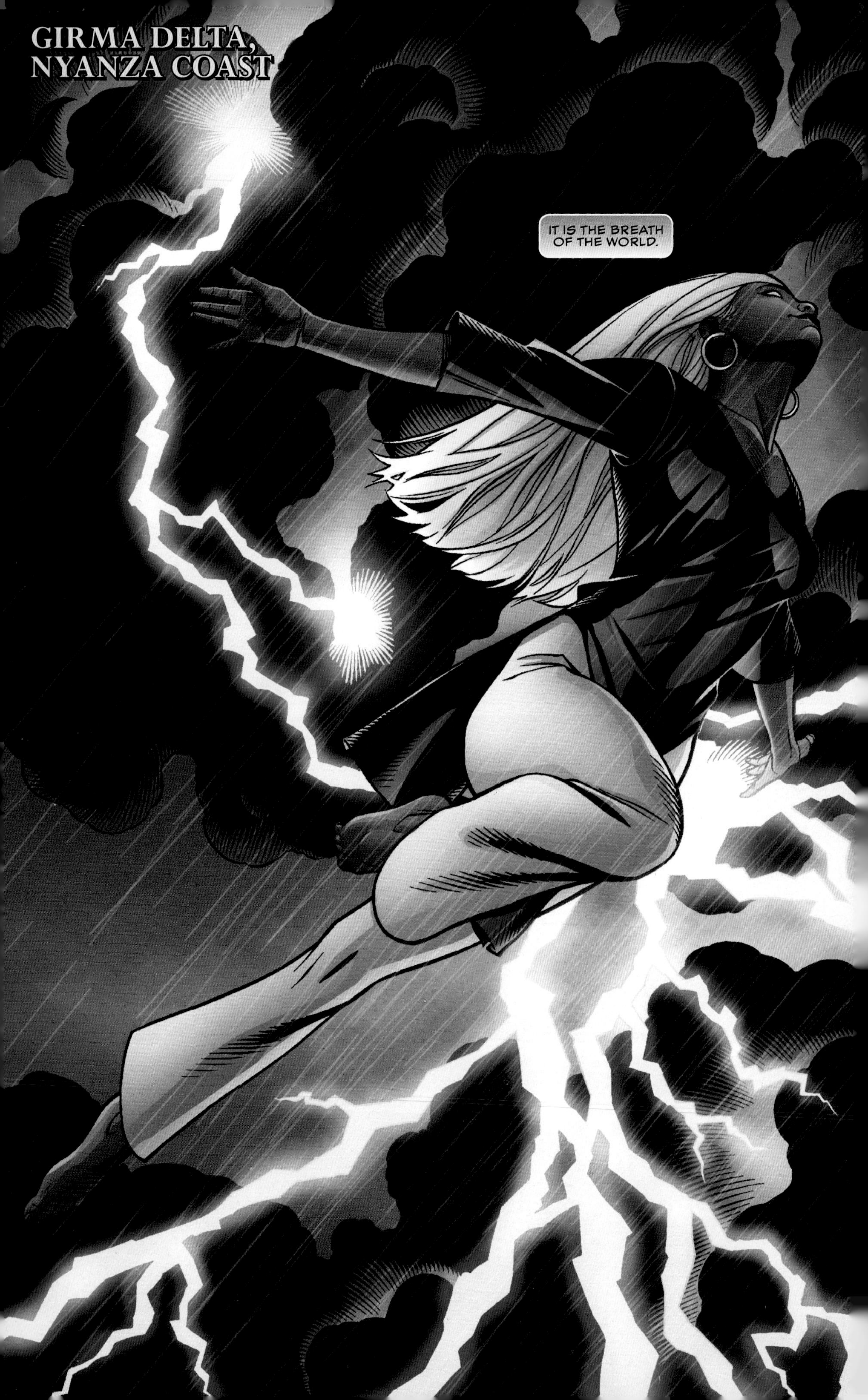
GIRMA DELTA,
NYANZA COAST
IT IS THE BREATH OF THE WORLD.

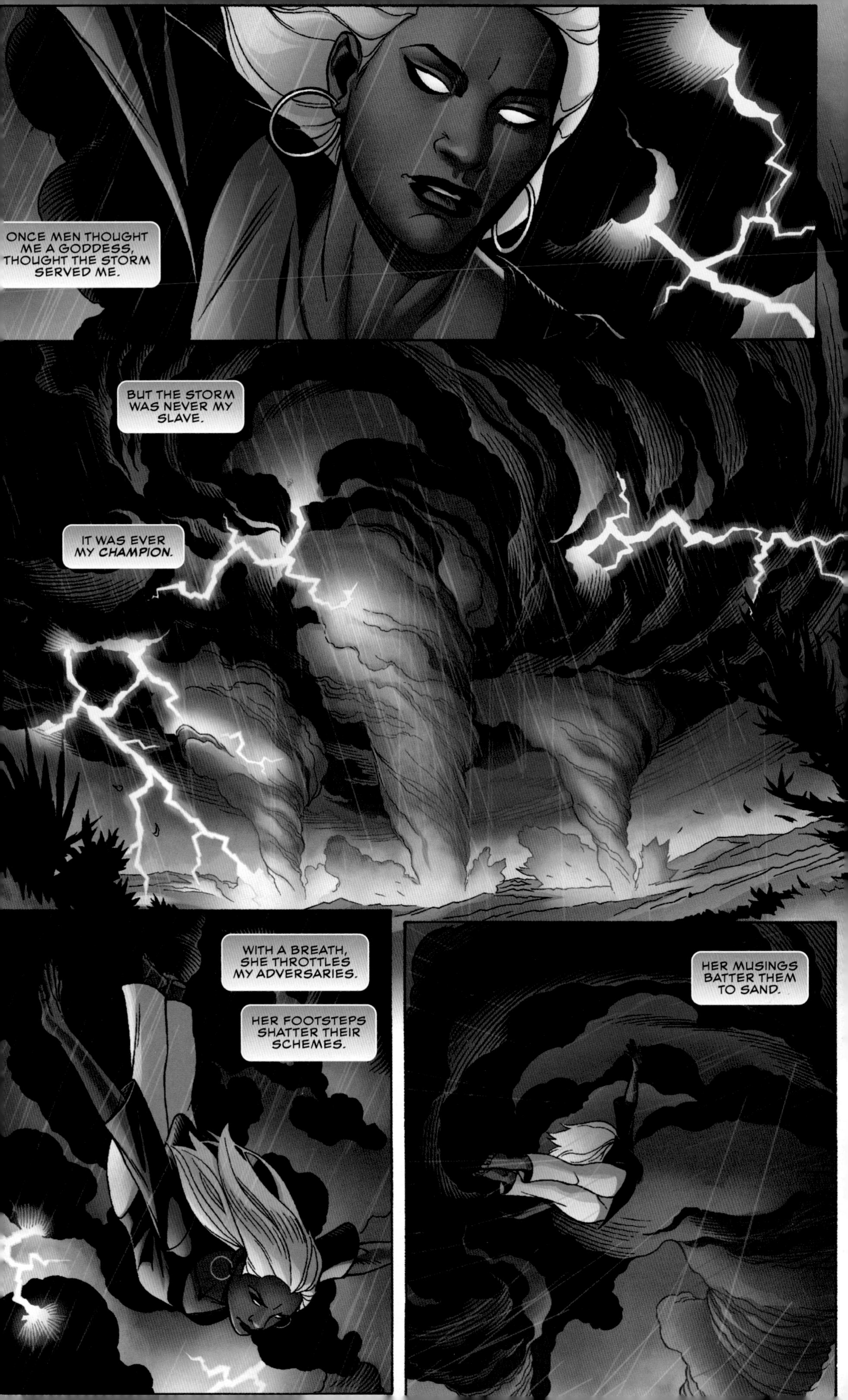
ONCE MEN THOUGHT ME A GODDESS, THOUGHT THE STORM SERVED ME.
BUT THE STORM WAS NEVER MY SLAVE.
IT WAS EVER MY CHAMPION.
WITH A BREATH, SHE THROTTLES MY ADVERSARIES.
HER FOOTSTEPS SHATTER THEIR SCHEMES.
HER MUSINGS BATTER THEM TO SAND.

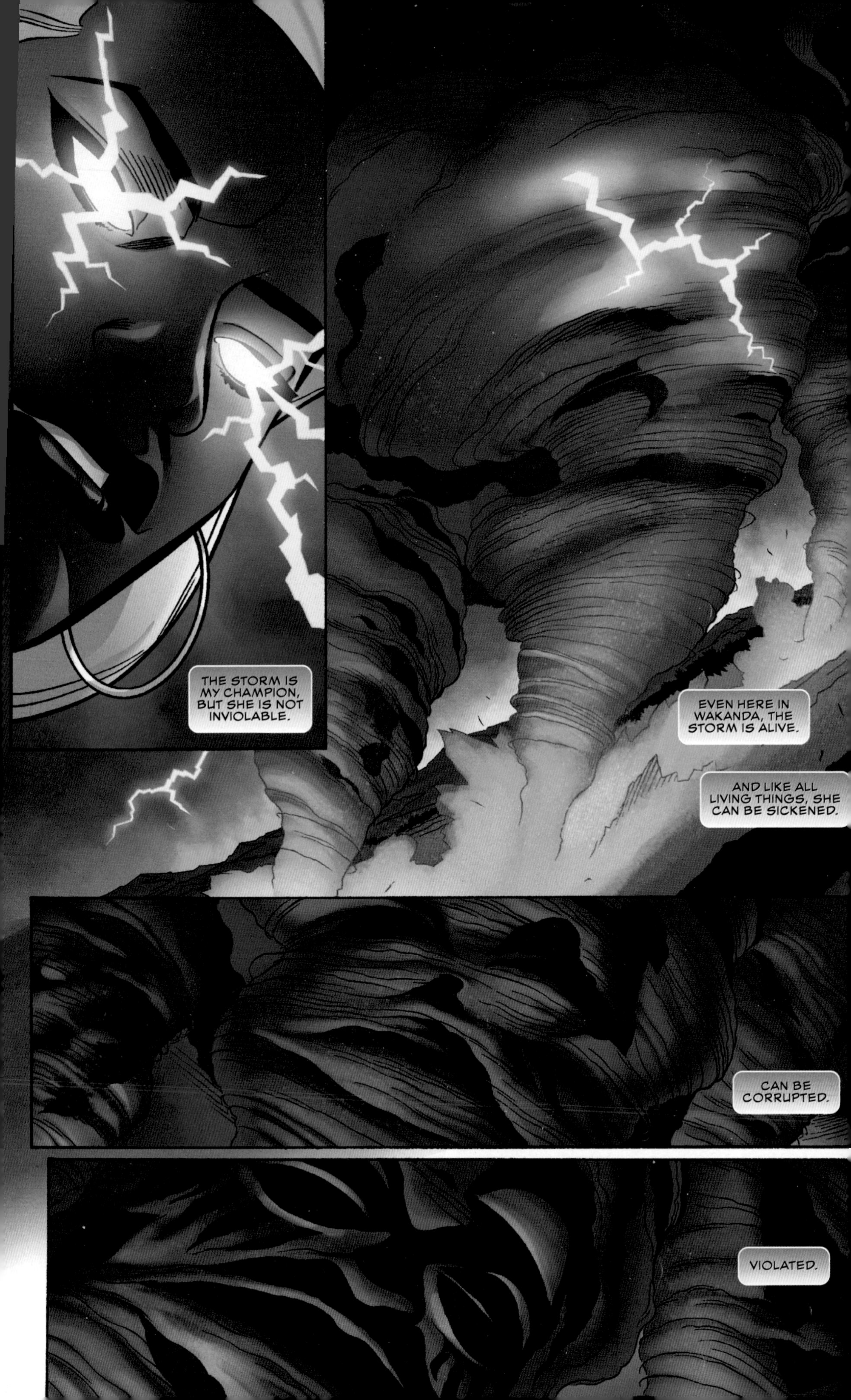
THE STORM IS MY CHAMPION, BUT SHE IS NOT INVIOLABLE.
EVEN HERE IN WAKANDA, THE STORM IS ALIVE.
AND LIKE ALL LIVING THINGS, SHE CAN BE SICKENED.
CAN BE CORRUPTED.
VIOLATED.

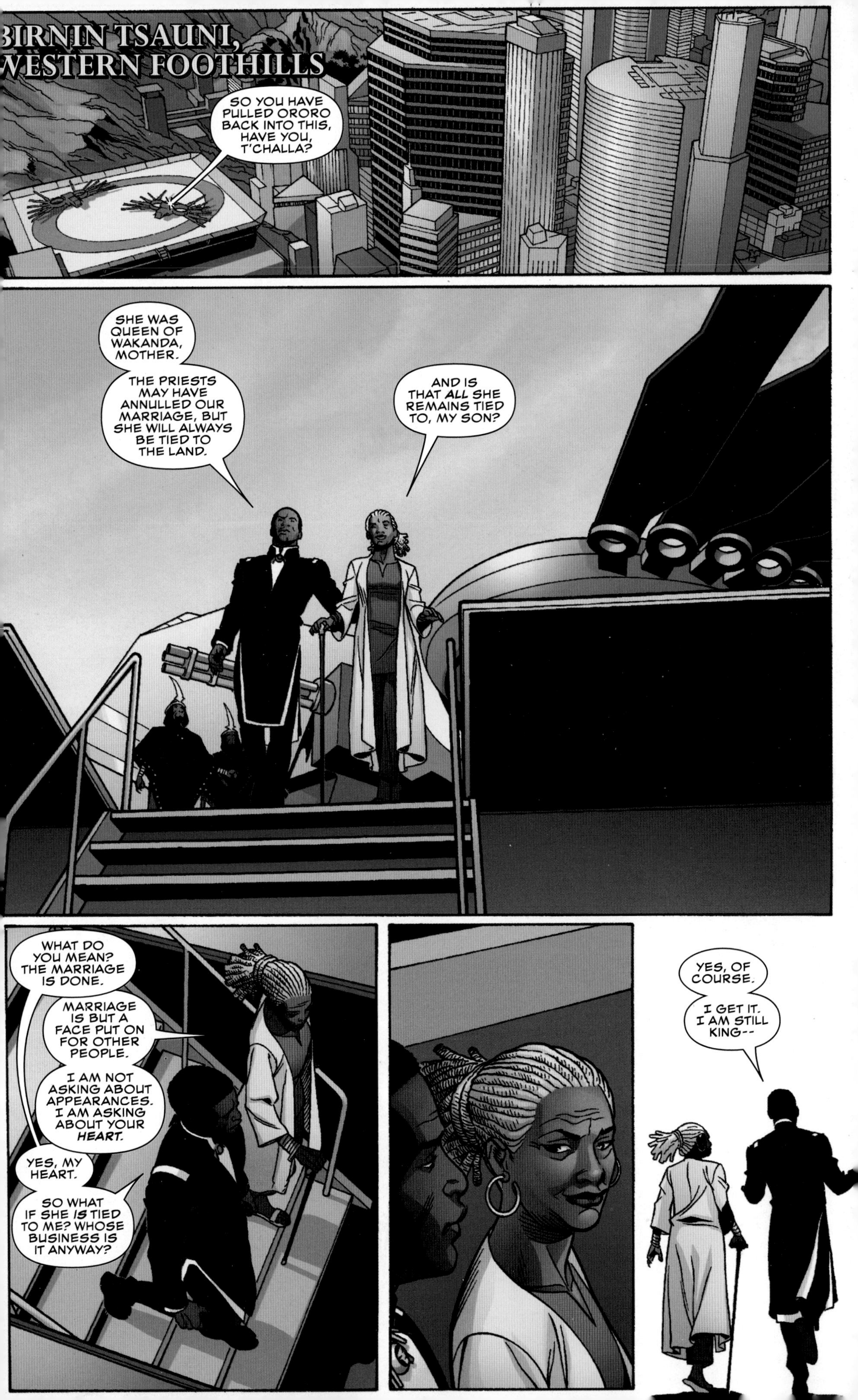

BIRNIN TSAUNI, WESTERN FOOTHILLS
SO YOU HAVE PULLED ORORO BACK INTO THIS, HAVE YOU, T'CHALLA?
SHE WAS QUEEN OF WAKANDA, MOTHER.
THE PRIESTS MAY HAVE ANNULLED OUR MARRIAGE, BUT SHE WILL ALWAYS BE TIED TO THE LAND.
AND IS THAT ALL SHE REMAINS TIED TO, MY SON?
WHAT DO YOU MEAN? THE MARRIAGE IS DONE.
MARRIAGE IS BUT A FACE PUT ON FOR OTHER PEOPLE.
I AM NOT ASKING ABOUT APPEARANCES. I AM ASKING ABOUT YOUR HEART.
YES, MY HEART.
SO WHAT IF SHE IS TIED TO ME? WHOSE BUSINESS IS IT ANYWAY?
YES, OF COURSE.
I GET IT. I AM STILL KING--

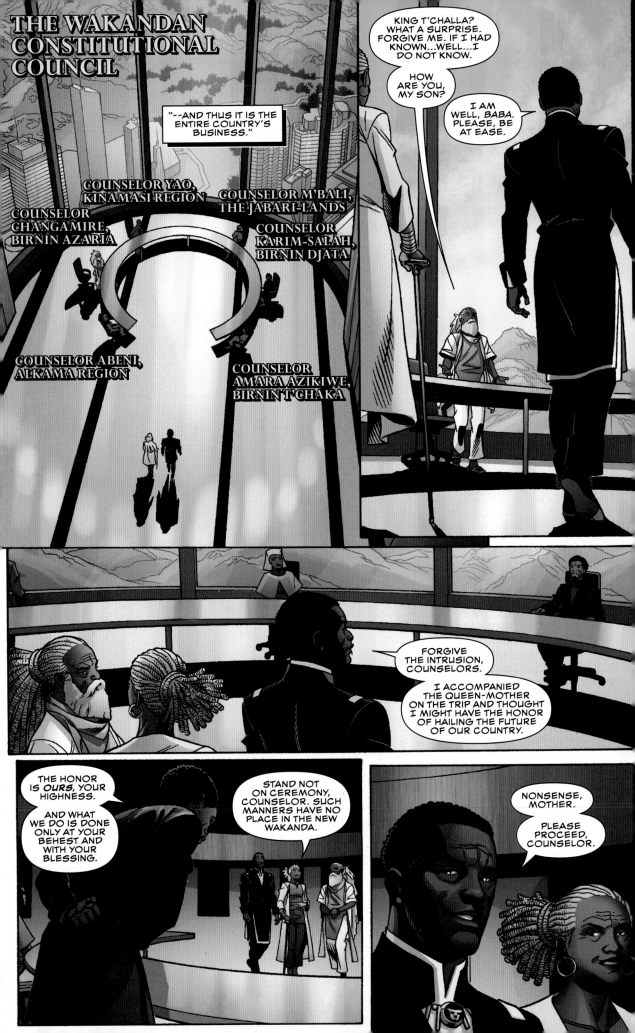

THE WAKANDAN
CONSTITUTIONAL
COUNCIL

"--AND THUS IT IS THE ENTIRE COUNTRY'S BUSINESS."

COUNSELOR YAO, KINAMASI REGION

COUNSELOR M'BALI, THE JABARI-LANDS

COUNSELOR CHANGAMIRE, BIRNIN AZARIA

COUNSELOR KARIM-SALAH, BIRNIN DJATA

COUNSELOR ABENI, ALKAMA REGION

COUNSELOR AMARA AZIKIWE, BIRNIN T'CHAKA

KING T'CHALLA? WHAT A SURPRISE. FORGIVE ME. IF I HAD KNOWN...WELL...I DO NOT KNOW.

HOW ARE YOU, MY SON?

I AM WELL, BABA. PLEASE, BE AT EASE.

FORGIVE THE INTRUSION, COUNSELORS.

I ACCOMPANIED THE QUEEN-MOTHER ON THE TRIP AND THOUGHT I MIGHT HAVE THE HONOR OF HAILING THE FUTURE OF OUR COUNTRY.

THE HONOR IS OURS, YOUR HIGHNESS.

AND WHAT WE DO IS DONE ONLY AT YOUR BEHEST AND WITH YOUR BLESSING.

STAND NOT ON CEREMONY, COUNSELOR. SUCH MANNERS HAVE NO PLACE IN THE NEW WAKANDA.

NONSENSE, MOTHER.

PLEASE PROCEED, COUNSELOR.

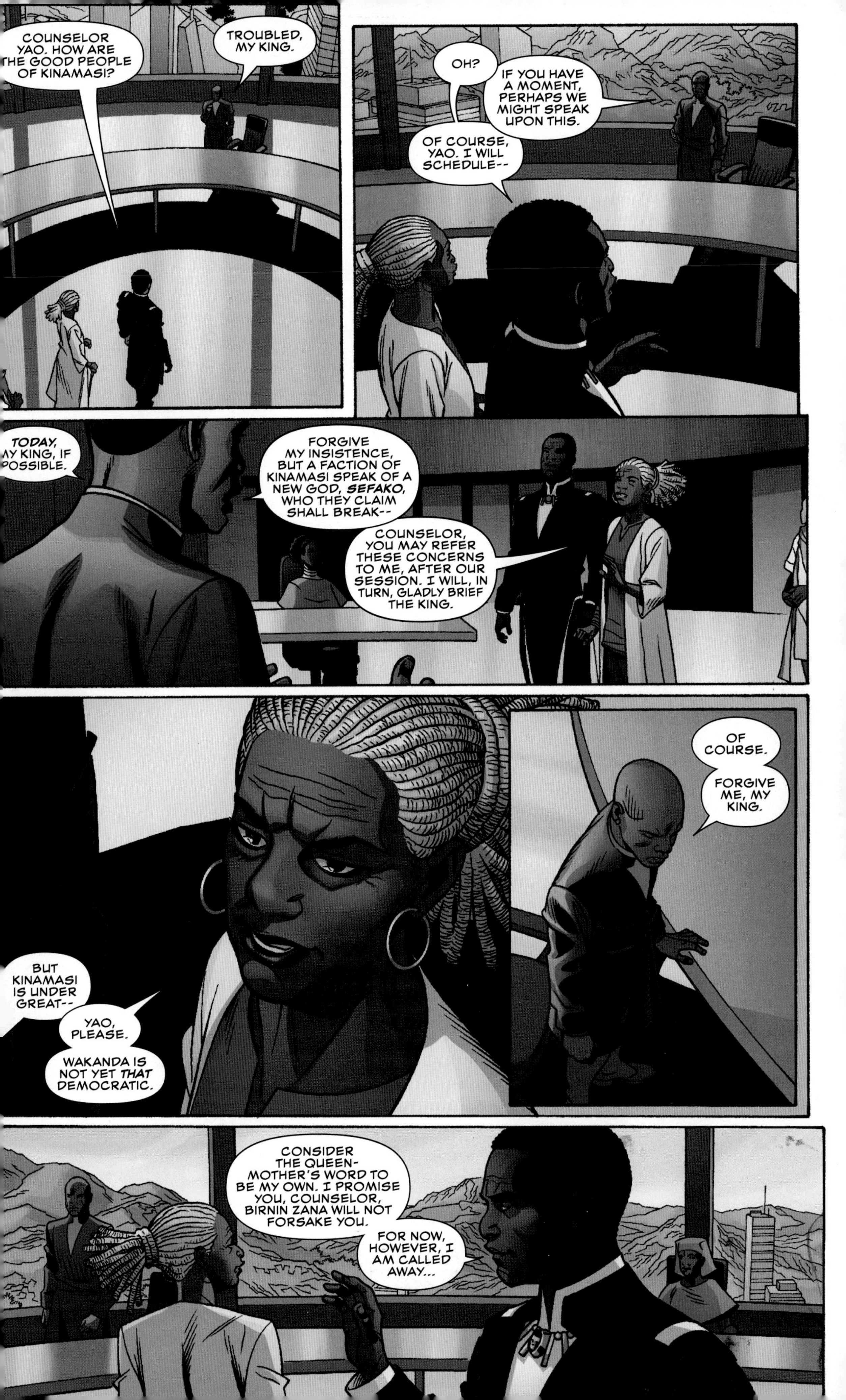

COUNSELOR YAO. HOW ARE THE GOOD PEOPLE OF KINAMASI?
TROUBLED, MY KING.
OH?
IF YOU HAVE A MOMENT, PERHAPS WE MIGHT SPEAK UPON THIS.
OF COURSE, YAO. I WILL SCHEDULE--
TODAY, MY KING, IF POSSIBLE.
FORGIVE MY INSISTENCE, BUT A FACTION OF KINAMASI SPEAK OF A NEW GOD, SEFAKO, WHO THEY CLAIM SHALL BREAK--
COUNSELOR, YOU MAY REFER THESE CONCERNS TO ME, AFTER OUR SESSION. I WILL, IN TURN, GLADLY BRIEF THE KING.
OF COURSE.
FORGIVE ME, MY KING.
BUT KINAMASI IS UNDER GREAT--
YAO, PLEASE.
WAKANDA IS NOT YET THAT DEMOCRATIC.
CONSIDER THE QUEEN-MOTHER'S WORD TO BE MY OWN. I PROMISE YOU, COUNSELOR, BIRNIN ZANA WILL NOT FORSAKE YOU.
FOR NOW, HOWEVER, I AM CALLED AWAY...

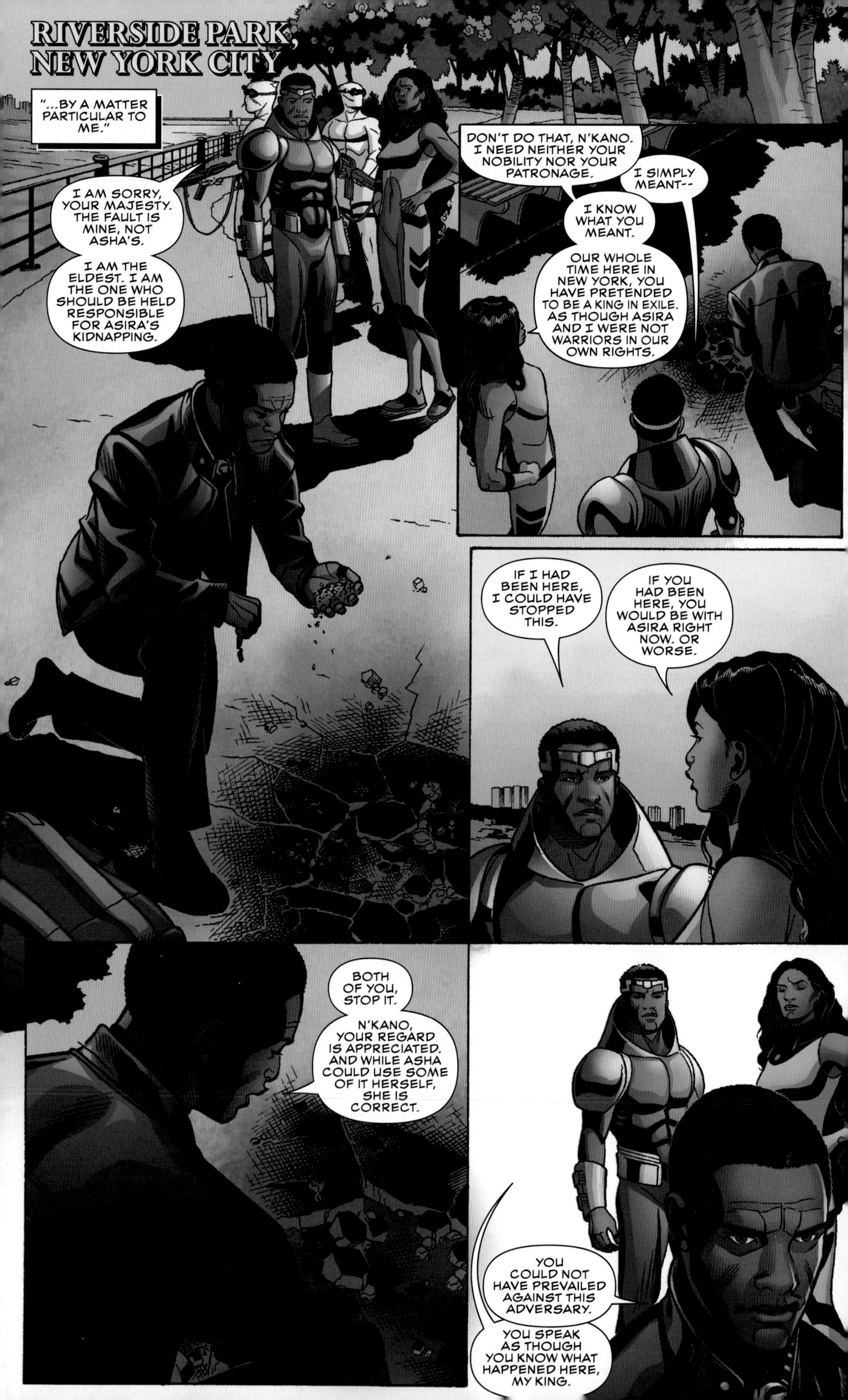
RIVERSIDE PARK, NEW YORK CITY
"...BY A MATTER PARTICULAR TO ME."
I AM SORRY, YOUR MAJESTY. THE FAULT IS MINE, NOT ASHA'S.
I AM THE ELDEST. I AM THE ONE WHO SHOULD BE HELD RESPONSIBLE FOR ASIRA'S KIDNAPPING.
DON'T DO THAT, N'KANO. I NEED NEITHER YOUR NOBILITY NOR YOUR PATRONAGE.
I SIMPLY MEANT--
I KNOW WHAT YOU MEANT.
OUR WHOLE TIME HERE IN NEW YORK, YOU HAVE PRETENDED TO BE A KING IN EXILE. AS THOUGH ASIRA AND I WERE NOT WARRIORS IN OUR OWN RIGHTS.
IF I HAD BEEN HERE, I COULD HAVE STOPPED THIS.
IF YOU HAD BEEN HERE, YOU WOULD BE WITH ASIRA RIGHT NOW. OR WORSE.
BOTH OF YOU, STOP IT.
N'KANO, YOUR REGARD IS APPRECIATED. AND WHILE ASHA COULD USE SOME OF IT HERSELF, SHE IS CORRECT.
YOU COULD NOT HAVE PREVAILED AGAINST THIS ADVERSARY.
YOU SPEAK AS THOUGH YOU KNOW WHAT HAPPENED HERE, MY KING.

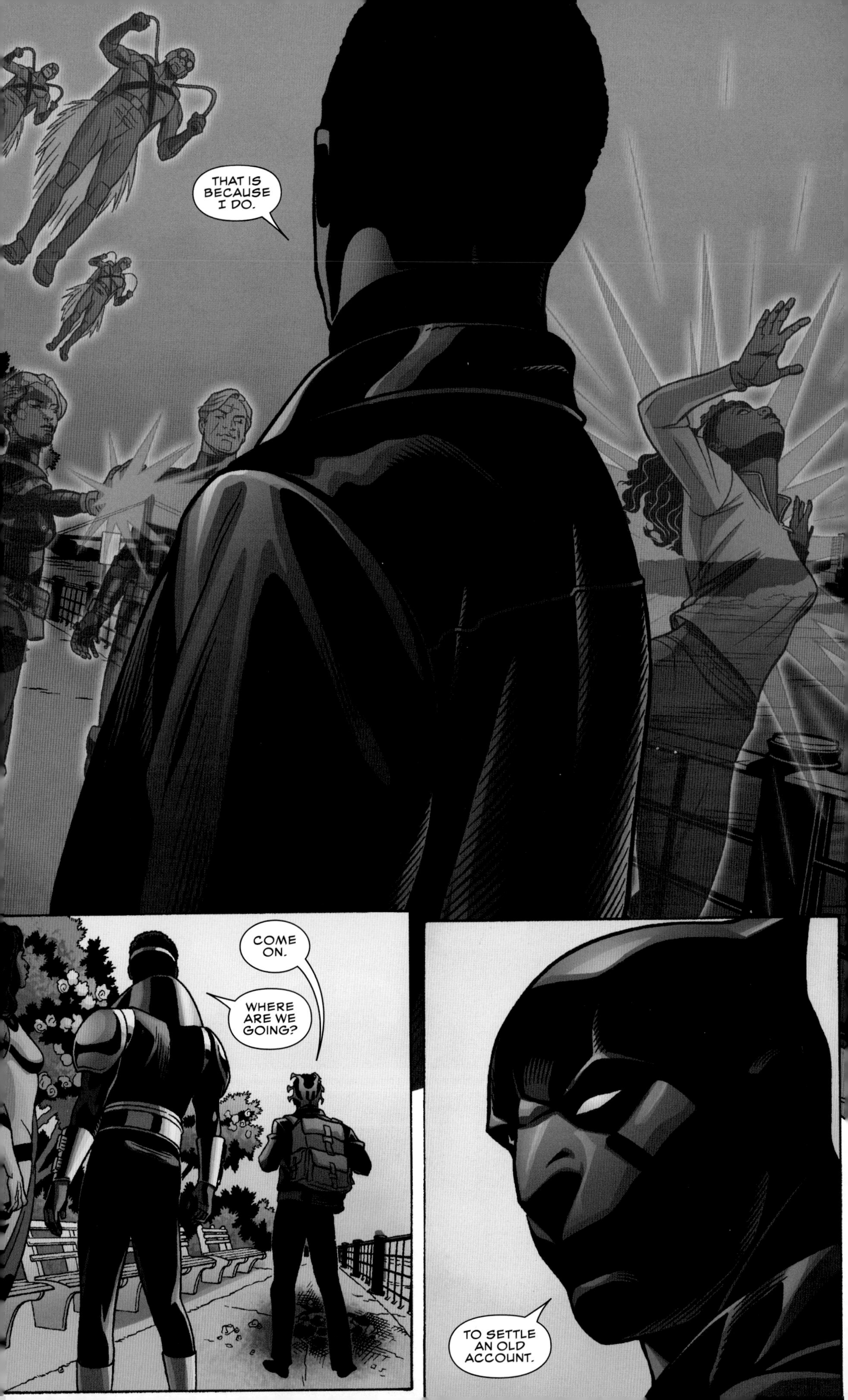
THAT IS BECAUSE I DO.
COME ON.
WHERE ARE WE GOING?
TO SETTLE AN OLD ACCOUNT.

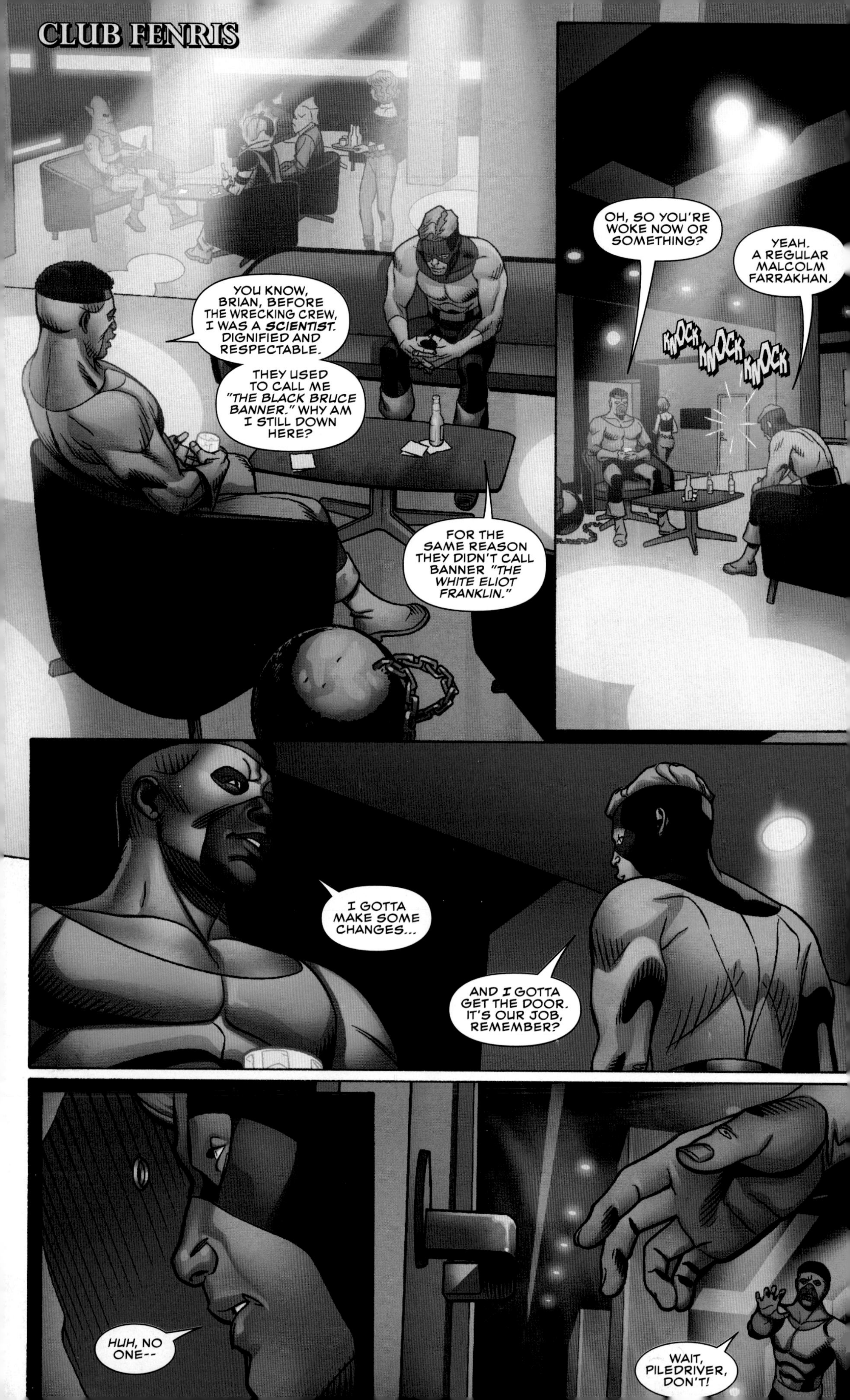
CLUB FENRIS
YOU KNOW, BRIAN, BEFORE THE WRECKING CREW, I WAS A SCIENTIST. DIGNIFIED AND RESPECTABLE.
THEY USED TO CALL ME "THE BLACK BRUCE BANNER." WHY AM I STILL DOWN HERE?
FOR THE SAME REASON THEY DIDN'T CALL BANNER "THE WHITE ELIOT FRANKLIN."
OH, SO YOU'RE WOKE NOW OR SOMETHING?
YEAH. A REGULAR MALCOLM FARRAKHAN.
KNOCK KNOCK KNOCK
I GOTTA MAKE SOME CHANGES...
AND I GOTTA GET THE DOOR. IT'S OUR JOB, REMEMBER?
HUH, NO ONE--
WAIT, PILEDRIVER, DON'T!

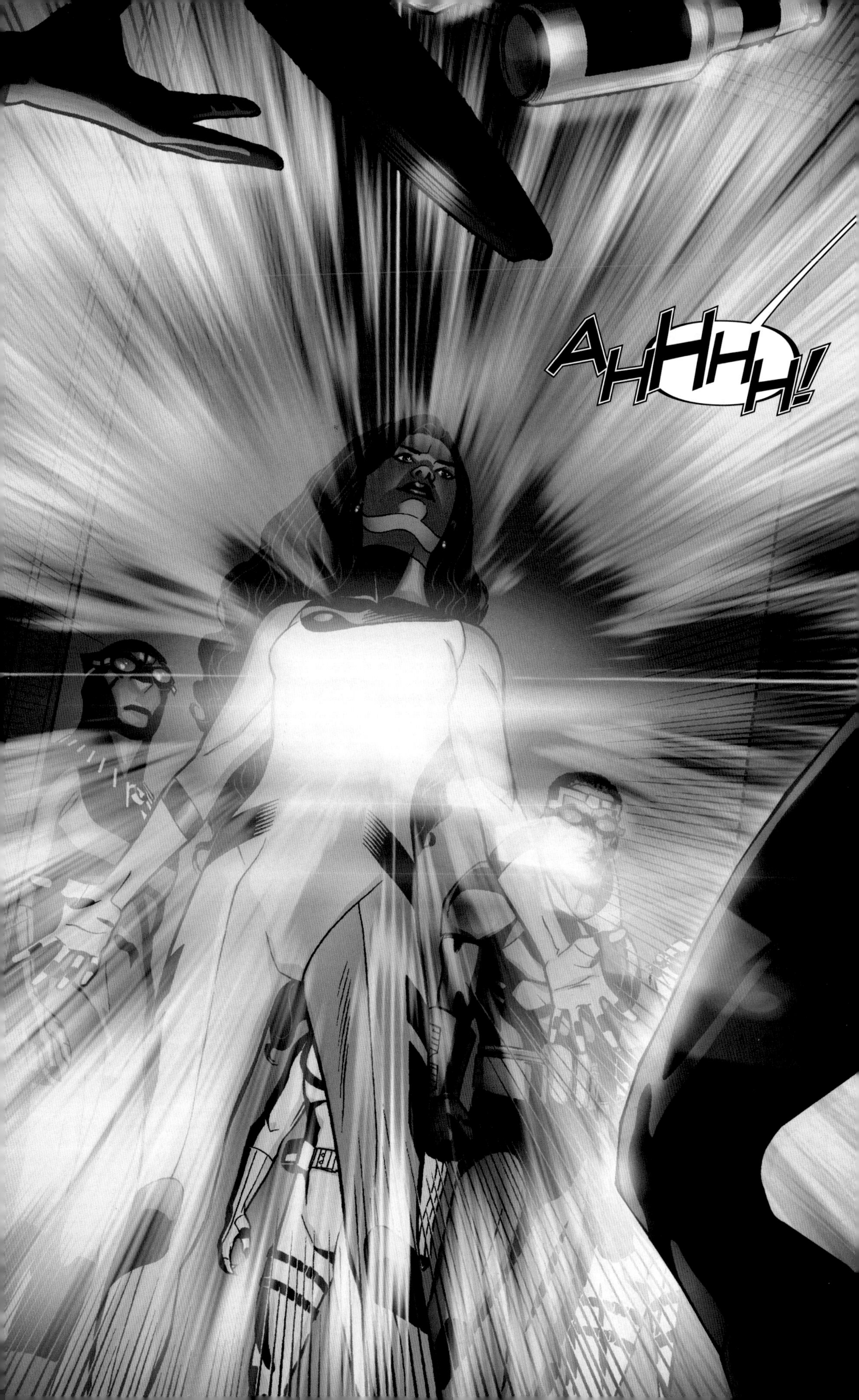
AHHHH!

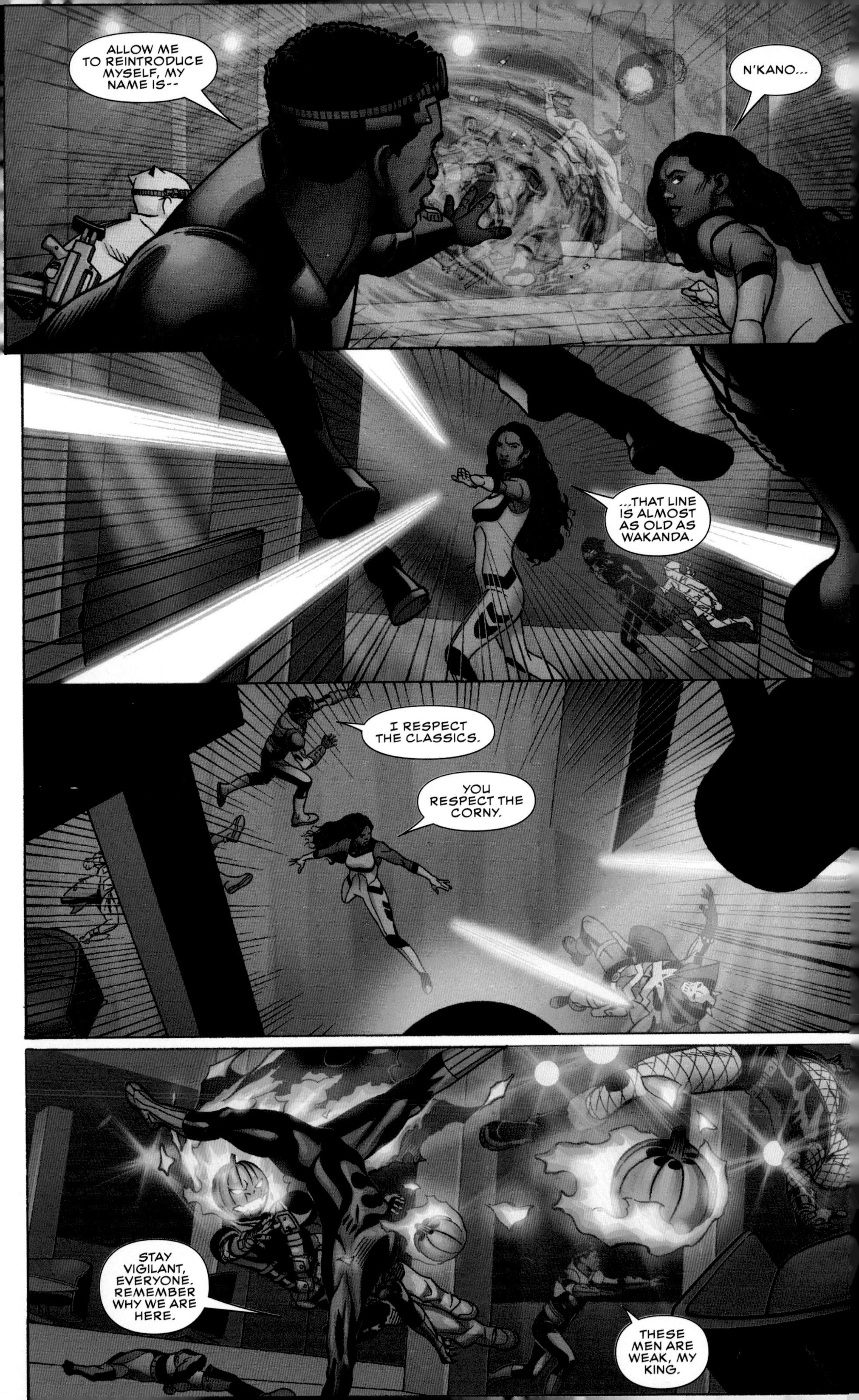
ALLOW ME TO REINTRODUCE MYSELF, MY NAME IS--
N'KANO...
...THAT LINE IS ALMOST AS OLD AS WAKANDA.
I RESPECT THE CLASSICS.
YOU RESPECT THE CORNY.
STAY VIGILANT, EVERYONE. REMEMBER WHY WE ARE HERE.
THESE MEN ARE WEAK, MY KING.

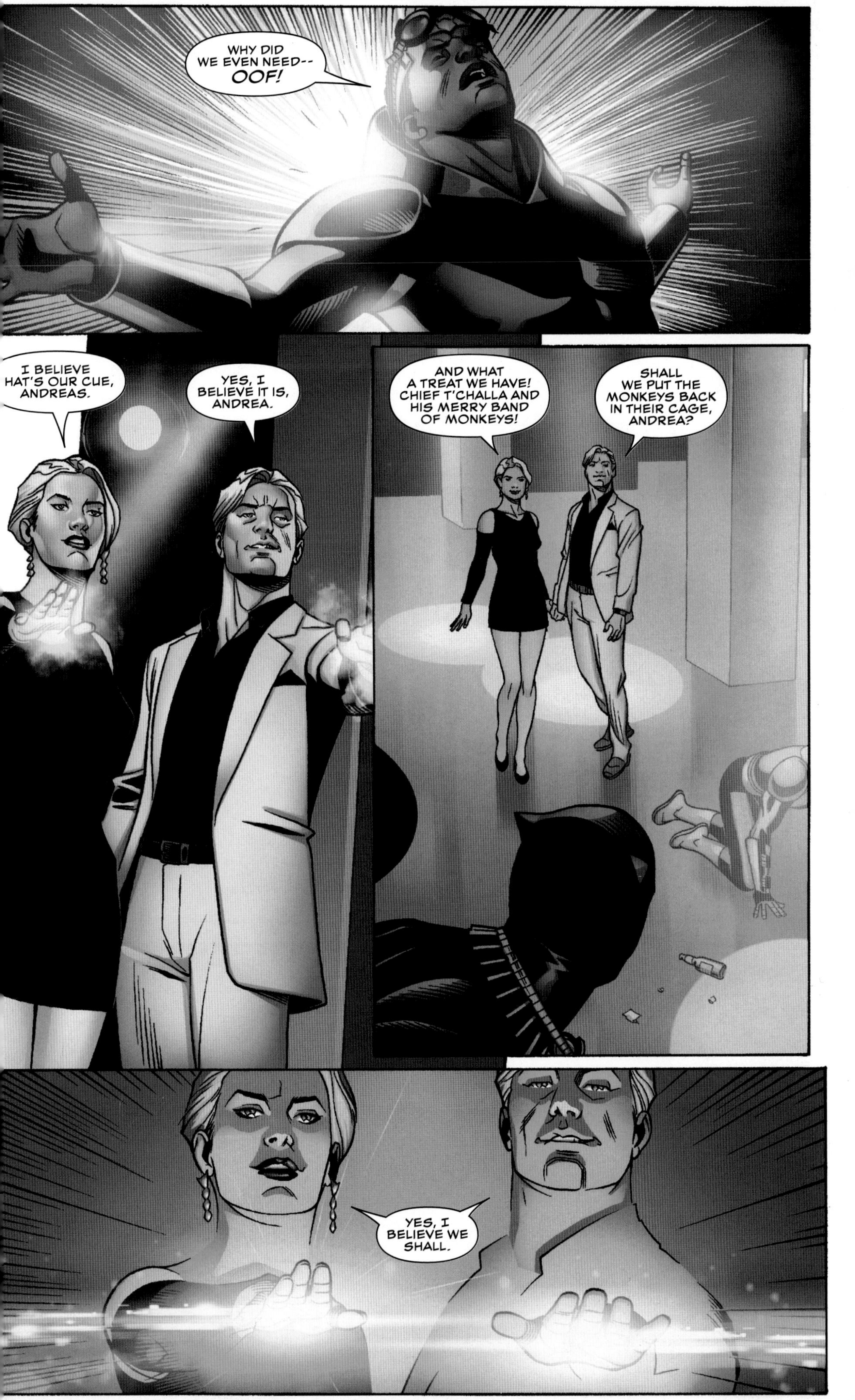
WHY DID WE EVEN NEED-- OOF!
I BELIEVE HAT'S OUR CUE, ANDREAS.
YES, I BELIEVE IT IS, ANDREA.
AND WHAT A TREAT WE HAVE! CHIEF T'CHALLA AND HIS MERRY BAND OF MONKEYS!
SHALL WE PUT THE MONKEYS BACK IN THEIR CAGE, ANDREA?
YES, I BELIEVE WE SHALL.

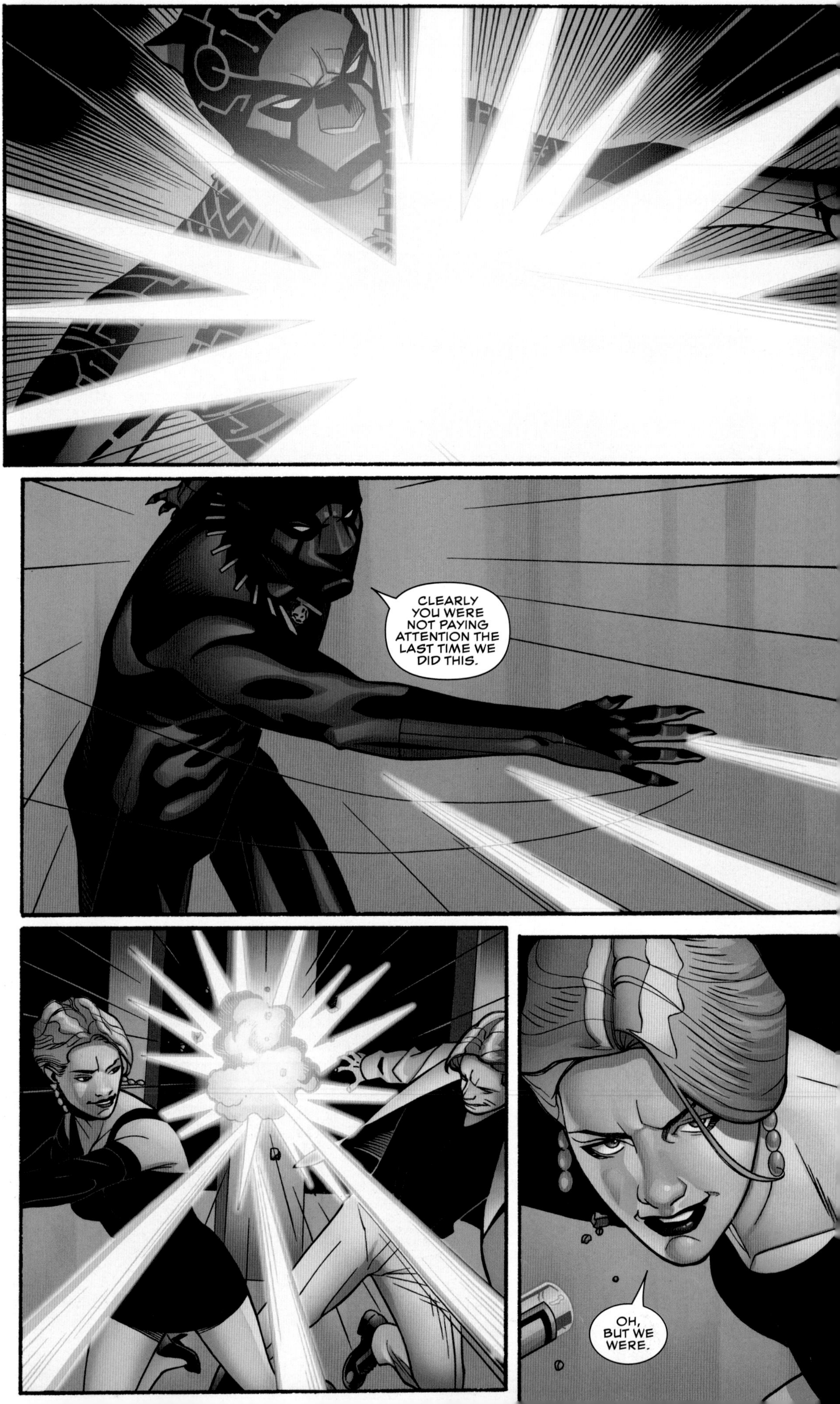
CLEARLY YOU WERE NOT PAYING ATTENTION THE LAST TIME WE DID THIS.
OH, BUT WE WERE.

YOU SHOULD NEVER HAVE COME HERE, T'CHALLA.

OUR HOUSE. OUR RULES.

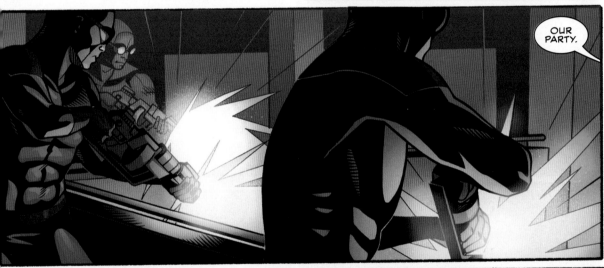

OUR PARTY.

HIS SUIT ABSORBS AND REFLECTS ENERGY, ANDREAS.

HOW ABOUT WE GIVE IT A STRESS TEST, ANDREA?

SO MUCH FOR YOUR SUIT, I GUESS.

WHAT NOW, CHIEF T'CHALLA?

WHAT, INDEED...

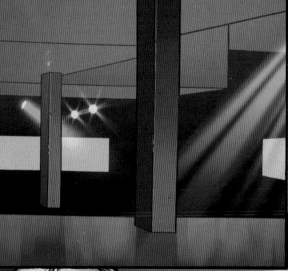

HEY... WHERE DID...?

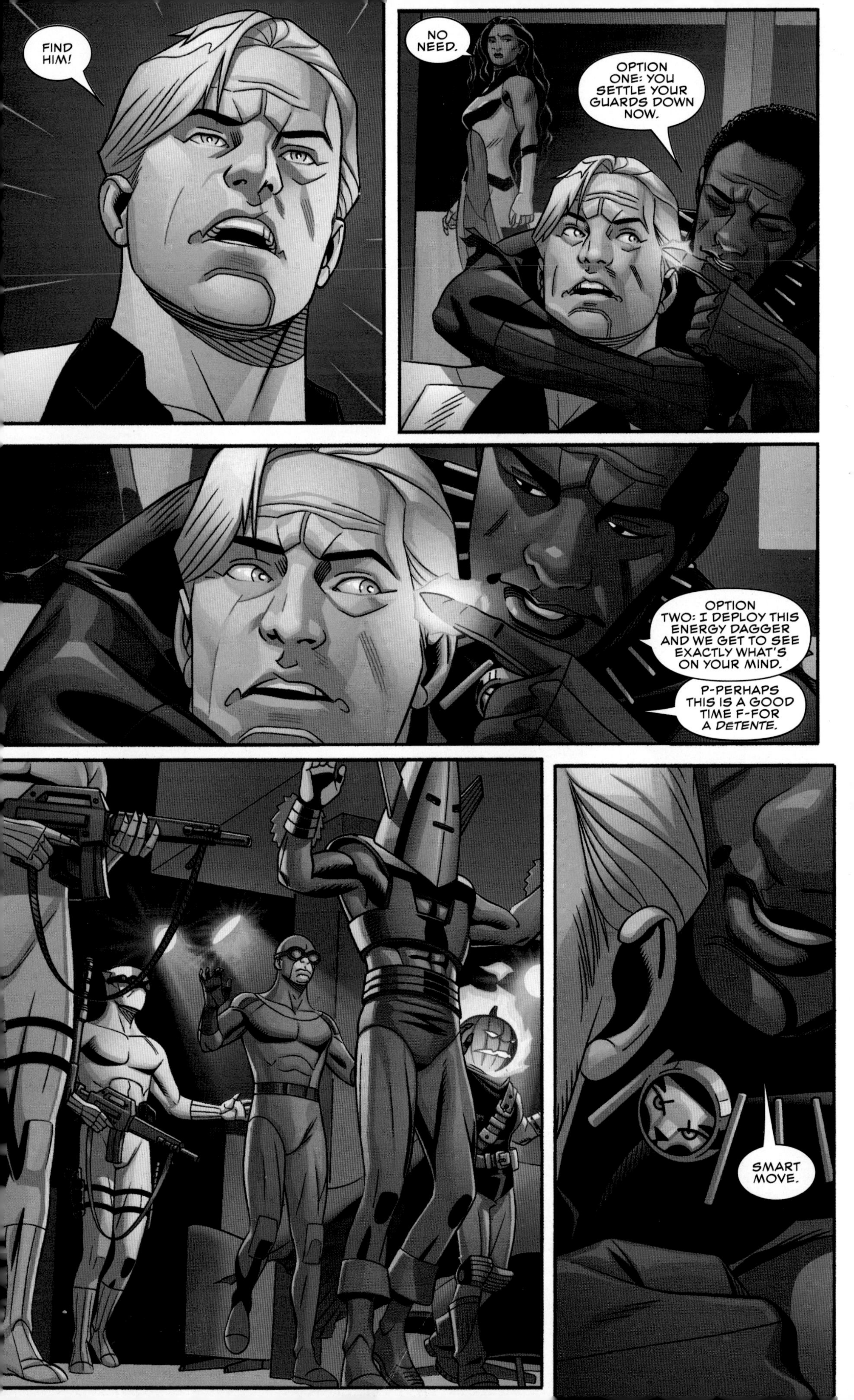
FIND HIM!
NO NEED.
OPTION ONE: YOU SETTLE YOUR GUARDS DOWN NOW.
OPTION TWO: I DEPLOY THIS ENERGY DAGGER AND WE GET TO SEE EXACTLY WHAT'S ON YOUR MIND.
P-PERHAPS THIS IS A GOOD TIME F-FOR A *DETENTE*.
SMART MOVE.

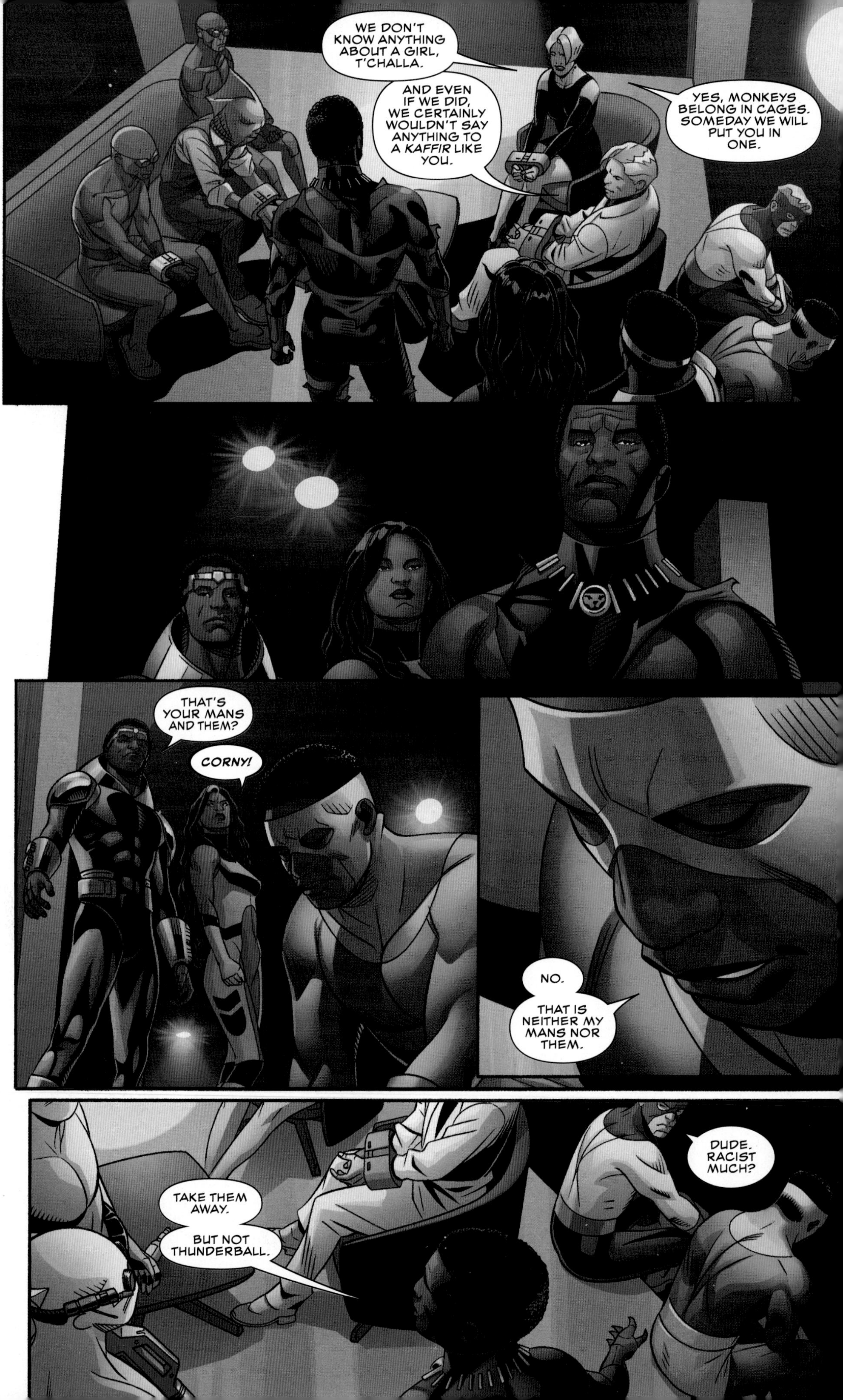
WE DON'T KNOW ANYTHING ABOUT A GIRL, T'CHALLA.
AND EVEN IF WE DID, WE CERTAINLY WOULDN'T SAY ANYTHING TO A *KAFFIR* LIKE YOU.
YES, MONKEYS BELONG IN CAGES. SOMEDAY WE WILL PUT YOU IN ONE.
THAT'S YOUR MANS AND THEM?
CORNY!
NO.
THAT IS NEITHER MY MANS NOR THEM.
TAKE THEM AWAY.
BUT NOT THUNDERBALL.
DUDE. RACIST MUCH?

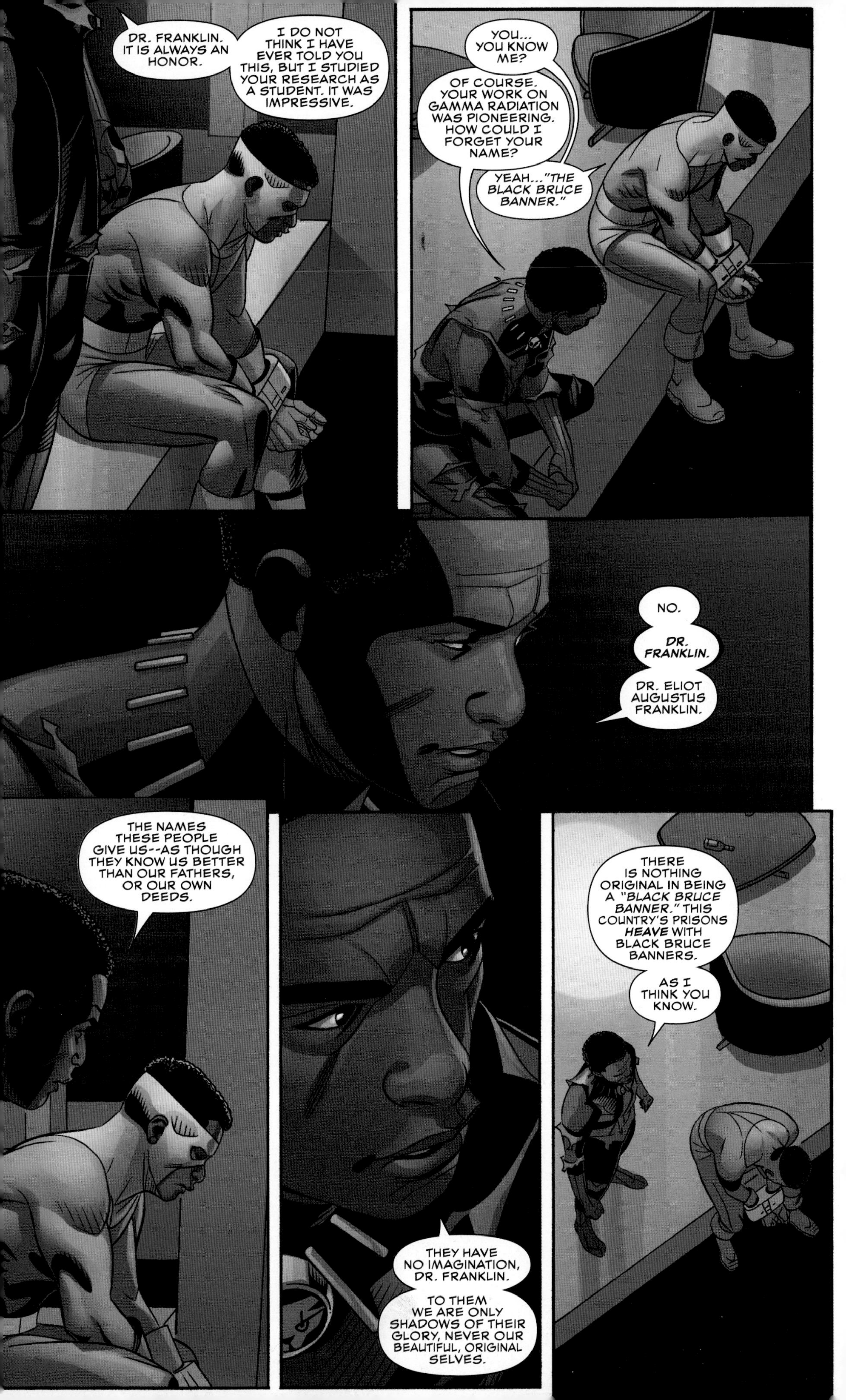
DR. FRANKLIN. IT IS ALWAYS AN HONOR.
I DO NOT THINK I HAVE EVER TOLD YOU THIS, BUT I STUDIED YOUR RESEARCH AS A STUDENT. IT WAS IMPRESSIVE.
YOU... YOU KNOW ME?
OF COURSE. YOUR WORK ON GAMMA RADIATION WAS PIONEERING. HOW COULD I FORGET YOUR NAME?
YEAH..."THE BLACK BRUCE BANNER."
NO.
DR. FRANKLIN.
DR. ELIOT AUGUSTUS FRANKLIN.
THE NAMES THESE PEOPLE GIVE US--AS THOUGH THEY KNOW US BETTER THAN OUR FATHERS, OR OUR OWN DEEDS.
THEY HAVE NO IMAGINATION, DR. FRANKLIN.
TO THEM WE ARE ONLY SHADOWS OF THEIR GLORY, NEVER OUR BEAUTIFUL, ORIGINAL SELVES.
THERE IS NOTHING ORIGINAL IN BEING A "BLACK BRUCE BANNER." THIS COUNTRY'S PRISONS HEAVE WITH BLACK BRUCE BANNERS.
AS I THINK YOU KNOW.

DR. FRANKLIN, I WILL BE BRIEF. TIME IS OF THE ESSENCE.

THE GIRL.

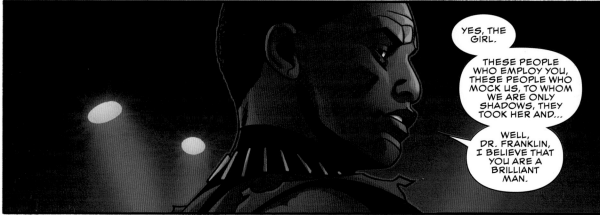

YES, THE GIRL.

THESE PEOPLE WHO EMPLOY YOU, THESE PEOPLE WHO MOCK US, TO WHOM WE ARE ONLY SHADOWS, THEY TOOK HER AND...

WELL, DR. FRANKLIN, I BELIEVE THAT YOU ARE A BRILLIANT MAN.

BUT MORE, I BELIEVE YOU WERE A GOOD MAN ONCE. AND THAT YOU MIGHT WELL BE ONE AGAIN.

YOU DO NOT HAVE TO ANSWER TO WHATEVER THEY CALL YOU, DR. FRANKLIN.

IT IS NOT TOO LATE TO RECOVER YOUR OWN NAME.

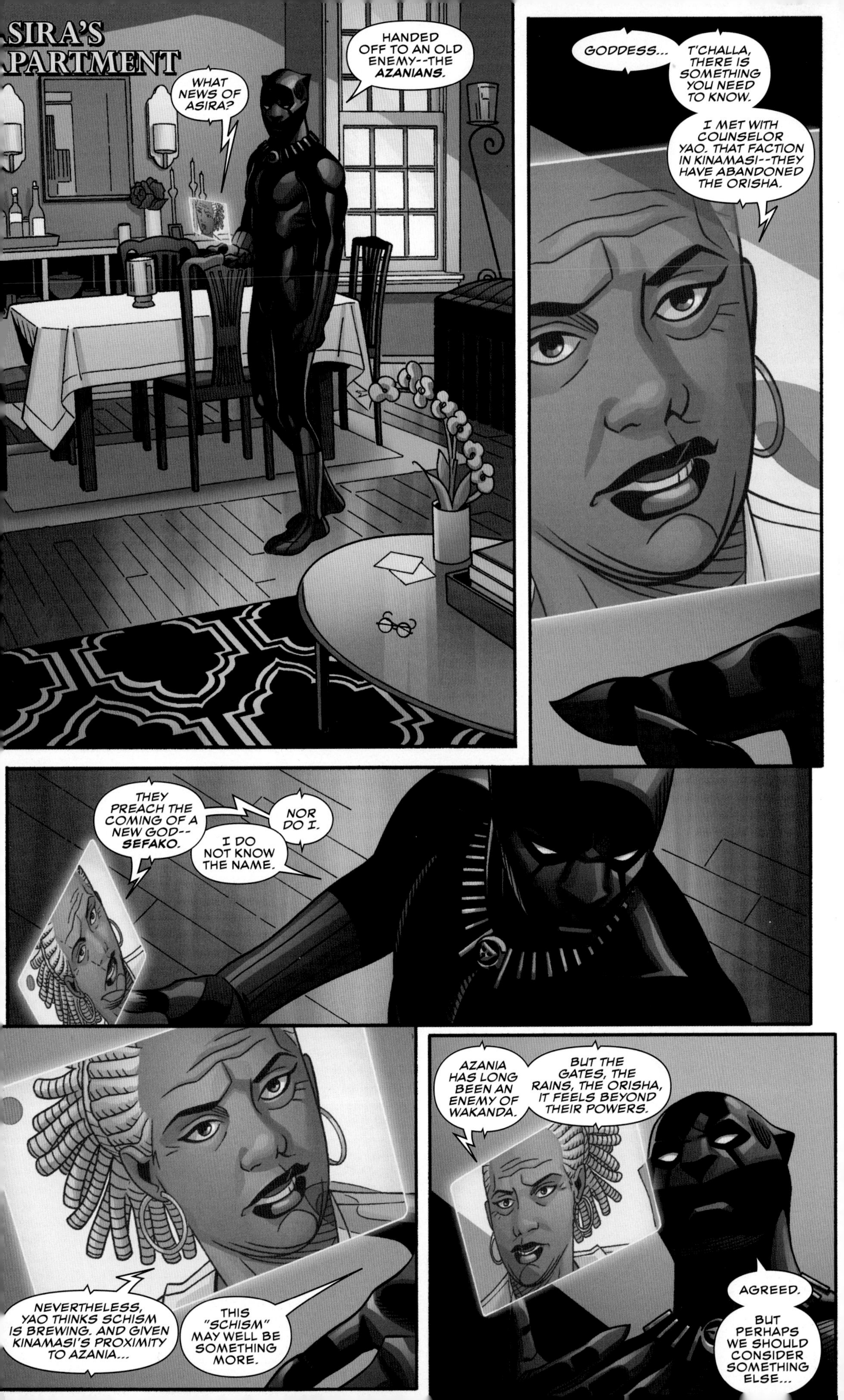
SIRA'S
PARTMENT
WHAT NEWS OF ASIRA?
HANDED OFF TO AN OLD ENEMY--THE AZANIANS.
GODDESS...
T'CHALLA, THERE IS SOMETHING YOU NEED TO KNOW.
I MET WITH COUNSELOR YAO. THAT FACTION IN KINAMASI--THEY HAVE ABANDONED THE ORISHA.
THEY PREACH THE COMING OF A NEW GOD--SEFAKO.
I DO NOT KNOW THE NAME.
NOR DO I.
NEVERTHELESS, YAO THINKS SCHISM IS BREWING. AND GIVEN KINAMASI'S PROXIMITY TO AZANIA...
THIS "SCHISM" MAY WELL BE SOMETHING MORE.
AZANIA HAS LONG BEEN AN ENEMY OF WAKANDA.
BUT THE GATES, THE RAINS, THE ORISHA, IT FEELS BEYOND THEIR POWERS.
AGREED.
BUT PERHAPS WE SHOULD CONSIDER SOMETHING ELSE...

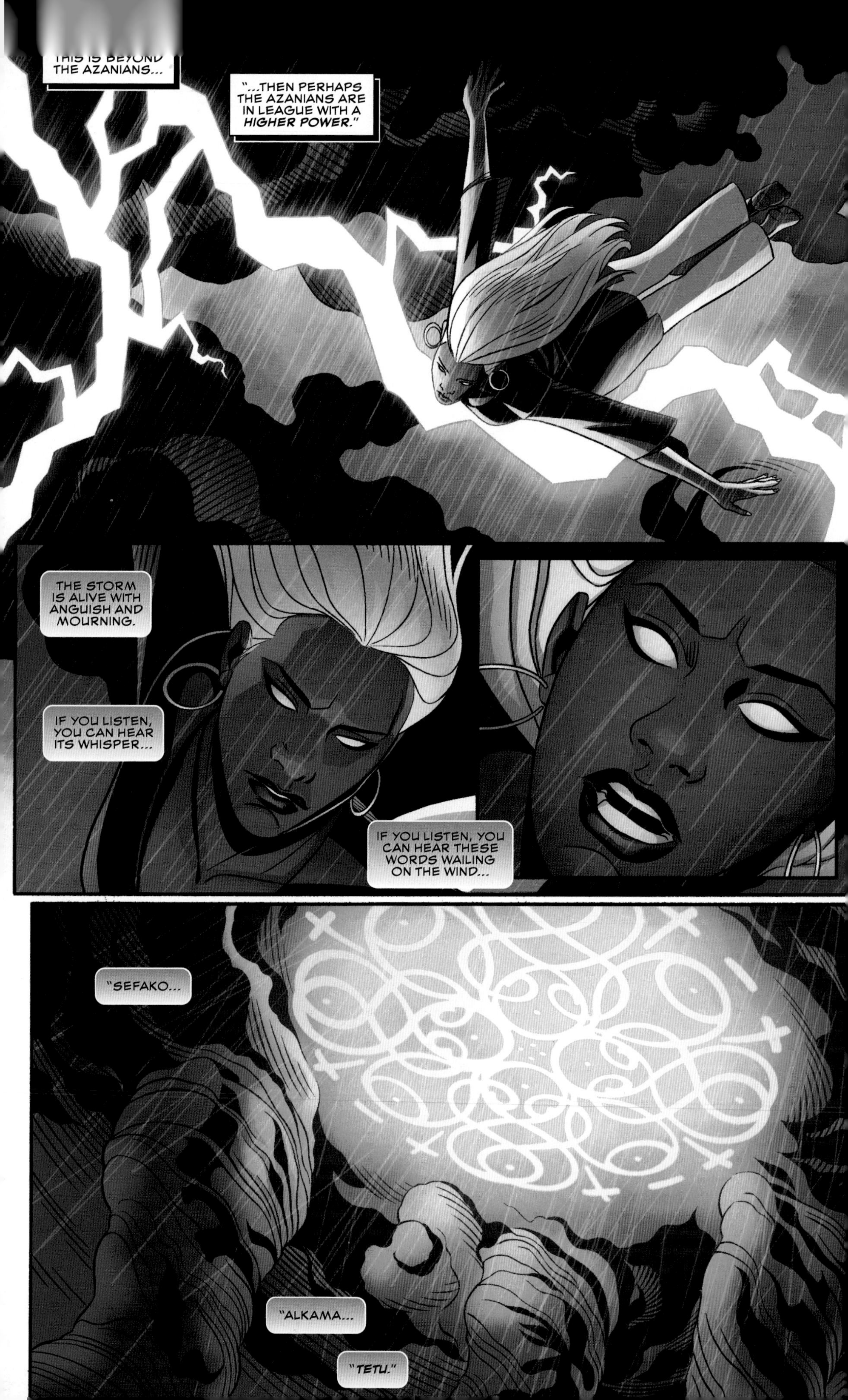
THIS IS BEYOND THE AZANIANS...
"...THEN PERHAPS THE AZANIANS ARE IN LEAGUE WITH A *HIGHER POWER.*"
THE STORM IS ALIVE WITH ANGUISH AND MOURNING.
IF YOU LISTEN, YOU CAN HEAR ITS WHISPER...
IF YOU LISTEN, YOU CAN HEAR THESE WORDS WAILING ON THE WIND...
"SEFAKO...
"ALKAMA...
"*TETU.*"

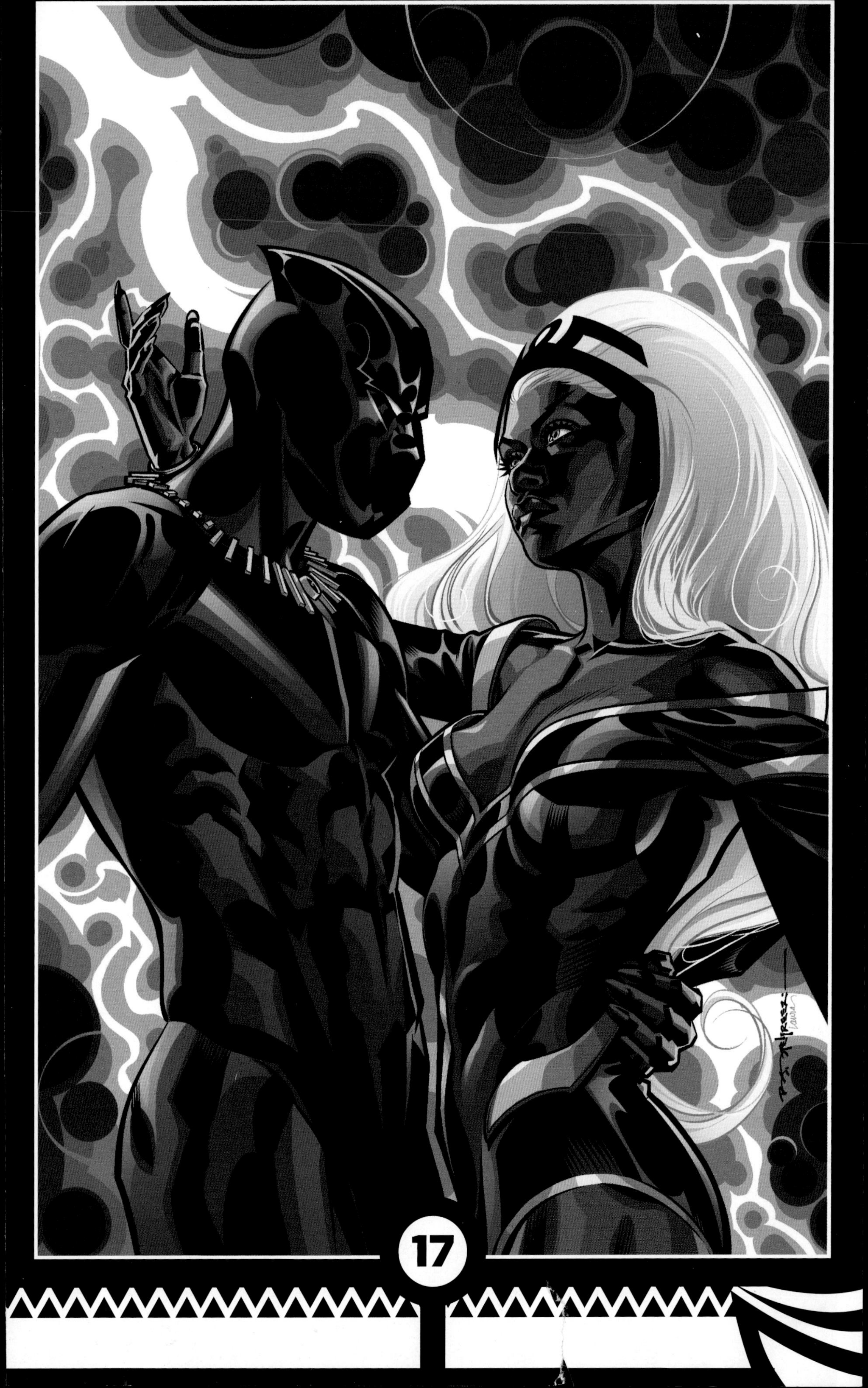
17

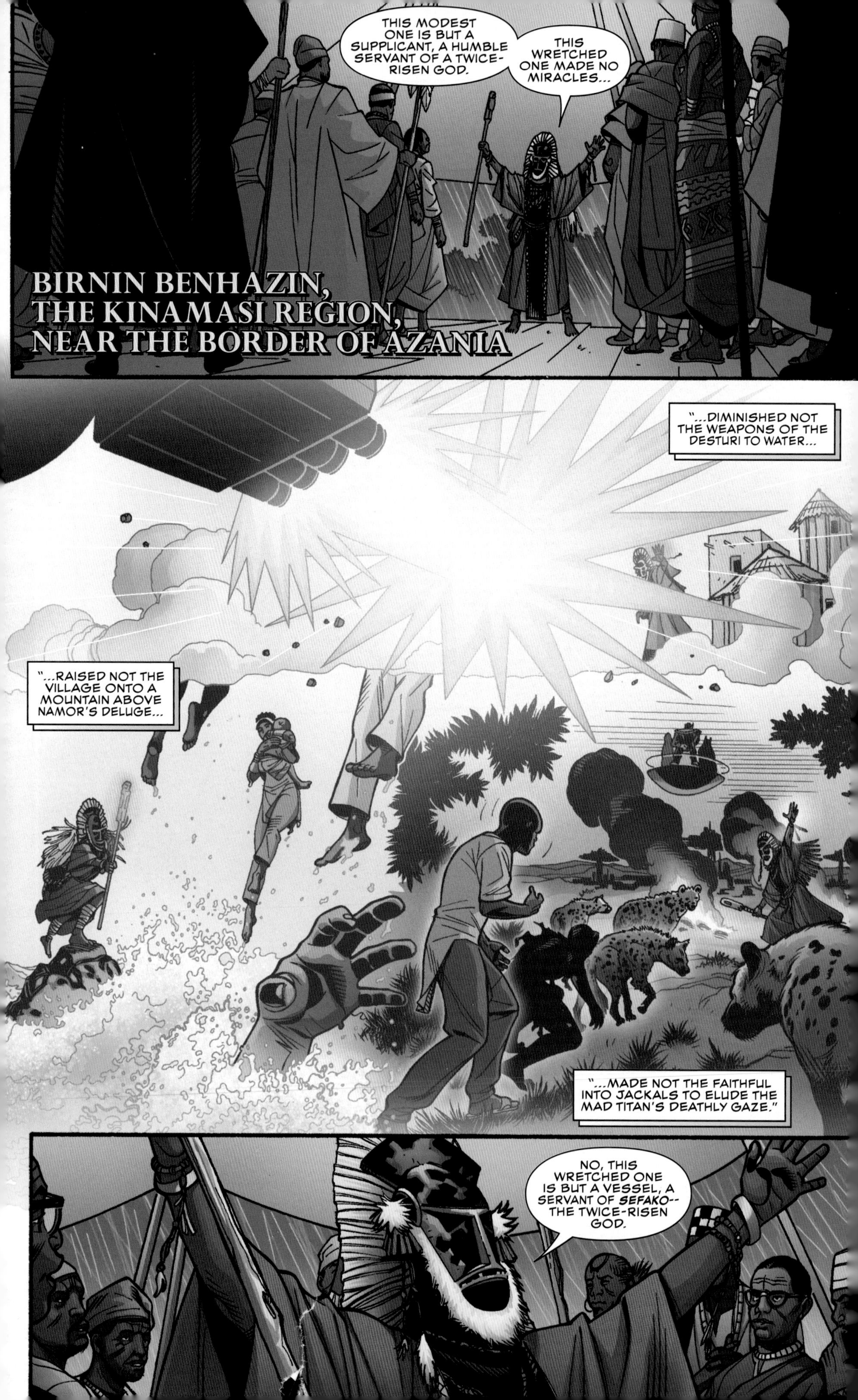

THIS MODEST ONE IS BUT A SUPPLICANT, A HUMBLE SERVANT OF A TWICE-RISEN GOD.
THIS WRETCHED ONE MADE NO MIRACLES...
BIRNIN BENHAZIN, THE KINAMASI REGION, NEAR THE BORDER OF AZANIA
"...DIMINISHED NOT THE WEAPONS OF THE DESTURI TO WATER...
"...RAISED NOT THE VILLAGE ONTO A MOUNTAIN ABOVE NAMOR'S DELUGE...
"...MADE NOT THE FAITHFUL INTO JACKALS TO ELUDE THE MAD TITAN'S DEATHLY GAZE."
NO, THIS WRETCHED ONE IS BUT A VESSEL, A SERVANT OF SEFAKO-- THE TWICE-RISEN GOD.

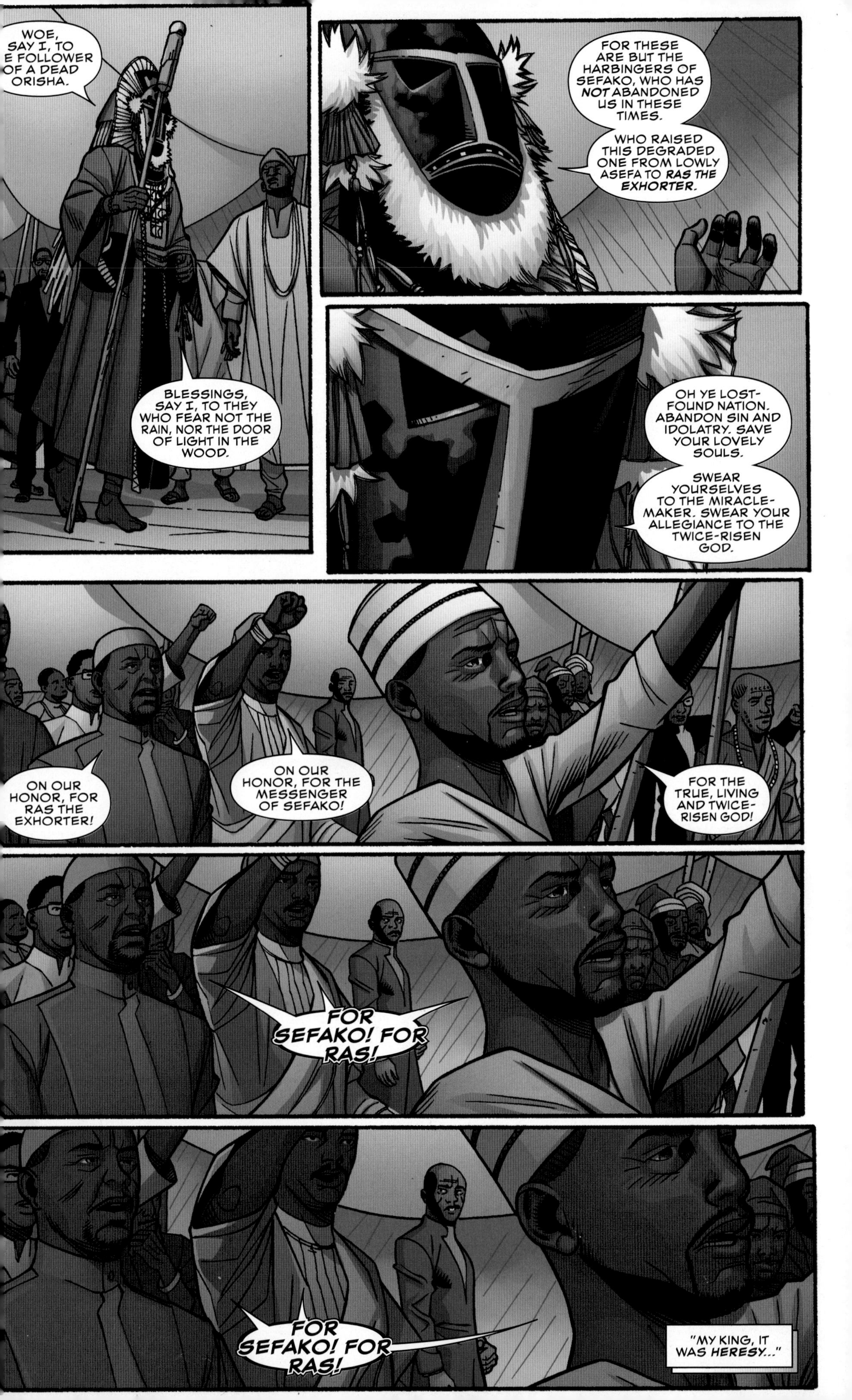
WOE, SAY I, TO E FOLLOWER OF A DEAD ORISHA.
BLESSINGS, SAY I, TO THEY WHO FEAR NOT THE RAIN, NOR THE DOOR OF LIGHT IN THE WOOD.
FOR THESE ARE BUT THE HARBINGERS OF SEFAKO, WHO HAS NOT ABANDONED US IN THESE TIMES.
WHO RAISED THIS DEGRADED ONE FROM LOWLY ASEFA TO RAS THE EXHORTER.
OH YE LOST-FOUND NATION. ABANDON SIN AND IDOLATRY. SAVE YOUR LOVELY SOULS.
SWEAR YOURSELVES TO THE MIRACLE-MAKER. SWEAR YOUR ALLEGIANCE TO THE TWICE-RISEN GOD.
ON OUR HONOR, FOR RAS THE EXHORTER!
ON OUR HONOR, FOR THE MESSENGER OF SEFAKO!
FOR THE TRUE, LIVING AND TWICE-RISEN GOD!
FOR SEFAKO! FOR RAS!
FOR SEFAKO! FOR RAS!
"MY KING, IT WAS HERESY..."

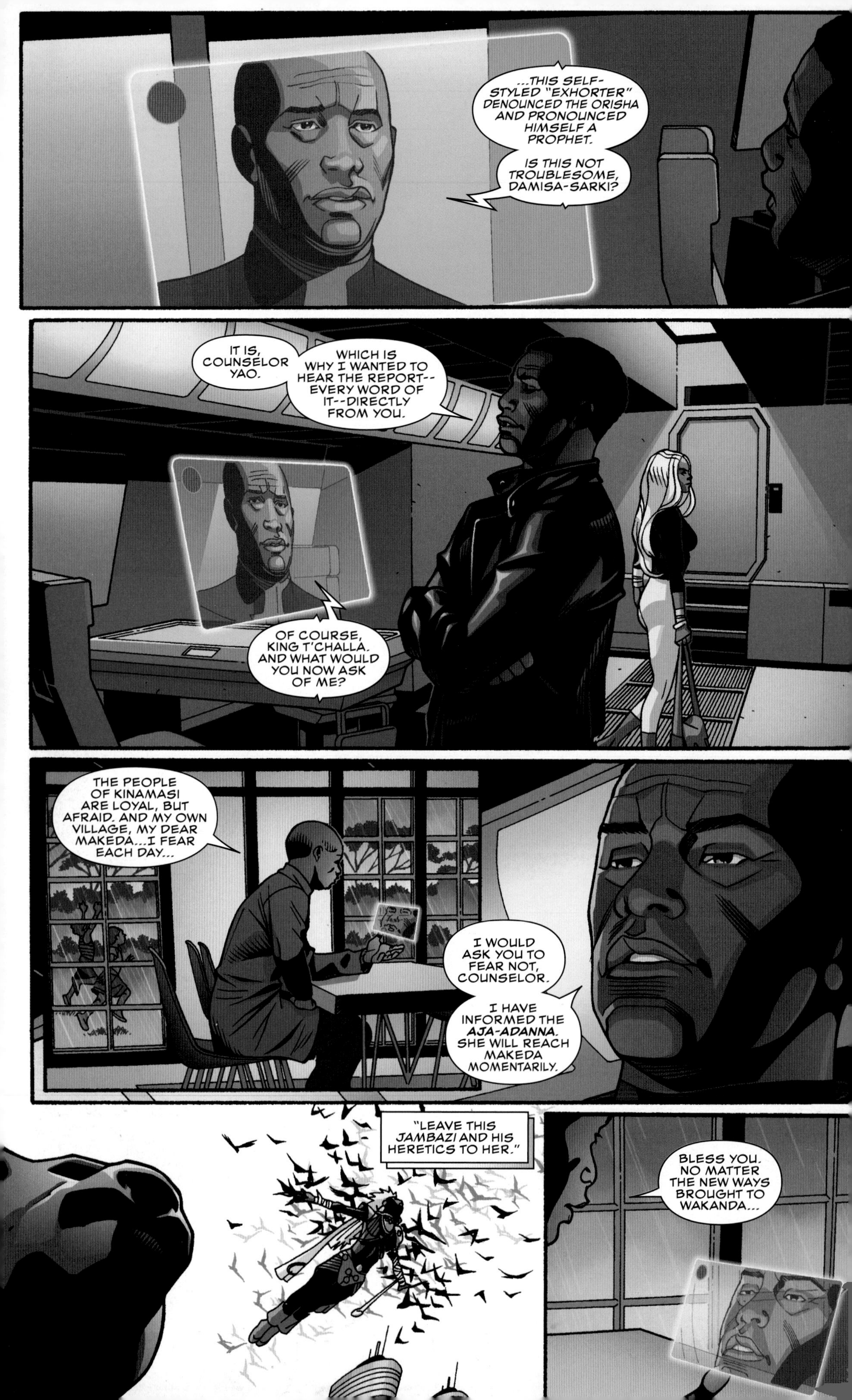

...THIS SELF-STYLED "EXHORTER" DENOUNCED THE ORISHA AND PRONOUNCED HIMSELF A PROPHET.
IS THIS NOT TROUBLESOME, DAMISA-SARKI?
IT IS, COUNSELOR YAO.
WHICH IS WHY I WANTED TO HEAR THE REPORT--EVERY WORD OF IT--DIRECTLY FROM YOU.
OF COURSE, KING T'CHALLA. AND WHAT WOULD YOU NOW ASK OF ME?
THE PEOPLE OF KINAMASI ARE LOYAL, BUT AFRAID. AND MY OWN VILLAGE, MY DEAR MAKEDA...I FEAR EACH DAY...
I WOULD ASK YOU TO FEAR NOT, COUNSELOR.
I HAVE INFORMED THE AJA-ADANNA. SHE WILL REACH MAKEDA MOMENTARILY.
"LEAVE THIS JAMBAZI AND HIS HERETICS TO HER."
BLESS YOU. NO MATTER THE NEW WAYS BROUGHT TO WAKANDA...

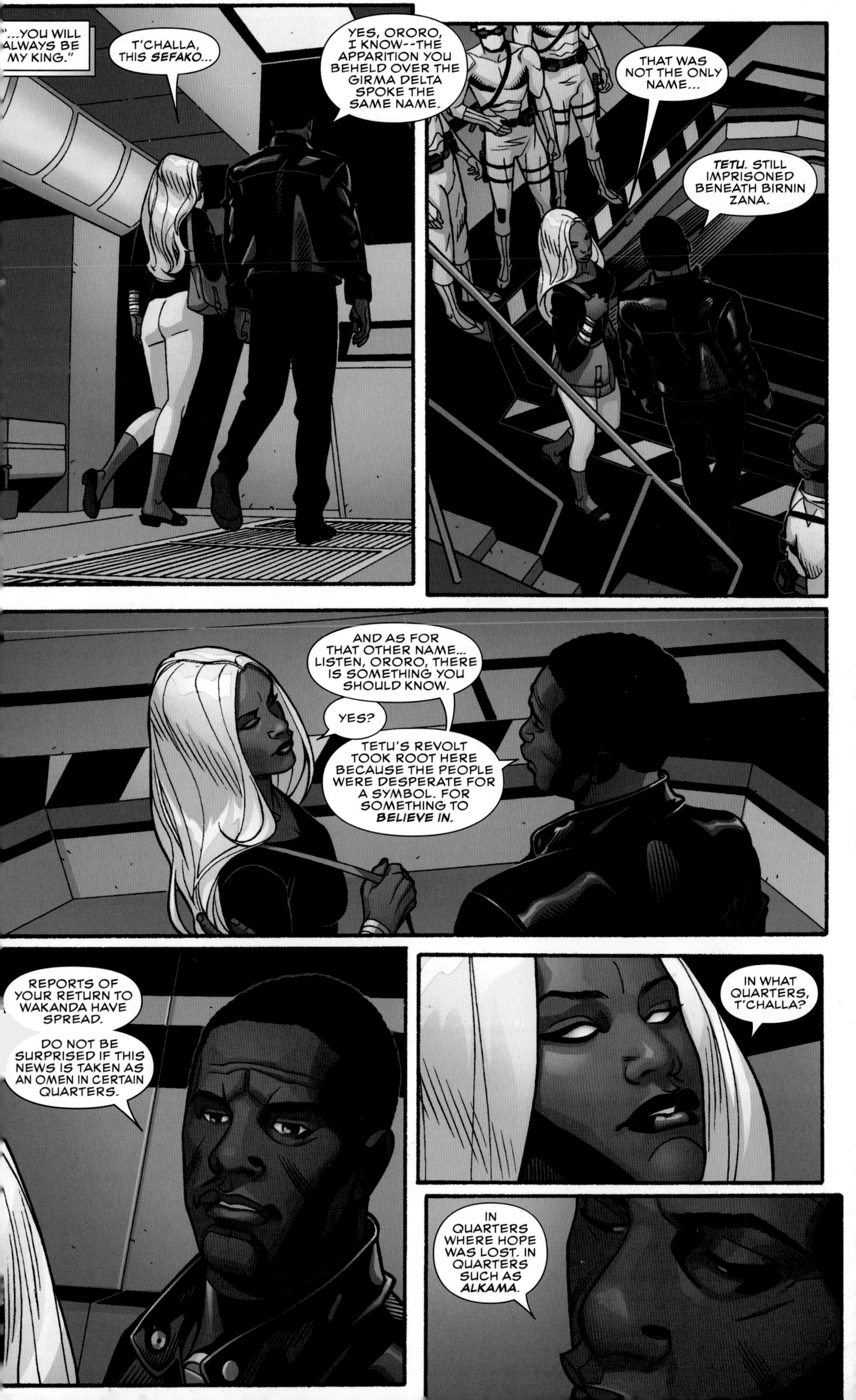
"...YOU WILL ALWAYS BE MY KING."
T'CHALLA, THIS SEFAKO...
YES, ORORO, I KNOW--THE APPARITION YOU BEHELD OVER THE GIRMA DELTA SPOKE THE SAME NAME.
THAT WAS NOT THE ONLY NAME...
TETU. STILL IMPRISONED BENEATH BIRNIN ZANA.
AND AS FOR THAT OTHER NAME... LISTEN, ORORO, THERE IS SOMETHING YOU SHOULD KNOW.
YES?
TETU'S REVOLT TOOK ROOT HERE BECAUSE THE PEOPLE WERE DESPERATE FOR A SYMBOL. FOR SOMETHING TO BELIEVE IN.
REPORTS OF YOUR RETURN TO WAKANDA HAVE SPREAD.
DO NOT BE SURPRISED IF THIS NEWS IS TAKEN AS AN OMEN IN CERTAIN QUARTERS.
IN WHAT QUARTERS, T'CHALLA?
IN QUARTERS WHERE HOPE WAS LOST. IN QUARTERS SUCH AS ALKAMA.

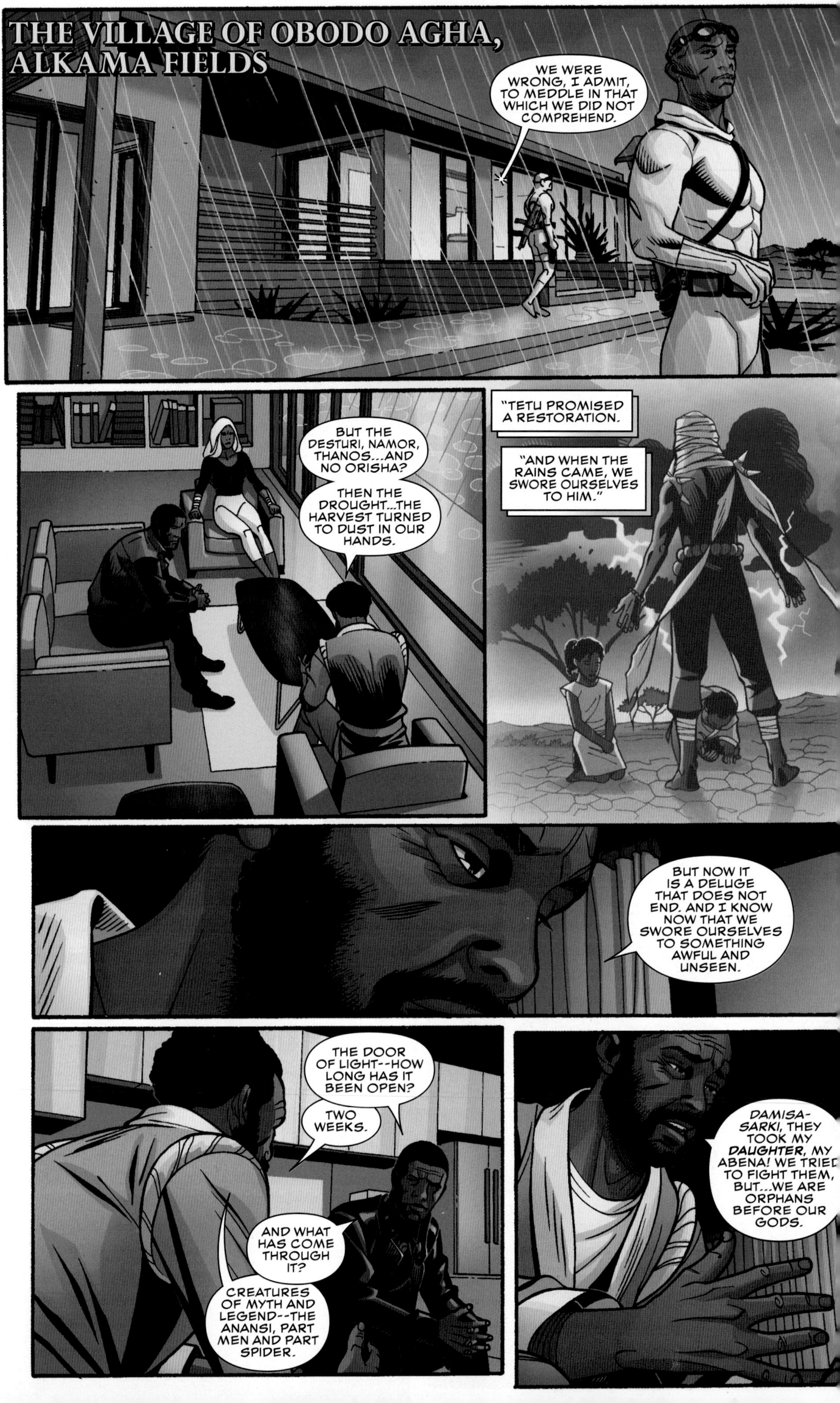
THE VILLAGE OF OBODO AGHA, ALKAMA FIELDS
WE WERE WRONG, I ADMIT, TO MEDDLE IN THAT WHICH WE DID NOT COMPREHEND.
BUT THE DESTURI, NAMOR, THANOS...AND NO ORISHA?
THEN THE DROUGHT...THE HARVEST TURNED TO DUST IN OUR HANDS.
"TETU PROMISED A RESTORATION.
"AND WHEN THE RAINS CAME, WE SWORE OURSELVES TO HIM."
BUT NOW IT IS A DELUGE THAT DOES NOT END. AND I KNOW NOW THAT WE SWORE OURSELVES TO SOMETHING AWFUL AND UNSEEN.
THE DOOR OF LIGHT--HOW LONG HAS IT BEEN OPEN?
TWO WEEKS.
AND WHAT HAS COME THROUGH IT?
CREATURES OF MYTH AND LEGEND--THE ANANSI, PART MEN AND PART SPIDER.
DAMISA-SARKI, THEY TOOK MY DAUGHTER, MY ABENA! WE TRIED TO FIGHT THEM, BUT...WE ARE ORPHANS BEFORE OUR GODS.

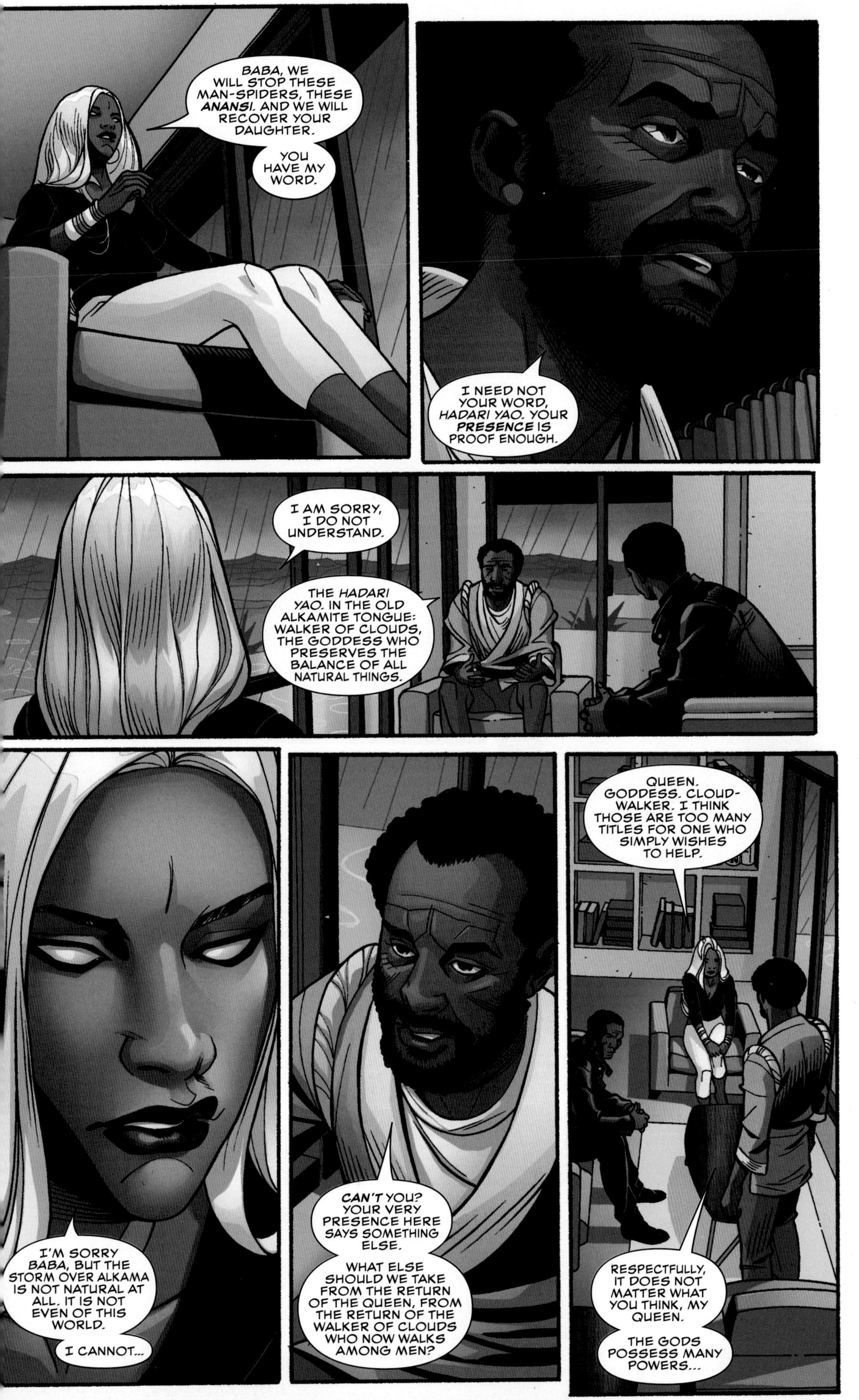
BABA, WE WILL STOP THESE MAN-SPIDERS, THESE ANANSI. AND WE WILL RECOVER YOUR DAUGHTER.
YOU HAVE MY WORD.
I NEED NOT YOUR WORD, HADARI YAO. YOUR PRESENCE IS PROOF ENOUGH.
I AM SORRY, I DO NOT UNDERSTAND.
THE HADARI YAO. IN THE OLD ALKAMITE TONGUE: WALKER OF CLOUDS, THE GODDESS WHO PRESERVES THE BALANCE OF ALL NATURAL THINGS.
I'M SORRY BABA, BUT THE STORM OVER ALKAMA IS NOT NATURAL AT ALL. IT IS NOT EVEN OF THIS WORLD.
I CANNOT...
CAN'T YOU? YOUR VERY PRESENCE HERE SAYS SOMETHING ELSE.
WHAT ELSE SHOULD WE TAKE FROM THE RETURN OF THE QUEEN, FROM THE RETURN OF THE WALKER OF CLOUDS WHO NOW WALKS AMONG MEN?
QUEEN. GODDESS. CLOUD-WALKER. I THINK THOSE ARE TOO MANY TITLES FOR ONE WHO SIMPLY WISHES TO HELP.
RESPECTFULLY, IT DOES NOT MATTER WHAT YOU THINK, MY QUEEN.
THE GODS POSSESS MANY POWERS...

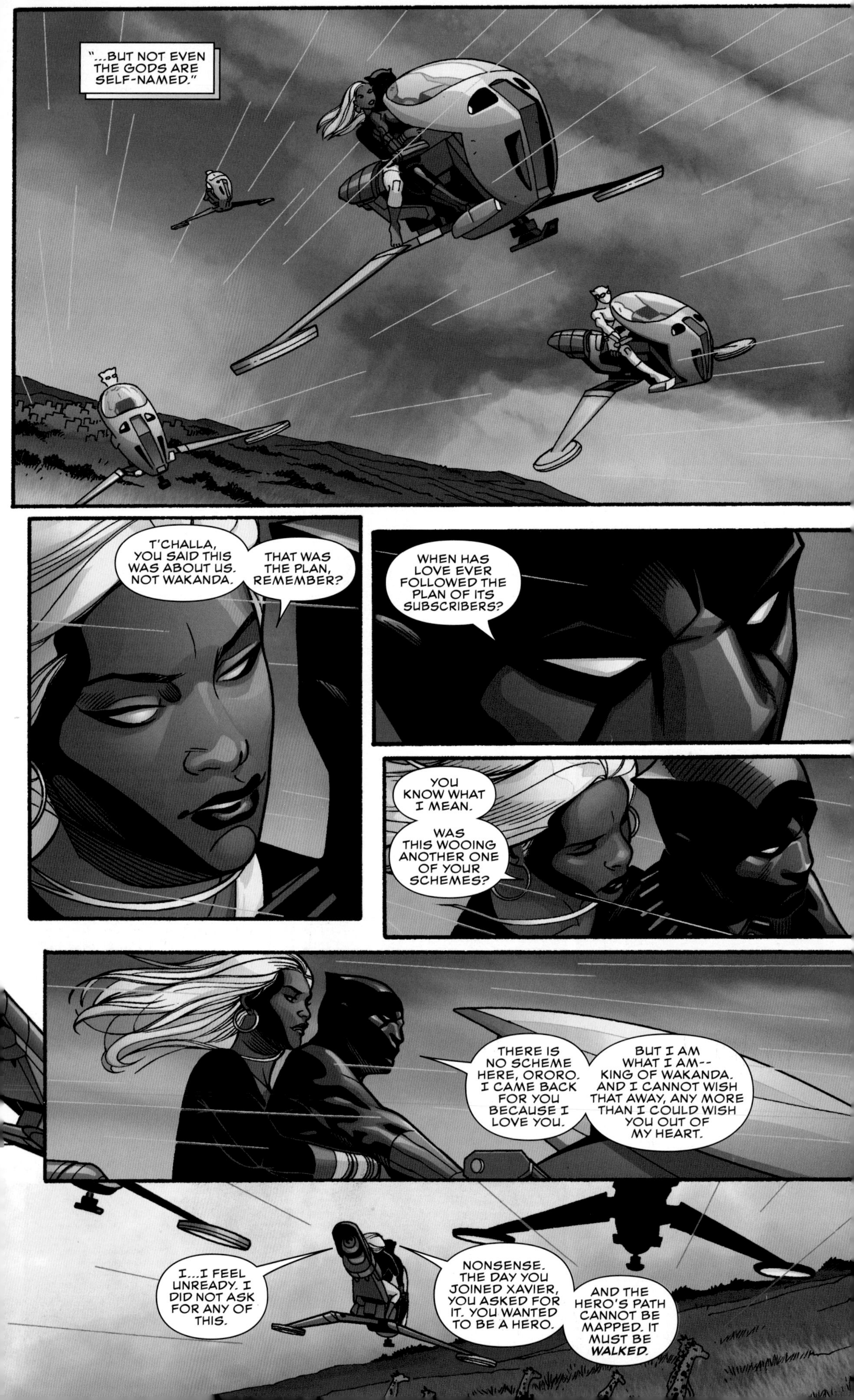
"...BUT NOT EVEN THE GODS ARE SELF-NAMED."
T'CHALLA, YOU SAID THIS WAS ABOUT US. NOT WAKANDA.
THAT WAS THE PLAN, REMEMBER?
WHEN HAS LOVE EVER FOLLOWED THE PLAN OF ITS SUBSCRIBERS?
YOU KNOW WHAT I MEAN.
WAS THIS WOOING ANOTHER ONE OF YOUR SCHEMES?
THERE IS NO SCHEME HERE, ORORO. I CAME BACK FOR YOU BECAUSE I LOVE YOU.
BUT I AM WHAT I AM-- KING OF WAKANDA. AND I CANNOT WISH THAT AWAY, ANY MORE THAN I COULD WISH YOU OUT OF MY HEART.
I...I FEEL UNREADY. I DID NOT ASK FOR ANY OF THIS.
NONSENSE. THE DAY YOU JOINED XAVIER, YOU ASKED FOR IT. YOU WANTED TO BE A HERO.
AND THE HERO'S PATH CANNOT BE MAPPED. IT MUST BE *WALKED*.

AND BY WHAT LAW SHOULD THAT PATH NOT RUN THROUGH WAKANDA?

THE GODS HAVE FORSAKEN THE PEOPLE. SOME OF THEM THINK THEIR KING HAS TOO. AND SO SOME OF THEM NOW LOOK TO *YOU.*

YOU SHOULD NOT TAKE THE FAITH OF PEOPLE LIGHTLY.

BELIEVE ME. I KNOW.

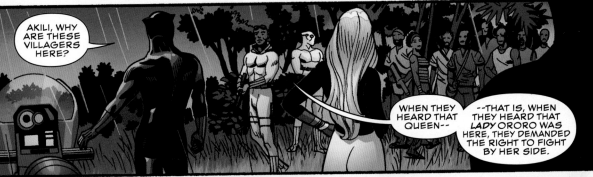

AKILI, WHY ARE THESE VILLAGERS HERE?

WHEN THEY HEARD THAT QUEEN--

--THAT IS, WHEN THEY HEARD THAT *LADY* ORORO WAS HERE, THEY DEMANDED THE RIGHT TO FIGHT BY HER SIDE.

IT IS HER! THE GODDESS, OUR QUEEN, HAS RETURNED!

THE ANANSI SHALL BE VANQUISHED!

HAIL DAMISA-SARKI! HAIL HADARI YAO!

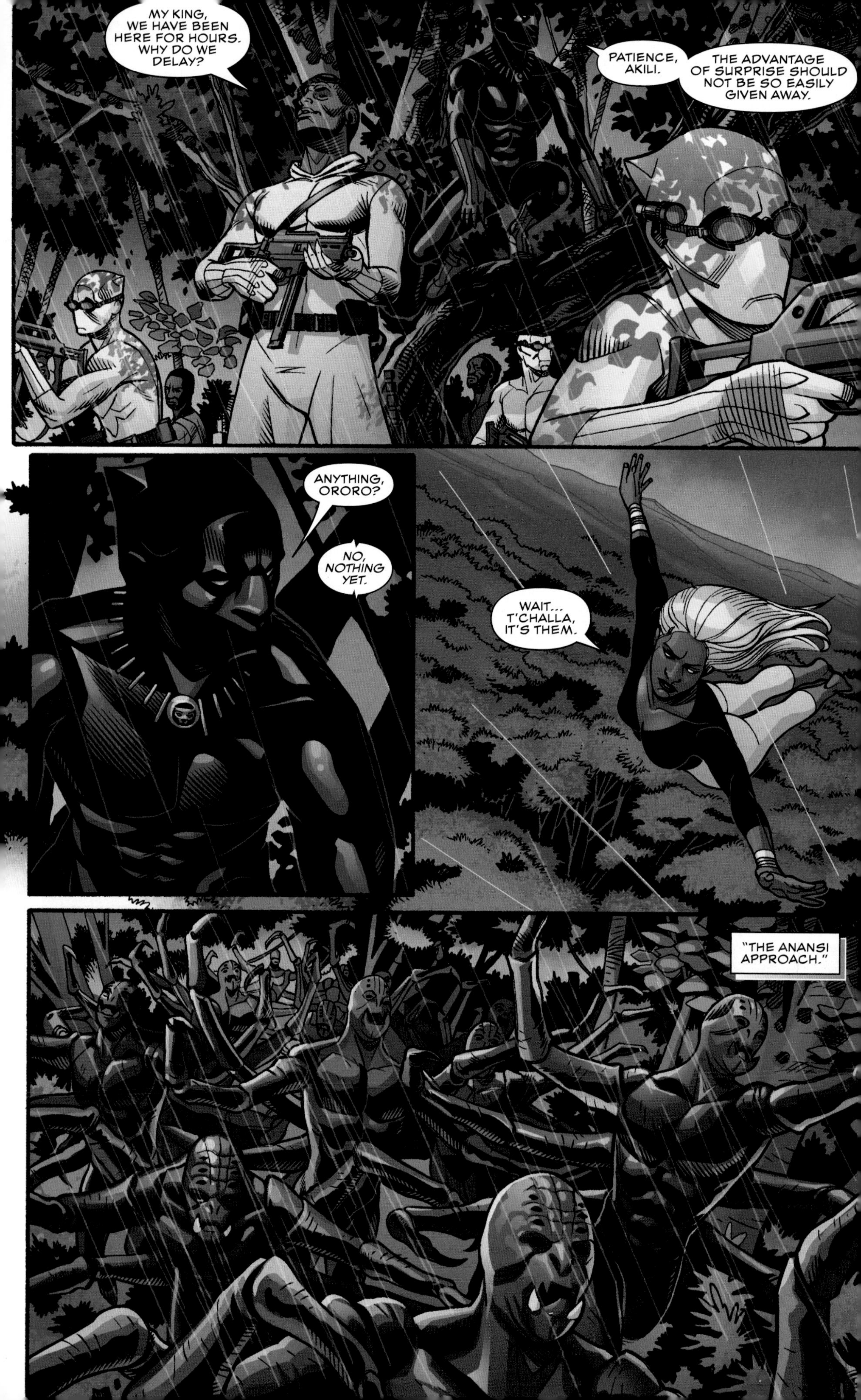
MY KING, WE HAVE BEEN HERE FOR HOURS. WHY DO WE DELAY?
PATIENCE, AKILI.
THE ADVANTAGE OF SURPRISE SHOULD NOT BE SO EASILY GIVEN AWAY.
ANYTHING, ORORO?
NO, NOTHING YET.
WAIT... T'CHALLA, IT'S THEM.
"THE ANANSI APPROACH."

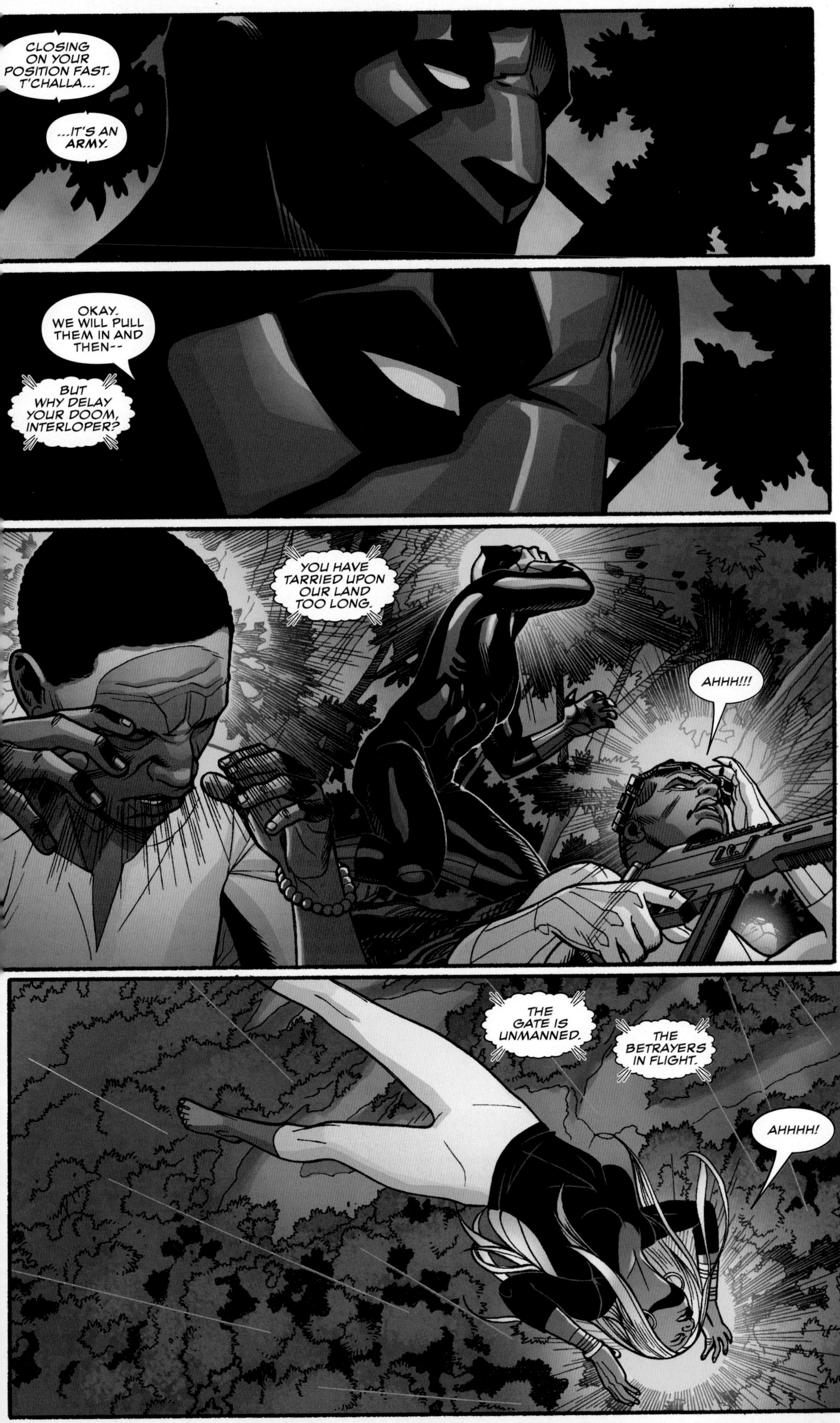
CLOSING ON YOUR POSITION FAST. T'CHALLA...
...IT'S AN ARMY.
OKAY. WE WILL PULL THEM IN AND THEN--
BUT WHY DELAY YOUR DOOM, INTERLOPER?
YOU HAVE TARRIED UPON OUR LAND TOO LONG.
AHHH!!!
THE GATE IS UNMANNED.
THE BETRAYERS IN FLIGHT.
AHHHH!

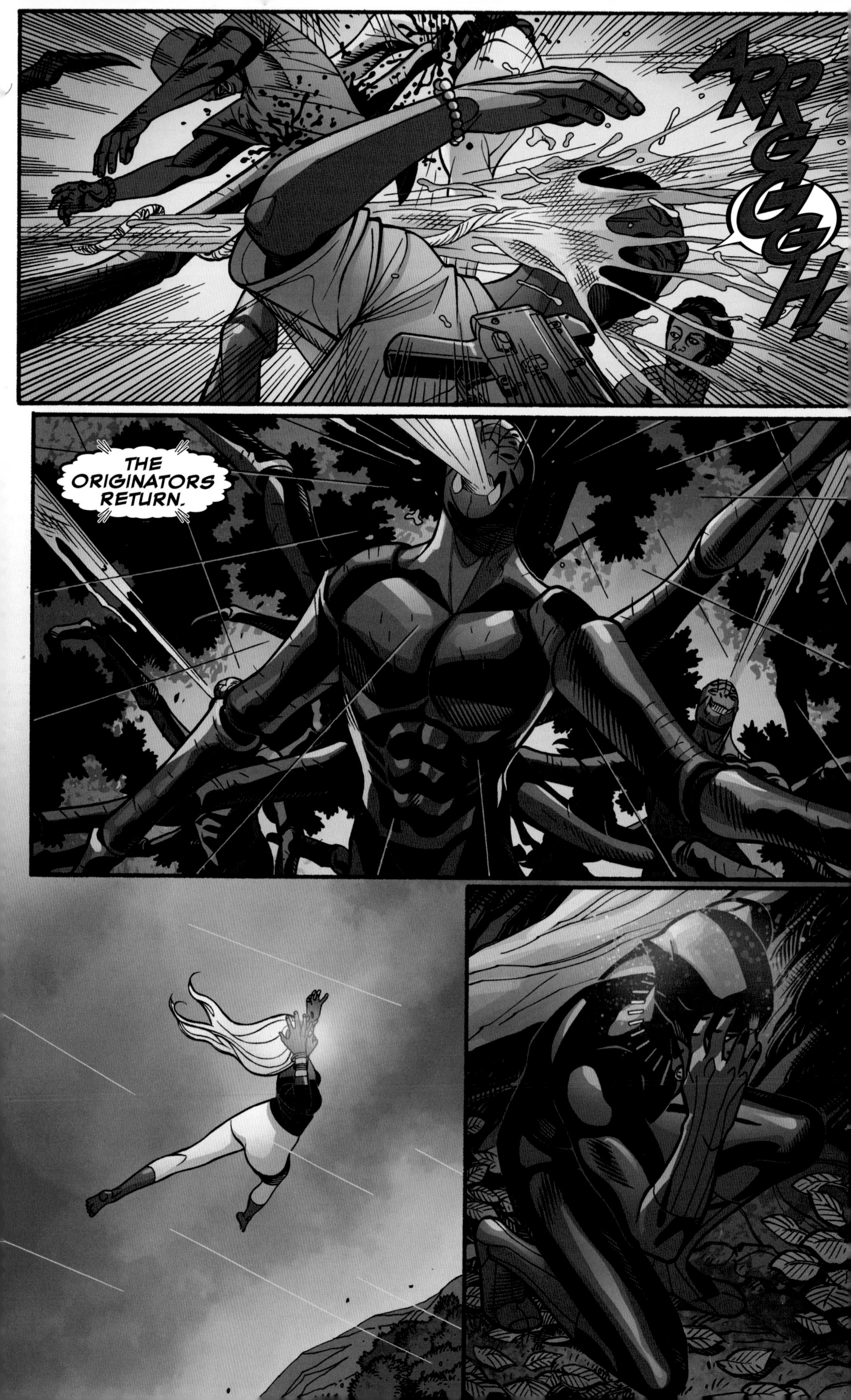
ARRGGGH!
THE ORIGINATORS RETURN.

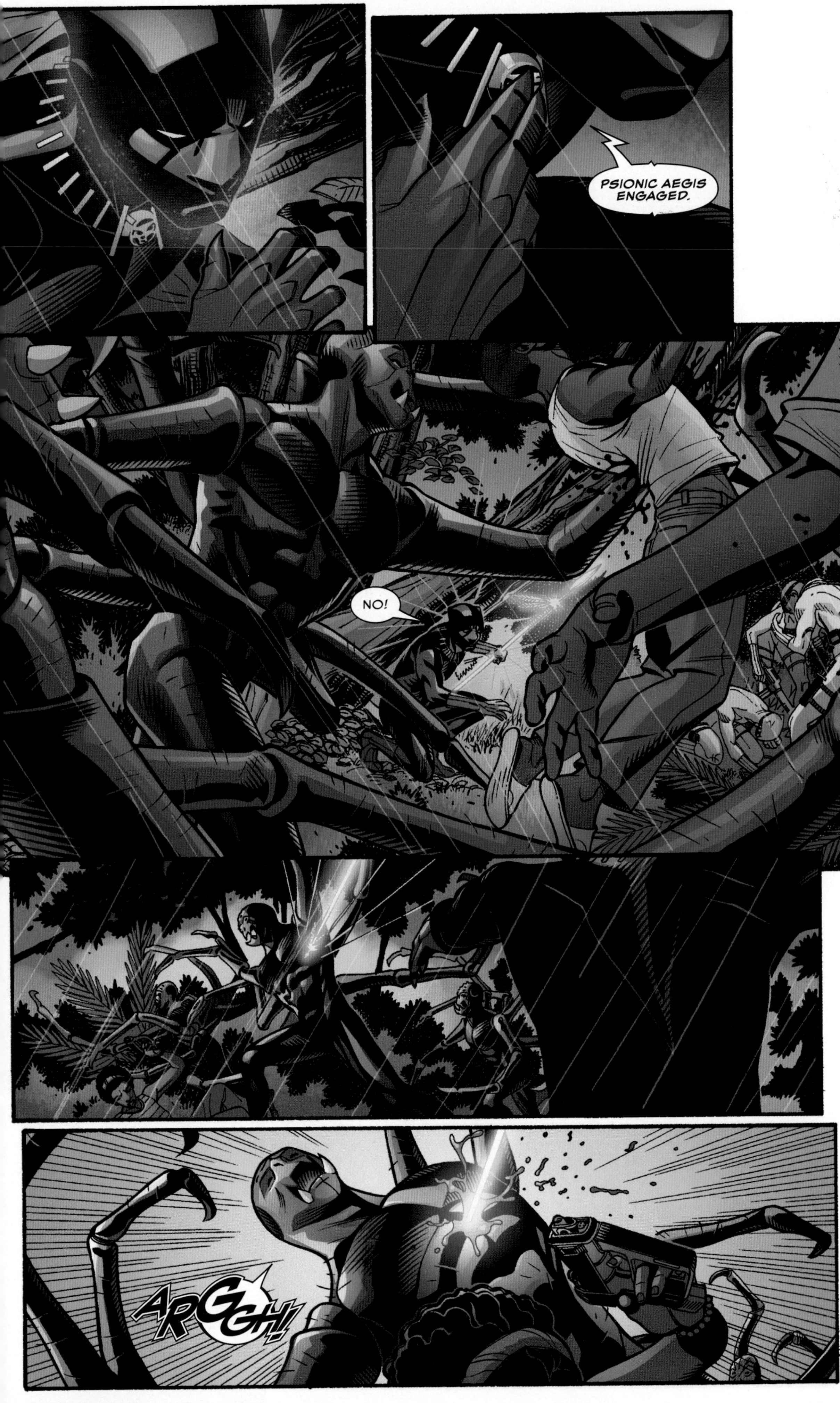
PSIONIC AEGIS ENGAGED.
NO!
ARGGH!

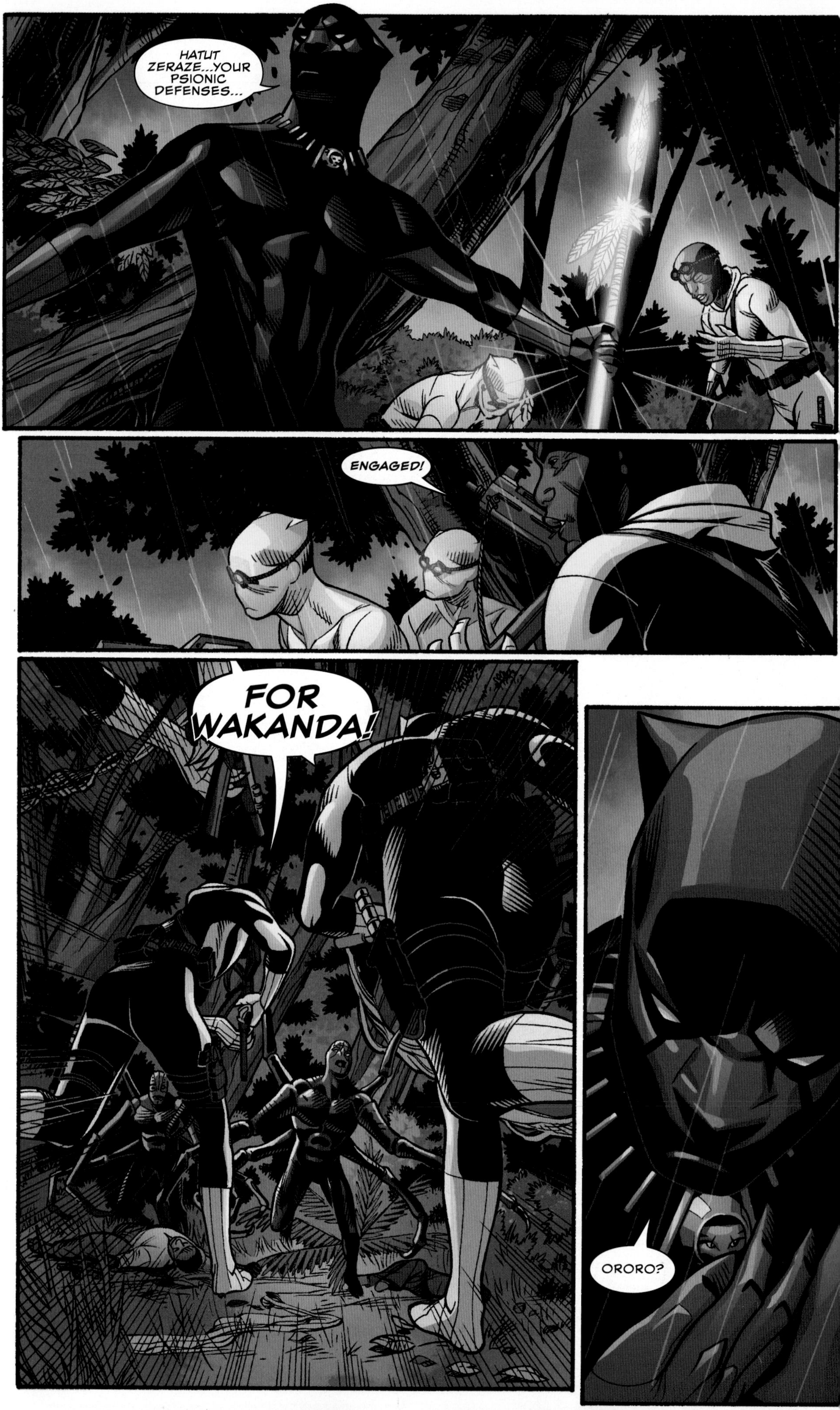
HATUT ZERAZE...YOUR PSIONIC DEFENSES...
ENGAGED!
FOR WAKANDA!
ORORO?

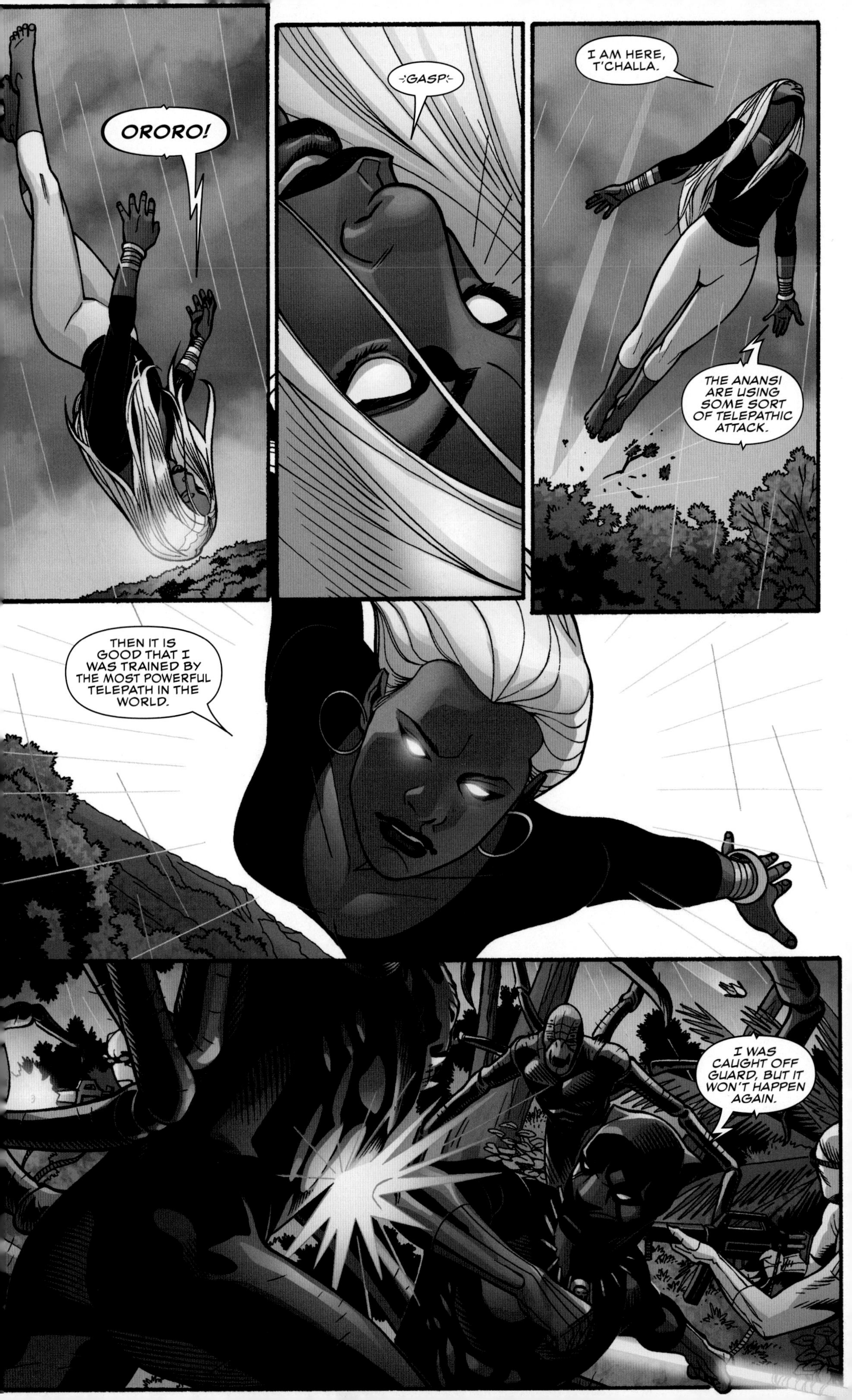
ORORO!
-GASP-
I AM HERE, T'CHALLA.
THE ANANSI ARE USING SOME SORT OF TELEPATHIC ATTACK.
THEN IT IS GOOD THAT I WAS TRAINED BY THE MOST POWERFUL TELEPATH IN THE WORLD.
I WAS CAUGHT OFF GUARD, BUT IT WON'T HAPPEN AGAIN.

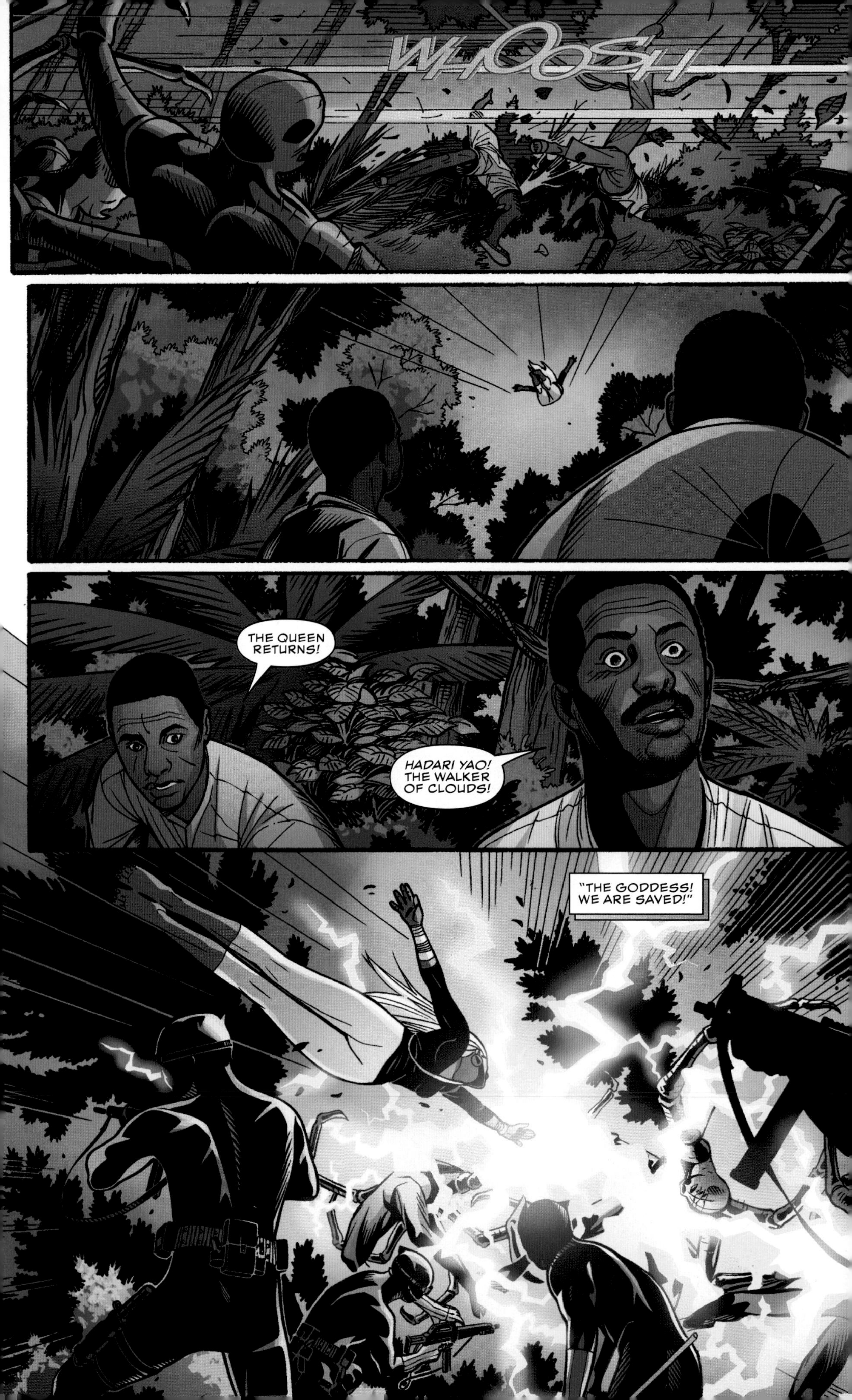
WHOOOSH
THE QUEEN RETURNS!
HADARI YAO! THE WALKER OF CLOUDS!
"THE GODDESS! WE ARE SAVED!"

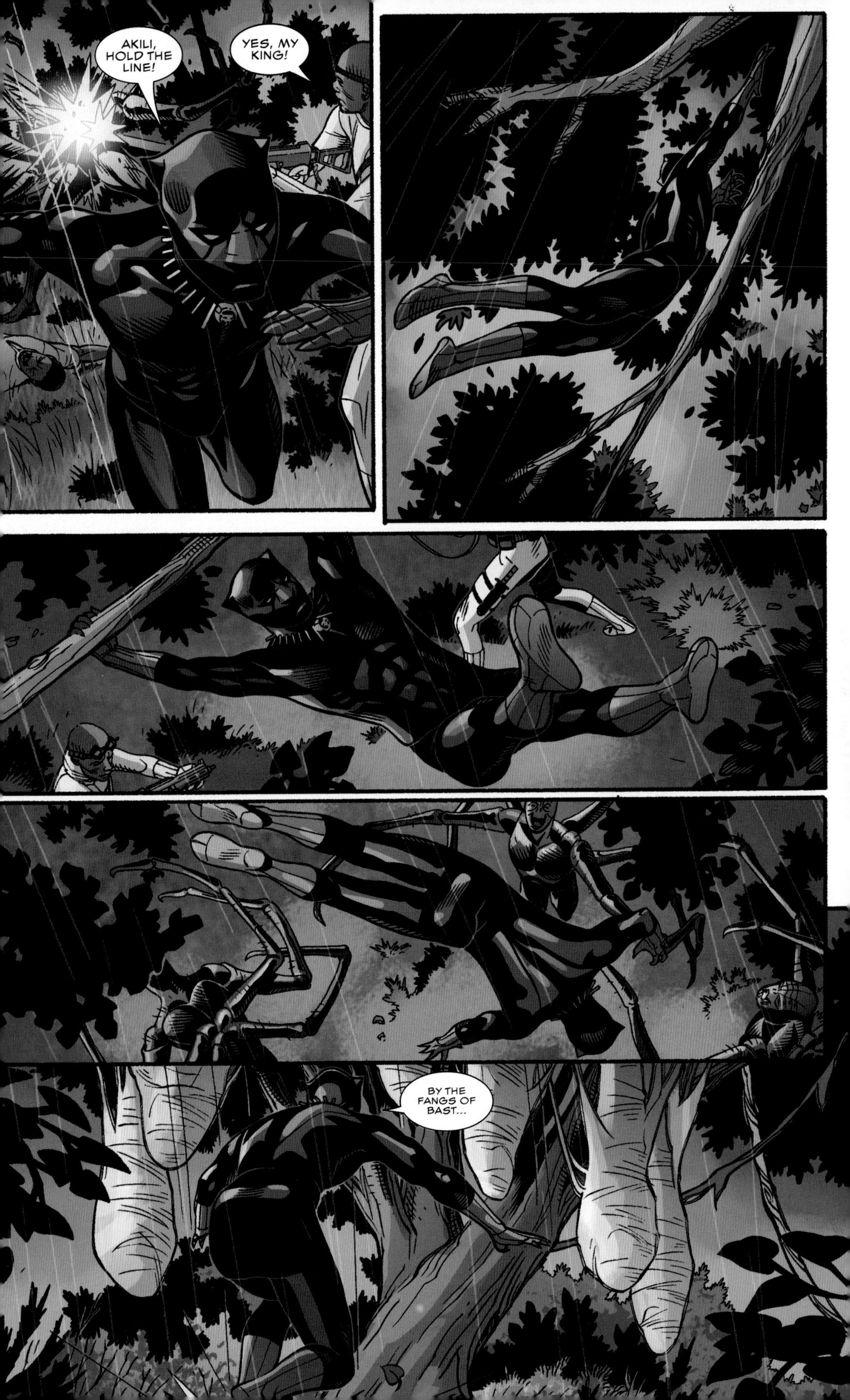
AKILI, HOLD THE LINE!
YES, MY KING!
BY THE FANGS OF BAST...

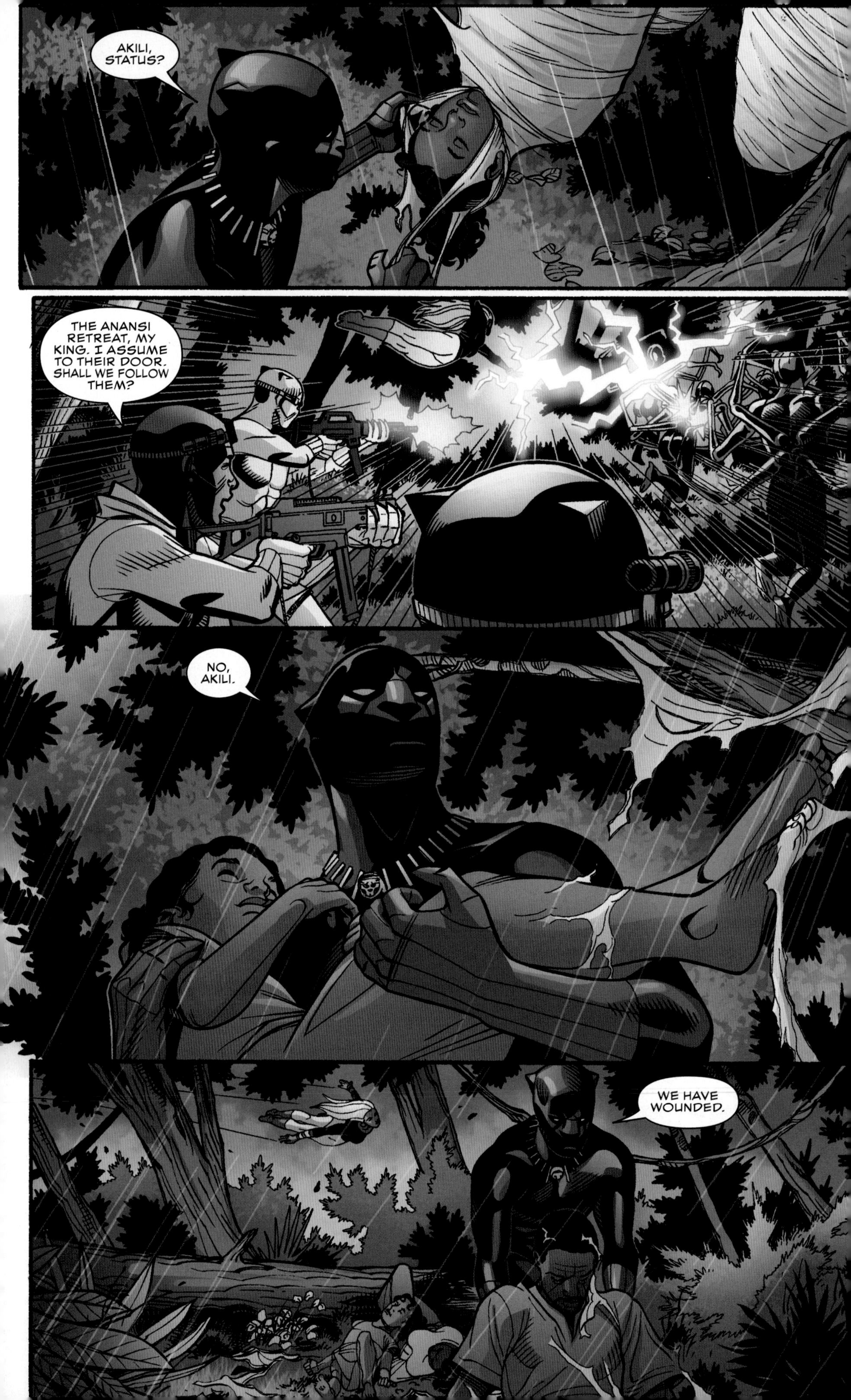
AKILI, STATUS?
THE ANANSI RETREAT, MY KING. I ASSUME TO THEIR DOOR. SHALL WE FOLLOW THEM?
NO, AKILI.
WE HAVE WOUNDED.

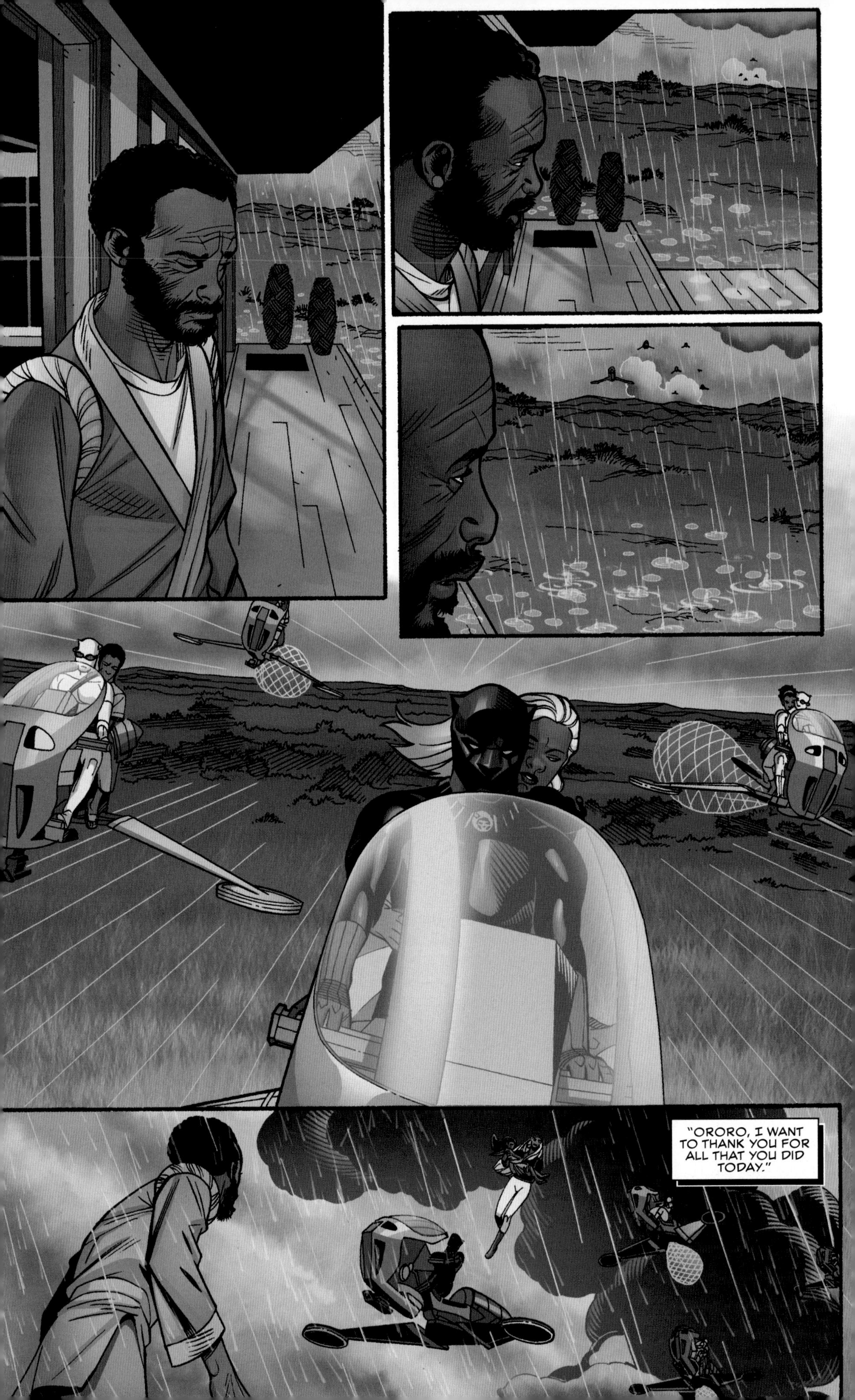
"ORORO, I WANT TO THANK YOU FOR ALL THAT YOU DID TODAY."

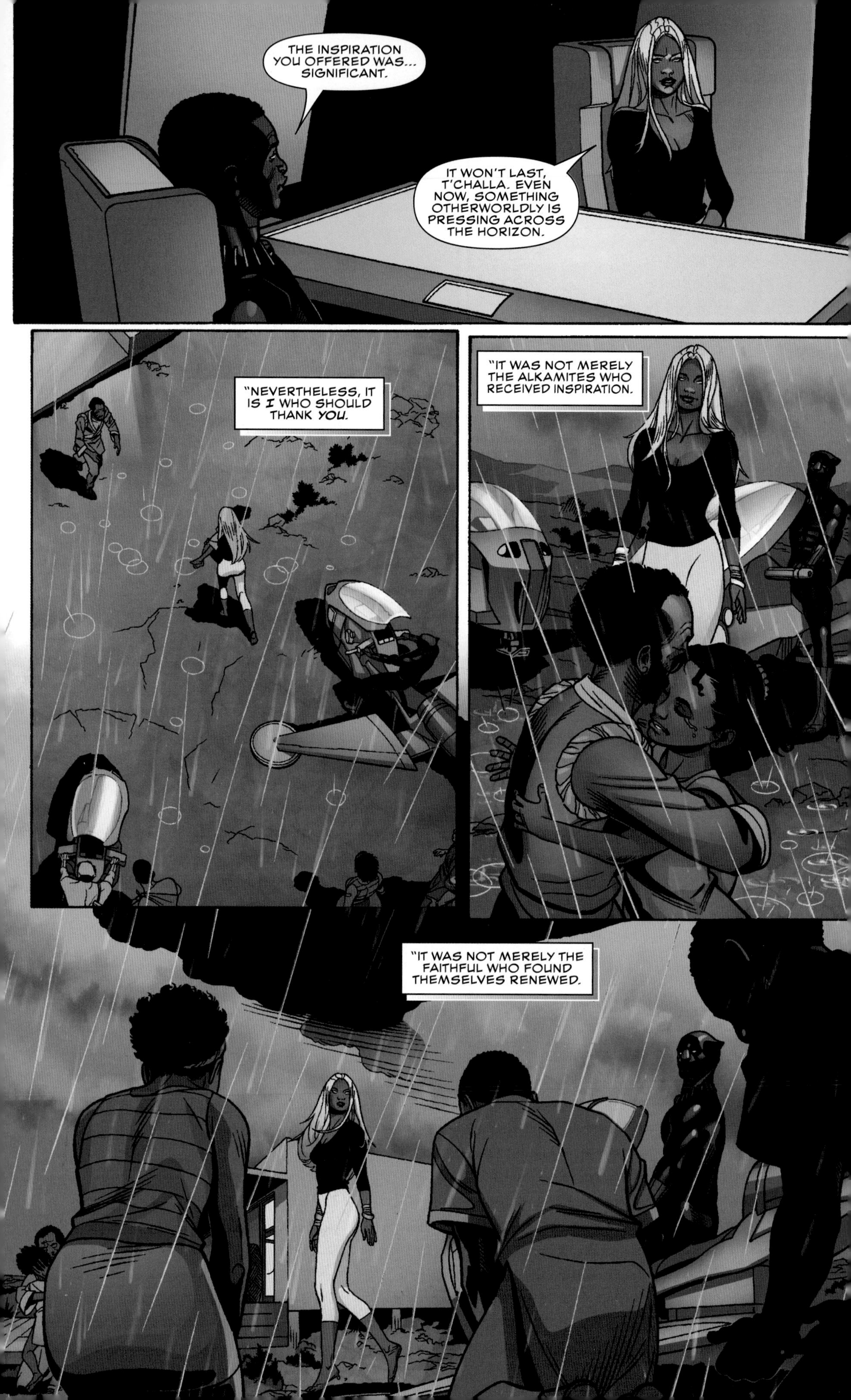
THE INSPIRATION YOU OFFERED WAS... SIGNIFICANT.
IT WON'T LAST, T'CHALLA. EVEN NOW, SOMETHING OTHERWORLDLY IS PRESSING ACROSS THE HORIZON.
"NEVERTHELESS, IT IS *I* WHO SHOULD THANK *YOU*.
"IT WAS NOT MERELY THE ALKAMITES WHO RECEIVED INSPIRATION.
"IT WAS NOT MERELY THE FAITHFUL WHO FOUND THEMSELVES RENEWED.

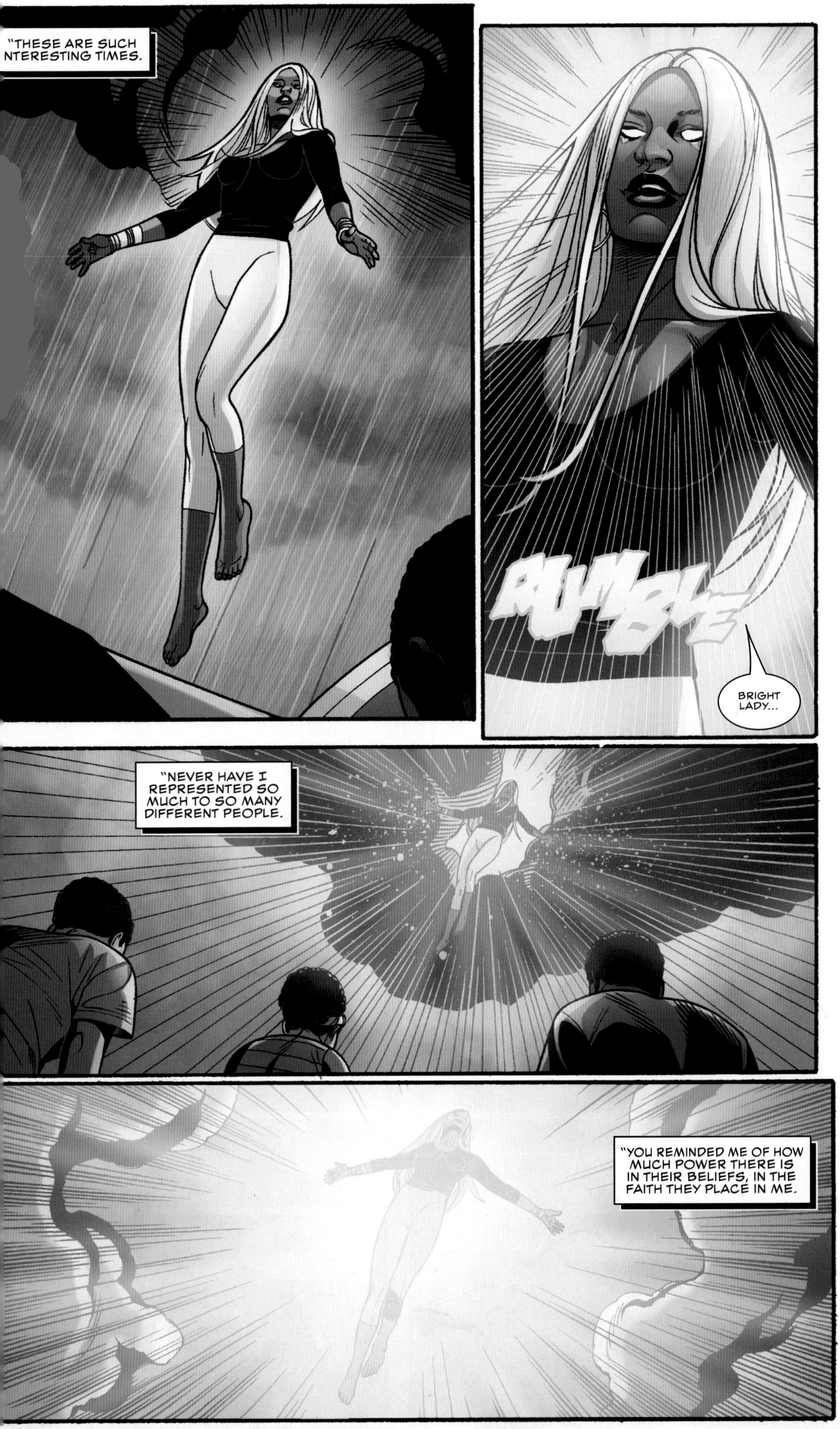
"THESE ARE SUCH NTERESTING TIMES.
RUMBLE
BRIGHT LADY...
"NEVER HAVE I REPRESENTED SO MUCH TO SO MANY DIFFERENT PEOPLE.
"YOU REMINDED ME OF HOW MUCH POWER THERE IS IN THEIR BELIEFS, IN THE FAITH THEY PLACE IN ME.

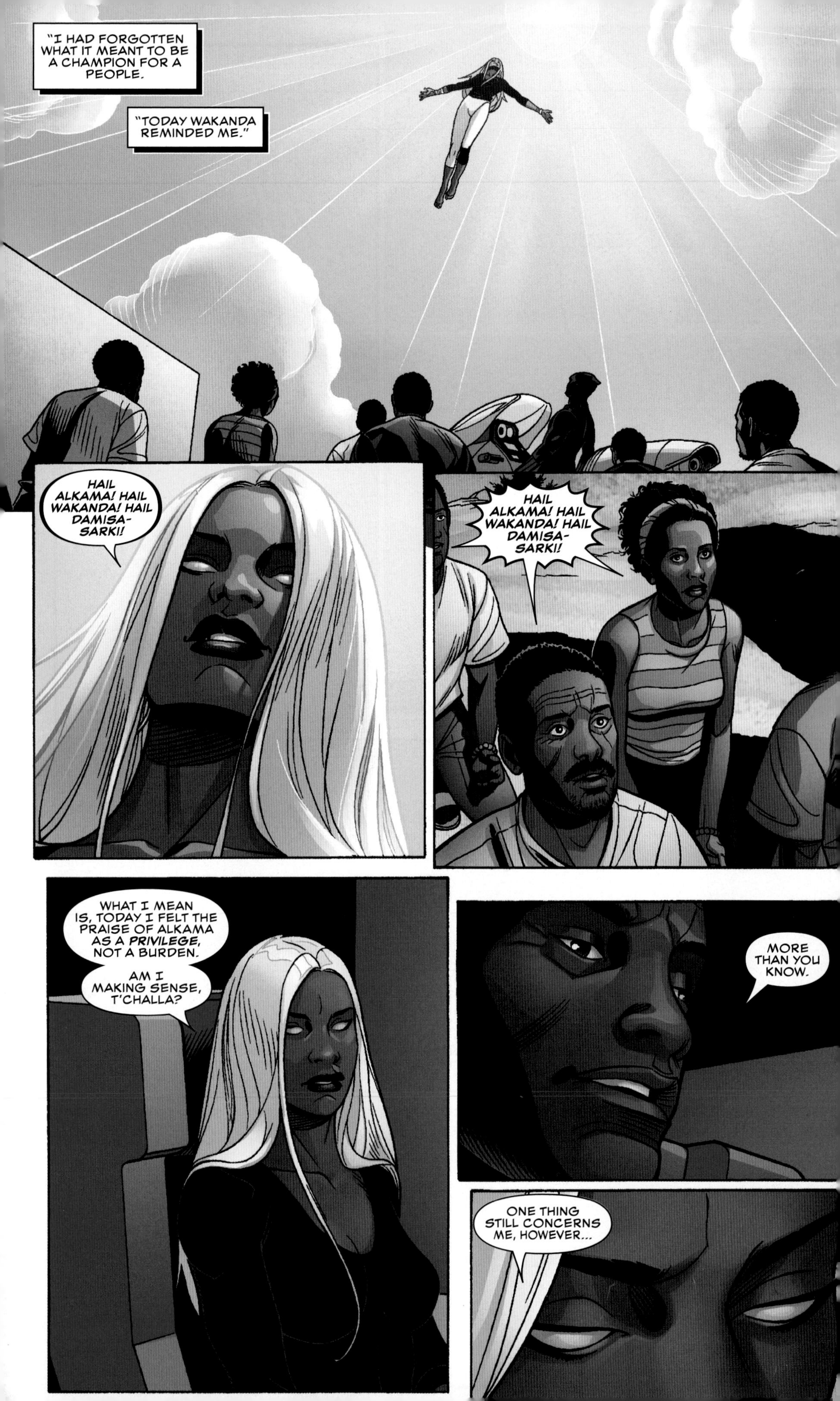
"I HAD FORGOTTEN WHAT IT MEANT TO BE A CHAMPION FOR A PEOPLE.
"TODAY WAKANDA REMINDED ME."
HAIL ALKAMA! HAIL WAKANDA! HAIL DAMISA-SARKI!
HAIL ALKAMA! HAIL WAKANDA! HAIL DAMISA-SARKI!
WHAT I MEAN IS, TODAY I FELT THE PRAISE OF ALKAMA AS A *PRIVILEGE*, NOT A BURDEN.
AM I MAKING SENSE, T'CHALLA?
MORE THAN YOU KNOW.
ONE THING STILL CONCERNS ME, HOWEVER...

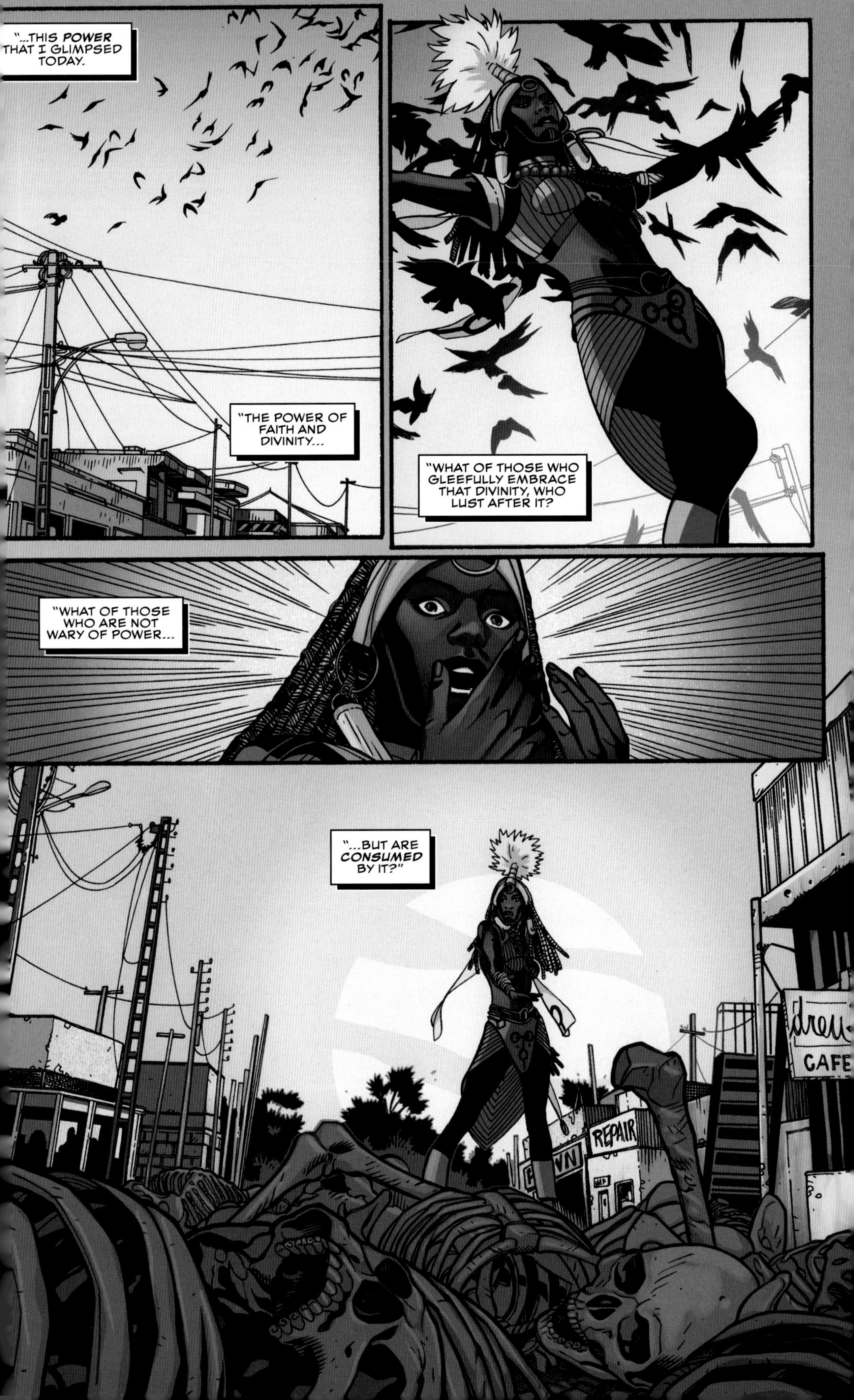
"...THIS POWER THAT I GLIMPSED TODAY.
"THE POWER OF FAITH AND DIVINITY...
"WHAT OF THOSE WHO GLEEFULLY EMBRACE THAT DIVINITY, WHO LUST AFTER IT?
"WHAT OF THOSE WHO ARE NOT WARY OF POWER...
"...BUT ARE CONSUMED BY IT?"
REPAIR
CAFE

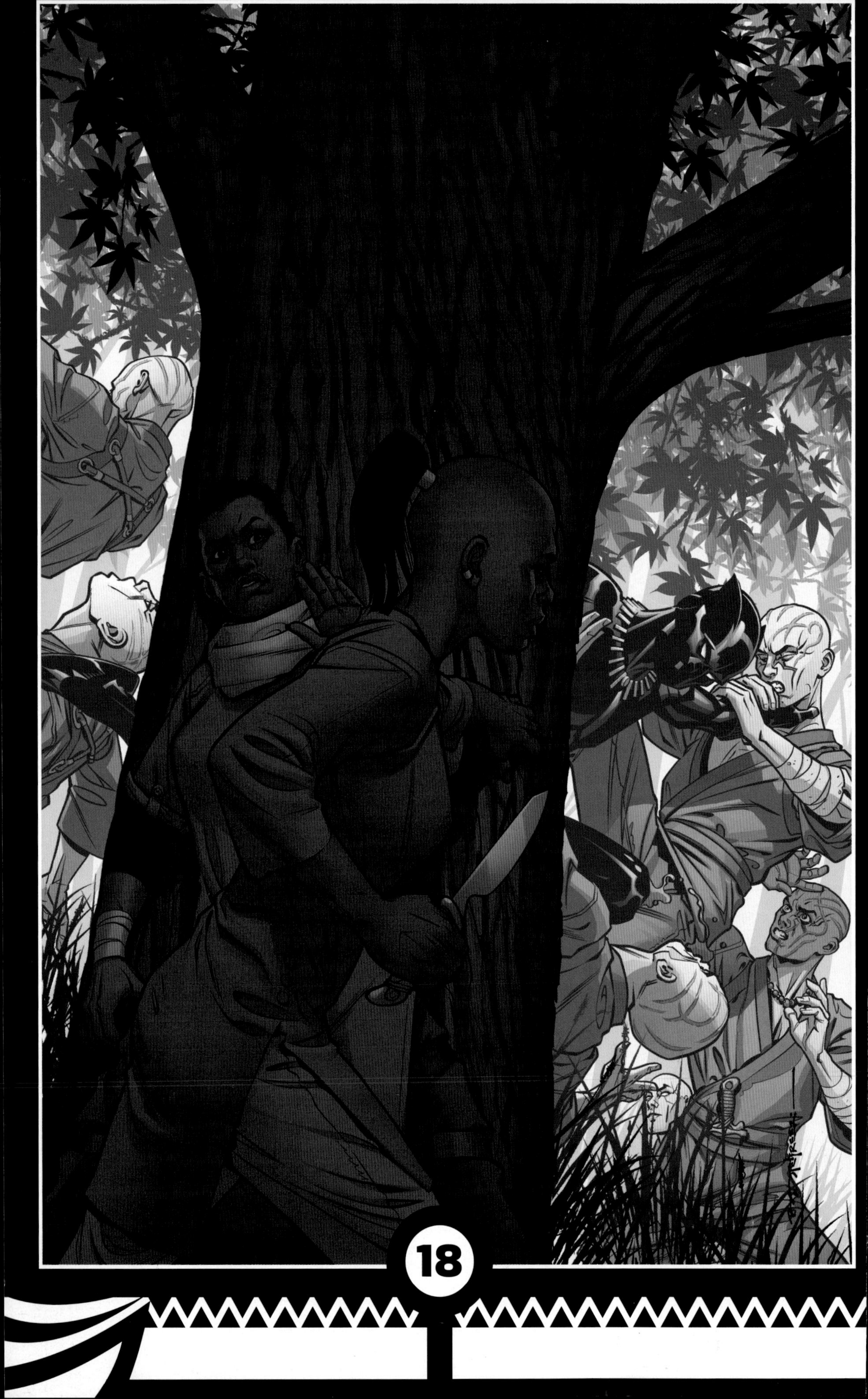
18

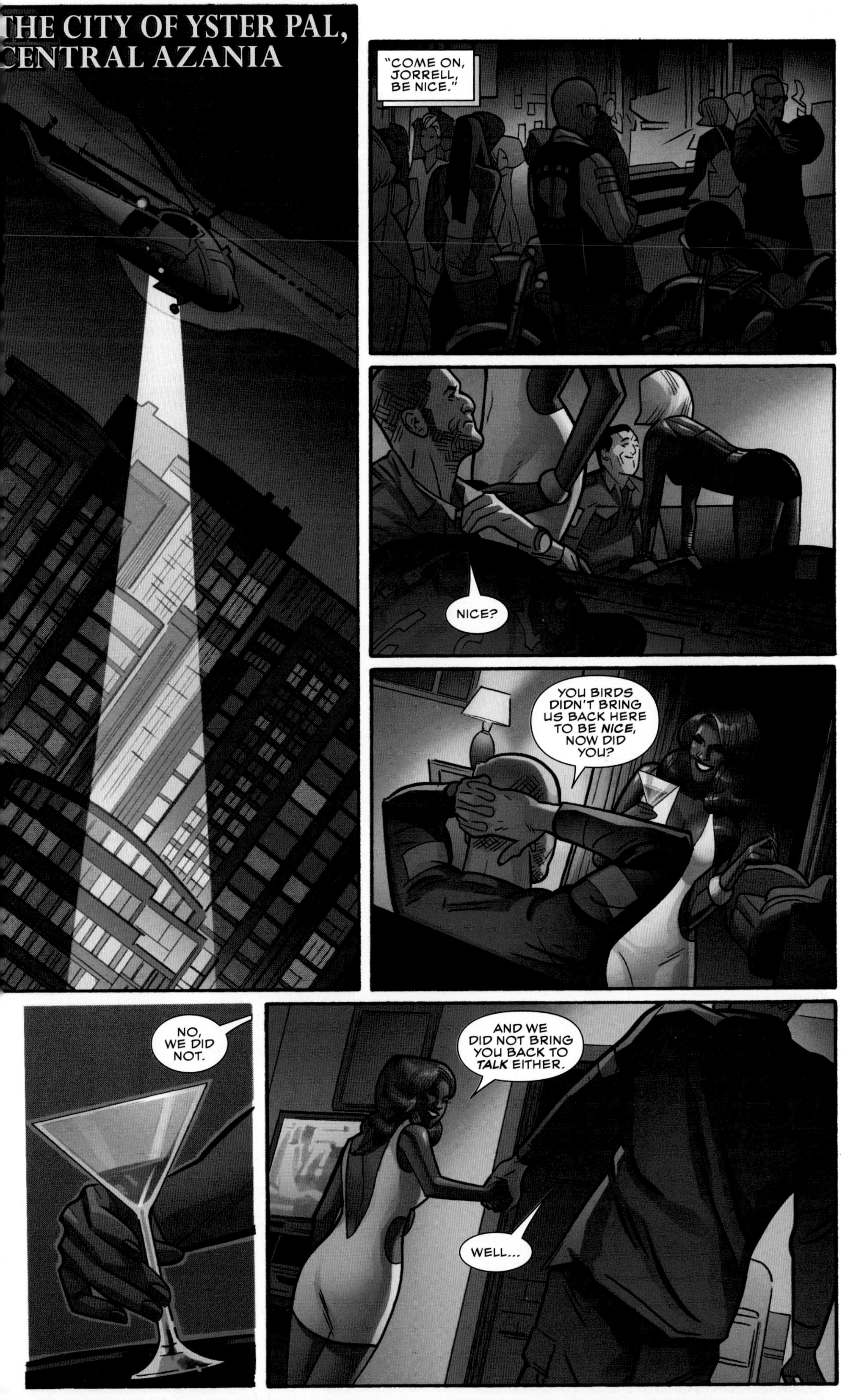
THE CITY OF YSTER PAL, CENTRAL AZANIA
"COME ON, JORRELL, BE NICE."
NICE?
YOU BIRDS DIDN'T BRING US BACK HERE TO BE NICE, NOW DID YOU?
NO, WE DID NOT.
AND WE DID NOT BRING YOU BACK TO TALK EITHER.
WELL...

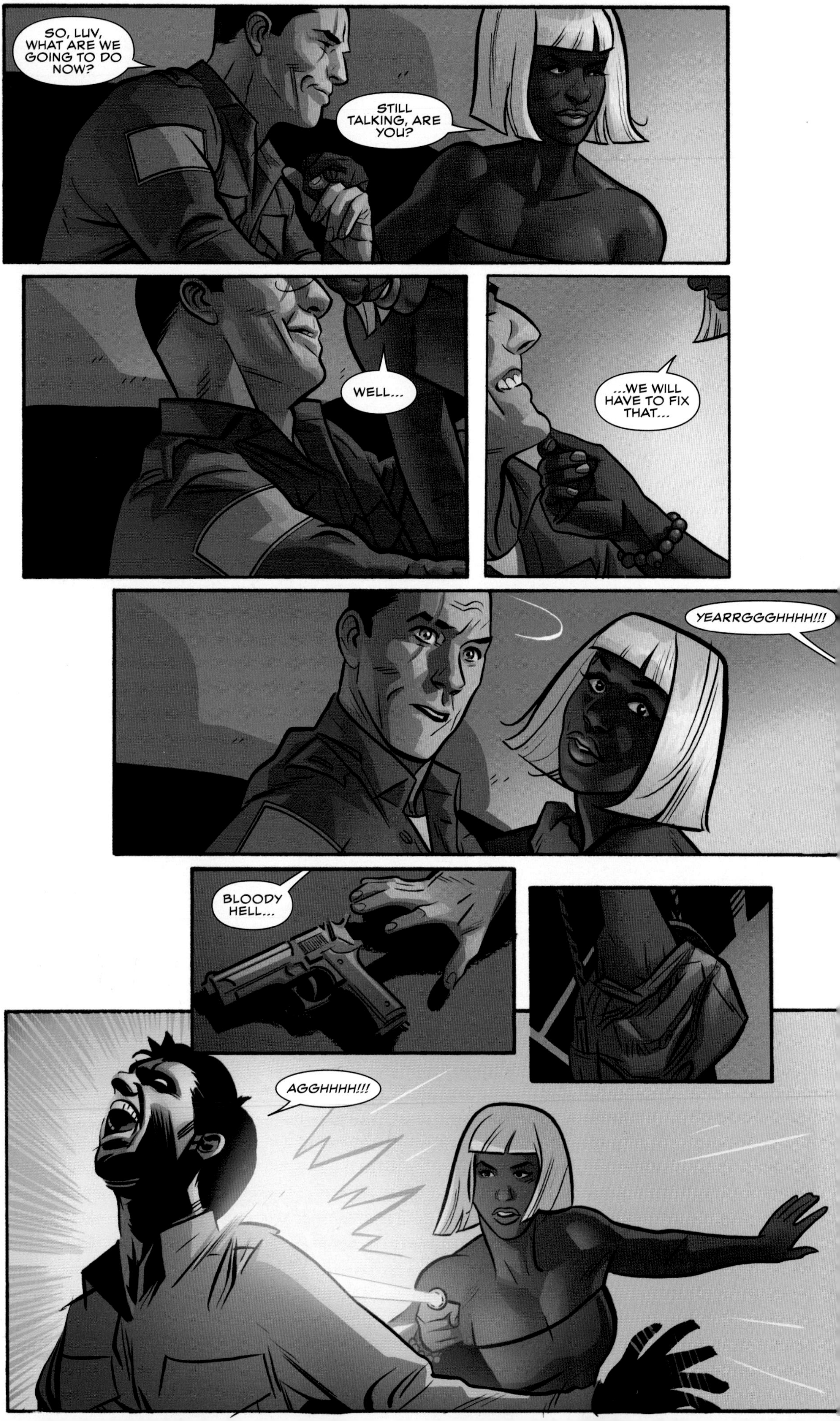
SO, LUV, WHAT ARE WE GOING TO DO NOW?
STILL TALKING, ARE YOU?
WELL...
...WE WILL HAVE TO FIX THAT...
YEARRGGGHHHH!!!
BLOODY HELL...
AGGHHHH!!!

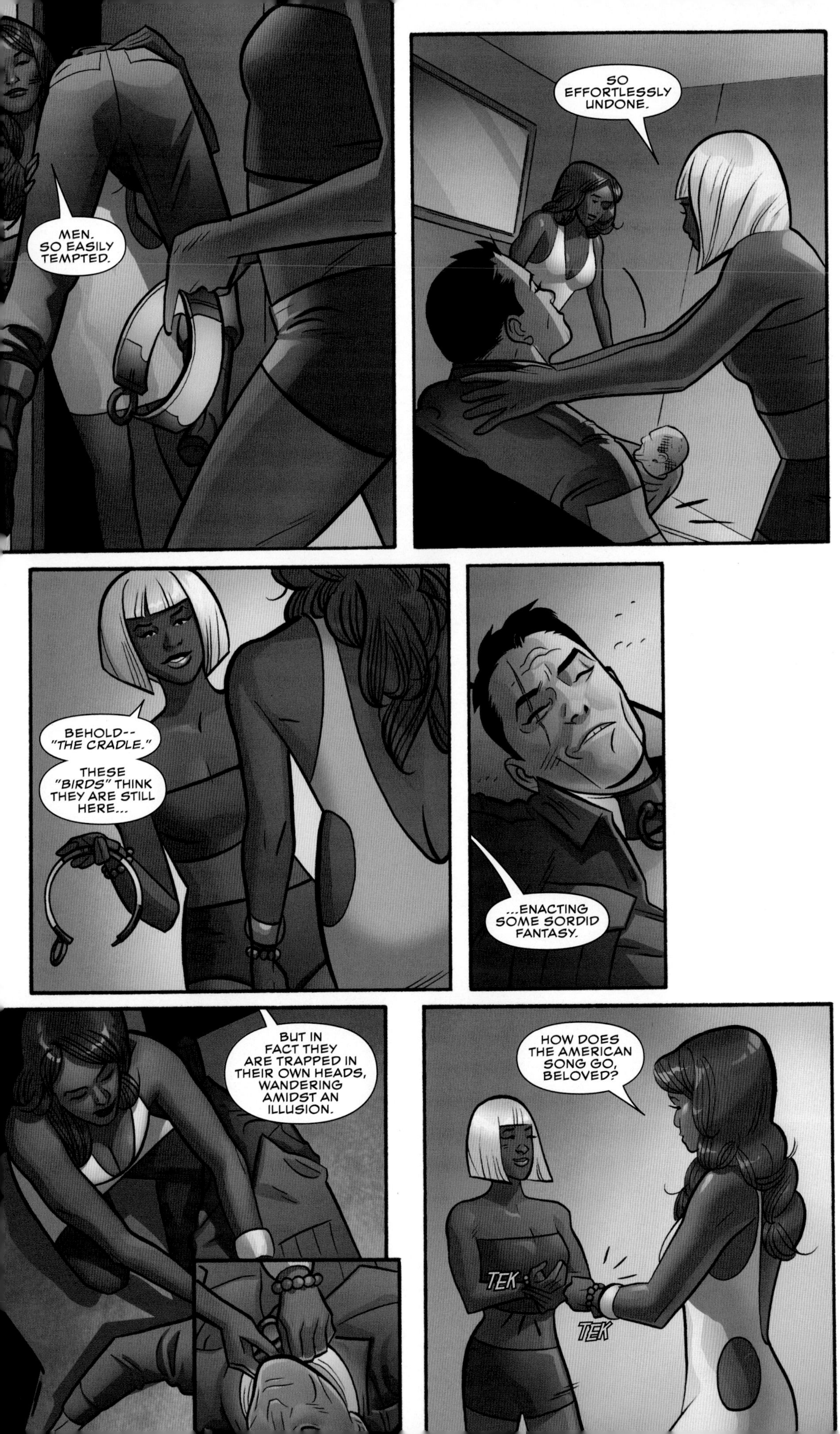

MEN. SO EASILY TEMPTED.
SO EFFORTLESSLY UNDONE.
BEHOLD-- "THE CRADLE."
THESE "BIRDS" THINK THEY ARE STILL HERE...
...ENACTING SOME SORDID FANTASY.
BUT IN FACT THEY ARE TRAPPED IN THEIR OWN HEADS, WANDERING AMIDST AN ILLUSION.
HOW DOES THE AMERICAN SONG GO, BELOVED?
TEK
TEK

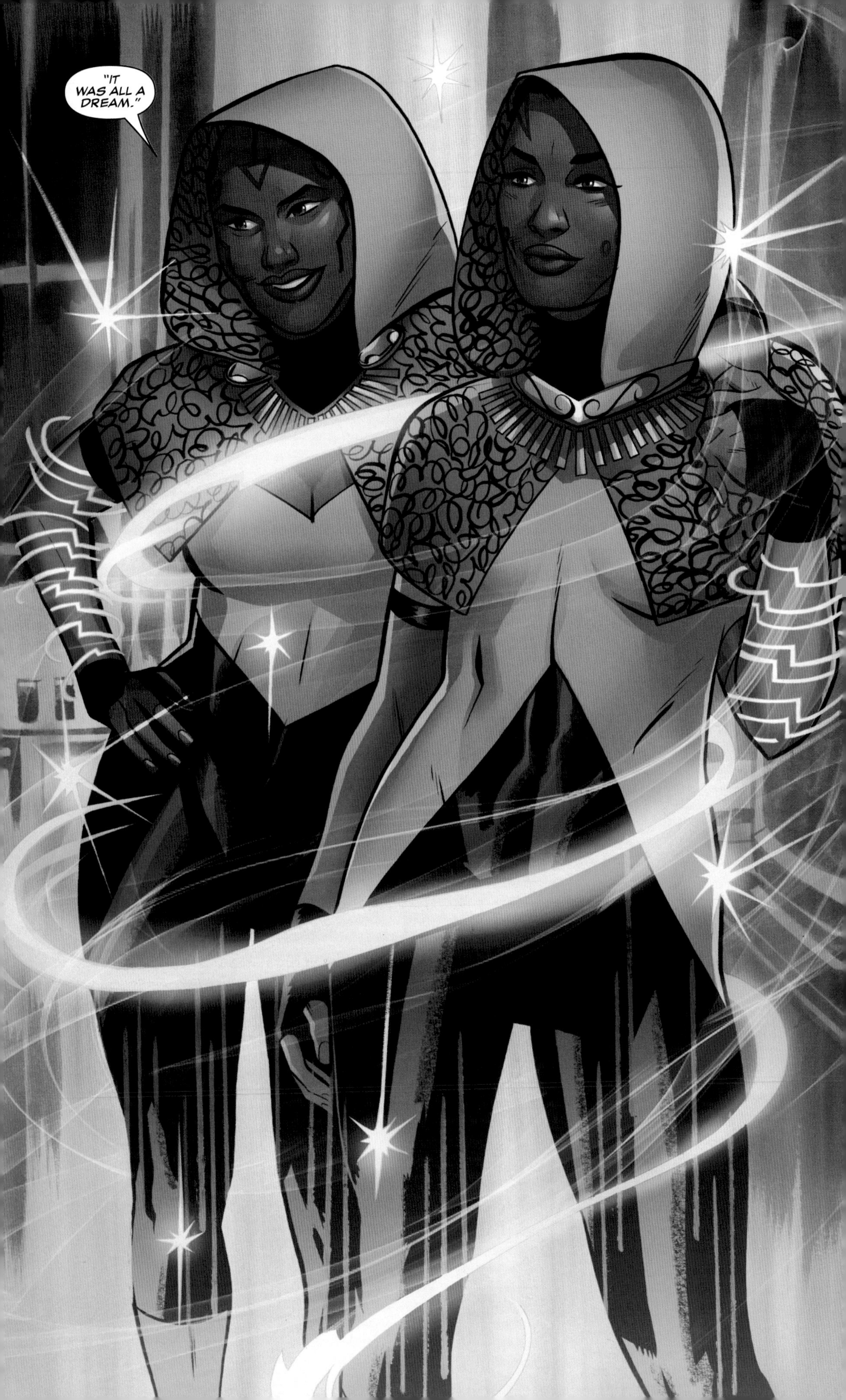
"IT WAS ALL A DREAM."

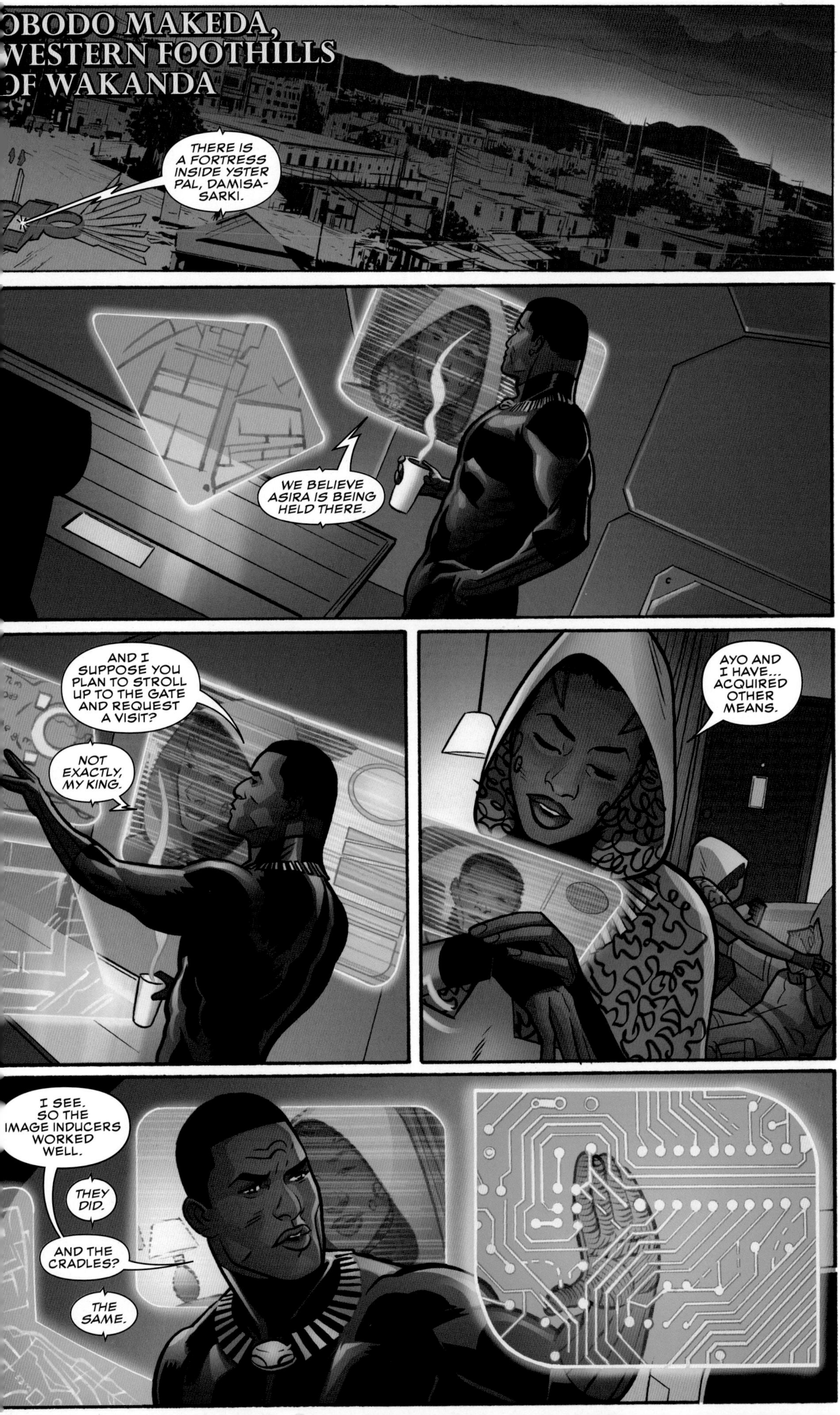
OBODO MAKEDA, WESTERN FOOTHILLS OF WAKANDA
THERE IS A FORTRESS INSIDE YSTER PAL, DAMISA-SARKI.
WE BELIEVE ASIRA IS BEING HELD THERE.
AND I SUPPOSE YOU PLAN TO STROLL UP TO THE GATE AND REQUEST A VISIT?
NOT EXACTLY, MY KING.
AYO AND I HAVE... ACQUIRED OTHER MEANS.
I SEE. SO THE IMAGE INDUCERS WORKED WELL.
THEY DID.
AND THE CRADLES?
THE SAME.

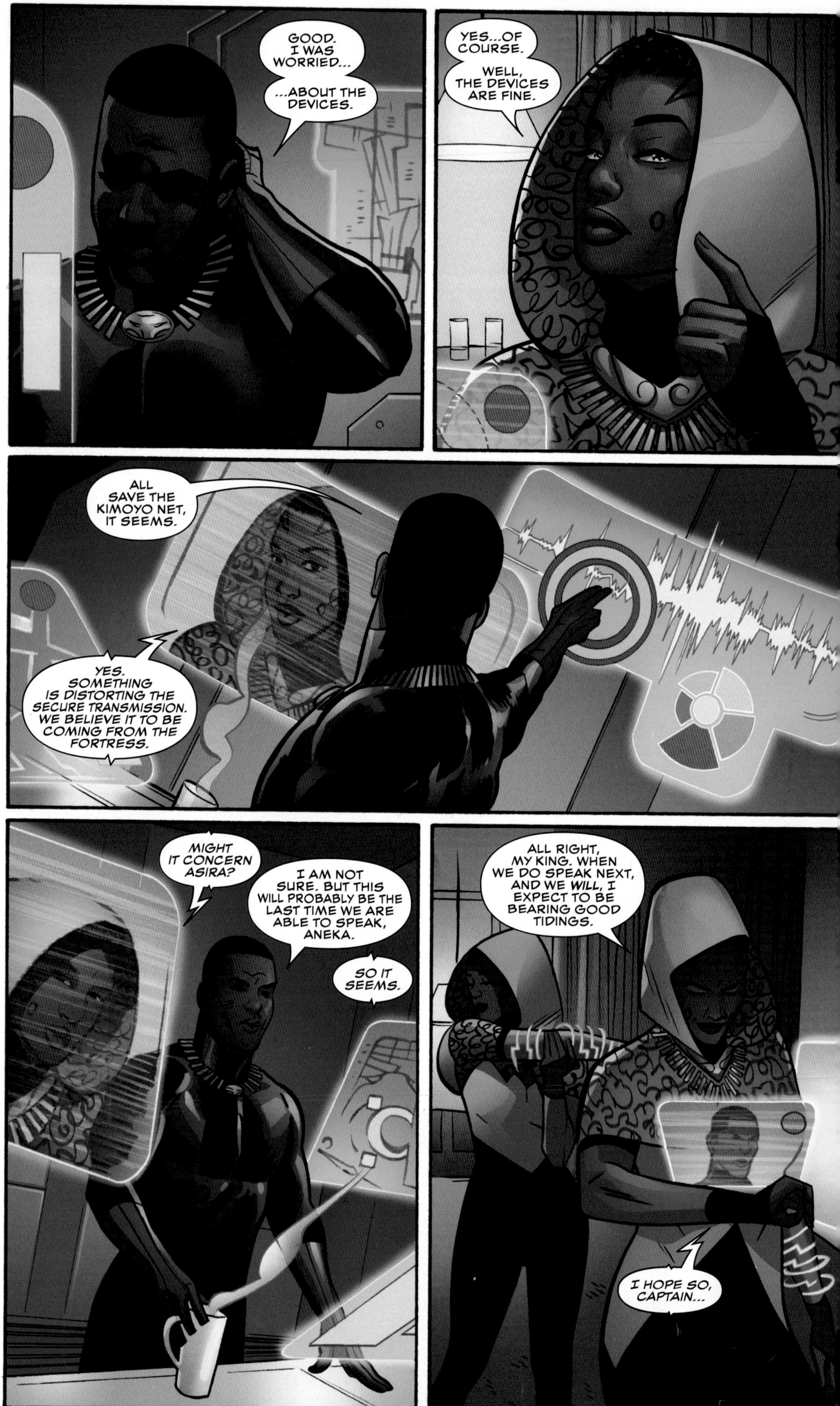
GOOD. I WAS WORRIED...
...ABOUT THE DEVICES.
YES...OF COURSE.
WELL, THE DEVICES ARE FINE.
ALL SAVE THE KIMOYO NET, IT SEEMS.
YES. SOMETHING IS DISTORTING THE SECURE TRANSMISSION. WE BELIEVE IT TO BE COMING FROM THE FORTRESS.
MIGHT IT CONCERN ASIRA?
I AM NOT SURE. BUT THIS WILL PROBABLY BE THE LAST TIME WE ARE ABLE TO SPEAK, ANEKA.
SO IT SEEMS.
ALL RIGHT, MY KING. WHEN WE DO SPEAK NEXT, AND WE WILL, I EXPECT TO BE BEARING GOOD TIDINGS.
I HOPE SO, CAPTAIN...

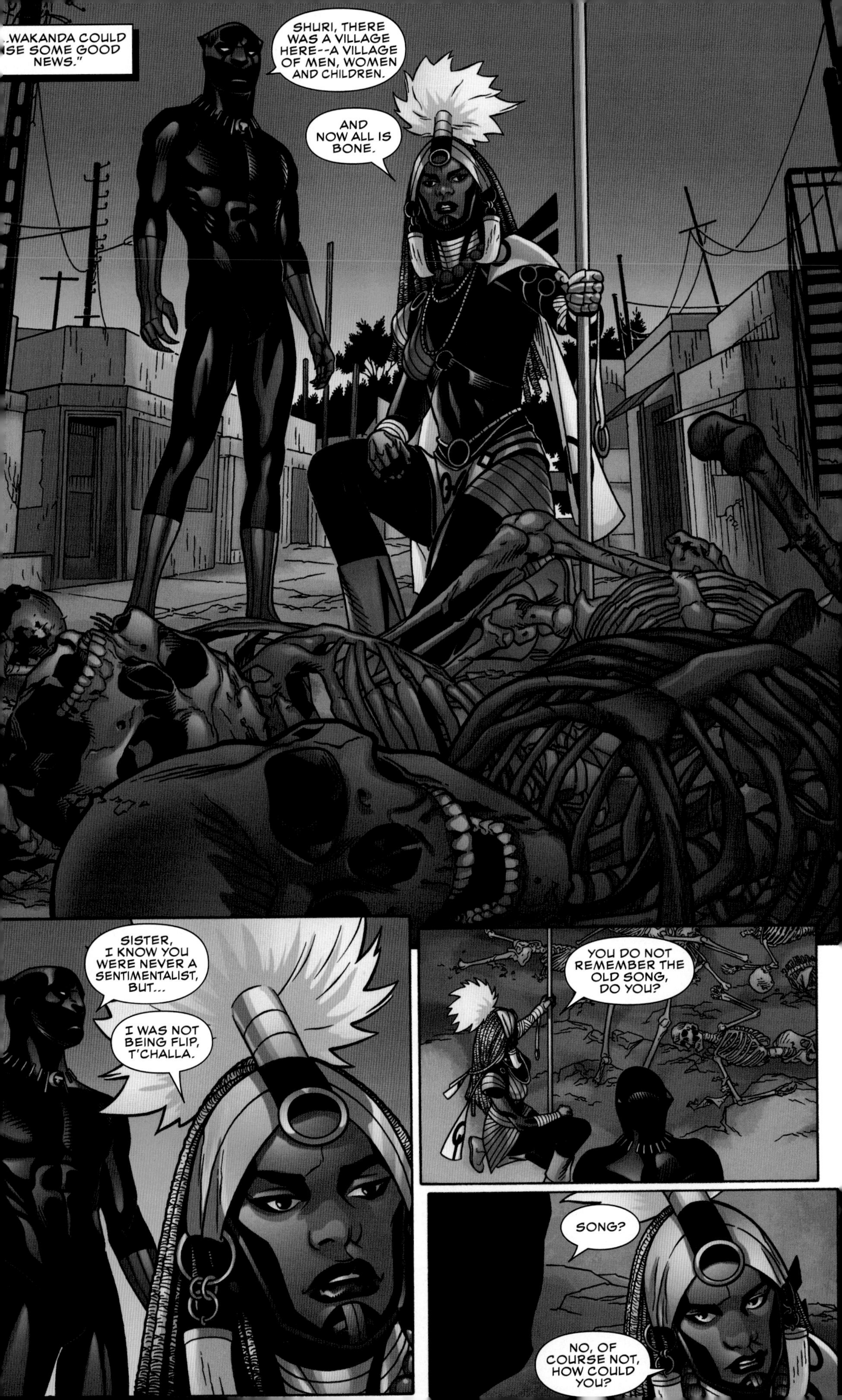
...WAKANDA COULD USE SOME GOOD NEWS."
SHURI, THERE WAS A VILLAGE HERE--A VILLAGE OF MEN, WOMEN AND CHILDREN.
AND NOW ALL IS BONE.
SISTER, I KNOW YOU WERE NEVER A SENTIMENTALIST, BUT...
I WAS NOT BEING FLIP, T'CHALLA.
YOU DO NOT REMEMBER THE OLD SONG, DO YOU?
SONG?
NO, OF COURSE NOT, HOW COULD YOU?

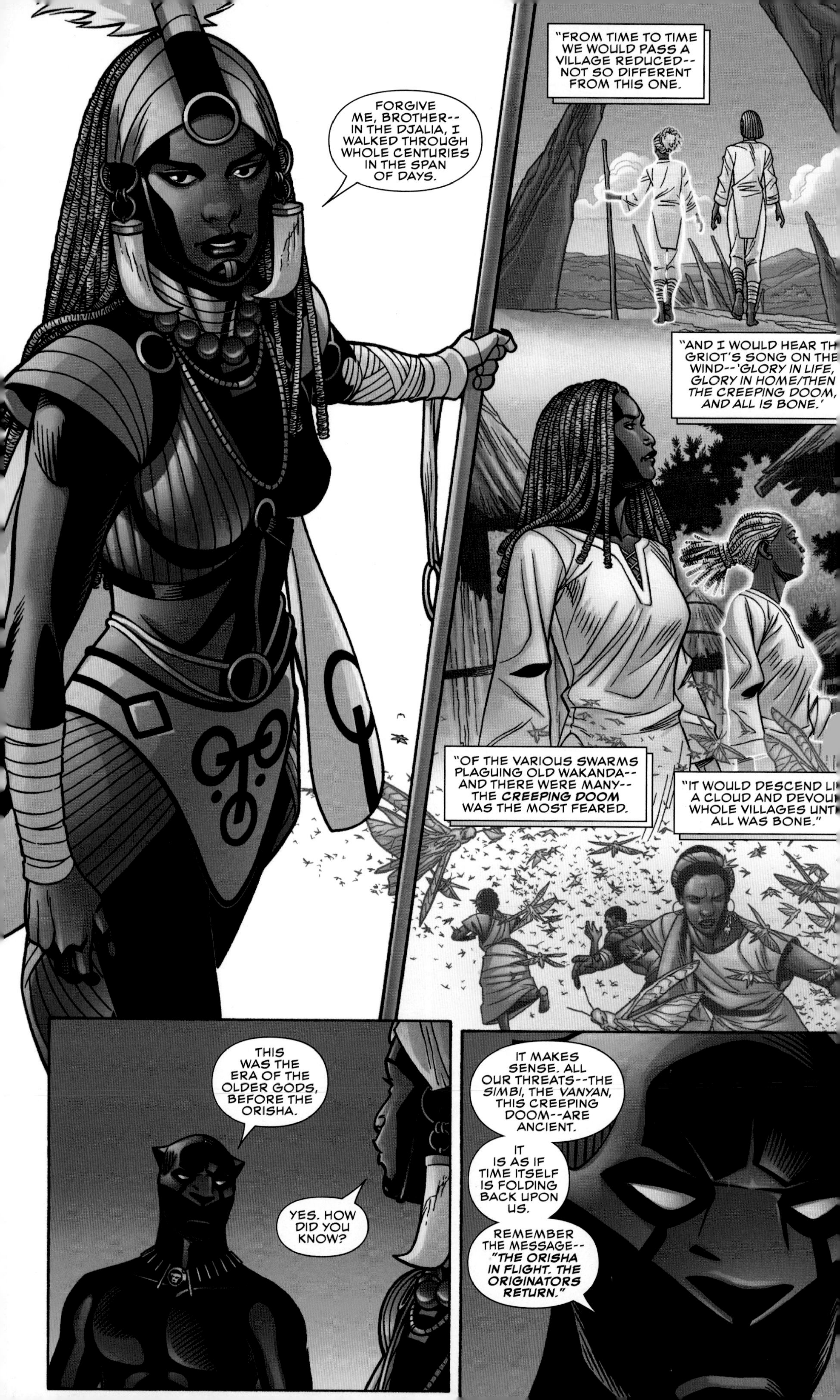
FORGIVE ME, BROTHER-- IN THE DJALIA, I WALKED THROUGH WHOLE CENTURIES IN THE SPAN OF DAYS.
"FROM TIME TO TIME WE WOULD PASS A VILLAGE REDUCED-- NOT SO DIFFERENT FROM THIS ONE.
"AND I WOULD HEAR TH GRIOT'S SONG ON THE WIND--'GLORY IN LIFE, GLORY IN HOME/THEN THE CREEPING DOOM, AND ALL IS BONE.'
"OF THE VARIOUS SWARMS PLAGUING OLD WAKANDA-- AND THERE WERE MANY-- THE CREEPING DOOM WAS THE MOST FEARED.
"IT WOULD DESCEND LI A CLOUD AND DEVOU WHOLE VILLAGES UNT ALL WAS BONE."
THIS WAS THE ERA OF THE OLDER GODS, BEFORE THE ORISHA.
YES. HOW DID YOU KNOW?
IT MAKES SENSE. ALL OUR THREATS--THE SIMBI, THE VANYAN, THIS CREEPING DOOM--ARE ANCIENT.
IT IS AS IF TIME ITSELF IS FOLDING BACK UPON US.
REMEMBER THE MESSAGE-- "THE ORISHA IN FLIGHT. THE ORIGINATORS RETURN."

HAS THIS RAS THE EXHORTER PLEDGED HIS LOYALTY TO THESE ORIGINATORS? TO HIS "LOST-FOUND GOD"?

AND WHAT IF THE ORISHA HAD BEEN HOLDING SOMETHING AT BAY? SOME THREAT FROM THE WAKANDAN PAST?

IF THIS WAS LIKE THE OTHERS, THEN THERE IS A DOOR NEARBY.

WAY AHEAD OF YOU, SISTER.

"THERE."

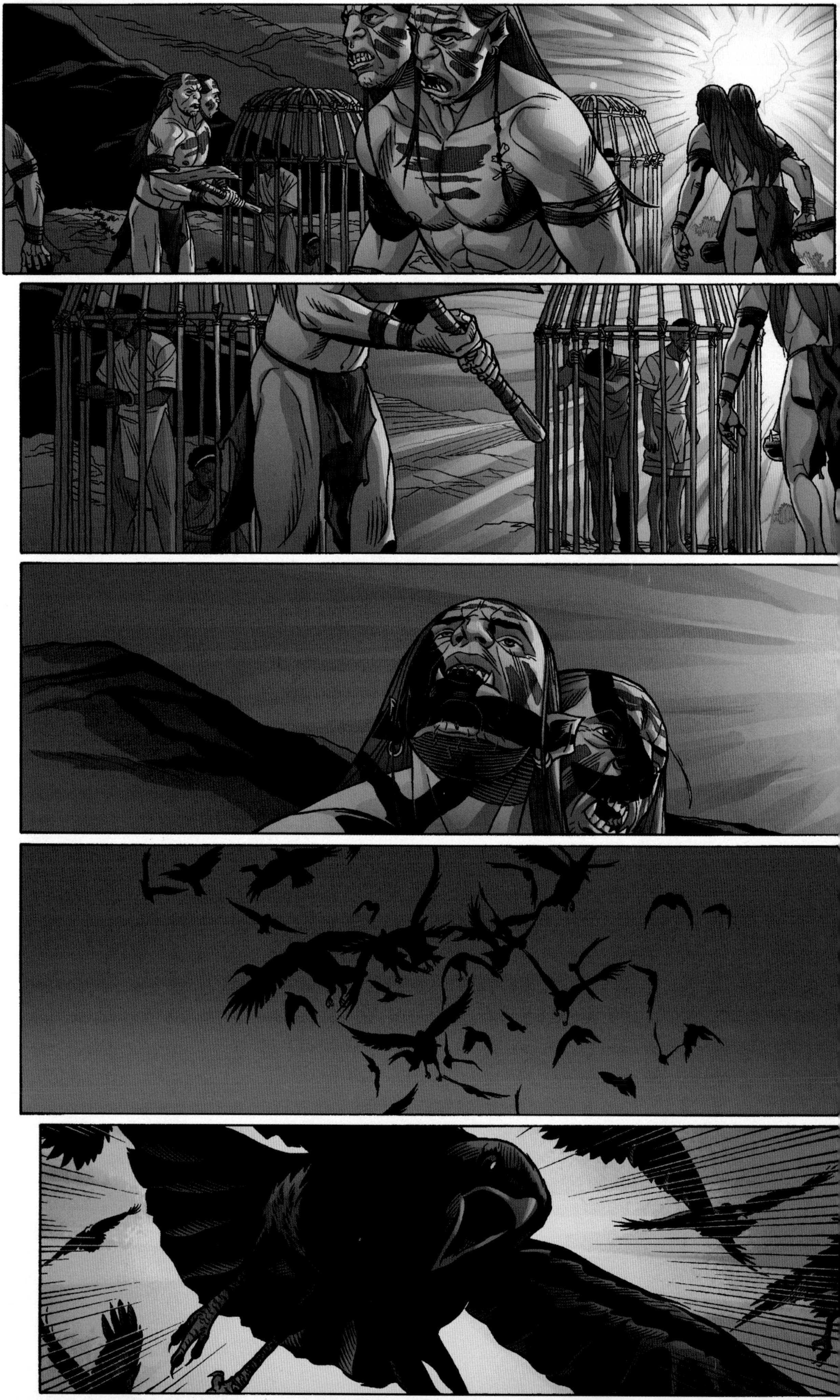

RUN. NOW.

ANGAAARGAAH!!

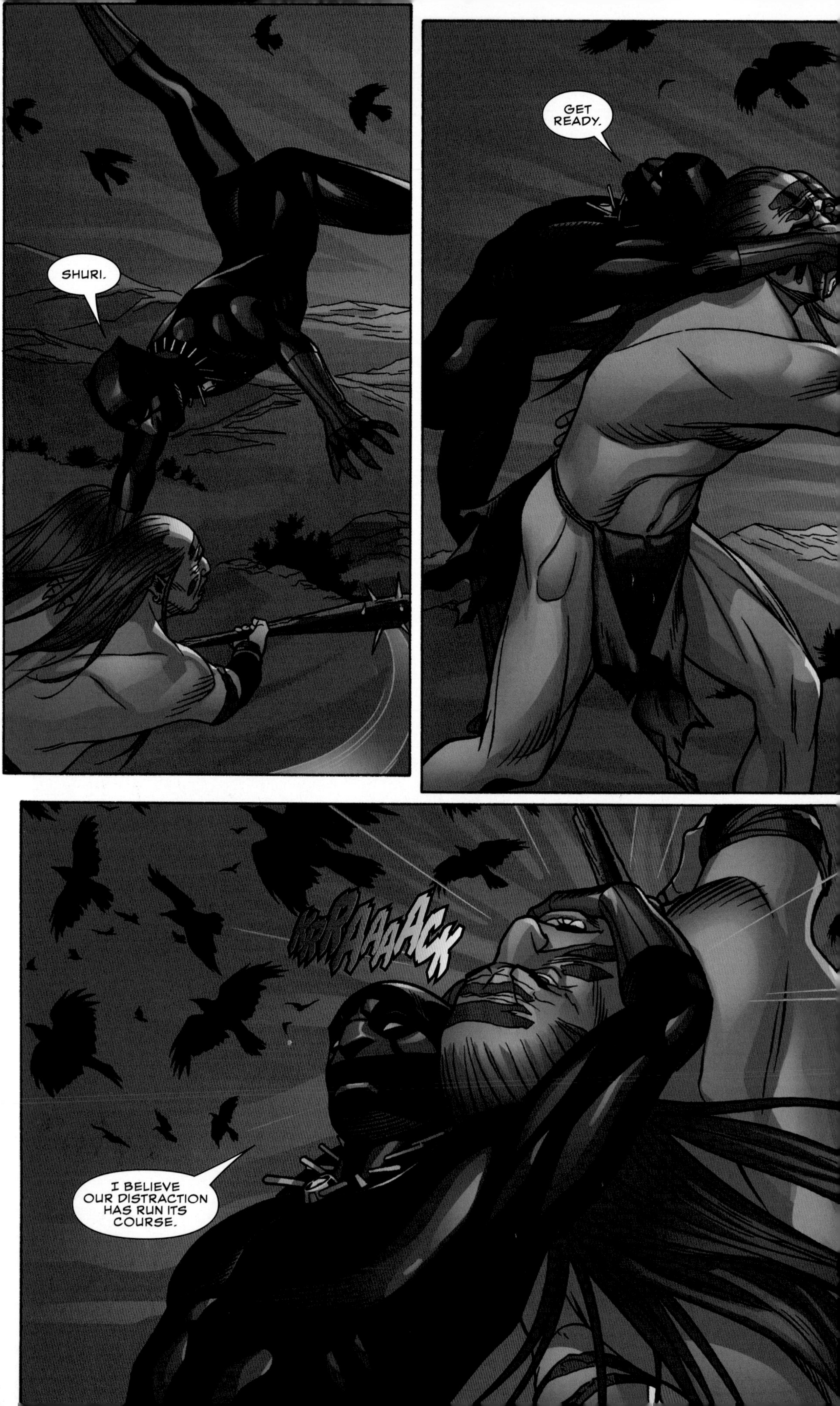
SHURI.
GET READY.
I BELIEVE OUR DISTRACTION HAS RUN ITS COURSE.

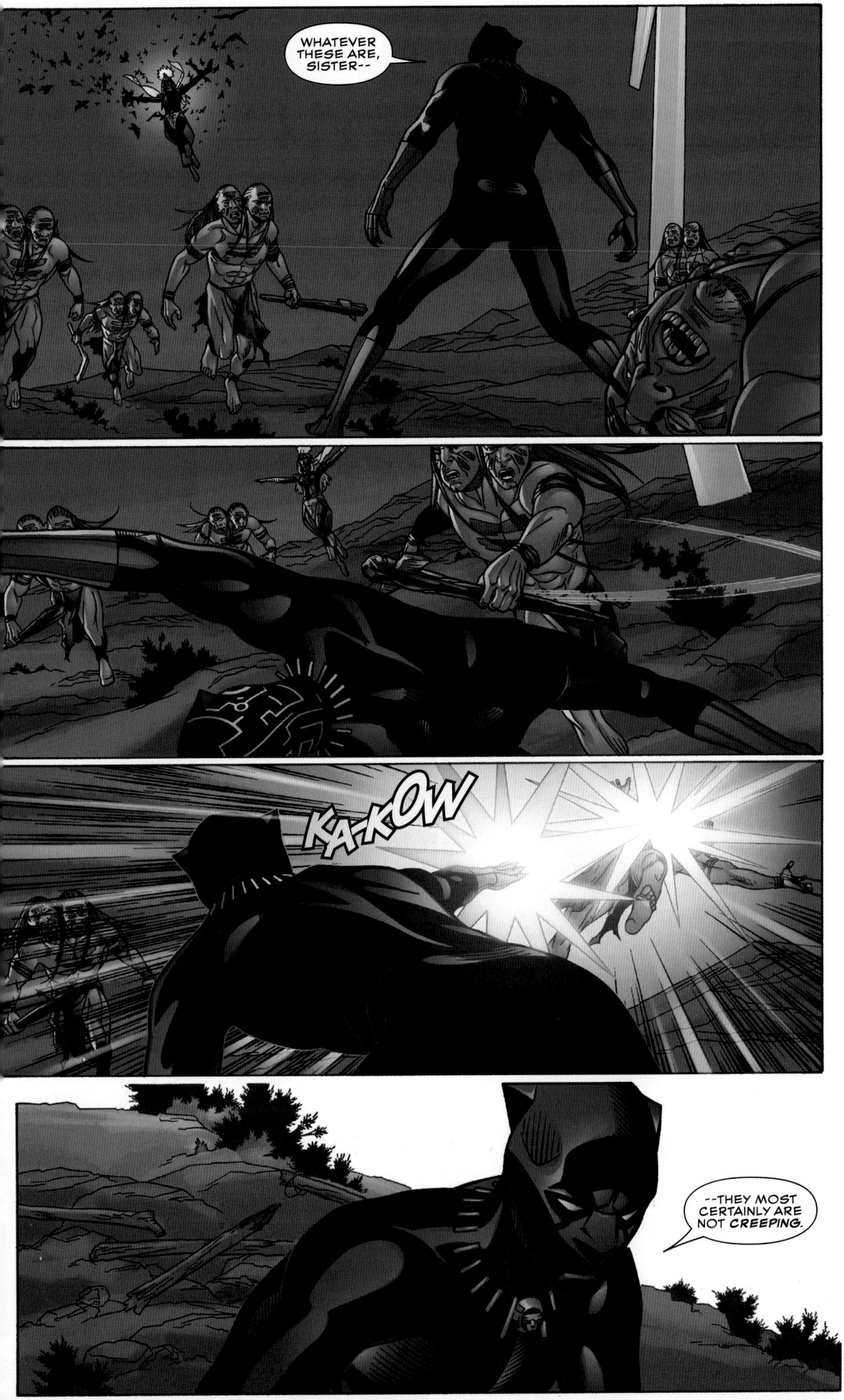
WHATEVER THESE ARE, SISTER--
KA-KOW
--THEY MOST CERTAINLY ARE NOT CREEPING.

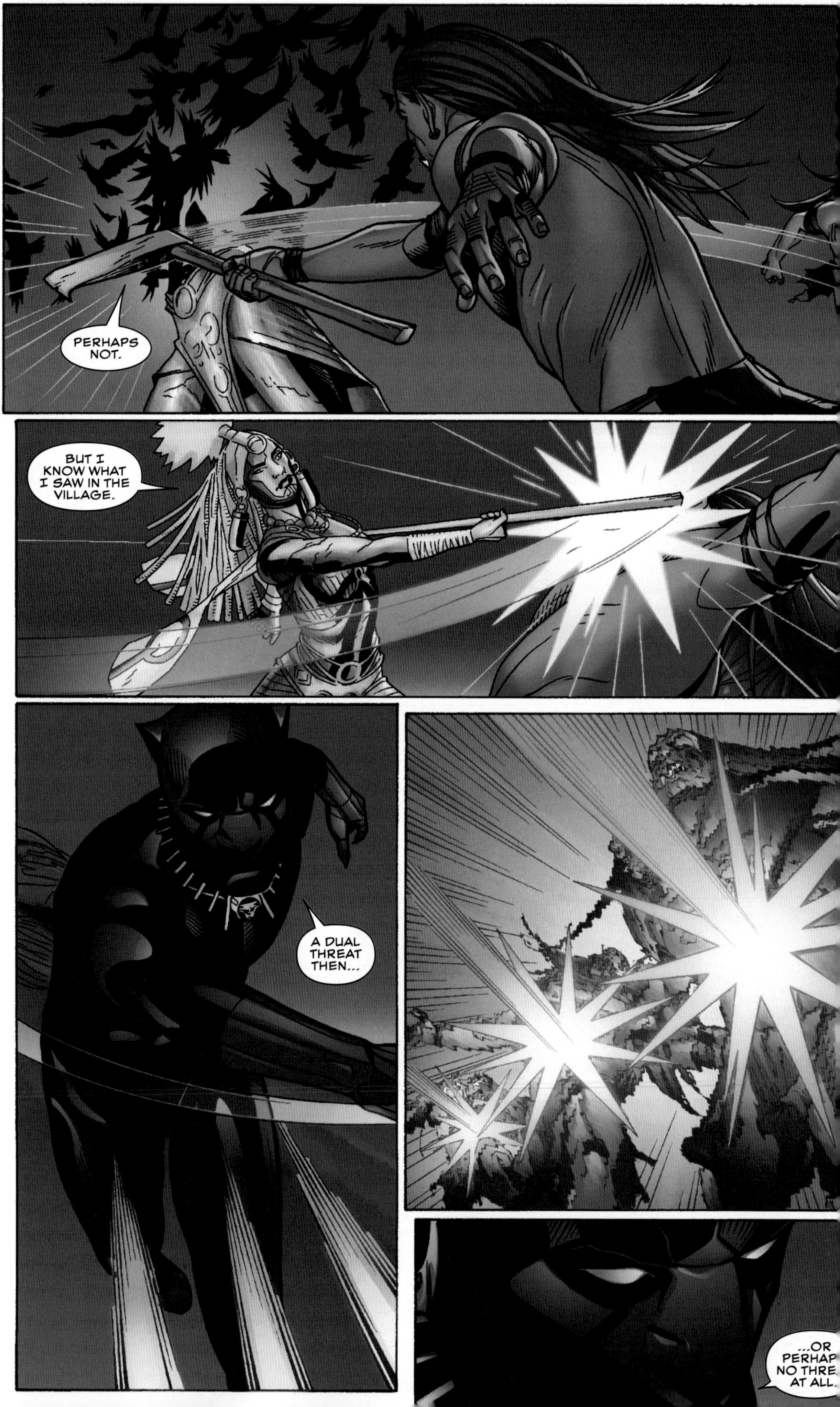
PERHAPS NOT.
BUT I KNOW WHAT I SAW IN THE VILLAGE.
A DUAL THREAT THEN...
...OR PERHAP NO THRE AT ALL.

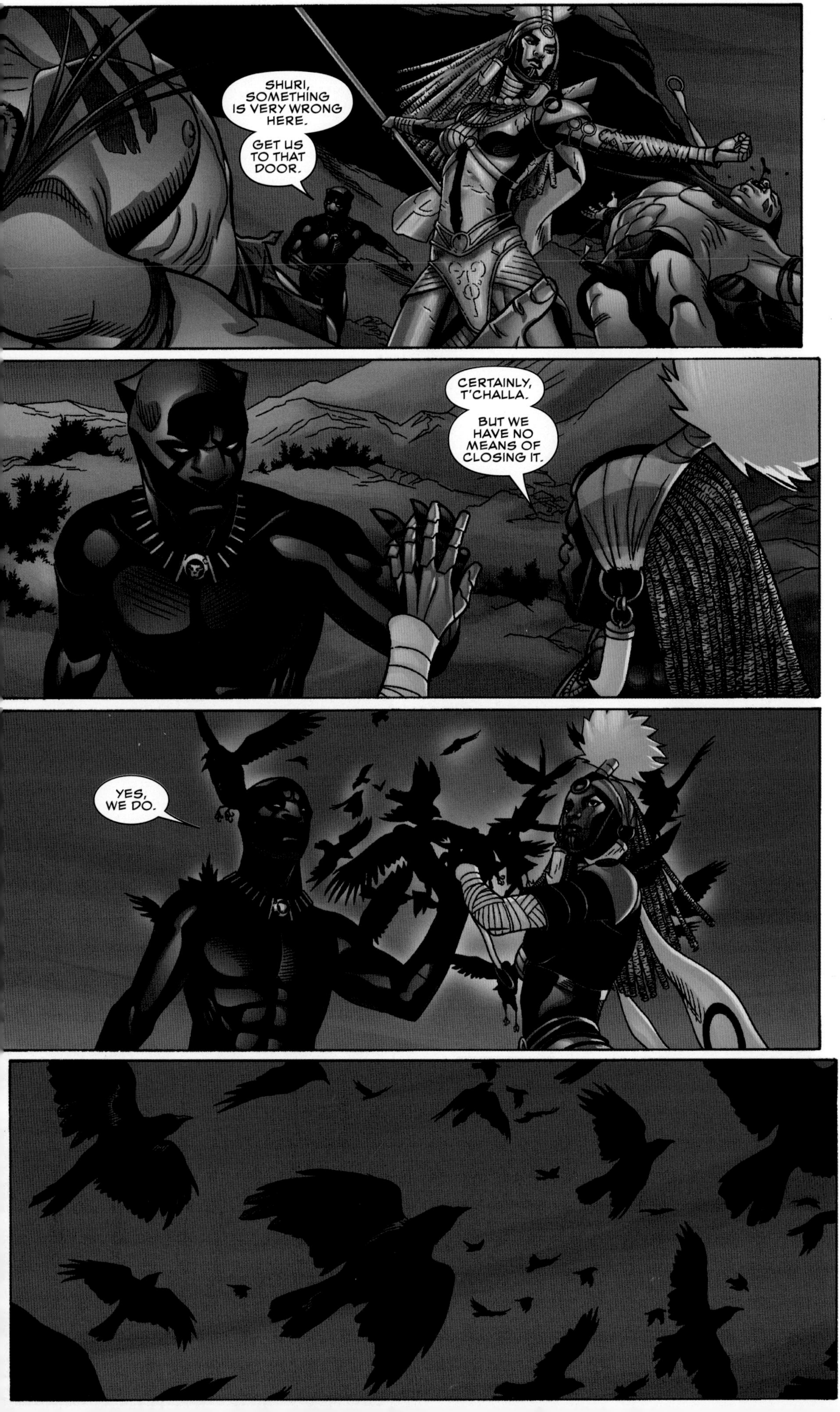
SHURI, SOMETHING IS VERY WRONG HERE.
GET US TO THAT DOOR.
CERTAINLY, T'CHALLA.
BUT WE HAVE NO MEANS OF CLOSING IT.
YES, WE DO.

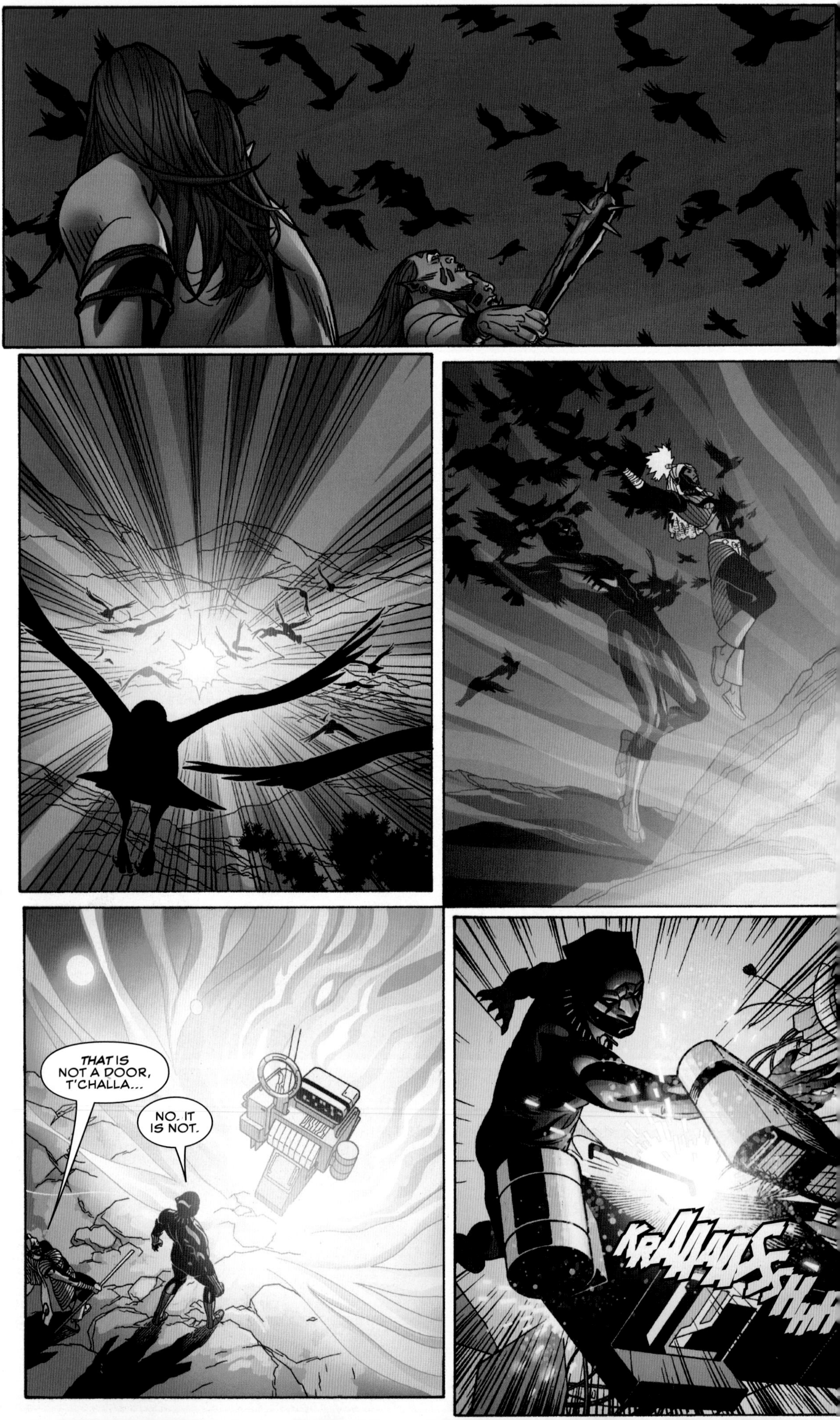

THAT IS NOT A DOOR, T'CHALLA...
NO. IT IS NOT.
KRAAAASHHH

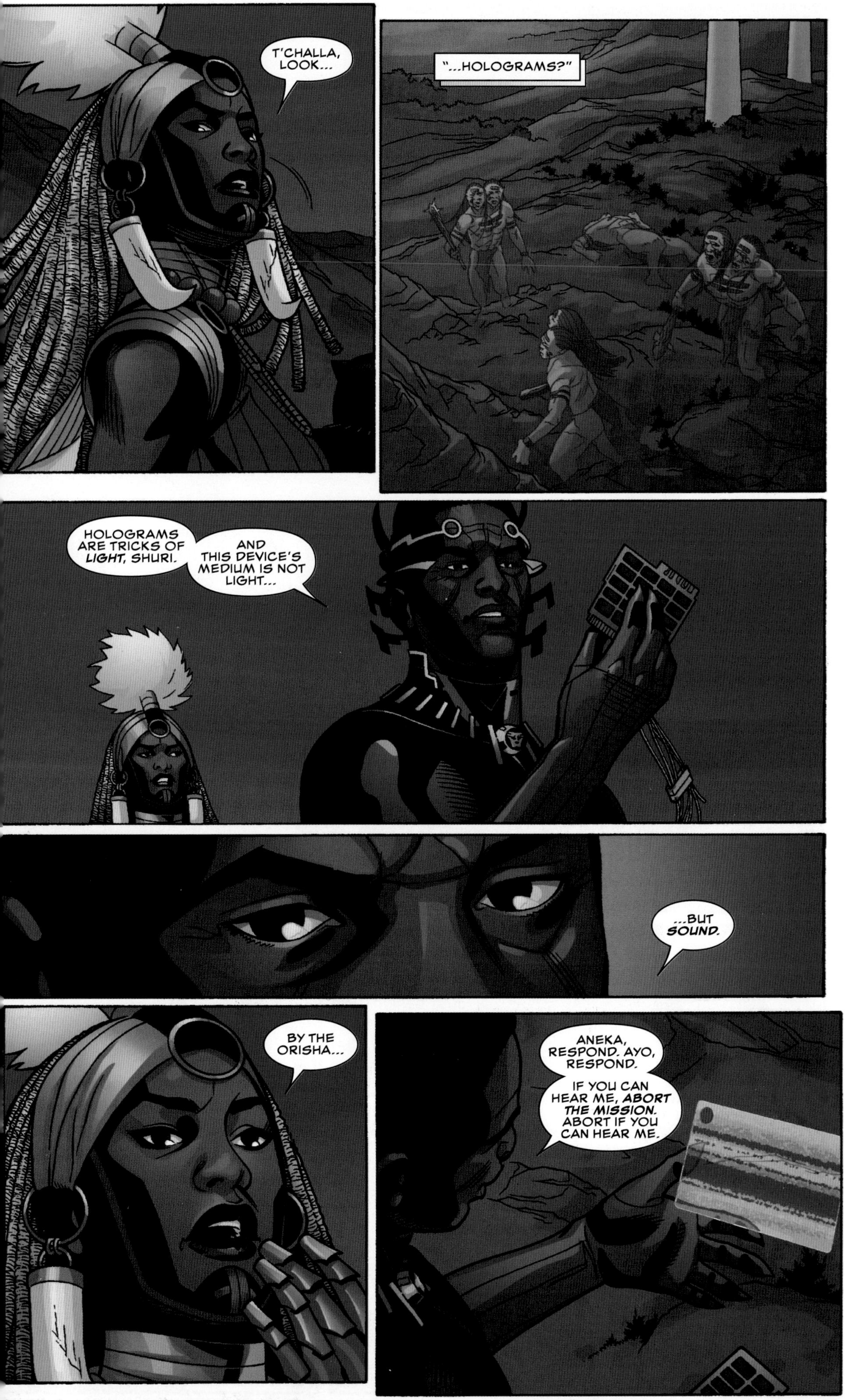
T'CHALLA, LOOK...
"...HOLOGRAMS?"
HOLOGRAMS ARE TRICKS OF *LIGHT*, SHURI.
AND THIS DEVICE'S MEDIUM IS NOT LIGHT...
...BUT *SOUND.*
BY THE ORISHA...
ANEKA, RESPOND. AYO, RESPOND.
IF YOU CAN HEAR ME, ***ABORT THE MISSION.*** ABORT IF YOU CAN HEAR ME.

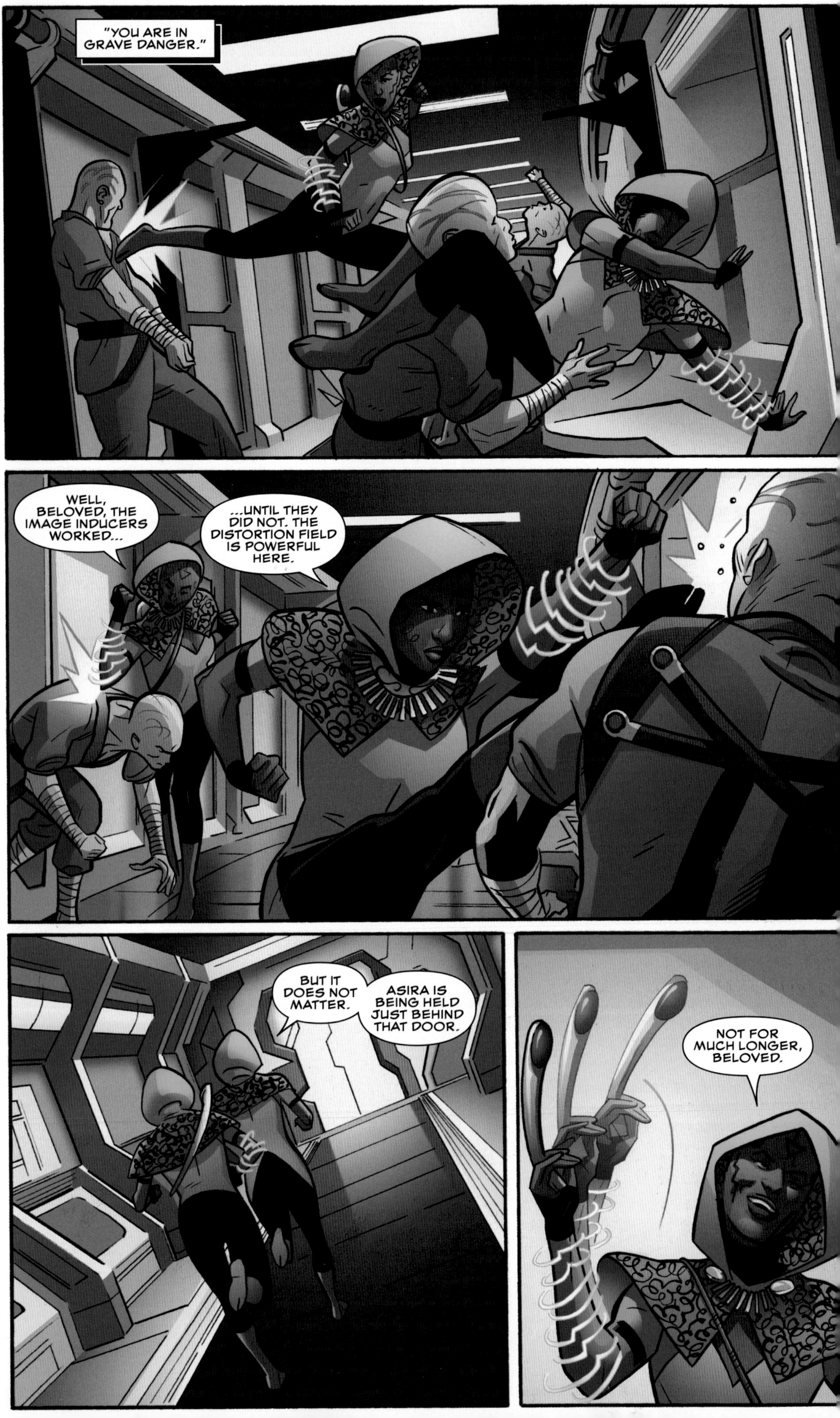
"YOU ARE IN GRAVE DANGER."
WELL, BELOVED, THE IMAGE INDUCERS WORKED...
...UNTIL THEY DID NOT. THE DISTORTION FIELD IS POWERFUL HERE.
BUT IT DOES NOT MATTER.
ASIRA IS BEING HELD JUST BEHIND THAT DOOR.
NOT FOR MUCH LONGER, BELOVED.

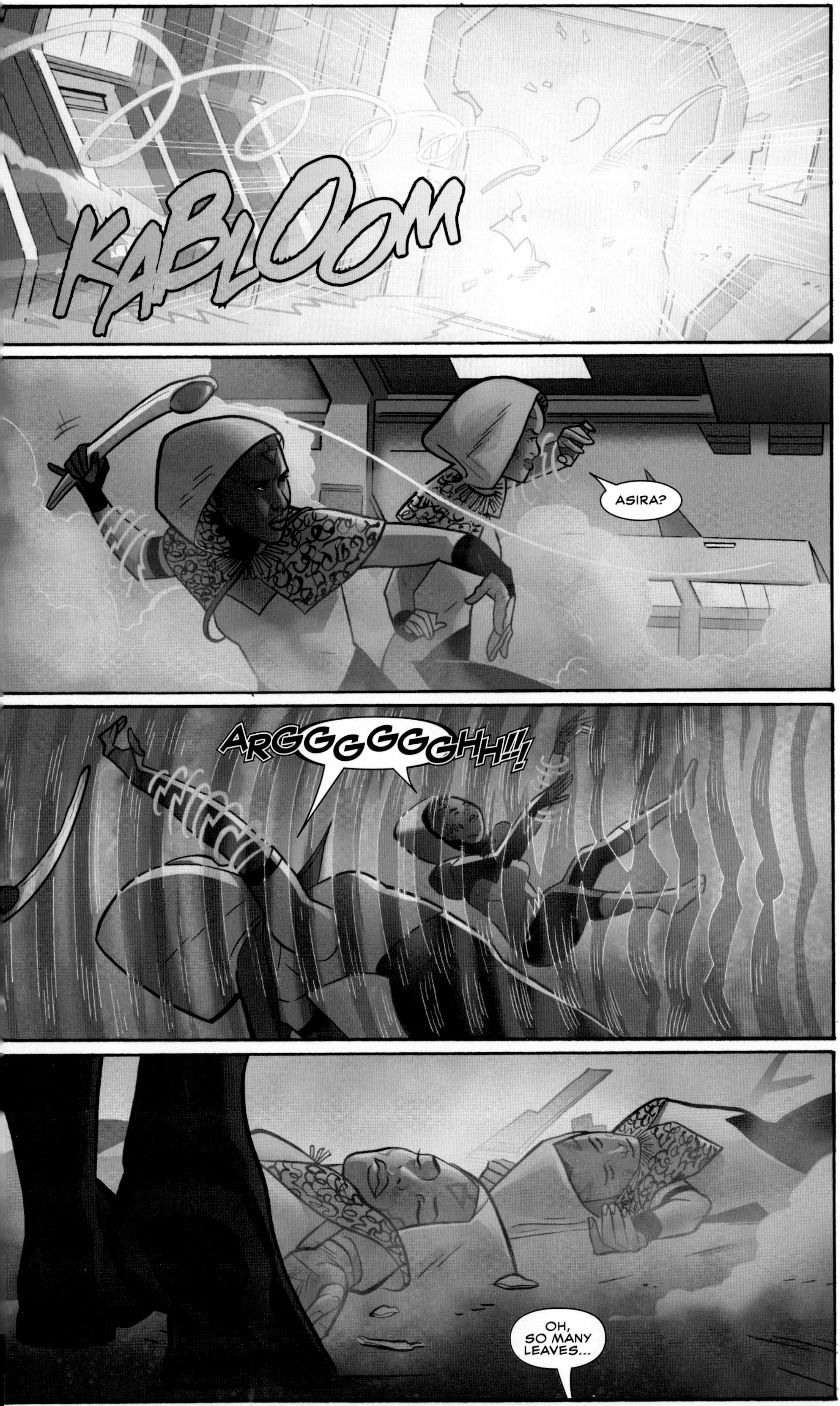
KABLOOM
ASIRA?
ARGGGGGGHH!!!
OH, SO MANY LEAVES...

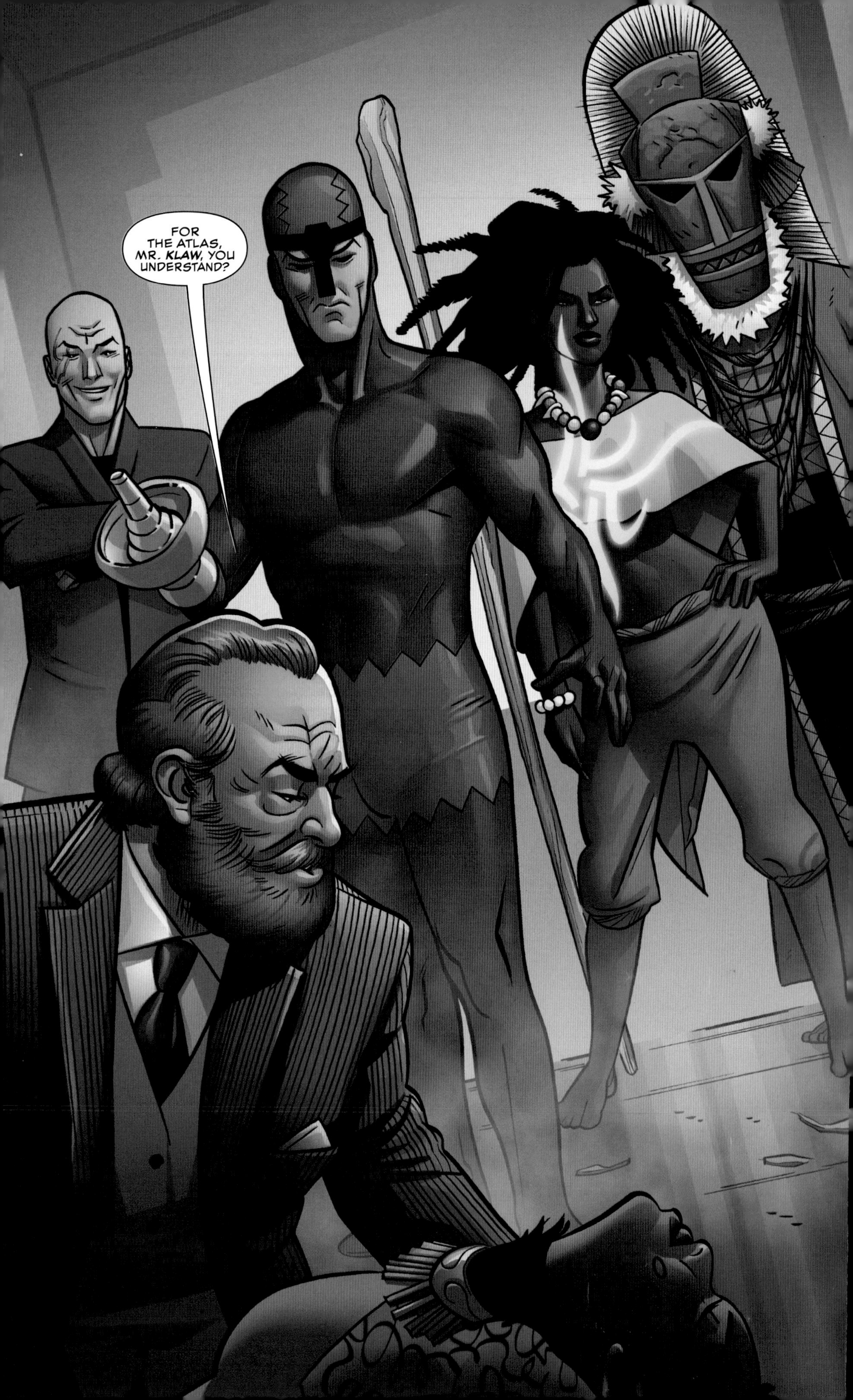
FOR THE ATLAS, MR. KLAW, YOU UNDERSTAND?

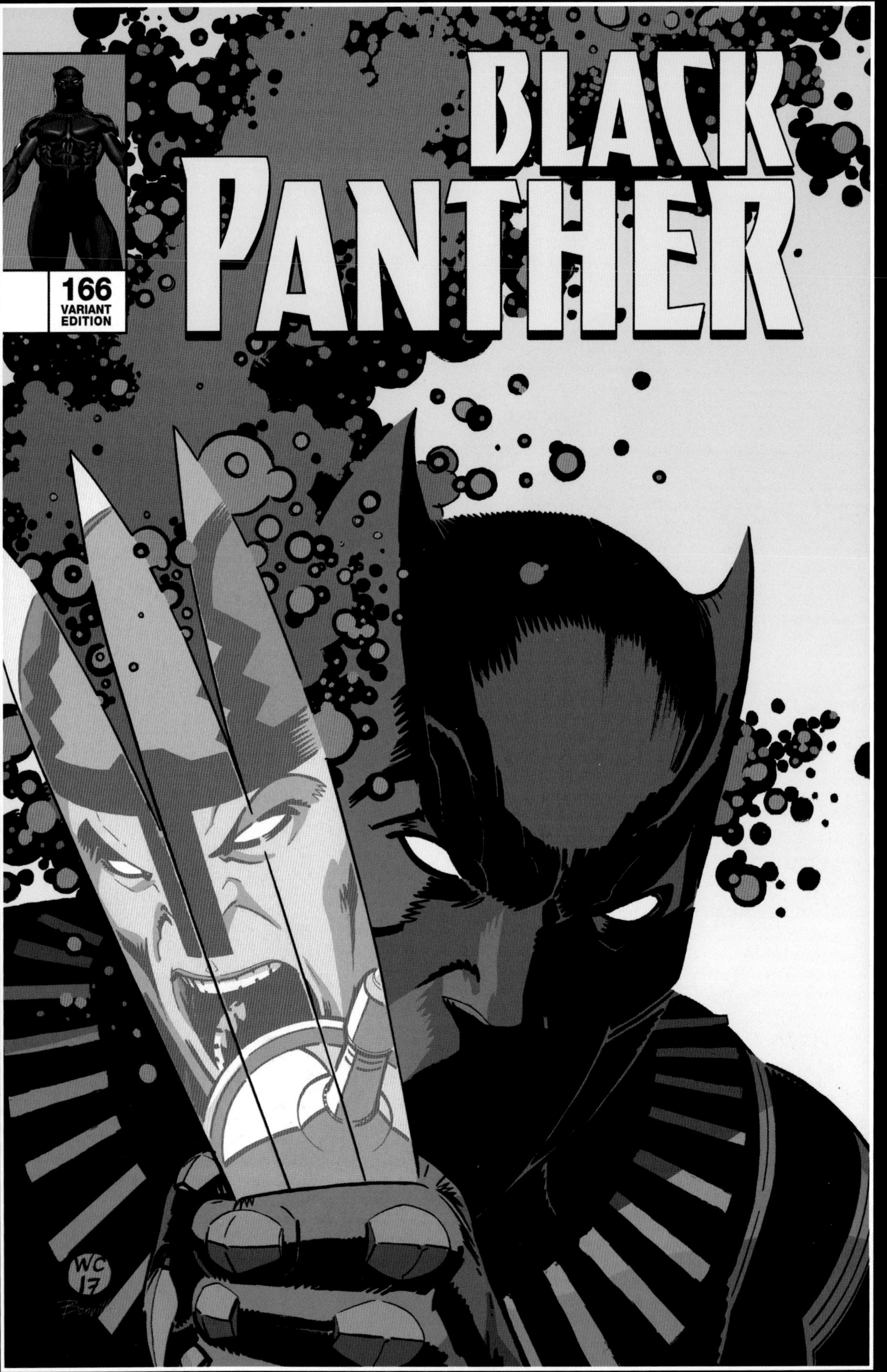
BLACK PANTHER
166
VARIANT EDITION
WC 17
Bonvill

#166 HOMAGE VARIANT BY **WES CRAIG** & **TAMRA BONVILLAIN**

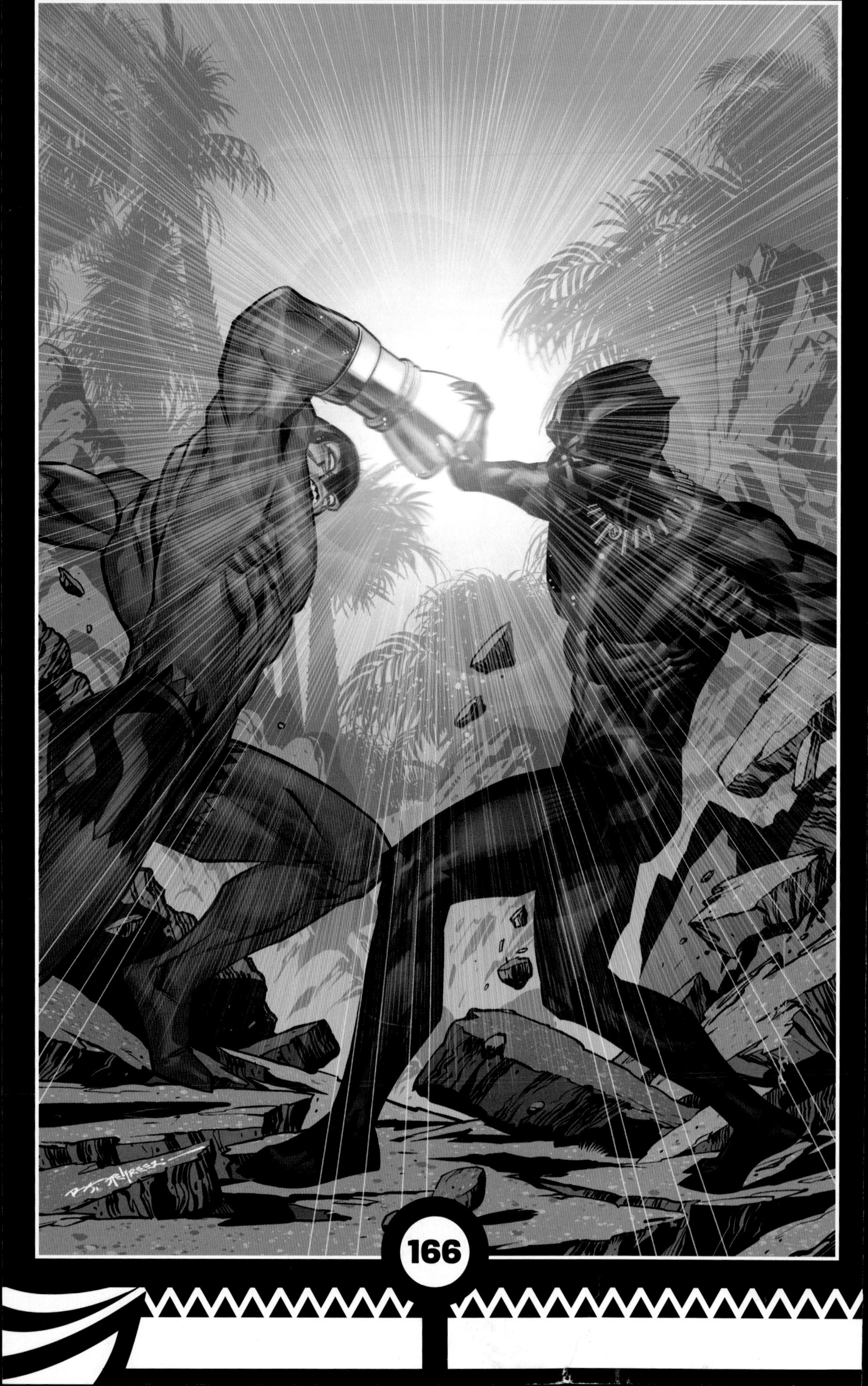

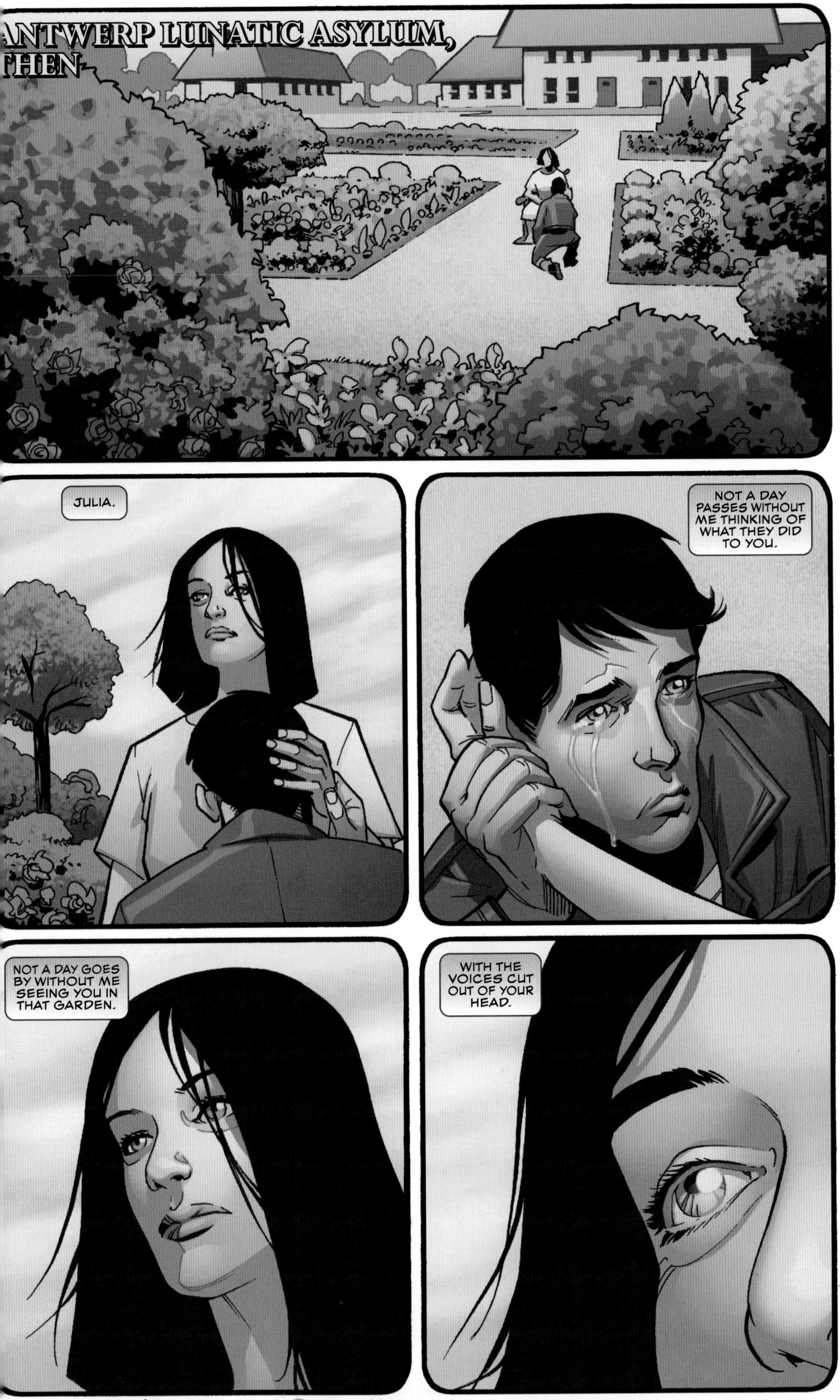
ANTWERP LUNATIC ASYLUM, THEN
JULIA.
NOT A DAY PASSES WITHOUT ME THINKING OF WHAT THEY DID TO YOU.
NOT A DAY GOES BY WITHOUT ME SEEING YOU IN THAT GARDEN.
WITH THE VOICES CUT OUT OF YOUR HEAD.

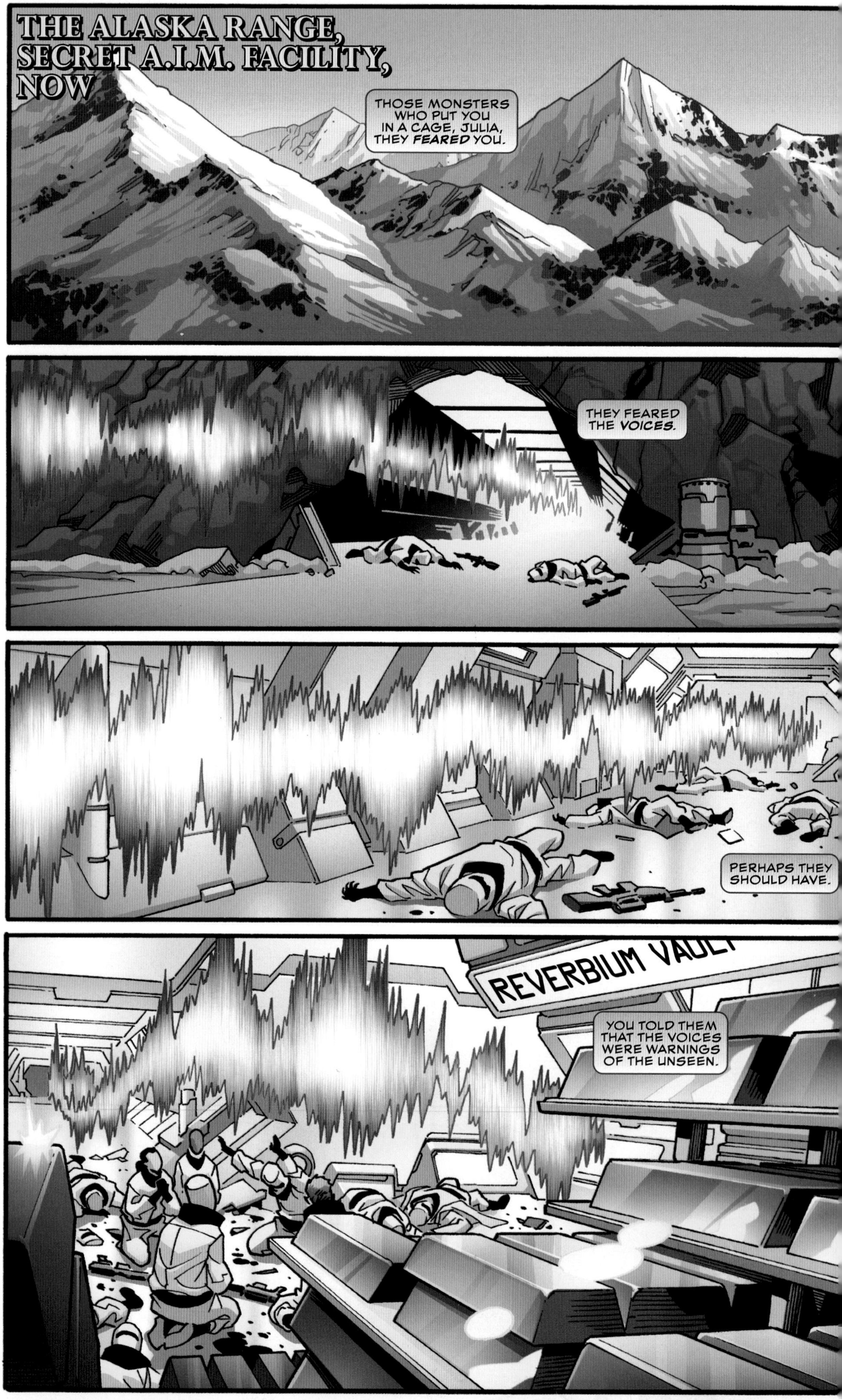
THE ALASKA RANGE, SECRET A.I.M. FACILITY, NOW
THOSE MONSTERS WHO PUT YOU IN A CAGE, JULIA, THEY FEARED YOU.
THEY FEARED THE VOICES.
PERHAPS THEY SHOULD HAVE.
REVERBIUM VAULT
YOU TOLD THEM THAT THE VOICES WERE WARNINGS OF THE UNSEEN.

THE REPROACH OF THE GODS.

I KNOW NOW THAT YOU WERE RIGHT, SISTER.

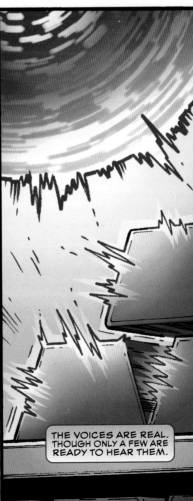

THE VOICES ARE REAL. THOUGH ONLY A FEW ARE READY TO HEAR THEM.

FOR WEEKS NOW, I HAVE BEEN THAT PARTICULAR VOICE.

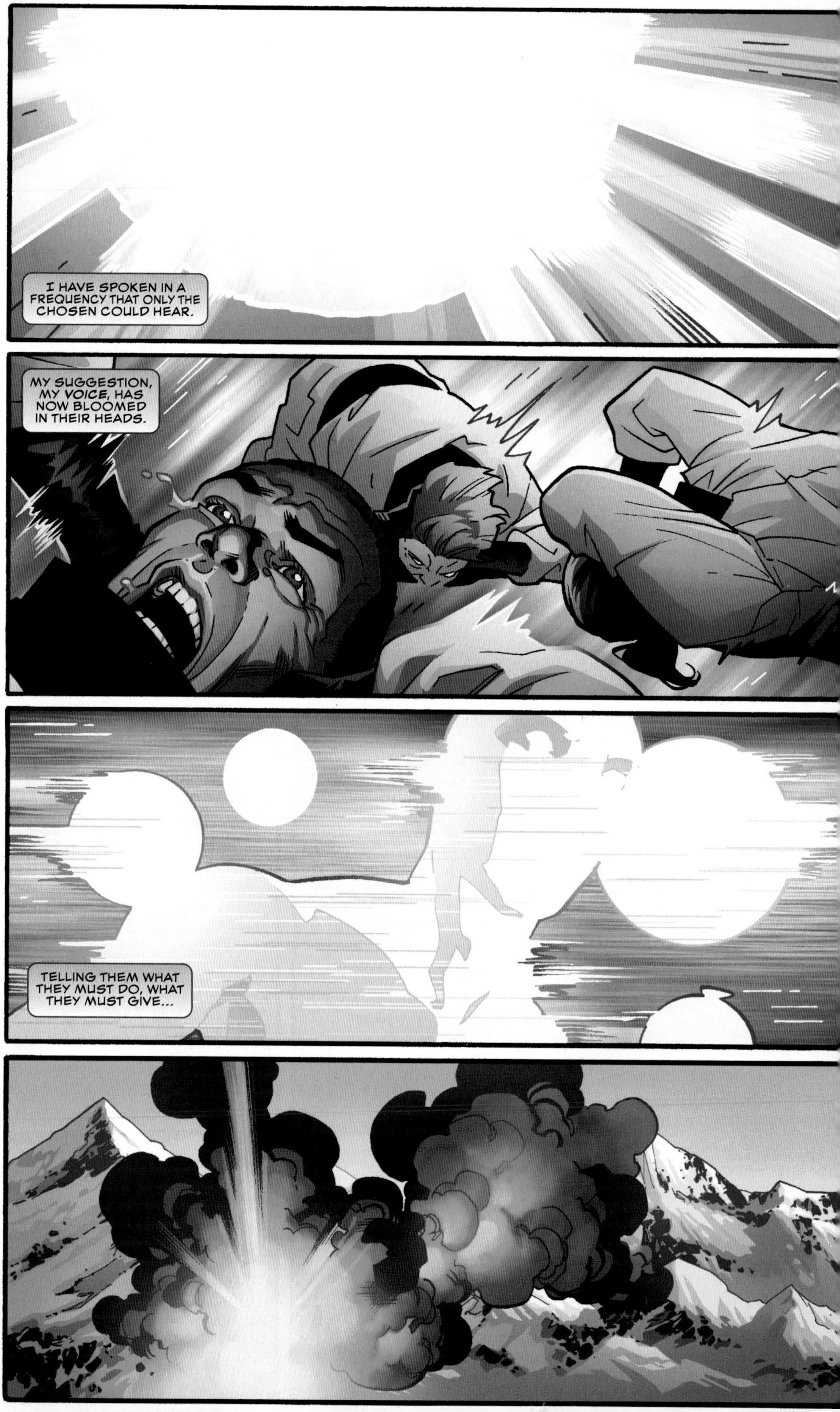
I HAVE SPOKEN IN A FREQUENCY THAT ONLY THE CHOSEN COULD HEAR.
MY SUGGESTION, MY *VOICE*, HAS NOW BLOOMED IN THEIR HEADS.
TELLING THEM WHAT THEY MUST DO, WHAT THEY MUST GIVE...

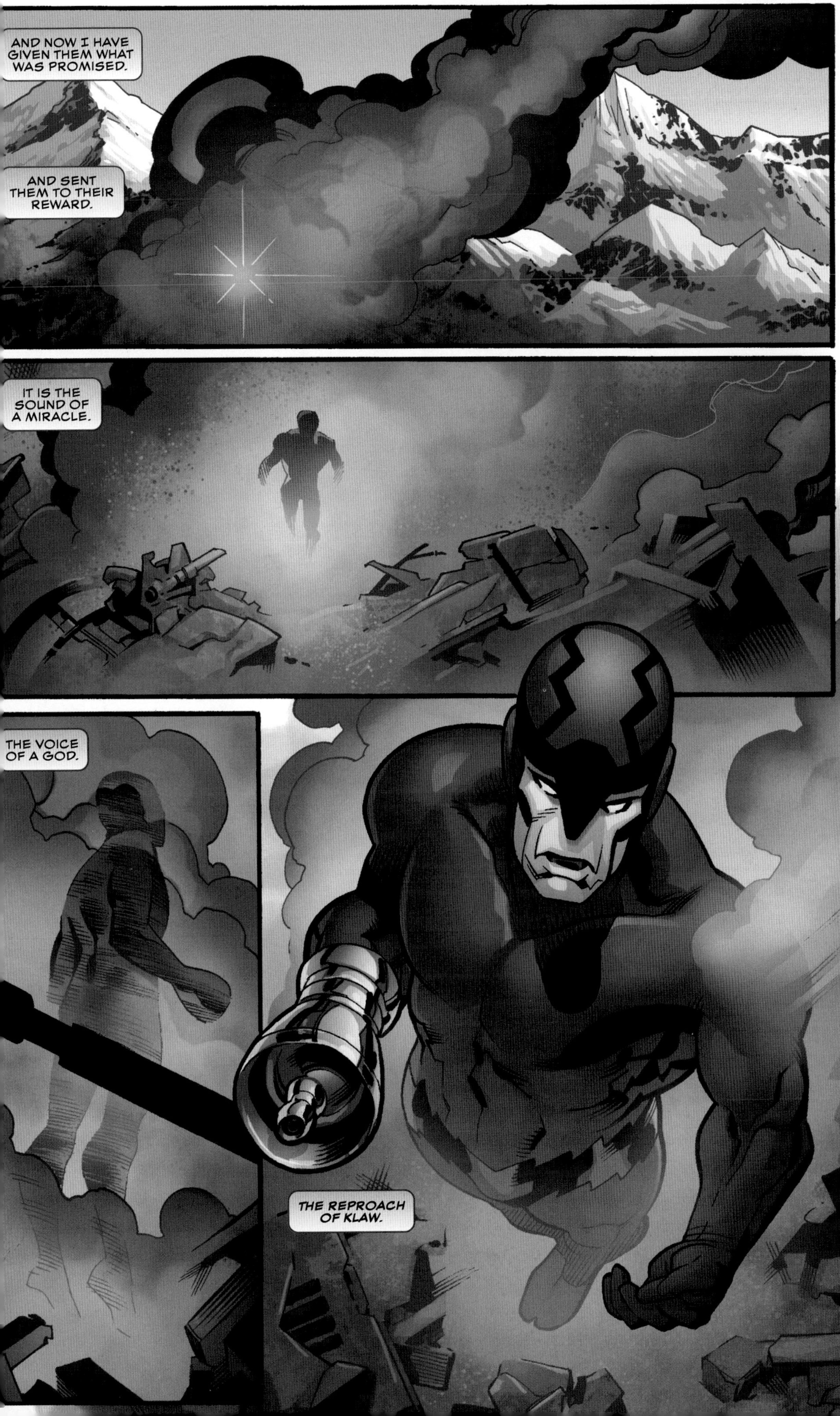
AND NOW I HAVE GIVEN THEM WHAT WAS PROMISED.
AND SENT THEM TO THEIR REWARD.
IT IS THE SOUND OF A MIRACLE.
THE VOICE OF A GOD.
THE REPROACH OF KLAW.

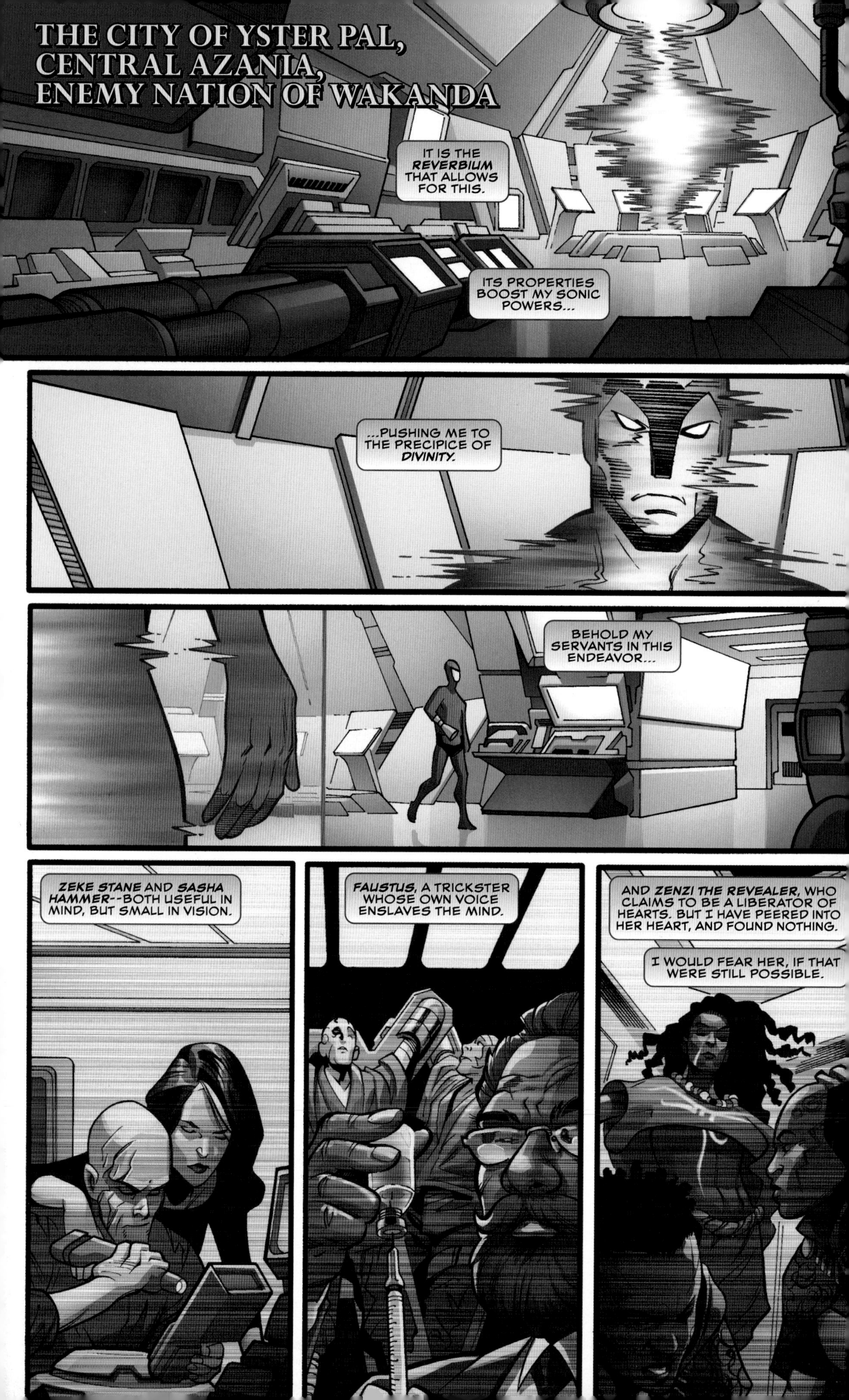
THE CITY OF YSTER PAL, CENTRAL AZANIA, ENEMY NATION OF WAKANDA
IT IS THE REVERBIUM THAT ALLOWS FOR THIS.
ITS PROPERTIES BOOST MY SONIC POWERS...
...PUSHING ME TO THE PRECIPICE OF DIVINITY.
BEHOLD MY SERVANTS IN THIS ENDEAVOR...
ZEKE STANE AND SASHA HAMMER--BOTH USEFUL IN MIND, BUT SMALL IN VISION.
FAUSTUS, A TRICKSTER WHOSE OWN VOICE ENSLAVES THE MIND.
AND ZENZI THE REVEALER, WHO CLAIMS TO BE A LIBERATOR OF HEARTS. BUT I HAVE PEERED INTO HER HEART, AND FOUND NOTHING.
I WOULD FEAR HER, IF THAT WERE STILL POSSIBLE.

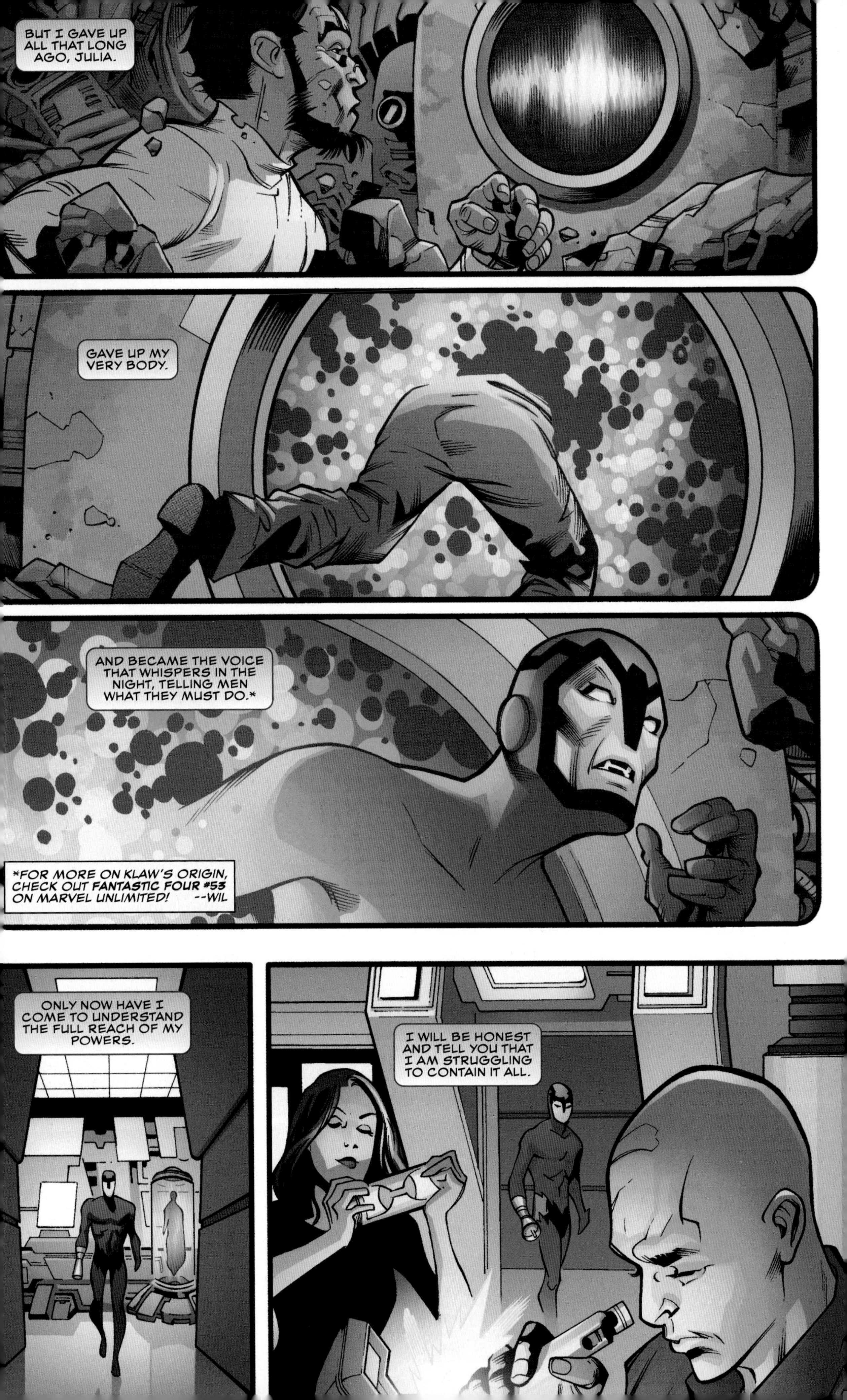
BUT I GAVE UP ALL THAT LONG AGO, JULIA.
GAVE UP MY VERY BODY.
AND BECAME THE VOICE THAT WHISPERS IN THE NIGHT, TELLING MEN WHAT THEY MUST DO.*
*FOR MORE ON KLAW'S ORIGIN, CHECK OUT FANTASTIC FOUR #53 ON MARVEL UNLIMITED! --WIL
ONLY NOW HAVE I COME TO UNDERSTAND THE FULL REACH OF MY POWERS.
I WILL BE HONEST AND TELL YOU THAT I AM STRUGGLING TO CONTAIN IT ALL.

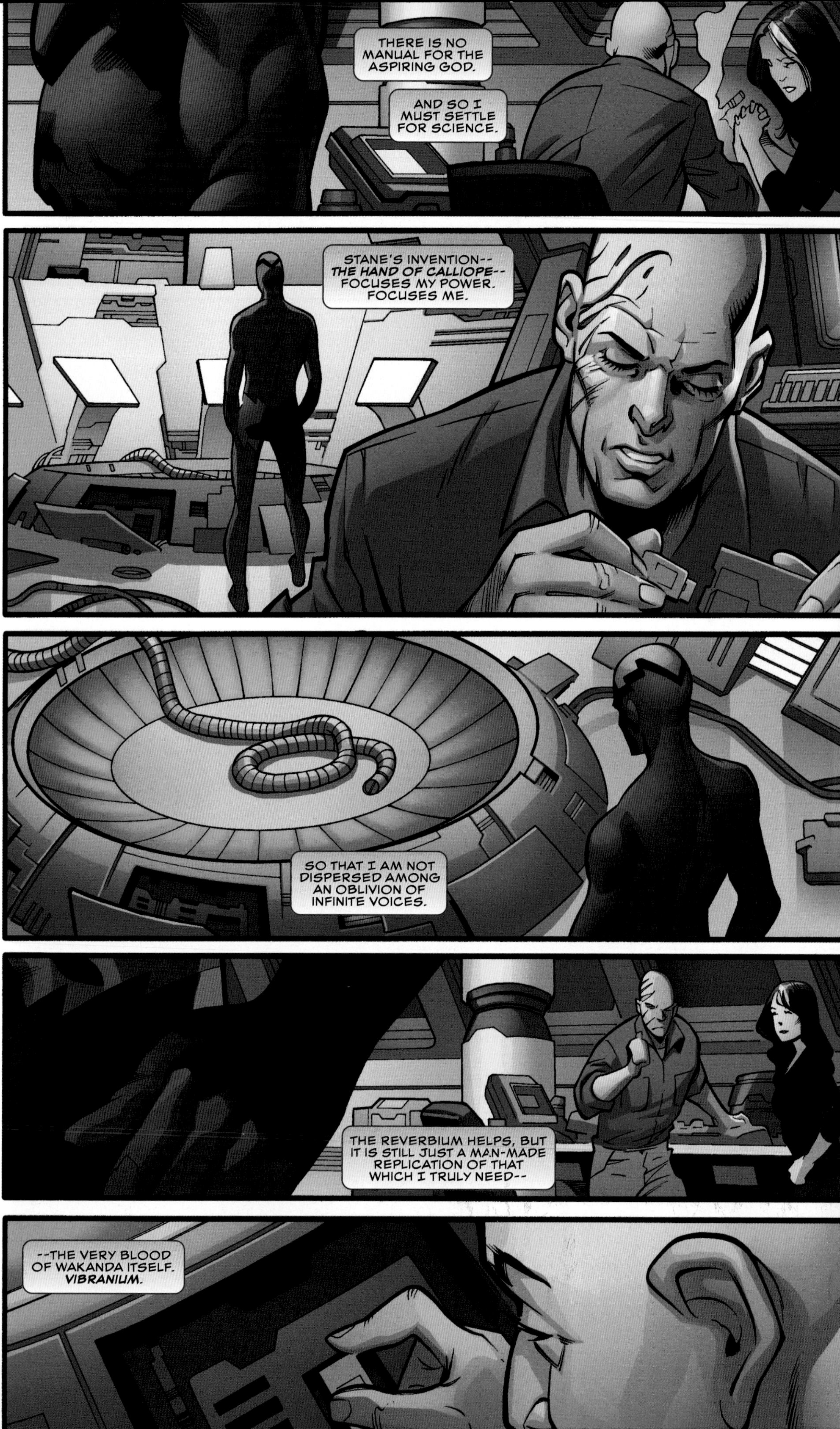
THERE IS NO MANUAL FOR THE ASPIRING GOD.
AND SO I MUST SETTLE FOR SCIENCE.
STANE'S INVENTION-- *THE HAND OF CALLIOPE*-- FOCUSES MY POWER. FOCUSES ME.
SO THAT I AM NOT DISPERSED AMONG AN OBLIVION OF INFINITE VOICES.
THE REVERBIUM HELPS, BUT IT IS STILL JUST A MAN-MADE REPLICATION OF THAT WHICH I TRULY NEED--
--THE VERY BLOOD OF WAKANDA ITSELF. **VIBRANIUM.**

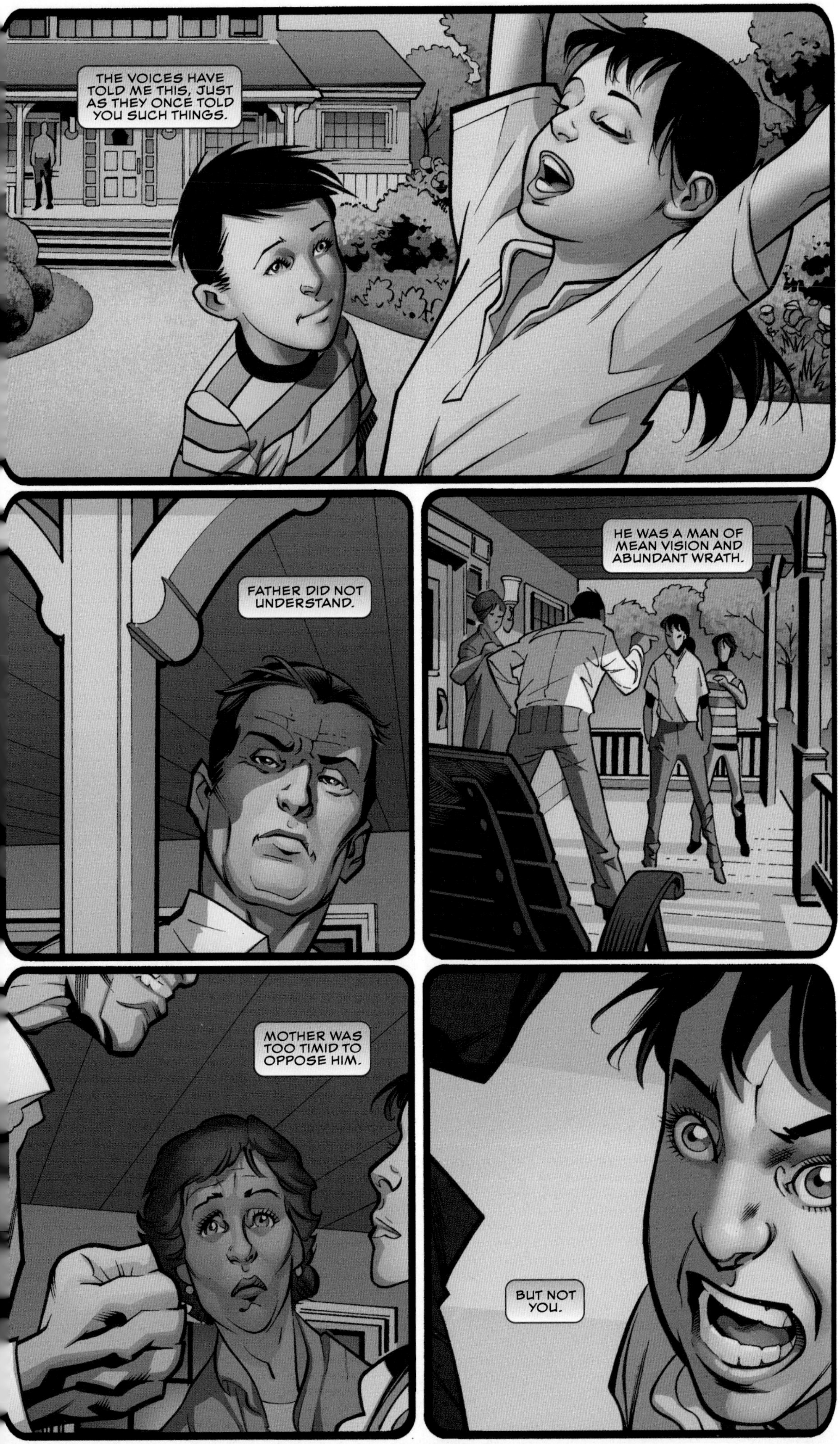
THE VOICES HAVE TOLD ME THIS, JUST AS THEY ONCE TOLD YOU SUCH THINGS.
FATHER DID NOT UNDERSTAND.
HE WAS A MAN OF MEAN VISION AND ABUNDANT WRATH.
MOTHER WAS TOO TIMID TO OPPOSE HIM.
BUT NOT YOU.

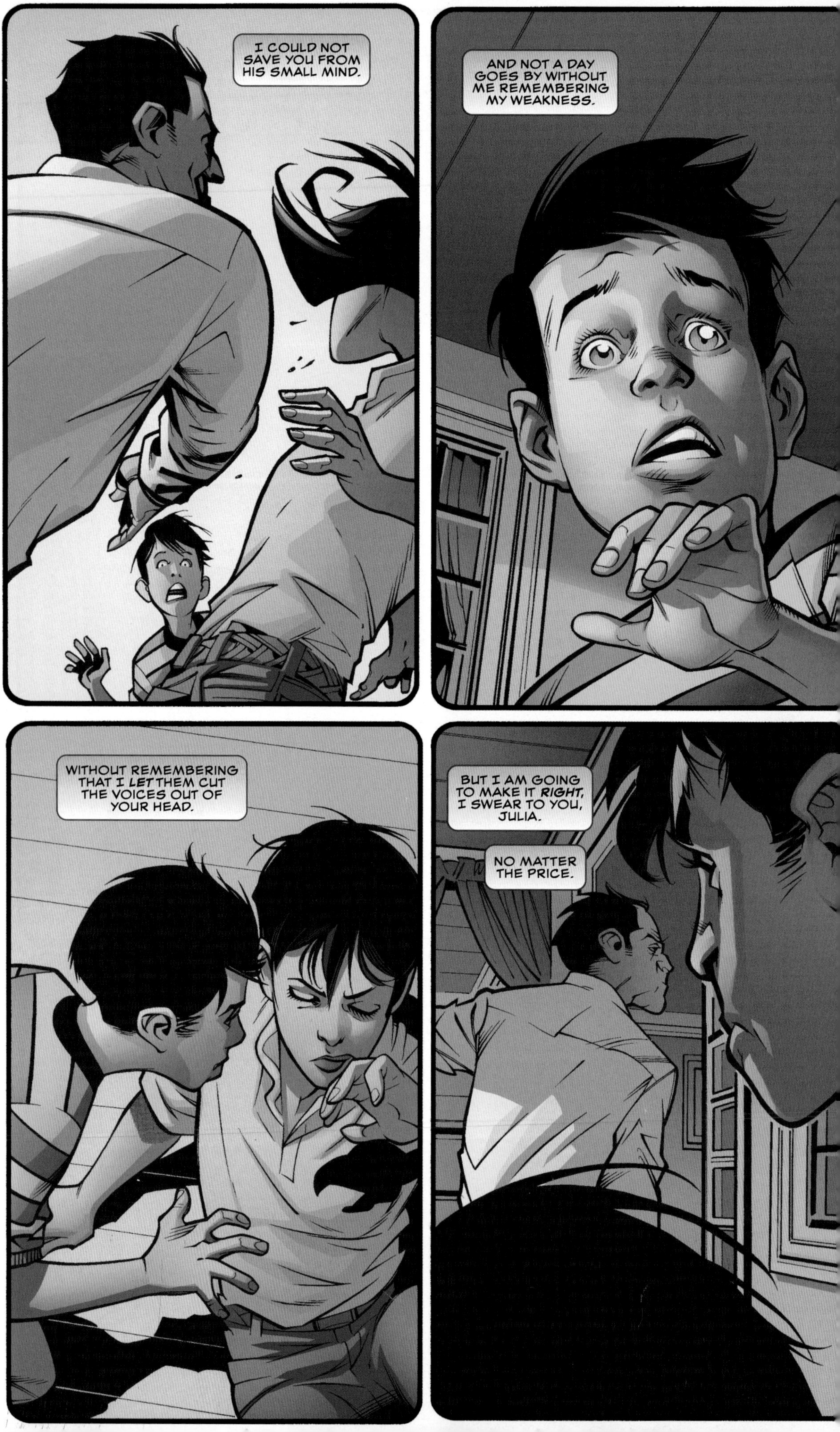
I COULD NOT SAVE YOU FROM HIS SMALL MIND.
AND NOT A DAY GOES BY WITHOUT ME REMEMBERING MY WEAKNESS.
WITHOUT REMEMBERING THAT I *LET* THEM CUT THE VOICES OUT OF YOUR HEAD.
BUT I AM GOING TO MAKE IT *RIGHT*, I SWEAR TO YOU, JULIA.
NO MATTER THE PRICE.

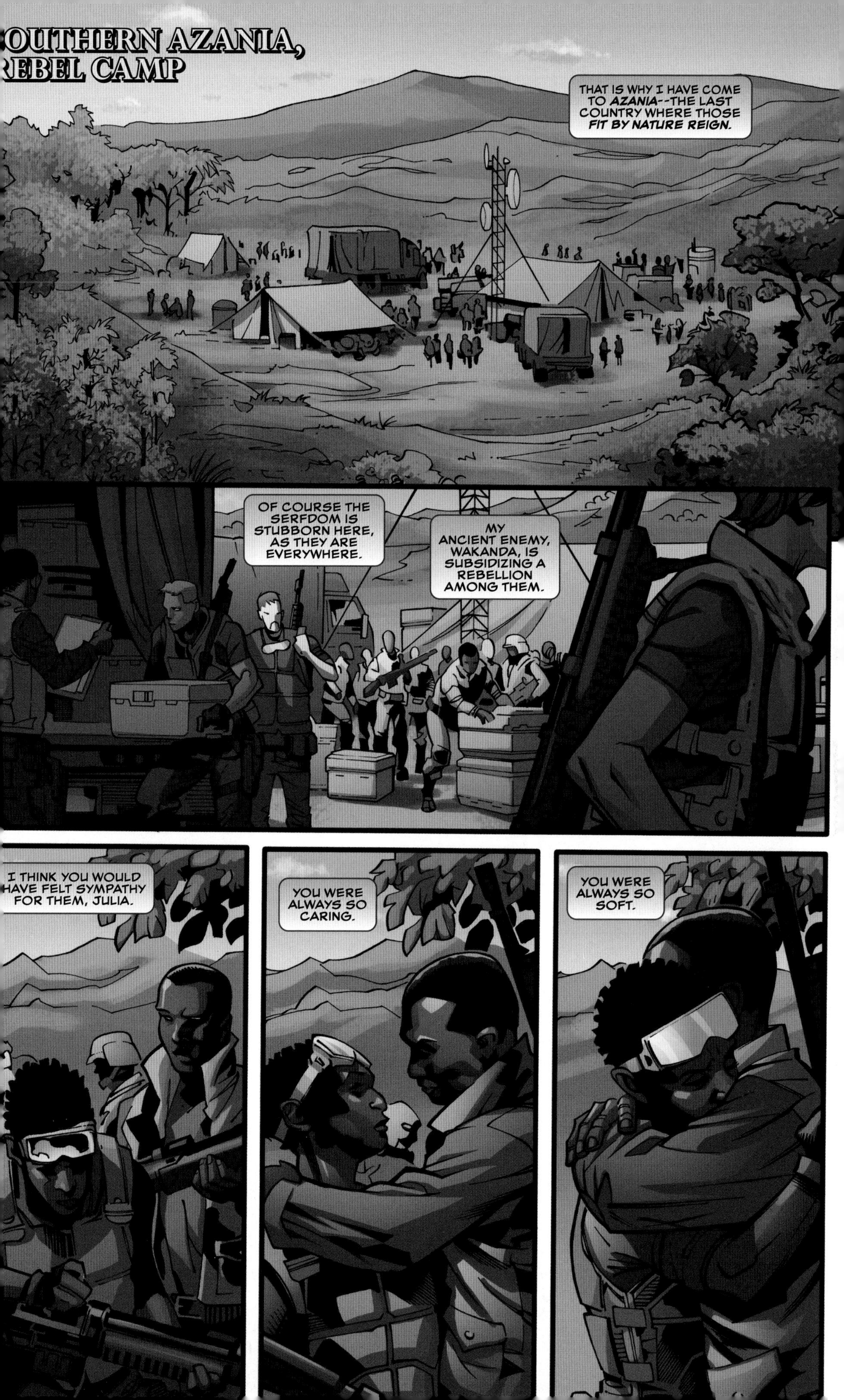
SOUTHERN AZANIA, REBEL CAMP
THAT IS WHY I HAVE COME TO AZANIA--THE LAST COUNTRY WHERE THOSE FIT BY NATURE REIGN.
OF COURSE THE SERFDOM IS STUBBORN HERE, AS THEY ARE EVERYWHERE.
MY ANCIENT ENEMY, WAKANDA, IS SUBSIDIZING A REBELLION AMONG THEM.
I THINK YOU WOULD HAVE FELT SYMPATHY FOR THEM, JULIA.
YOU WERE ALWAYS SO CARING.
YOU WERE ALWAYS SO SOFT.

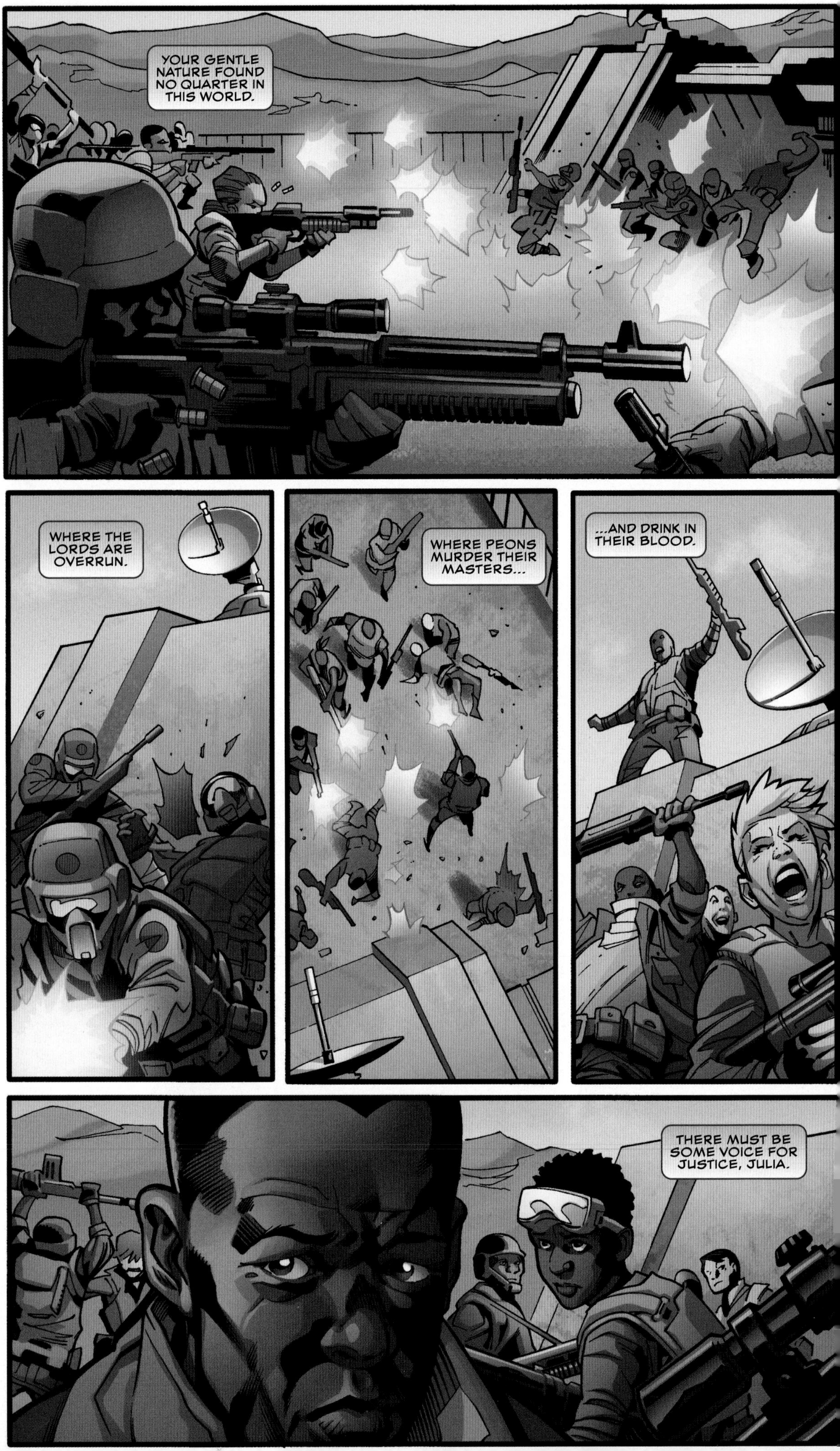
YOUR GENTLE NATURE FOUND NO QUARTER IN THIS WORLD.
WHERE THE LORDS ARE OVERRUN.
WHERE PEONS MURDER THEIR MASTERS...
...AND DRINK IN THEIR BLOOD.
THERE MUST BE SOME VOICE FOR JUSTICE, JULIA.

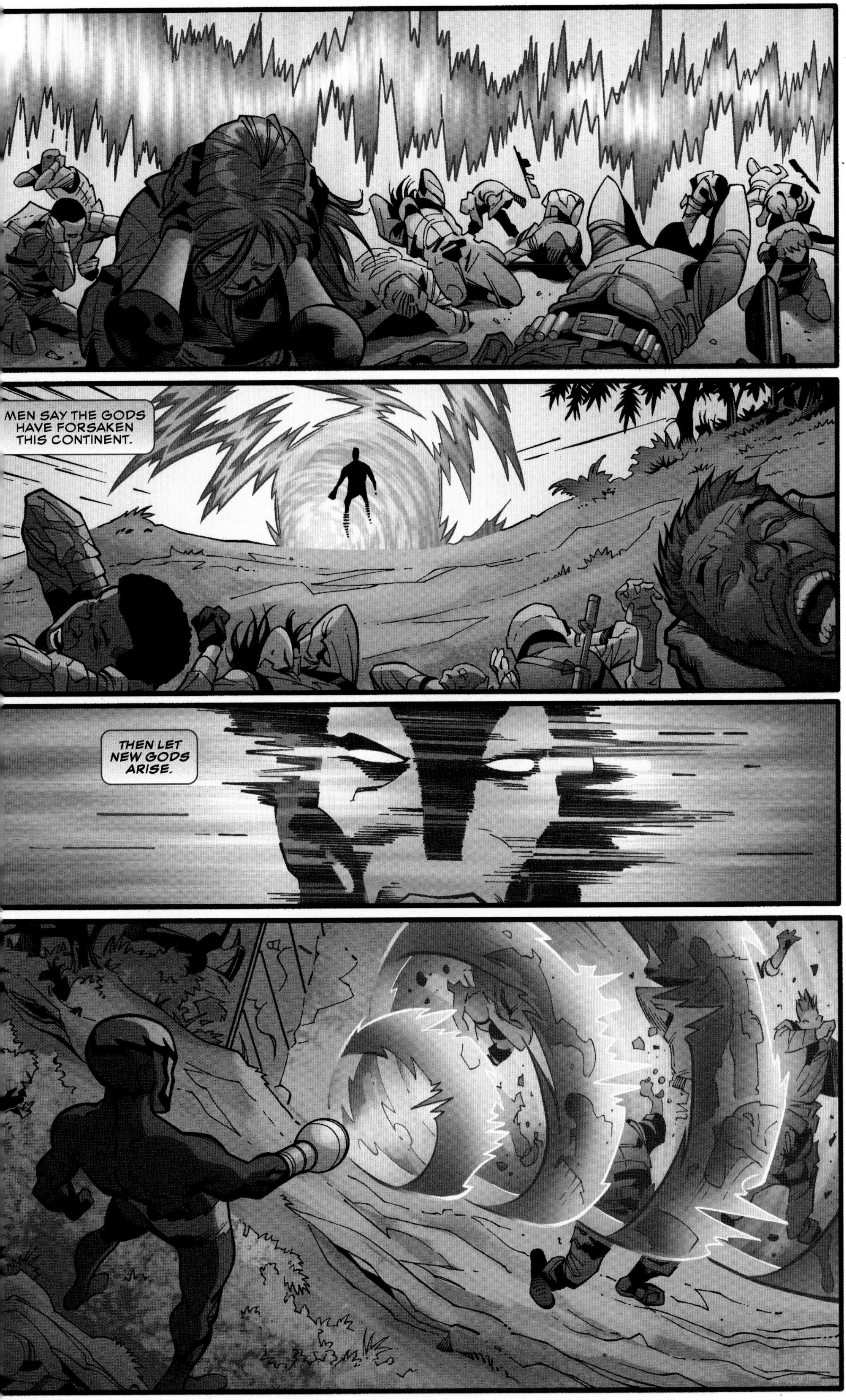
MEN SAY THE GODS HAVE FORSAKEN THIS CONTINENT.
THEN LET NEW GODS ARISE.

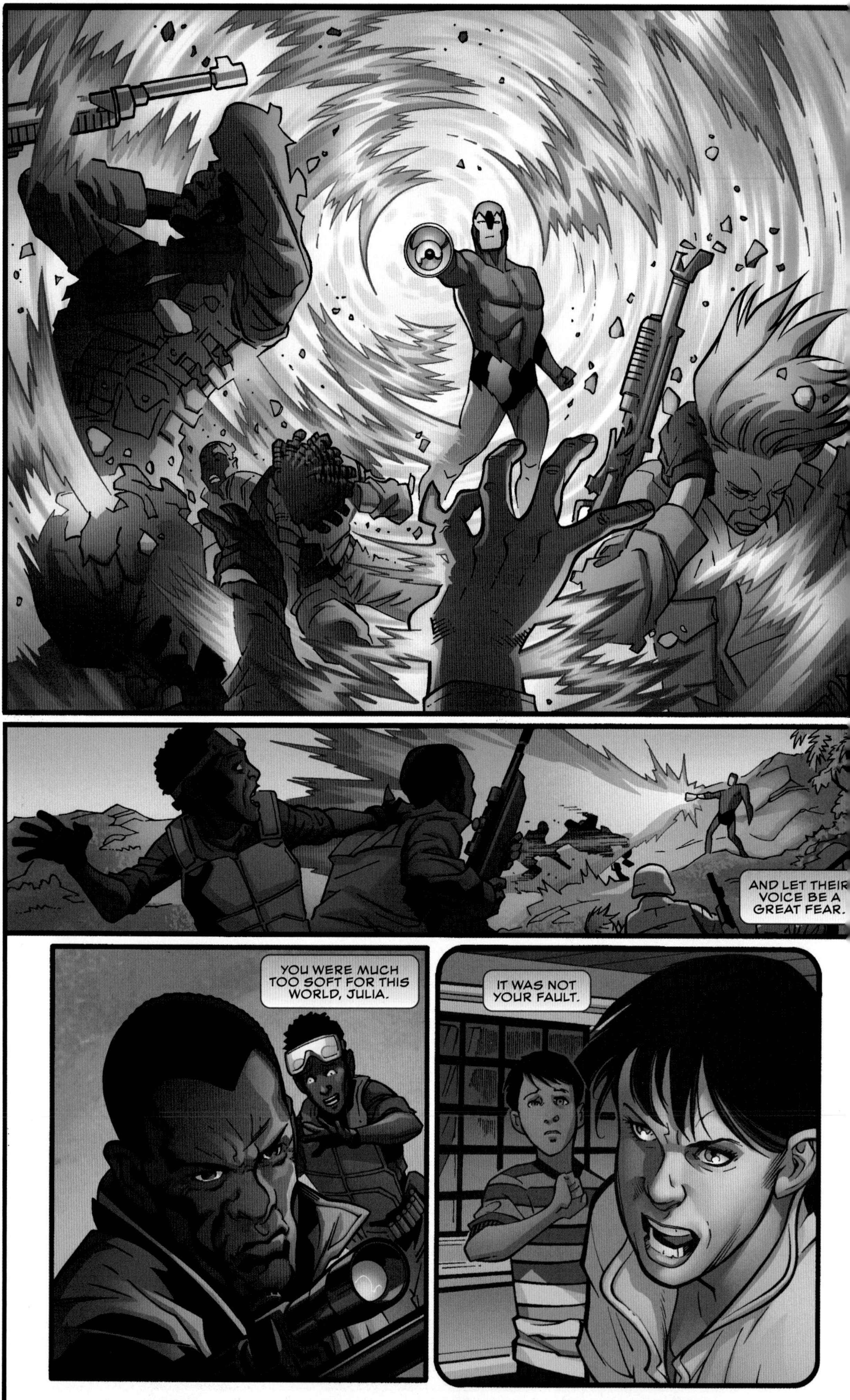
AND LET THEIR VOICE BE A GREAT FEAR.
YOU WERE MUCH TOO SOFT FOR THIS WORLD, JULIA.
IT WAS NOT YOUR FAULT.

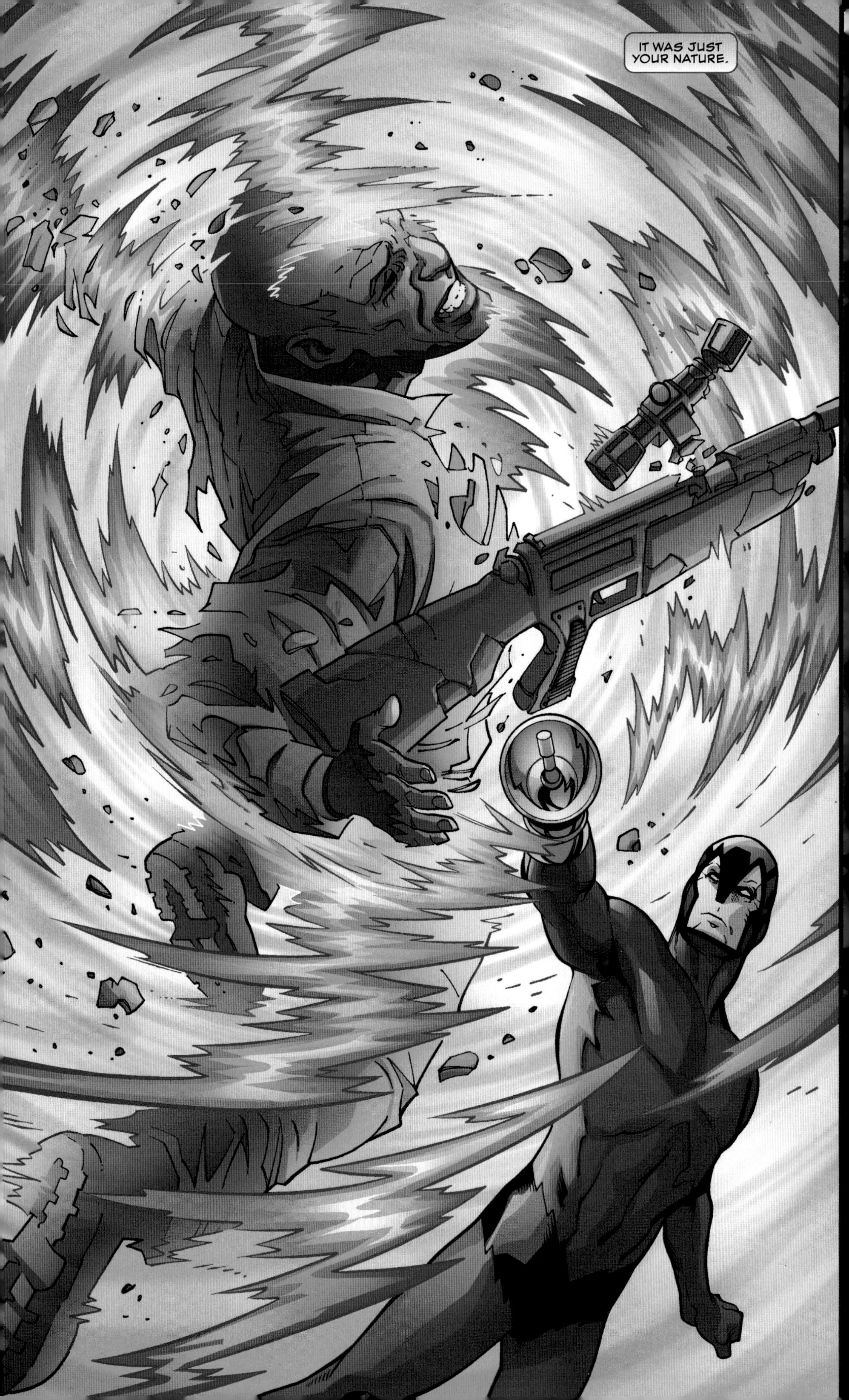
IT WAS JUST YOUR NATURE.

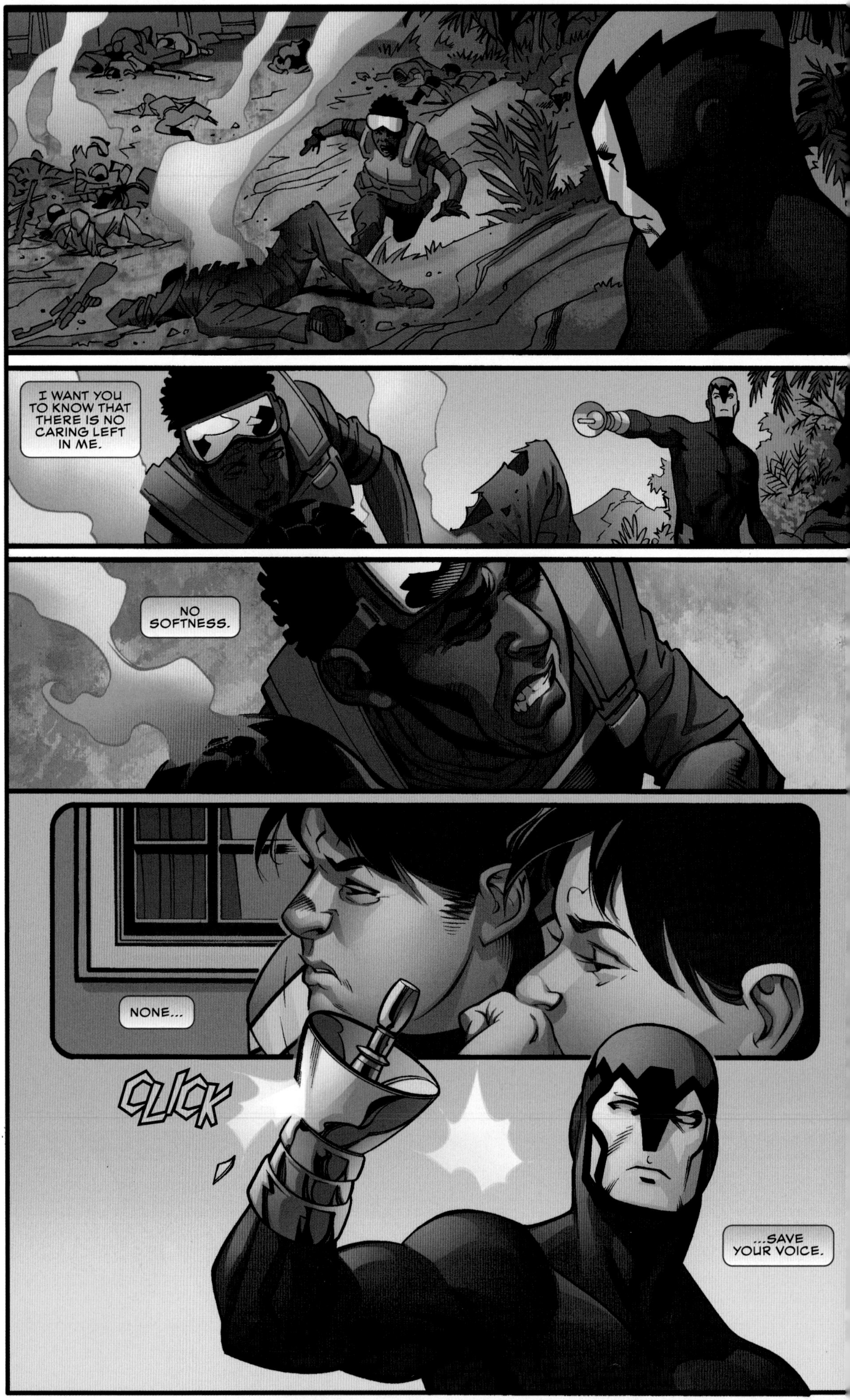
I WANT YOU TO KNOW THAT THERE IS NO CARING LEFT IN ME.
NO SOFTNESS.
NONE...
CLICK
...SAVE YOUR VOICE.

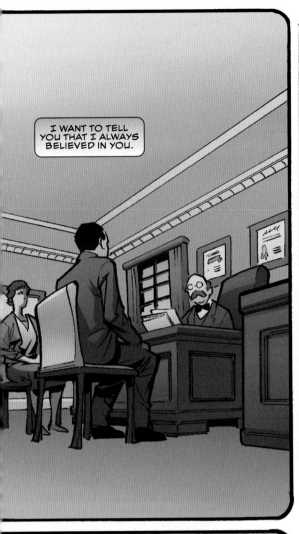

I WANT TO TELL YOU THAT I ALWAYS BELIEVED IN YOU.

THAT I BELIEVED IN THE VOICES WHEN OTHERS DID NOT.

AND THAT THE DAY THEY CARVED THE VOICES OUT OF YOUR HEAD...

ANTWERP ASYLUM

TRANSORBITAL LOBOTOMY

...WAS THE DAY THEY CARVED THE GOD OUT OF THEIR OWN HEARTS.

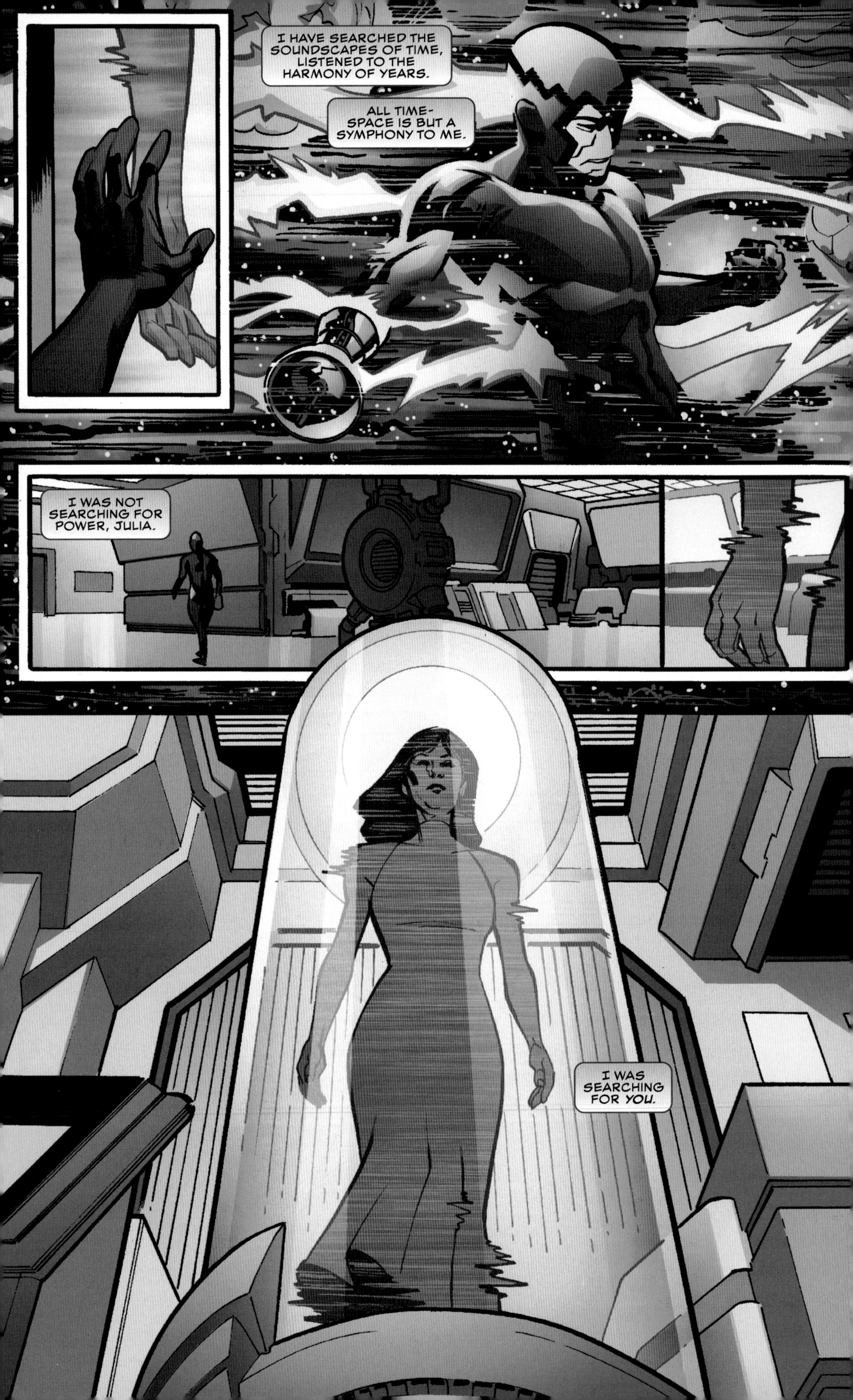
I HAVE SEARCHED THE SOUNDSCAPES OF TIME, LISTENED TO THE HARMONY OF YEARS.
ALL TIME-SPACE IS BUT A SYMPHONY TO ME.
I WAS NOT SEARCHING FOR POWER, JULIA.
I WAS SEARCHING FOR *YOU*.

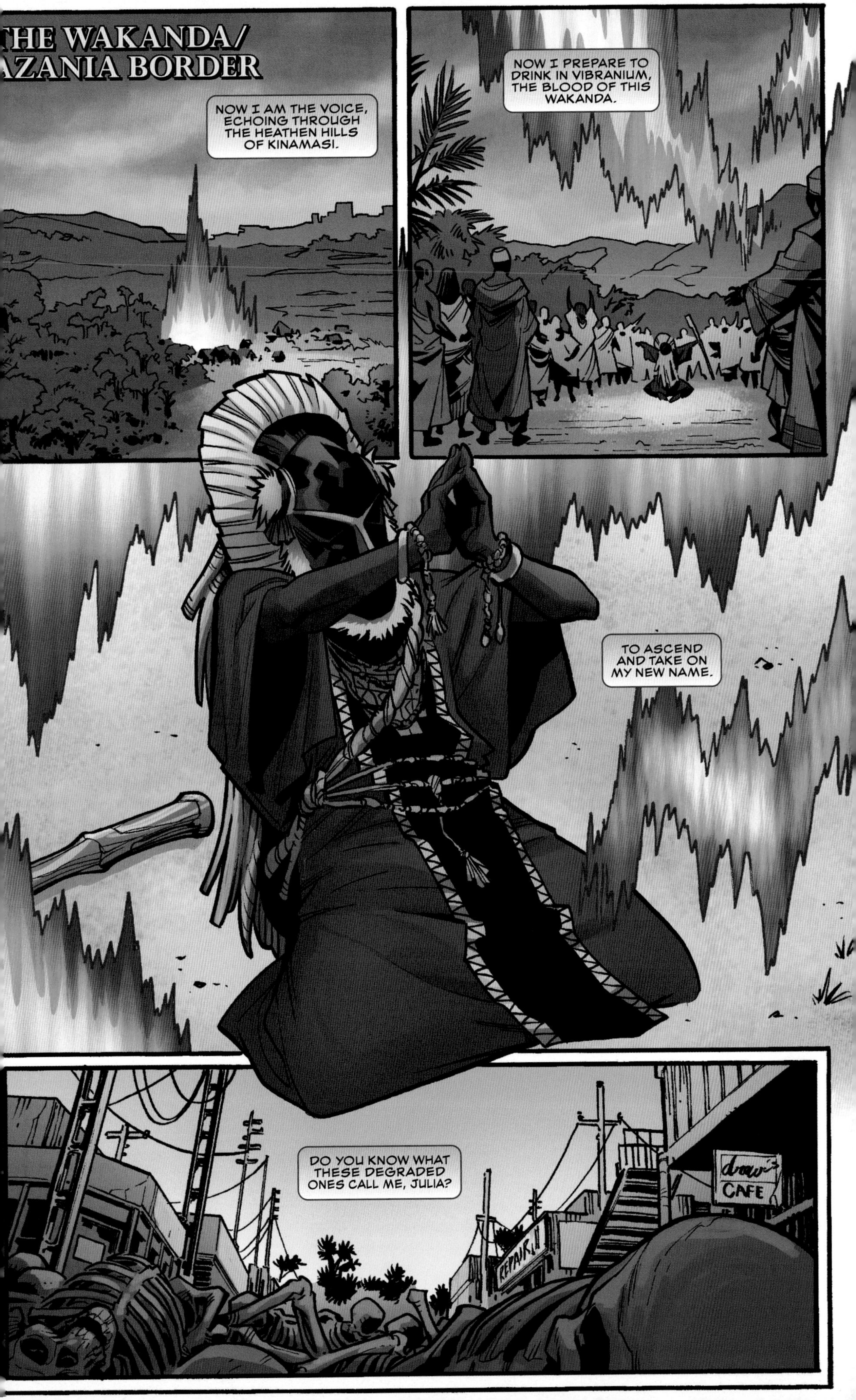
THE WAKANDA/
AZANIA BORDER
NOW I AM THE VOICE, ECHOING THROUGH THE HEATHEN HILLS OF KINAMASI.
NOW I PREPARE TO DRINK IN VIBRANIUM, THE BLOOD OF THIS WAKANDA.
TO ASCEND AND TAKE ON MY NEW NAME.
DO YOU KNOW WHAT THESE DEGRADED ONES CALL ME, JULIA?
REPAIR
CAFE

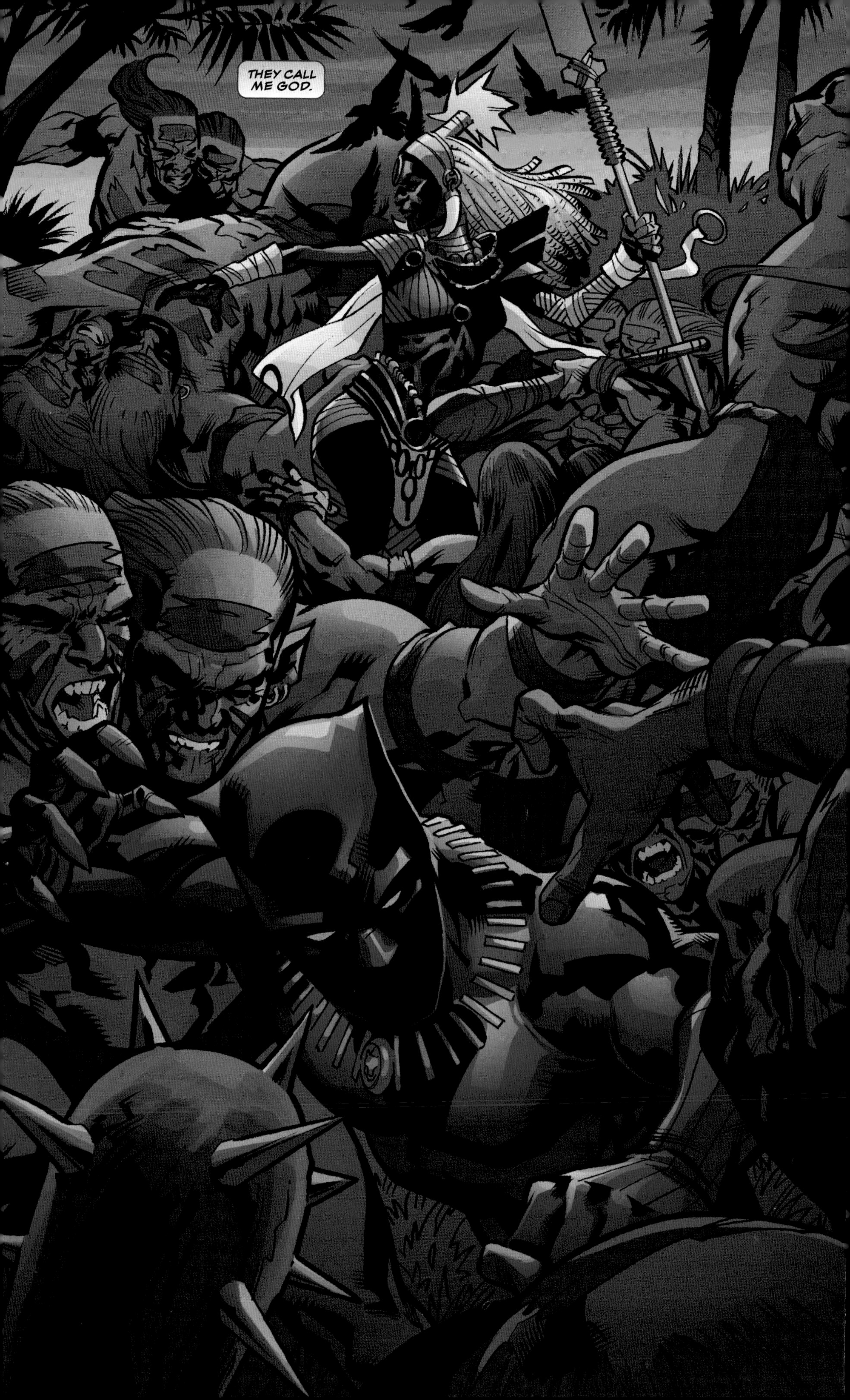
THEY CALL ME GOD.

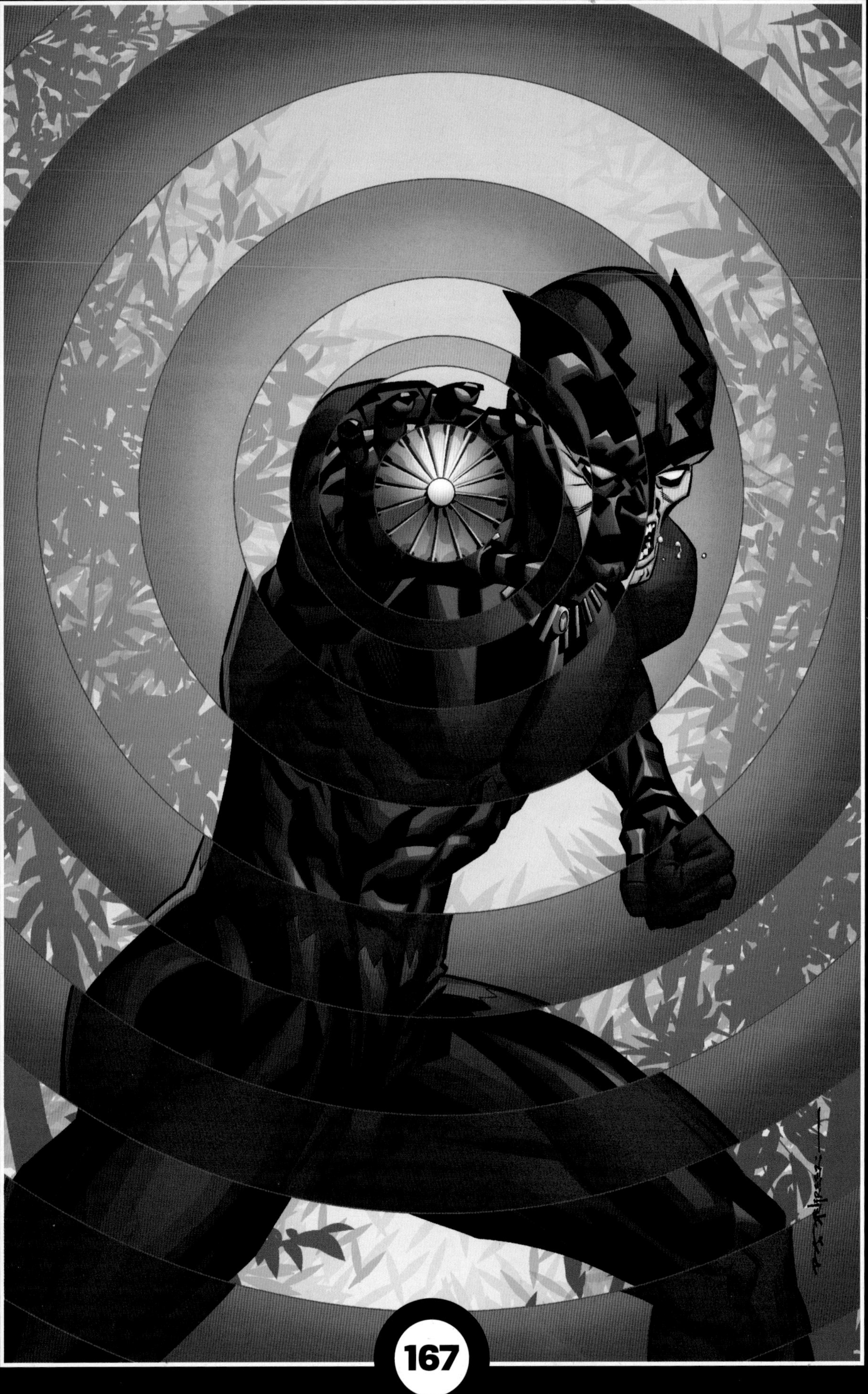

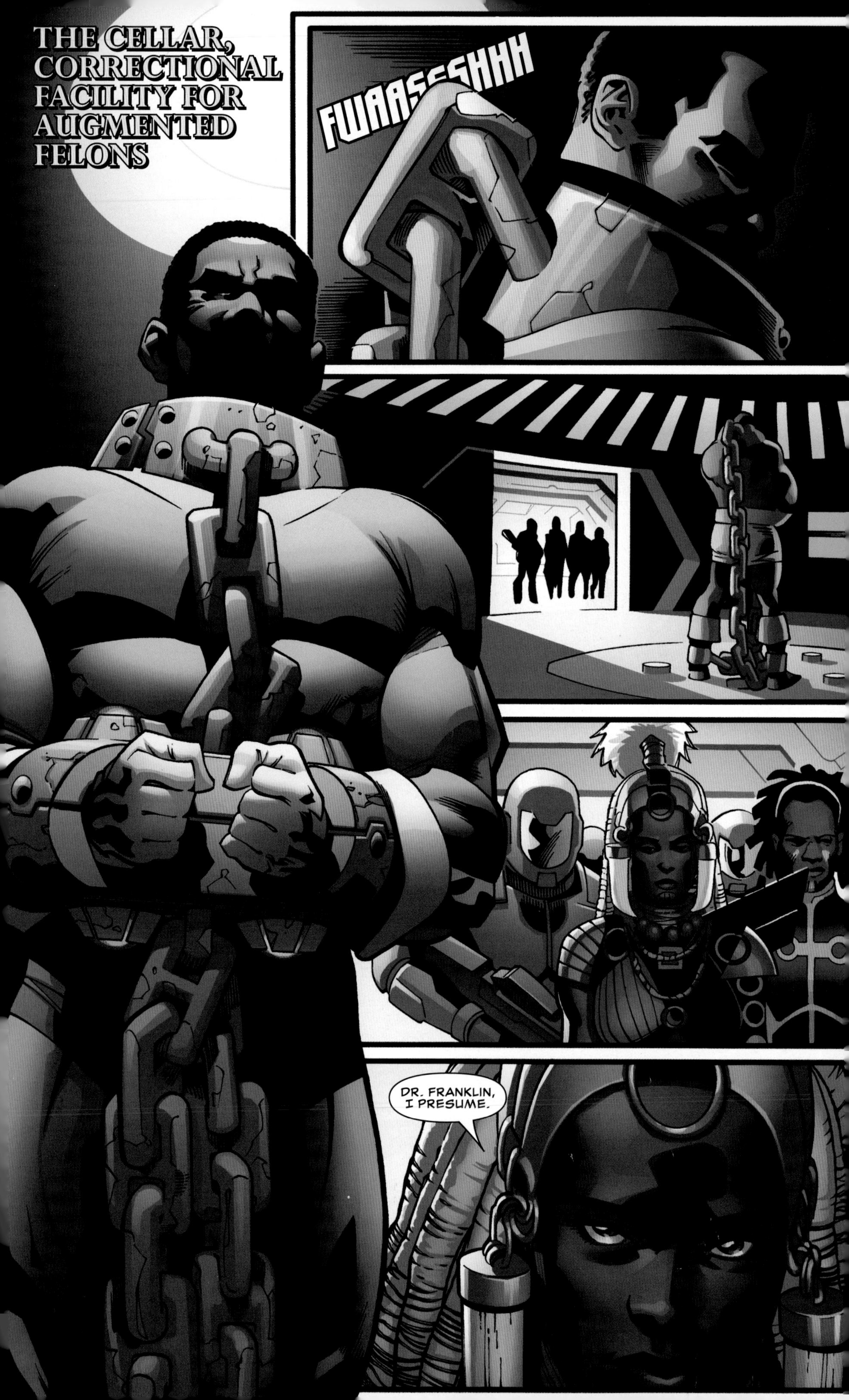
THE CELLAR, CORRECTIONAL FACILITY FOR AUGMENTED FELONS
FWAASSSHHH
DR. FRANKLIN, I PRESUME.

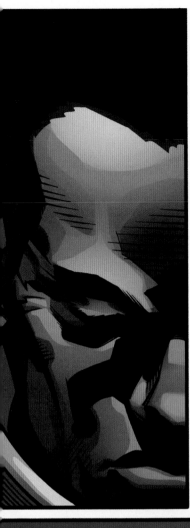

SELF-PITY? THAT WILL NOT DO.

YOU MUST KNOW THIS, BECAUSE YOU MUST KNOW ME. AND IF NOT ME, THEN YOU MUST KNOW WHAT I REPRESENT.

THE PANTHER.

YES. THE PANTHER. THERE WAS AN AGREEMENT, WAS THERE NOT?*

*SEE BLACK PANTHER #16.
—WIL

SHUN INIQUITY. MAKE PENANCE. WAIT FOR THE PANTHER'S SIGN.

WHAT HAPPENED, DR. FRANKLIN?

I FELL BACK. I THOUGHT I WAS OUT OF THE HOLE, AND I FELL RIGHT BACK.

YOU'D BE SURPRISED HOW EASY IT IS TO FALL BACK.

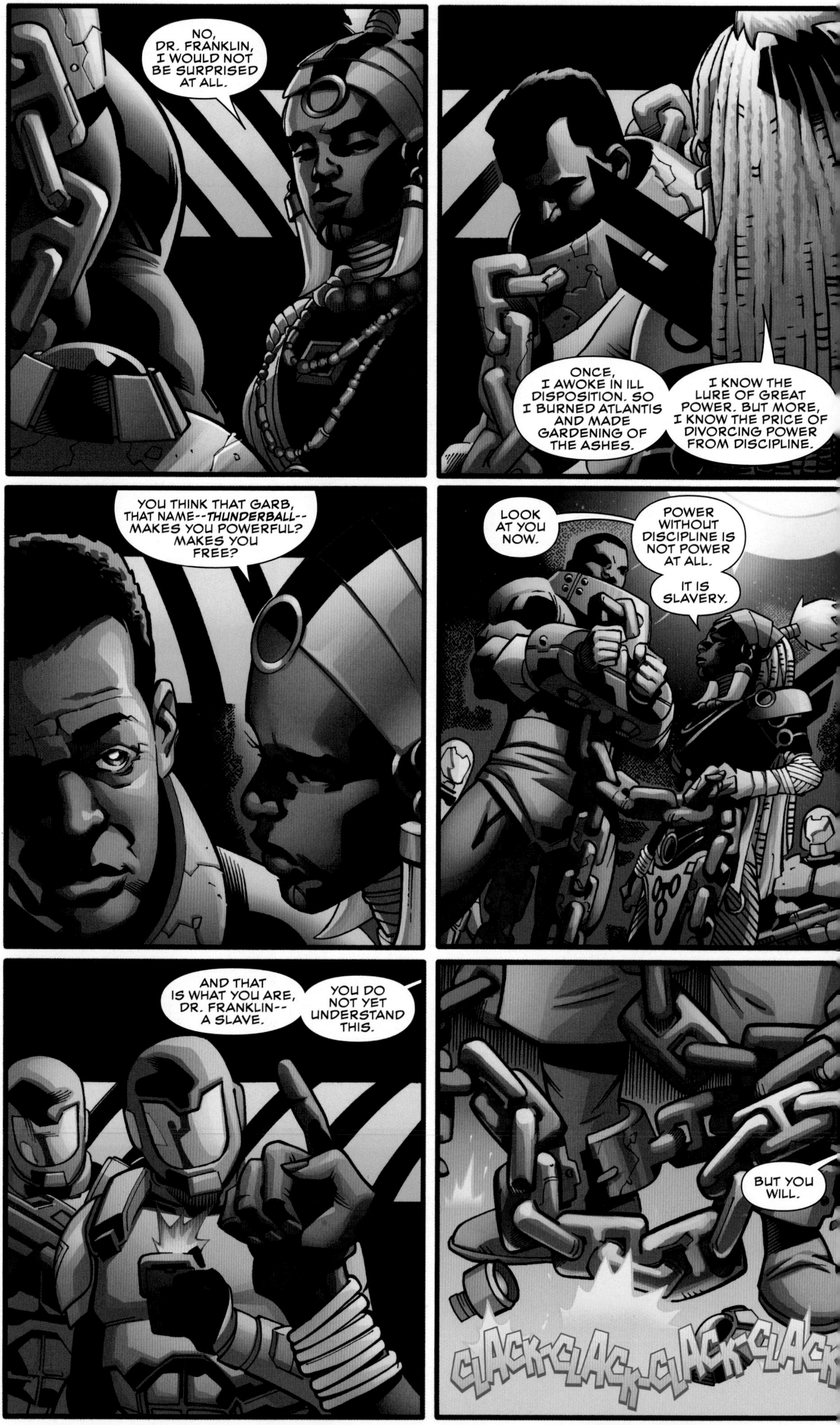
NO, DR. FRANKLIN, I WOULD NOT BE SURPRISED AT ALL.
ONCE, I AWOKE IN ILL DISPOSITION. SO I BURNED ATLANTIS AND MADE GARDENING OF THE ASHES.
I KNOW THE LURE OF GREAT POWER. BUT MORE, I KNOW THE PRICE OF DIVORCING POWER FROM DISCIPLINE.
YOU THINK THAT GARB, THAT NAME--THUNDERBALL--MAKES YOU POWERFUL? MAKES YOU FREE?
LOOK AT YOU NOW.
POWER WITHOUT DISCIPLINE IS NOT POWER AT ALL.
IT IS SLAVERY.
AND THAT IS WHAT YOU ARE, DR. FRANKLIN--A SLAVE.
YOU DO NOT YET UNDERSTAND THIS.
BUT YOU WILL.
CLACK-CLACK-CLACK-CLACK

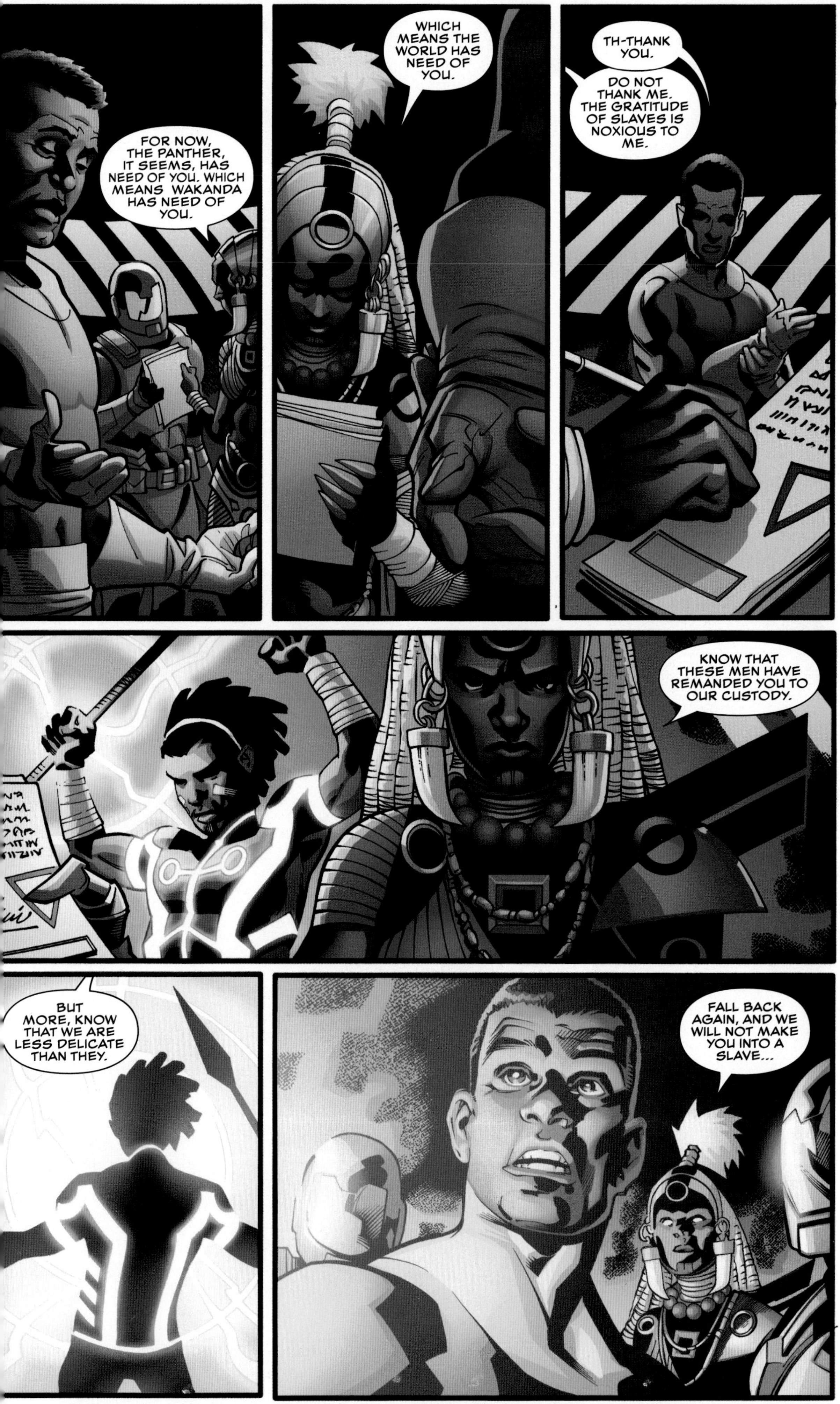
FOR NOW, THE PANTHER, IT SEEMS, HAS NEED OF YOU. WHICH MEANS WAKANDA HAS NEED OF YOU.
WHICH MEANS THE WORLD HAS NEED OF YOU.
TH-THANK YOU.
DO NOT THANK ME. THE GRATITUDE OF SLAVES IS NOXIOUS TO ME.
KNOW THAT THESE MEN HAVE REMANDED YOU TO OUR CUSTODY.
BUT MORE, KNOW THAT WE ARE LESS DELICATE THAN THEY.
FALL BACK AGAIN, AND WE WILL NOT MAKE YOU INTO A SLAVE...

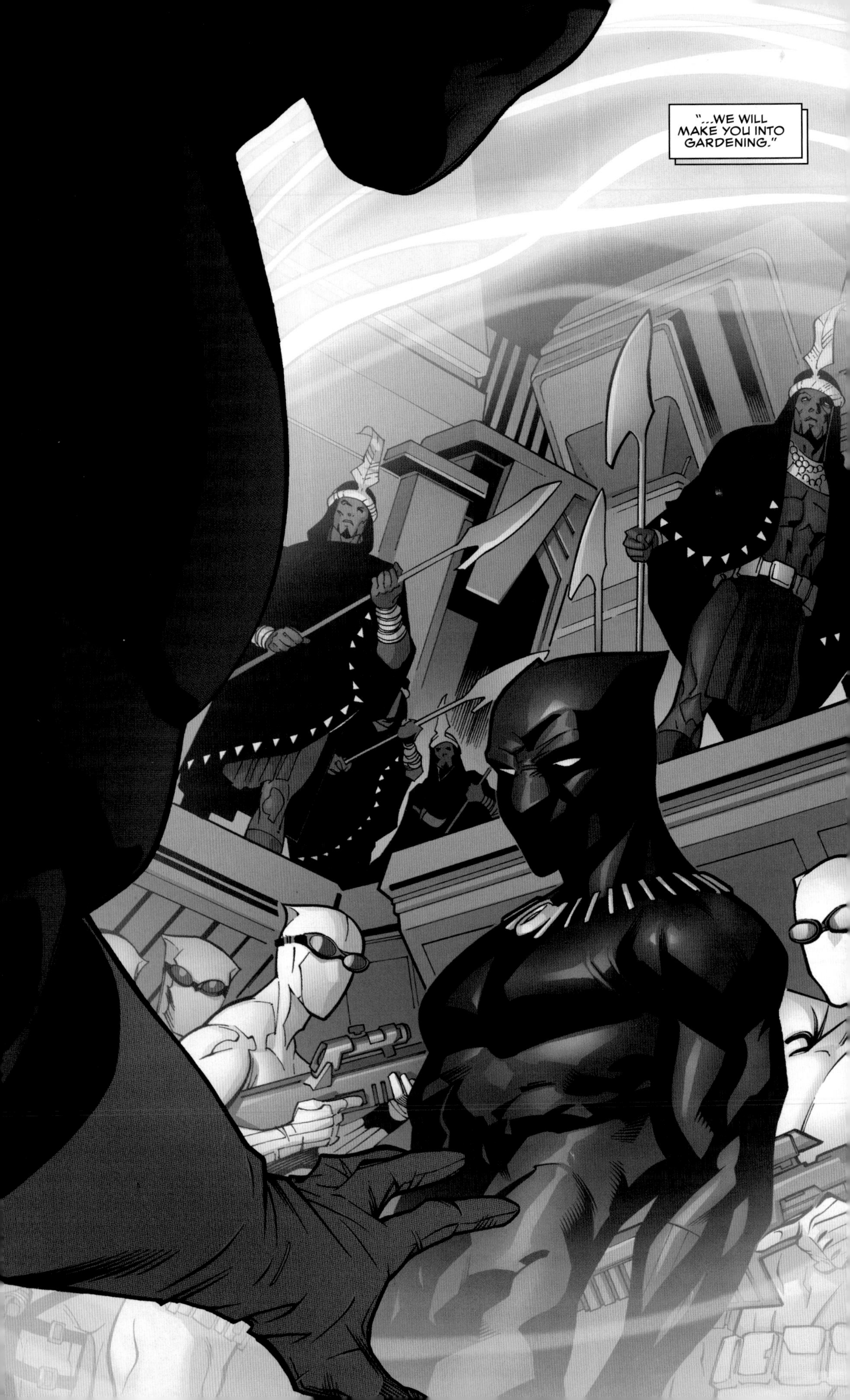
"...WE WILL MAKE YOU INTO GARDENING."

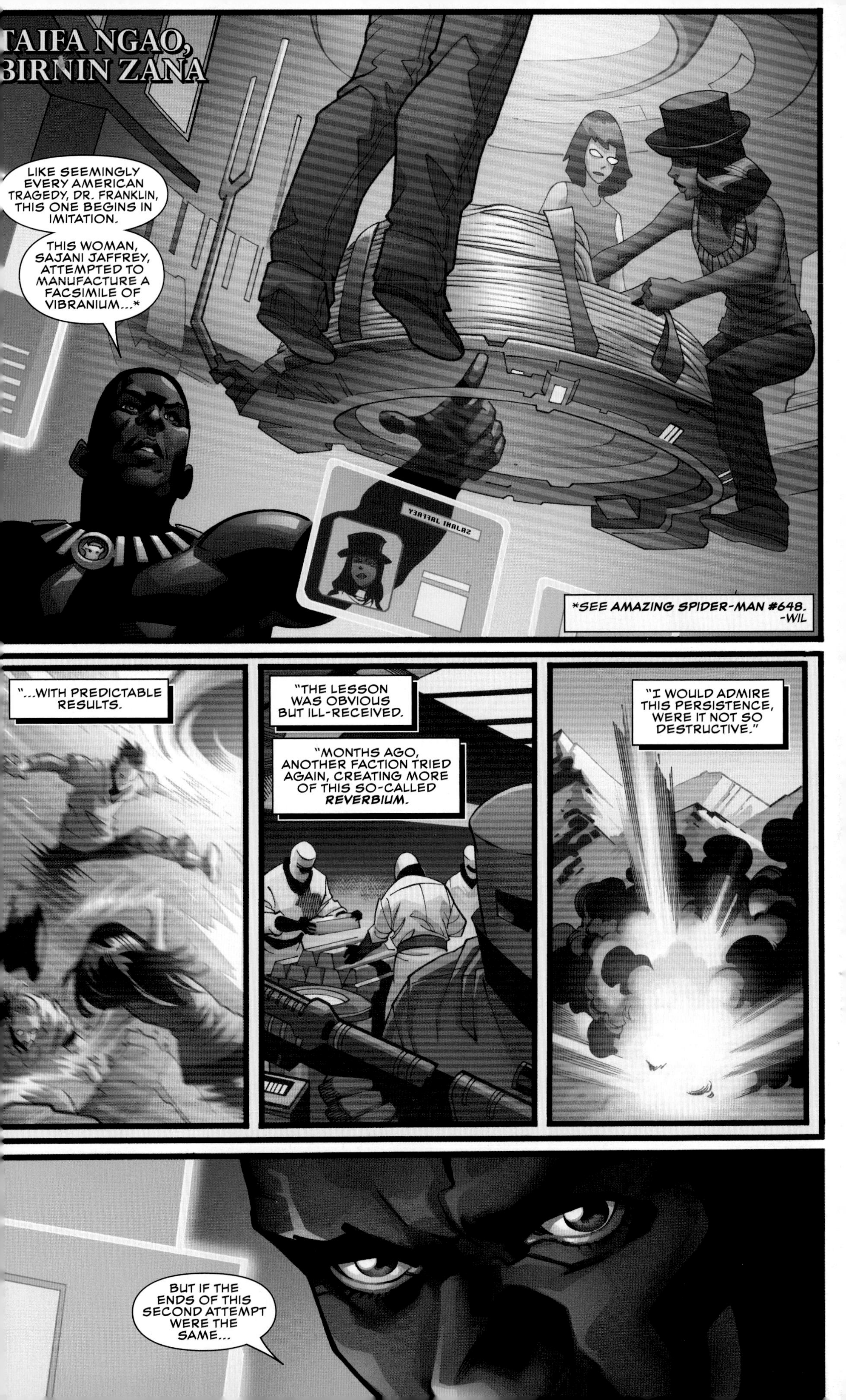
TAIFA NGAO, BIRNIN ZANA
LIKE SEEMINGLY EVERY AMERICAN TRAGEDY, DR. FRANKLIN, THIS ONE BEGINS IN IMITATION.
THIS WOMAN, SAJANI JAFFREY, ATTEMPTED TO MANUFACTURE A FACSIMILE OF VIBRANIUM...*
SAJANI JAFFREY
*SEE AMAZING SPIDER-MAN #648. -WIL
"...WITH PREDICTABLE RESULTS.
"THE LESSON WAS OBVIOUS BUT ILL-RECEIVED.
"MONTHS AGO, ANOTHER FACTION TRIED AGAIN, CREATING MORE OF THIS SO-CALLED REVERBIUM.
"I WOULD ADMIRE THIS PERSISTENCE, WERE IT NOT SO DESTRUCTIVE."
BUT IF THE ENDS OF THIS SECOND ATTEMPT WERE THE SAME...

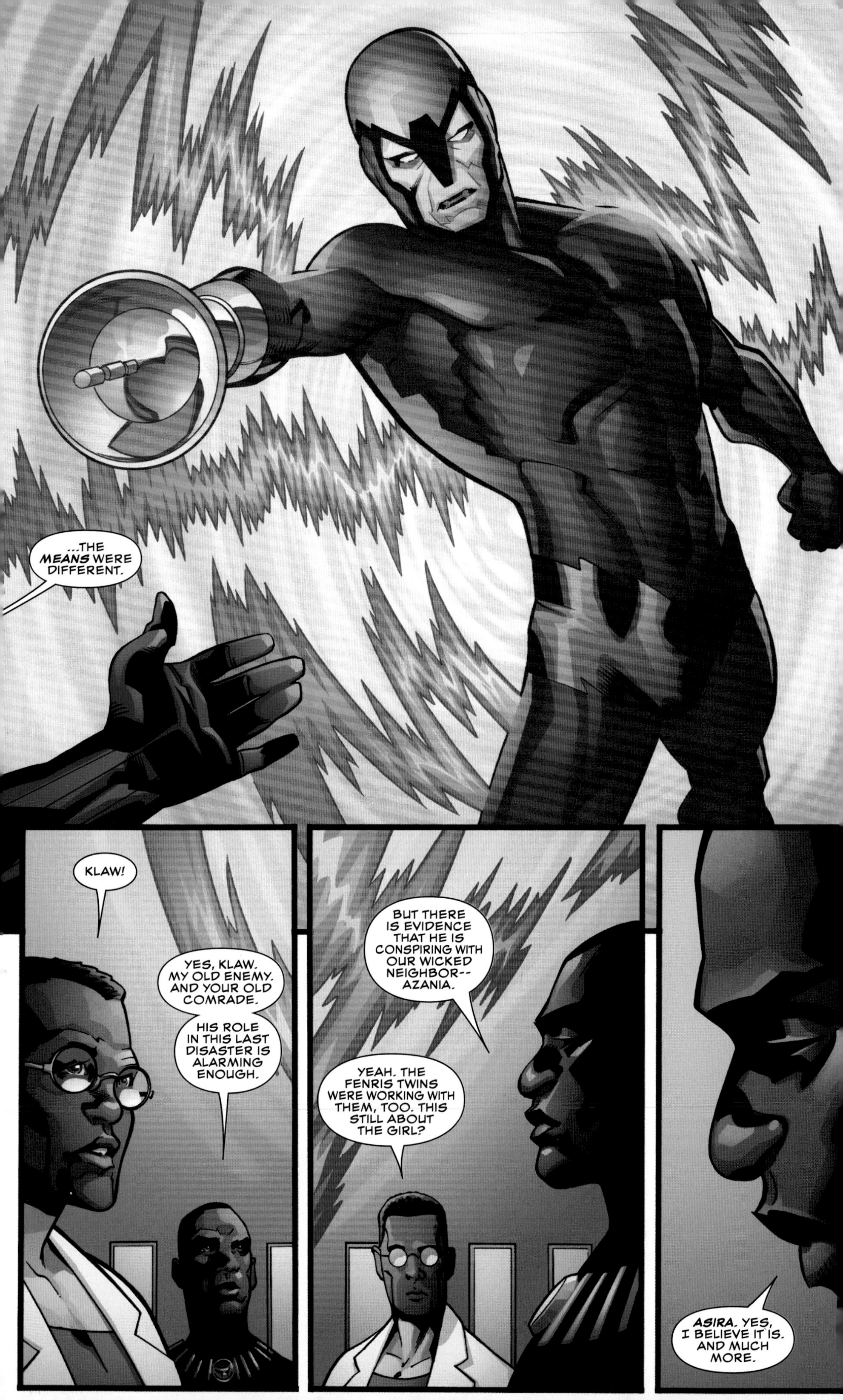
...THE MEANS WERE DIFFERENT.
KLAW!
YES, KLAW. MY OLD ENEMY. AND YOUR OLD COMRADE.
HIS ROLE IN THIS LAST DISASTER IS ALARMING ENOUGH.
BUT THERE IS EVIDENCE THAT HE IS CONSPIRING WITH OUR WICKED NEIGHBOR-- AZANIA.
YEAH. THE FENRIS TWINS WERE WORKING WITH THEM, TOO. THIS STILL ABOUT THE GIRL?
ASIRA. YES, I BELIEVE IT IS. AND MUCH MORE.

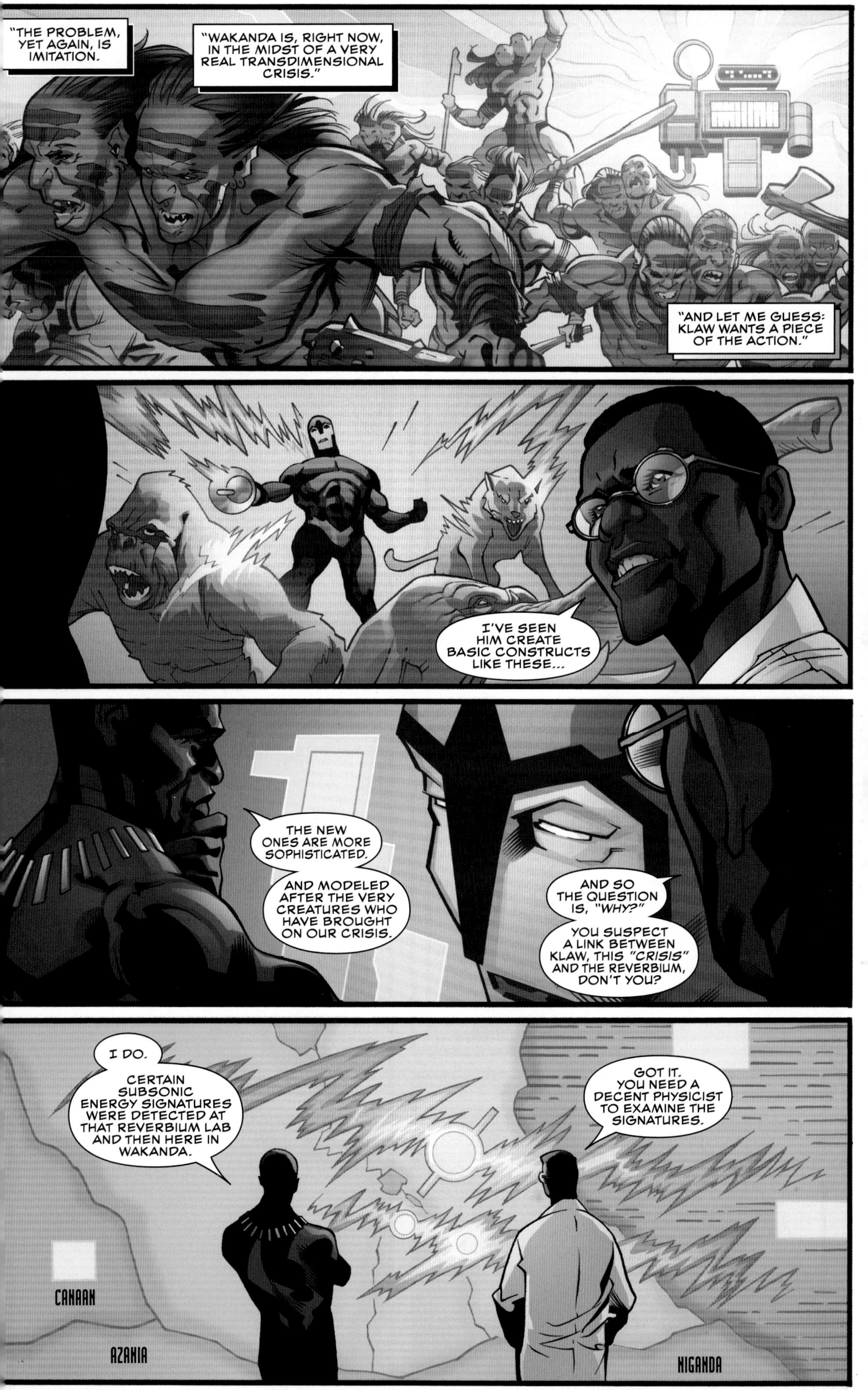
"THE PROBLEM, YET AGAIN, IS IMITATION.
"WAKANDA IS, RIGHT NOW, IN THE MIDST OF A VERY REAL TRANSDIMENSIONAL CRISIS."
"AND LET ME GUESS: KLAW WANTS A PIECE OF THE ACTION."
I'VE SEEN HIM CREATE BASIC CONSTRUCTS LIKE THESE...
THE NEW ONES ARE MORE SOPHISTICATED.
AND MODELED AFTER THE VERY CREATURES WHO HAVE BROUGHT ON OUR CRISIS.
AND SO THE QUESTION IS, "WHY?"
YOU SUSPECT A LINK BETWEEN KLAW, THIS "CRISIS" AND THE REVERBIUM, DON'T YOU?
I DO.
CERTAIN SUBSONIC ENERGY SIGNATURES WERE DETECTED AT THAT REVERBIUM LAB AND THEN HERE IN WAKANDA.
GOT IT. YOU NEED A DECENT PHYSICIST TO EXAMINE THE SIGNATURES.
CANAAN
AZANIA
NIGANDA

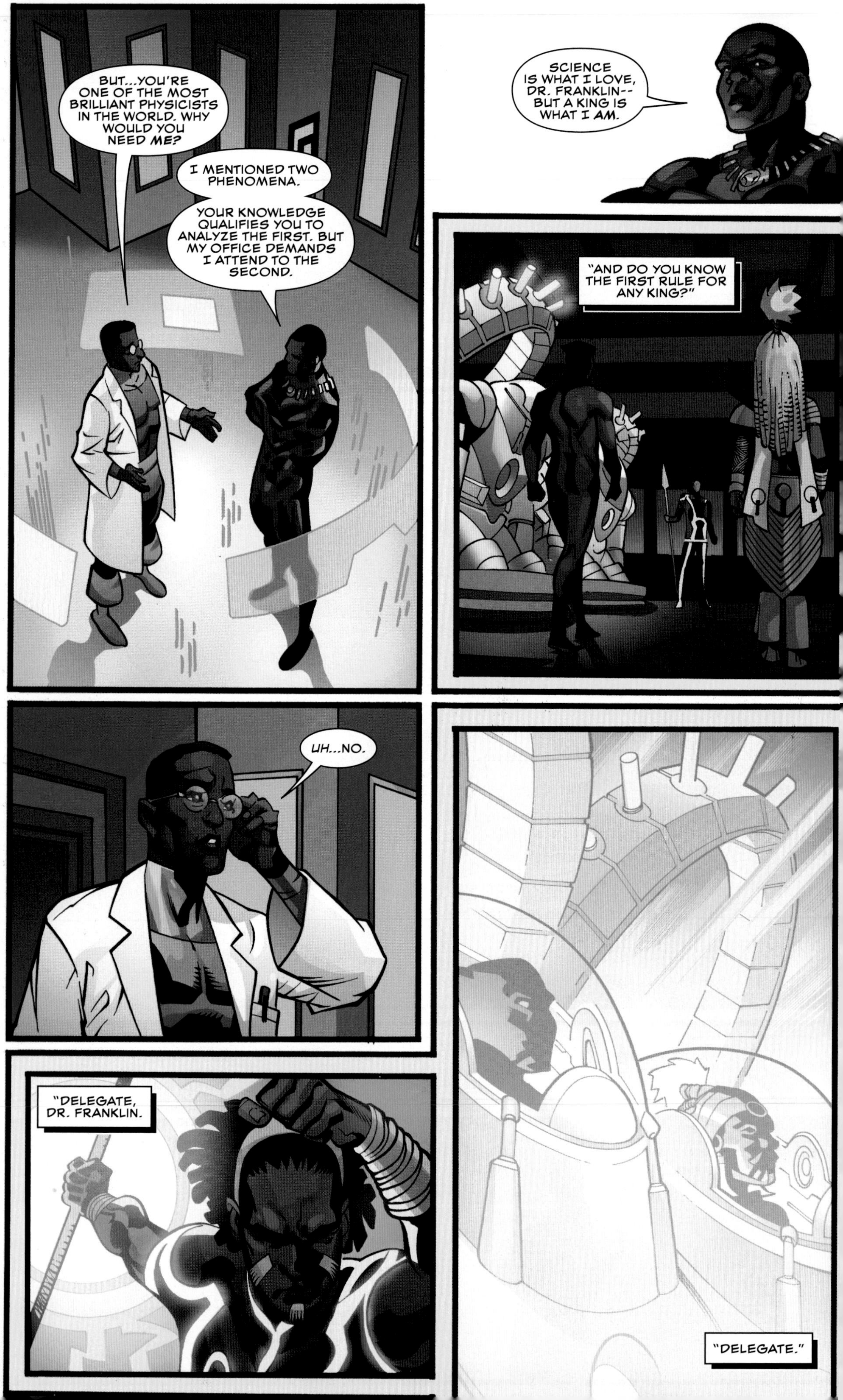
BUT...YOU'RE ONE OF THE MOST BRILLIANT PHYSICISTS IN THE WORLD. WHY WOULD YOU NEED *ME*?
I MENTIONED TWO PHENOMENA.
YOUR KNOWLEDGE QUALIFIES YOU TO ANALYZE THE FIRST. BUT MY OFFICE DEMANDS I ATTEND TO THE SECOND.
SCIENCE IS WHAT I LOVE, DR. FRANKLIN-- BUT A KING IS WHAT I *AM*.
"AND DO YOU KNOW THE FIRST RULE FOR ANY KING?"
UH...NO.
"DELEGATE, DR. FRANKLIN.
"DELEGATE."

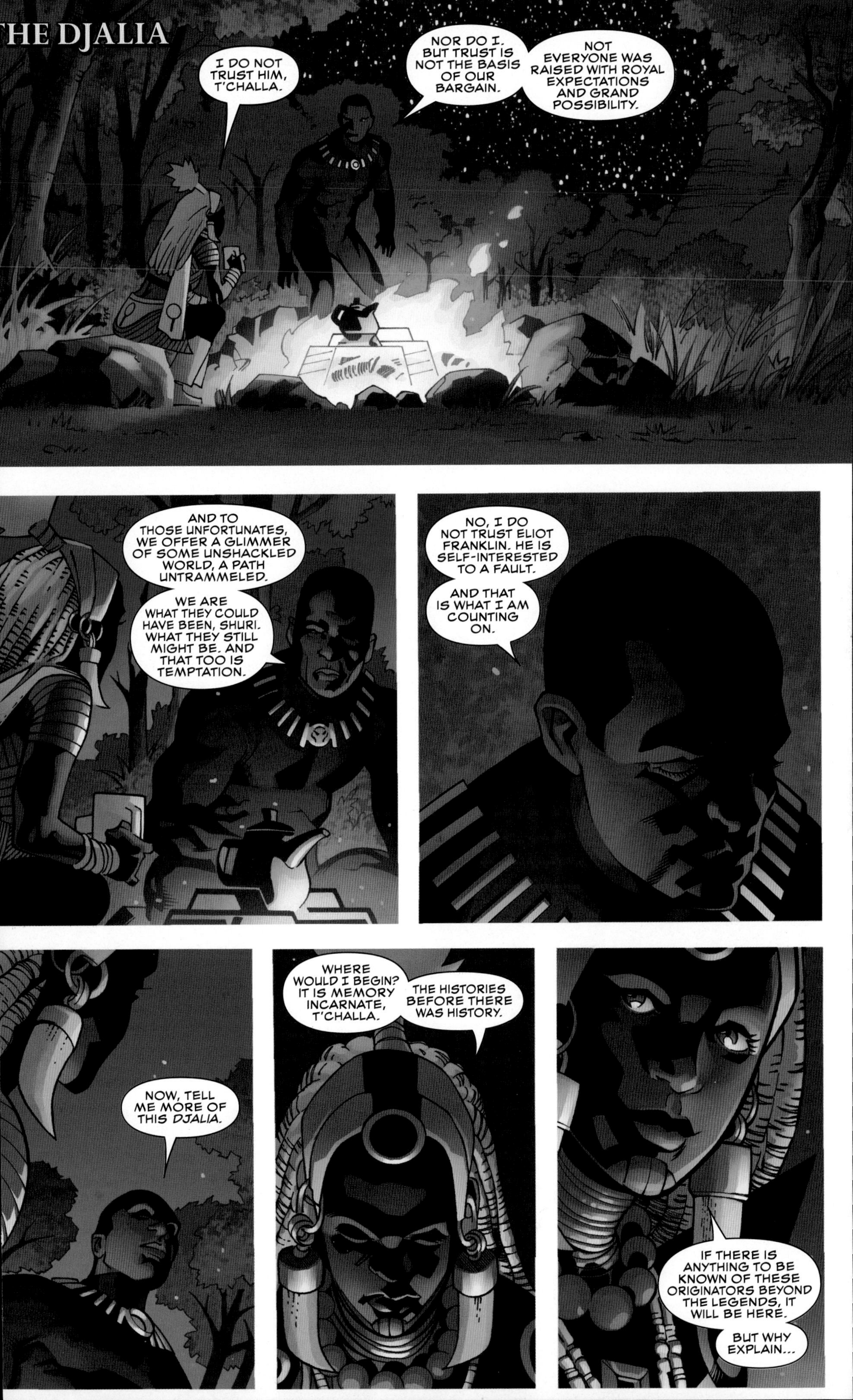
THE DJALIA
I DO NOT TRUST HIM, T'CHALLA.
NOR DO I. BUT TRUST IS NOT THE BASIS OF OUR BARGAIN.
NOT EVERYONE WAS RAISED WITH ROYAL EXPECTATIONS AND GRAND POSSIBILITY.
AND TO THOSE UNFORTUNATES, WE OFFER A GLIMMER OF SOME UNSHACKLED WORLD, A PATH UNTRAMMELED.
WE ARE WHAT THEY COULD HAVE BEEN, SHURI. WHAT THEY STILL MIGHT BE. AND THAT TOO IS TEMPTATION.
NO, I DO NOT TRUST ELIOT FRANKLIN. HE IS SELF-INTERESTED TO A FAULT.
AND THAT IS WHAT I AM COUNTING ON.
NOW, TELL ME MORE OF THIS *DJALIA*.
WHERE WOULD I BEGIN? IT IS MEMORY INCARNATE, T'CHALLA.
THE HISTORIES BEFORE THERE WAS HISTORY.
IF THERE IS ANYTHING TO BE KNOWN OF THESE ORIGINATORS BEYOND THE LEGENDS, IT WILL BE HERE.
BUT WHY EXPLAIN...

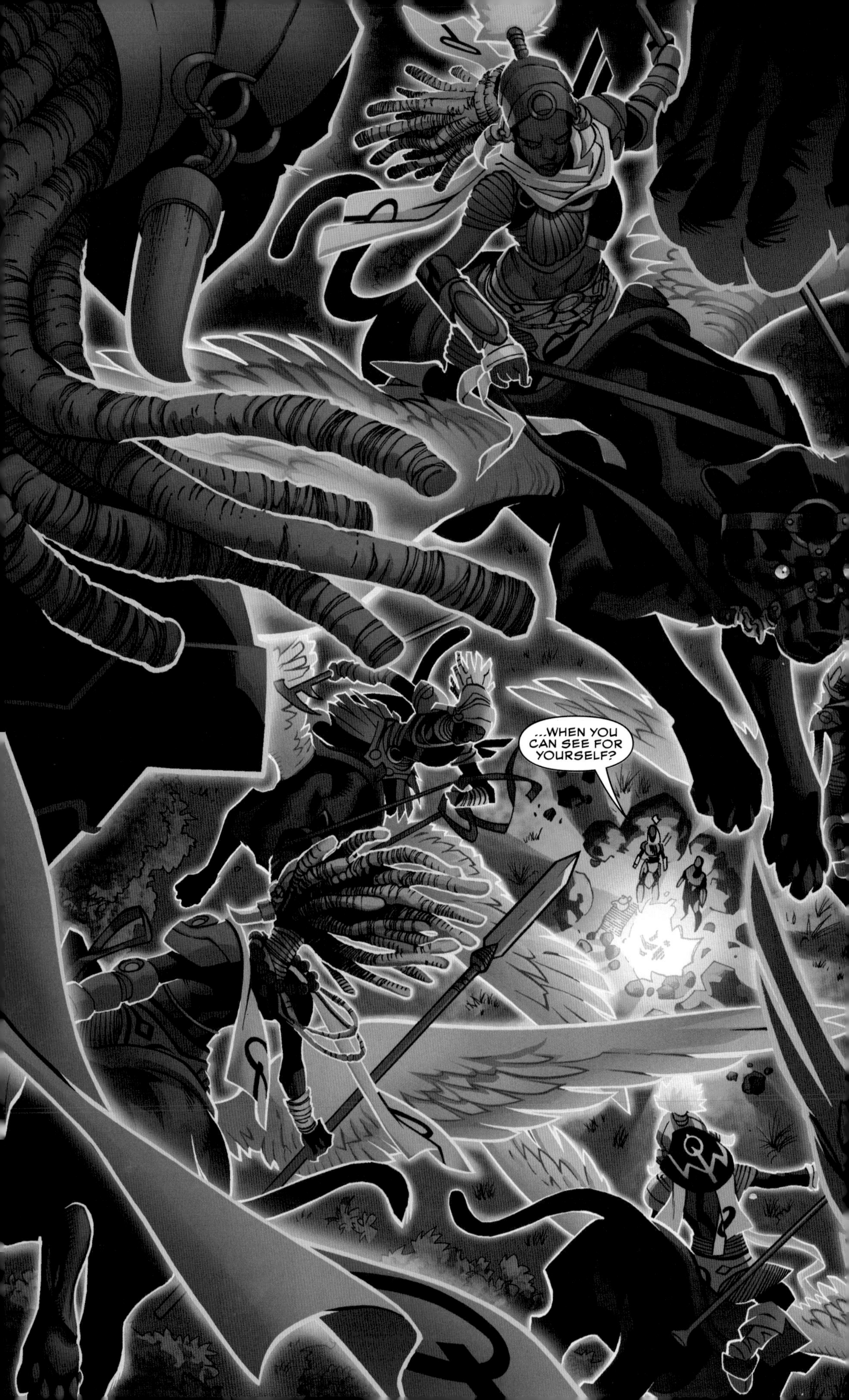
...WHEN YOU CAN SEE FOR YOURSELF?

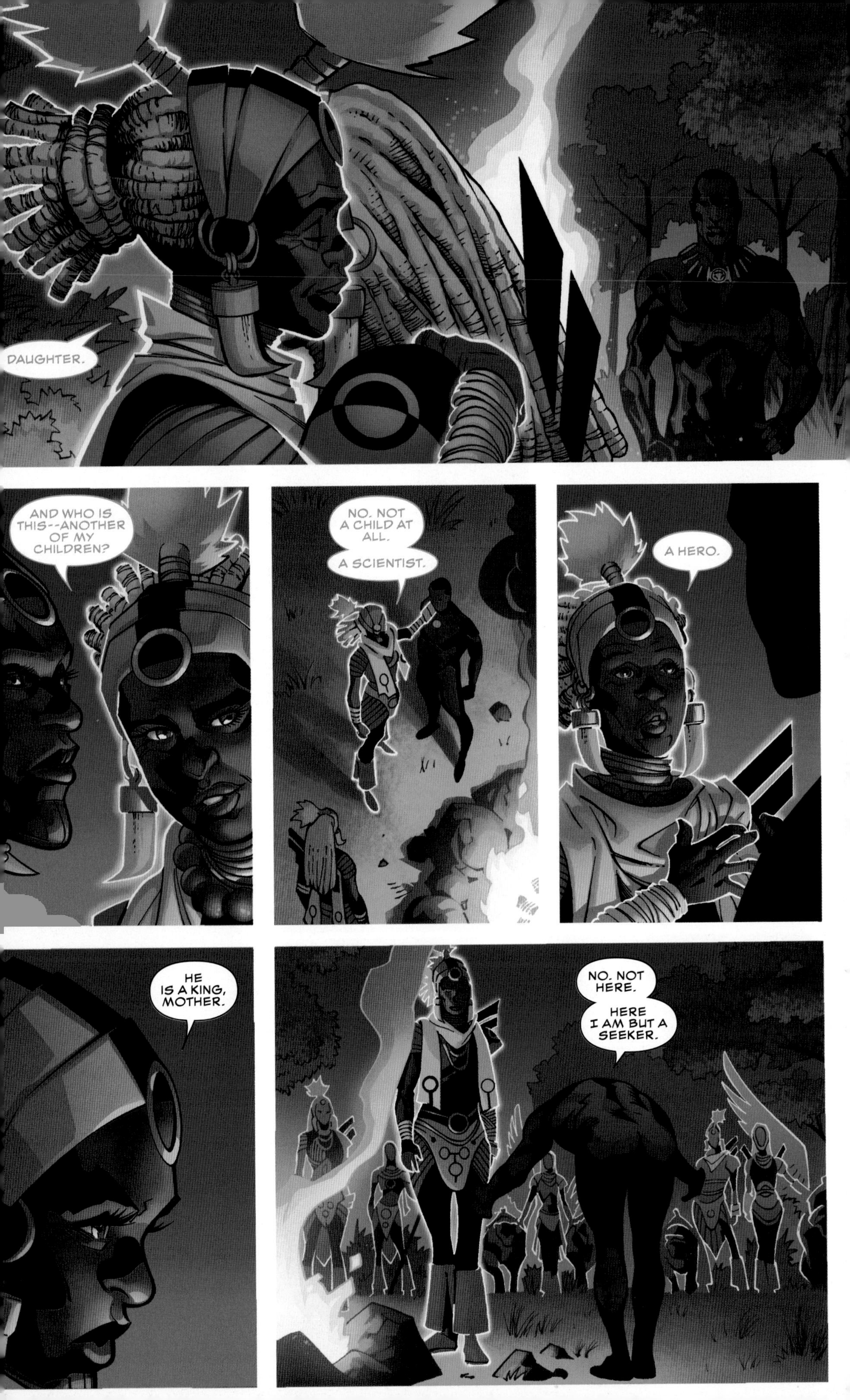
DAUGHTER.
AND WHO IS THIS--ANOTHER OF MY CHILDREN?
NO. NOT A CHILD AT ALL.
A SCIENTIST.
A HERO.
HE IS A KING, MOTHER.
NO. NOT HERE.
HERE I AM BUT A SEEKER.

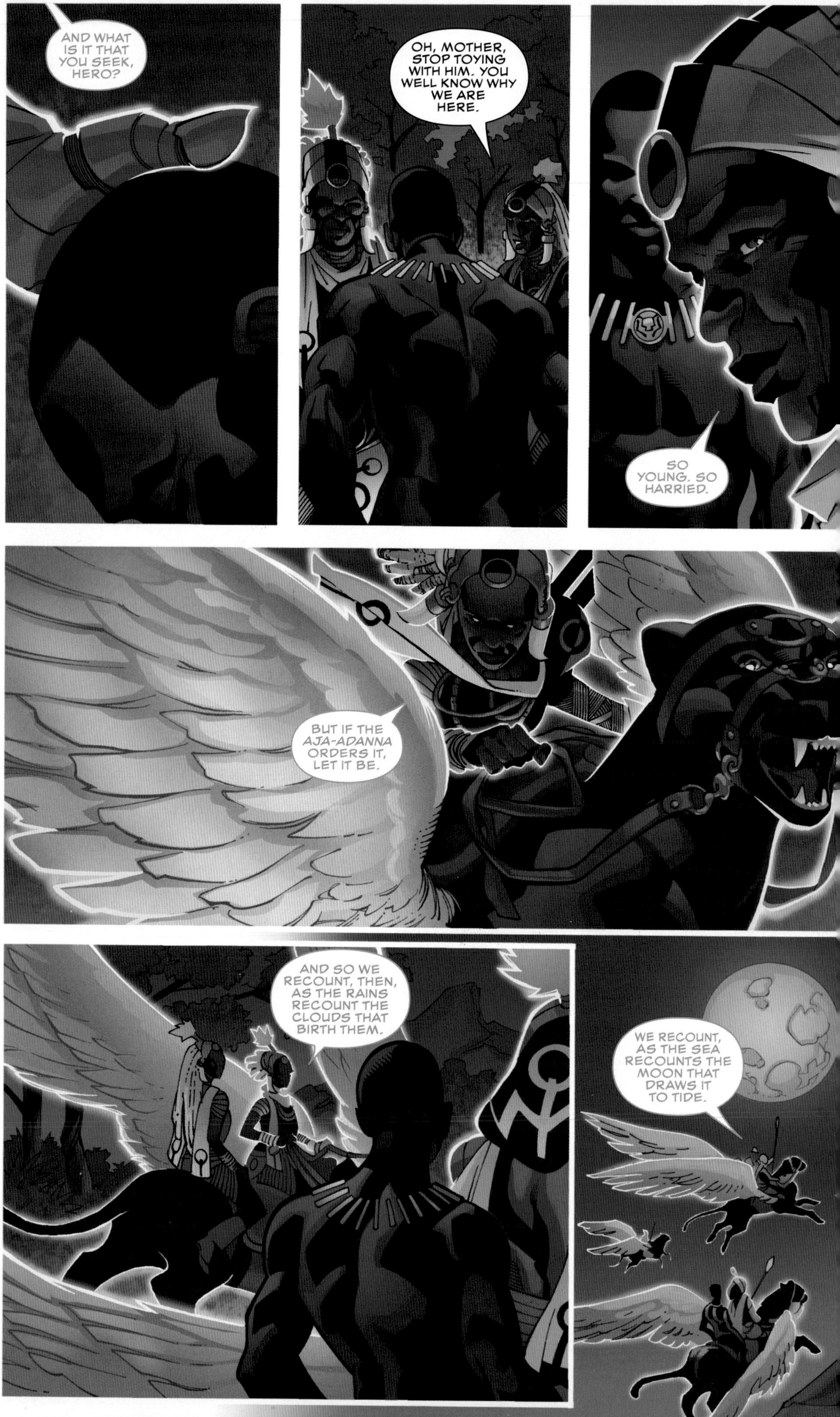
AND WHAT IS IT THAT YOU SEEK, HERO?
OH, MOTHER, STOP TOYING WITH HIM. YOU WELL KNOW WHY WE ARE HERE.
SO YOUNG. SO HARRIED.
BUT IF THE *AJA-ADANNA* ORDERS IT, LET IT BE.
AND SO WE RECOUNT, THEN, AS THE RAINS RECOUNT THE CLOUDS THAT BIRTH THEM.
WE RECOUNT, AS THE SEA RECOUNTS THE MOON THAT DRAWS IT TO TIDE.

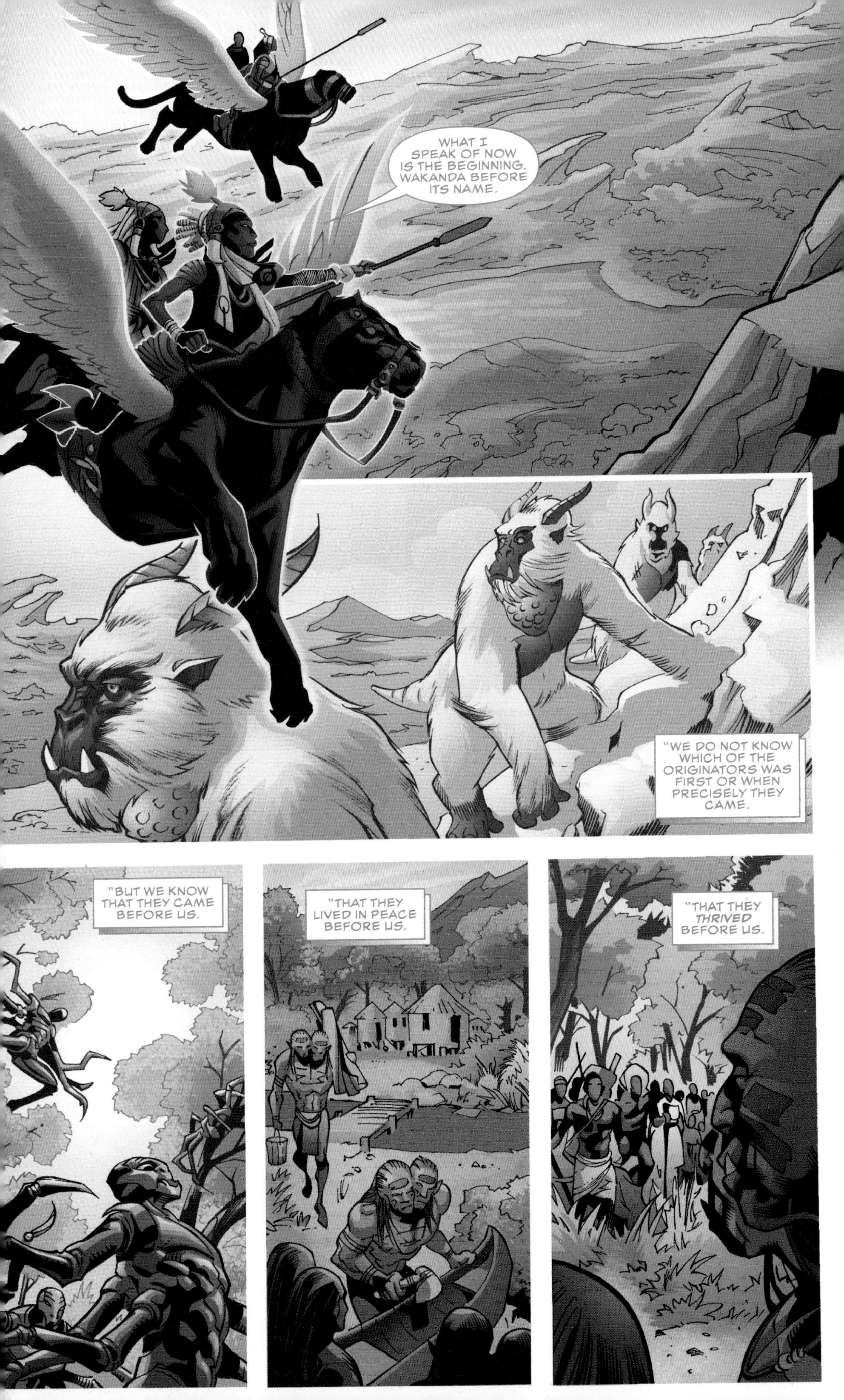
WHAT I SPEAK OF NOW IS THE BEGINNING. WAKANDA BEFORE ITS NAME.
"WE DO NOT KNOW WHICH OF THE ORIGINATORS WAS FIRST OR WHEN PRECISELY THEY CAME.
"BUT WE KNOW THAT THEY CAME BEFORE US.
"THAT THEY LIVED IN PEACE BEFORE US.
"THAT THEY *THRIVED* BEFORE US.

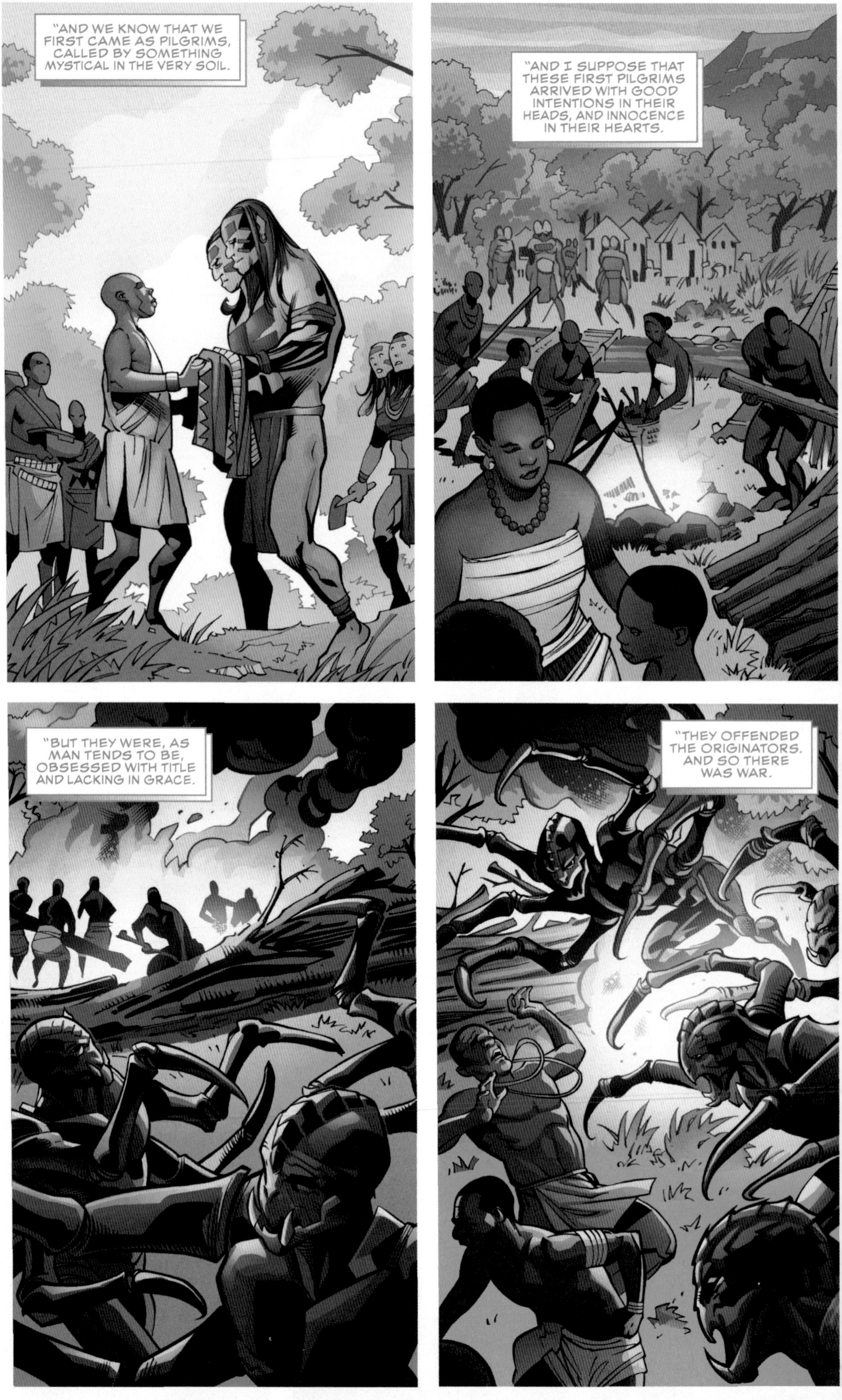
"AND WE KNOW THAT WE FIRST CAME AS PILGRIMS, CALLED BY SOMETHING MYSTICAL IN THE VERY SOIL.
"AND I SUPPOSE THAT THESE FIRST PILGRIMS ARRIVED WITH GOOD INTENTIONS IN THEIR HEADS, AND INNOCENCE IN THEIR HEARTS.
"BUT THEY WERE, AS MAN TENDS TO BE, OBSESSED WITH TITLE AND LACKING IN GRACE.
"THEY OFFENDED THE ORIGINATORS. AND SO THERE WAS WAR.

"THE PILGRIMS WERE ROUTED AT FIRST.

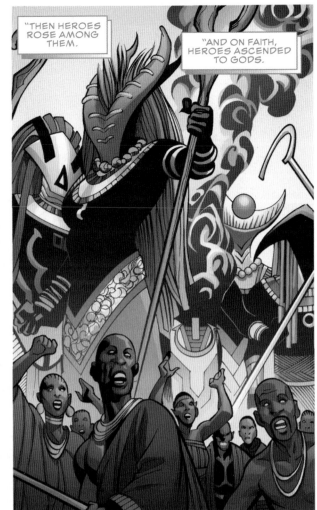

"THEN HEROES ROSE AMONG THEM.

"AND ON FAITH, HEROES ASCENDED TO GODS.

KOKOU, THE EVER-BURNING.

"MUJAJI, THE LIFE-GIVER.

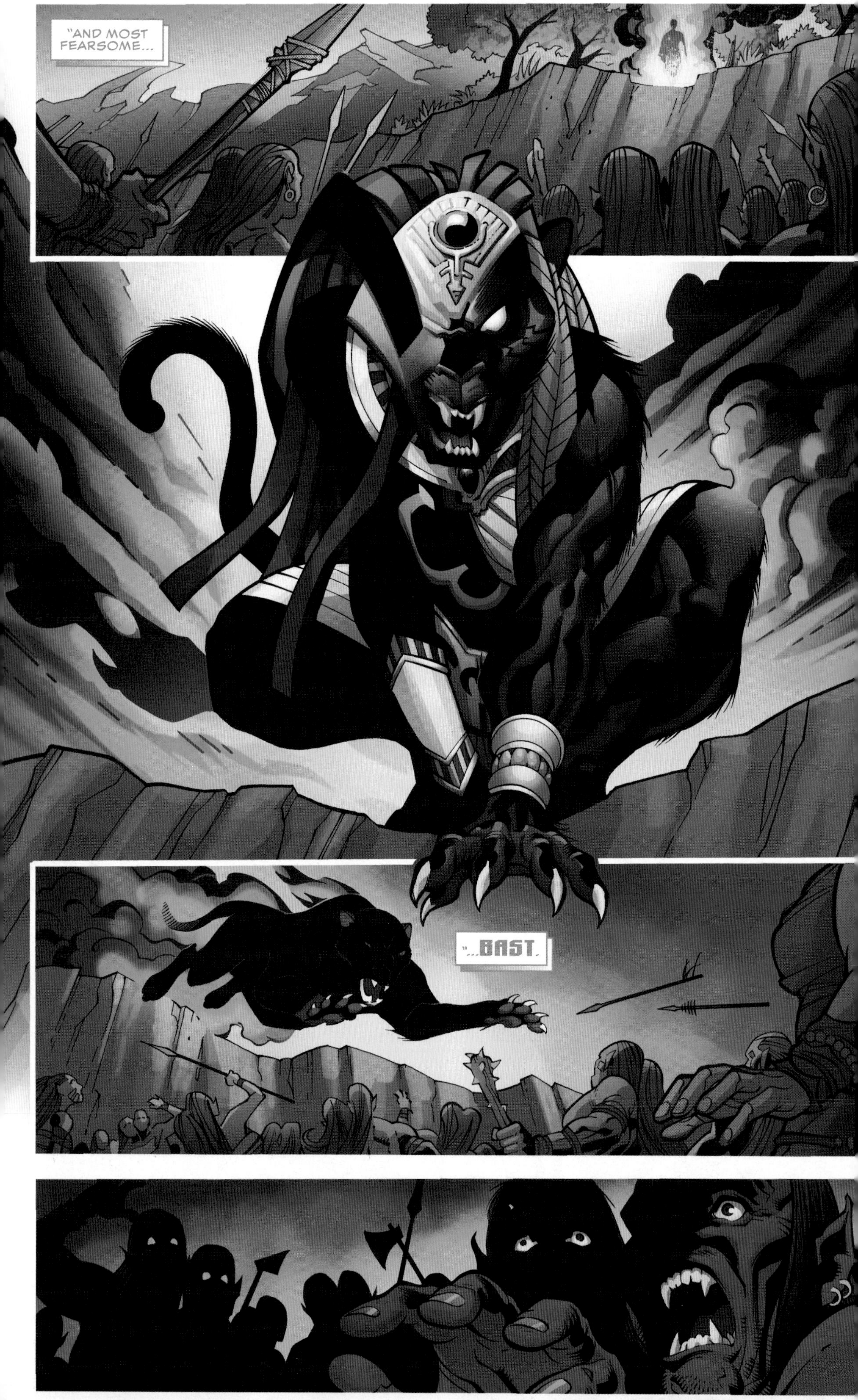
"AND MOST FEARSOME...
"...BAST."

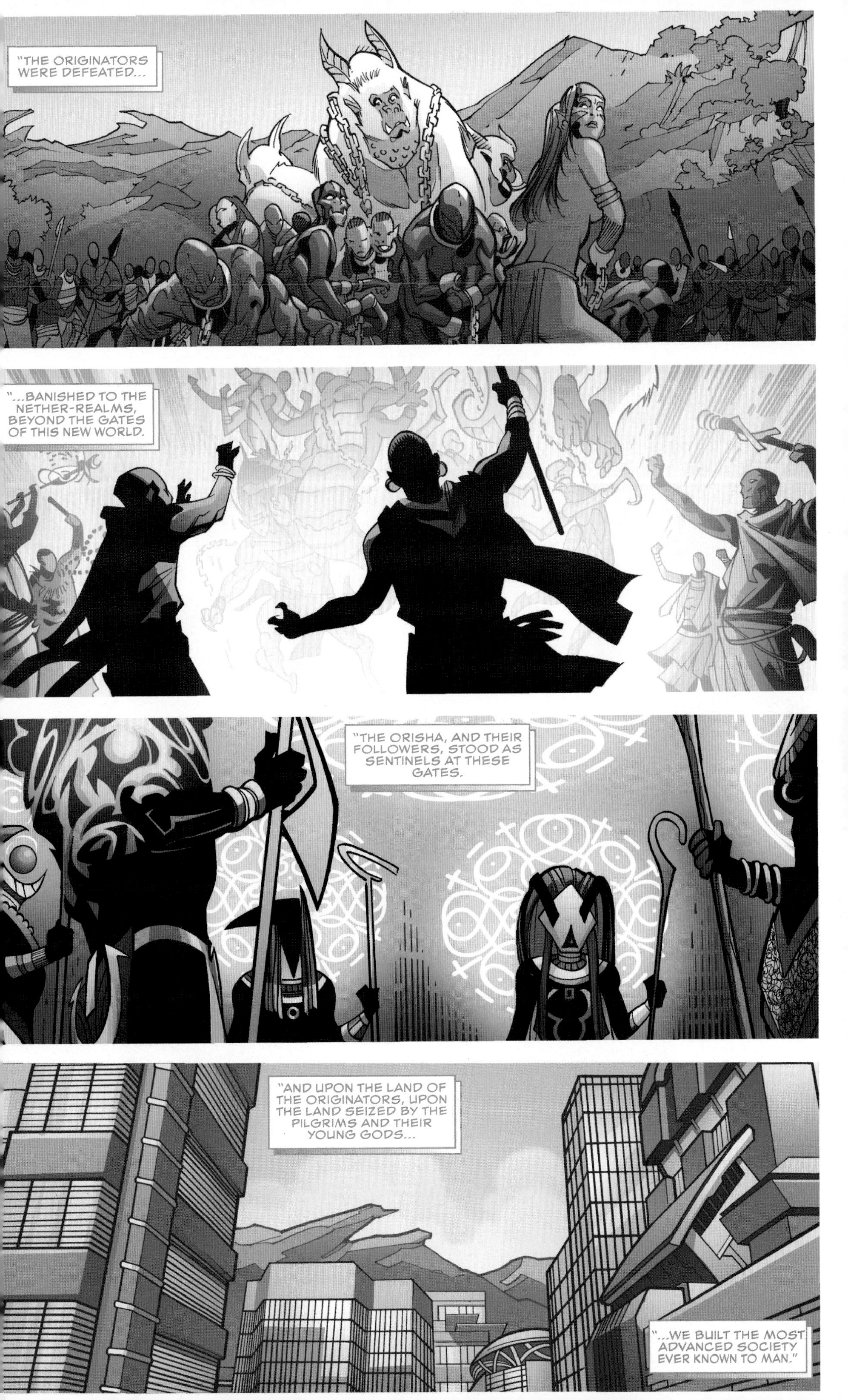
"THE ORIGINATORS WERE DEFEATED...
"...BANISHED TO THE NETHER-REALMS, BEYOND THE GATES OF THIS NEW WORLD.
"THE ORISHA, AND THEIR FOLLOWERS, STOOD AS SENTINELS AT THESE GATES.
"AND UPON THE LAND OF THE ORIGINATORS, UPON THE LAND SEIZED BY THE PILGRIMS AND THEIR YOUNG GODS...
"...WE BUILT THE MOST ADVANCED SOCIETY EVER KNOWN TO MAN."

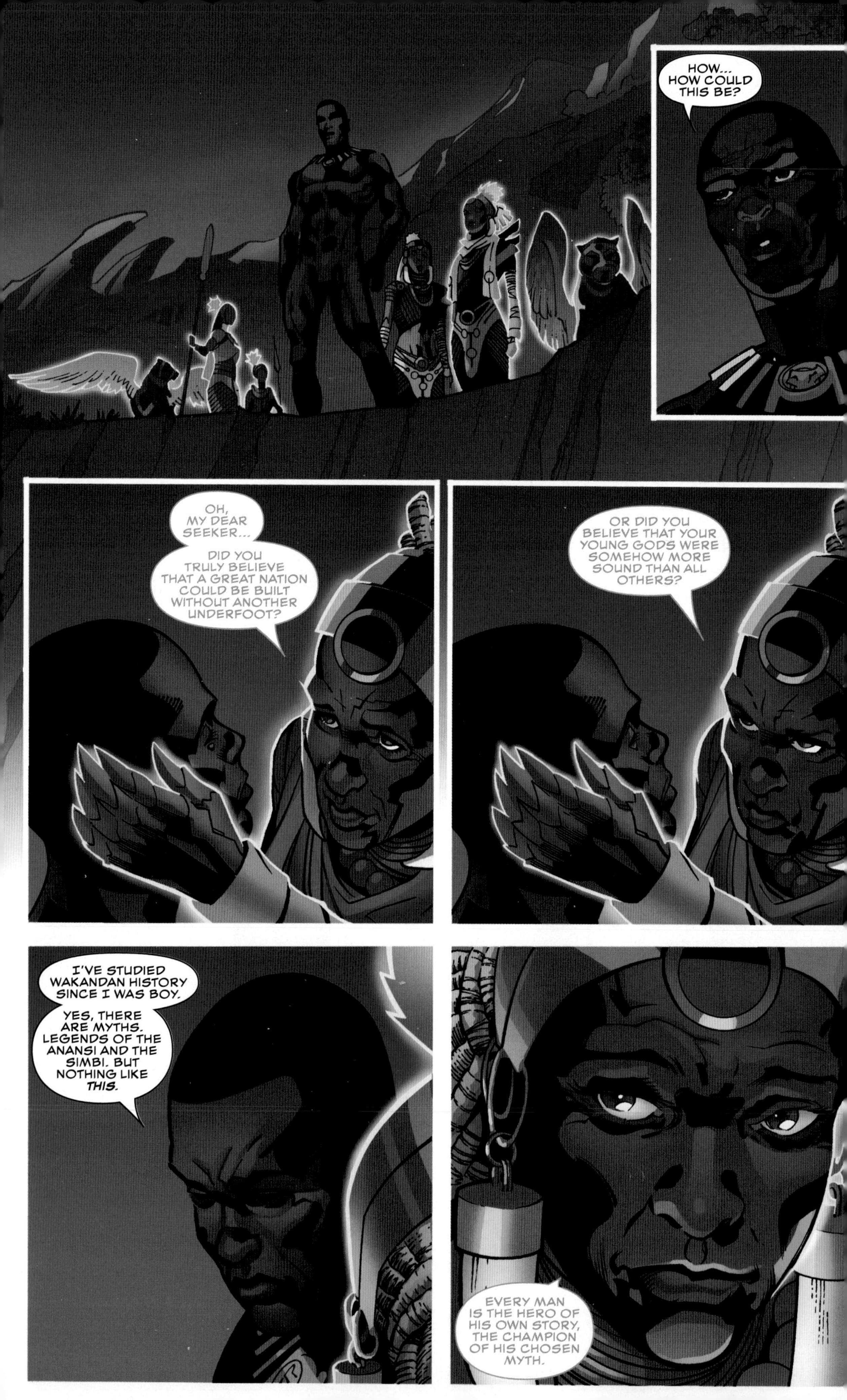
HOW... HOW COULD THIS BE?
OH, MY DEAR SEEKER...
DID YOU TRULY BELIEVE THAT A GREAT NATION COULD BE BUILT WITHOUT ANOTHER UNDERFOOT?
OR DID YOU BELIEVE THAT YOUR YOUNG GODS WERE SOMEHOW MORE SOUND THAN ALL OTHERS?
I'VE STUDIED WAKANDAN HISTORY SINCE I WAS BOY.
YES, THERE ARE MYTHS. LEGENDS OF THE ANANSI AND THE SIMBI. BUT NOTHING LIKE *THIS*.
EVERY MAN IS THE HERO OF HIS OWN STORY, THE CHAMPION OF HIS CHOSEN MYTH.

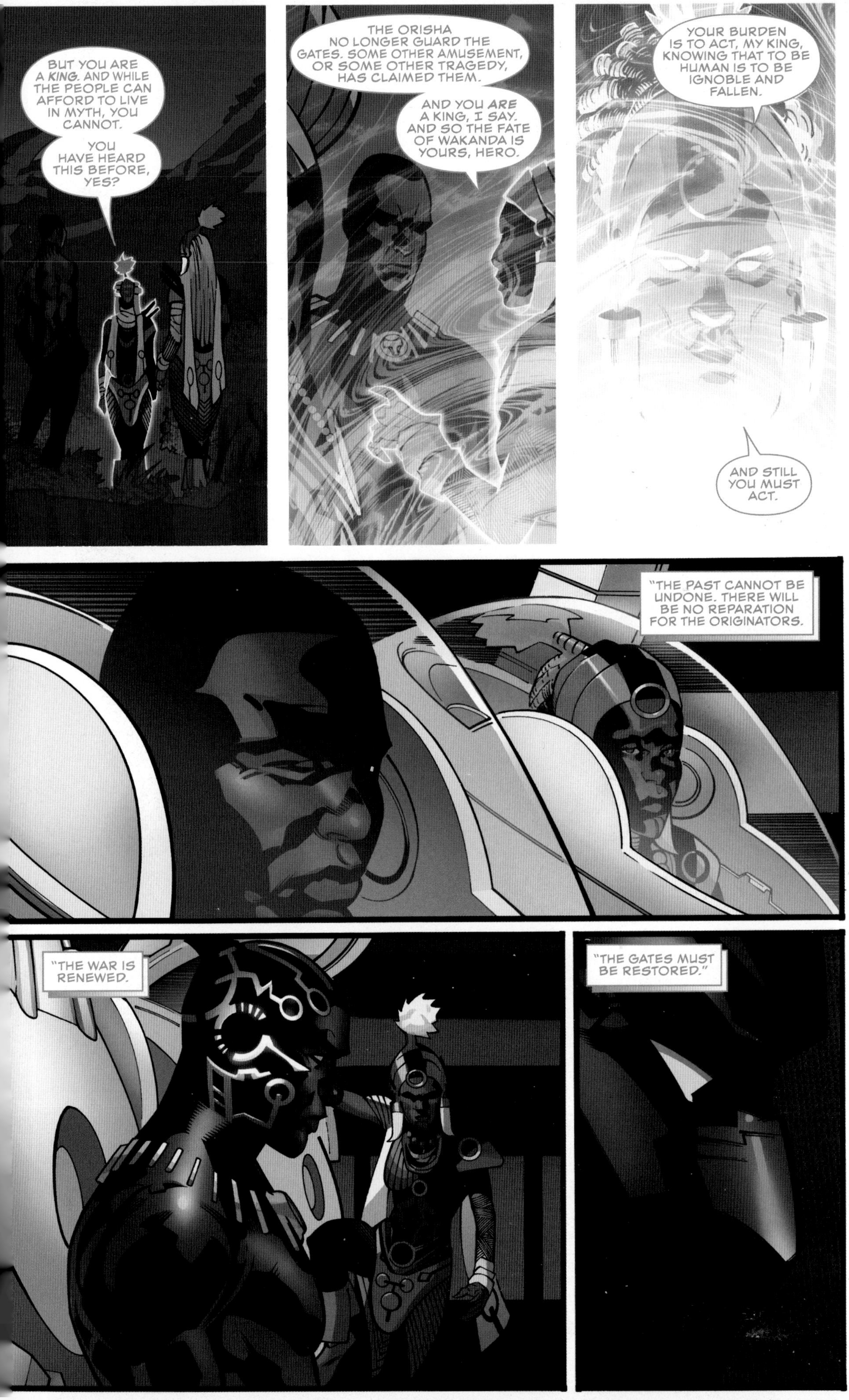
BUT YOU ARE A KING. AND WHILE THE PEOPLE CAN AFFORD TO LIVE IN MYTH, YOU CANNOT.
YOU HAVE HEARD THIS BEFORE, YES?
THE ORISHA NO LONGER GUARD THE GATES. SOME OTHER AMUSEMENT, OR SOME OTHER TRAGEDY, HAS CLAIMED THEM.
AND YOU ARE A KING, I SAY. AND SO THE FATE OF WAKANDA IS YOURS, HERO.
YOUR BURDEN IS TO ACT, MY KING, KNOWING THAT TO BE HUMAN IS TO BE IGNOBLE AND FALLEN.
AND STILL YOU MUST ACT.
"THE PAST CANNOT BE UNDONE. THERE WILL BE NO REPARATION FOR THE ORIGINATORS.
"THE WAR IS RENEWED.
"THE GATES MUST BE RESTORED."

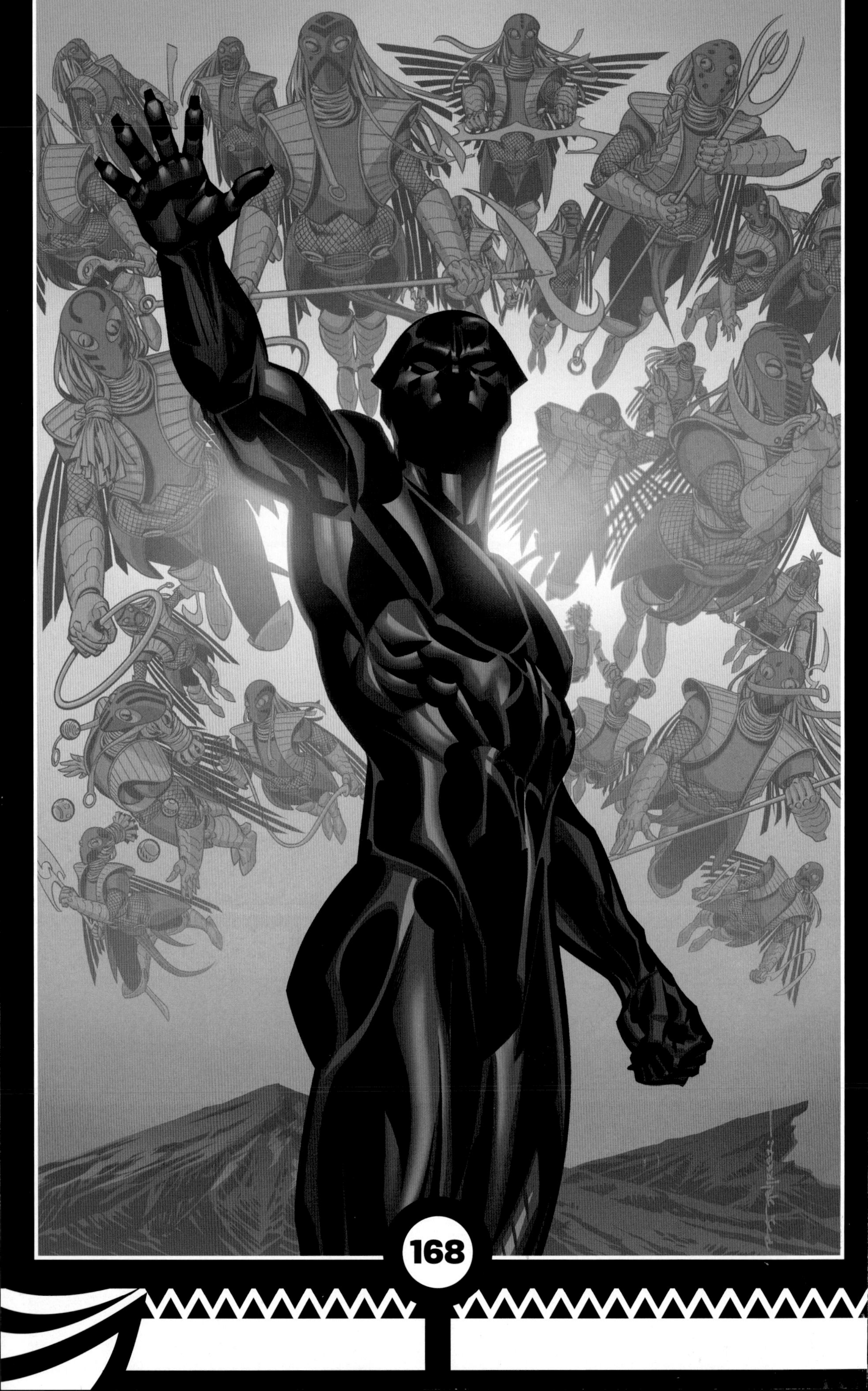

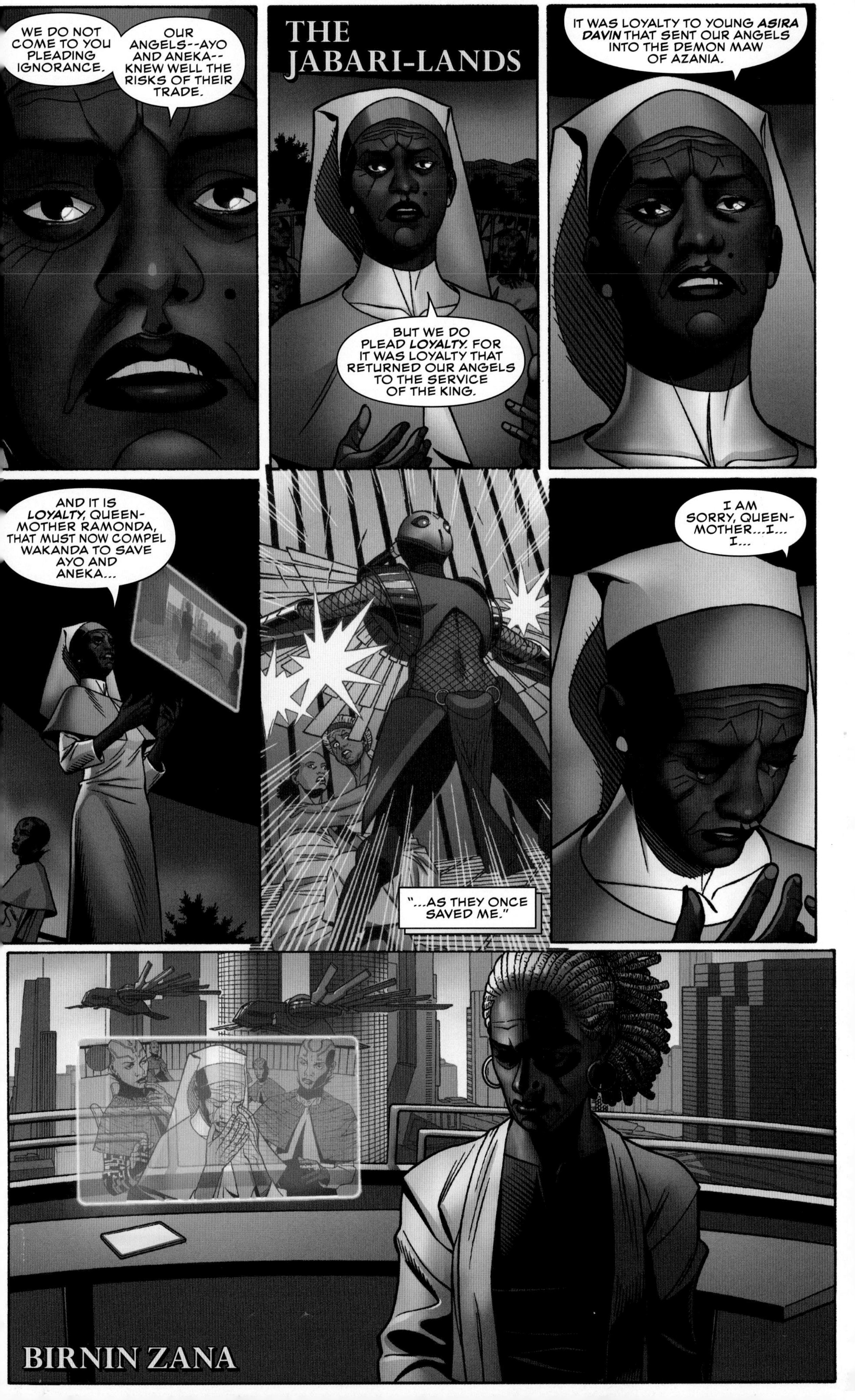
WE DO NOT COME TO YOU PLEADING IGNORANCE.
OUR ANGELS--AYO AND ANEKA--KNEW WELL THE RISKS OF THEIR TRADE.
THE JABARI-LANDS
BUT WE DO PLEAD LOYALTY. FOR IT WAS LOYALTY THAT RETURNED OUR ANGELS TO THE SERVICE OF THE KING.
IT WAS LOYALTY TO YOUNG ASIRA DAVIN THAT SENT OUR ANGELS INTO THE DEMON MAW OF AZANIA.
AND IT IS LOYALTY, QUEEN-MOTHER RAMONDA, THAT MUST NOW COMPEL WAKANDA TO SAVE AYO AND ANEKA...
"...AS THEY ONCE SAVED ME."
I AM SORRY, QUEEN-MOTHER...I... I...
BIRNIN ZANA

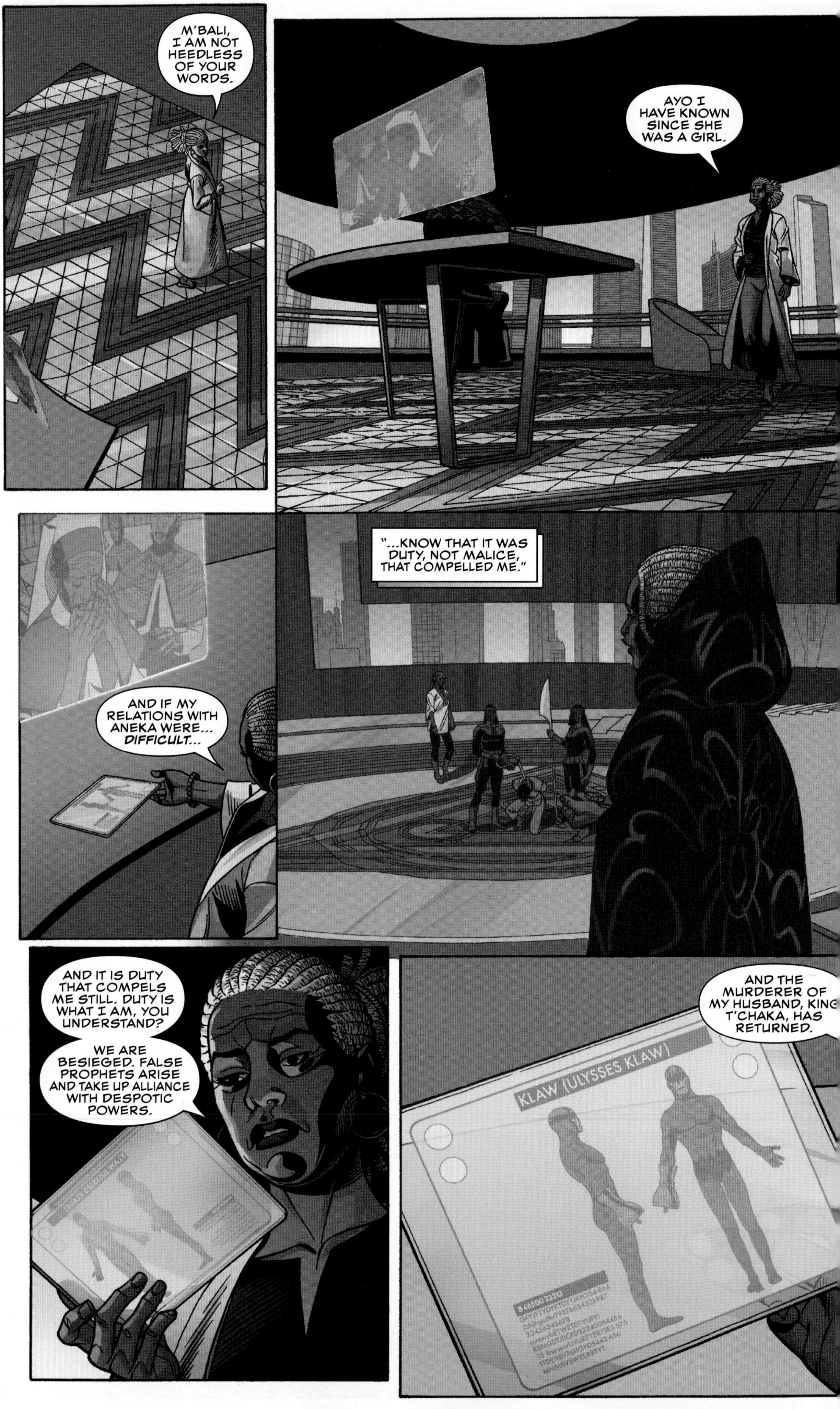
M'BALI, I AM NOT HEEDLESS OF YOUR WORDS.
AYO I HAVE KNOWN SINCE SHE WAS A GIRL.
AND IF MY RELATIONS WITH ANEKA WERE... *DIFFICULT*...
"...KNOW THAT IT WAS DUTY, NOT MALICE, THAT COMPELLED ME."
AND IT IS DUTY THAT COMPELS ME STILL. DUTY IS WHAT I AM, YOU UNDERSTAND?
WE ARE BESIEGED. FALSE PROPHETS ARISE AND TAKE UP ALLIANCE WITH DESPOTIC POWERS.
AND THE MURDERER OF MY HUSBAND, KING T'CHAKA, HAS RETURNED.
KLAW (ULYSSES KLAW)

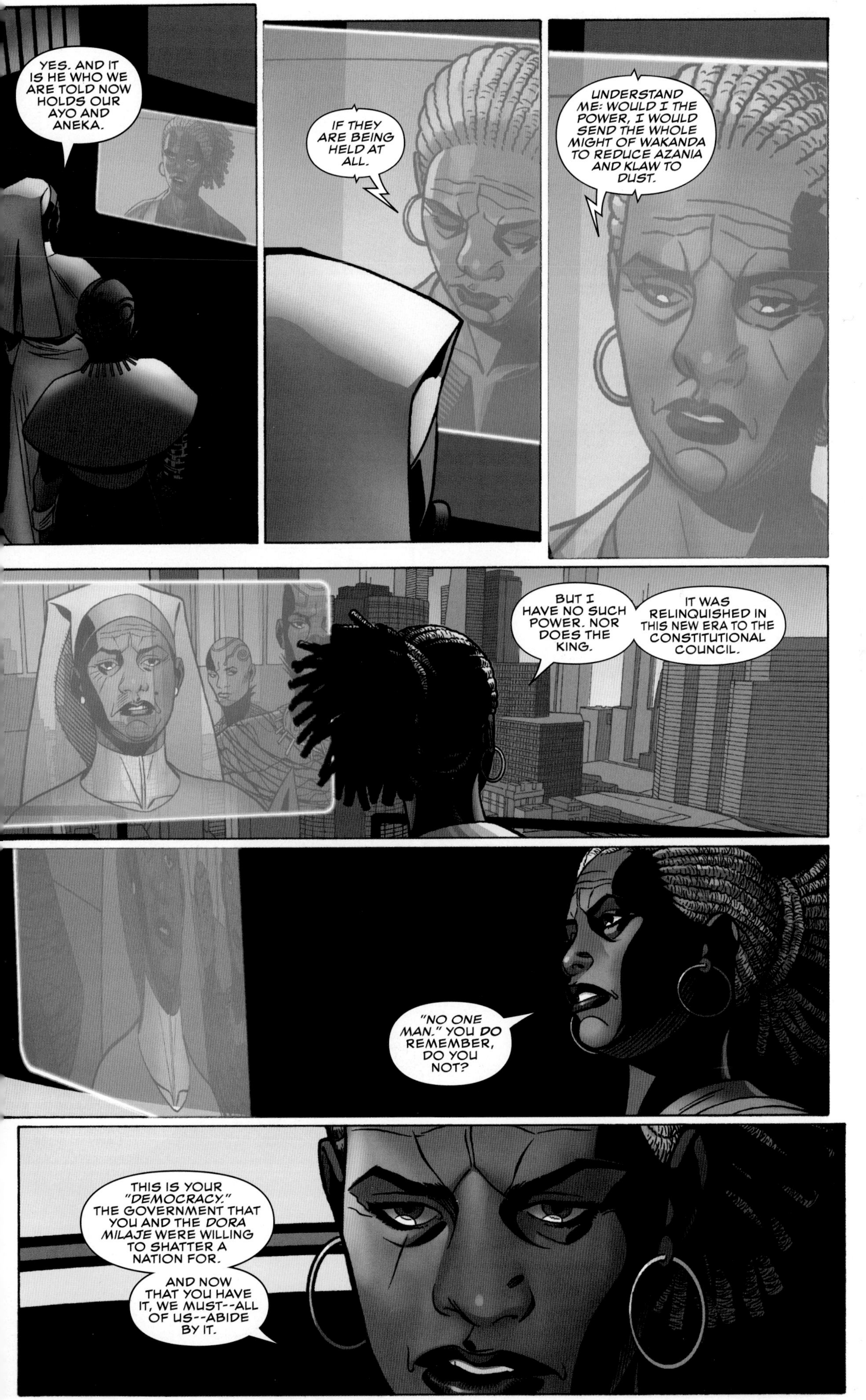
YES. AND IT IS HE WHO WE ARE TOLD NOW HOLDS OUR AYO AND ANEKA.
IF THEY ARE BEING HELD AT ALL.
UNDERSTAND ME: WOULD I THE POWER, I WOULD SEND THE WHOLE MIGHT OF WAKANDA TO REDUCE AZANIA AND KLAW TO DUST.
BUT I HAVE NO SUCH POWER. NOR DOES THE KING.
IT WAS RELINQUISHED IN THIS NEW ERA TO THE CONSTITUTIONAL COUNCIL.
"NO ONE MAN." YOU DO REMEMBER, DO YOU NOT?
THIS IS YOUR "DEMOCRACY." THE GOVERNMENT THAT YOU AND THE DORA MILAJE WERE WILLING TO SHATTER A NATION FOR.
AND NOW THAT YOU HAVE IT, WE MUST--ALL OF US--ABIDE BY IT.

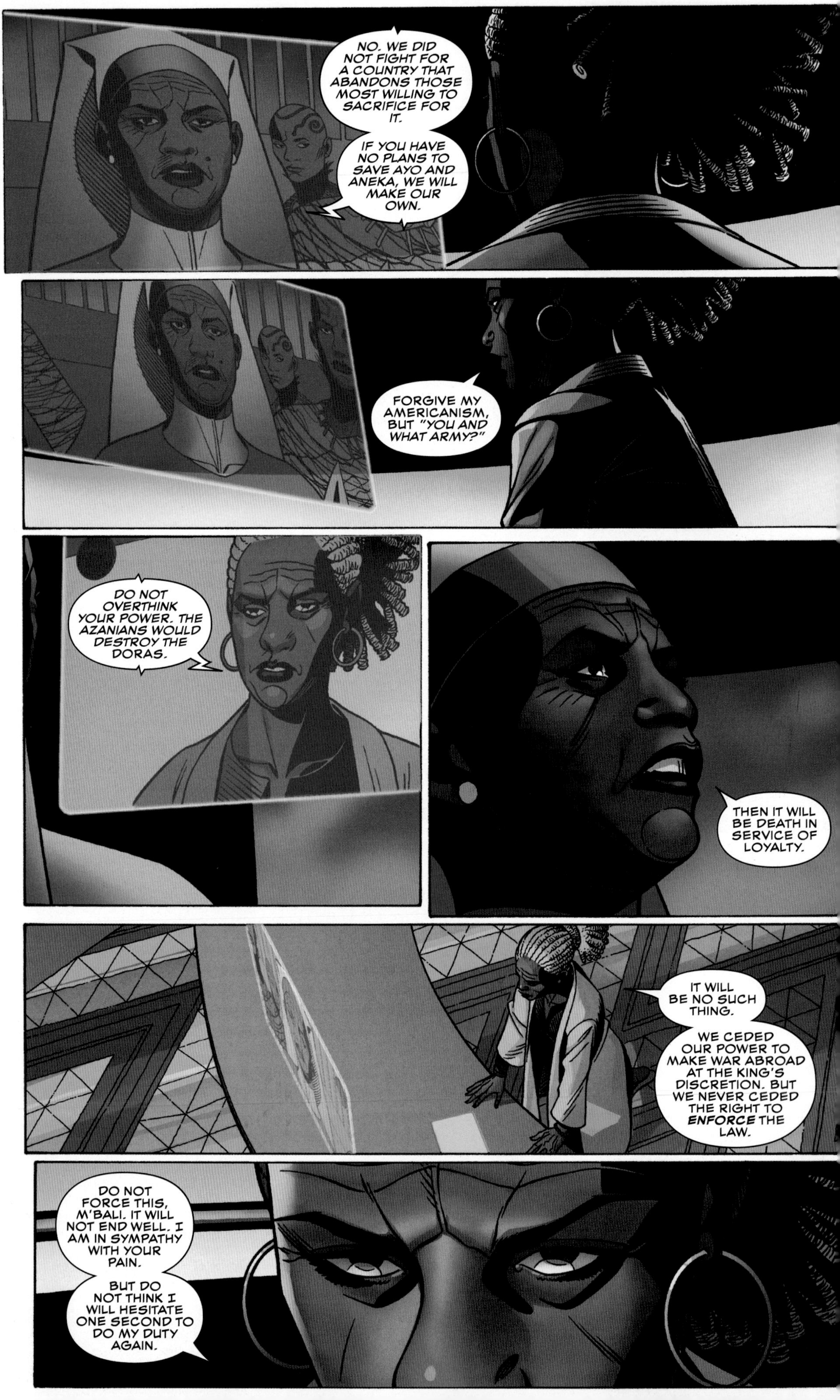
NO. WE DID NOT FIGHT FOR A COUNTRY THAT ABANDONS THOSE MOST WILLING TO SACRIFICE FOR IT.
IF YOU HAVE NO PLANS TO SAVE AYO AND ANEKA, WE WILL MAKE OUR OWN.
FORGIVE MY AMERICANISM, BUT "YOU AND WHAT ARMY?"
DO NOT OVERTHINK YOUR POWER. THE AZANIANS WOULD DESTROY THE DORAS.
THEN IT WILL BE DEATH IN SERVICE OF LOYALTY.
IT WILL BE NO SUCH THING.
WE CEDED OUR POWER TO MAKE WAR ABROAD AT THE KING'S DISCRETION. BUT WE NEVER CEDED THE RIGHT TO ENFORCE THE LAW.
DO NOT FORCE THIS, M'BALI. IT WILL NOT END WELL. I AM IN SYMPATHY WITH YOUR PAIN.
BUT DO NOT THINK I WILL HESITATE ONE SECOND TO DO MY DUTY AGAIN.

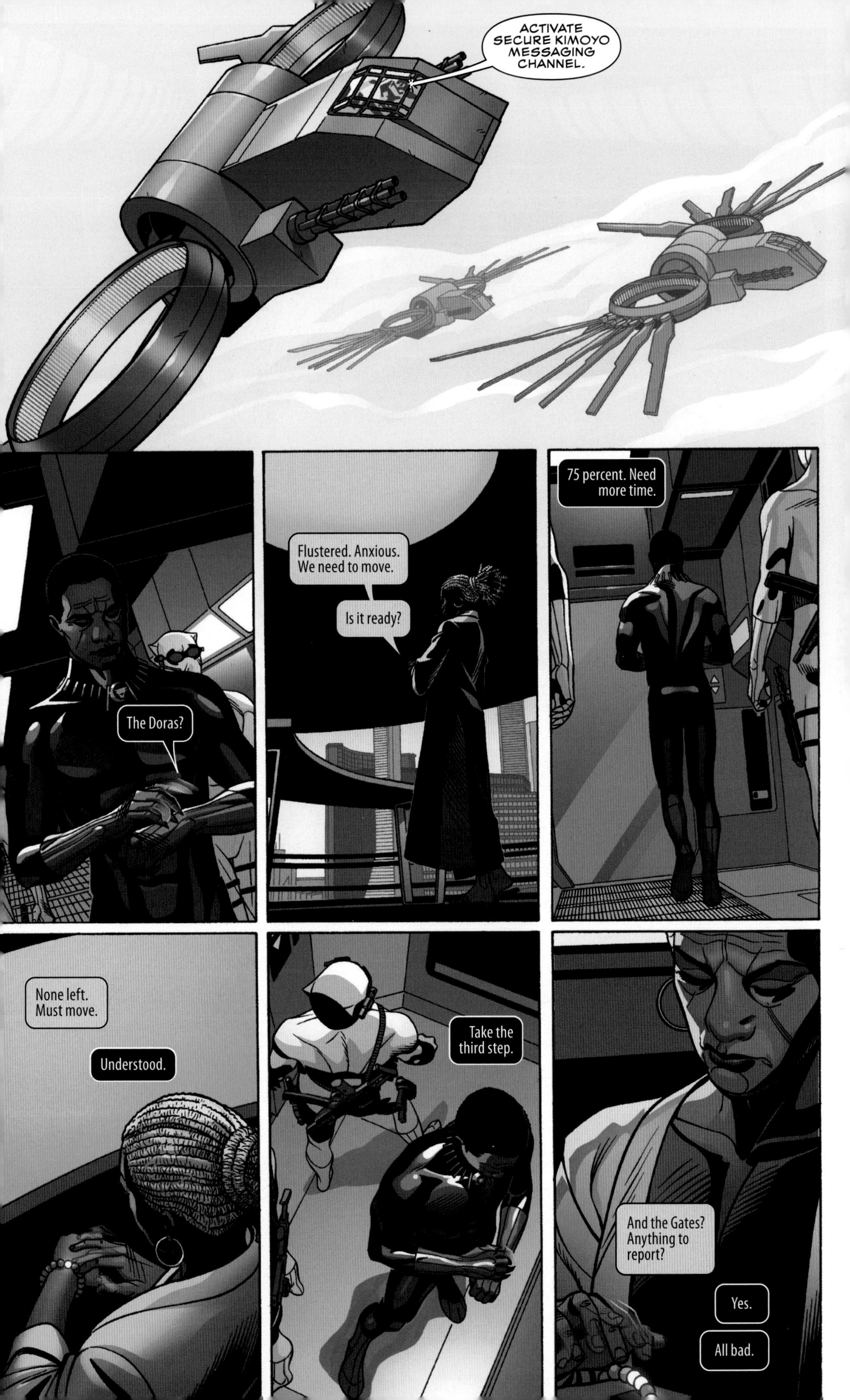
ACTIVATE SECURE KIMOYO MESSAGING CHANNEL.
The Doras?
Flustered. Anxious. We need to move.
Is it ready?
75 percent. Need more time.
None left. Must move.
Understood.
Take the third step.
And the Gates? Anything to report?
Yes.
All bad.

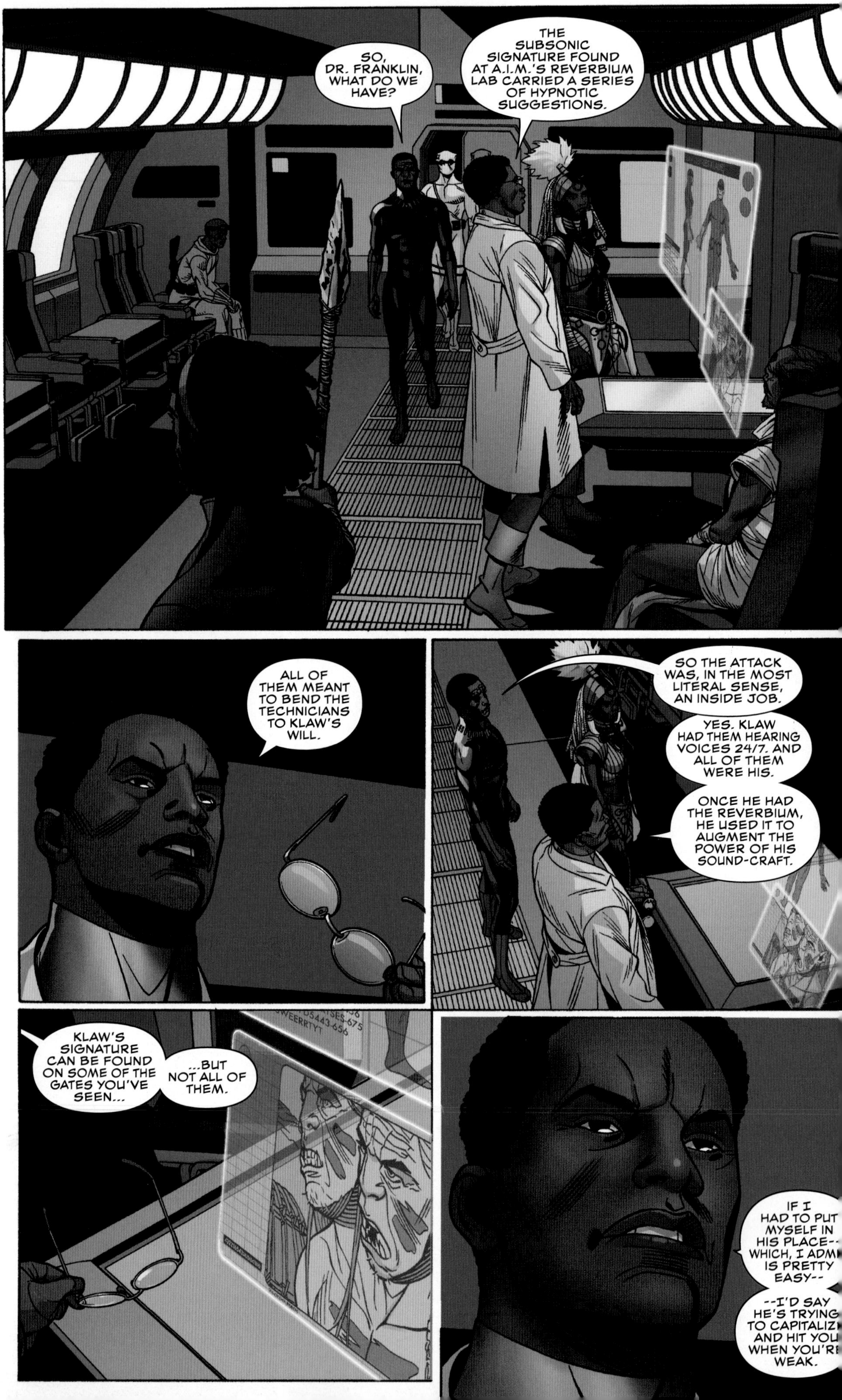

SO, DR. FRANKLIN, WHAT DO WE HAVE?
THE SUBSONIC SIGNATURE FOUND AT A.I.M.'S REVERBIUM LAB CARRIED A SERIES OF HYPNOTIC SUGGESTIONS.
ALL OF THEM MEANT TO BEND THE TECHNICIANS TO KLAW'S WILL.
SO THE ATTACK WAS, IN THE MOST LITERAL SENSE, AN INSIDE JOB.
YES. KLAW HAD THEM HEARING VOICES 24/7. AND ALL OF THEM WERE HIS.
ONCE HE HAD THE REVERBIUM, HE USED IT TO AUGMENT THE POWER OF HIS SOUND-CRAFT.
KLAW'S SIGNATURE CAN BE FOUND ON SOME OF THE GATES YOU'VE SEEN...
...BUT NOT ALL OF THEM.
IF I HAD TO PUT MYSELF IN HIS PLACE-- WHICH, I ADM IS PRETTY EASY--
--I'D SAY HE'S TRYING TO CAPITALIZ AND HIT YOU WHEN YOU'R WEAK.

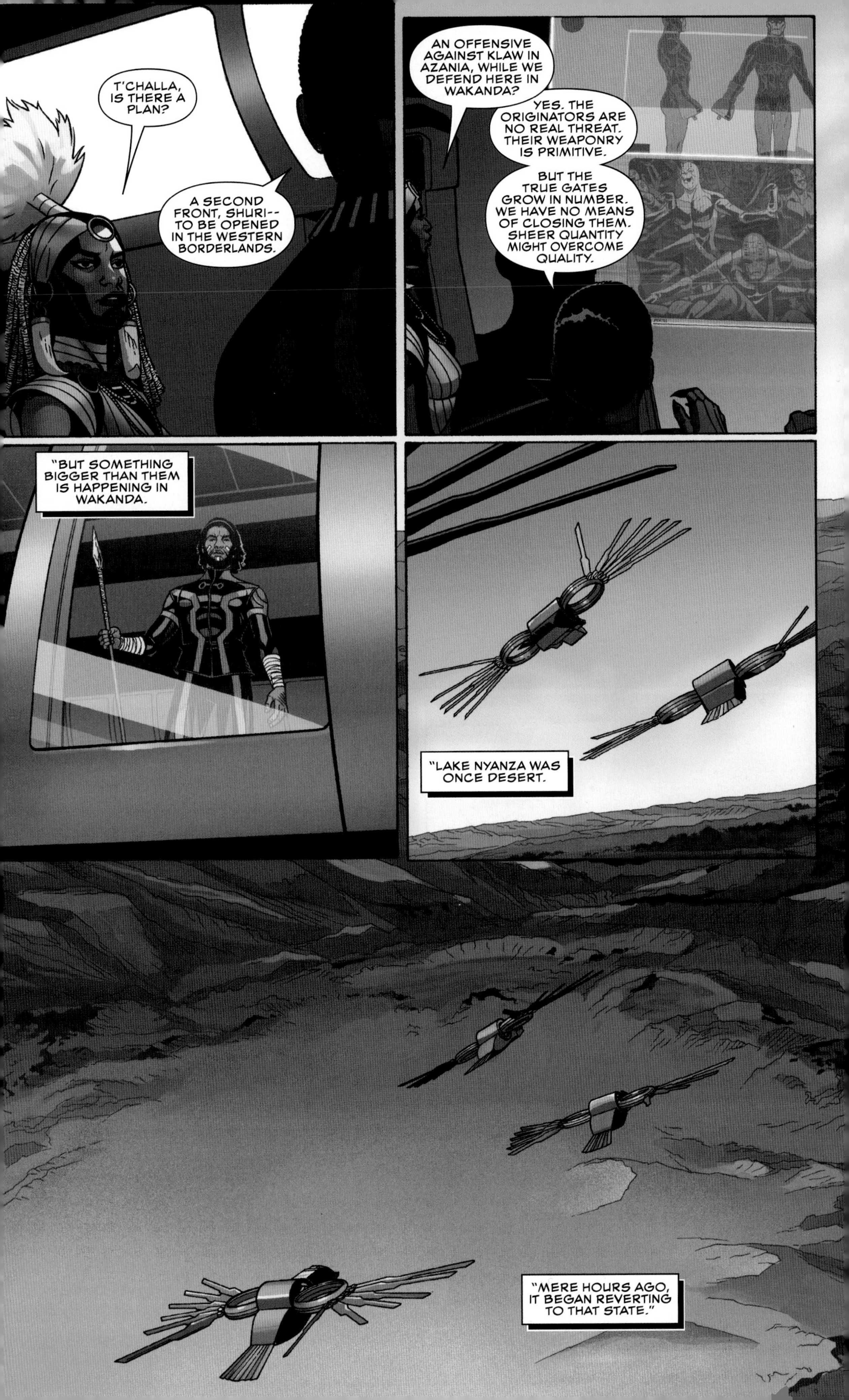
T'CHALLA, IS THERE A PLAN?
A SECOND FRONT, SHURI-- TO BE OPENED IN THE WESTERN BORDERLANDS.
AN OFFENSIVE AGAINST KLAW IN AZANIA, WHILE WE DEFEND HERE IN WAKANDA?
YES. THE ORIGINATORS ARE NO REAL THREAT. THEIR WEAPONRY IS PRIMITIVE.
BUT THE TRUE GATES GROW IN NUMBER. WE HAVE NO MEANS OF CLOSING THEM. SHEER QUANTITY MIGHT OVERCOME QUALITY.
"BUT SOMETHING BIGGER THAN THEM IS HAPPENING IN WAKANDA.
"LAKE NYANZA WAS ONCE DESERT.
"MERE HOURS AGO, IT BEGAN REVERTING TO THAT STATE."

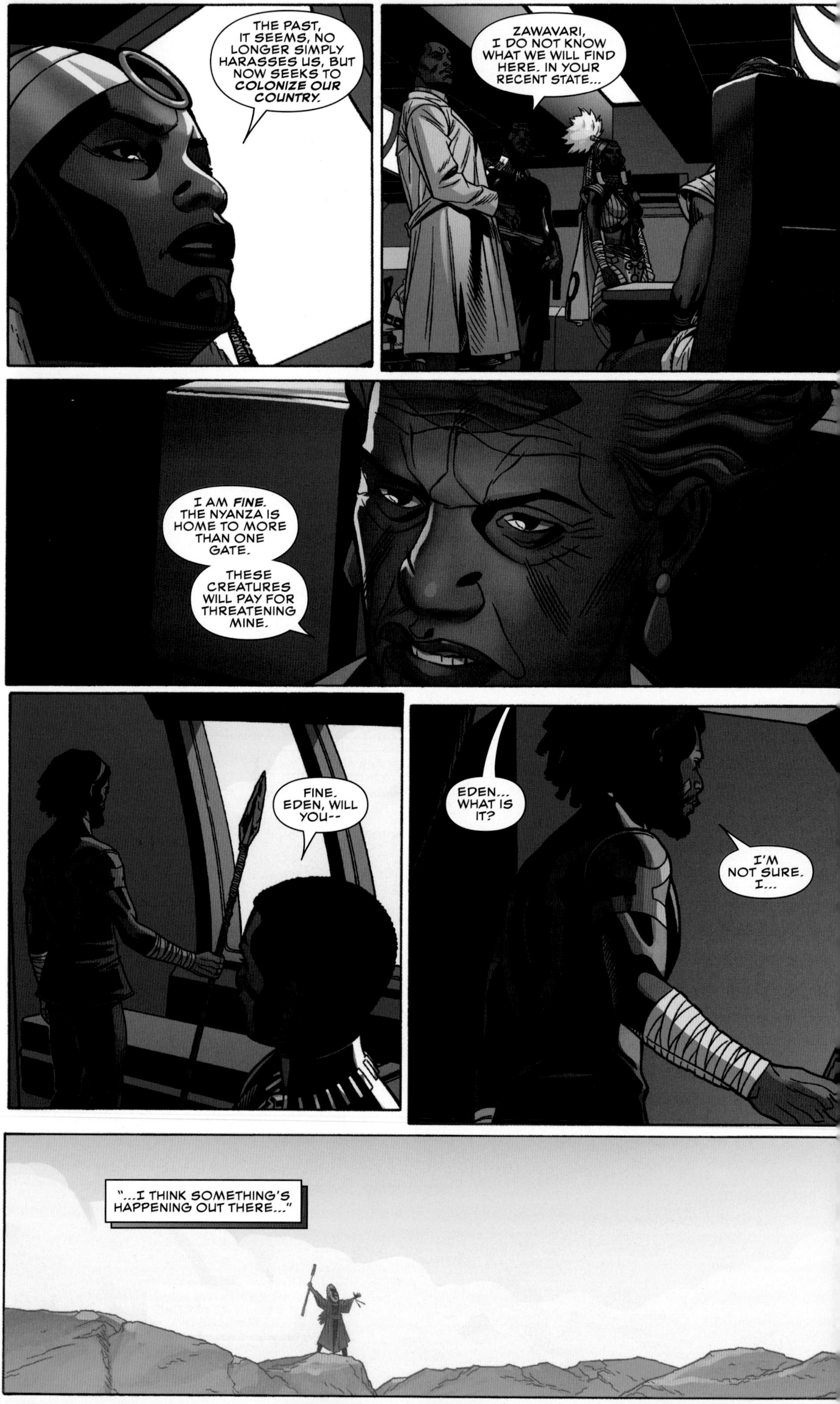
THE PAST, IT SEEMS, NO LONGER SIMPLY HARASSES US, BUT NOW SEEKS TO COLONIZE OUR COUNTRY.
ZAWAVARI, I DO NOT KNOW WHAT WE WILL FIND HERE. IN YOUR RECENT STATE...
I AM FINE. THE NYANZA IS HOME TO MORE THAN ONE GATE.
THESE CREATURES WILL PAY FOR THREATENING MINE.
FINE. EDEN, WILL YOU--
EDEN... WHAT IS IT?
I'M NOT SURE. I...
"...I THINK SOMETHING'S HAPPENING OUT THERE..."

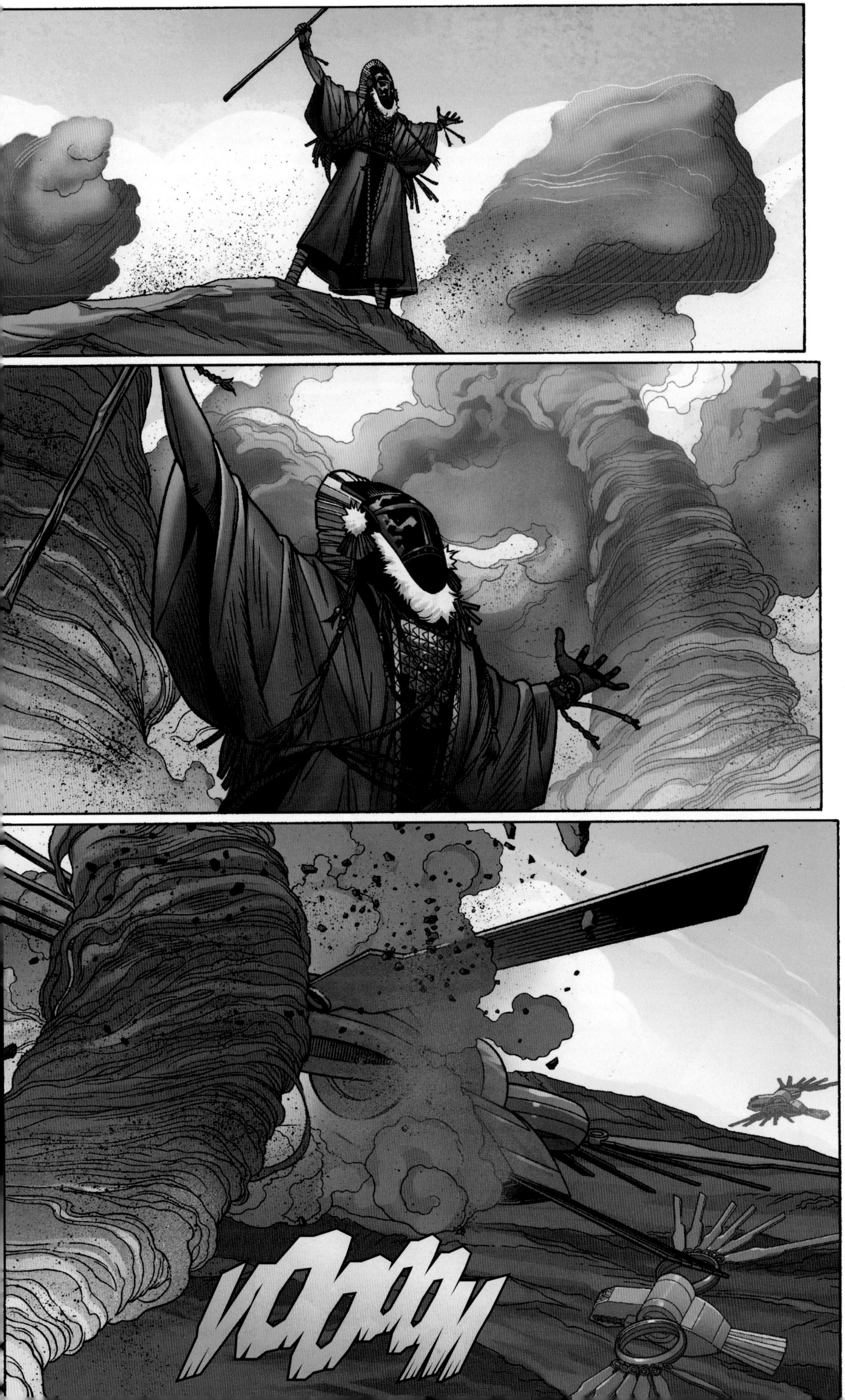
VOOOOM

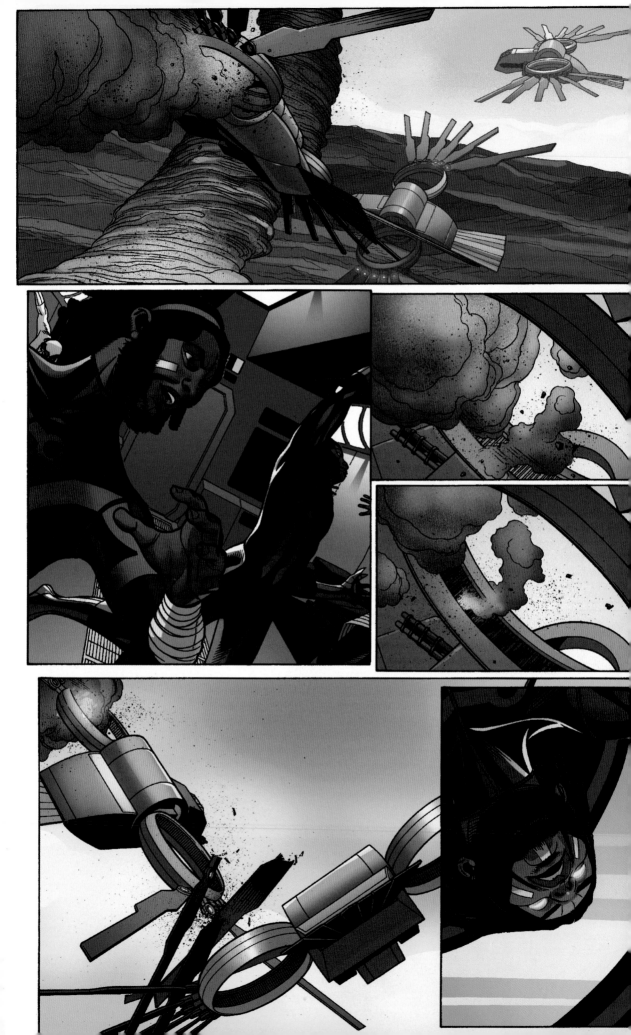

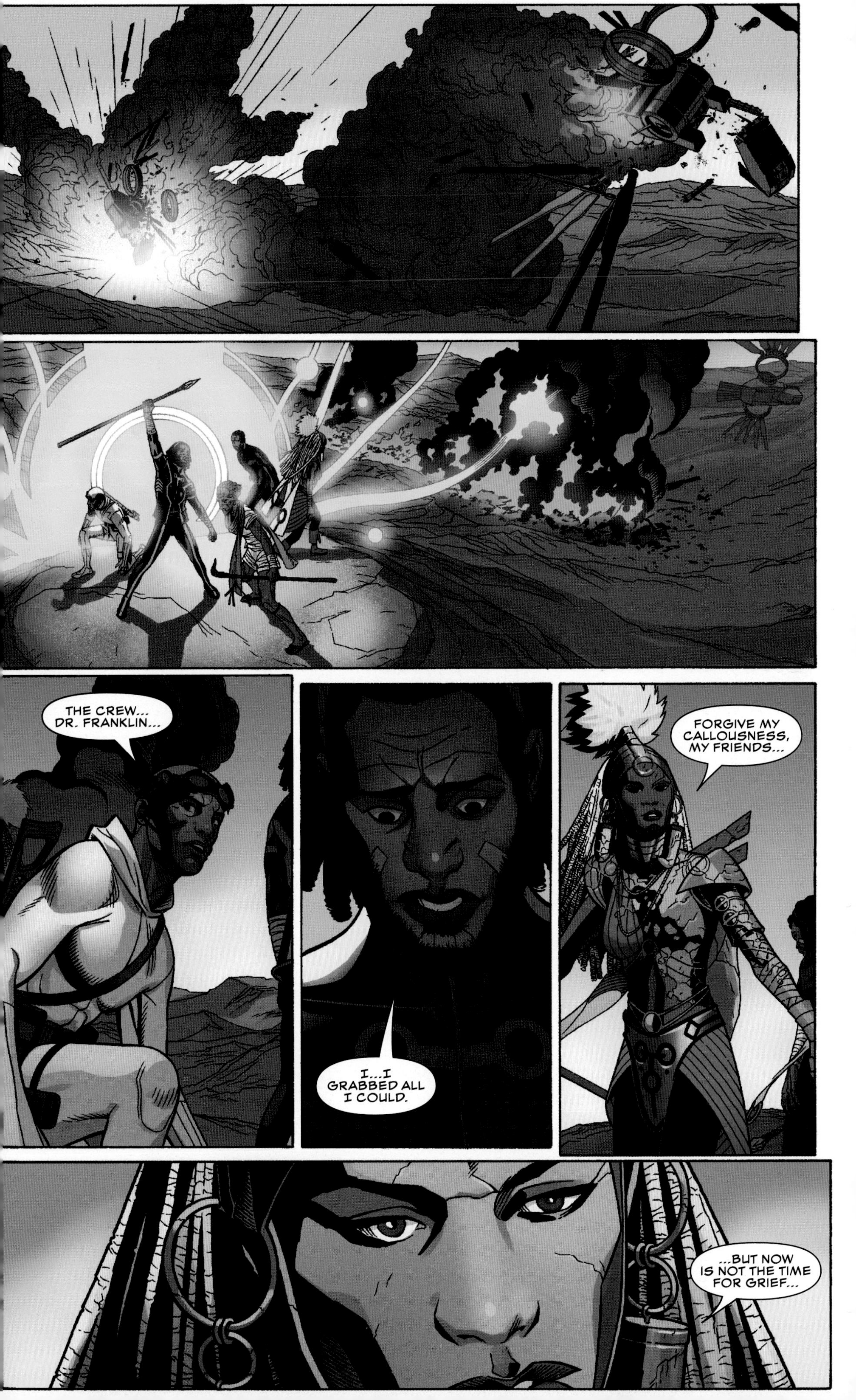
THE CREW... DR. FRANKLIN...
I...I GRABBED ALL I COULD.
FORGIVE MY CALLOUSNESS, MY FRIENDS...
...BUT NOW IS NOT THE TIME FOR GRIEF...

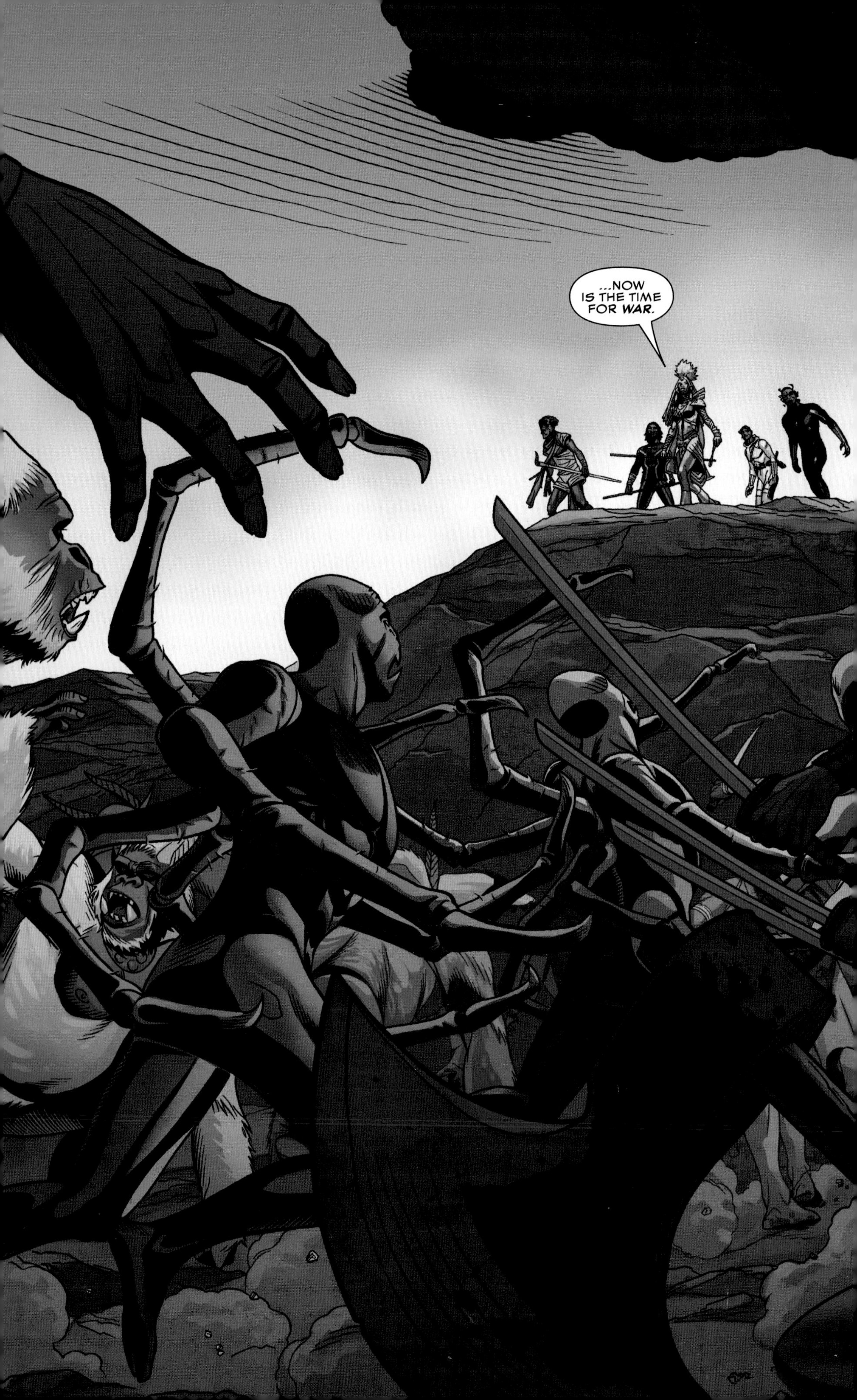
...NOW IS THE TIME FOR WAR.

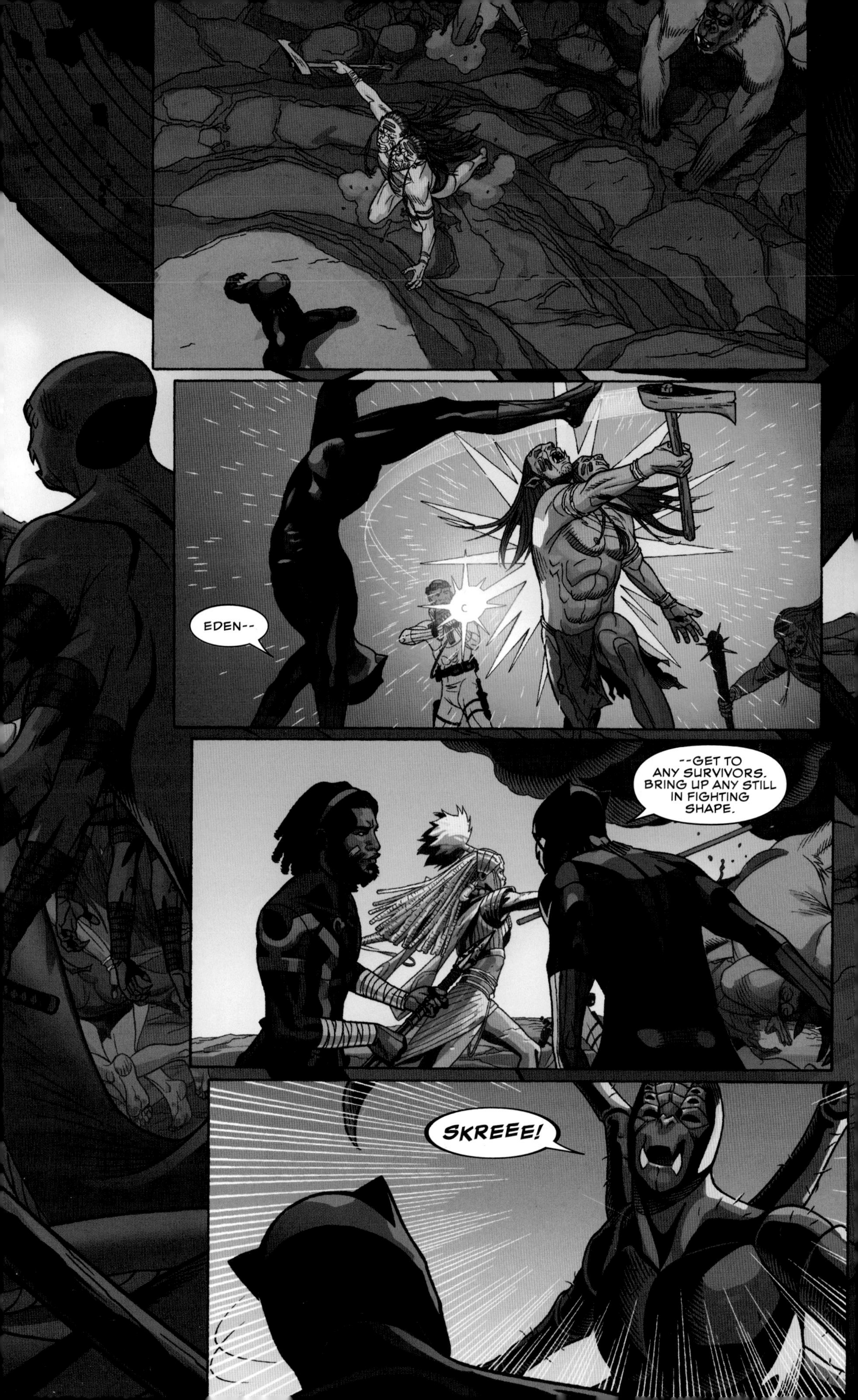
EDEN--
--GET TO ANY SURVIVORS. BRING UP ANY STILL IN FIGHTING SHAPE.
SKREEE!

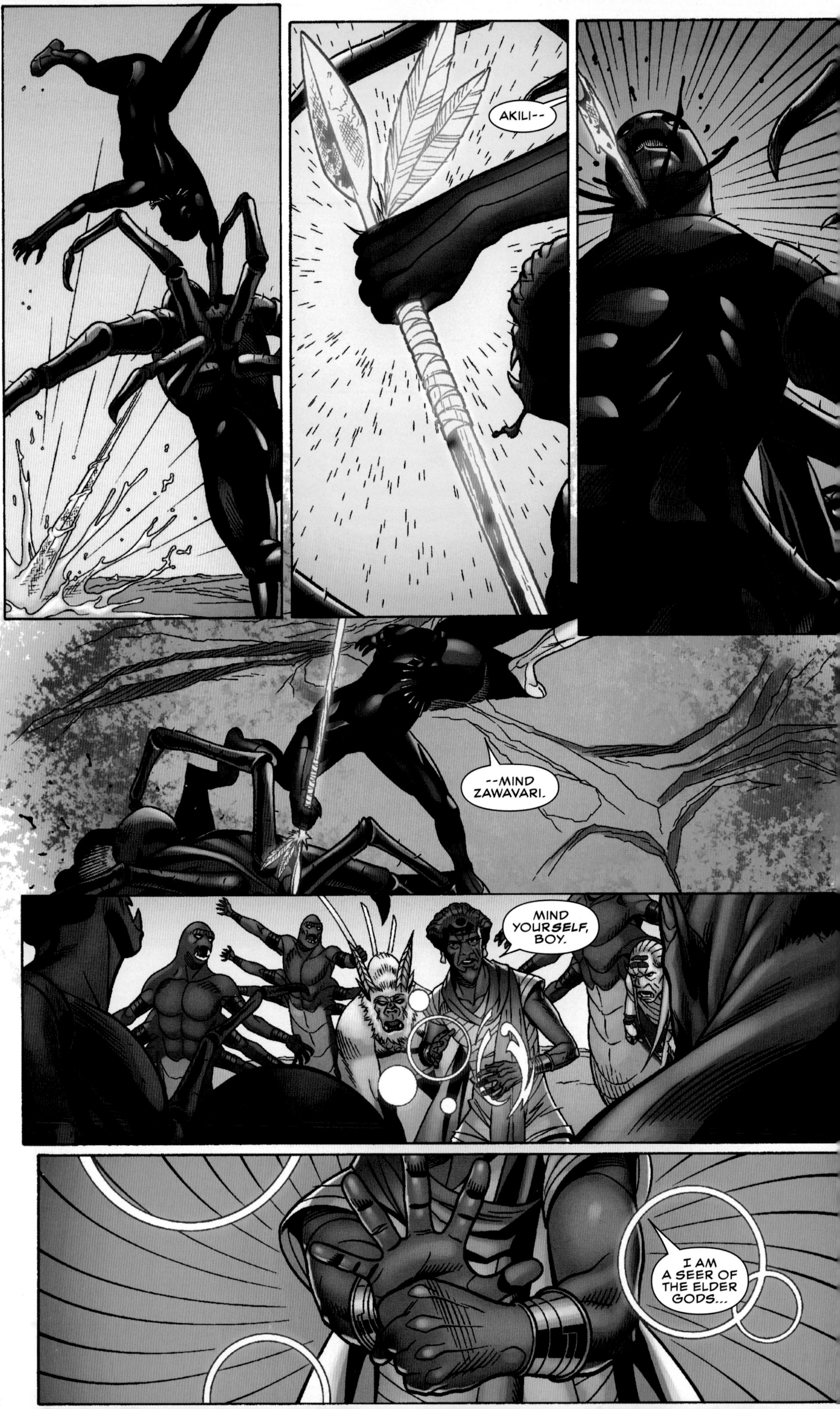
AKILI--
--MIND ZAWAVARI.
MIND YOURSELF, BOY.
I AM A SEER OF THE ELDER GODS...

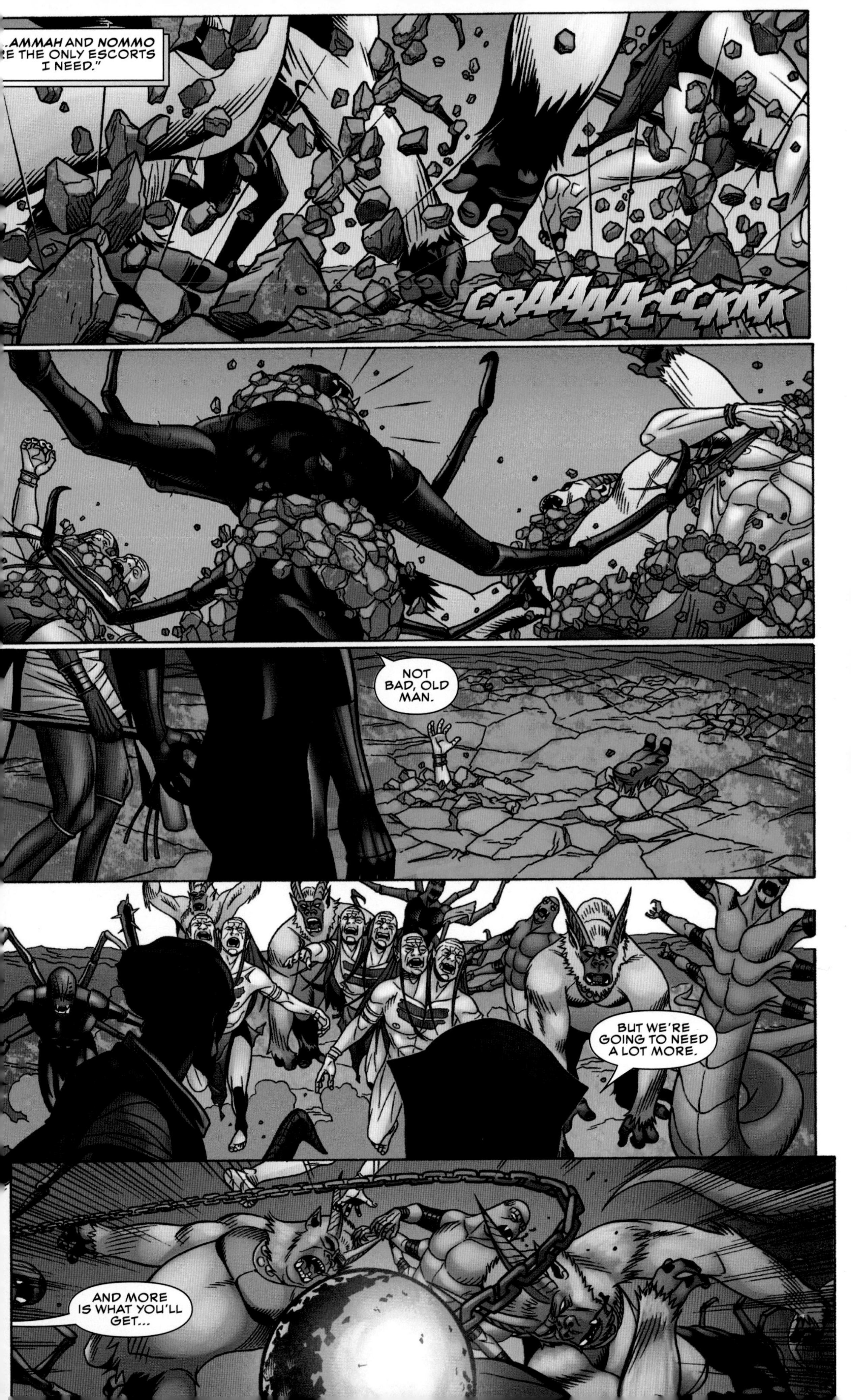
"...AMMAH AND NOMMO ARE THE ONLY ESCORTS I NEED."
CRAAAACCKKK
NOT BAD, OLD MAN.
BUT WE'RE GOING TO NEED A LOT MORE.
AND MORE IS WHAT YOU'LL GET...

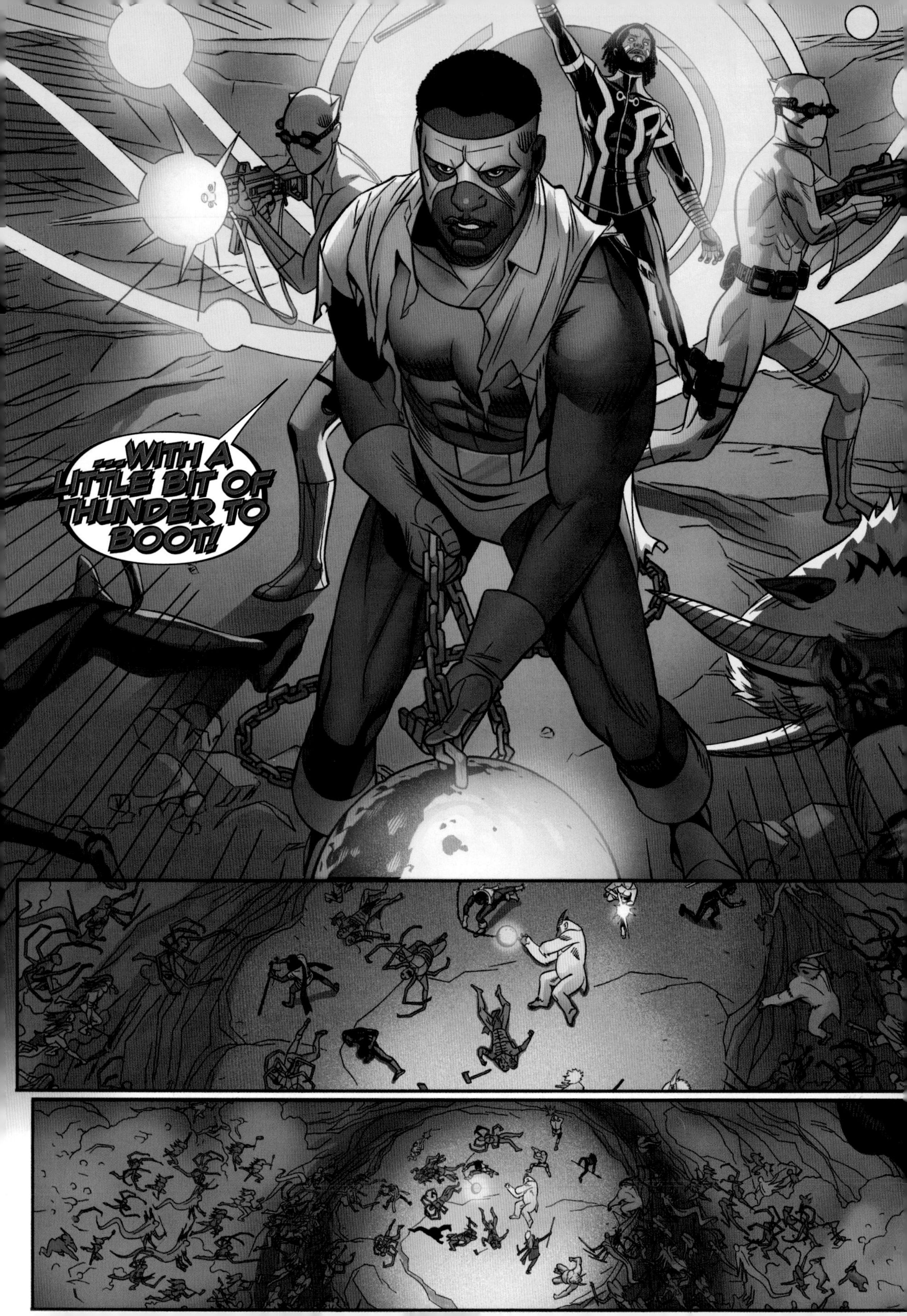
...WITH A LITTLE BIT OF THUNDER TO BOOT!

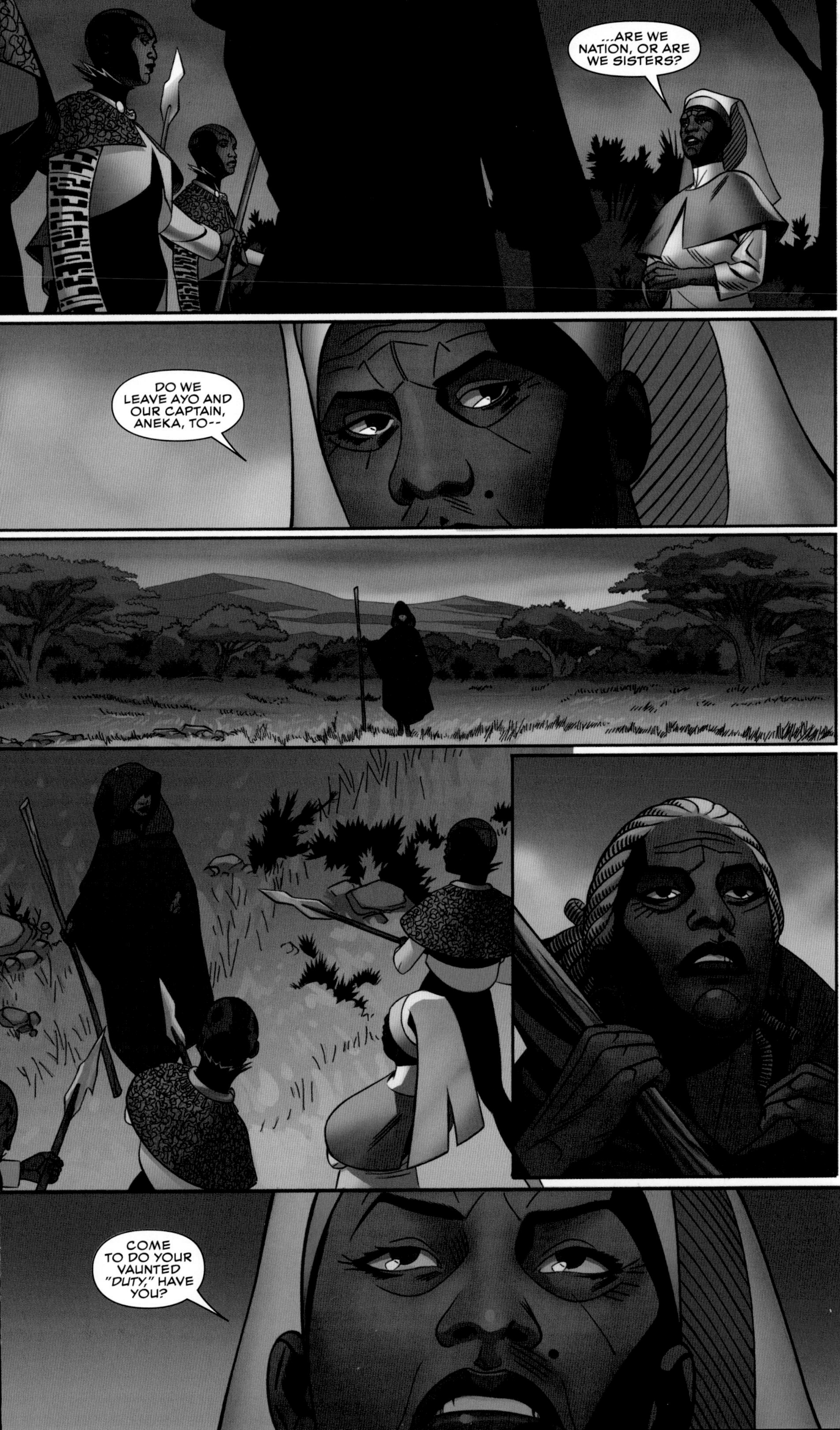
...ARE WE NATION, OR ARE WE SISTERS?
DO WE LEAVE AYO AND OUR CAPTAIN, ANEKA, TO--
COME TO DO YOUR VAUNTED "DUTY," HAVE YOU?

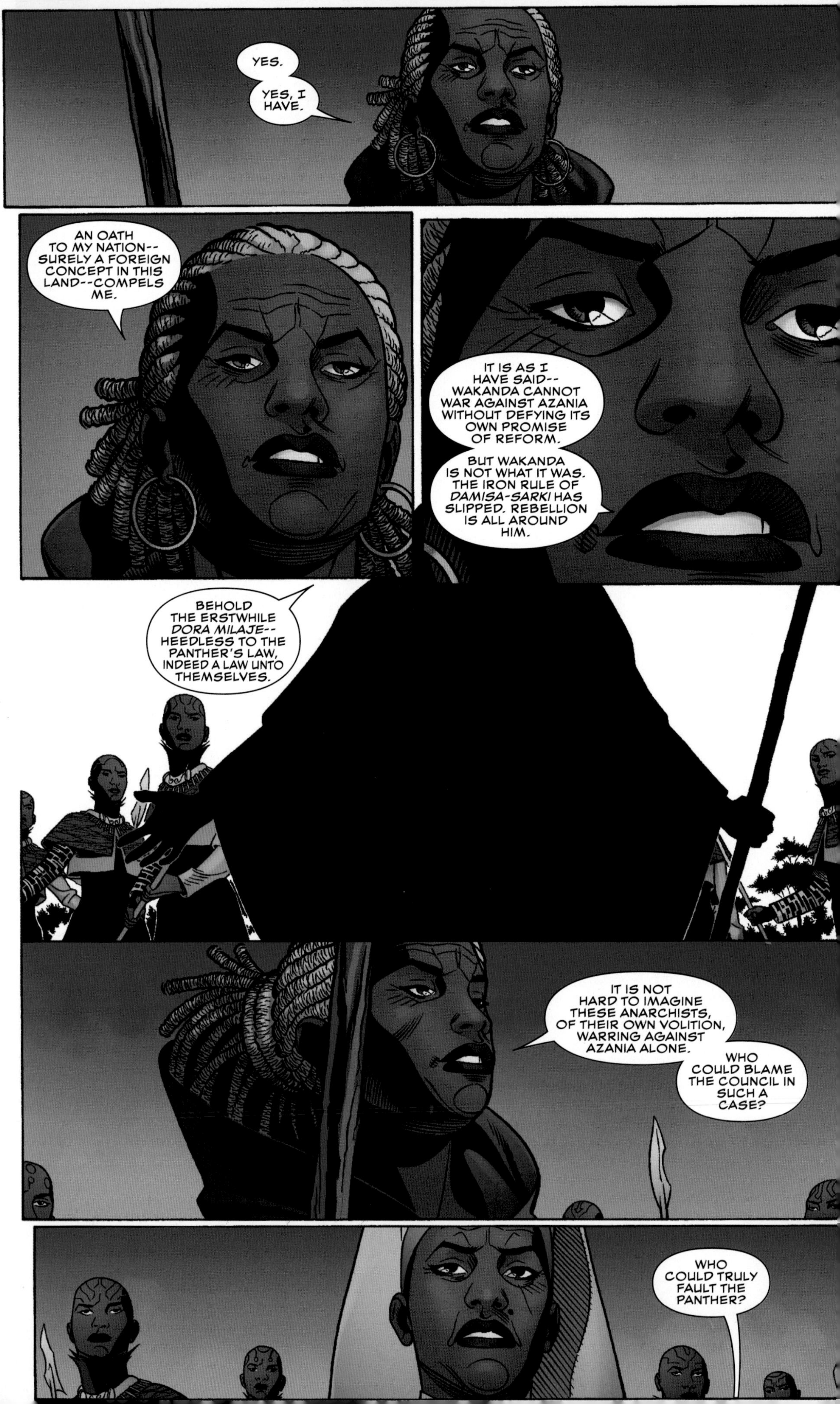
YES.
YES, I HAVE.
AN OATH TO MY NATION--SURELY A FOREIGN CONCEPT IN THIS LAND--COMPELS ME.
IT IS AS I HAVE SAID--WAKANDA CANNOT WAR AGAINST AZANIA WITHOUT DEFYING ITS OWN PROMISE OF REFORM.
BUT WAKANDA IS NOT WHAT IT WAS. THE IRON RULE OF *DAMISA-SARKI* HAS SLIPPED. REBELLION IS ALL AROUND HIM.
BEHOLD THE ERSTWHILE *DORA MILAJE*--HEEDLESS TO THE PANTHER'S LAW, INDEED A LAW UNTO THEMSELVES.
IT IS NOT HARD TO IMAGINE THESE ANARCHISTS, OF THEIR OWN VOLITION, WARRING AGAINST AZANIA ALONE.
WHO COULD BLAME THE COUNCIL IN SUCH A CASE?
WHO COULD TRULY FAULT THE PANTHER?

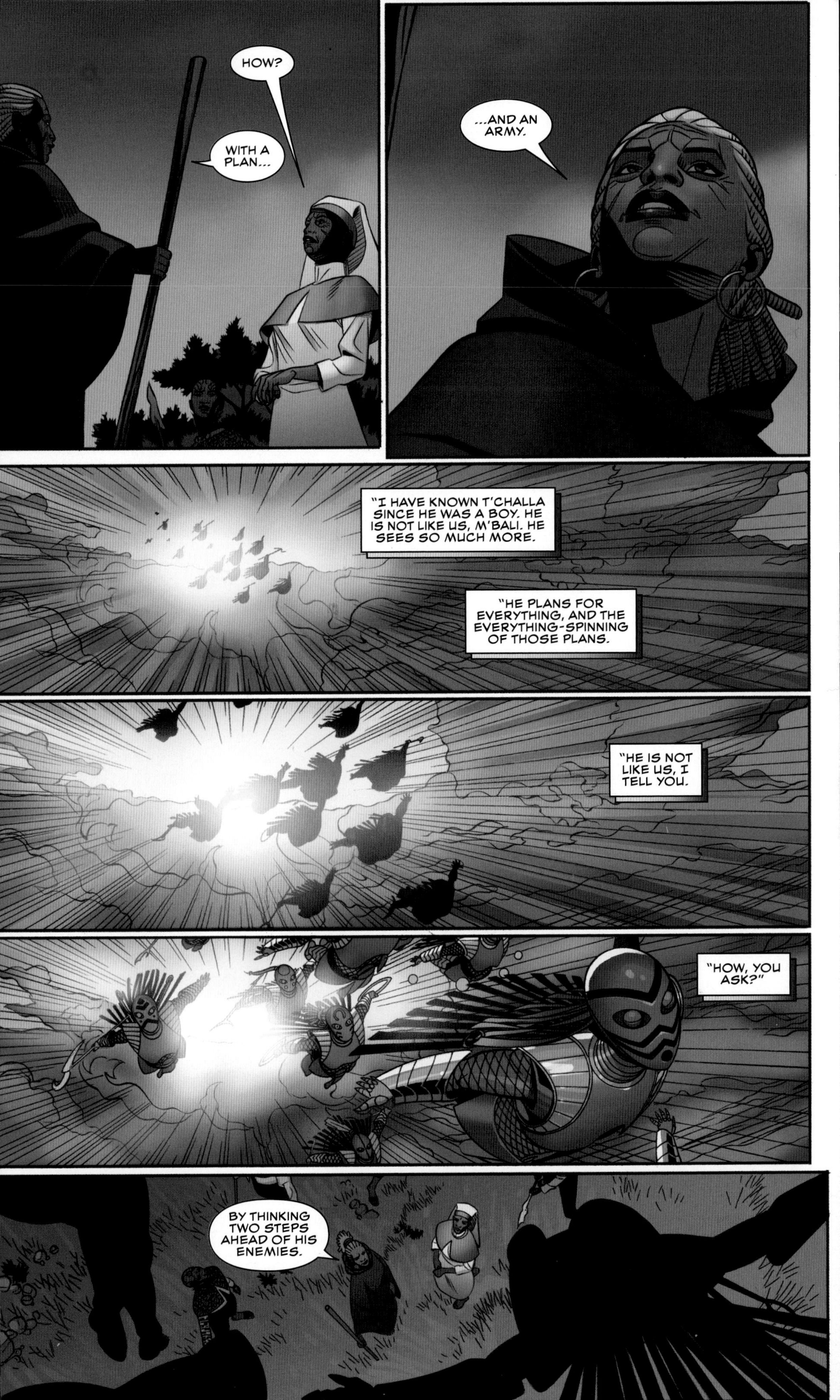

HOW?
WITH A PLAN...
...AND AN ARMY.
"I HAVE KNOWN T'CHALLA SINCE HE WAS A BOY. HE IS NOT LIKE US, M'BALI. HE SEES SO MUCH MORE.
"HE PLANS FOR EVERYTHING, AND THE EVERYTHING-SPINNING OF THOSE PLANS.
"HE IS NOT LIKE US, I TELL YOU.
"HOW, YOU ASK?"
BY THINKING TWO STEPS AHEAD OF HIS ENEMIES.

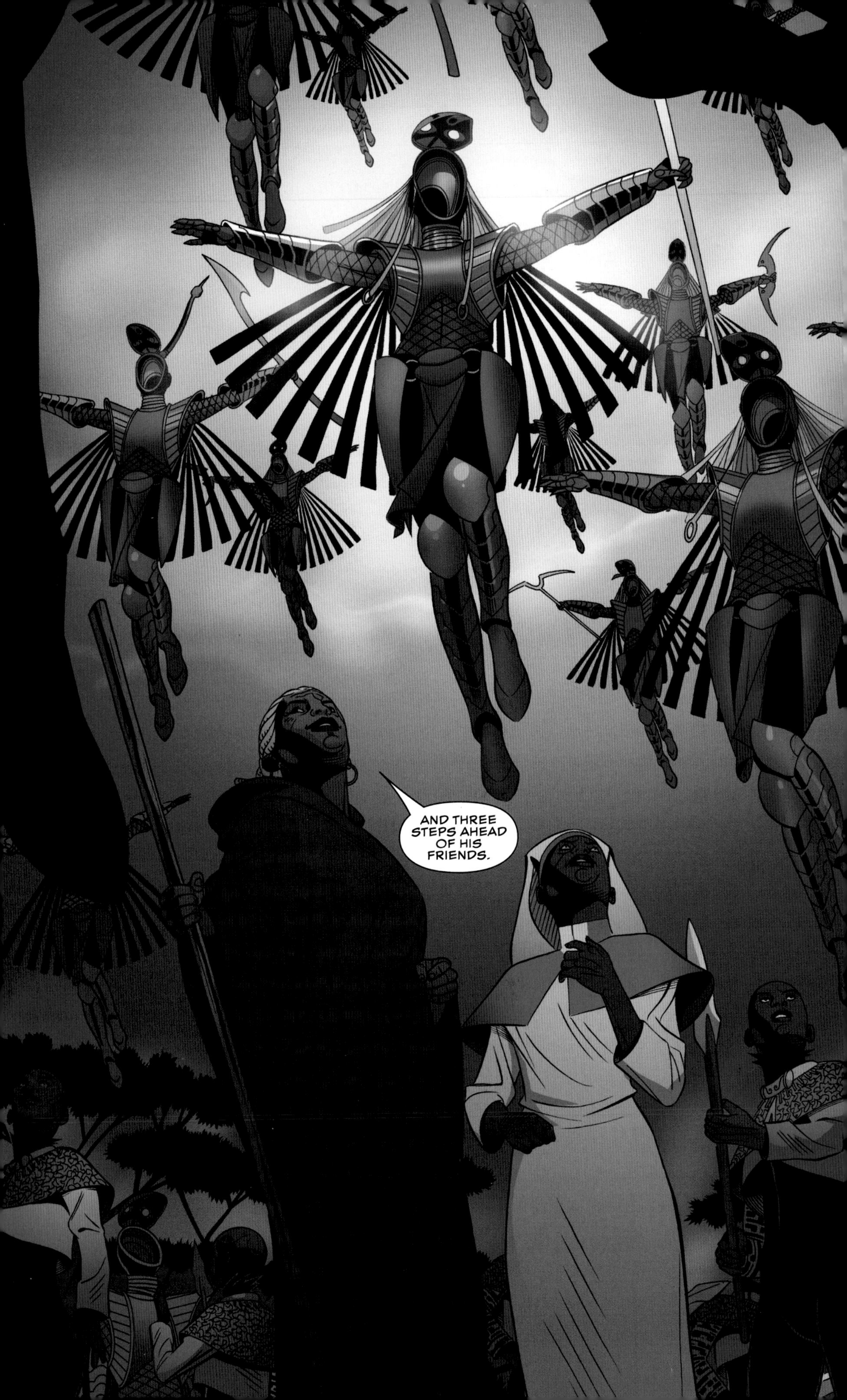
AND THREE STEPS AHEAD OF HIS FRIENDS.

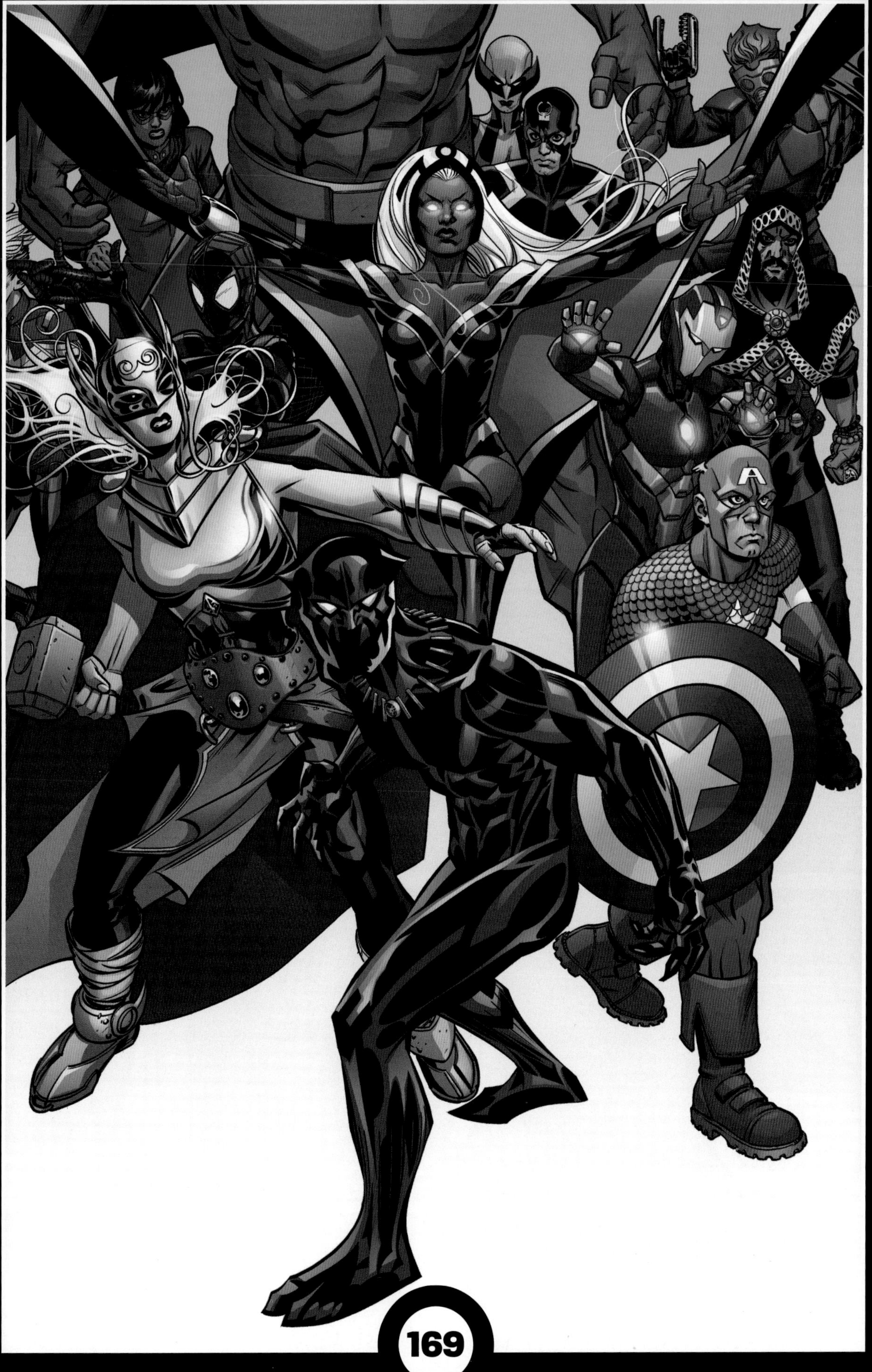

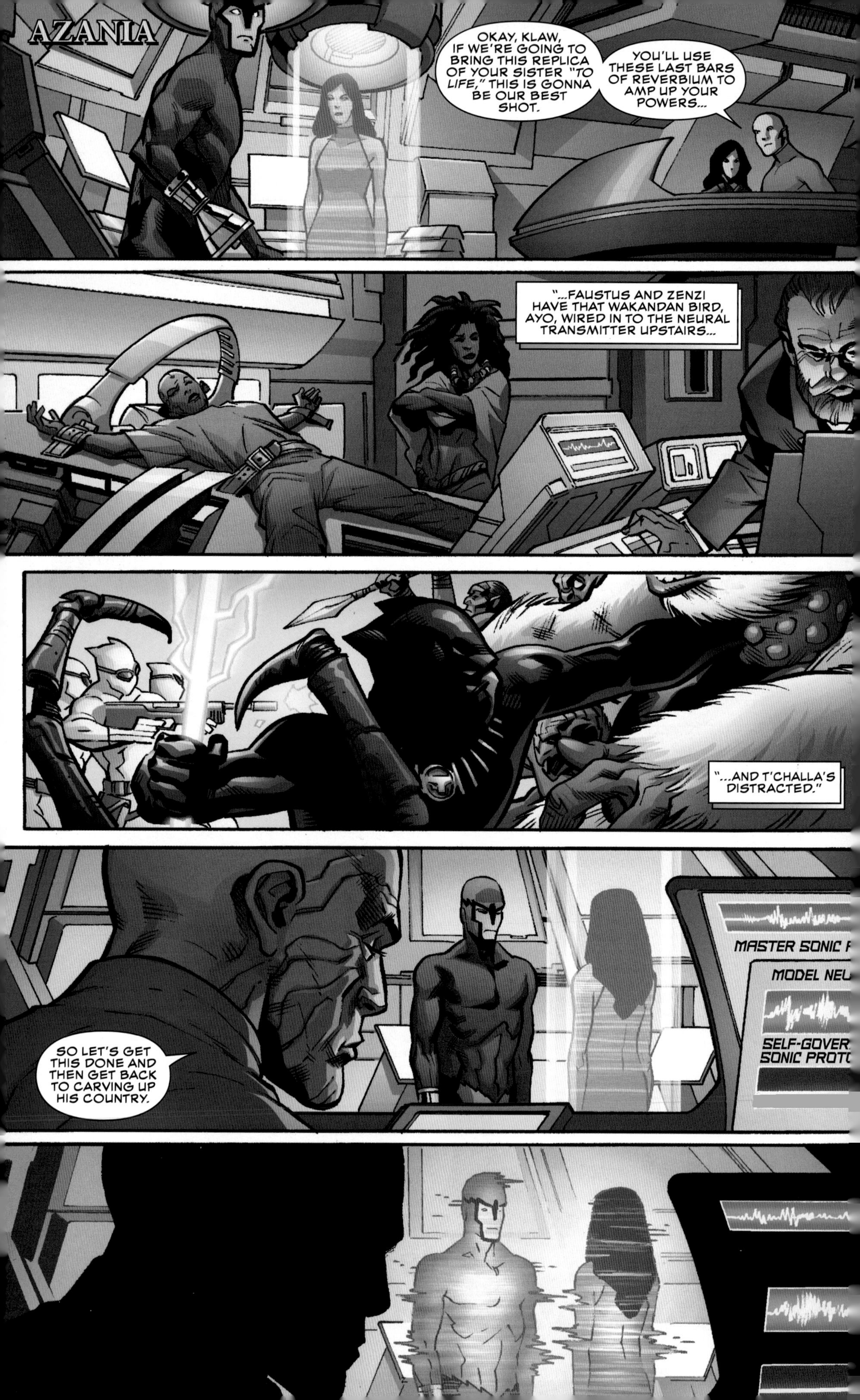
AZANIA
OKAY, KLAW, IF WE'RE GOING TO BRING THIS REPLICA OF YOUR SISTER "TO LIFE," THIS IS GONNA BE OUR BEST SHOT.
YOU'LL USE THESE LAST BARS OF REVERBIUM TO AMP UP YOUR POWERS...
"...FAUSTUS AND ZENZI HAVE THAT WAKANDAN BIRD, AYO, WIRED IN TO THE NEURAL TRANSMITTER UPSTAIRS...
"...AND T'CHALLA'S DISTRACTED."
MASTER SONIC
MODEL NEU
SELF-GOVER
SONIC PROT
SO LET'S GET THIS DONE AND THEN GET BACK TO CARVING UP HIS COUNTRY.

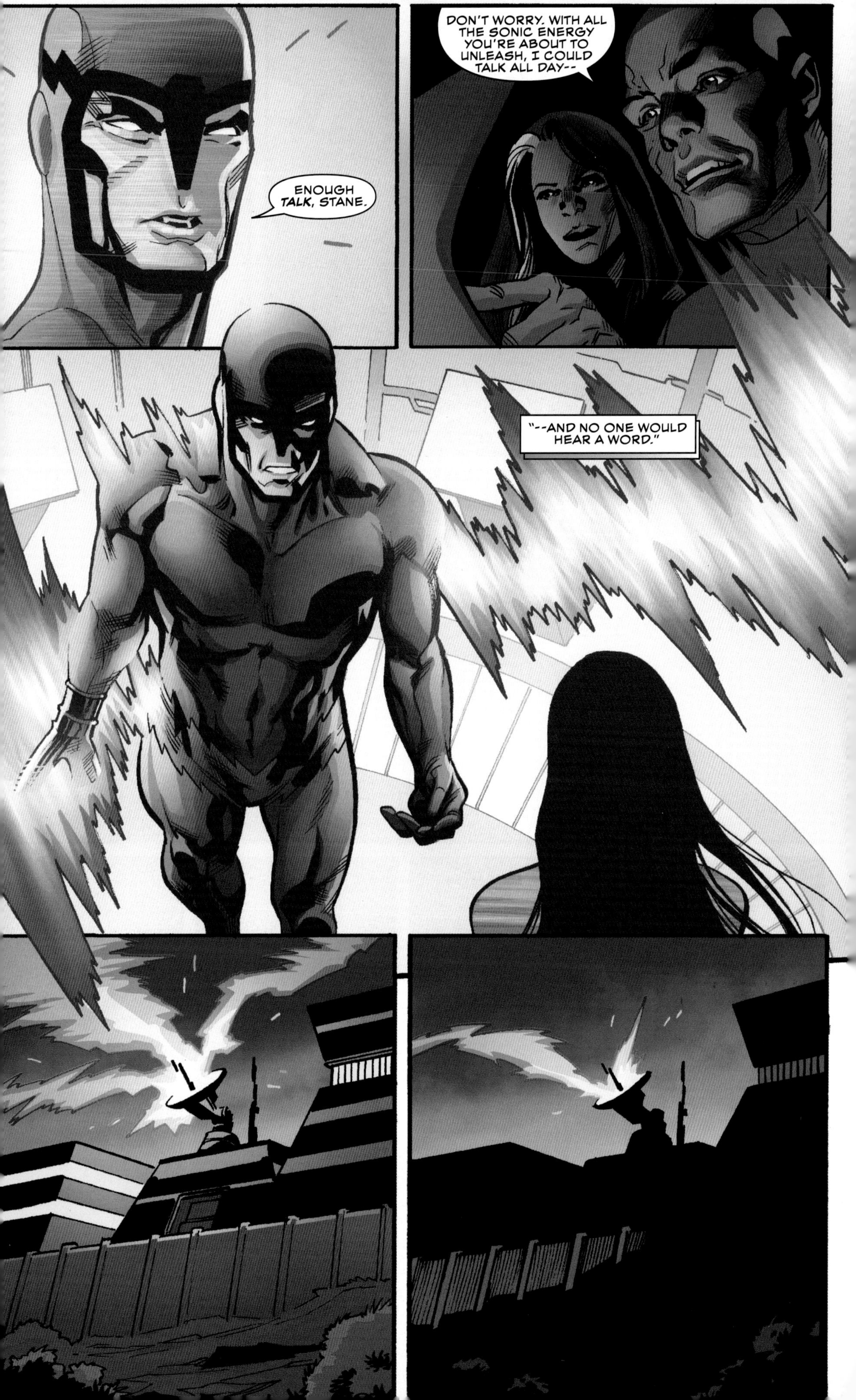
ENOUGH TALK, STANE.
DON'T WORRY. WITH ALL THE SONIC ENERGY YOU'RE ABOUT TO UNLEASH, I COULD TALK ALL DAY--
"--AND NO ONE WOULD HEAR A WORD."

C'MON, BOYS, LET'S HURRY UP AND GET THIS ONE TO HER CELL.

FAUSTUS TOOK HER GIRLFRIEND UPSTAIRS FOR "EXAMINATION."

HEY, MAYBE WE'LL GET OUR OWN SHOT AT

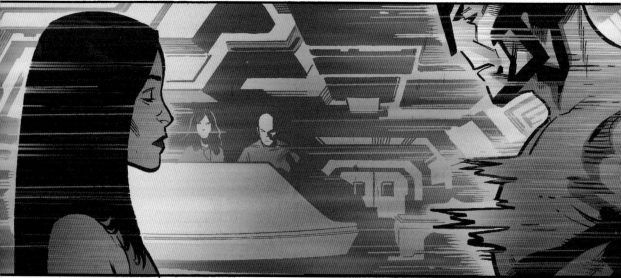

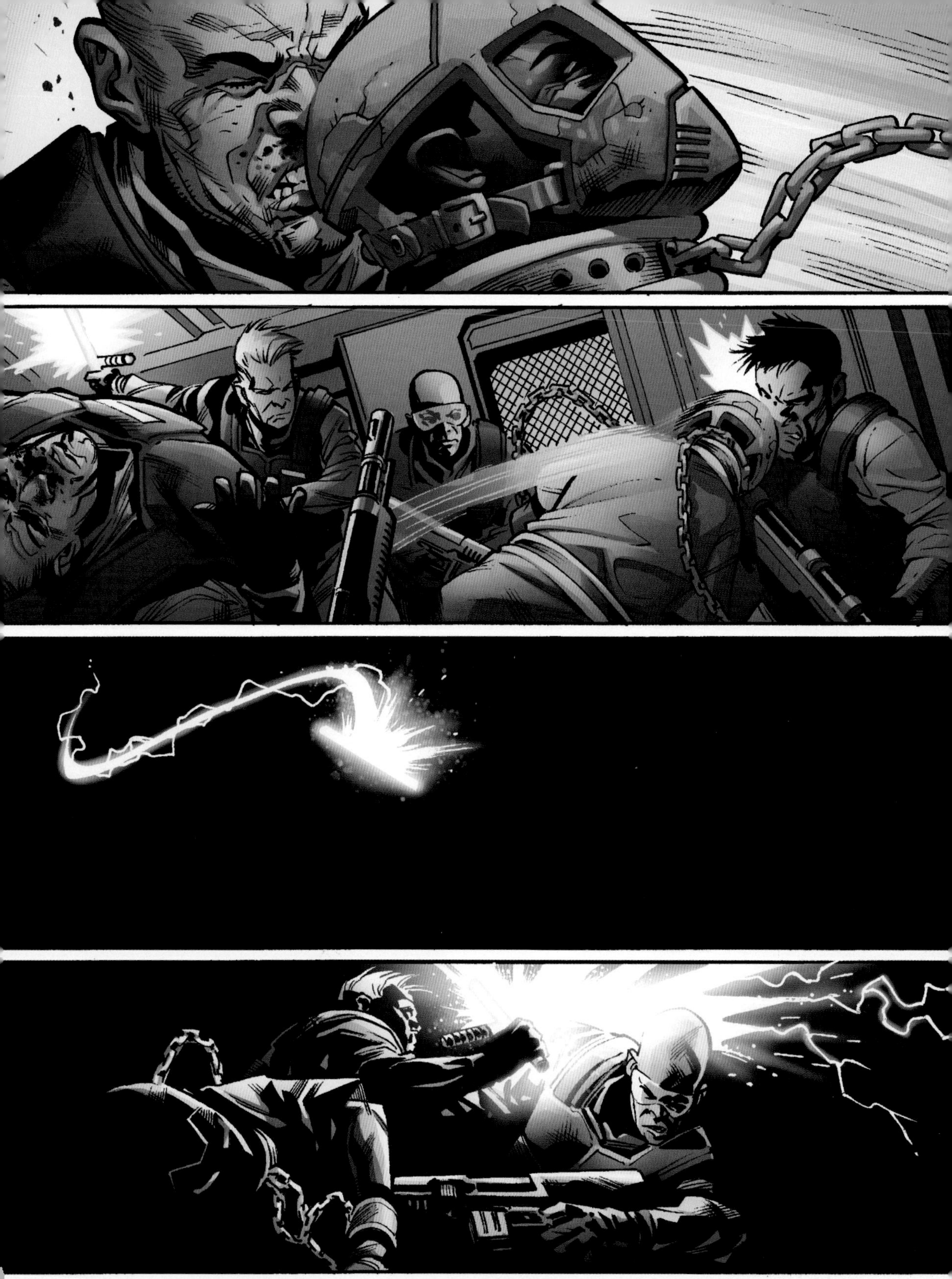

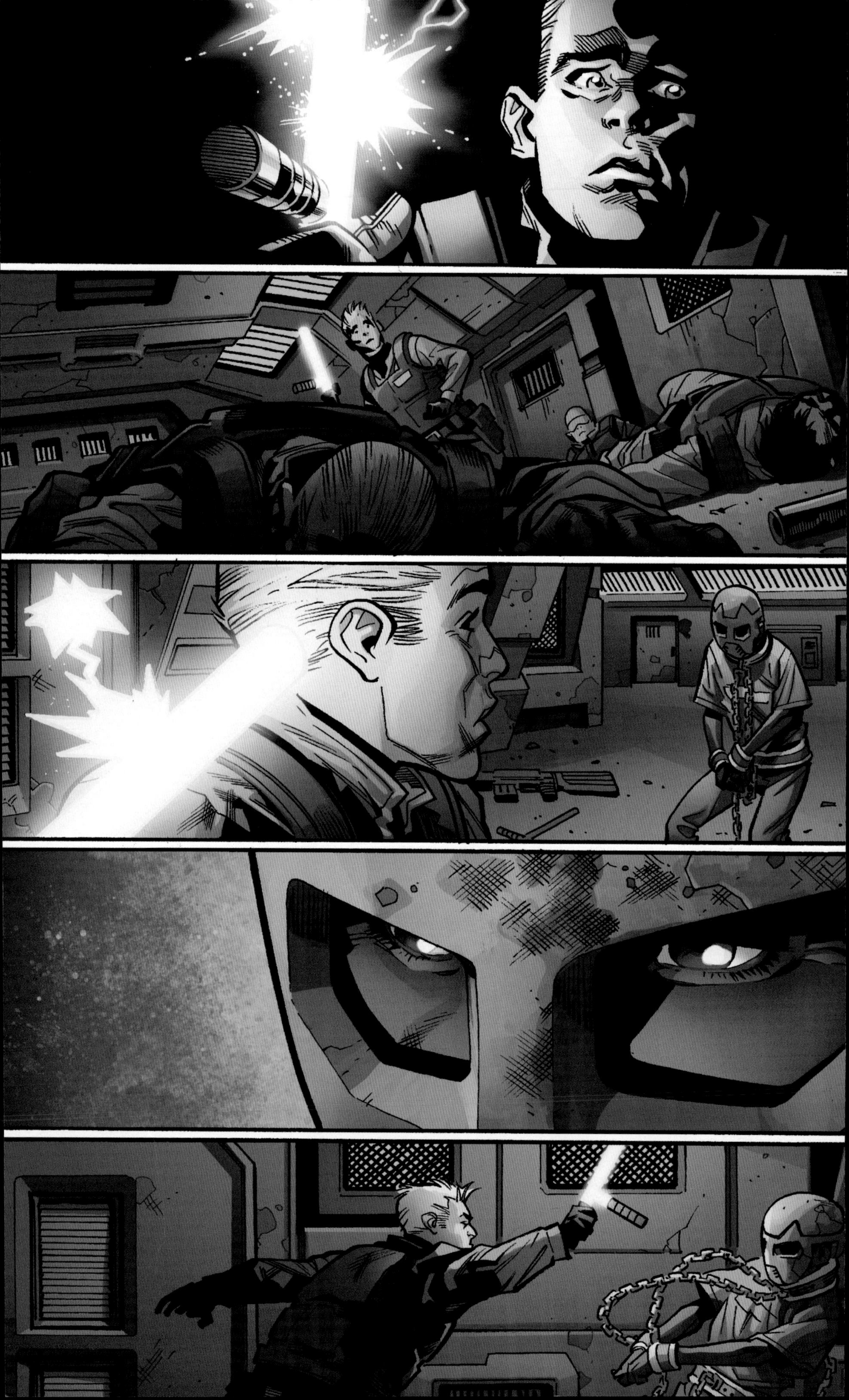

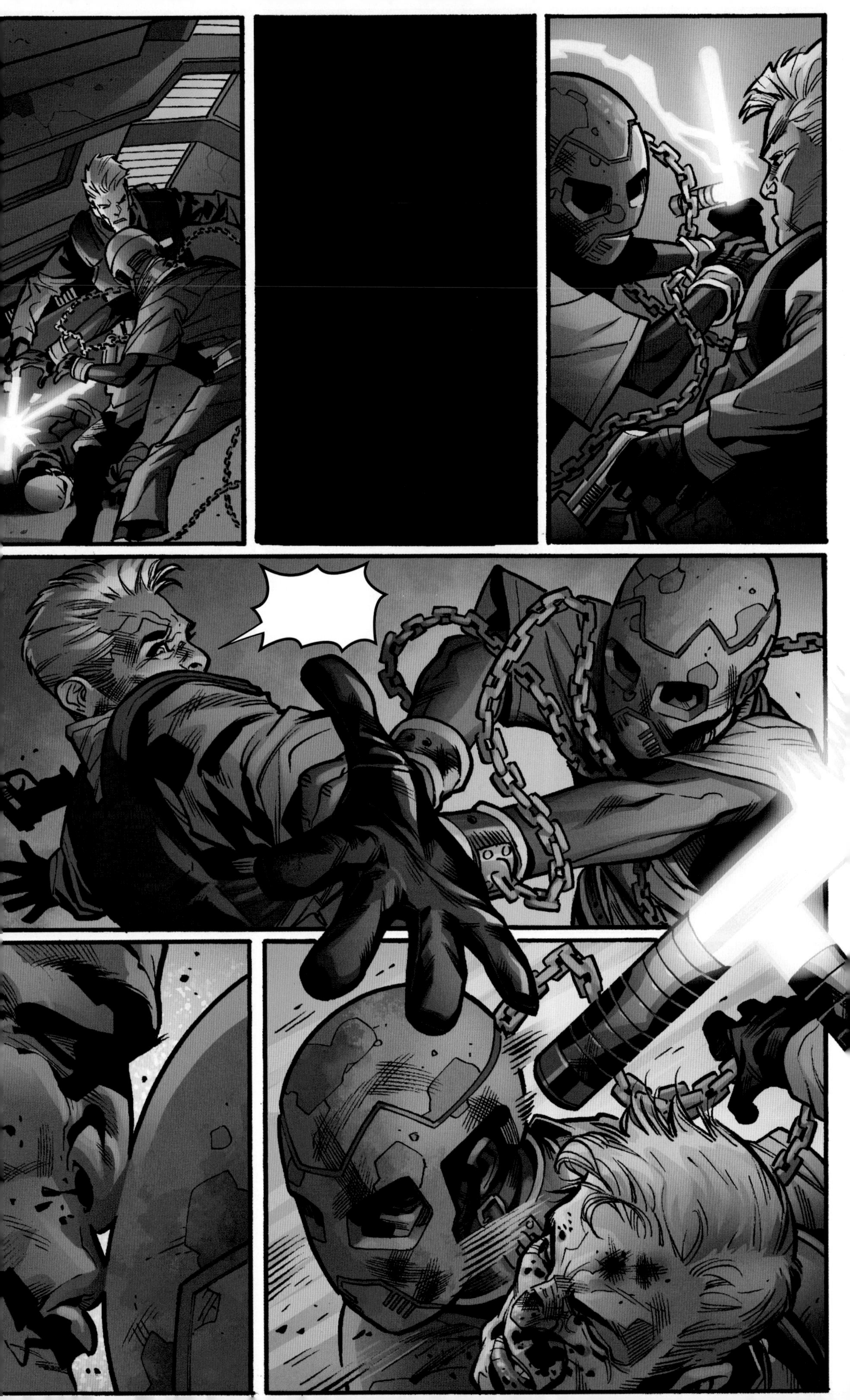

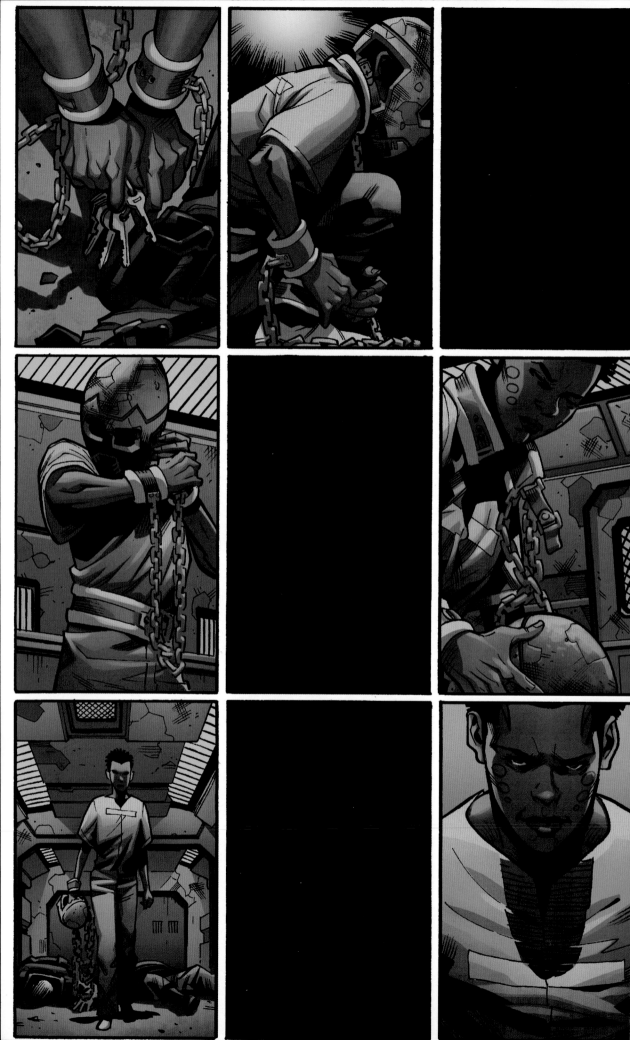

ALERT

!

INVASION COMMENCING-- ASSISTANCE REQUESTED

SITUATION CRITICAL

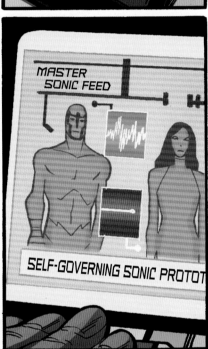

MASTER SONIC FEED

SELF-GOVERNING SONIC PROTOT

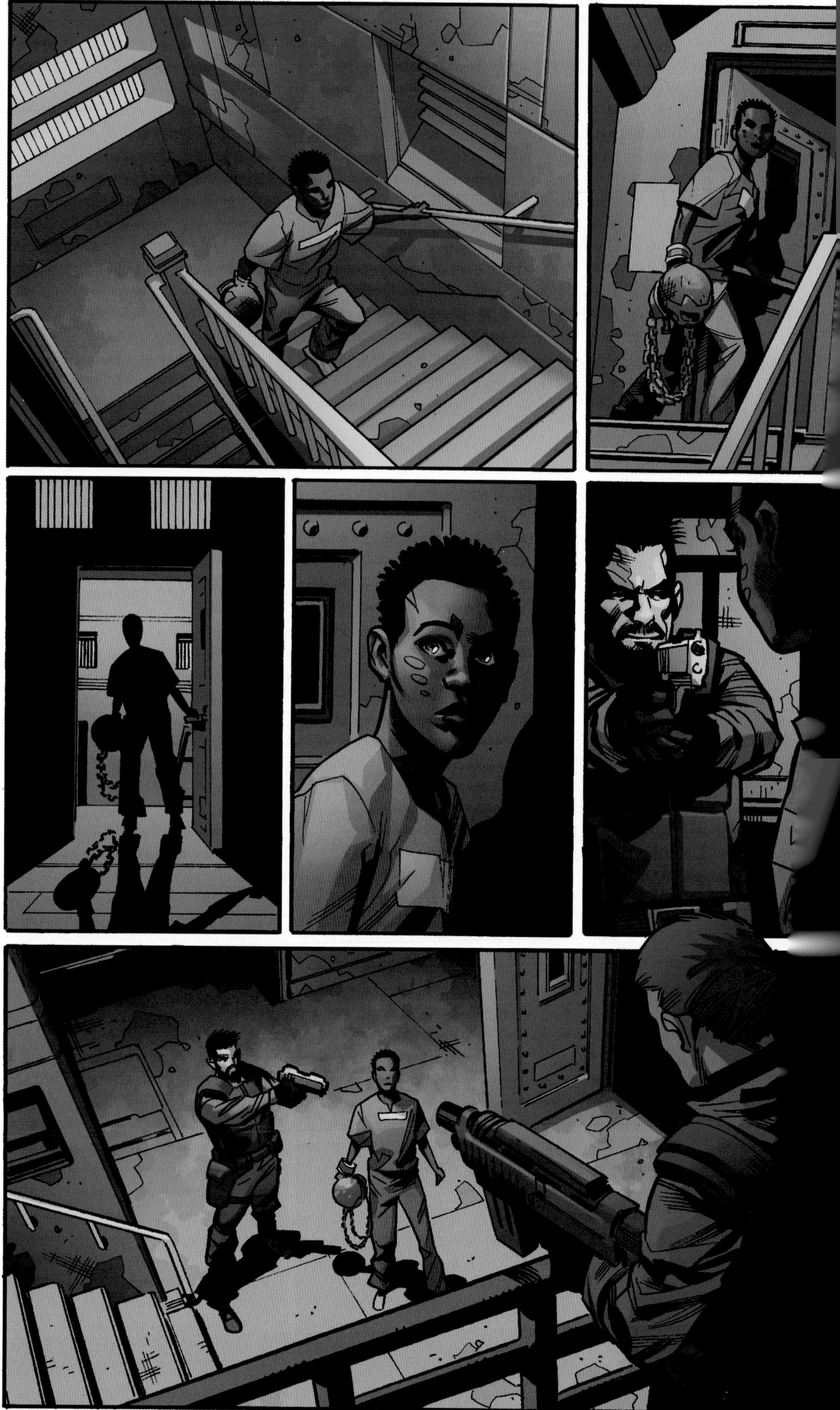

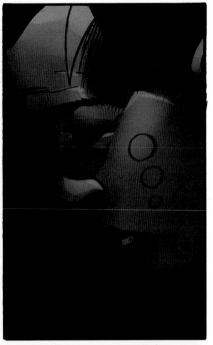

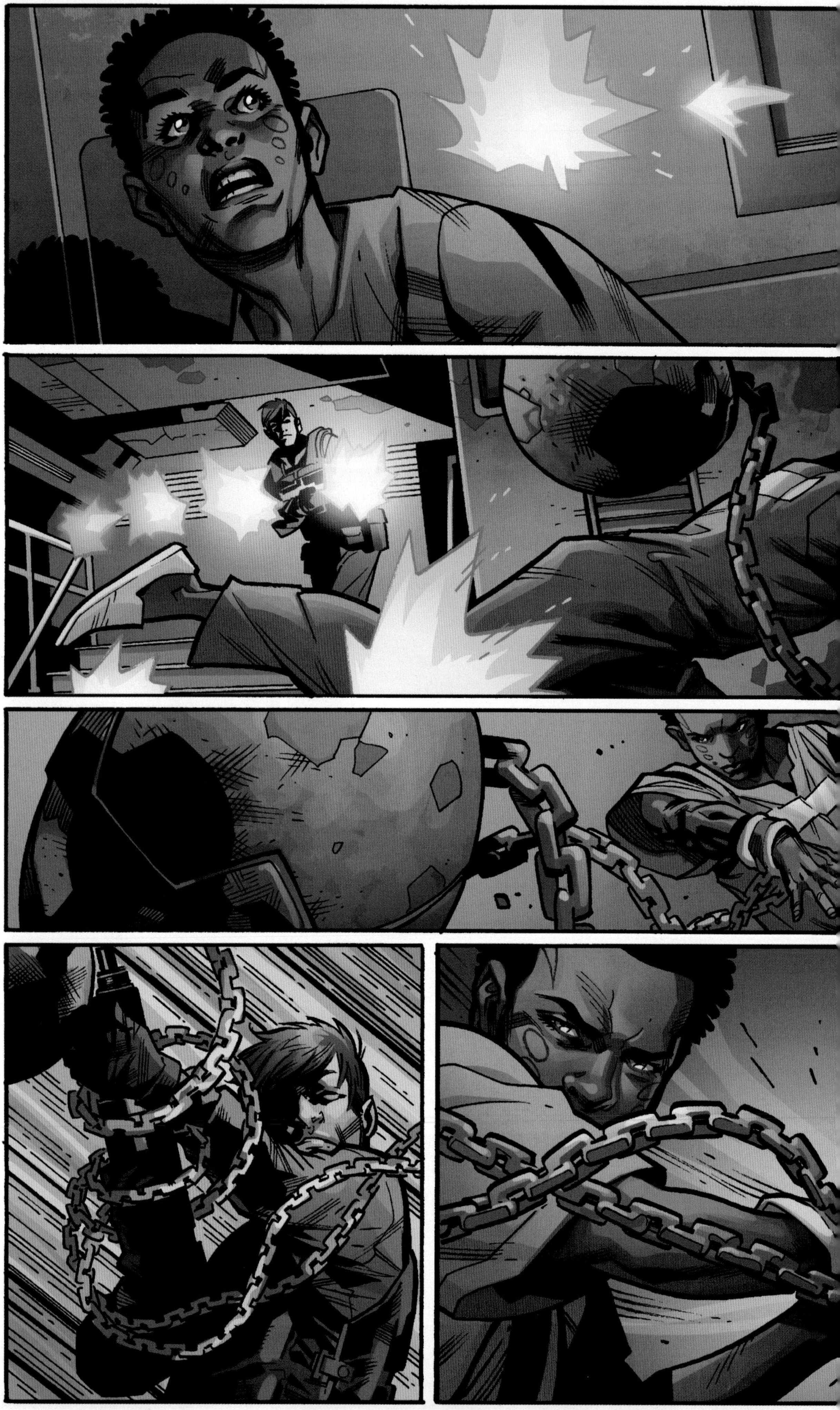

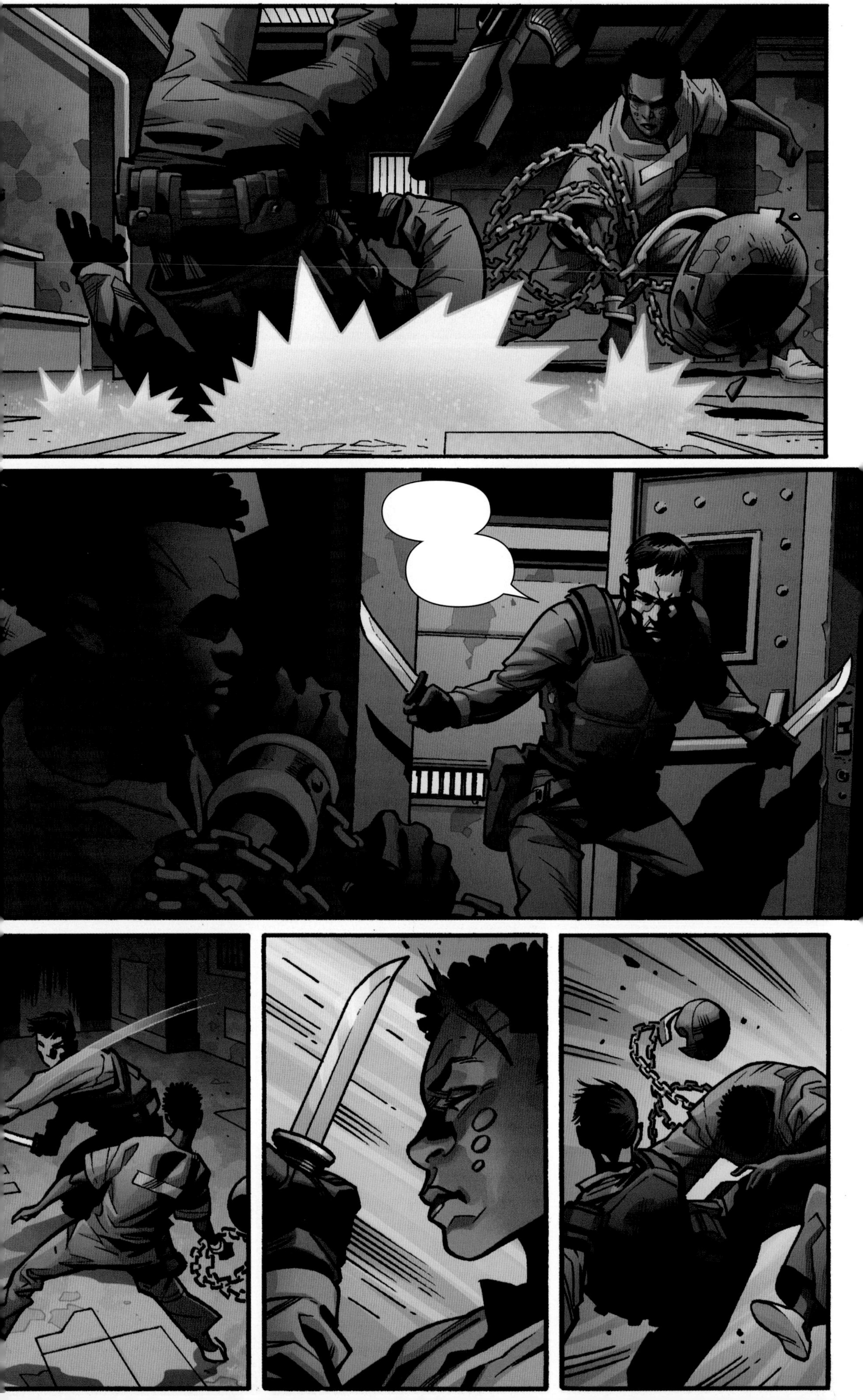

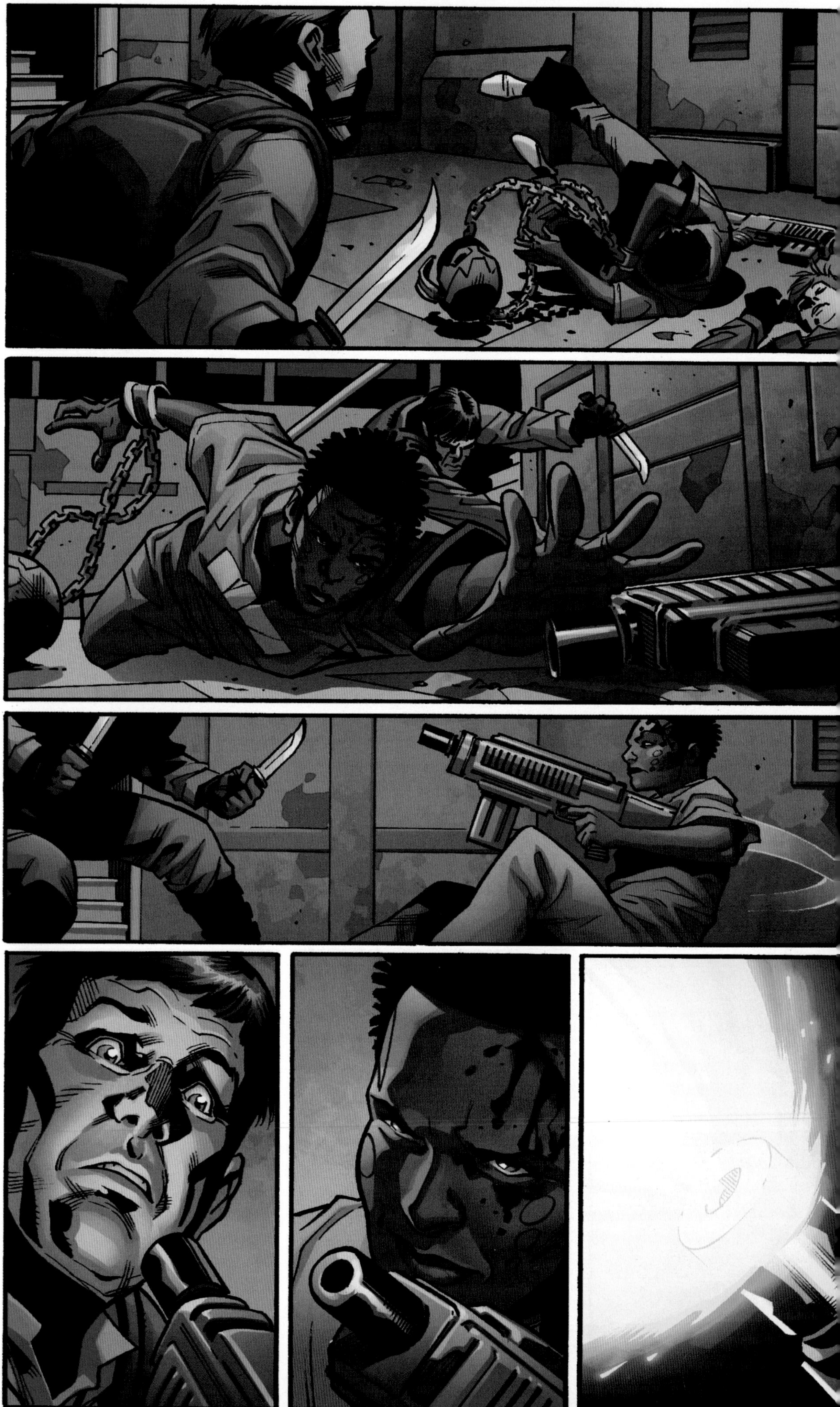

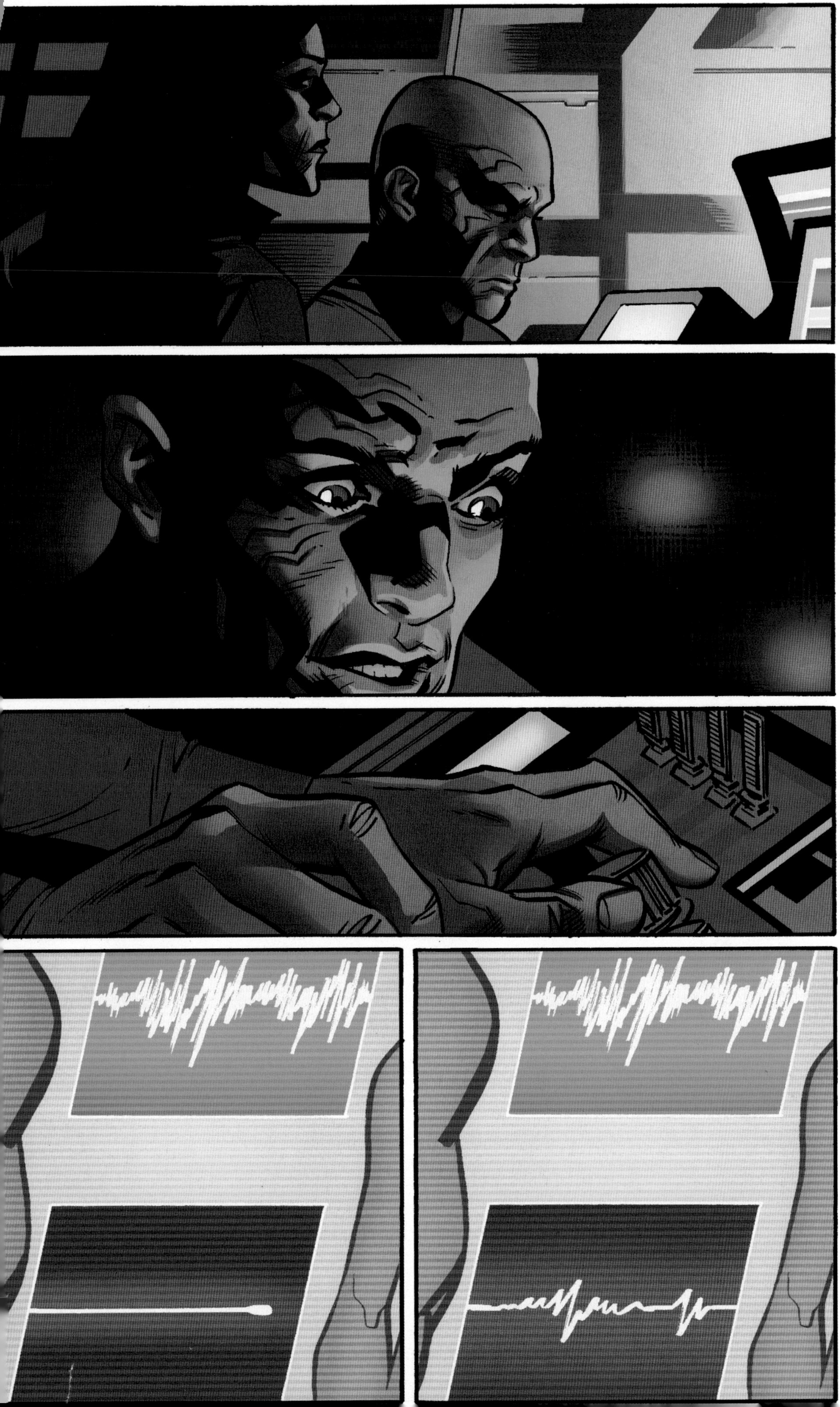

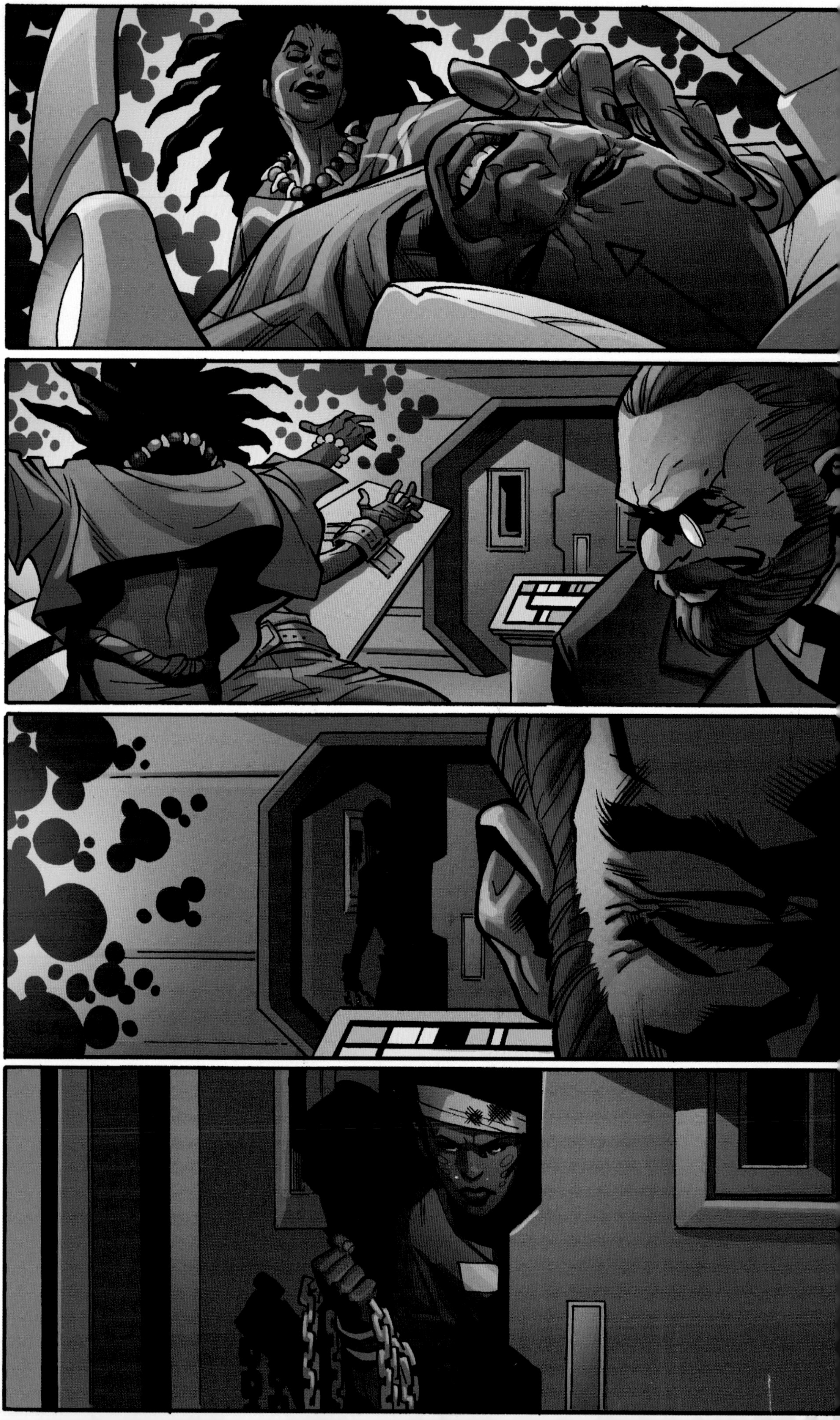

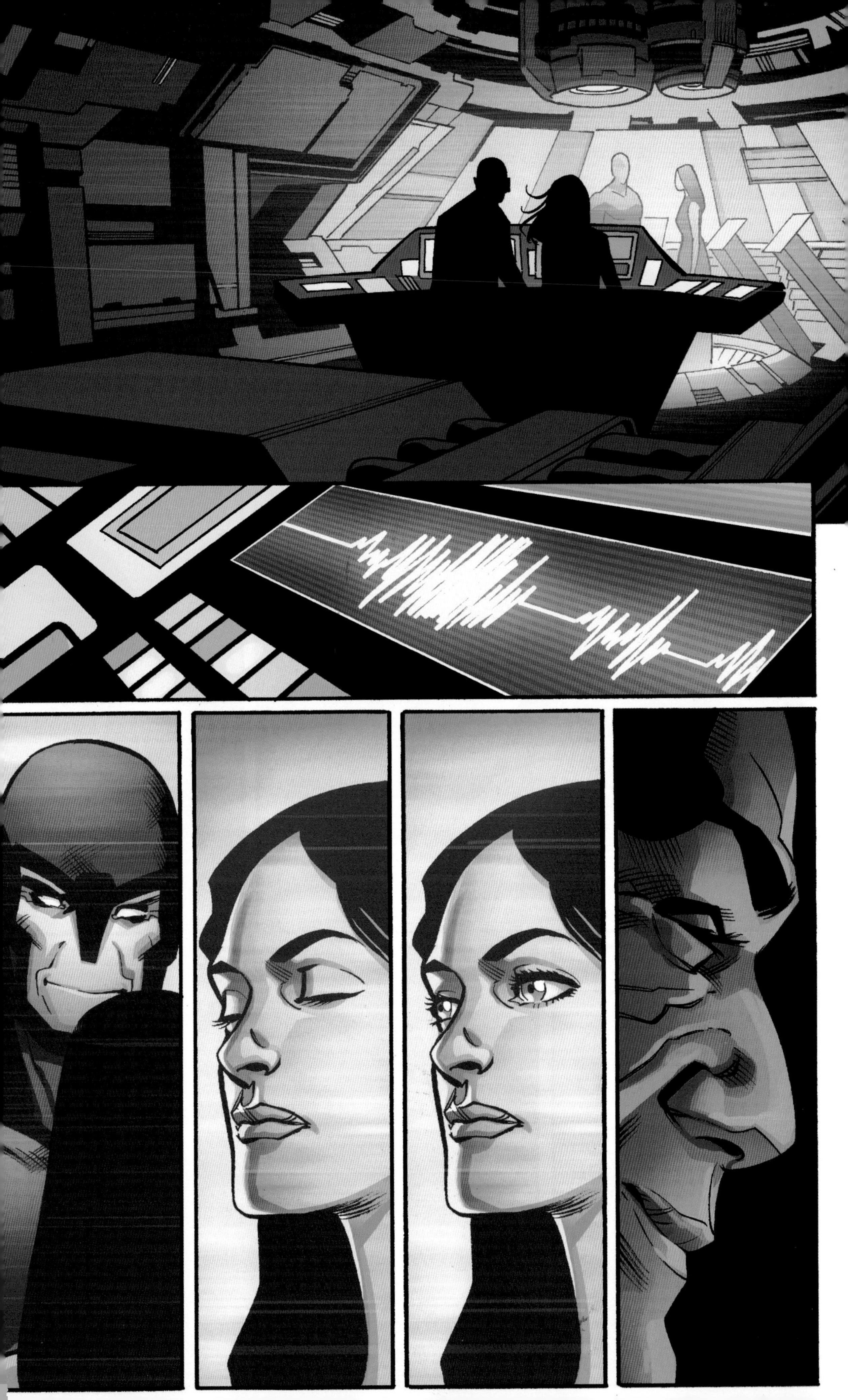

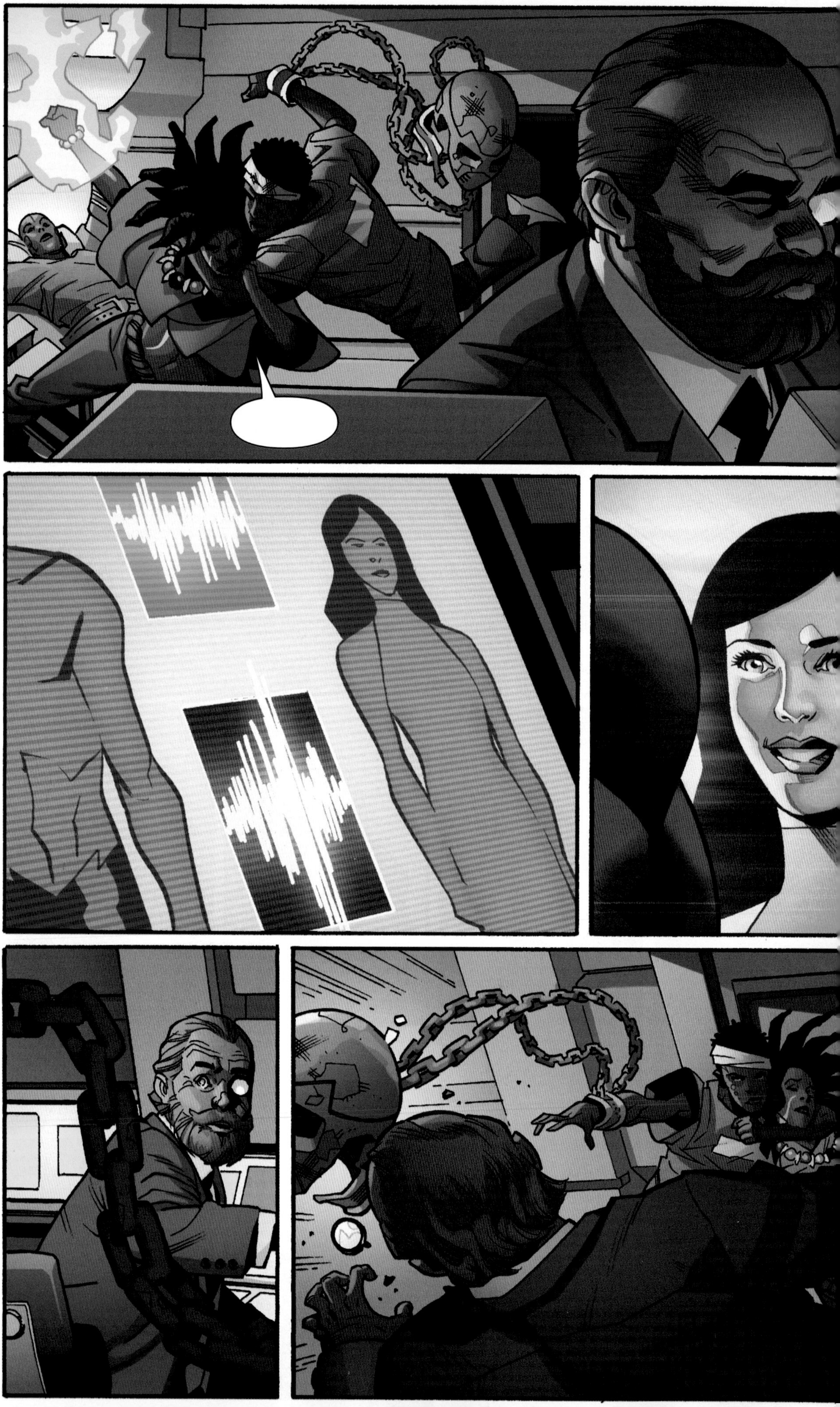

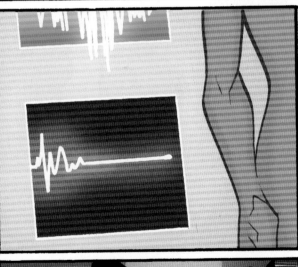

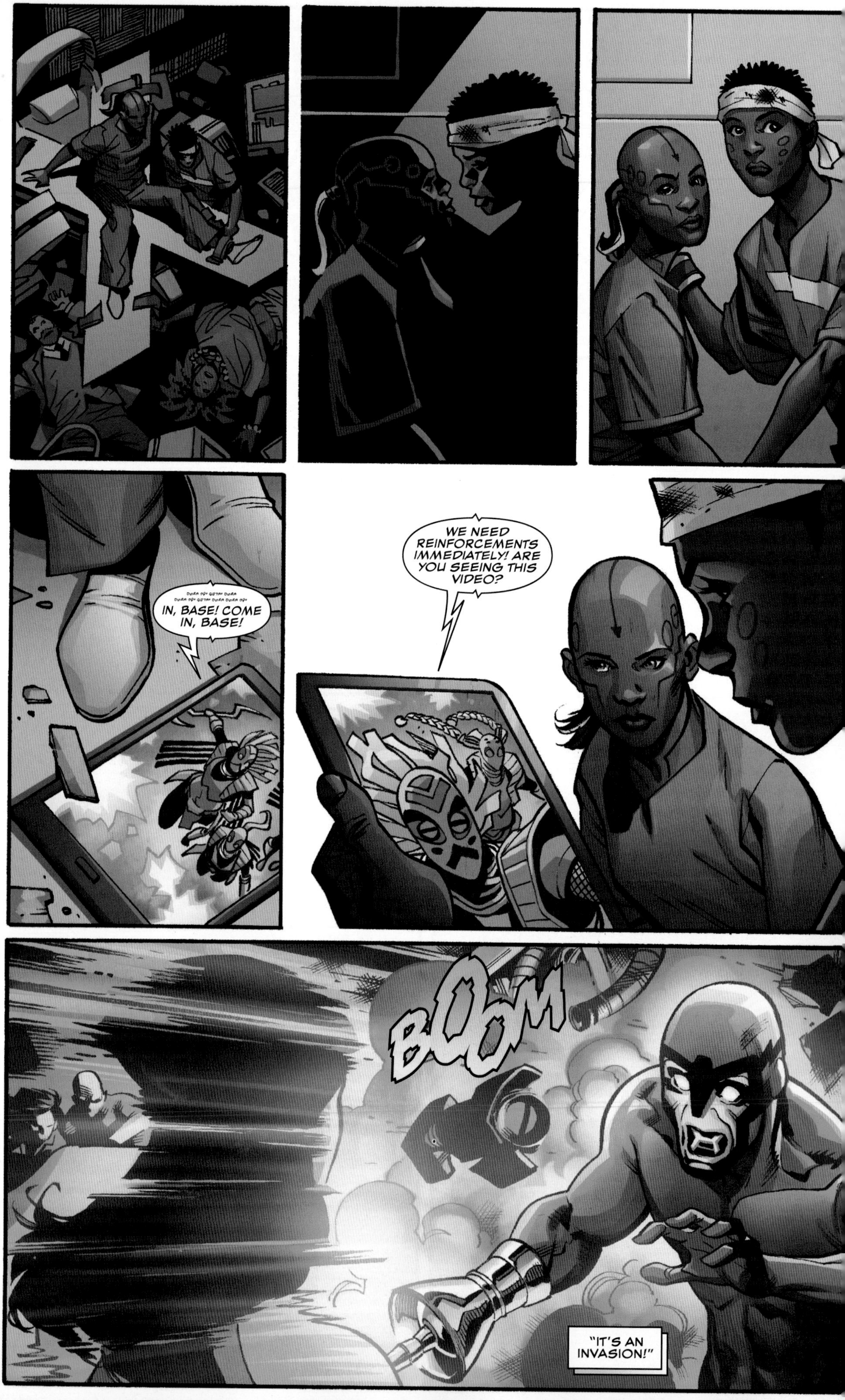

IN, BASE! COME IN, BASE!
WE NEED REINFORCEMENTS IMMEDIATELY! ARE YOU SEEING THIS VIDEO?
BOOM
"IT'S AN INVASION!"

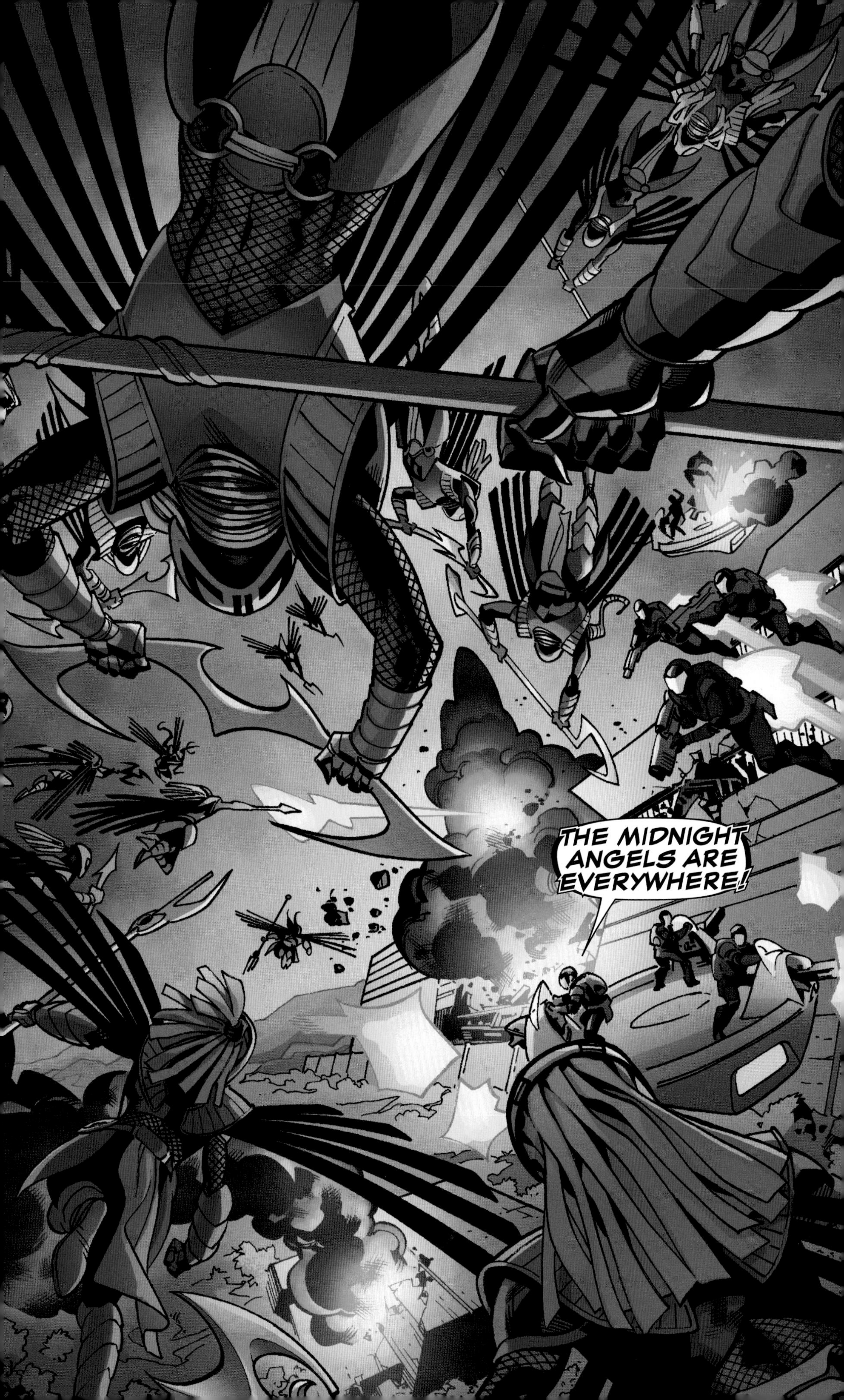
THE MIDNIGHT ANGELS ARE EVERYWHERE!

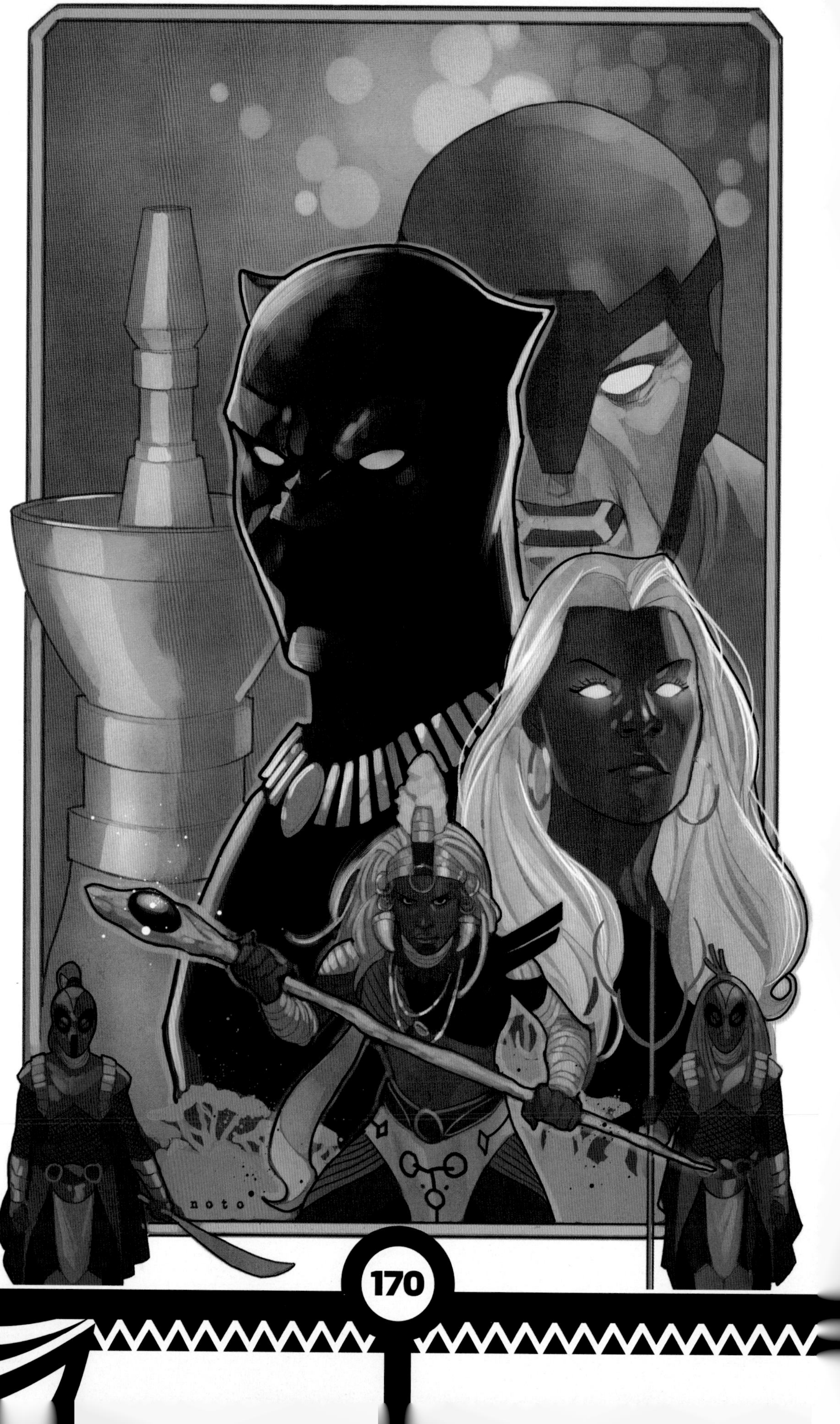
noto
170

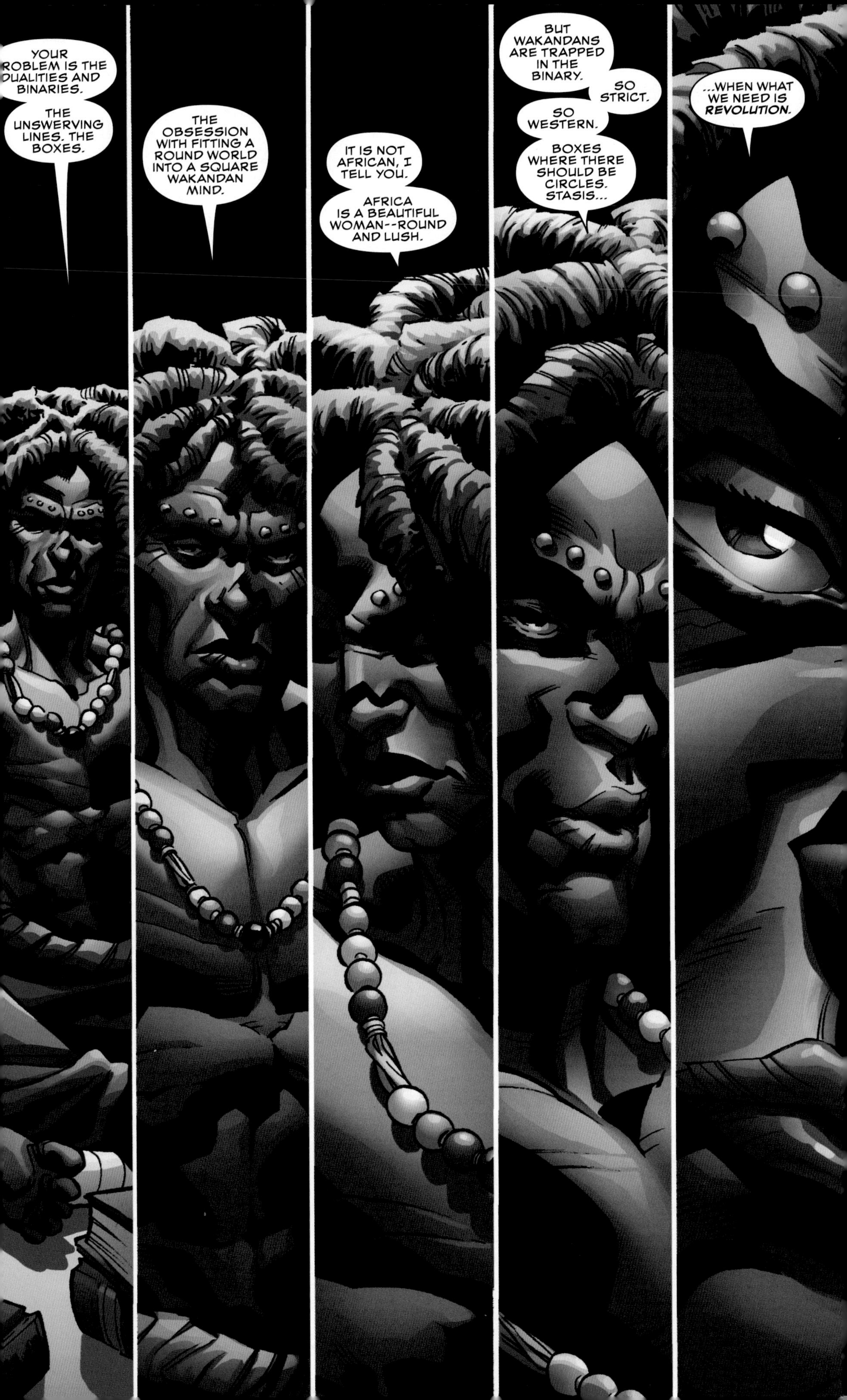
YOUR PROBLEM IS THE DUALITIES AND BINARIES.
THE UNSWERVING LINES. THE BOXES.
THE OBSESSION WITH FITTING A ROUND WORLD INTO A SQUARE WAKANDAN MIND.
IT IS NOT AFRICAN, I TELL YOU.
AFRICA IS A BEAUTIFUL WOMAN--ROUND AND LUSH.
BUT WAKANDANS ARE TRAPPED IN THE BINARY.
SO STRICT.
SO WESTERN.
BOXES WHERE THERE SHOULD BE CIRCLES. STASIS...
...WHEN WHAT WE NEED IS REVOLUTION.

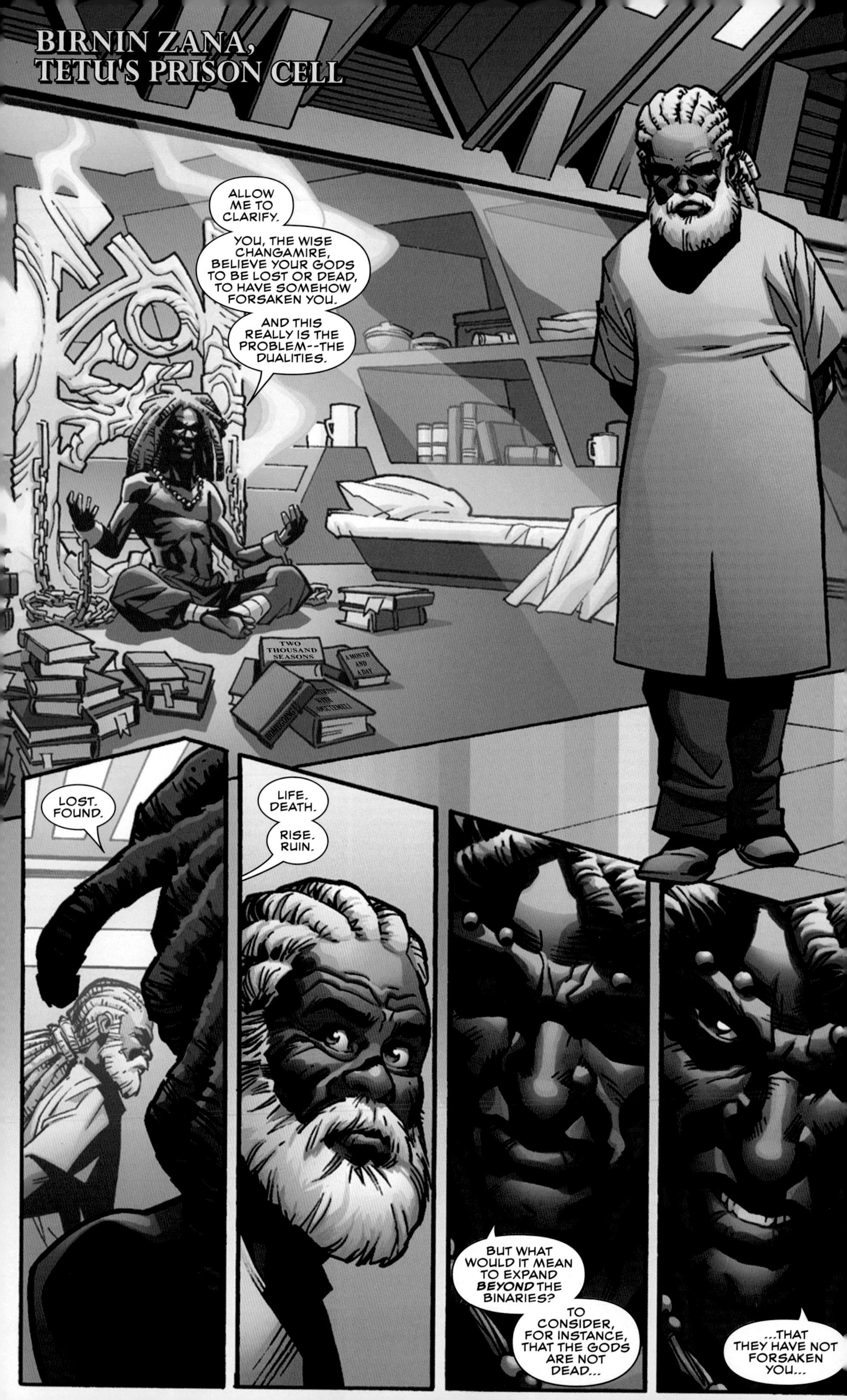
BIRNIN ZANA, TETU'S PRISON CELL
ALLOW ME TO CLARIFY.
YOU, THE WISE CHANGAMIRE, BELIEVE YOUR GODS TO BE LOST OR DEAD, TO HAVE SOMEHOW FORSAKEN YOU.
AND THIS REALLY IS THE PROBLEM--THE DUALITIES.
TWO THOUSAND SEASONS
A MONTH AND A DAY
HOMEGOING
LOST. FOUND.
LIFE. DEATH.
RISE. RUIN.
BUT WHAT WOULD IT MEAN TO EXPAND *BEYOND* THE BINARIES?
TO CONSIDER, FOR INSTANCE, THAT THE GODS ARE NOT DEAD...
...THAT THEY HAVE NOT FORSAKEN YOU...

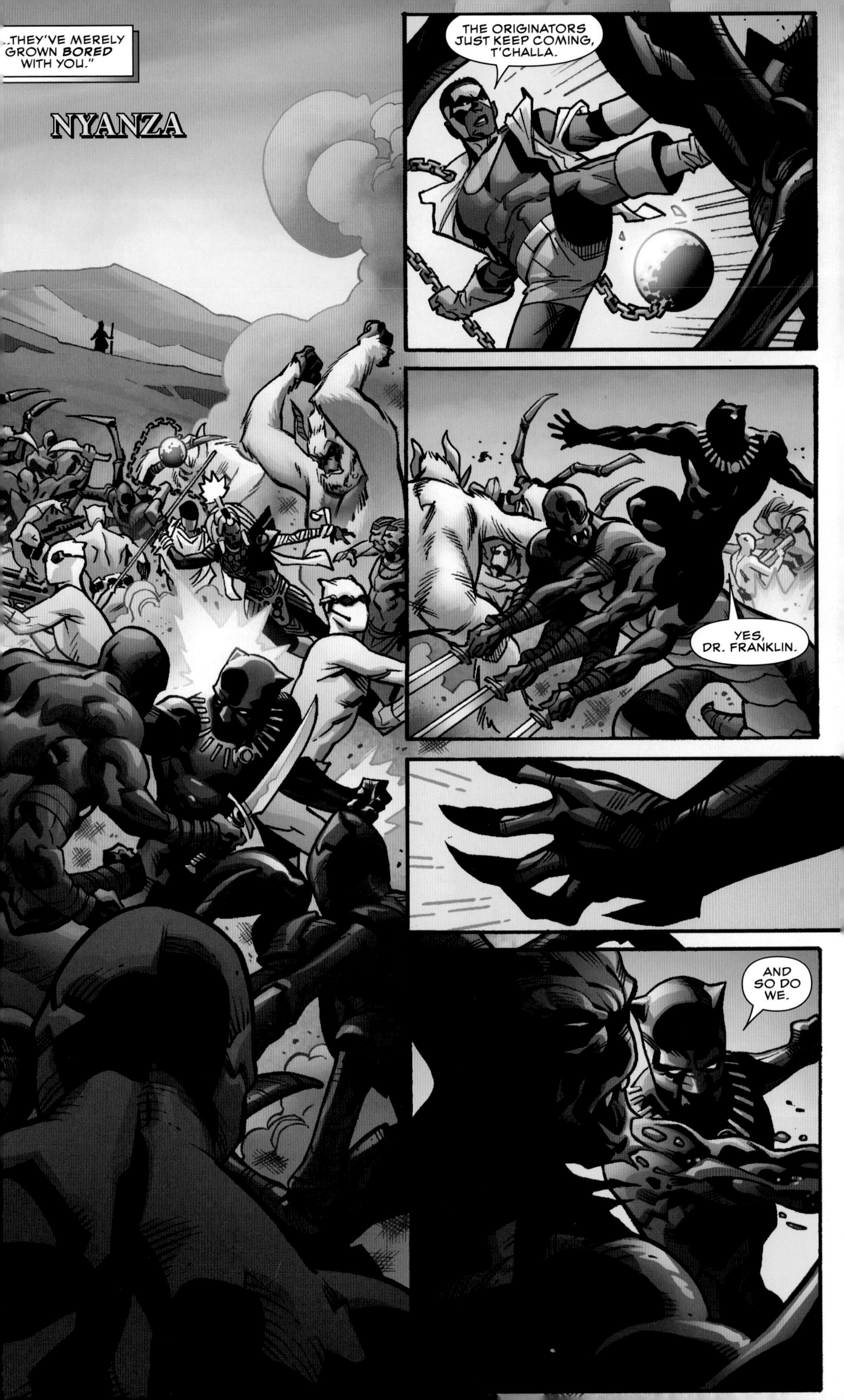
"...THEY'VE MERELY GROWN *BORED* WITH YOU."
NYANZA
THE ORIGINATORS JUST KEEP COMING, T'CHALLA.
YES, DR. FRANKLIN.
AND SO DO WE.

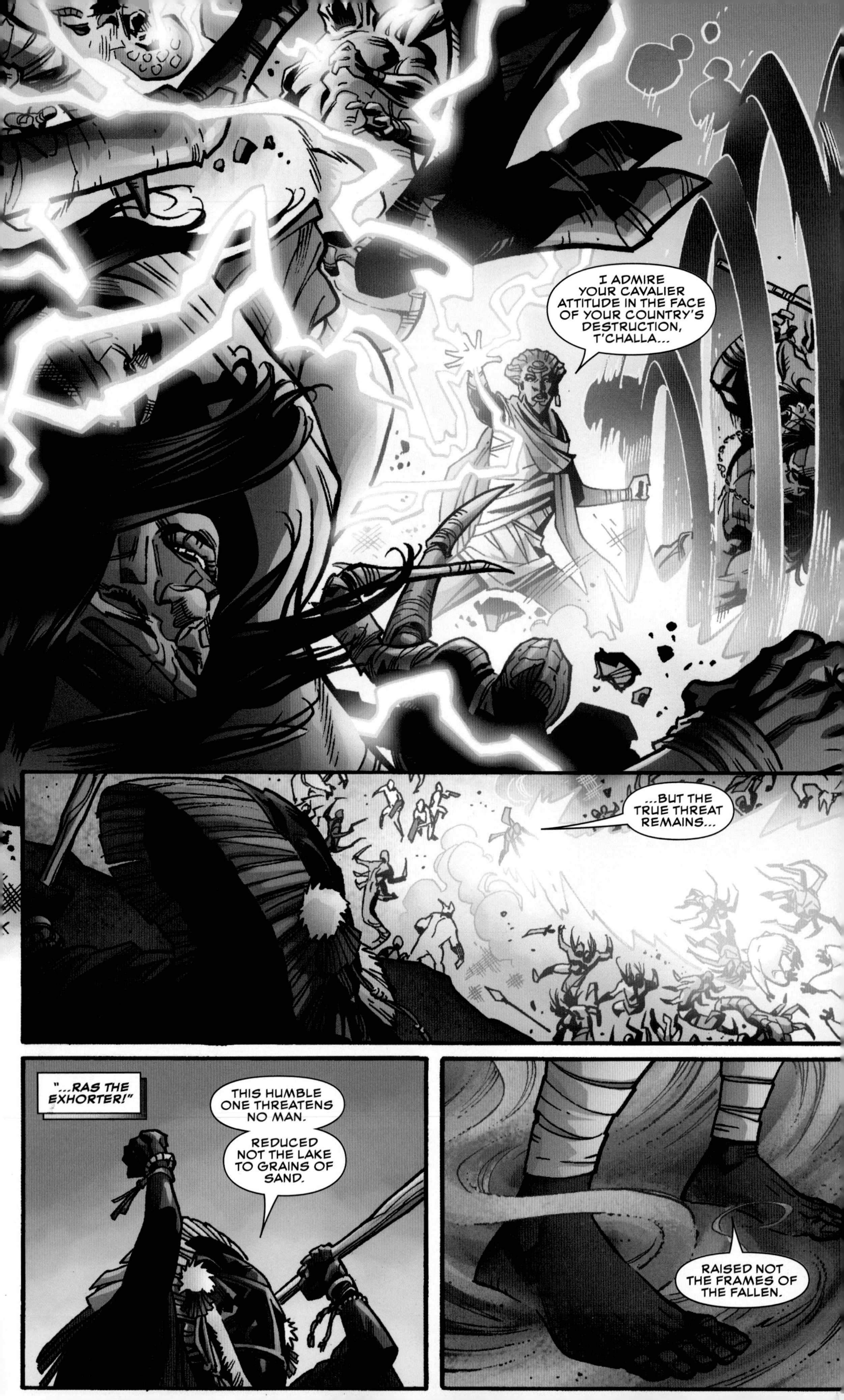
I ADMIRE YOUR CAVALIER ATTITUDE IN THE FACE OF YOUR COUNTRY'S DESTRUCTION, T'CHALLA...
...BUT THE TRUE THREAT REMAINS...
"...RAS THE EXHORTER!"
THIS HUMBLE ONE THREATENS NO MAN.
REDUCED NOT THE LAKE TO GRAINS OF SAND.
RAISED NOT THE FRAMES OF THE FALLEN.

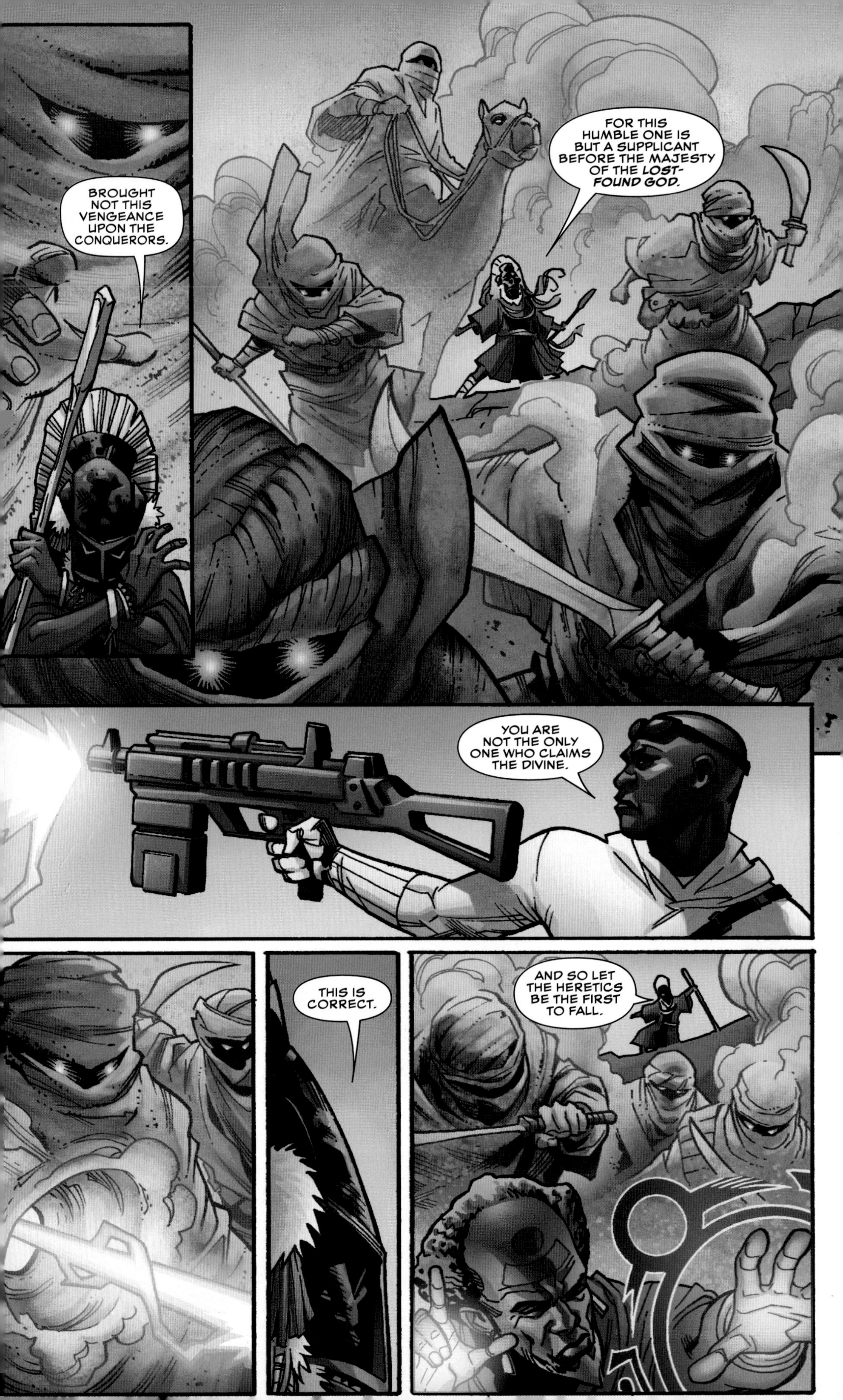
BROUGHT NOT THIS VENGEANCE UPON THE CONQUERORS.
FOR THIS HUMBLE ONE IS BUT A SUPPLICANT BEFORE THE MAJESTY OF THE *LOST-FOUND GOD.*
YOU ARE NOT THE ONLY ONE WHO CLAIMS THE DIVINE.
THIS IS CORRECT.
AND SO LET THE HERETICS BE THE FIRST TO FALL.

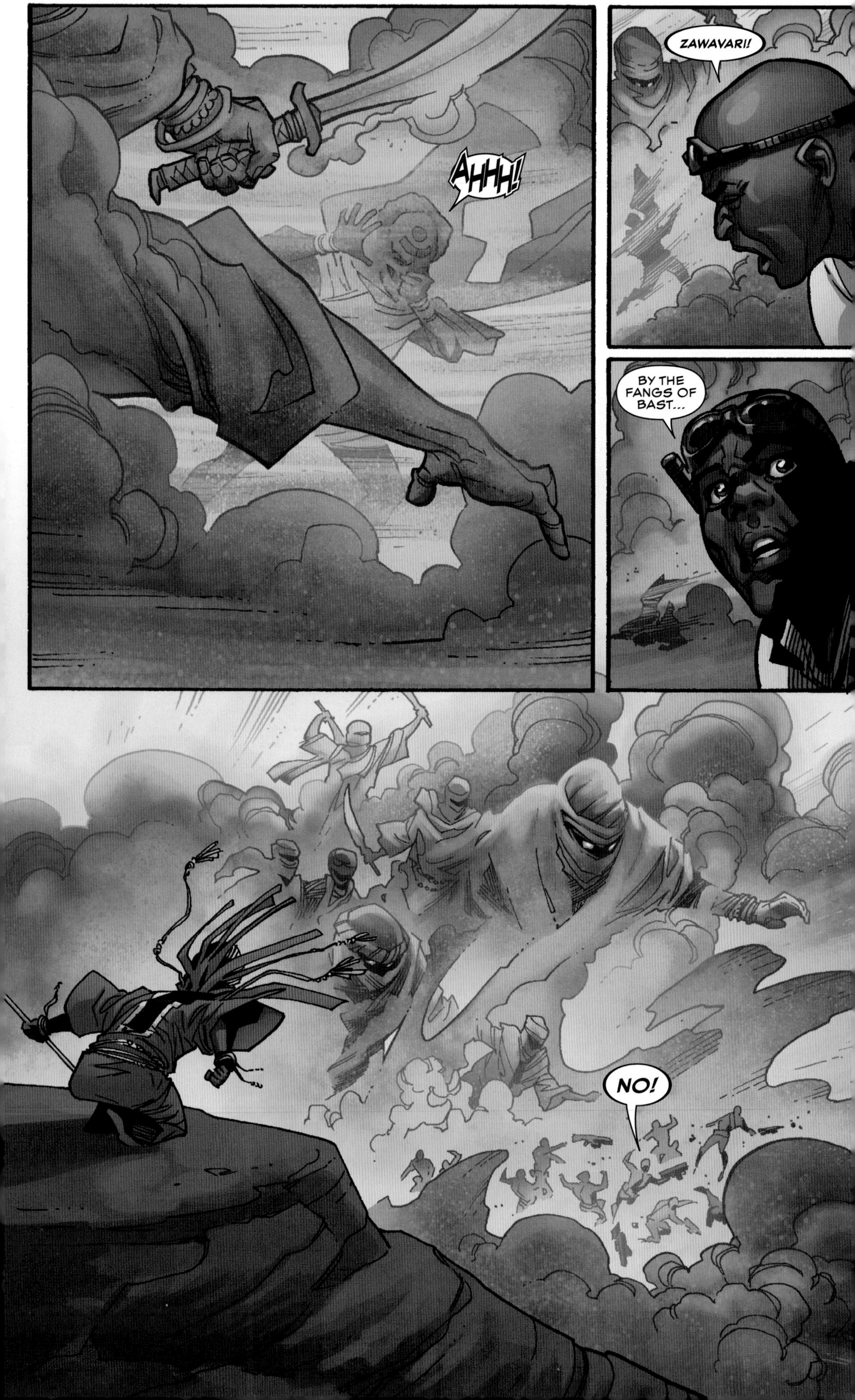
AHHH!
ZAWAVARI!
BY THE FANGS OF BAST...
NO!

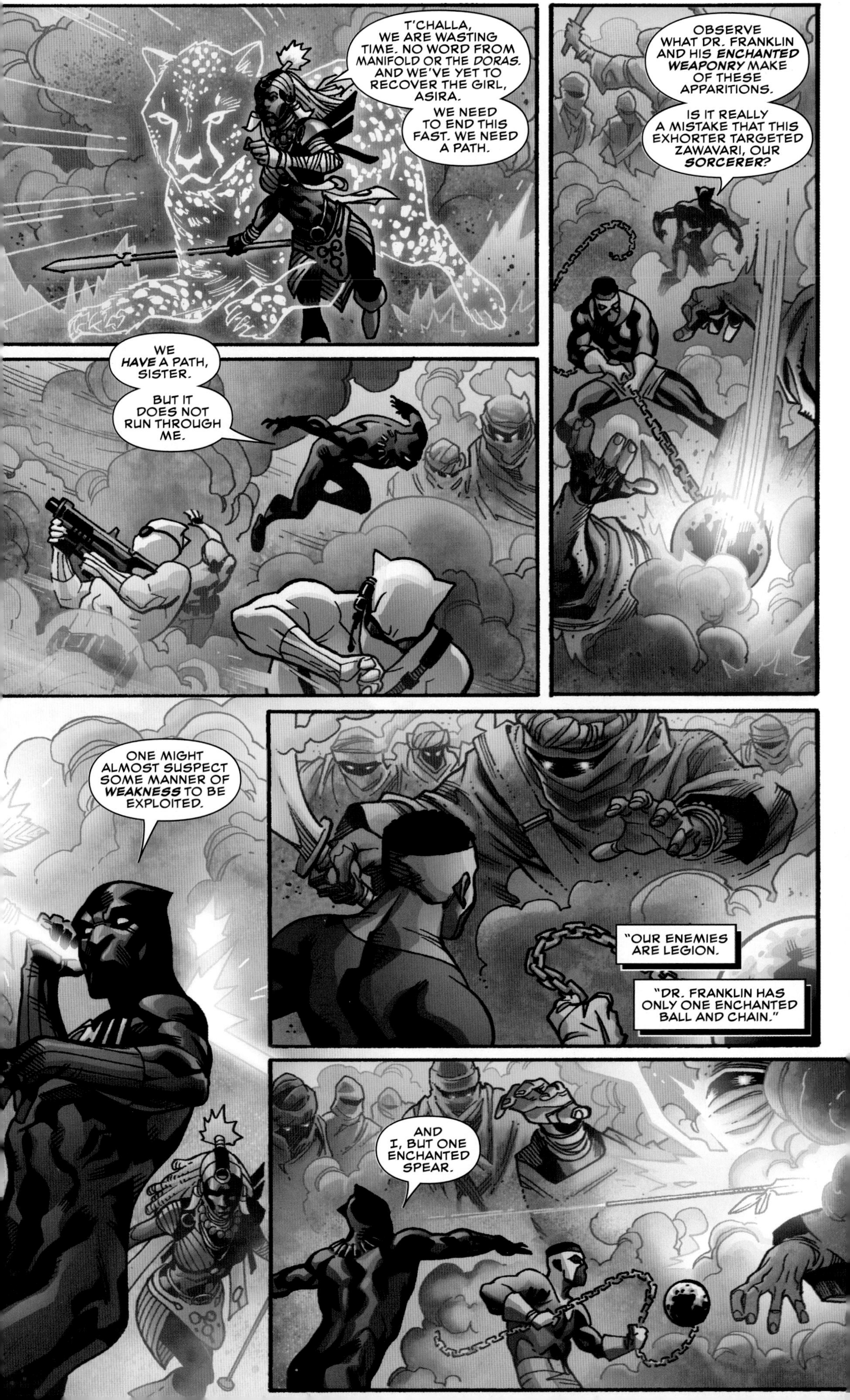

T'CHALLA, WE ARE WASTING TIME. NO WORD FROM MANIFOLD OR THE *DORAS*. AND WE'VE YET TO RECOVER THE GIRL, ASIRA.
WE NEED TO END THIS FAST. WE NEED A PATH.
OBSERVE WHAT DR. FRANKLIN AND HIS ***ENCHANTED WEAPONRY*** MAKE OF THESE APPARITIONS.
IS IT REALLY A MISTAKE THAT THIS EXHORTER TARGETED ZAWAVARI, OUR ***SORCERER***?
WE ***HAVE*** A PATH, SISTER.
BUT IT DOES NOT RUN THROUGH ME.
ONE MIGHT ALMOST SUSPECT SOME MANNER OF ***WEAKNESS*** TO BE EXPLOITED.
"OUR ENEMIES ARE LEGION.
"DR. FRANKLIN HAS ONLY ONE ENCHANTED BALL AND CHAIN."
AND I, BUT ONE ENCHANTED SPEAR.

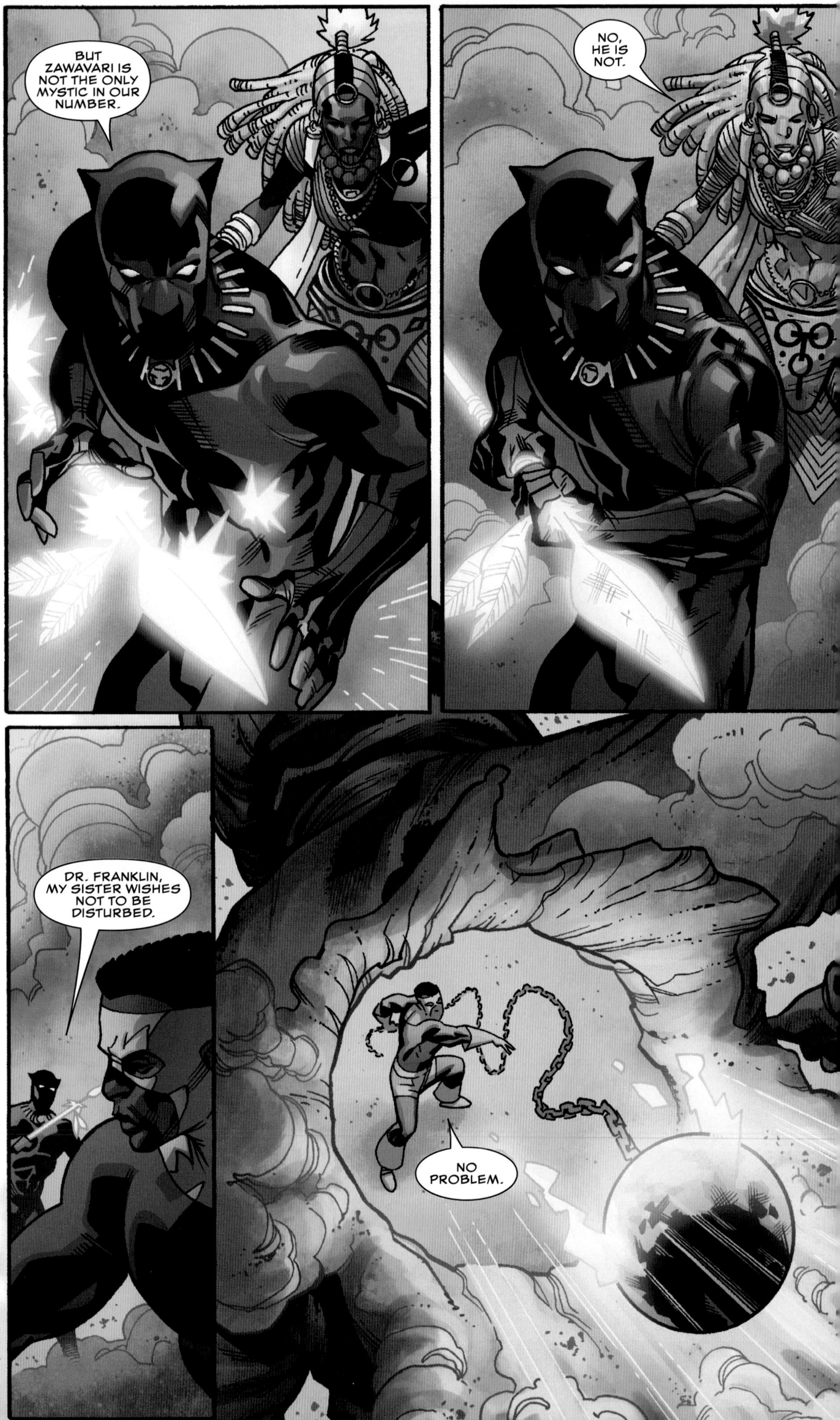

BUT ZAWAVARI IS NOT THE ONLY MYSTIC IN OUR NUMBER.
NO, HE IS NOT.
DR. FRANKLIN, MY SISTER WISHES NOT TO BE DISTURBED.
NO PROBLEM.

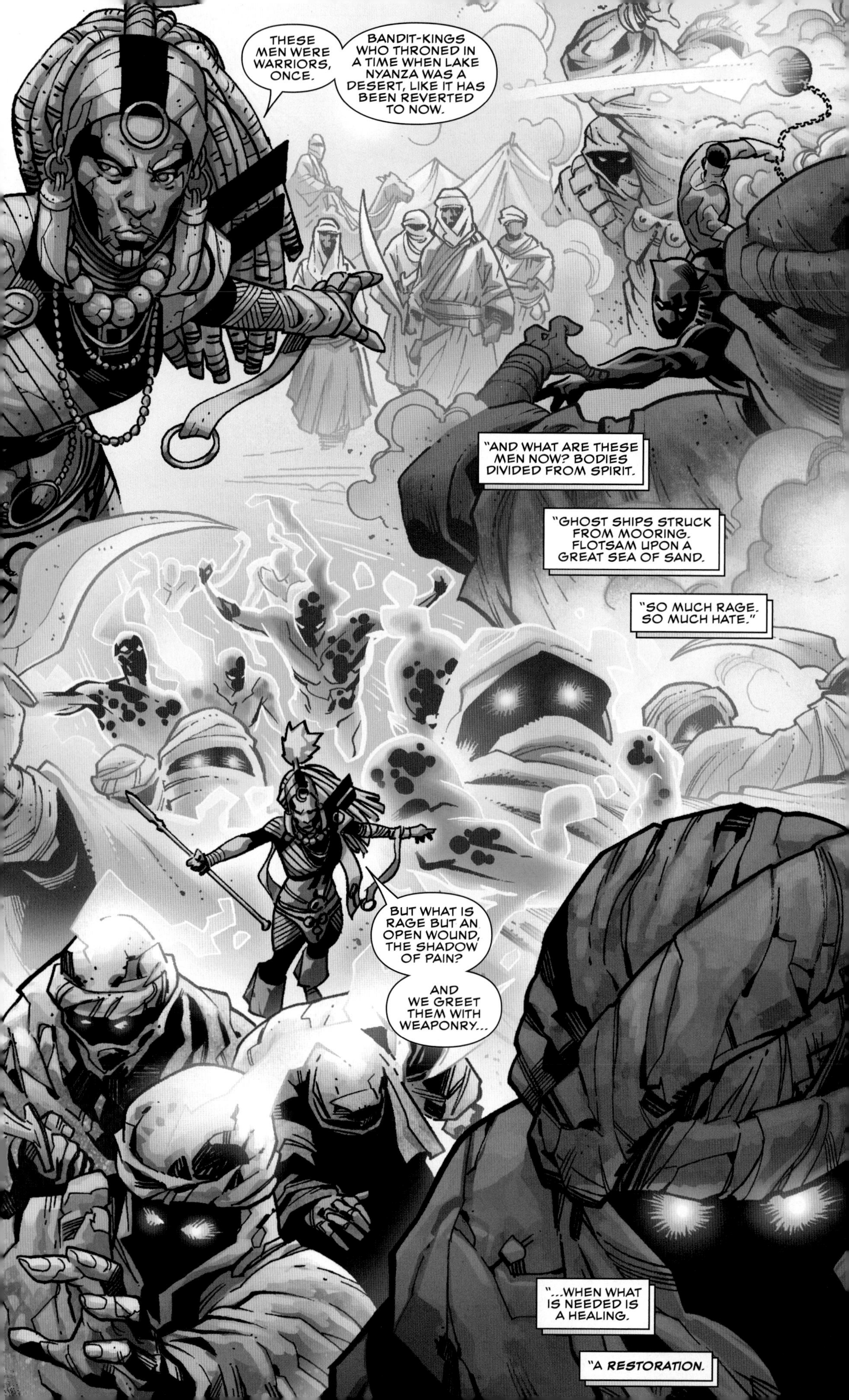
THESE MEN WERE WARRIORS, ONCE.
BANDIT-KINGS WHO THRONED IN A TIME WHEN LAKE NYANZA WAS A DESERT, LIKE IT HAS BEEN REVERTED TO NOW.
"AND WHAT ARE THESE MEN NOW? BODIES DIVIDED FROM SPIRIT.
"GHOST SHIPS STRUCK FROM MOORING. FLOTSAM UPON A GREAT SEA OF SAND.
"SO MUCH RAGE. SO MUCH HATE."
BUT WHAT IS RAGE BUT AN OPEN WOUND, THE SHADOW OF PAIN?
AND WE GREET THEM WITH WEAPONRY...
"...WHEN WHAT IS NEEDED IS A HEALING.
"A RESTORATION.

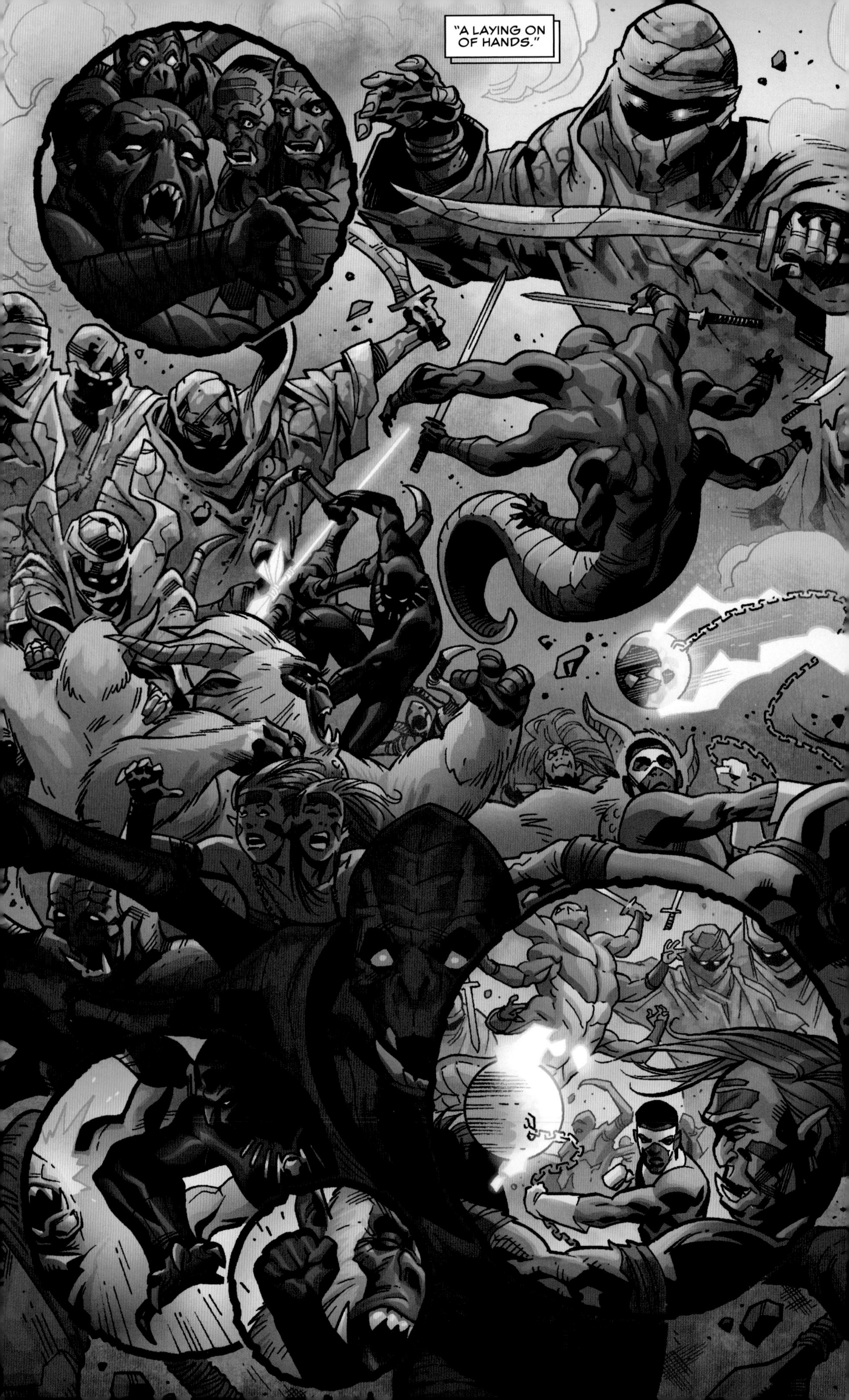
"A LAYING ON OF HANDS."

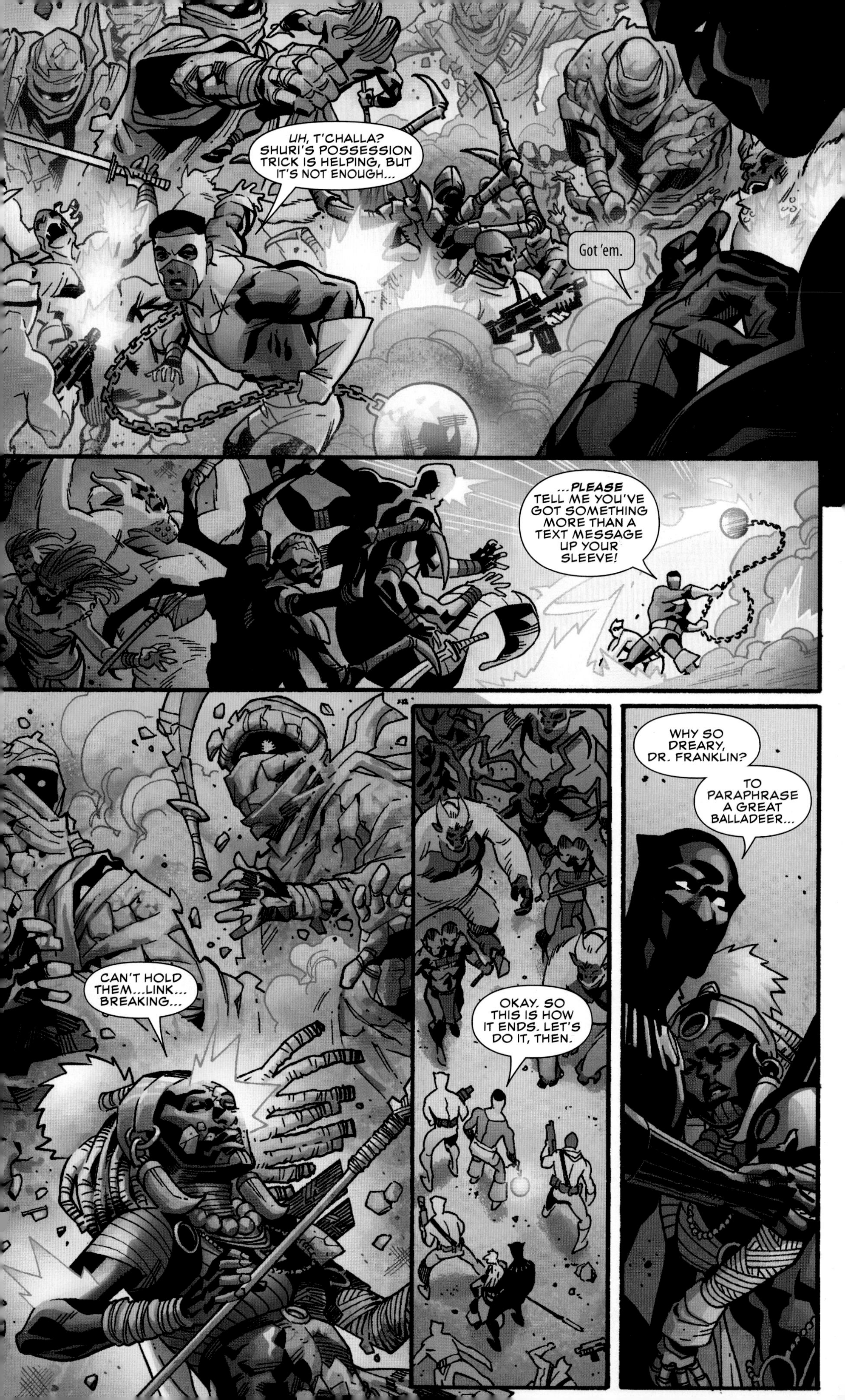
UH, T'CHALLA? SHURI'S POSSESSION TRICK IS HELPING, BUT IT'S NOT ENOUGH...
Got 'em.
...PLEASE TELL ME YOU'VE GOT SOMETHING MORE THAN A TEXT MESSAGE UP YOUR SLEEVE!
CAN'T HOLD THEM...LINK... BREAKING...
OKAY. SO THIS IS HOW IT ENDS. LET'S DO IT, THEN.
WHY SO DREARY, DR. FRANKLIN?
TO PARAPHRASE A GREAT BALLADEER...

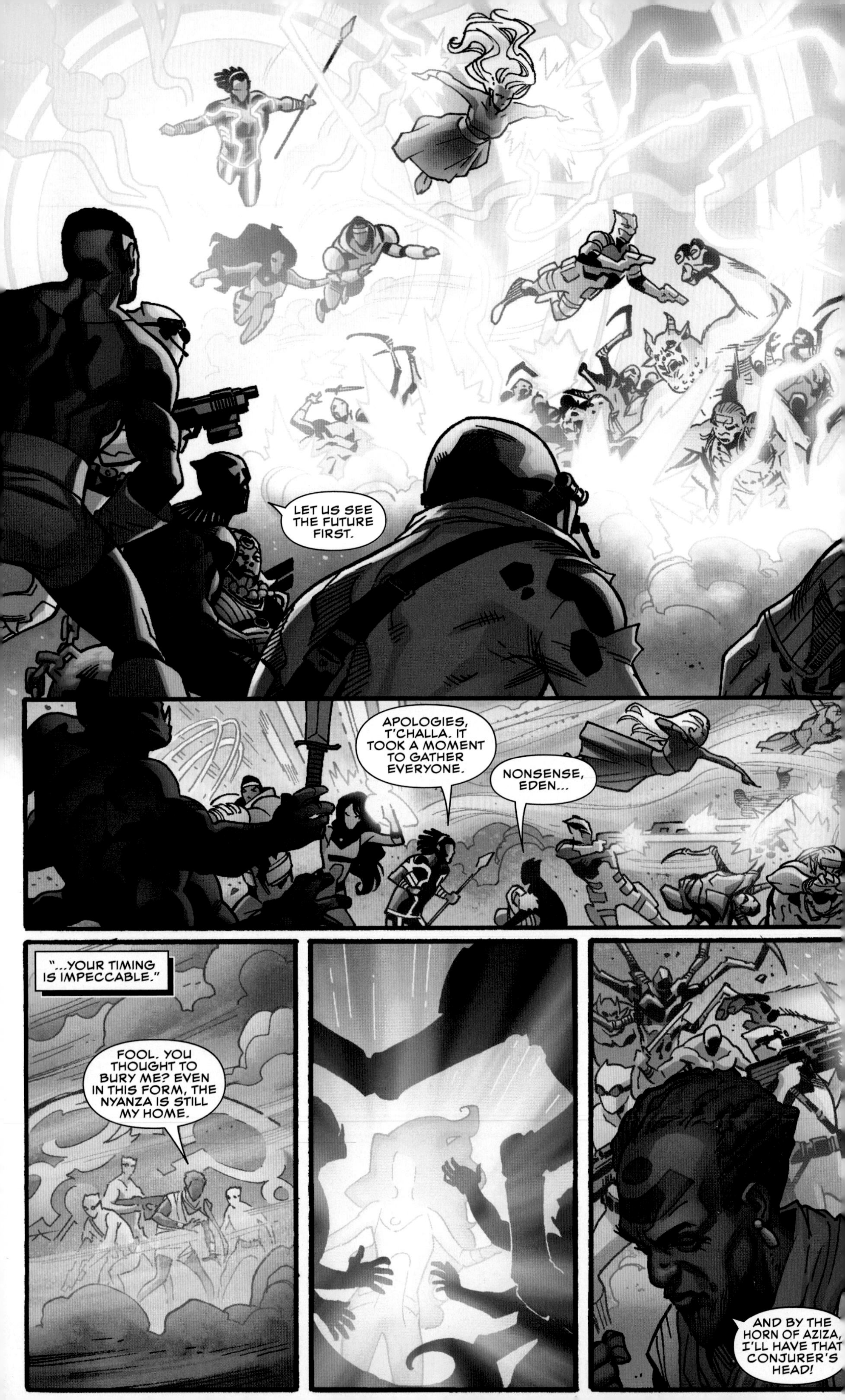
LET US SEE THE FUTURE FIRST.
APOLOGIES, T'CHALLA. IT TOOK A MOMENT TO GATHER EVERYONE.
NONSENSE, EDEN...
"...YOUR TIMING IS IMPECCABLE."
FOOL. YOU THOUGHT TO BURY ME? EVEN IN THIS FORM, THE NYANZA IS STILL MY HOME.
AND BY THE HORN OF AZIZA, I'LL HAVE THAT CONJURER'S HEAD!

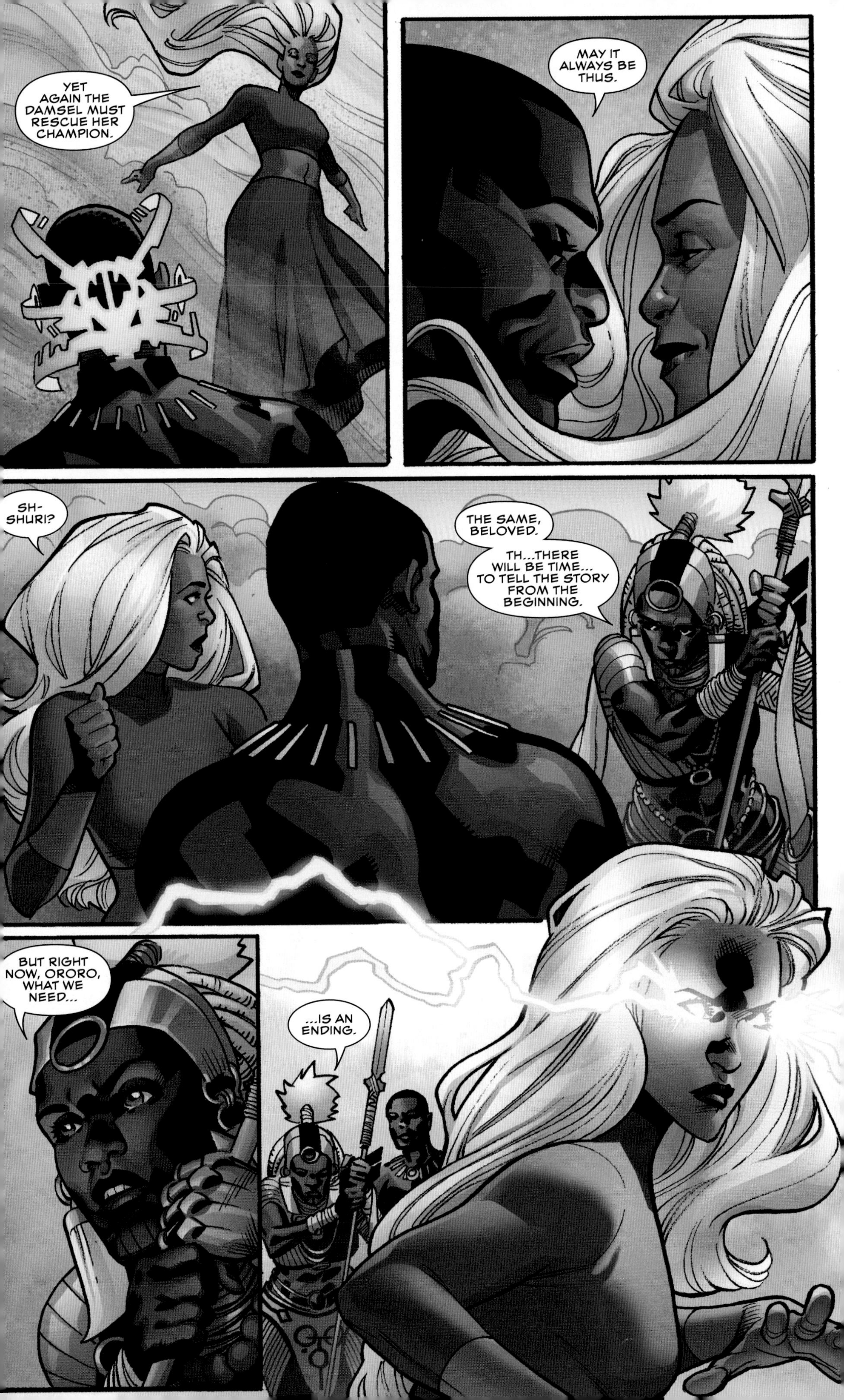

YET AGAIN THE DAMSEL MUST RESCUE HER CHAMPION.
MAY IT ALWAYS BE THUS.
SH-SHURI?
THE SAME, BELOVED.
TH...THERE WILL BE TIME... TO TELL THE STORY FROM THE BEGINNING.
BUT RIGHT NOW, ORORO, WHAT WE NEED...
...IS AN ENDING.

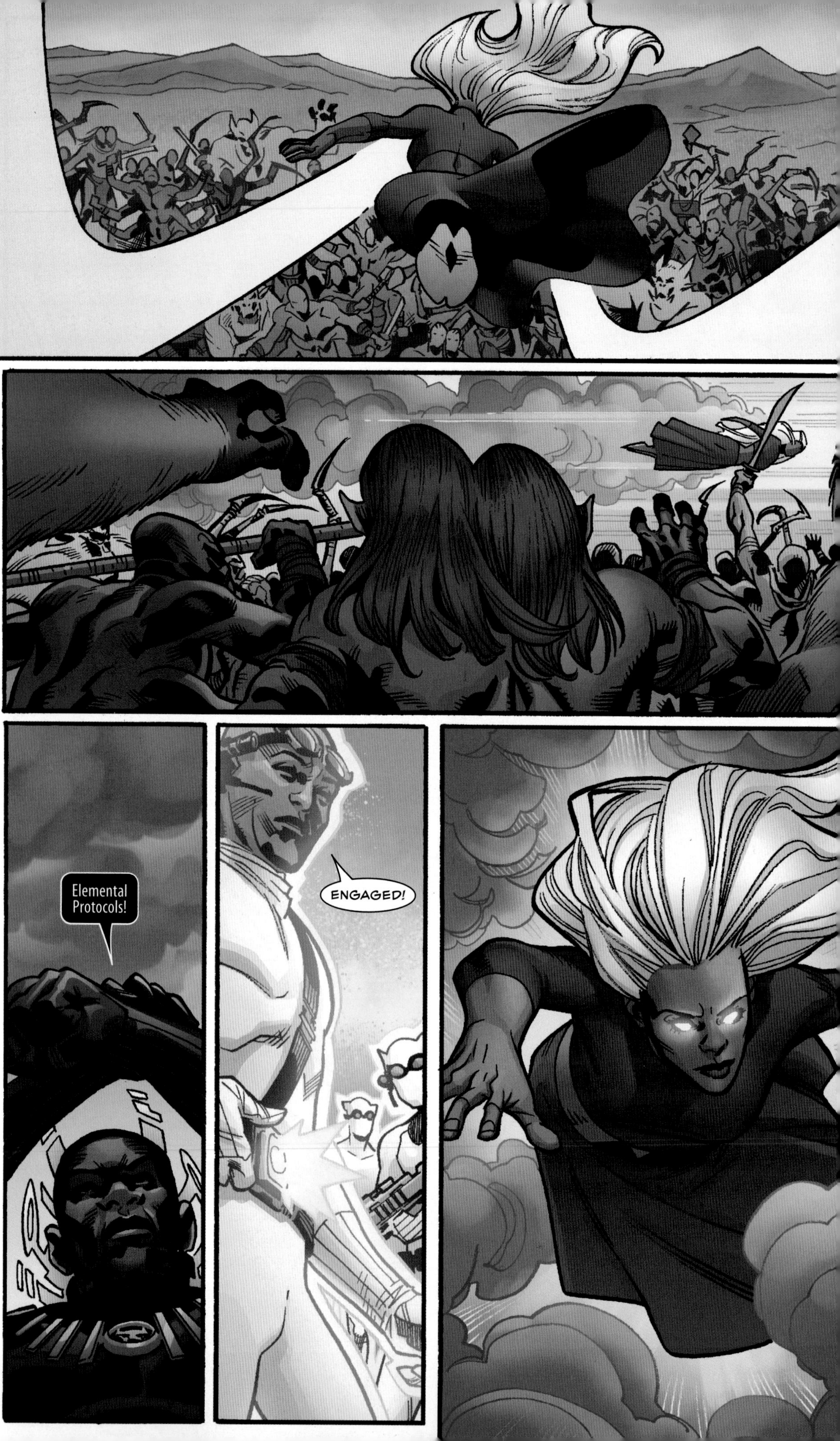
Elemental Protocols!
ENGAGED!

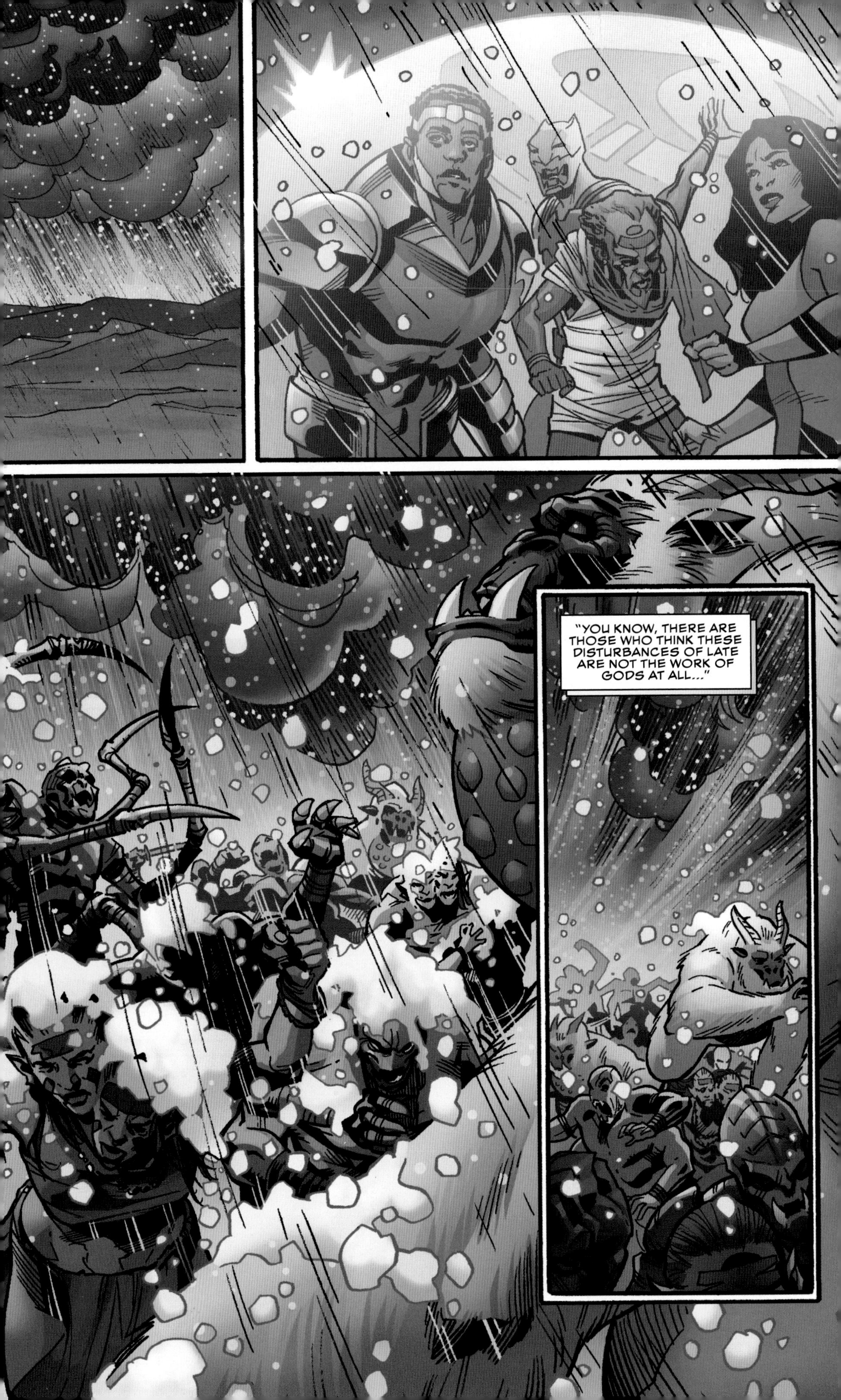
"YOU KNOW, THERE ARE THOSE WHO THINK THESE DISTURBANCES OF LATE ARE NOT THE WORK OF GODS AT ALL..."

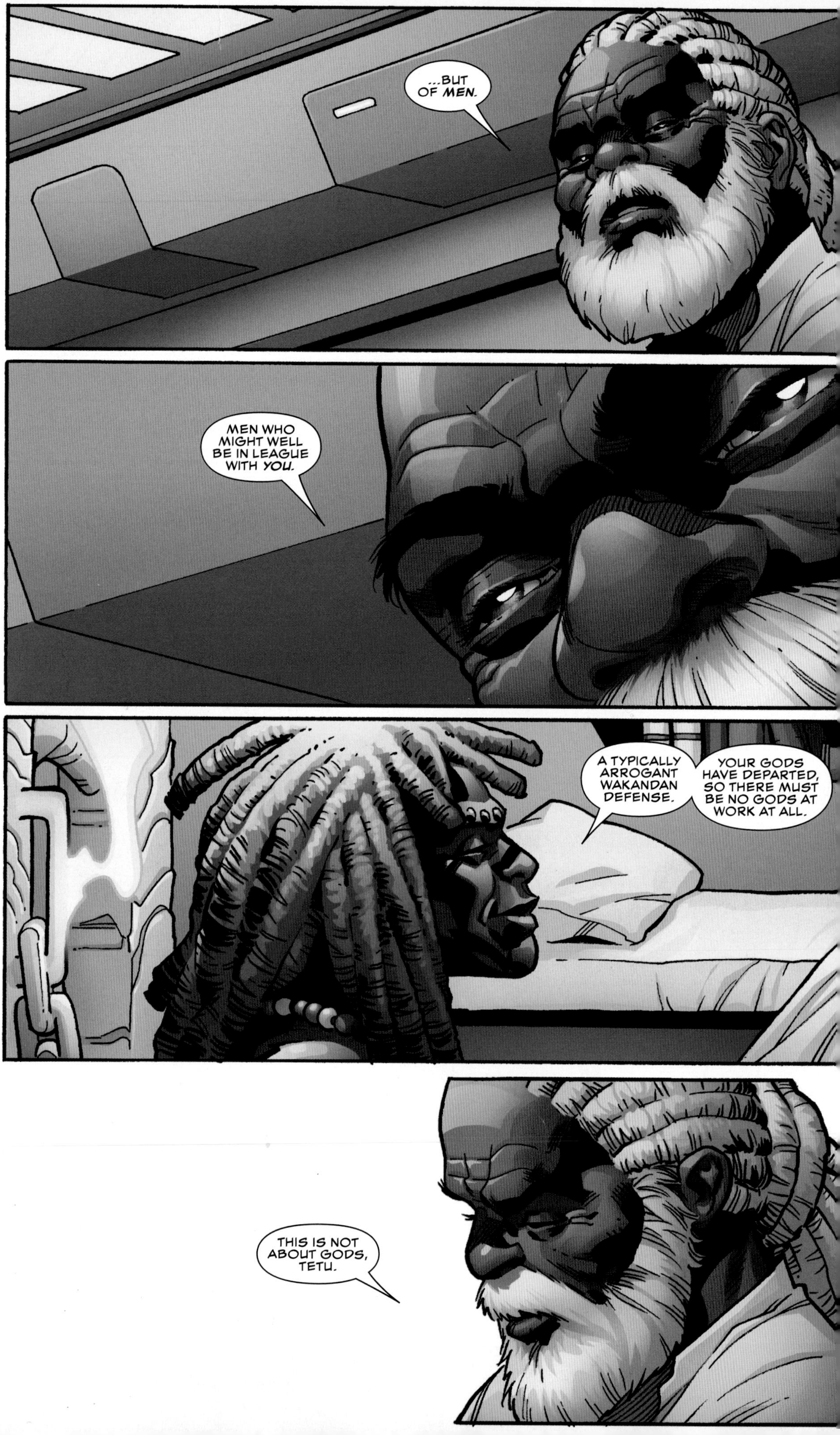
...BUT OF MEN.
MEN WHO MIGHT WELL BE IN LEAGUE WITH YOU.
A TYPICALLY ARROGANT WAKANDAN DEFENSE.
YOUR GODS HAVE DEPARTED, SO THERE MUST BE NO GODS AT WORK AT ALL.
THIS IS NOT ABOUT GODS, TETU.

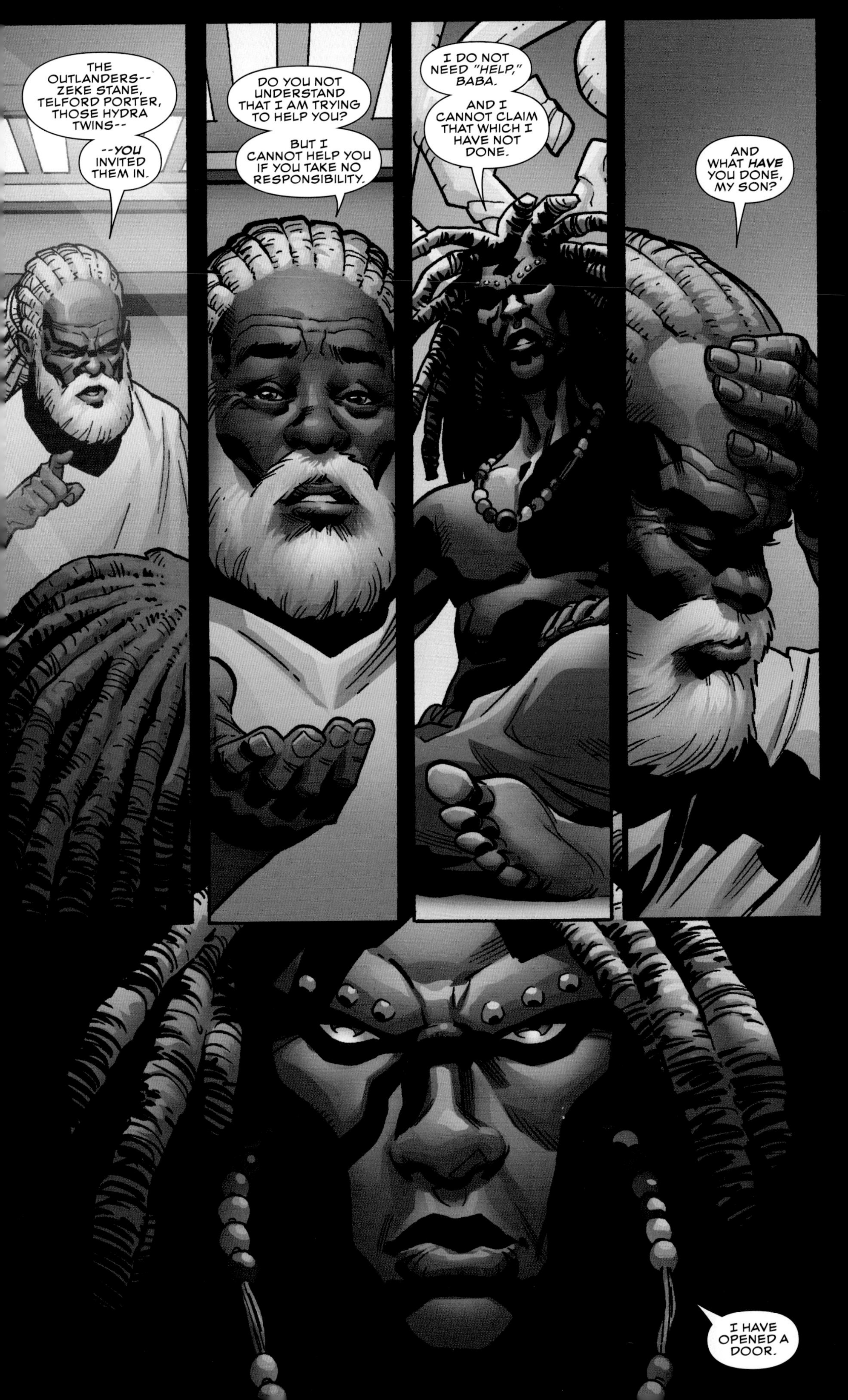

THE OUTLANDERS-- ZEKE STANE, TELFORD PORTER, THOSE HYDRA TWINS--
--YOU INVITED THEM IN.
DO YOU NOT UNDERSTAND THAT I AM TRYING TO HELP YOU?
BUT I CANNOT HELP YOU IF YOU TAKE NO RESPONSIBILITY.
I DO NOT NEED "HELP," BABA.
AND I CANNOT CLAIM THAT WHICH I HAVE NOT DONE.
AND WHAT HAVE YOU DONE, MY SON?
I HAVE OPENED A DOOR.

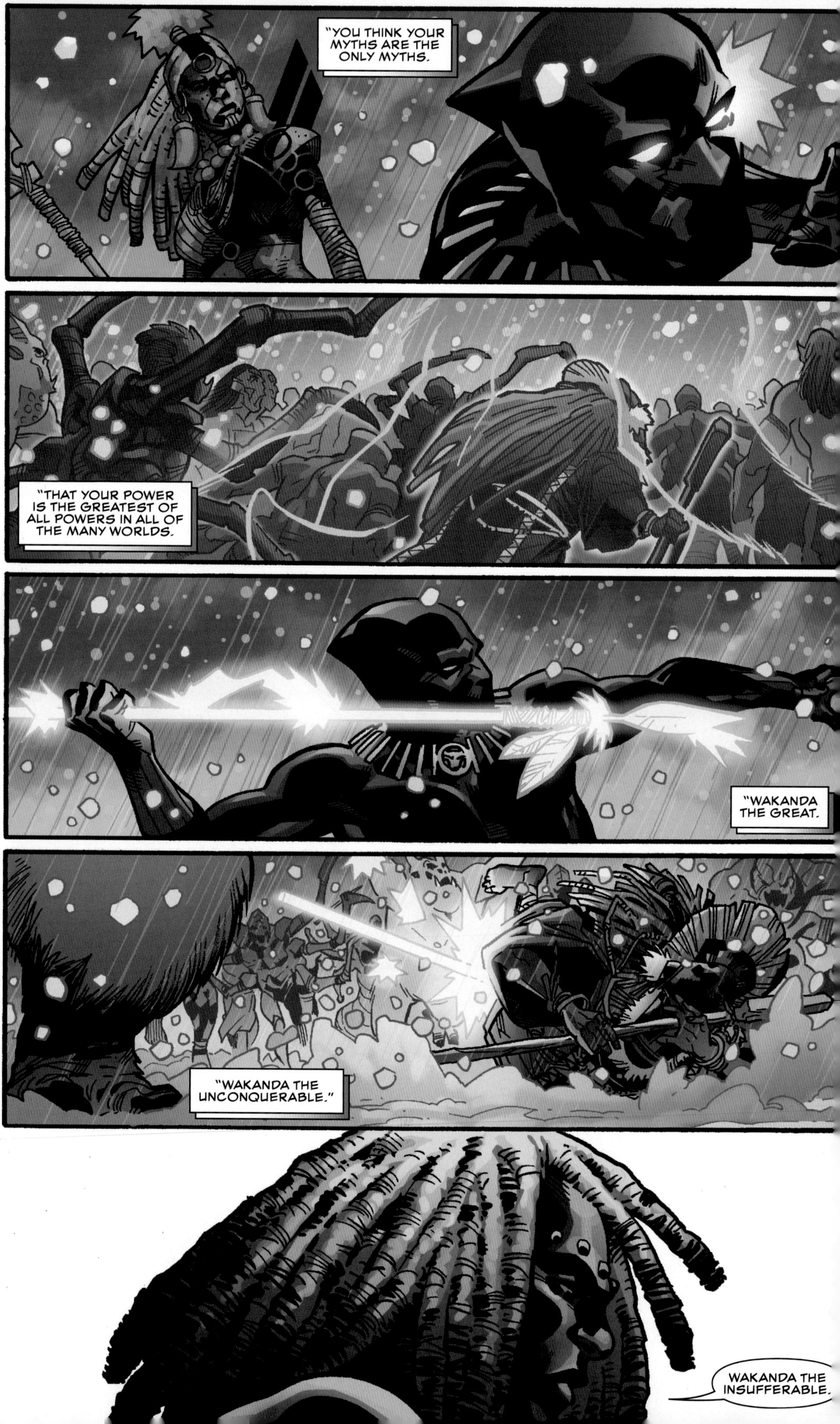
"YOU THINK YOUR MYTHS ARE THE ONLY MYTHS.
"THAT YOUR POWER IS THE GREATEST OF ALL POWERS IN ALL OF THE MANY WORLDS.
"WAKANDA THE GREAT.
"WAKANDA THE UNCONQUERABLE."
WAKANDA THE INSUFFERABLE.

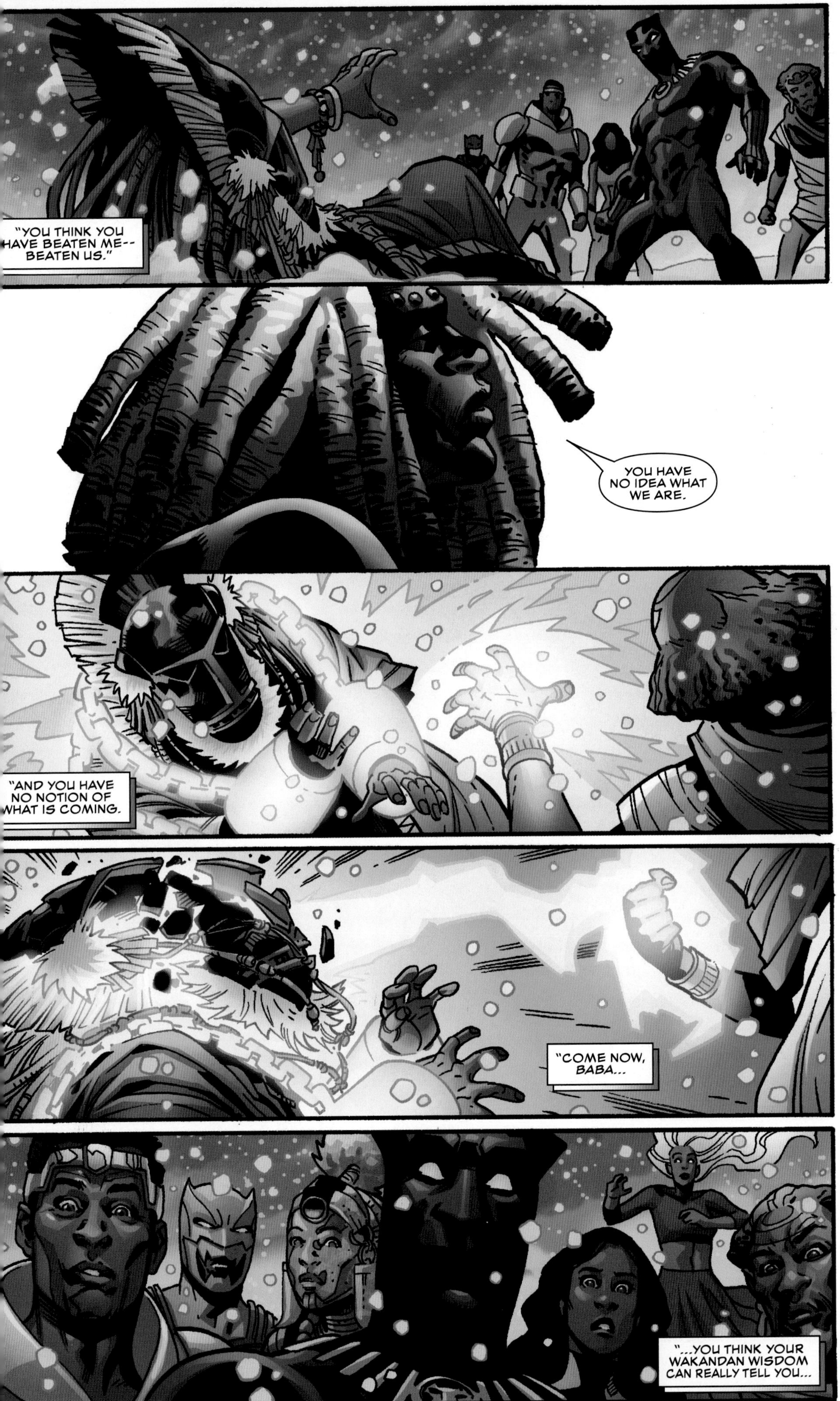
"YOU THINK YOU HAVE BEATEN ME-- BEATEN US."
YOU HAVE NO IDEA WHAT WE ARE.
"AND YOU HAVE NO NOTION OF WHAT IS COMING.
"COME NOW, BABA...
"...YOU THINK YOUR WAKANDAN WISDOM CAN REALLY TELL YOU...

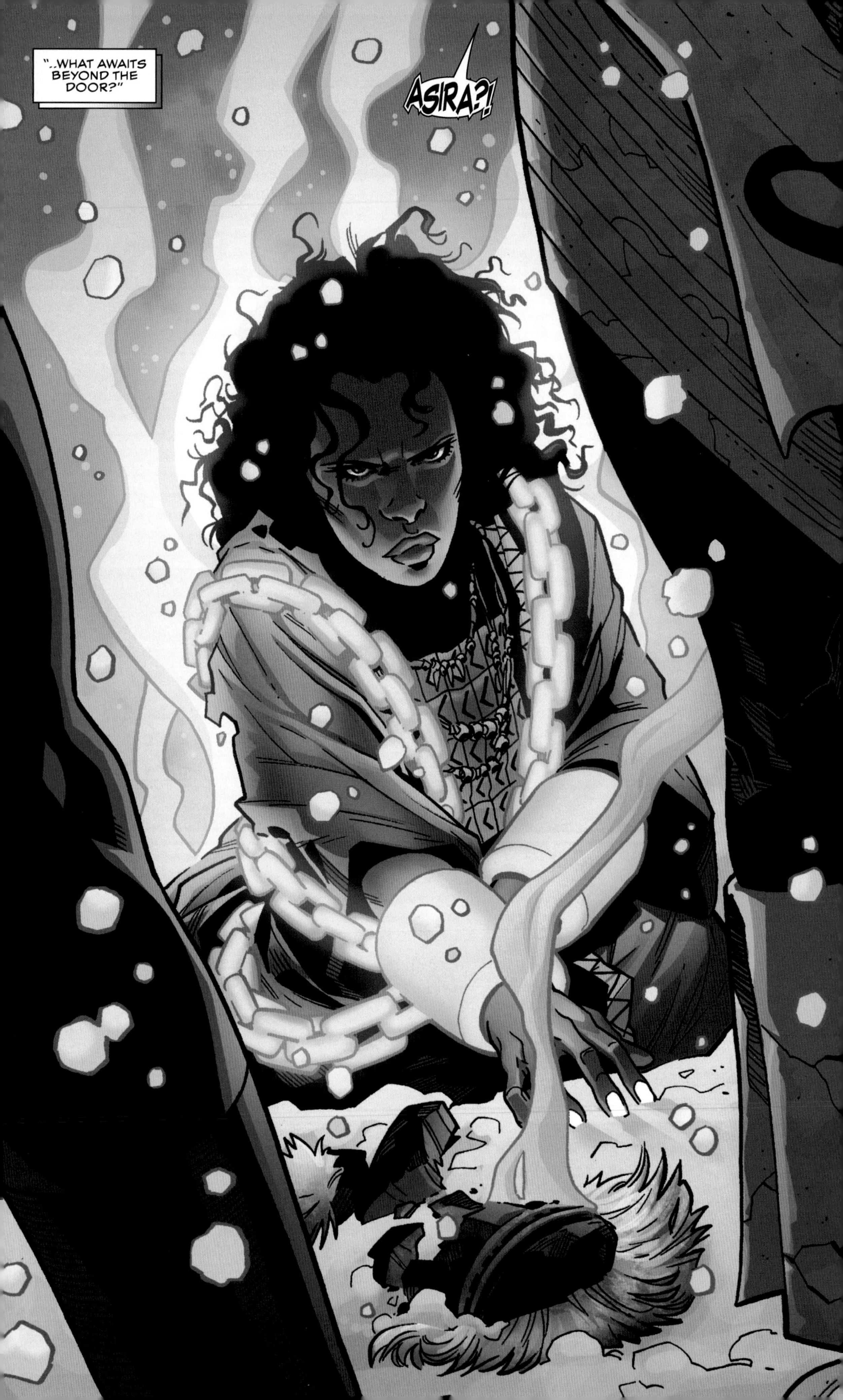
"..WHAT AWAITS BEYOND THE DOOR?"
ASIRA?!

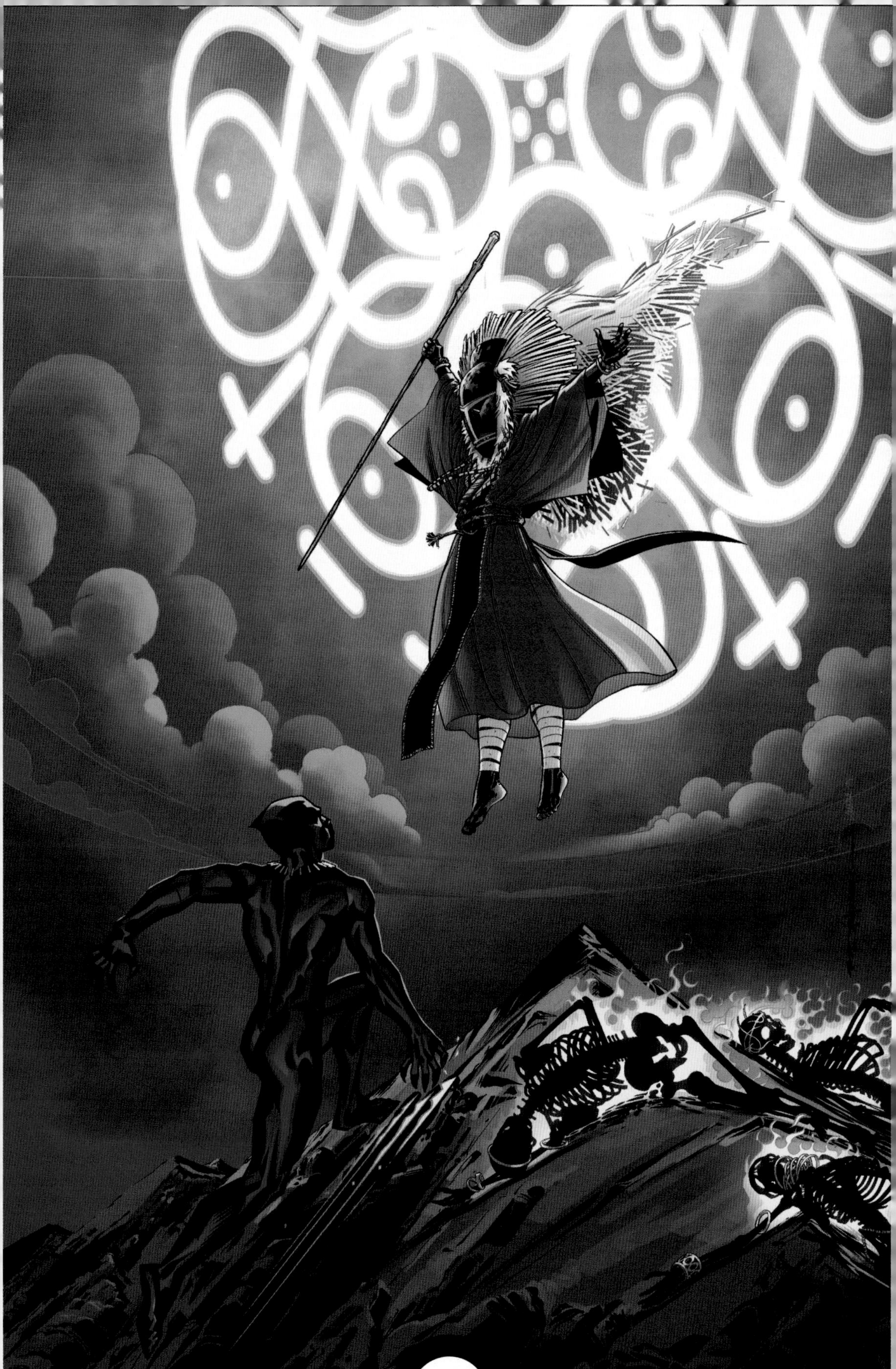

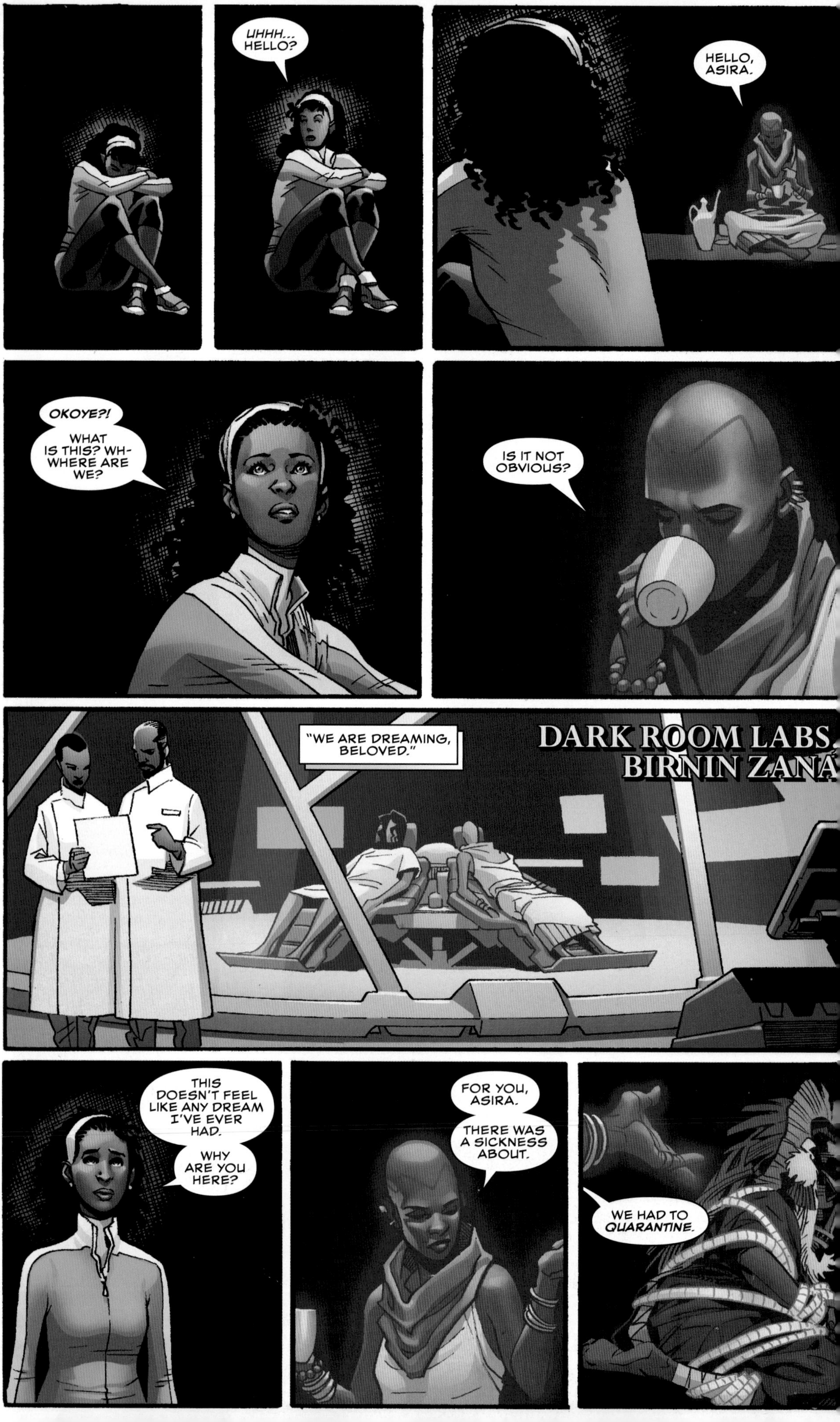
UHHH... HELLO?
HELLO, ASIRA.
OKOYE?!
WHAT IS THIS? WH-WHERE ARE WE?
IS IT NOT OBVIOUS?
DARK ROOM LABS, BIRNIN ZANA
"WE ARE DREAMING, BELOVED."
THIS DOESN'T FEEL LIKE ANY DREAM I'VE EVER HAD.
WHY ARE YOU HERE?
FOR YOU, ASIRA.
THERE WAS A SICKNESS ABOUT.
WE HAD TO *QUARANTINE*.

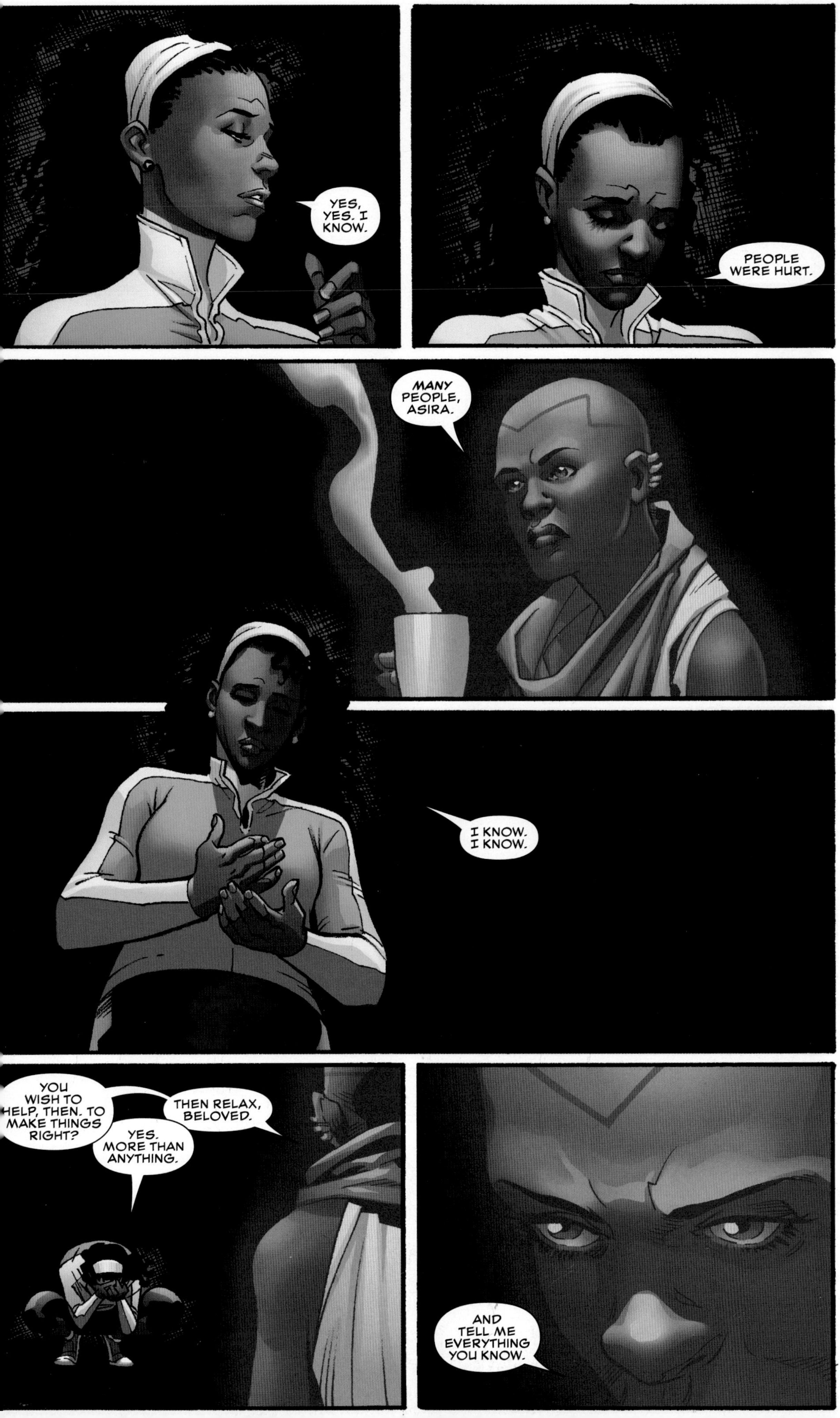
YES, YES. I KNOW.
PEOPLE WERE HURT.
MANY PEOPLE, ASIRA.
I KNOW. I KNOW.
YOU WISH TO HELP, THEN. TO MAKE THINGS RIGHT?
YES. MORE THAN ANYTHING.
THEN RELAX, BELOVED.
AND TELL ME EVERYTHING YOU KNOW.

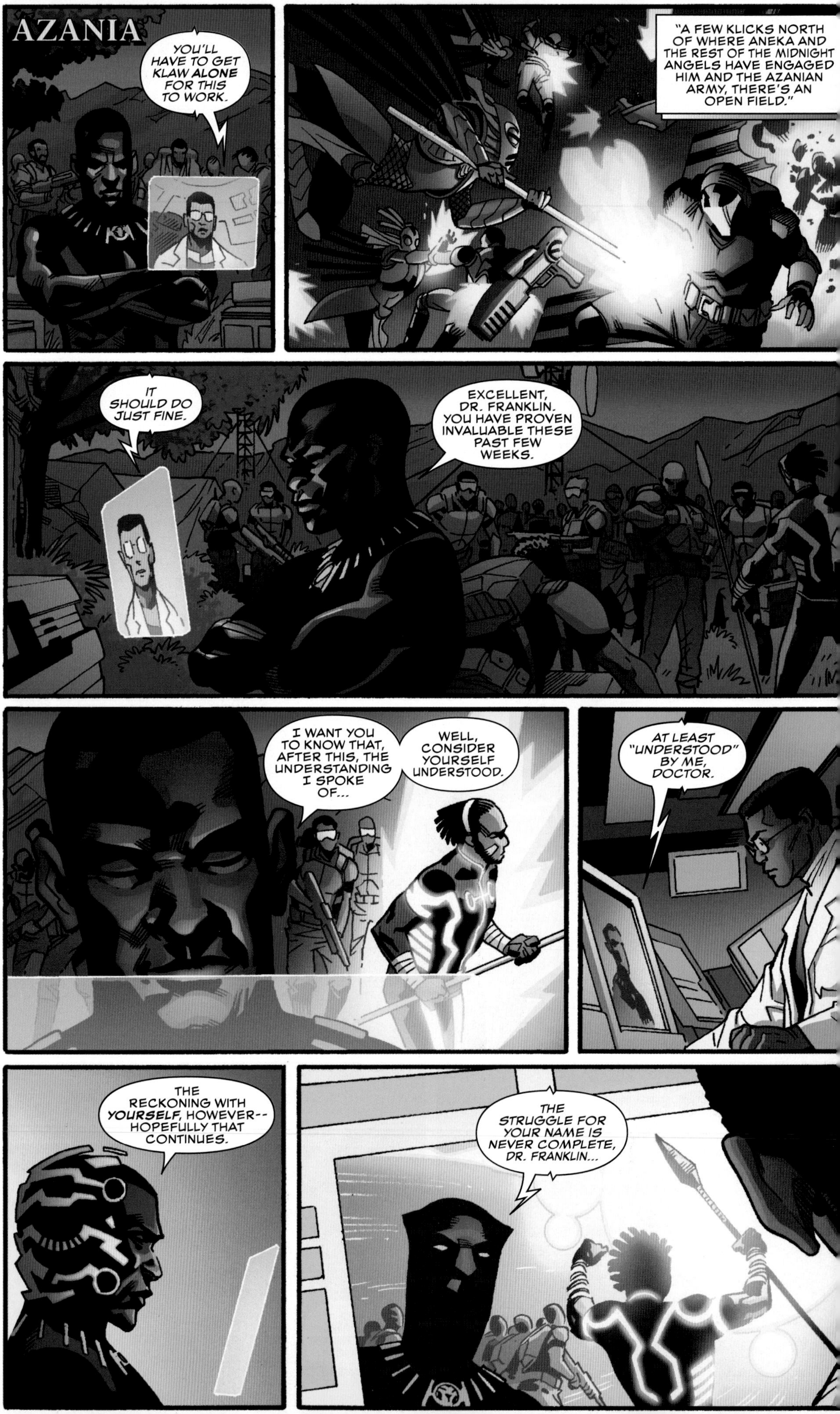
AZANIA
YOU'LL HAVE TO GET KLAW ALONE FOR THIS TO WORK.
"A FEW KLICKS NORTH OF WHERE ANEKA AND THE REST OF THE MIDNIGHT ANGELS HAVE ENGAGED HIM AND THE AZANIAN ARMY, THERE'S AN OPEN FIELD."
IT SHOULD DO JUST FINE.
EXCELLENT, DR. FRANKLIN. YOU HAVE PROVEN INVALUABLE THESE PAST FEW WEEKS.
I WANT YOU TO KNOW THAT, AFTER THIS, THE UNDERSTANDING I SPOKE OF...
WELL, CONSIDER YOURSELF UNDERSTOOD.
AT LEAST "UNDERSTOOD" BY ME, DOCTOR.
THE RECKONING WITH YOURSELF, HOWEVER--HOPEFULLY THAT CONTINUES.
THE STRUGGLE FOR YOUR NAME IS NEVER COMPLETE, DR. FRANKLIN...

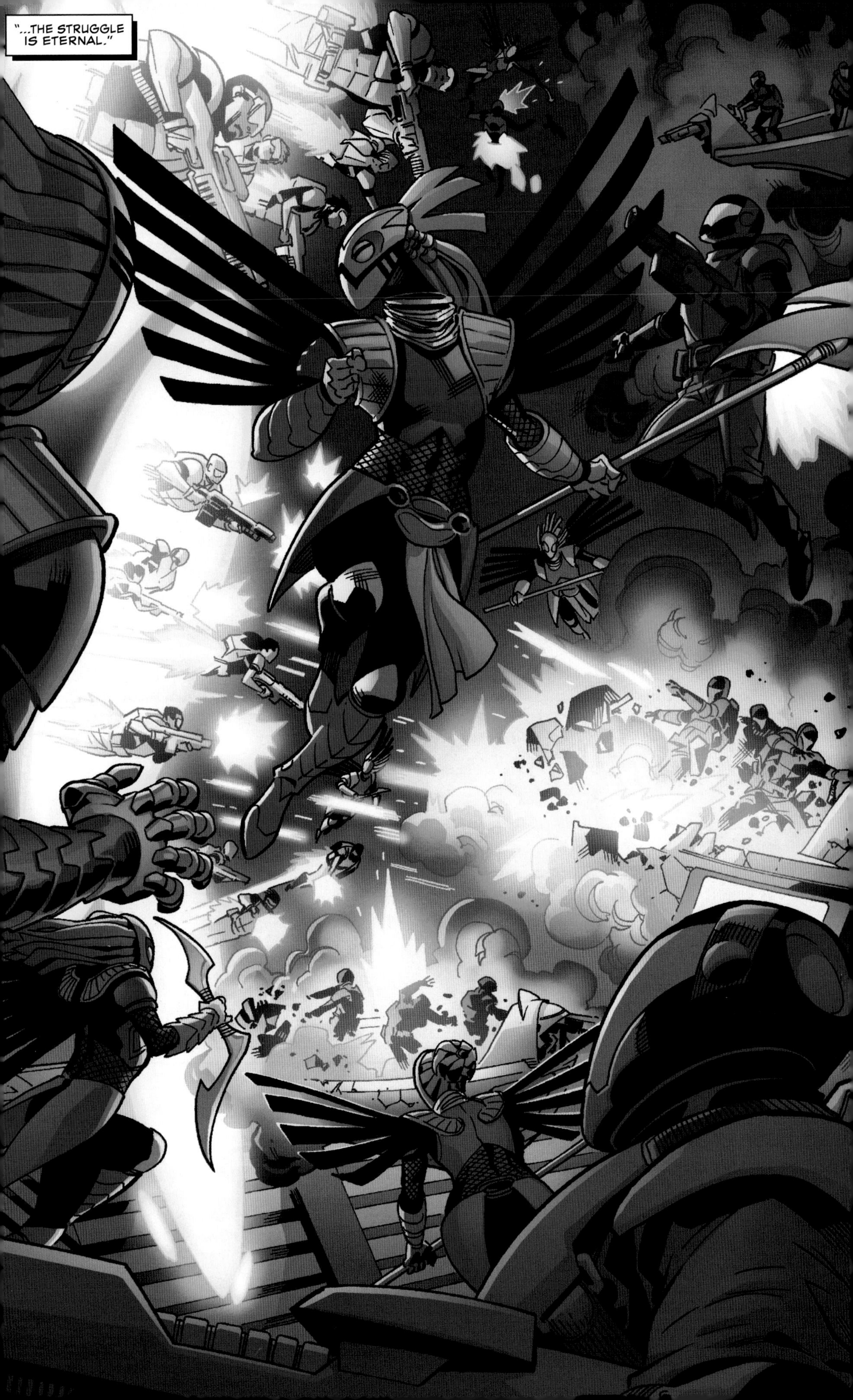
"...THE STRUGGLE IS ETERNAL."

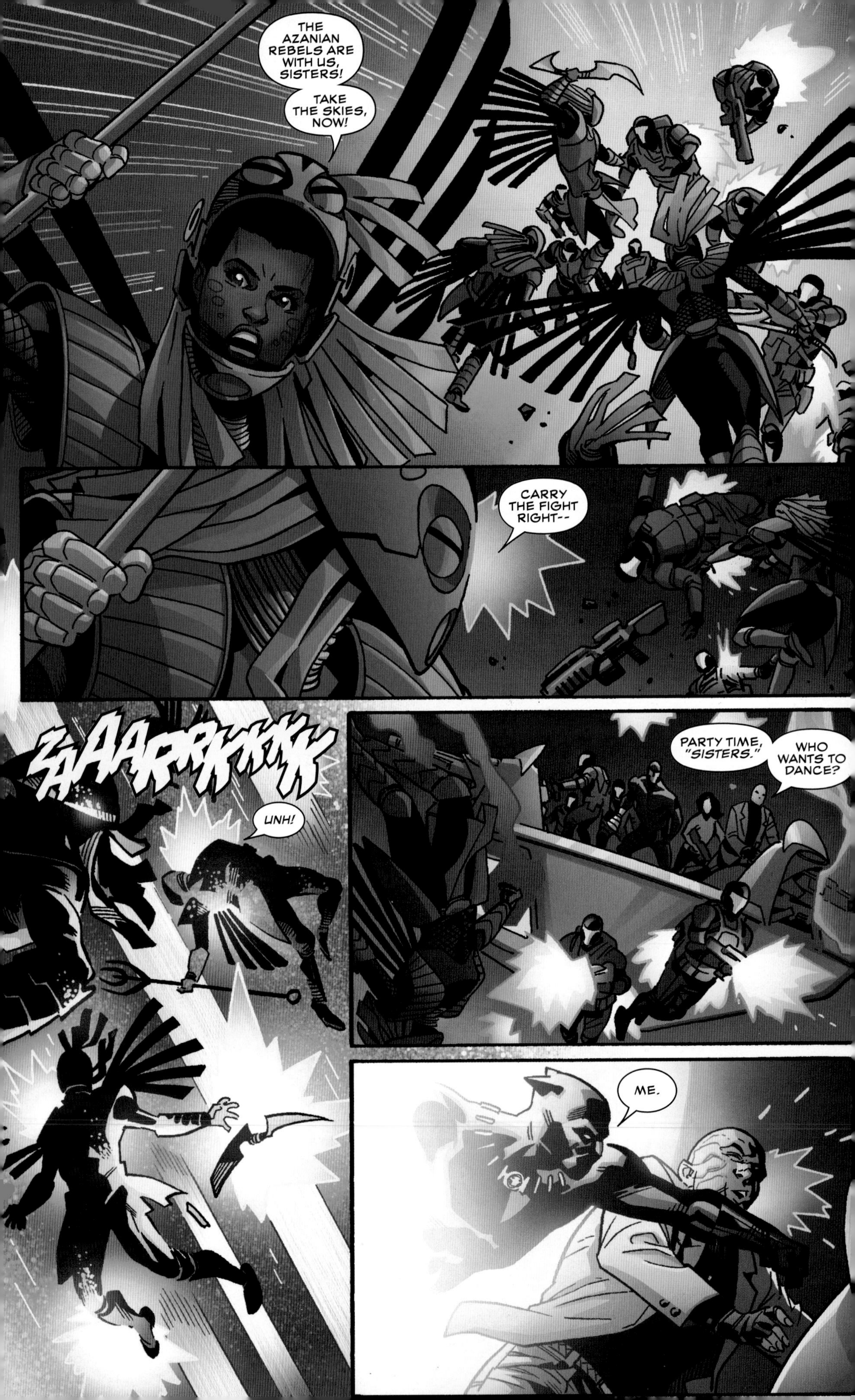
THE AZANIAN REBELS ARE WITH US, SISTERS!
TAKE THE SKIES, NOW!
CARRY THE FIGHT RIGHT--
ZAAARKKKK
UNH!
PARTY TIME, "SISTERS."
WHO WANTS TO DANCE?
ME.

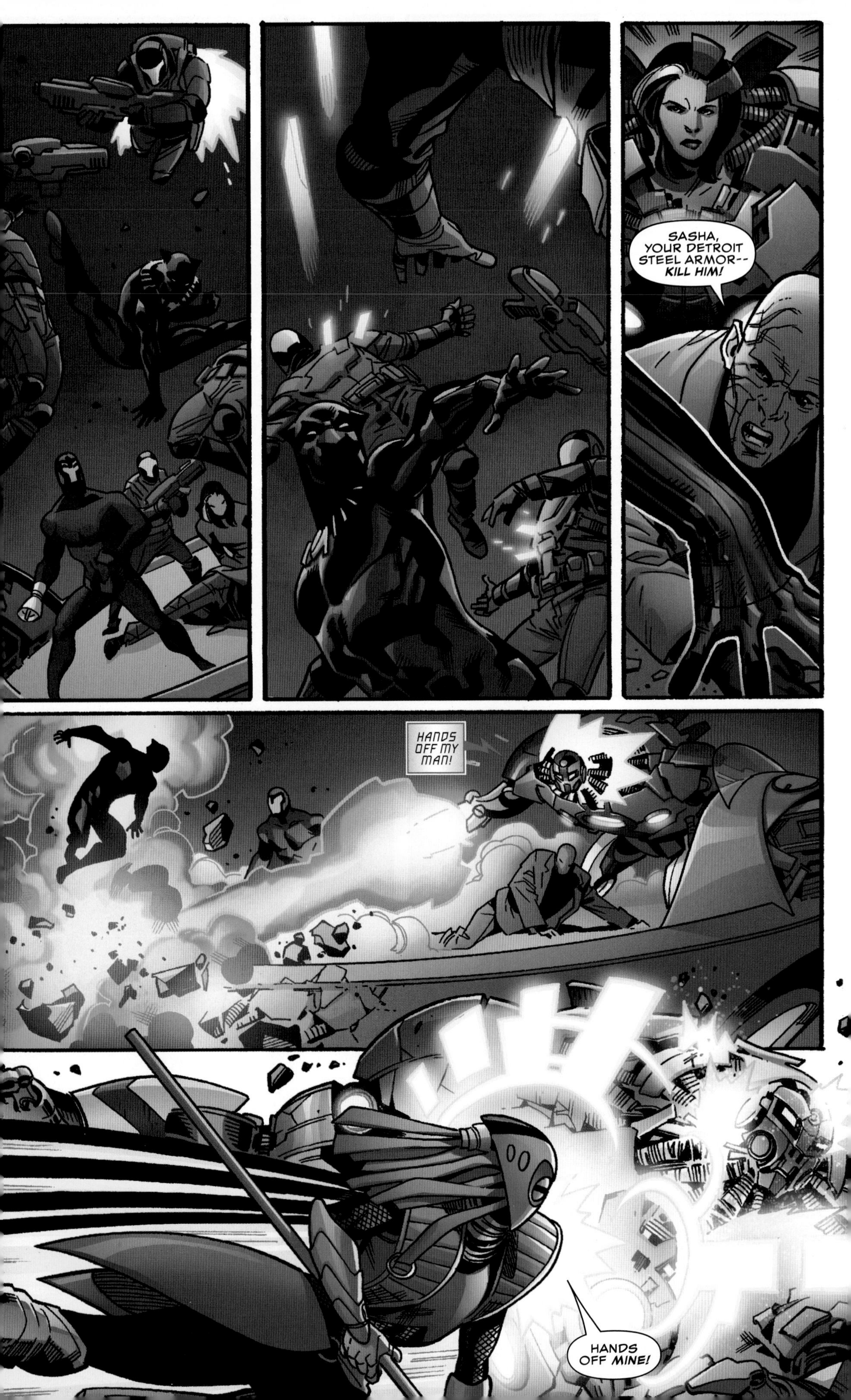
SASHA, YOUR DETROIT STEEL ARMOR-- KILL HIM!
HANDS OFF MY MAN!
HANDS OFF MINE!

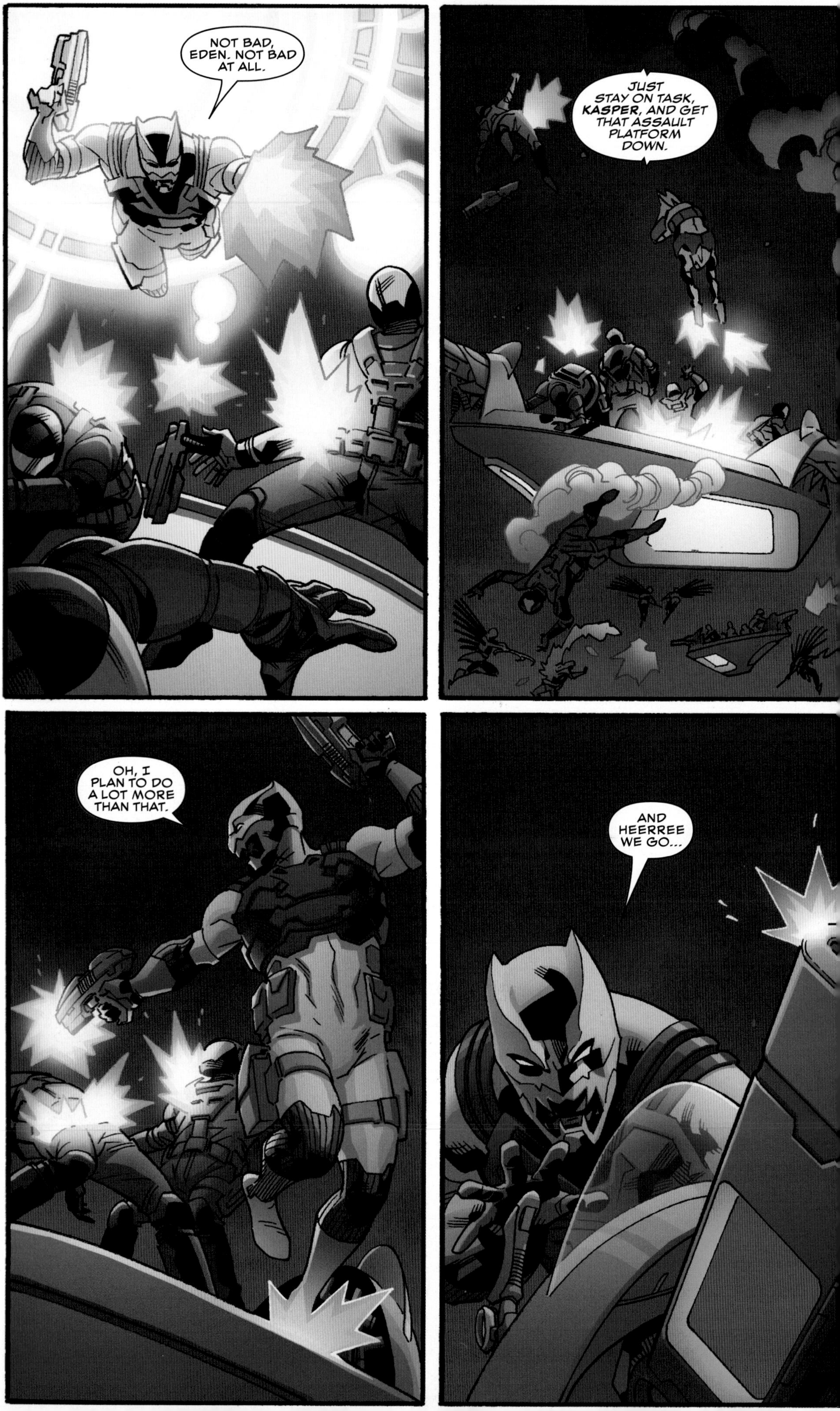
NOT BAD, EDEN. NOT BAD AT ALL.
JUST STAY ON TASK, KASPER, AND GET THAT ASSAULT PLATFORM DOWN.
OH, I PLAN TO DO A LOT MORE THAN THAT.
AND HEERREE WE GO...

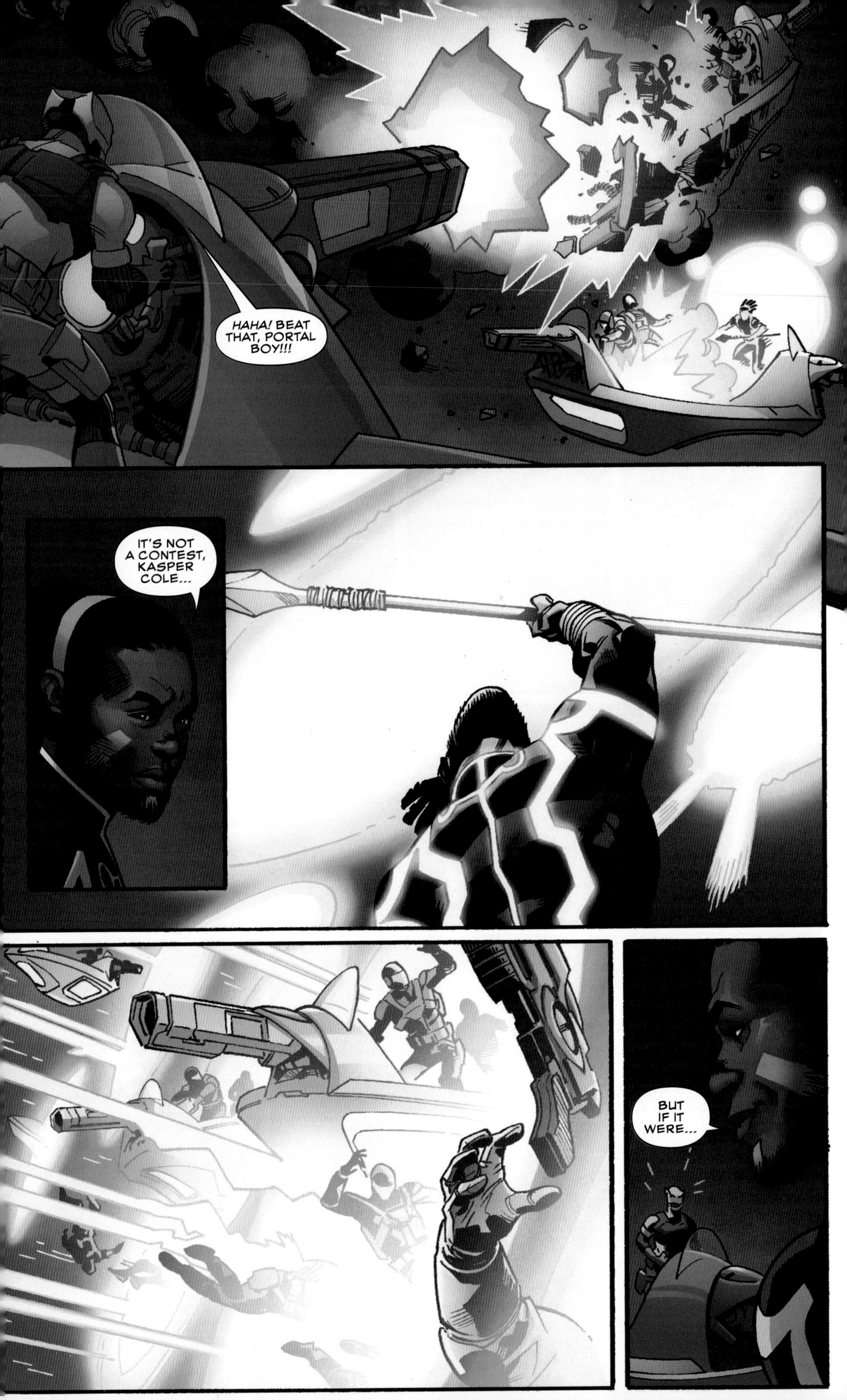
HAHA! BEAT THAT, PORTAL BOY!!!
IT'S NOT A CONTEST, KASPER COLE...
BUT IF IT WERE...

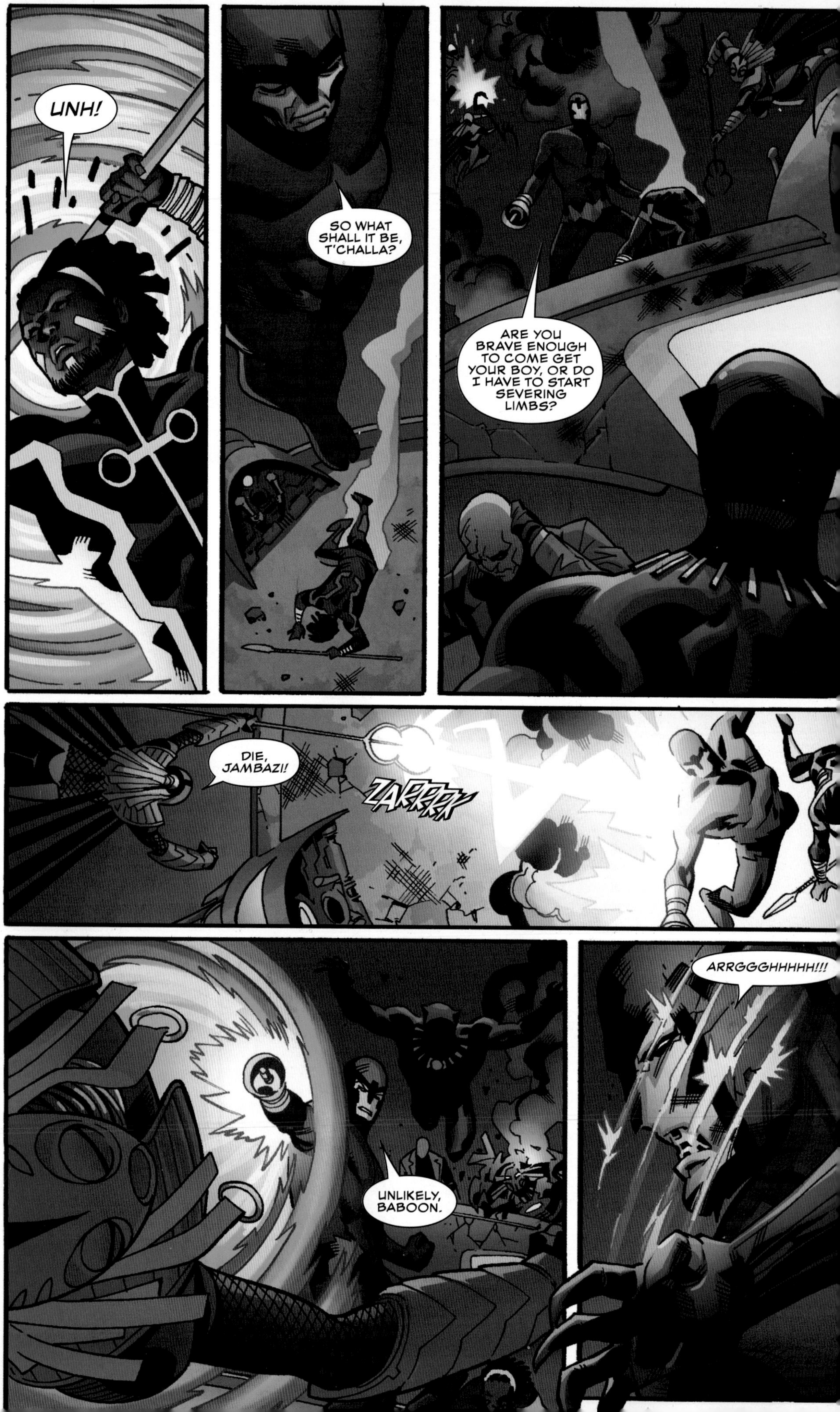
UNH!
SO WHAT SHALL IT BE, T'CHALLA?
ARE YOU BRAVE ENOUGH TO COME GET YOUR BOY, OR DO I HAVE TO START SEVERING LIMBS?
DIE, JAMBAZI!
ZAKRRRK
UNLIKELY, BABOON.
ARRGGGHHHHH!!!

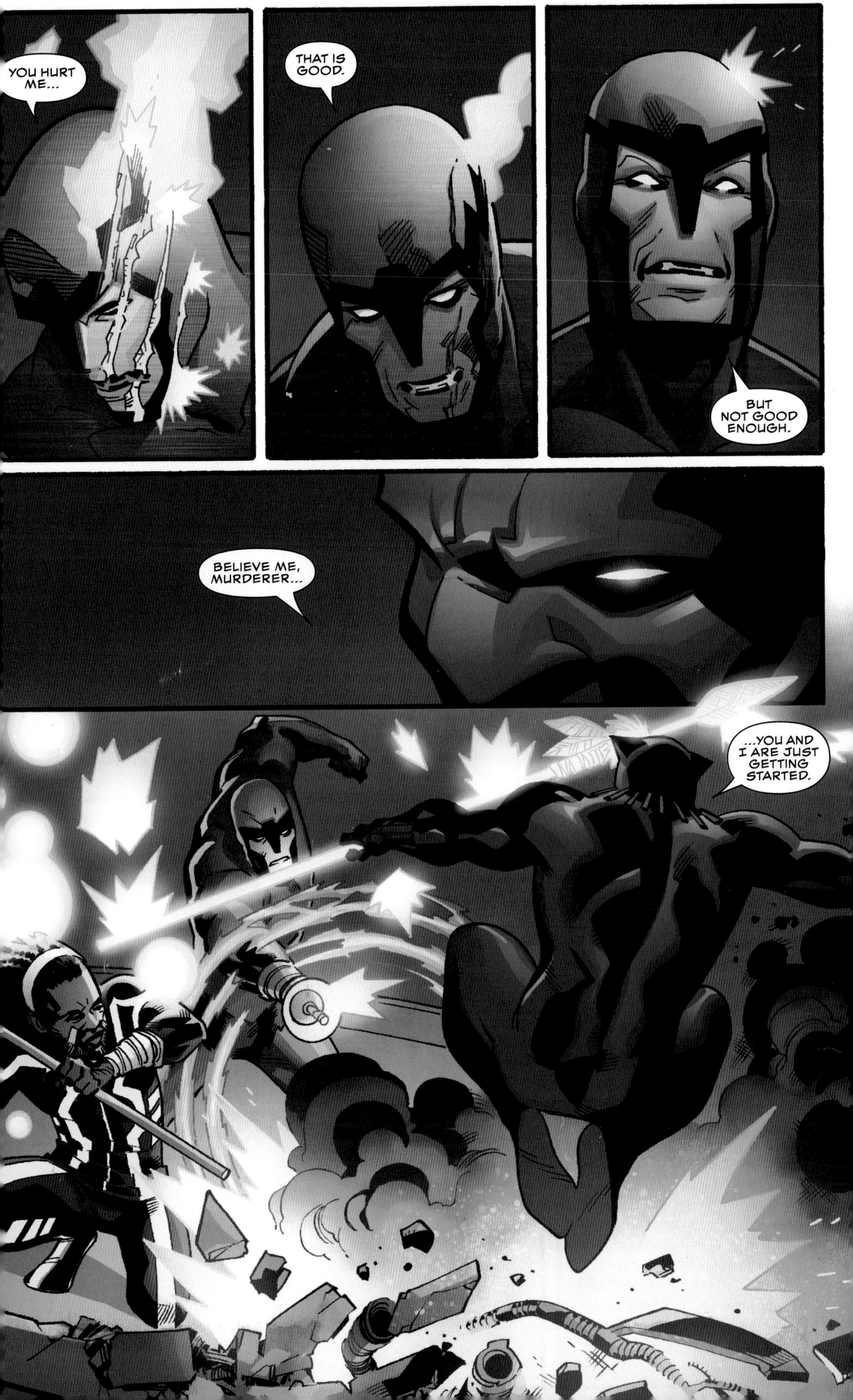
YOU HURT ME...
THAT IS GOOD.
BUT NOT GOOD ENOUGH.
BELIEVE ME, MURDERER...
...YOU AND I ARE JUST GETTING STARTED.

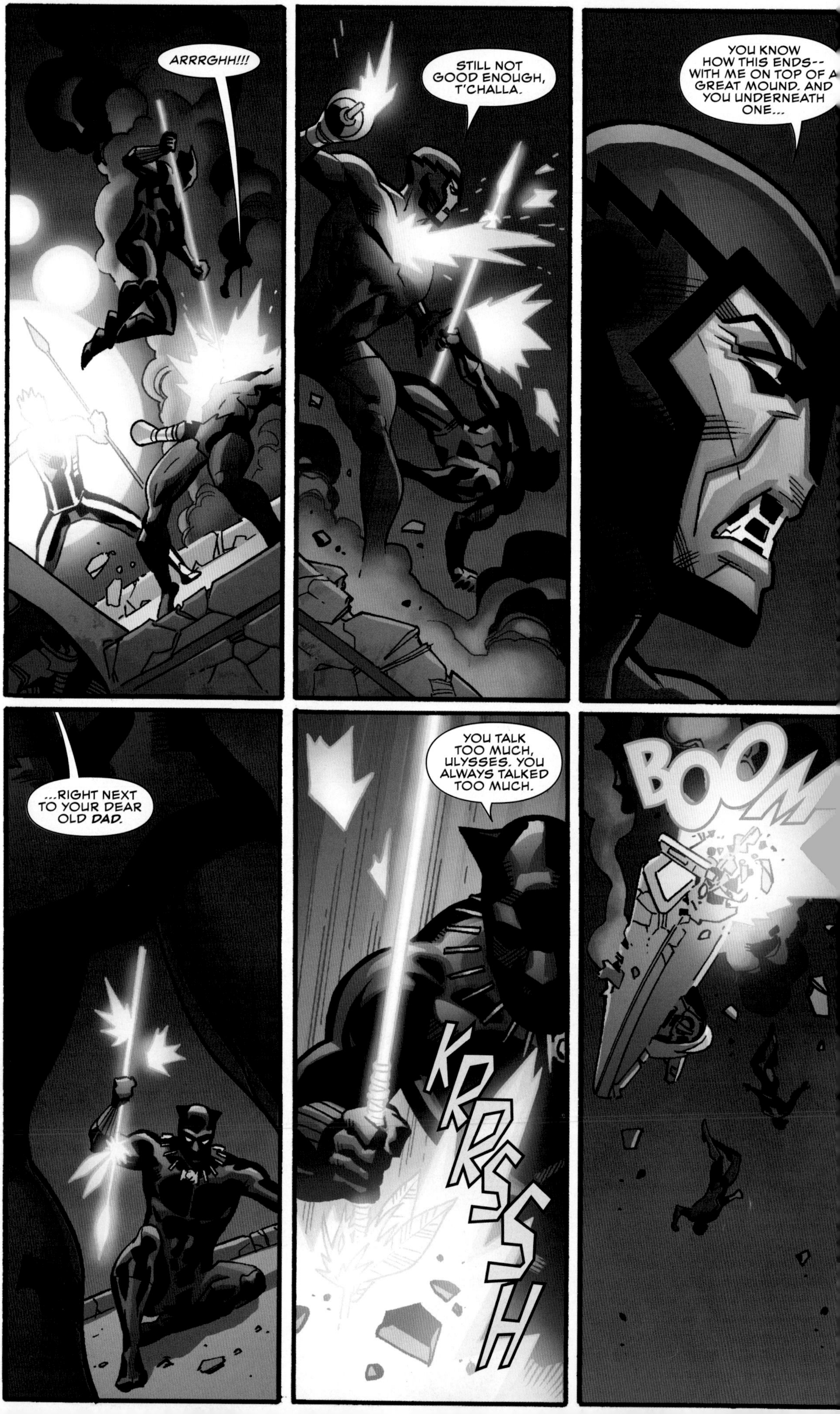
ARRRGHH!!!
STILL NOT GOOD ENOUGH, T'CHALLA.
YOU KNOW HOW THIS ENDS-- WITH ME ON TOP OF A GREAT MOUND. AND YOU UNDERNEATH ONE...
...RIGHT NEXT TO YOUR DEAR OLD DAD.
YOU TALK TOO MUCH, ULYSSES. YOU ALWAYS TALKED TOO MUCH.
KRSSSH
BOOM

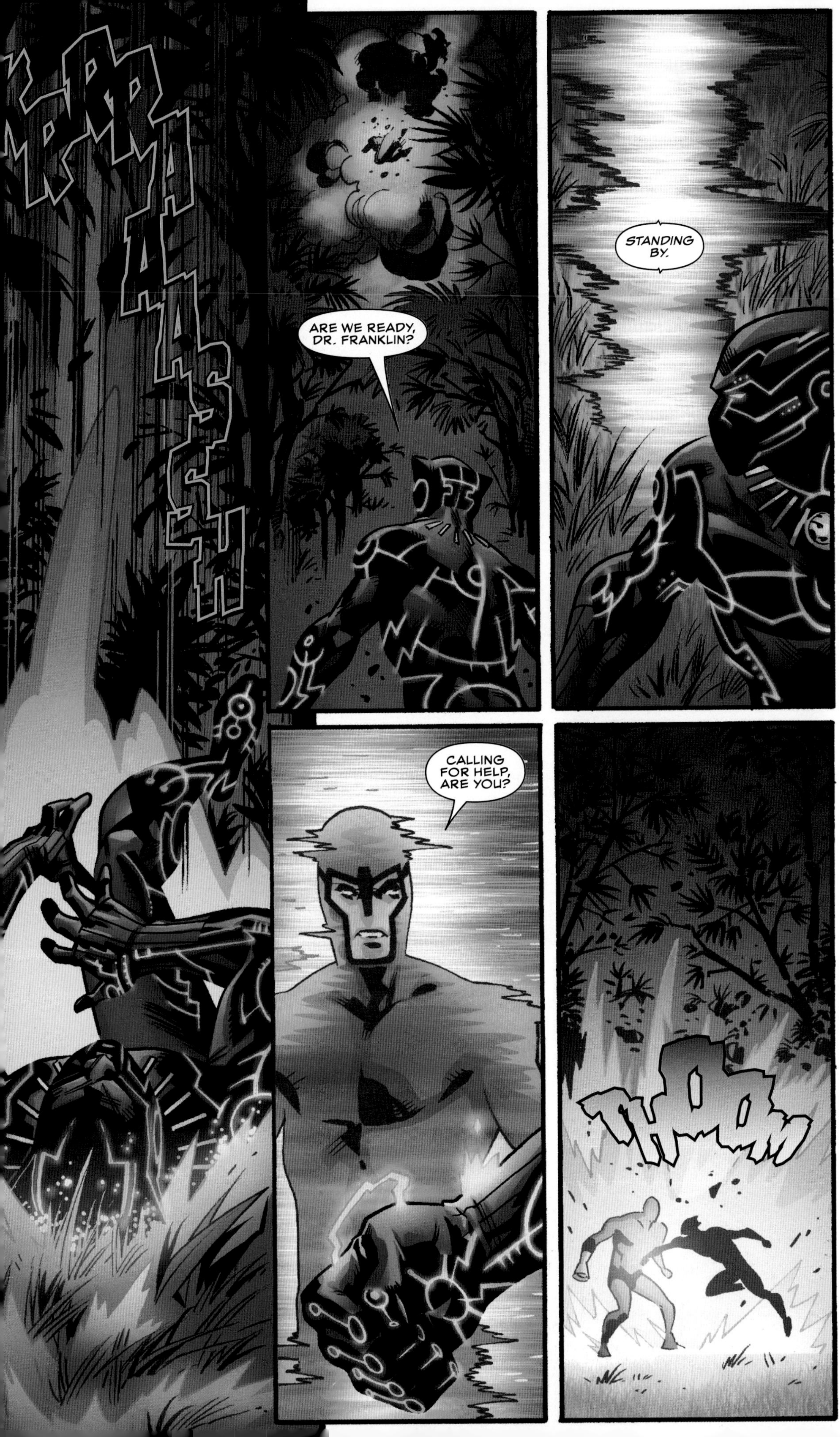
KRRAAASH
ARE WE READY, DR. FRANKLIN?
STANDING BY.
CALLING FOR HELP, ARE YOU?
THOOM

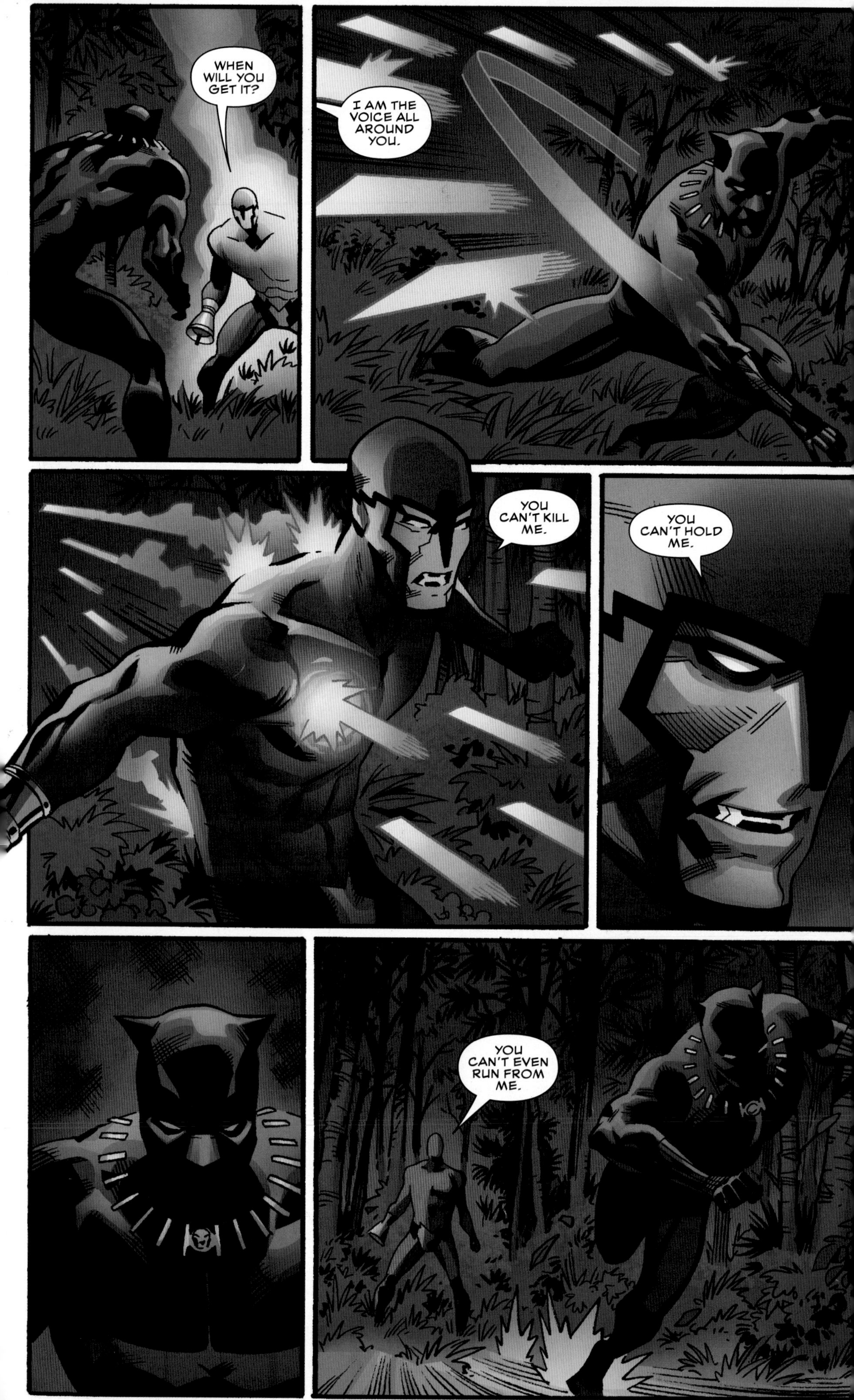
WHEN WILL YOU GET IT?
I AM THE VOICE ALL AROUND YOU.
YOU CAN'T KILL ME.
YOU CAN'T HOLD ME.
YOU CAN'T EVEN RUN FROM ME.

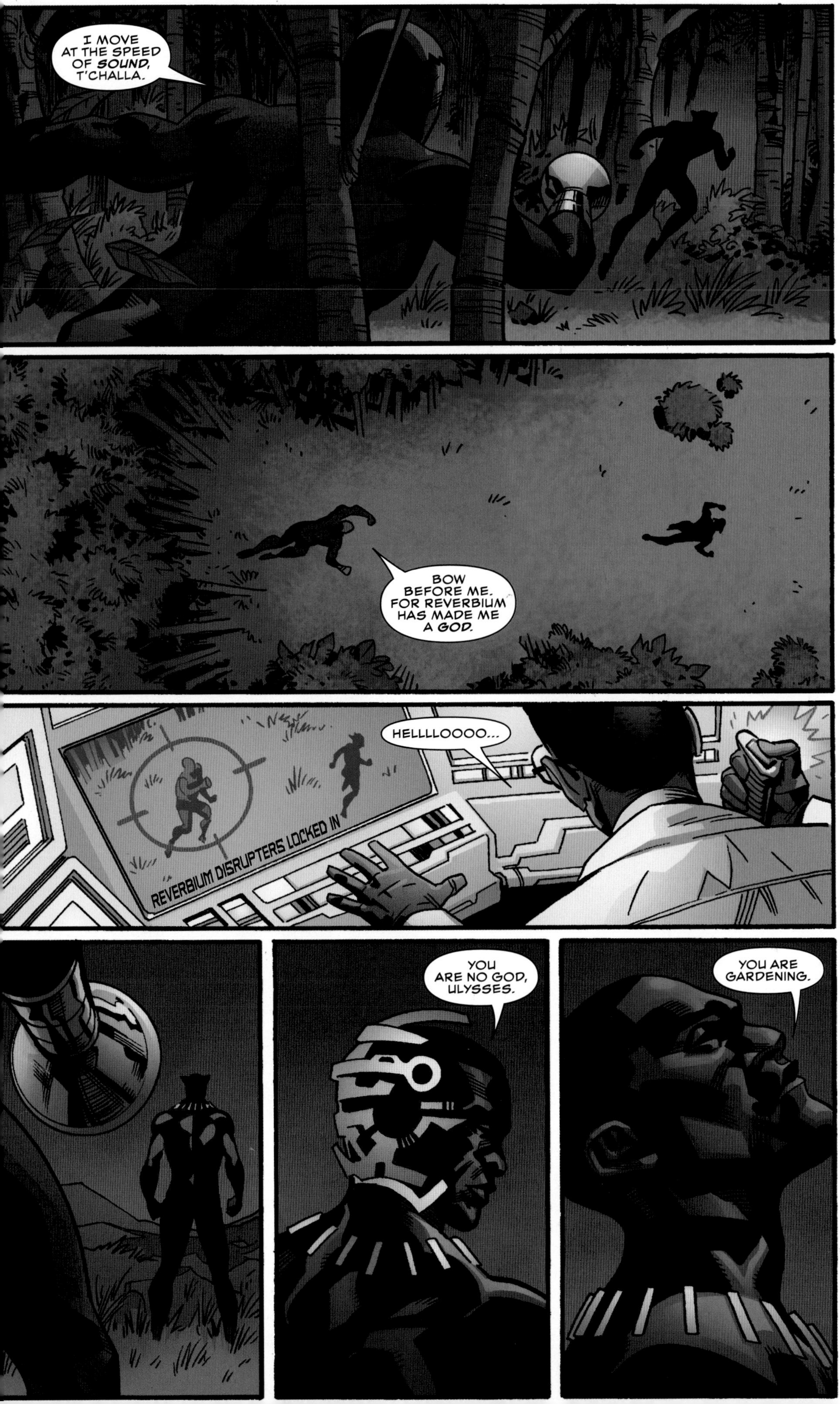
I MOVE AT THE SPEED OF SOUND, T'CHALLA.
BOW BEFORE ME. FOR REVERBIUM HAS MADE ME A GOD.
HELLLLOOOO...
REVERBIUM DISRUPTERS LOCKED IN
YOU ARE NO GOD, ULYSSES.
YOU ARE GARDENING.

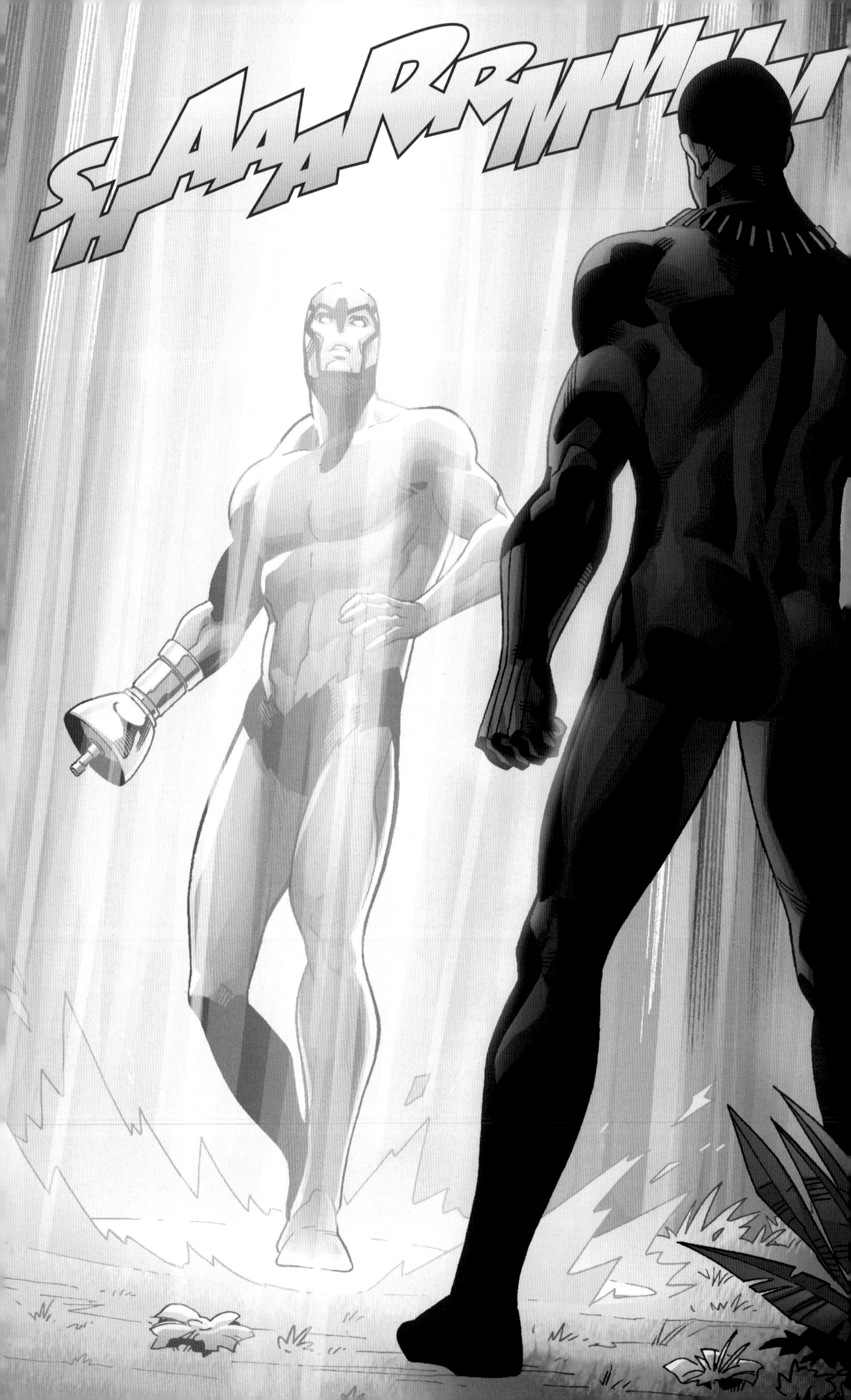
SHAARRMMM

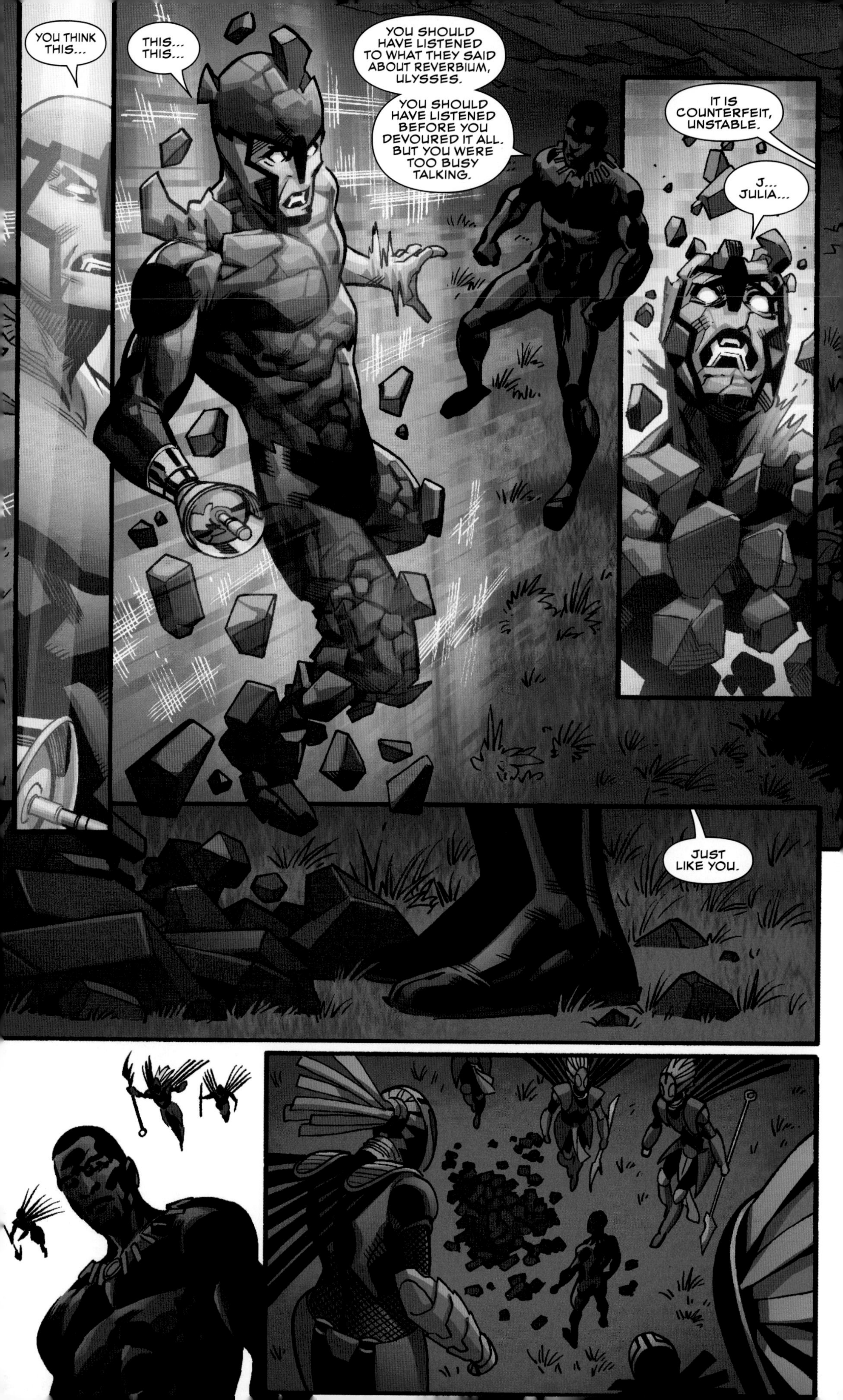
YOU THINK THIS...
THIS... THIS...
YOU SHOULD HAVE LISTENED TO WHAT THEY SAID ABOUT REVERBIUM, ULYSSES.
YOU SHOULD HAVE LISTENED BEFORE YOU DEVOURED IT ALL. BUT YOU WERE TOO BUSY TALKING.
IT IS COUNTERFEIT, UNSTABLE.
J... JULIA...
JUST LIKE YOU.

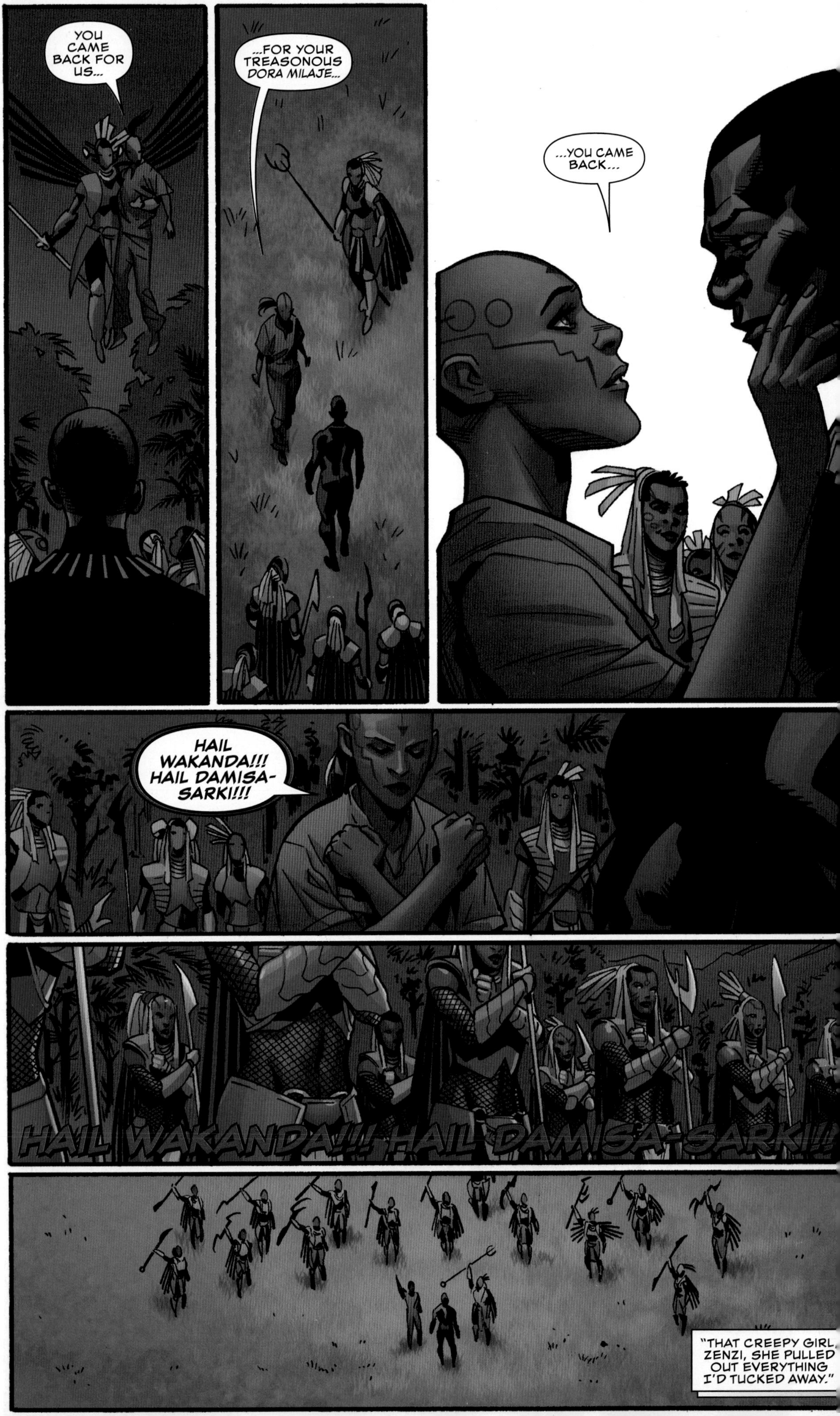
YOU CAME BACK FOR US...
...FOR YOUR TREASONOUS DORA MILAJE...
...YOU CAME BACK...
HAIL WAKANDA!!! HAIL DAMISA-SARKI!!!
HAIL WAKANDA!!! HAIL DAMISA-SARKI!!!
"THAT CREEPY GIRL ZENZI, SHE PULLED OUT EVERYTHING I'D TUCKED AWAY."

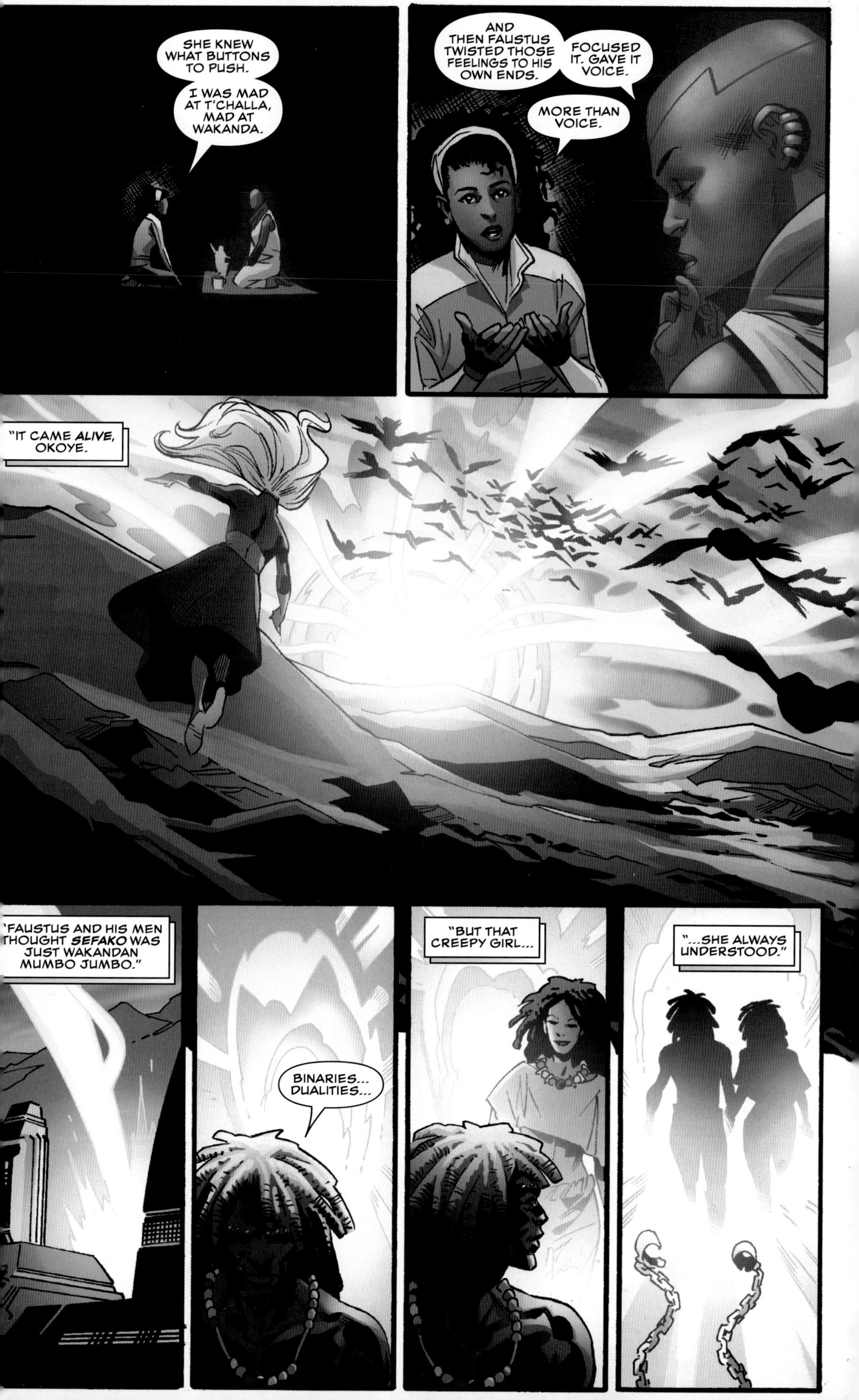
SHE KNEW WHAT BUTTONS TO PUSH.
I WAS MAD AT T'CHALLA, MAD AT WAKANDA.
AND THEN FAUSTUS TWISTED THOSE FEELINGS TO HIS OWN ENDS.
FOCUSED IT. GAVE IT VOICE.
MORE THAN VOICE.
"IT CAME *ALIVE*, OKOYE.
"FAUSTUS AND HIS MEN THOUGHT *SEFAKO* WAS JUST WAKANDAN MUMBO JUMBO."
BINARIES... DUALITIES...
"BUT THAT CREEPY GIRL...
"...SHE ALWAYS UNDERSTOOD."

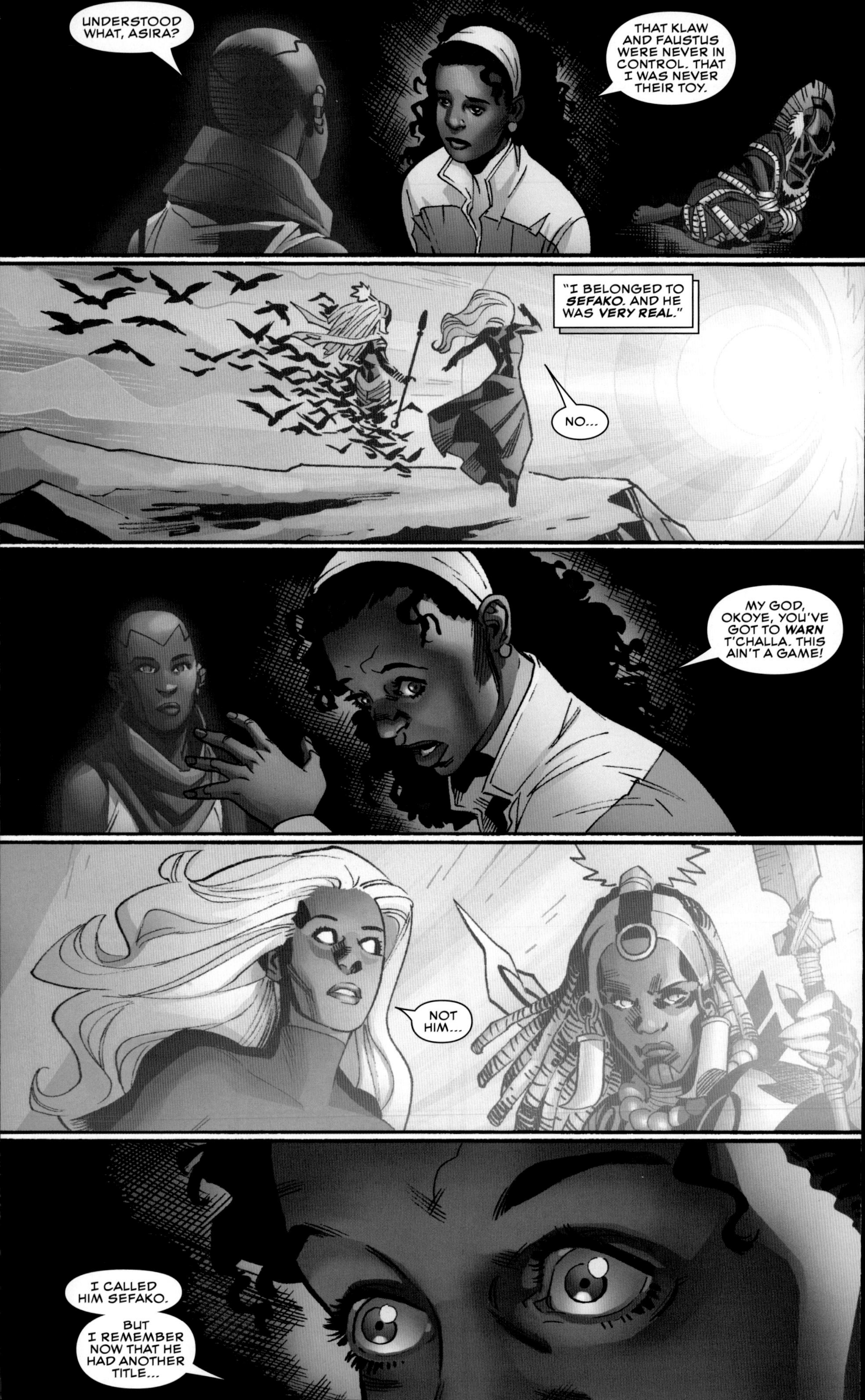
UNDERSTOOD WHAT, ASIRA?
THAT KLAW AND FAUSTUS WERE NEVER IN CONTROL. THAT I WAS NEVER THEIR TOY.
"I BELONGED TO SEFAKO. AND HE WAS VERY REAL."
NO...
MY GOD, OKOYE, YOU'VE GOT TO WARN T'CHALLA. THIS AIN'T A GAME!
NOT HIM...
I CALLED HIM SEFAKO.
BUT I REMEMBER NOW THAT HE HAD ANOTHER TITLE...

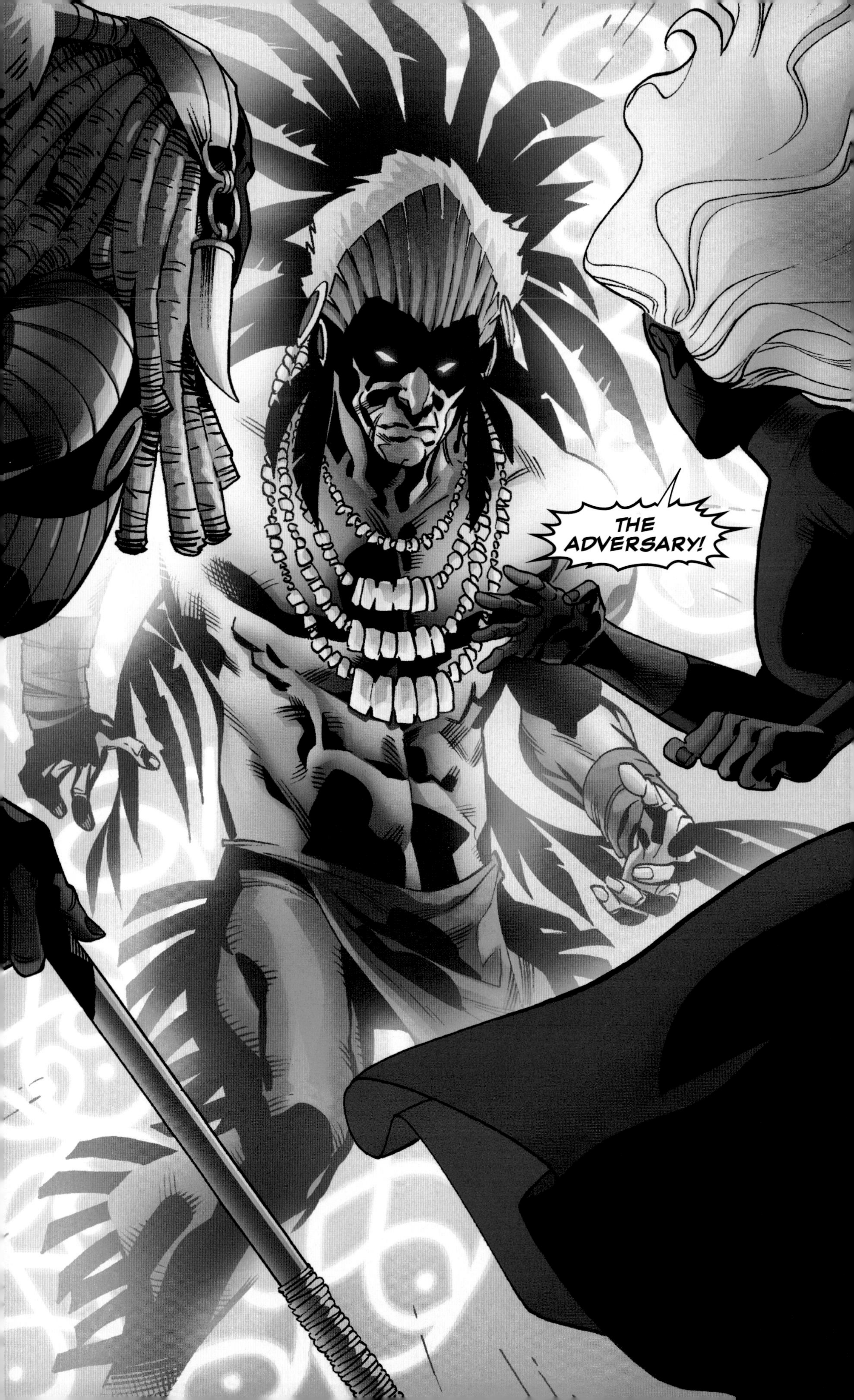
THE ADVERSARY!

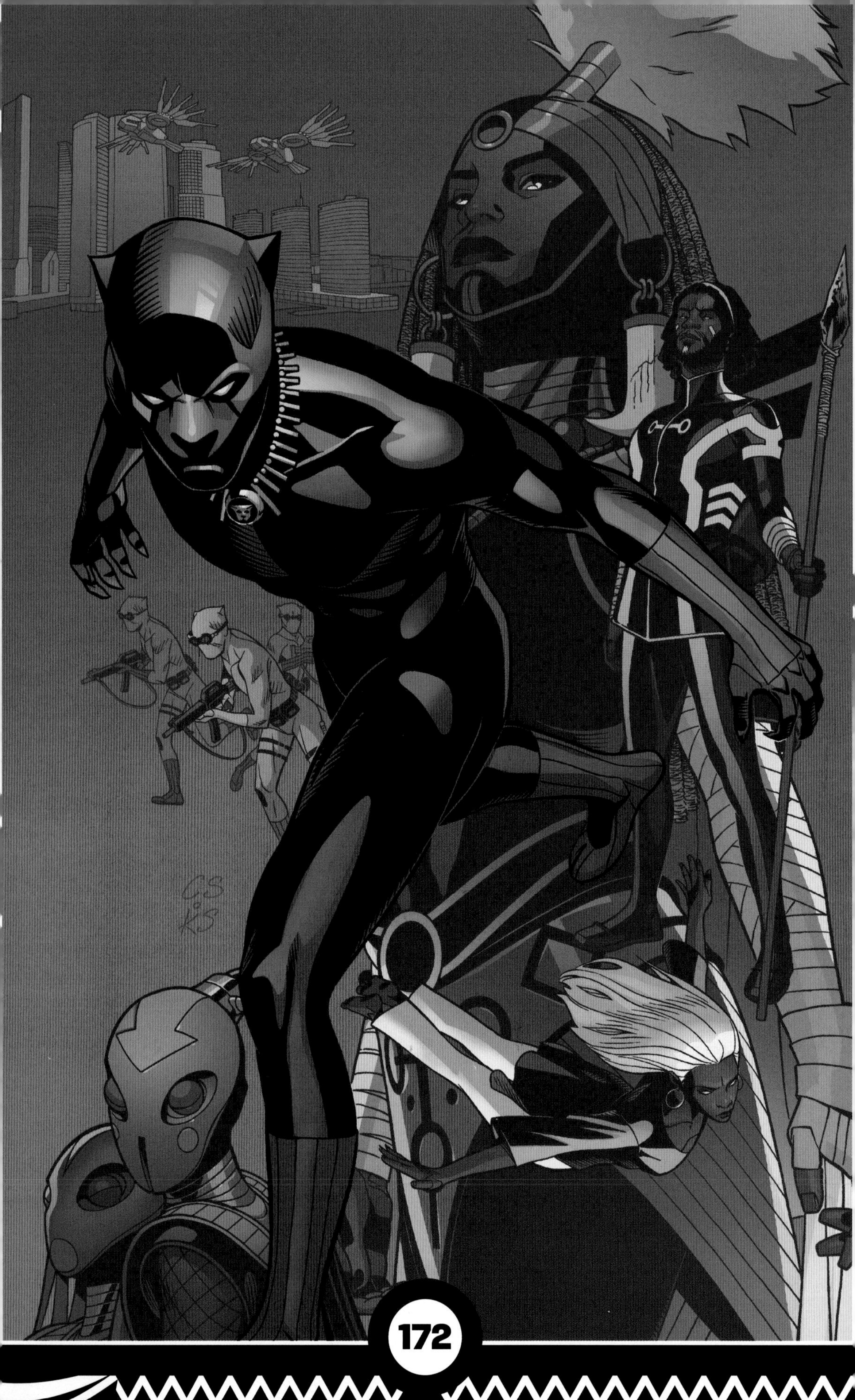

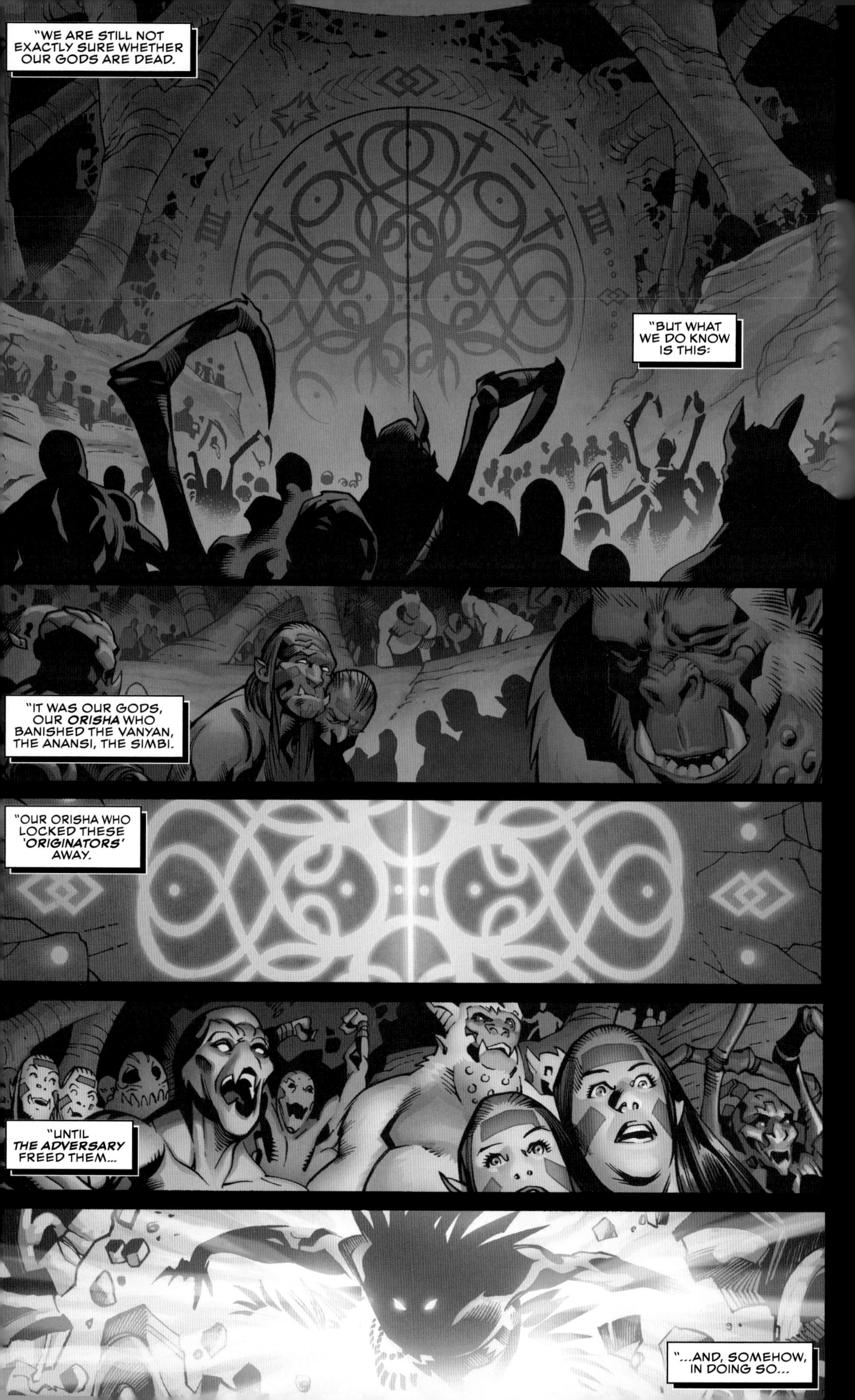
"WE ARE STILL NOT EXACTLY SURE WHETHER OUR GODS ARE DEAD.
"BUT WHAT WE DO KNOW IS THIS:
"IT WAS OUR GODS, OUR ORISHA WHO BANISHED THE VANYAN, THE ANANSI, THE SIMBI.
"OUR ORISHA WHO LOCKED THESE 'ORIGINATORS' AWAY.
"UNTIL THE ADVERSARY FREED THEM...
"...AND, SOMEHOW, IN DOING SO...

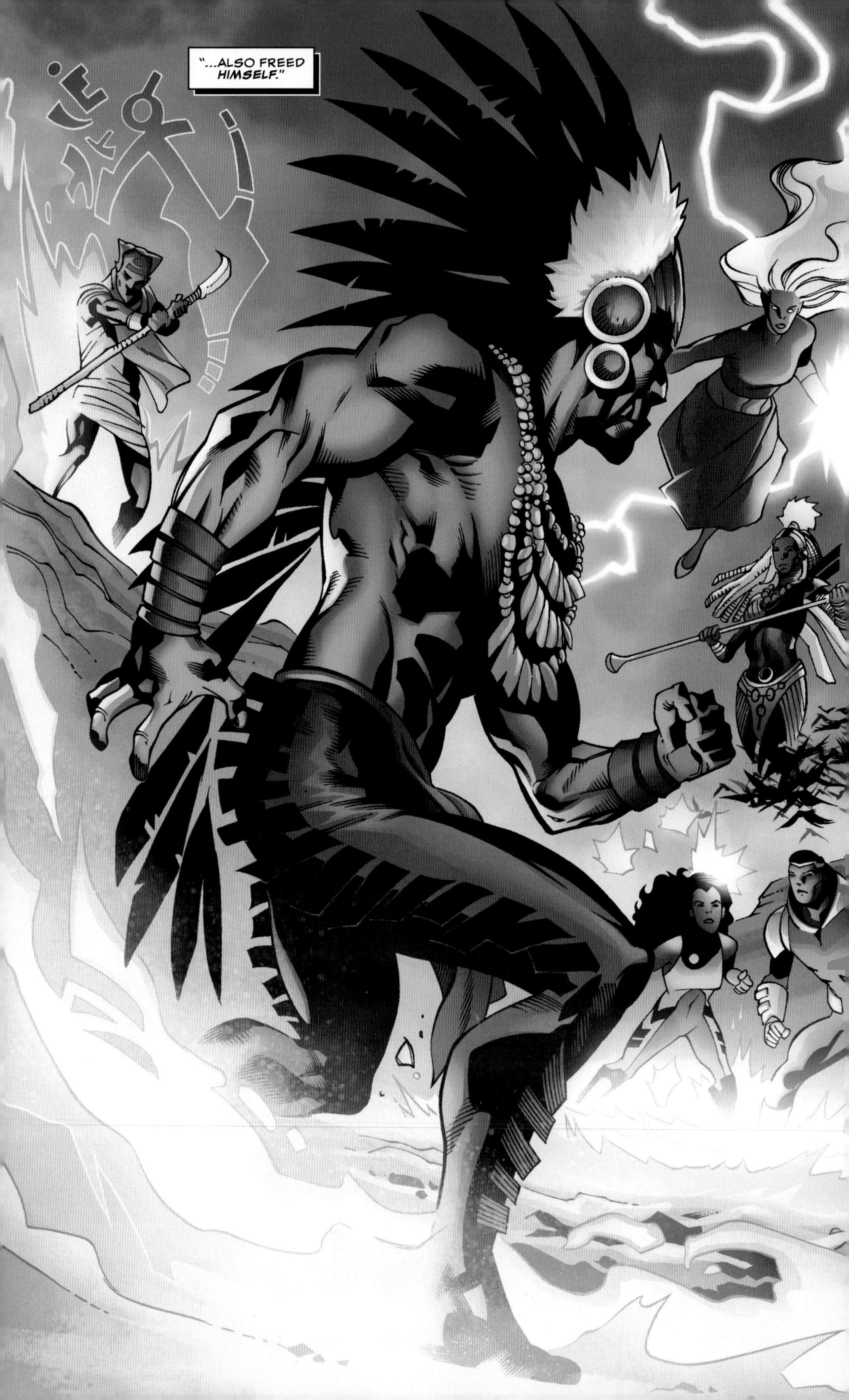
"...ALSO FREED HIMSELF."

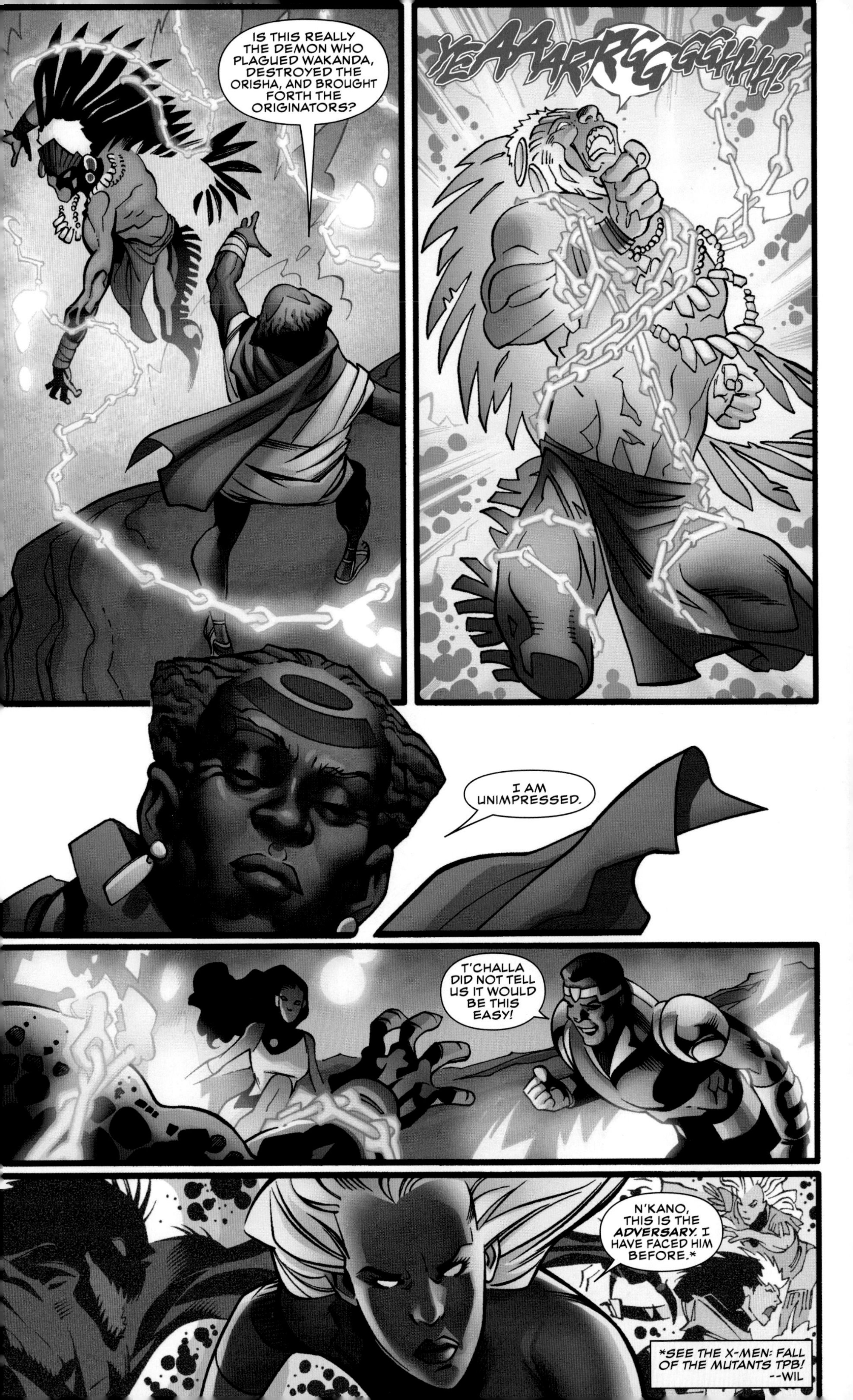
IS THIS REALLY THE DEMON WHO PLAGUED WAKANDA, DESTROYED THE ORISHA, AND BROUGHT FORTH THE ORIGINATORS?
YEAAARRGGGHHH!
I AM UNIMPRESSED.
T'CHALLA DID NOT TELL US IT WOULD BE THIS EASY!
N'KANO, THIS IS THE ADVERSARY. I HAVE FACED HIM BEFORE.*
*SEE THE X-MEN: FALL OF THE MUTANTS TPB! --WIL

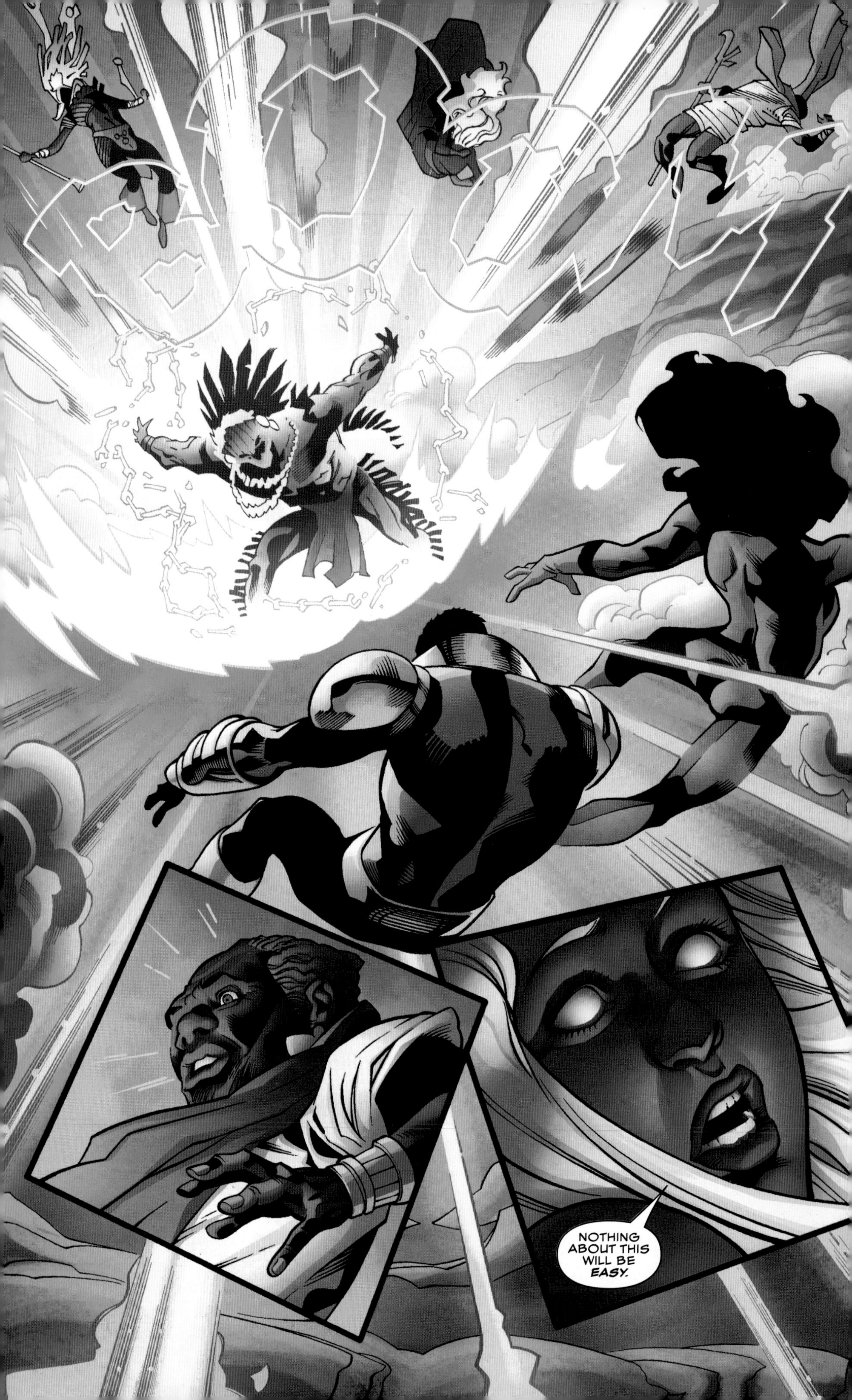
NOTHING ABOUT THIS WILL BE EASY.

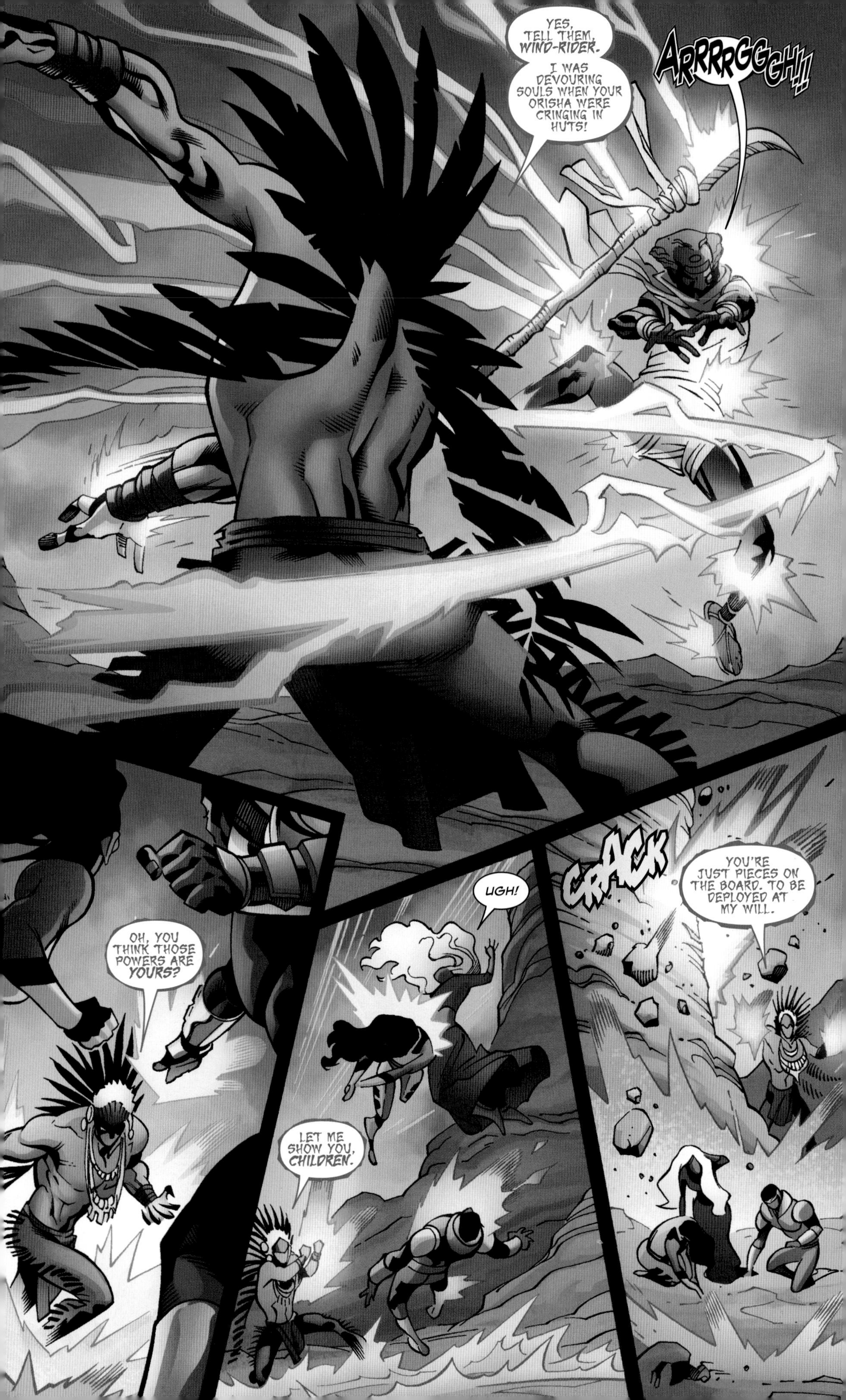
YES, TELL THEM, WIND-RIDER.
I WAS DEVOURING SOULS WHEN YOUR ORISHA WERE CRINGING IN HUTS!
ARRRRGGGH!!
OH, YOU THINK THOSE POWERS ARE YOURS?
UGH!
LET ME SHOW YOU, CHILDREN.
CRACK
YOU'RE JUST PIECES ON THE BOARD. TO BE DEPLOYED AT MY WILL.

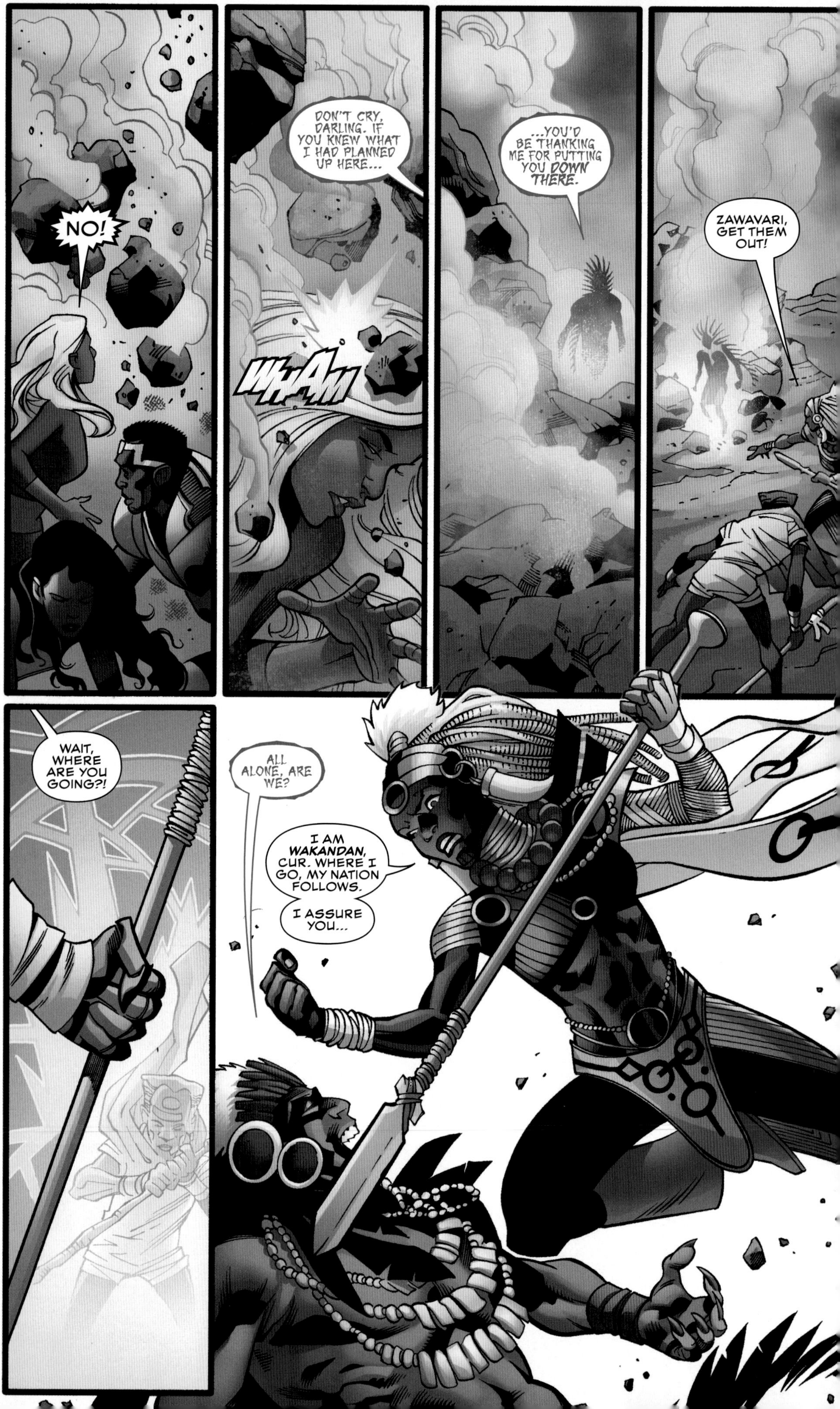
NO!
DON'T CRY, DARLING. IF YOU KNEW WHAT I HAD PLANNED UP HERE...
WHAM
...YOU'D BE THANKING ME FOR PUTTING YOU DOWN THERE.
ZAWAVARI, GET THEM OUT!
WAIT, WHERE ARE YOU GOING?!
ALL ALONE, ARE WE?
I AM WAKANDAN, CUR. WHERE I GO, MY NATION FOLLOWS.
I ASSURE YOU...

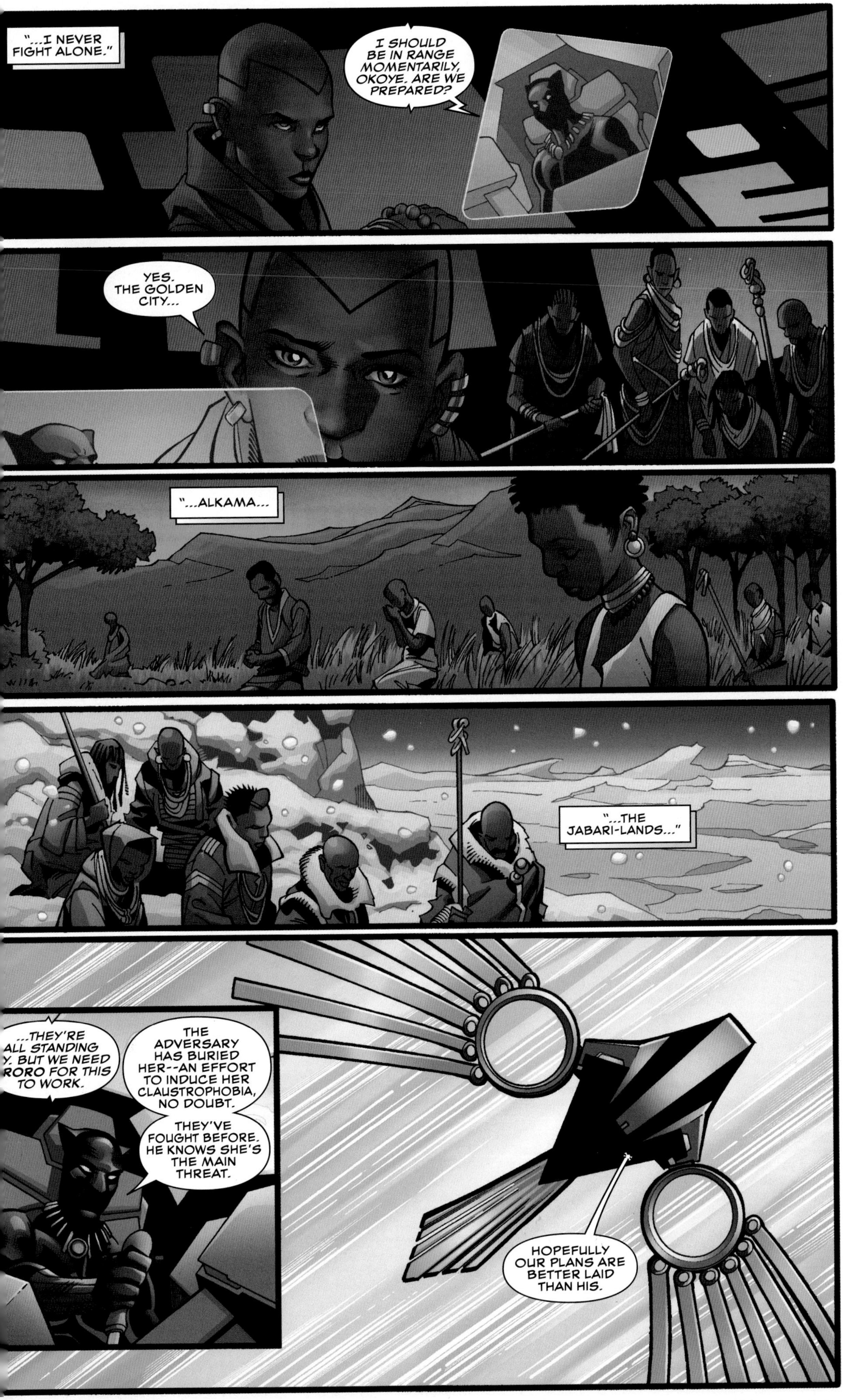

"...I NEVER FIGHT ALONE."
I SHOULD BE IN RANGE MOMENTARILY, OKOYE. ARE WE PREPARED?
YES. THE GOLDEN CITY...
"...ALKAMA...
"...THE JABARI-LANDS..."
...THEY'RE ALL STANDING BY. BUT WE NEED RORO FOR THIS TO WORK.
THE ADVERSARY HAS BURIED HER--AN EFFORT TO INDUCE HER CLAUSTROPHOBIA, NO DOUBT.
THEY'VE FOUGHT BEFORE. HE KNOWS SHE'S THE MAIN THREAT.
HOPEFULLY OUR PLANS ARE BETTER LAID THAN HIS.

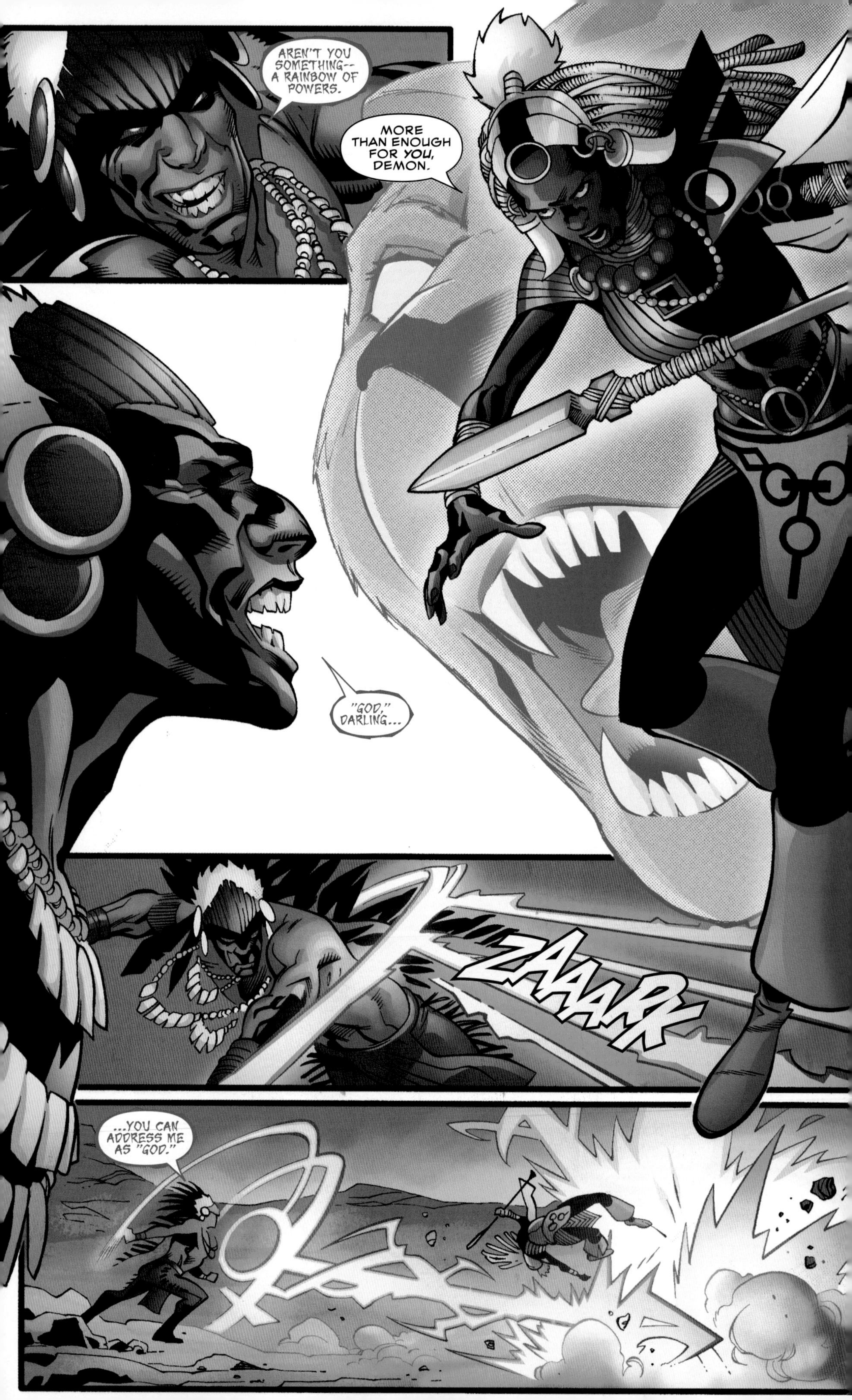
AREN'T YOU SOMETHING-- A RAINBOW OF POWERS.
MORE THAN ENOUGH FOR YOU, DEMON.
"GOD," DARLING...
ZAAARK
...YOU CAN ADDRESS ME AS "GOD."

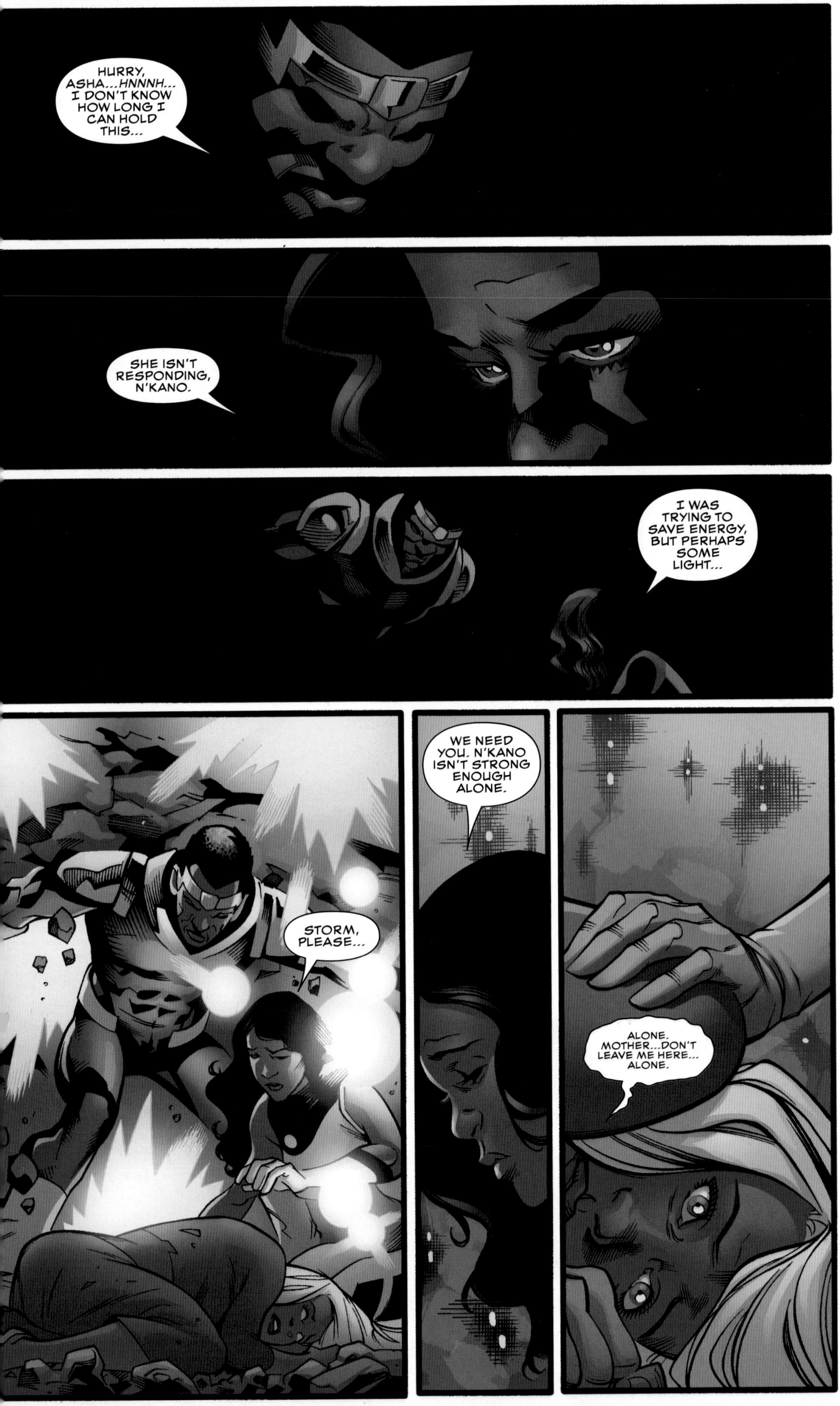
HURRY, ASHA...*HNNNH*... I DON'T KNOW HOW LONG I CAN HOLD THIS...
SHE ISN'T RESPONDING, N'KANO.
I WAS TRYING TO SAVE ENERGY, BUT PERHAPS SOME LIGHT...
STORM, PLEASE...
WE NEED YOU. N'KANO ISN'T STRONG ENOUGH ALONE.
ALONE. MOTHER...DON'T LEAVE ME HERE... ALONE.

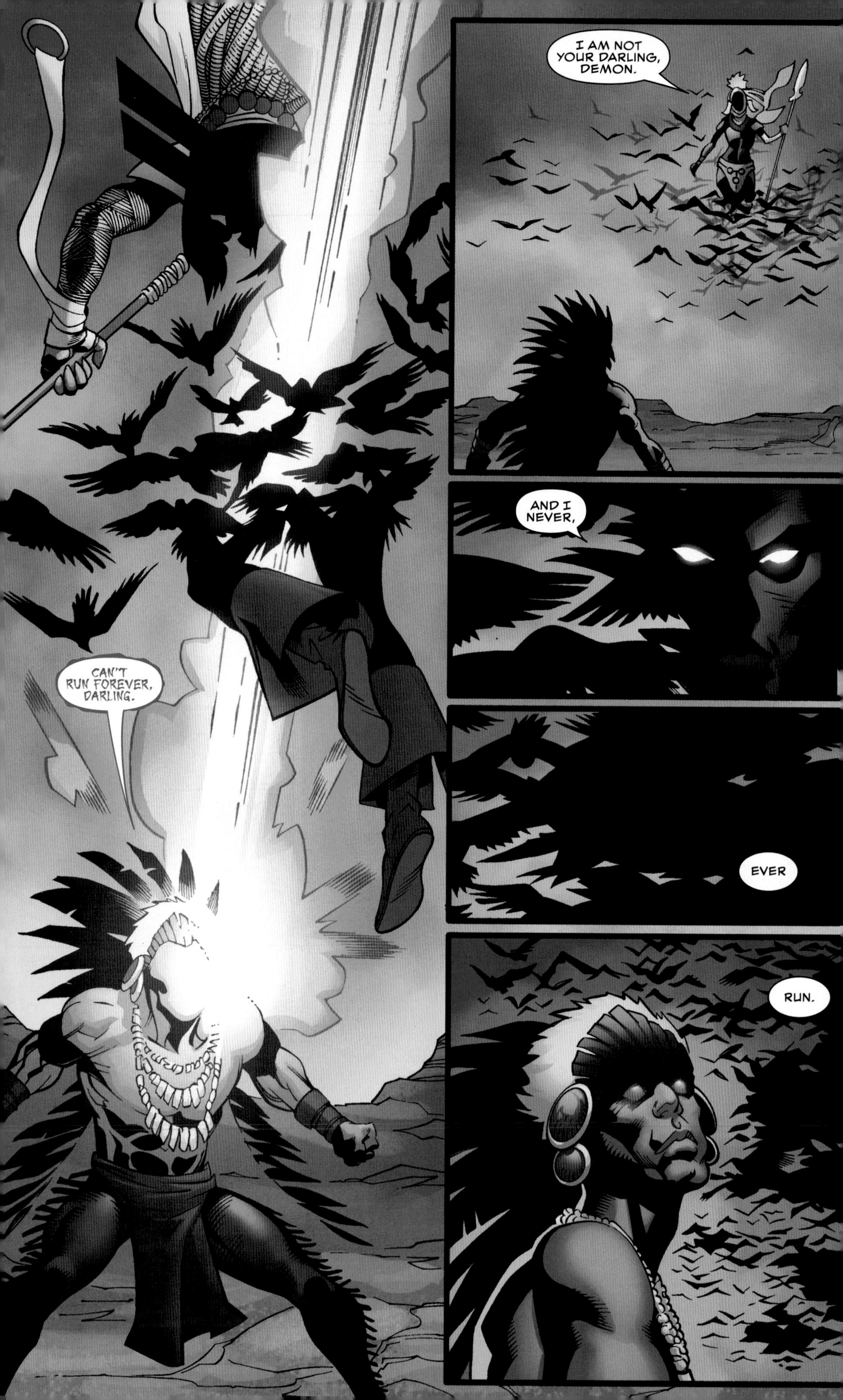
I AM NOT YOUR DARLING, DEMON.
CAN'T RUN FOREVER, DARLING.
AND I NEVER,
EVER
RUN.

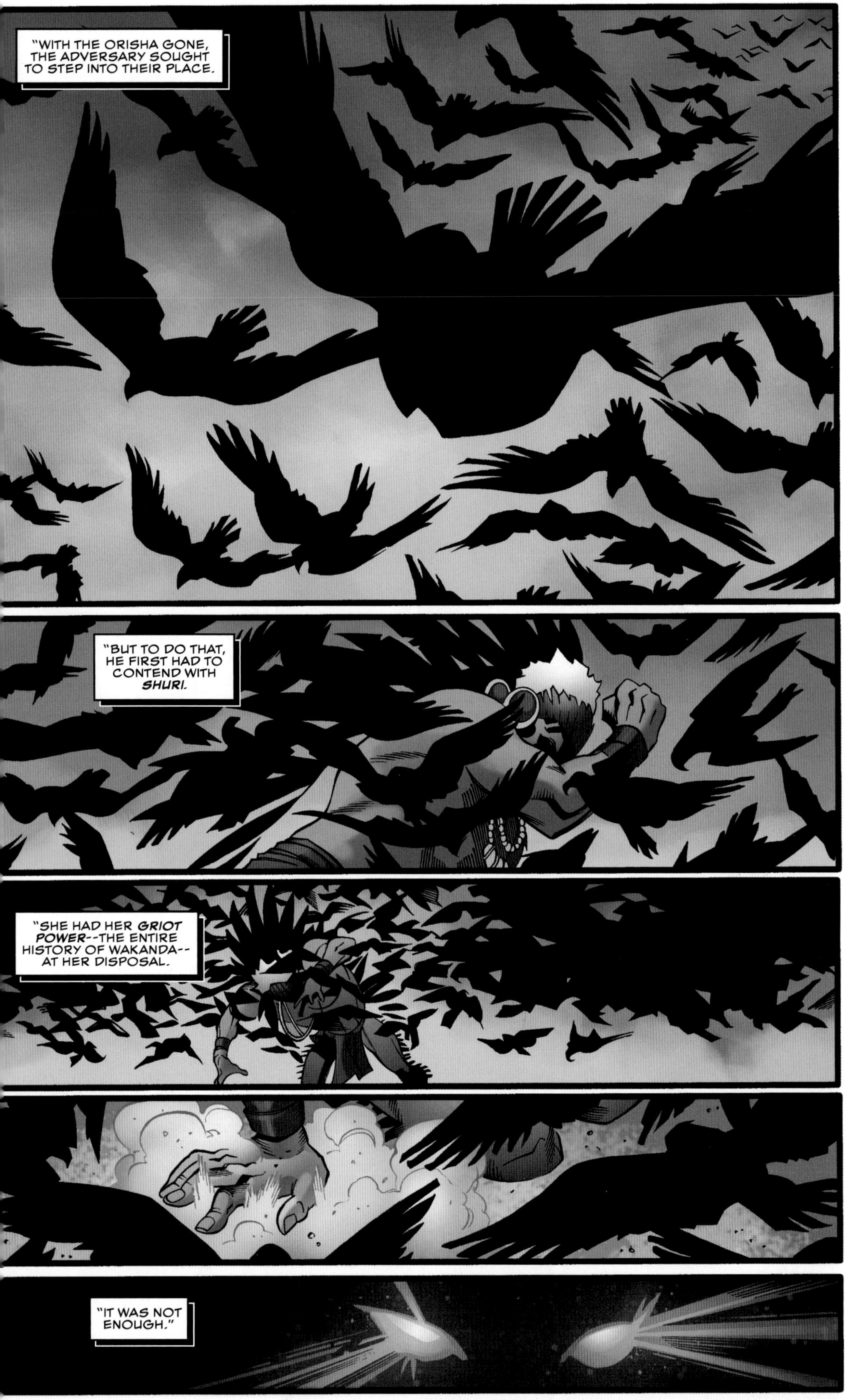
"WITH THE ORISHA GONE, THE ADVERSARY SOUGHT TO STEP INTO THEIR PLACE.
"BUT TO DO THAT, HE FIRST HAD TO CONTEND WITH *SHURI*.
"SHE HAD HER *GRIOT POWER*--THE ENTIRE HISTORY OF WAKANDA--AT HER DISPOSAL.
"IT WAS NOT ENOUGH."

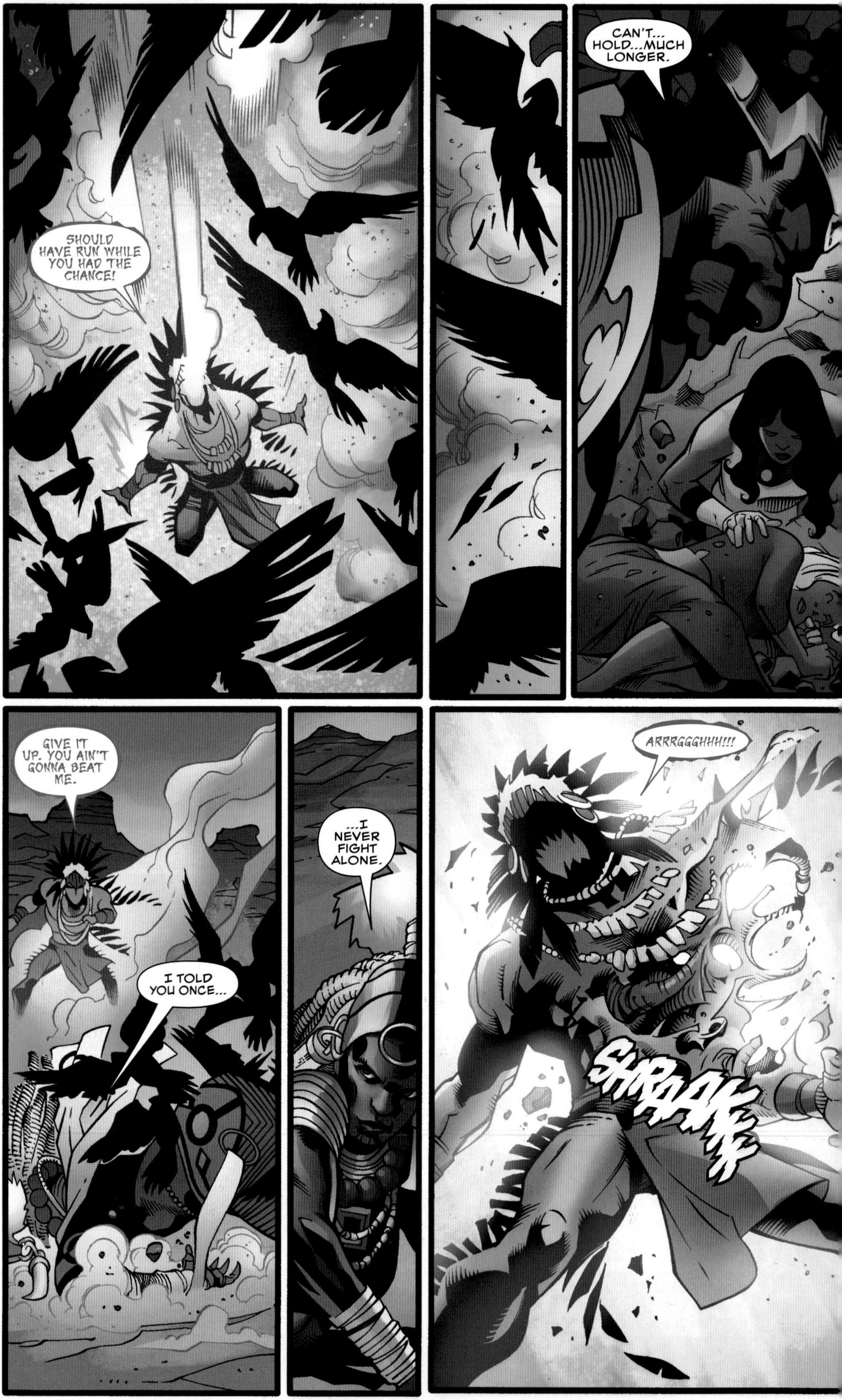
SHOULD HAVE RUN WHILE YOU HAD THE CHANCE!
CAN'T... HOLD...MUCH LONGER.
GIVE IT UP. YOU AIN'T GONNA BEAT ME.
I TOLD YOU ONCE...
...I NEVER FIGHT ALONE.
ARRRGGGHHH!!!
SHRAAK

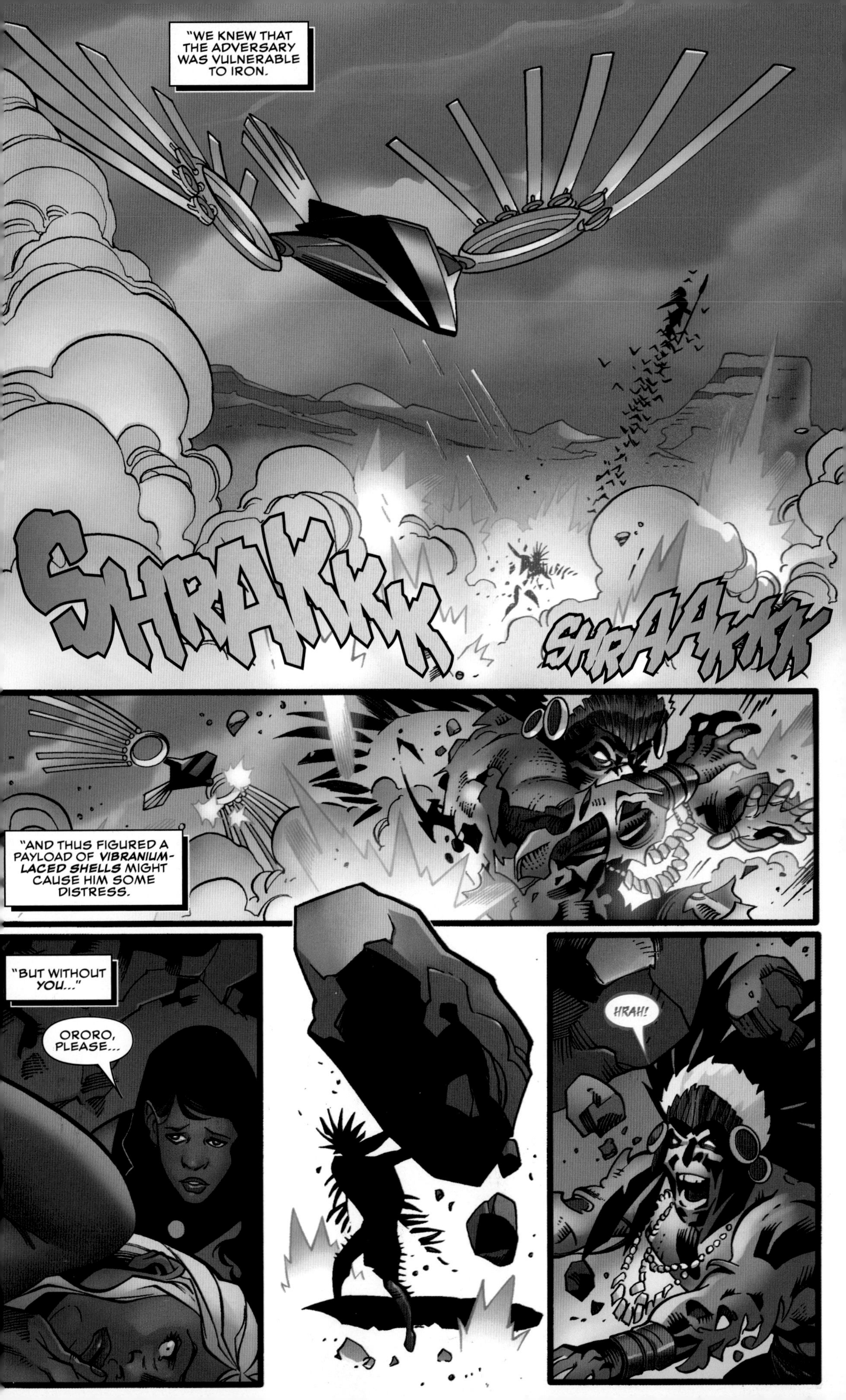
"WE KNEW THAT THE ADVERSARY WAS VULNERABLE TO IRON.
SHRAKKK
SHRAAKKK
"AND THUS FIGURED A PAYLOAD OF *VIBRANIUM-LACED SHELLS* MIGHT CAUSE HIM SOME DISTRESS.
"BUT WITHOUT *YOU*..."
ORORO, PLEASE...
HRAH!

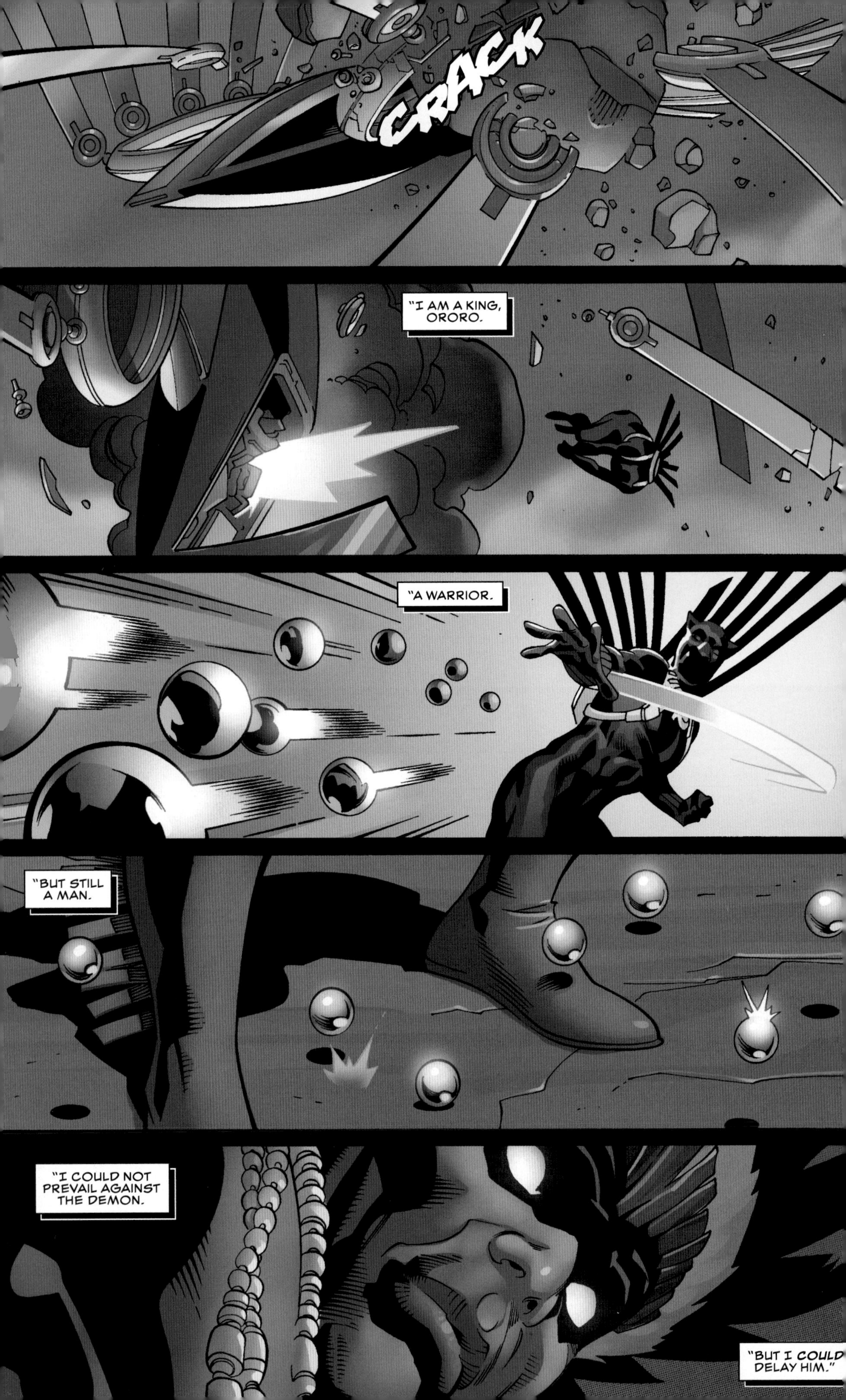
CRACK
"I AM A KING, ORORO.
"A WARRIOR.
"BUT STILL A MAN.
"I COULD NOT PREVAIL AGAINST THE DEMON.
"BUT I COULD DELAY HIM."

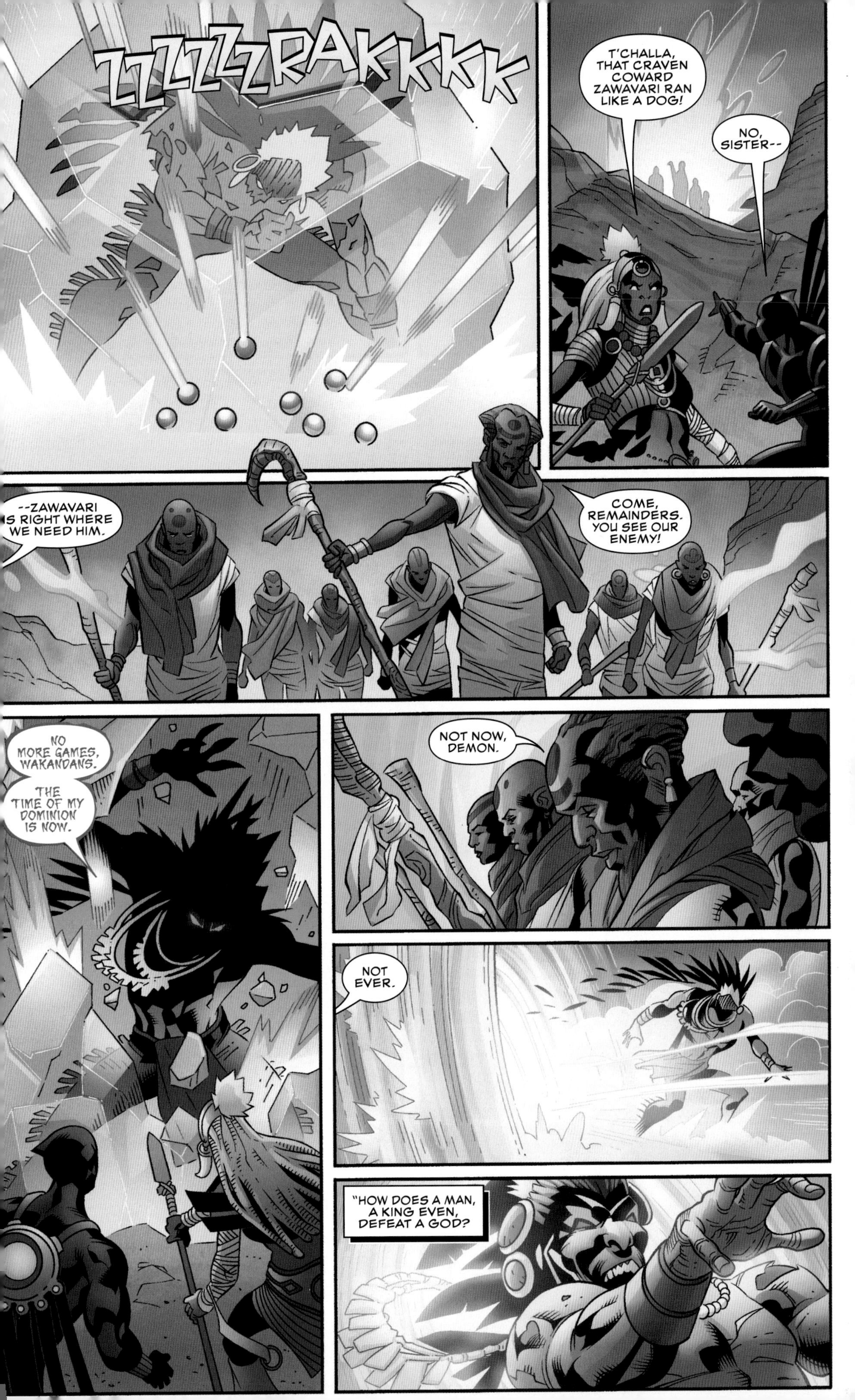
ZZZZZZRAKKKKK
T'CHALLA, THAT CRAVEN COWARD ZAWAVARI RAN LIKE A DOG!
NO, SISTER--
--ZAWAVARI IS RIGHT WHERE WE NEED HIM.
COME, REMAINDERS. YOU SEE OUR ENEMY!
NO MORE GAMES, WAKANDANS.
THE TIME OF MY DOMINION IS NOW.
NOT NOW, DEMON.
NOT EVER.
"HOW DOES A MAN, A KING EVEN, DEFEAT A GOD?

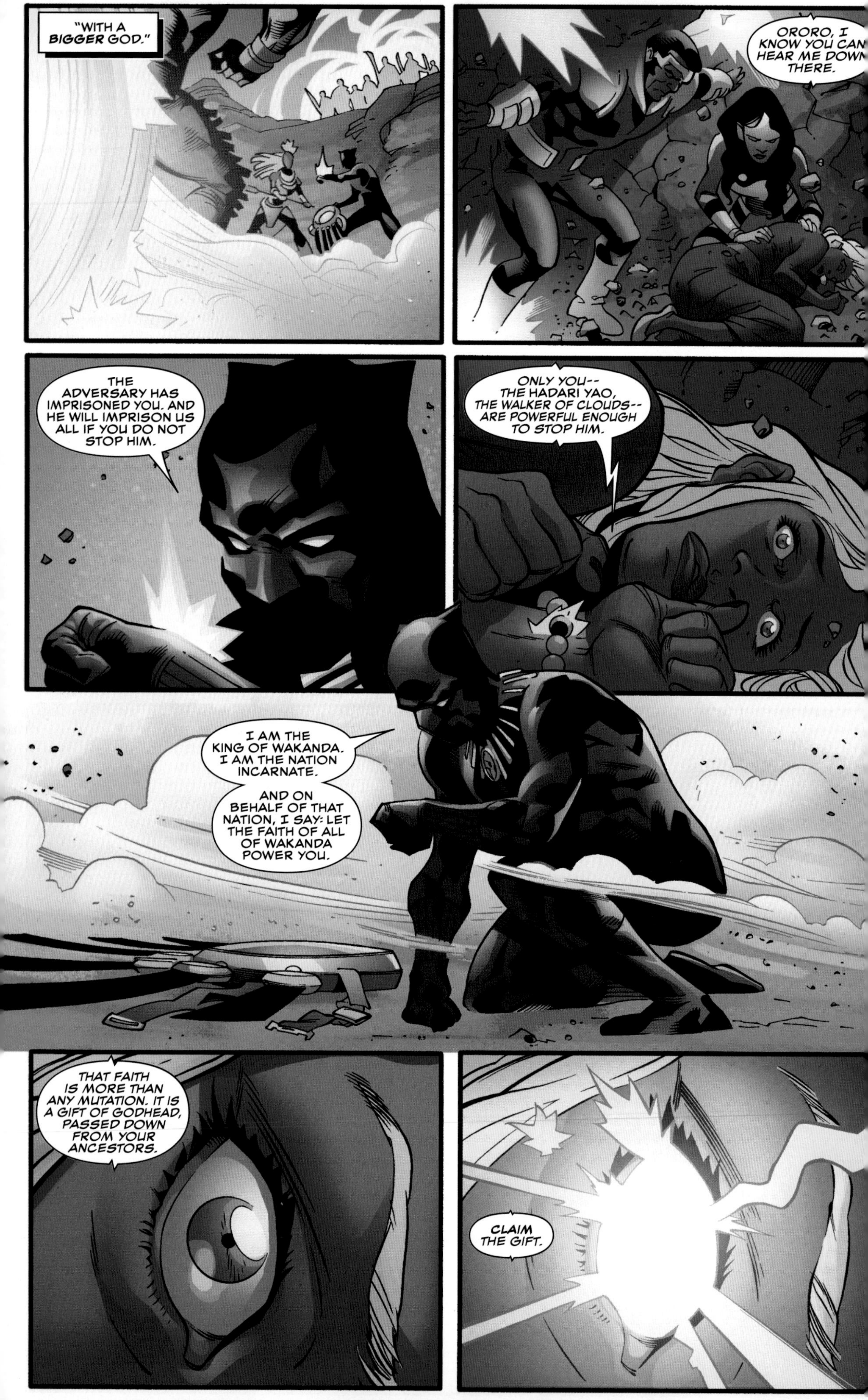
"WITH A BIGGER GOD."
ORORO, I KNOW YOU CAN HEAR ME DOWN THERE.
THE ADVERSARY HAS IMPRISONED YOU. AND HE WILL IMPRISON US ALL IF YOU DO NOT STOP HIM.
ONLY YOU-- THE HADARI YAO, THE WALKER OF CLOUDS-- ARE POWERFUL ENOUGH TO STOP HIM.
I AM THE KING OF WAKANDA. I AM THE NATION INCARNATE.
AND ON BEHALF OF THAT NATION, I SAY: LET THE FAITH OF ALL OF WAKANDA POWER YOU.
THAT FAITH IS MORE THAN ANY MUTATION. IT IS A GIFT OF GODHEAD, PASSED DOWN FROM YOUR ANCESTORS.
CLAIM THE GIFT.

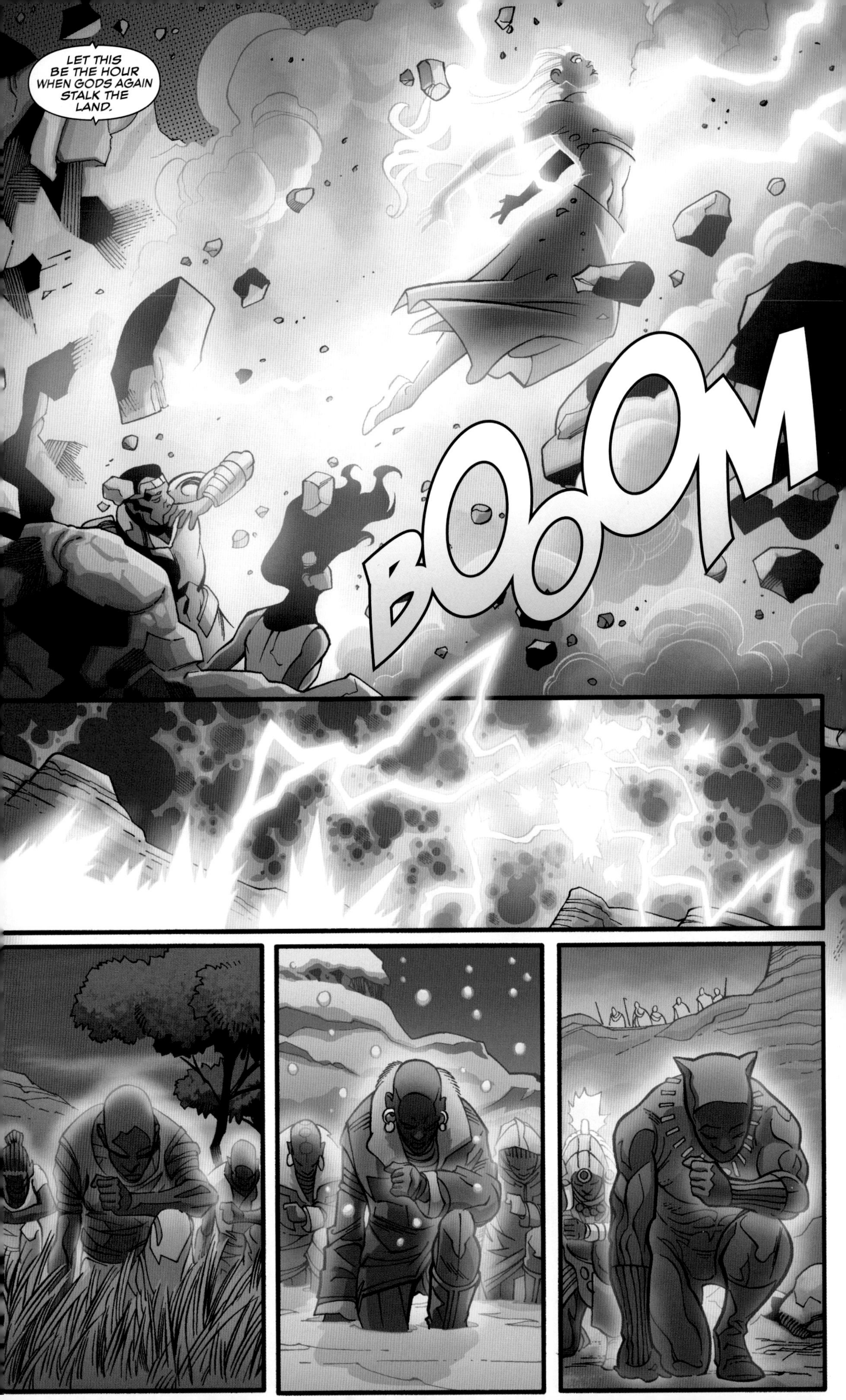
LET THIS BE THE HOUR WHEN GODS AGAIN STALK THE LAND.
BOOOM

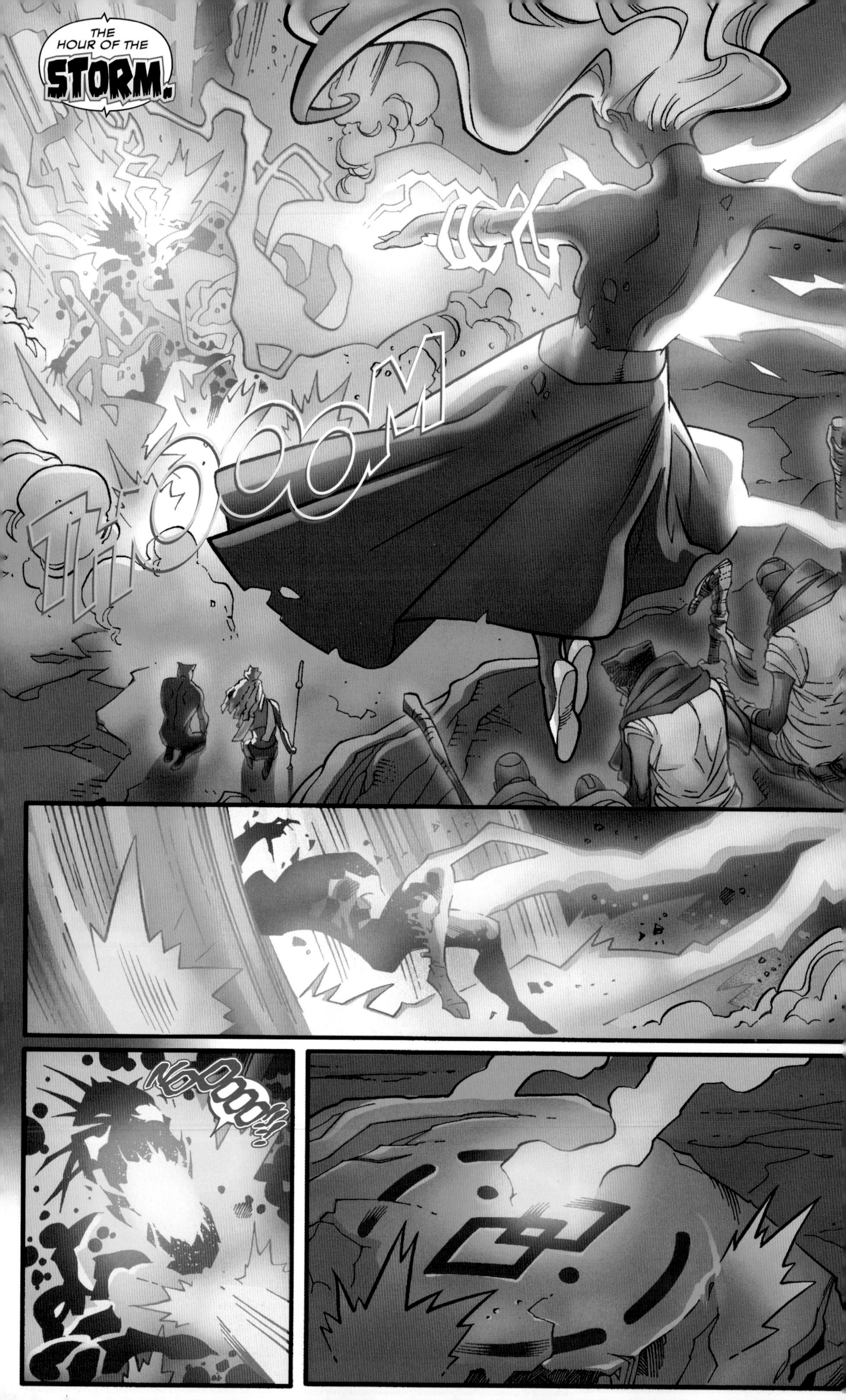
THE HOUR OF THE STORM.
THOOOOM
NOOOOO!!

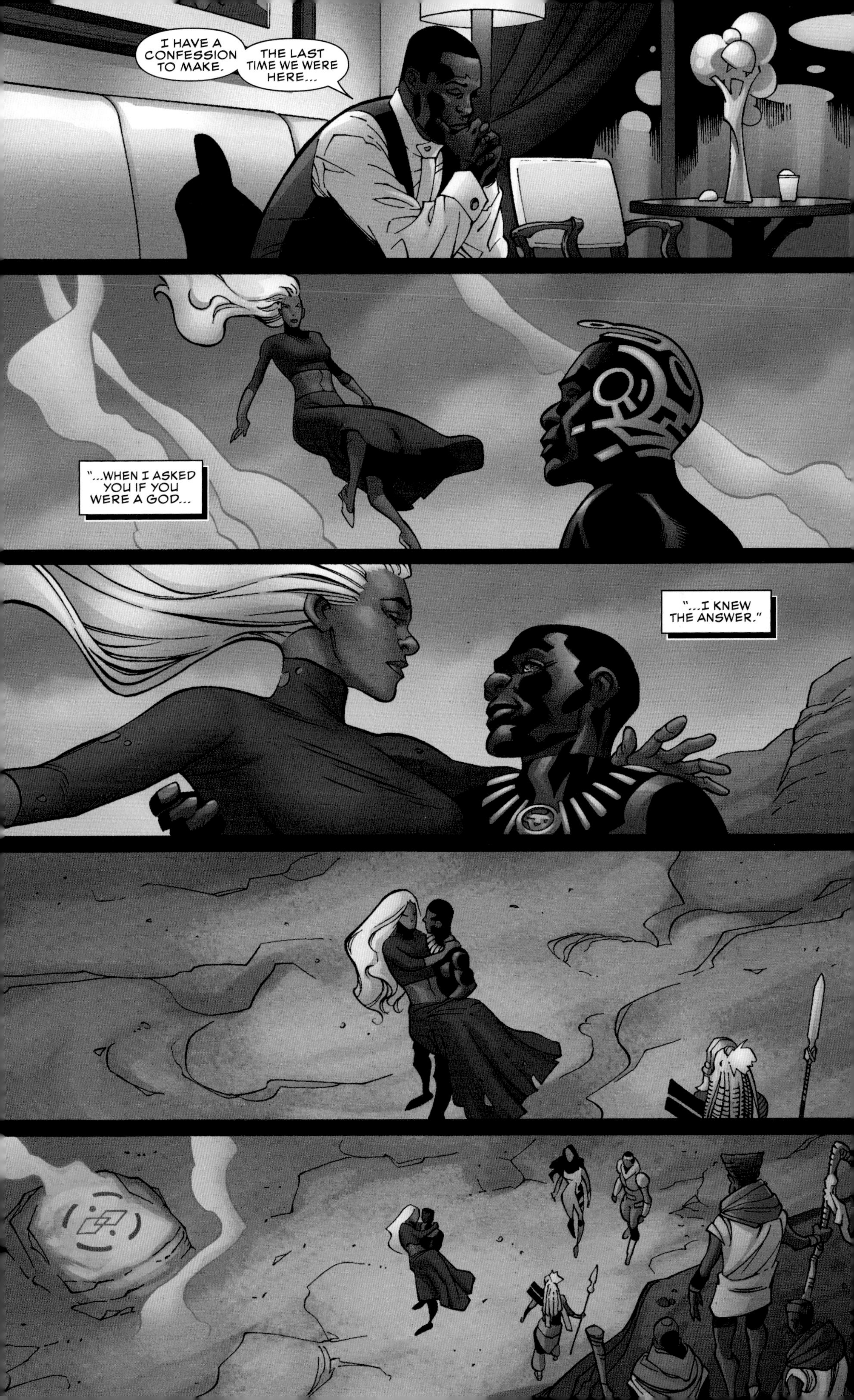
I HAVE A CONFESSION TO MAKE.
THE LAST TIME WE WERE HERE...
"...WHEN I ASKED YOU IF YOU WERE A GOD...
"...I KNEW THE ANSWER."

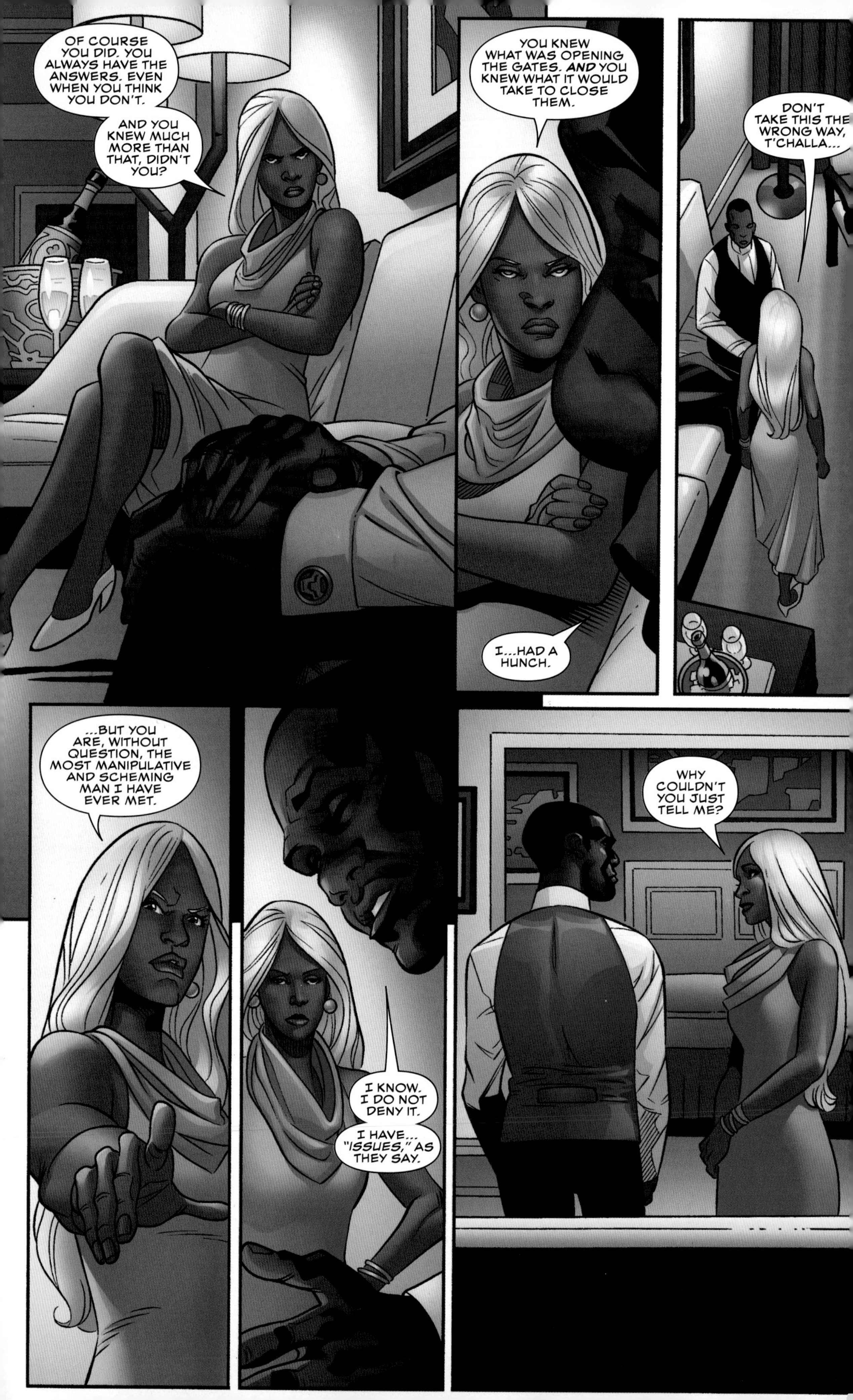
OF COURSE YOU DID. YOU ALWAYS HAVE THE ANSWERS. EVEN WHEN YOU THINK YOU DON'T.
AND YOU KNEW MUCH MORE THAN THAT, DIDN'T YOU?
YOU KNEW WHAT WAS OPENING THE GATES. AND YOU KNEW WHAT IT WOULD TAKE TO CLOSE THEM.
I...HAD A HUNCH.
DON'T TAKE THIS THE WRONG WAY, T'CHALLA...
...BUT YOU ARE, WITHOUT QUESTION, THE MOST MANIPULATIVE AND SCHEMING MAN I HAVE EVER MET.
I KNOW. I DO NOT DENY IT.
I HAVE... "ISSUES," AS THEY SAY.
WHY COULDN'T YOU JUST TELL ME?

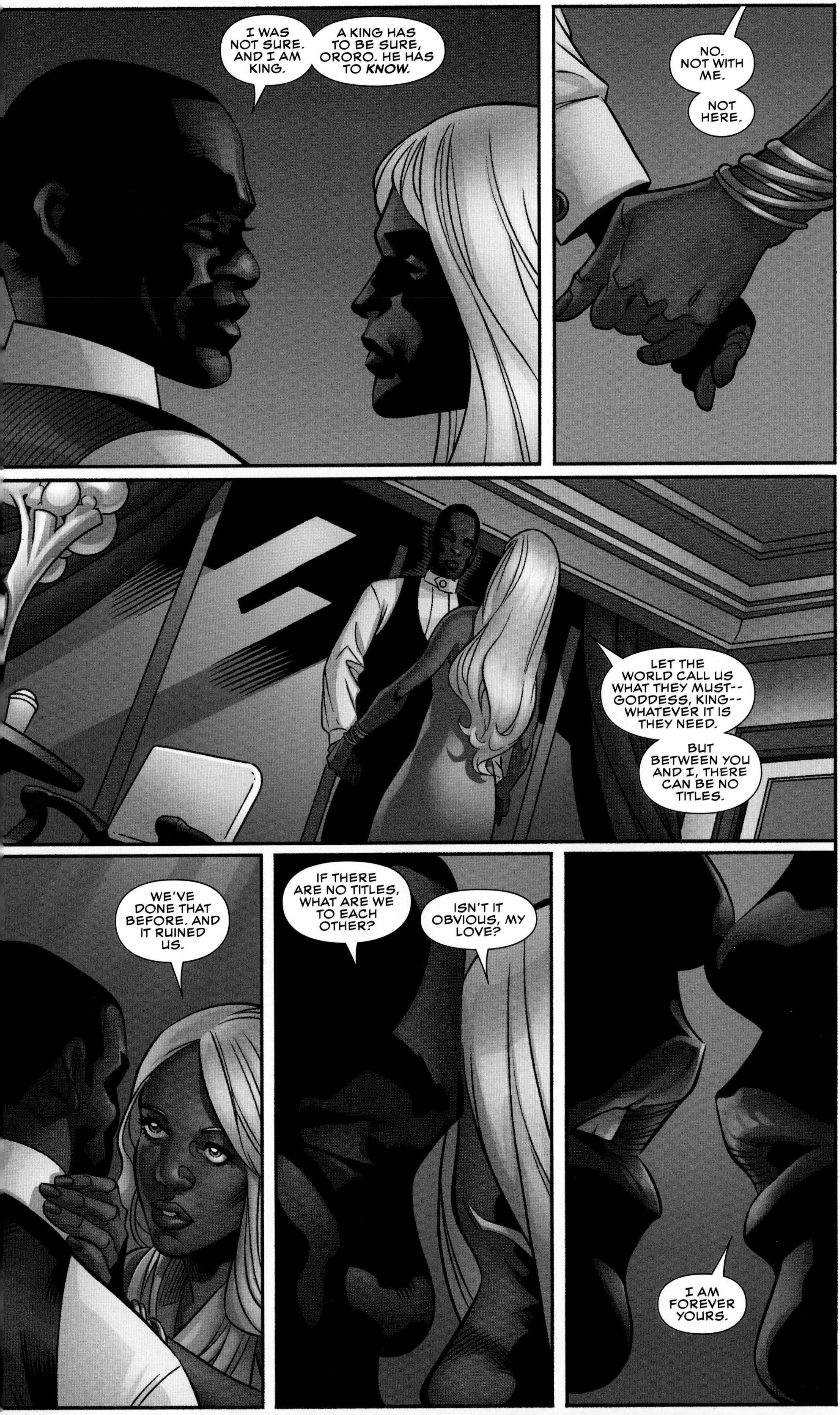
I WAS NOT SURE. AND I AM KING.
A KING HAS TO BE SURE, ORORO. HE HAS TO *KNOW.*
NO. NOT WITH ME.
NOT HERE.
LET THE WORLD CALL US WHAT THEY MUST-- GODDESS, KING-- WHATEVER IT IS THEY NEED.
BUT BETWEEN YOU AND I, THERE CAN BE NO TITLES.
WE'VE DONE THAT BEFORE. AND IT RUINED US.
IF THERE ARE NO TITLES, WHAT ARE WE TO EACH OTHER?
ISN'T IT OBVIOUS, MY LOVE?
I AM FOREVER YOURS.

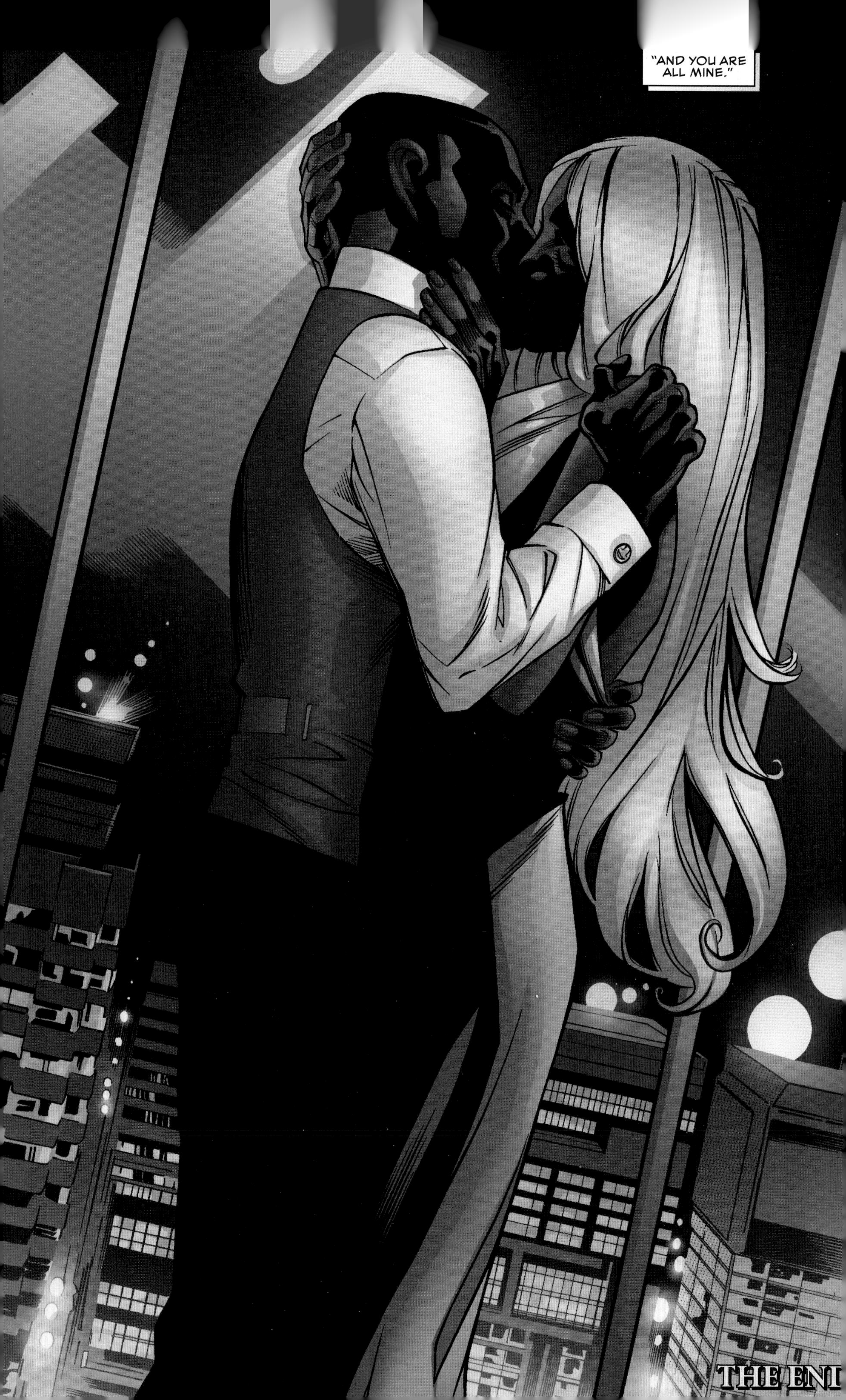
"AND YOU ARE ALL MINE."
THE END

Send your emails to mheroes@marvel.com and mark them "okay to print."

...llo, readers! Soon after they ...th attended the premiere of the ...ACK PANTHER movie earlier this ...nth, we got Ta-Nehisi Coates ...d Ryan Coogler, the director and ...-writer of the movie, together ...have a conversation about all ...ings Panther!

...-NEHISI COATES: Hey, what's up, ...y?

...AN COOGLER: Hey, what's ...ppening, boss?

...ATES: How you feeling, man?

...OGLER: I'm good, man.

...RVEL: Ryan, could you speak ...how the Black Panther comics ...general and Ta-Nehisi's run ...ecifically informed the movie?

...OGLER: Yeah, I mean they informed ...tremendously. When I got the gig, ...e first thing that I did was try to ...ad as many of the runs as possible. ...got access to the job really before ...ord dropped of Ta-Nehisi and Brian ...elfreeze doing the comic, so where ...was really digging in was some of ...e older stuff, and really getting into ...e Priest run and the Hickman [NEW ...VENGERS] run.

...d then I started to see what Ta-...ehisi was doing with the project, you ...ow, he was posting things online ...the months before the release of ...ACK PANTHER #1]. So I was seeing ...me of Brian Stelfreeze's early ...esign work, and I was just really ...oved by it. I thought it was just so ...teresting. I was reading Ta-Nehisi a ...t at the time, his non-fiction work, ...s essays, his book. I was really ...terested in what he and Brian were ...ping to be doing. I love Brian's work ...at he had done before coming on to ...ANTHER.

...thought it was interesting that the ...ief creative forces for what was ...appening in the comic and how ...was gonna look were these two ...rican American men of stature ...the industry. I thought that was ...ally interesting, and I could tell that ...e character was being written and ...rawn with that kind of reverence, ...d there was an energy around it in ...e comic world.

...RVEL: And you guys started ...mmunicating soon after that, right?

COATES: Yeah, and It turns out that Ryan was a cat who not just was a tremendous filmmaker, but his heart and the generosity of his soul just came across in the conversation. It was something just to hear how Ryan's mind worked.

I told Ryan this before, but I haven't had the courage yet to watch *Fruitvale Station*. I know it's a great movie, but it's a topic that's hard for me. But I watched *Creed*, man, and when I thought about Ryan doing Panther, the level of sensitivity that Ryan brought and nuance to basic character--somebody was going to do that in Wakanda? Have all the action and everything, but also have that character? Man, I was so excited about that. And he fulfilled it, he really did.

MARVEL: Ta-Nehisi, in your comics, and Ryan, in your movie, the women of Wakanda play such a large role-- why was that so important to you both?

COOGLER: That was some of my favorite stuff in Ta-Nehisi's run, with the Midnight Angels and how the *Dora [Milaje]* were represented. And I always wanted to make a film that really showed all aspects of black women. I got to do it a little bit in *Creed*, but with the characters that you have in the world of Black Panther-- with the *Dora Milaje*, with the queen mother Ramonda, with Shuri, and with Nakia and Okoye--you can really get that opportunity.

I really wanted to try to have women who speak to the themes of the film, who personally had their own arcs in the film, and who really speak to the fact that a society--an African society or any society--doesn't function without women carrying tremendous weight. T'Challa is a great king, but he can't be that without the women in his life. So that was kind of my perspective.

But Ta-Nehisi's work with the *Dora* and the Midnight Angels and the agency he gave them in his book, it was really an incredible jumping-off point.

COATES: Like Ryan, I've always wanted to do something that allows you to explore the world of black women and explore some of the issues that come with that. When I came into the run with BLACK

PANTHER, a lot of his supporting cast was actually dead, and it just so happened that a lot of the characters who were still alive were women.

And there had been that beautiful moment in Jonathan Hickman's run on NEW AVENGERS where T'Challa had to leave Shuri [NEW AVENGERS #24]. And one of the things that Ryan does beautifully in the film is that this is about a young king who's trying to learn how to wear the crown, and even though T'Challa is not a particularly young king in Hickman's run, a huge part of that is about that. I think Ryan's literally got a line in the movie where he says, "It's hard for a good man to be a king."

So when you had so many women in the cast, in terms of the ratio, and you had this case where my man had left his sister basically because he had to be king--it just felt like the natural place for tension. It felt natural to ask how would the *Dora Milaje* feel in this situation, how would his relationship be with his sister, how would he feel about that. So it really was the perfect opportunity to explore it.

And in terms of black women, some of the fight scenes in the film, like the ones with Okoye and Nakia, I just don't think you've seen two black women like that before! And there's not just fights, there's humor! It's not like they walk in and they're just badasses, there's humor between them! And there's that thing called the "Bechdel Test," how you can judge the complexity of the women characters--do they talk to each other about something else besides the men? There's all these instances between Nakia and Okoye where you get their own internal lives and their own internal motivations. So I appreciate Ryan saying that he saw some of that in the comic books, but he took it to another level. He really did.

MARVEL: Telling super hero stories was an unexpected move for both of you. You were both at a point where it seemed like you could go anywhere in terms of career direction. Can you talk about why you made your respective decisions and what the experience has been like?

COOGLER: I've always loved comic books. I think my love of comics goes back as far as my love of movies, possibly further back. And I loved when they would make cartoons about the comic books, I loved it when they made movies about the books. Once I realized that I wanted to be filmmaker, I started to gravitate toward films that dealt with more realism and international cinema that dealt with almost like a documentary-style realism, so those were the types of films I started to make. But I always felt all this love for big event movies that were inspired by comic books. I loved *Iron Man*. I loved *Batman Begins* and the *Dark Knight*, these movies that Nolan was putting out.

And I still would go to Comic-Con, you know what I mean, and sit in Hall H and watch them present these big, huge movies. And that was always something I wanted to do one day. So for me, the passion was always there. I know Ta-Nehisi will want to speak to that.

COATES: Yeah, it's the same way. My love of comic books is at least as old as my love of novels. It was in comic books that I first saw certain big words, you know what I mean? Like that Chris Claremont was using. [laughter] So when I got asked, I mean, I was blown away.

MARVEL: Ta-Nehisi, your BLACK PANTHER #1 was the highest ordered comic of 2016, and Ryan, your movie is already setting preorder ticket sale records. Why do you guys think that these characters are connecting with people so much? Would they always have? And why now?

COOGLER: In the case of the film, I think that it always would have connected, I truly do. In Ta-Nehisi's case, I think that it's a little different. When he wrote *Between the World and Me*, when that book was released, he operated in a cultural space that was very unique. And for him to transition to comics at that time, after the release of *Between the World and Me*, and to do it with this specific comic book, which has a history of being almost like the exclusive comic book where you could address some of these issues of colonization and African heritage head-on--it was a zeitgeist thing, man. And Brian Stelfreeze, he's somebody who's so respected in the comic book world--the fact that he and Ta-Nehisi were teaming up, it was a historic thing at the time for comic books.

As far as the film goes, T'Challa is such an interesting character, and there's this dynamic where we've got audiences who have seen several different types of super hero movies at this point, it's become a thing that's commonplace. I think the audiences have kind of grown tired of seeing the same old thing, and the idea of a super hero movie where you can still see things blow up and explode but you get it with a different flavor, you get it with something that feels unique, that feels special, feels of a moment--that makes Black Panther feel very special in the audience's eyes. But I think that if it came out at any time, it would be a good time, it would be a special time, but right now--

COATES: Ryan, you don't think there was something going on, though? Like, to push it a little further, do you think there was something that was happening right now that allowed Marvel to even greenlight that movie? To even decide to make a Black Panther movie, like at this point?

COOGLER: I'm sorry, Ta-Nehisi, you saying, like, do I think that there's something going on in the culture?

COATES: Yeah, like, in the broader culture, or even in our culture. Like, do you think they would have greenlit it, I don't know, even like twenty years ago, ten years ago? I mean, it's a radical thing to say, "Yo, I'm gonna tell the story of this black super hero and I'm gonna do it in the country, I'm going to do it in Wakanda, and it's going to be basically all black people in the movie." You know what I mean? So for someone like Disney to be like, "Yeah, all right, we doing that," you think there's something going on there?

COOGLER: I think it was a combination of a lot of things. I think it's the company Disney being at a point of confidence, trying to take risks. I think it's Marvel Studios. But I do think it's the cultural space as well, with internet and social media, these forms of communication, seeing the impact that people of color have on the market. Look at the *Fast and Furious* franchise, right?

COATES: Right, right.

COOGLER: You look at it and you see how profitable it is when you have a

film that has such broad inclusivi and seeing how that film series ju travels. You look at *Straight Ou Compton*, you see how financia successful that was. The business there, and I think it makes compani realize, "Oh yeah, we might be able do this." You won't find a compa that's more confident right now a a company that's smarter right nc than Disney.

COATES: So how do you feel nc after the premiere the other night? the weight still on your shoulders? A you feeling like you did somethin Are you happy yet? How you feelin

COOGLER: At premieres, you got room full of people who want the fi to work, you know what I'm sayin Everybody here wants the film work. They want to watch a goc movie. They want to see somethir that is going to make them proud. makes you incredibly nervous, ma and you don't know if the respons is real or not. But I'll tell you now th that night, the Panther premiere, th experience... Man, that's one I'm goi to remember for the rest of my life. I still trying to process it now.

COATES: You know what amaze me, man? How intellectually on-poi your whole cast was. You know wh I'm saying? This was not just a jc for them. They were very, very kee and aware of what it meant politica for this movie to be out there. It wa an impressive achievement, ma and they are an impressive bunch appreciate it a lot that my family an can share in it. It was incredible, ma Truly incredible.

COOGLER: Aw, man, right on, right o Right on, Ta-Nehisi, I appreciate you

Our thanks to Ta-Nehisi and Rya for making the time!

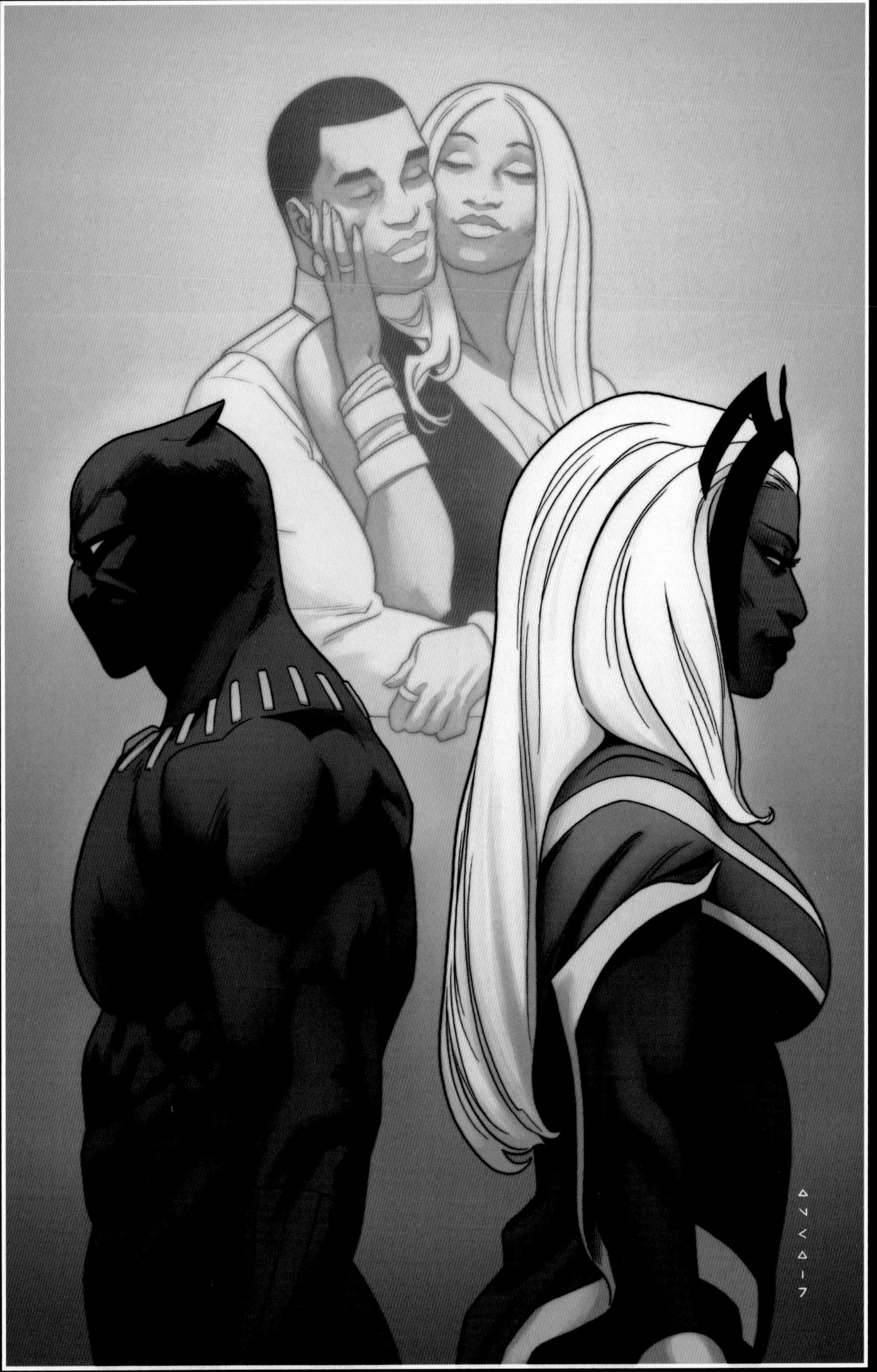

#13 VARIANT BY **KRIS ANKA**

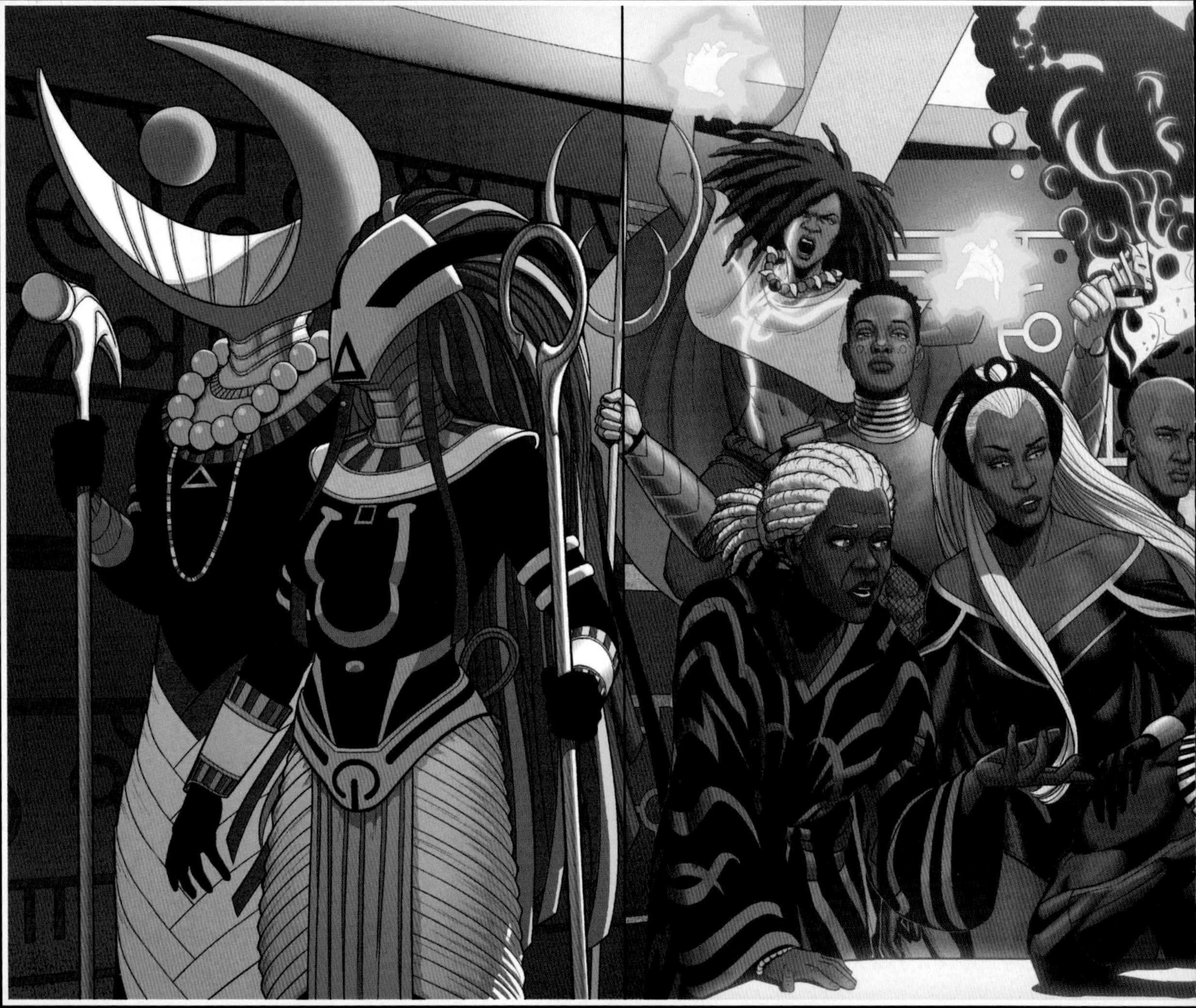

#13-16 COMBINED VARIANTS BY **JAMIE McKELVIE** & **MATTHEW WILSON**

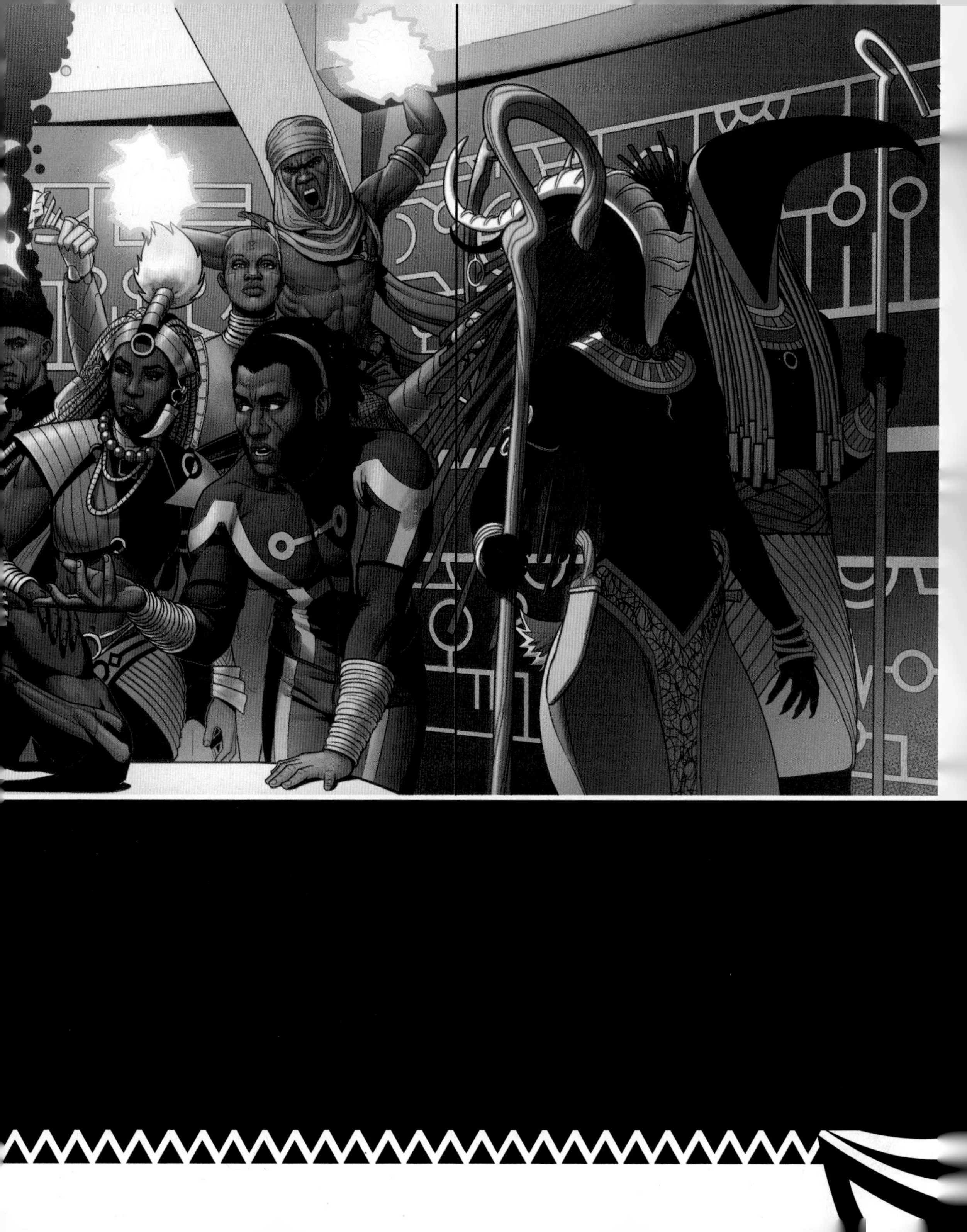

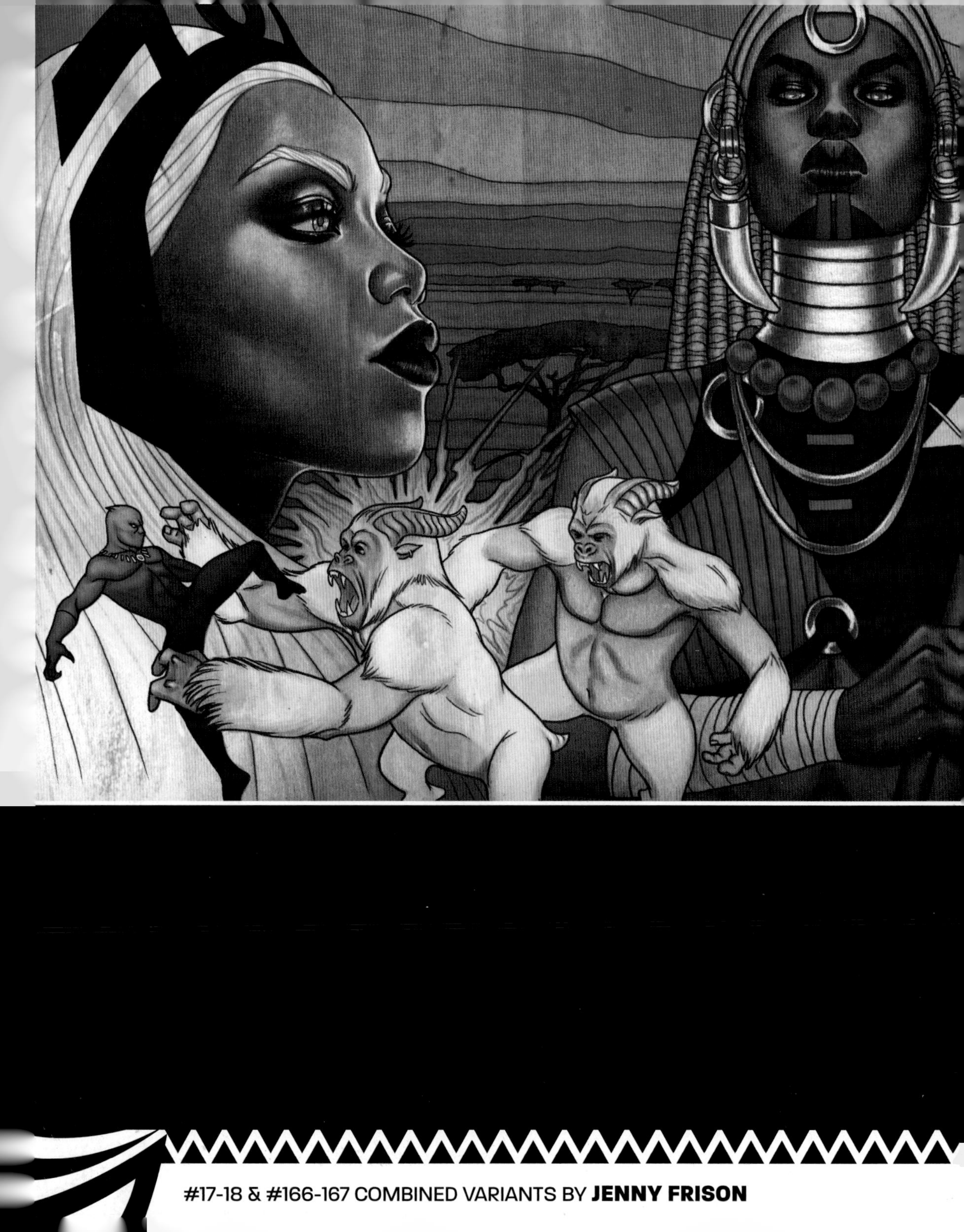

#17-18 & #166-167 COMBINED VARIANTS BY **JENNY FRISON**

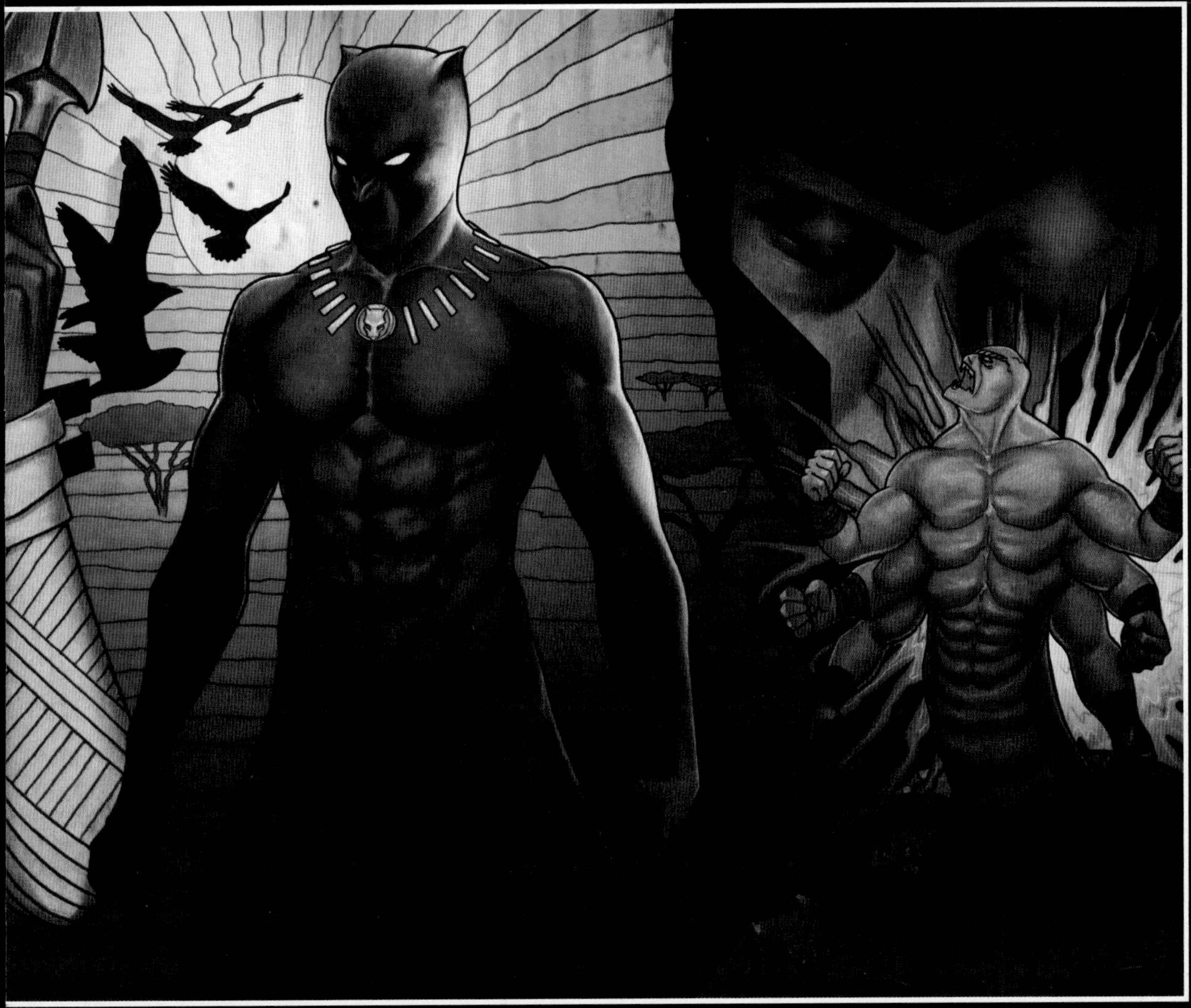

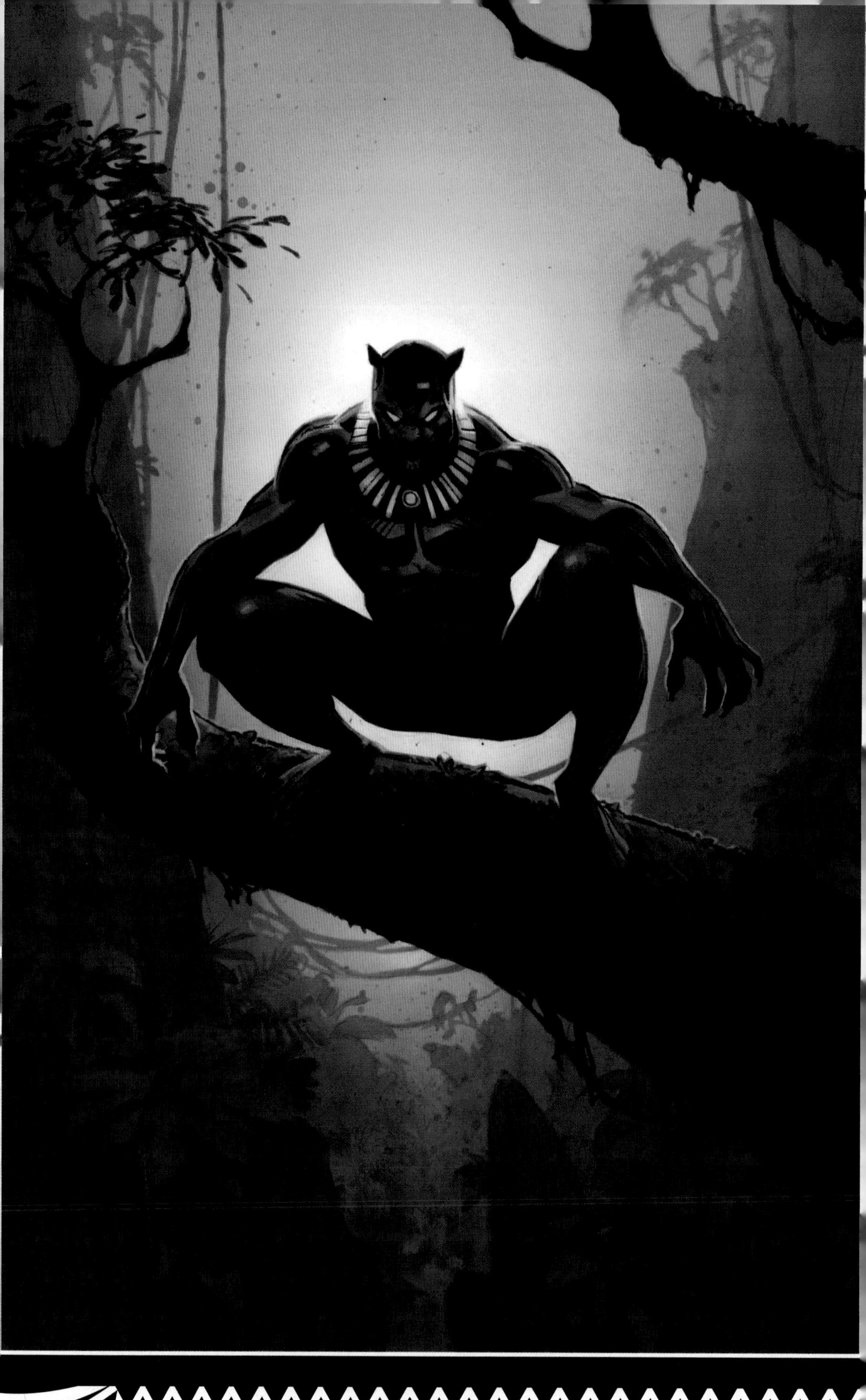

#14 VARIANT BY **ANDREW ROBINSON**

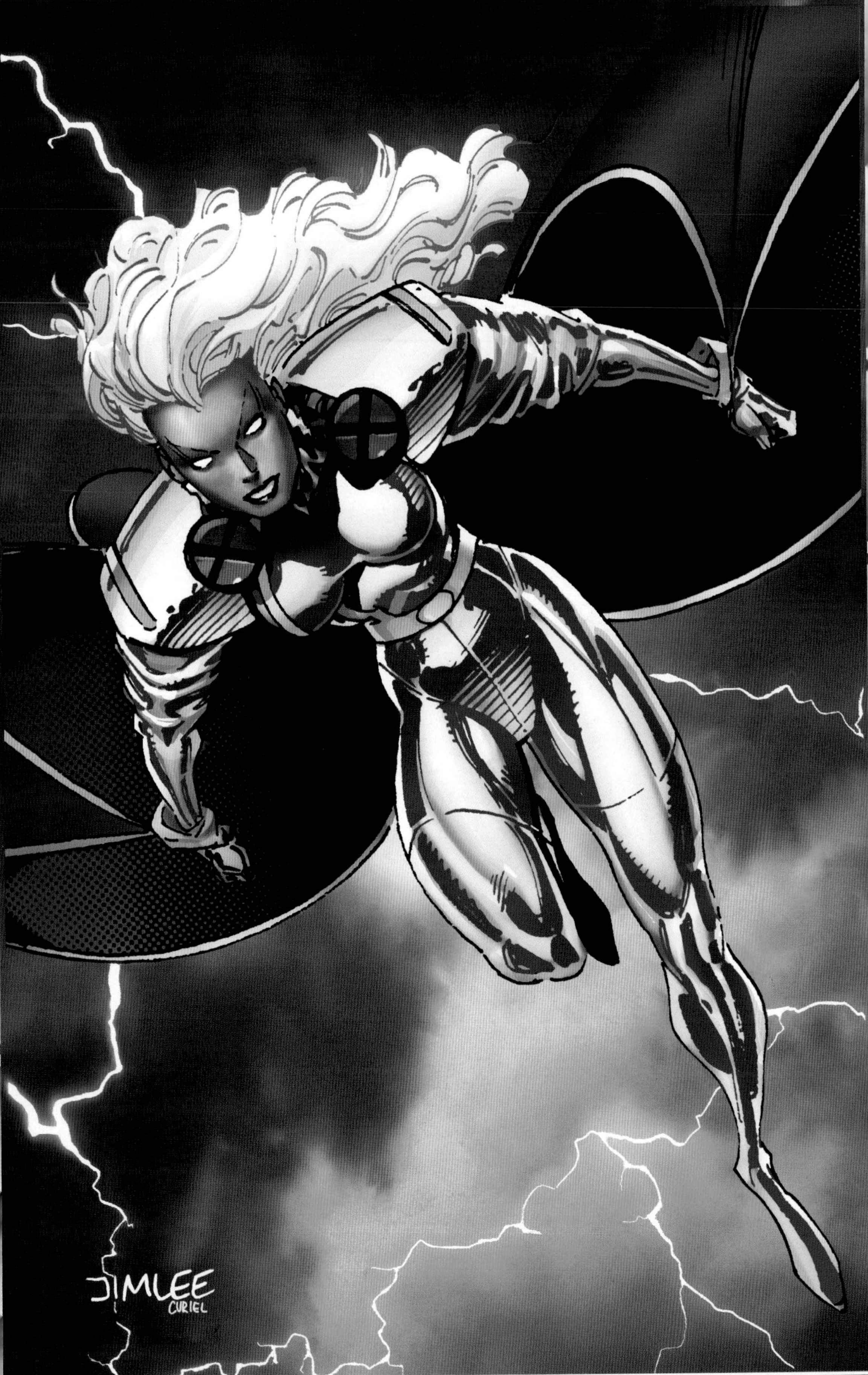
JIMLEE
CURIEL

#16 VARIANT BY **JIM LEE** & **DAVID CURIEL** WITH **JOE FRONTIRRE**

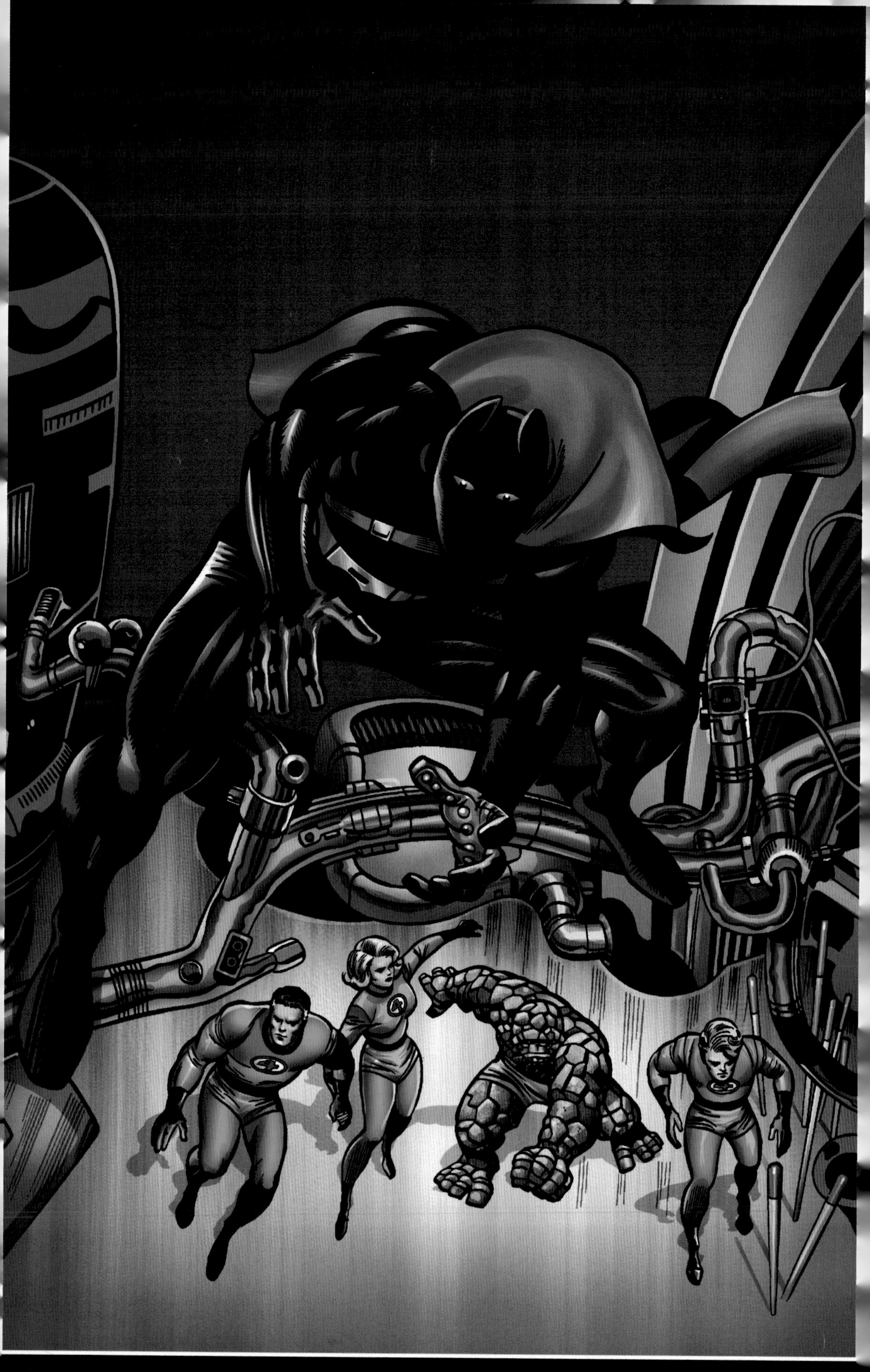

#16 KIRBY 100 VARIANT BY **JACK KIRBY, JOE SINNOTT**
& **PAUL MOUNTS** WITH **JOE FRONTIRRE**

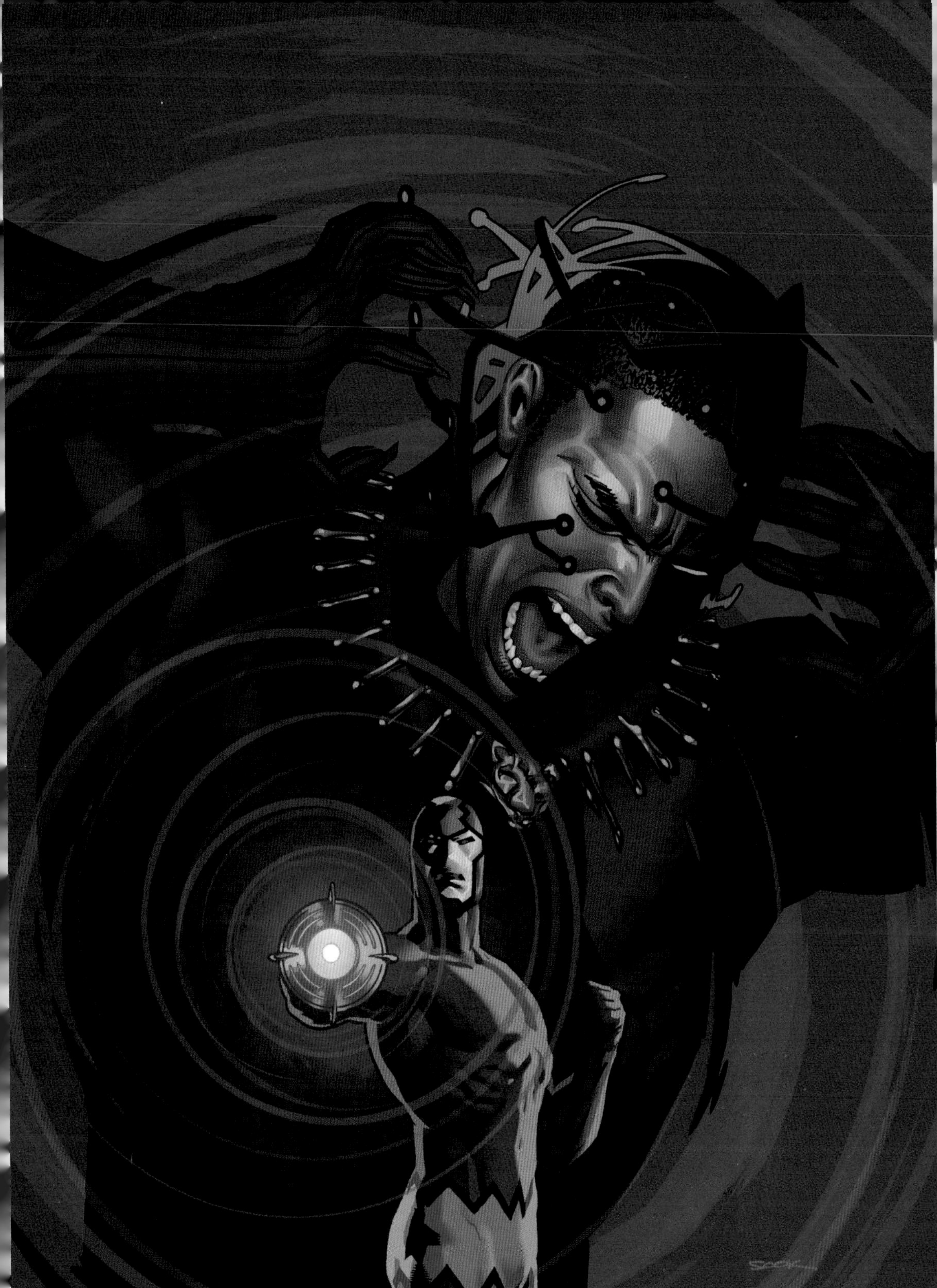

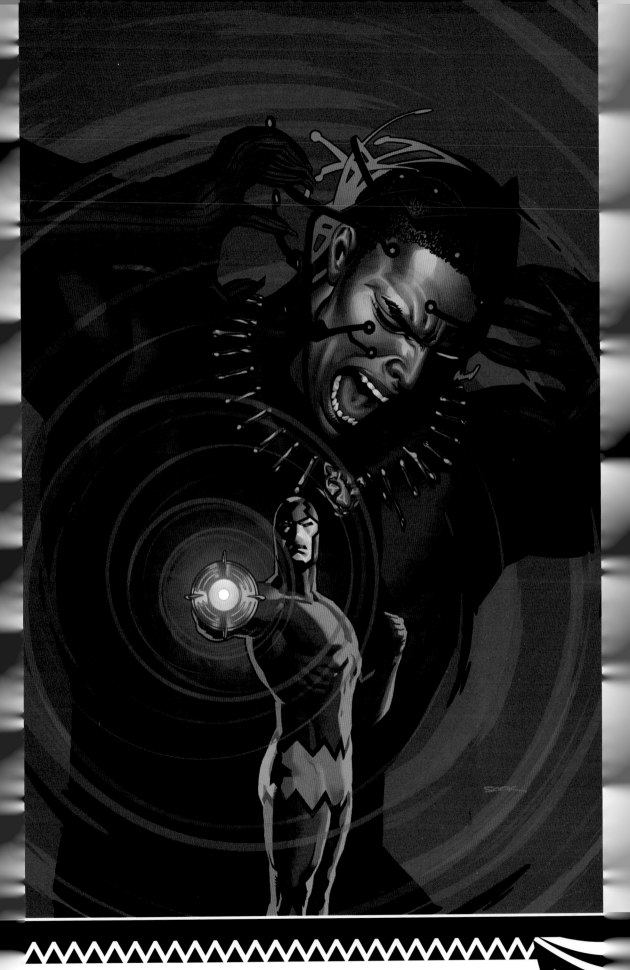

#166 VARIANT BY **RYAN SOOK**

BLACK PANTHER

HOW TO DRAW BLACK PANTHER IN SIX EASY STEPS!

BY CHIP "FAT CAT WHAT HATES MONDAYS" ZDARSKY

Wow! A "sketch variant cover"! You must be very excited! To prepare you to draw your very own SOMETIMES KING OF WAKANDA, here's a fun and informative step-by-step guide!

1

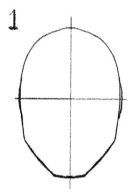

Black Panther has a strong jaw, so his head outline should be like an oval with some sharper edges defining the bottom half!

2

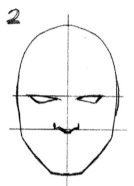

Don't be afraid to use lines to figure out the positions of his eyes and nose! Eyes are usually halfway down the face and noses a quarter of the way up the face!

3

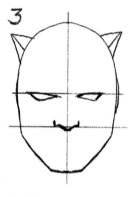

As a billionaire super hero, pointy ears are a must. Have them protrude at a slight angle to retain their catlike quality!

4

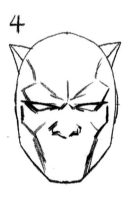

Since his mask is mostly featureless, be sure to lightly highlight contours of his face!

5

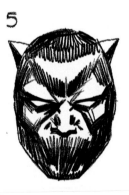

Add more detail, deepening the shape of his head through the mask!

6

Fill it all in black!

#166 HOW TO DRAW VARIANT BY **CHIP ZDARSKY**

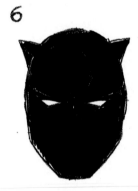

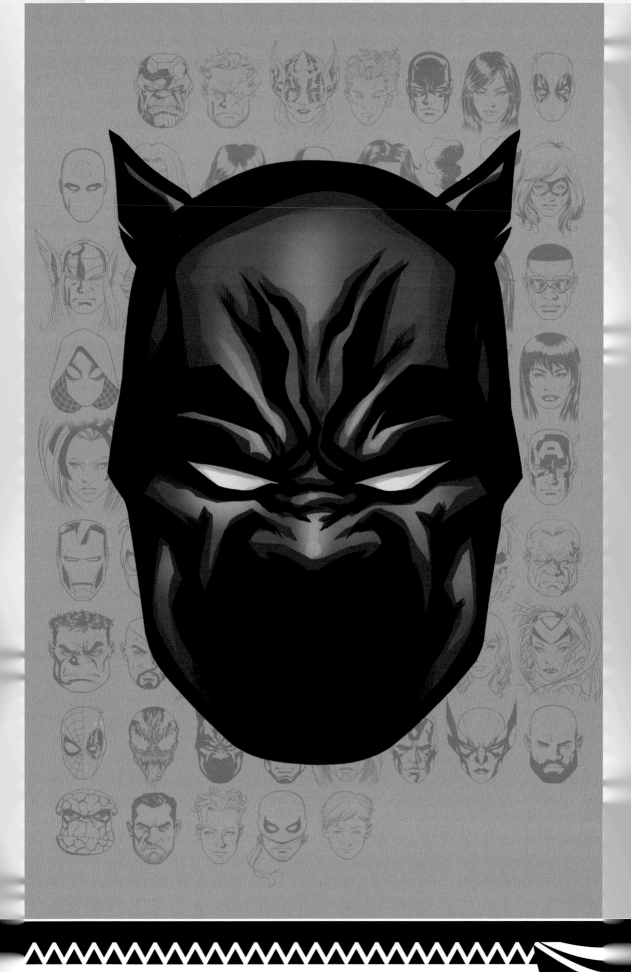

166 LEGACY HEADSHOT VARIANT BY **MIKE McKONE** & **RACHELLE ROSENBERG**

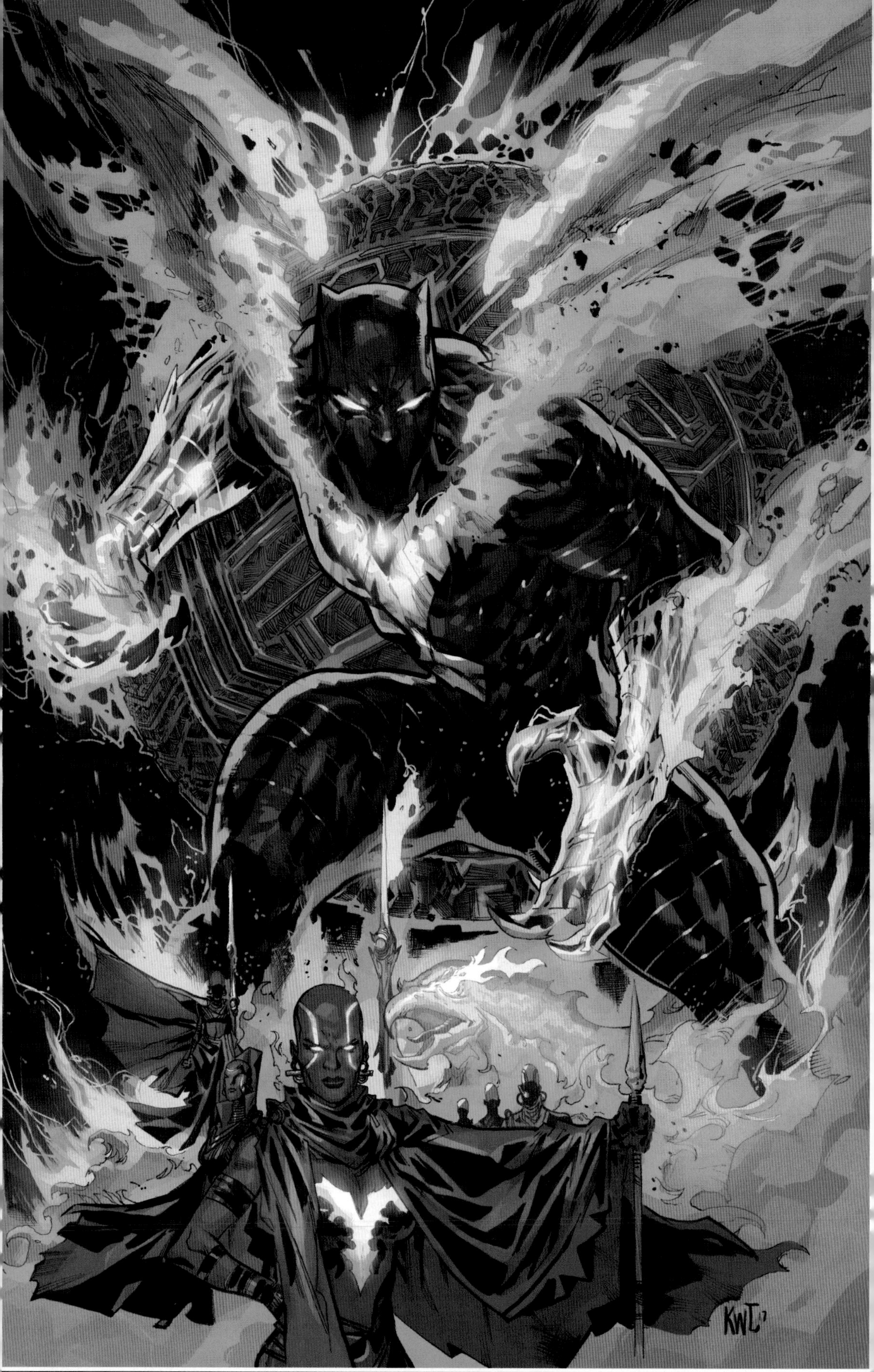

#168 PHOENIX VARIANT BY **KEN LASHLEY** & **MATT MILLA**

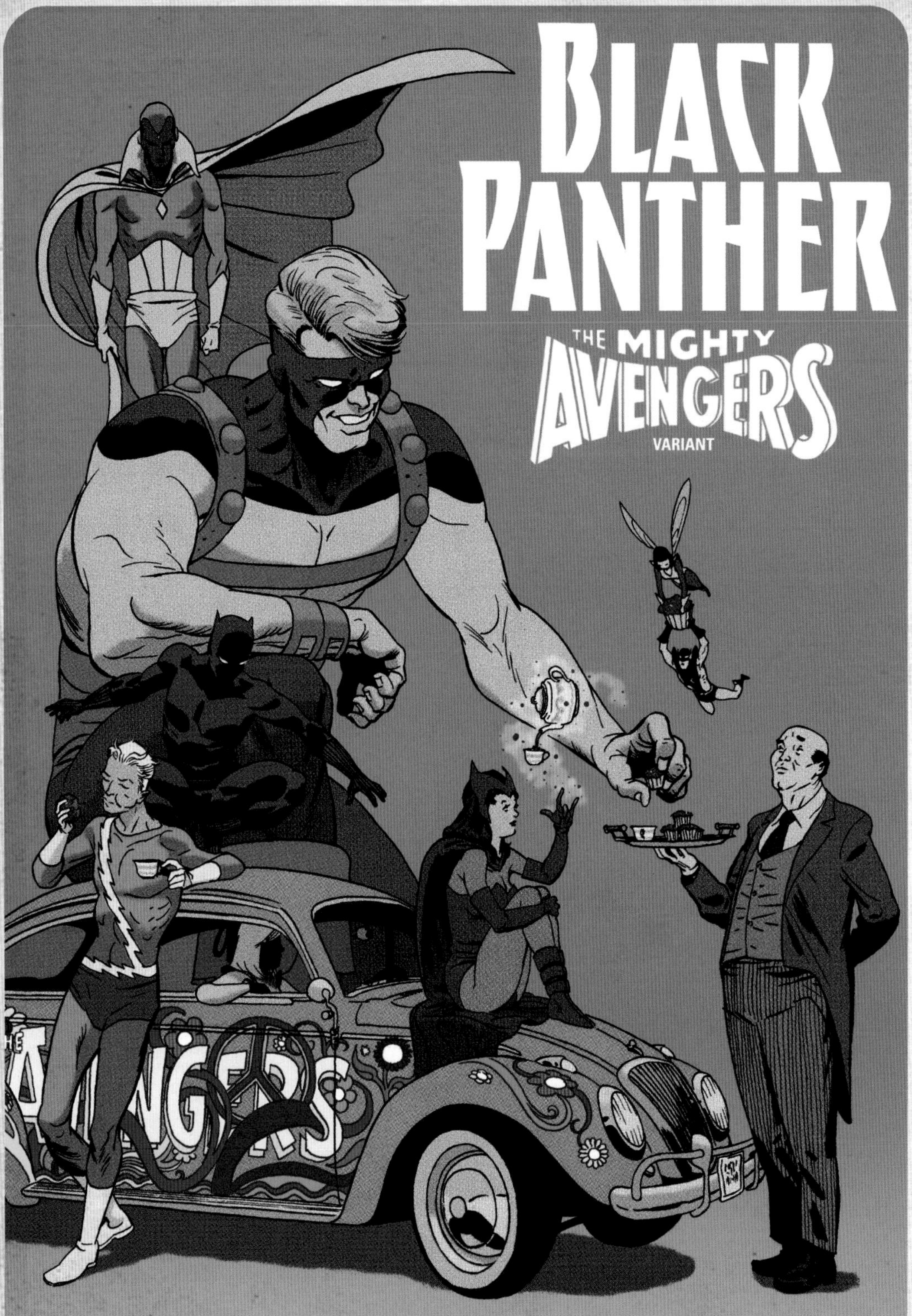
BLACK PANTHER
THE MIGHTY AVENGERS
VARIANT

#169 AVENGERS VARIANT BY **MARCOS MARTIN**

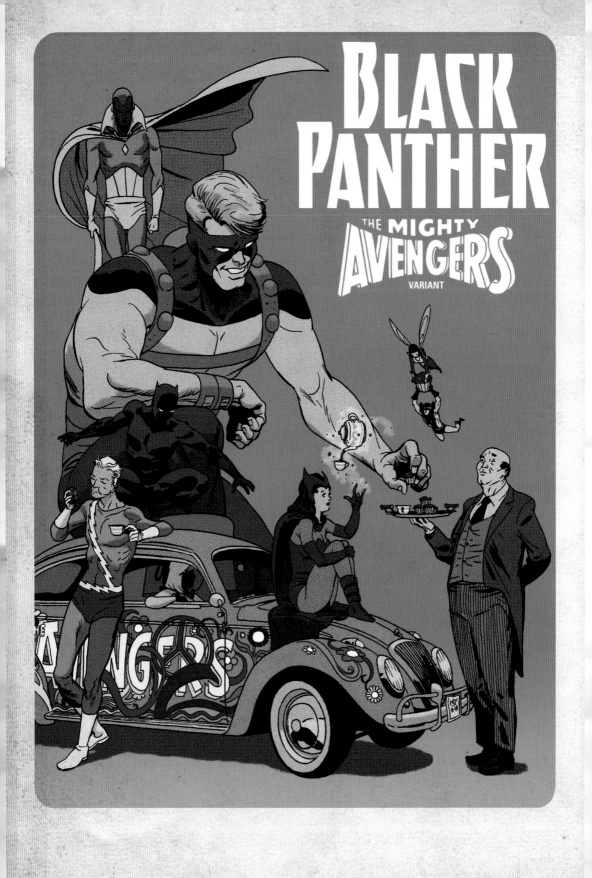

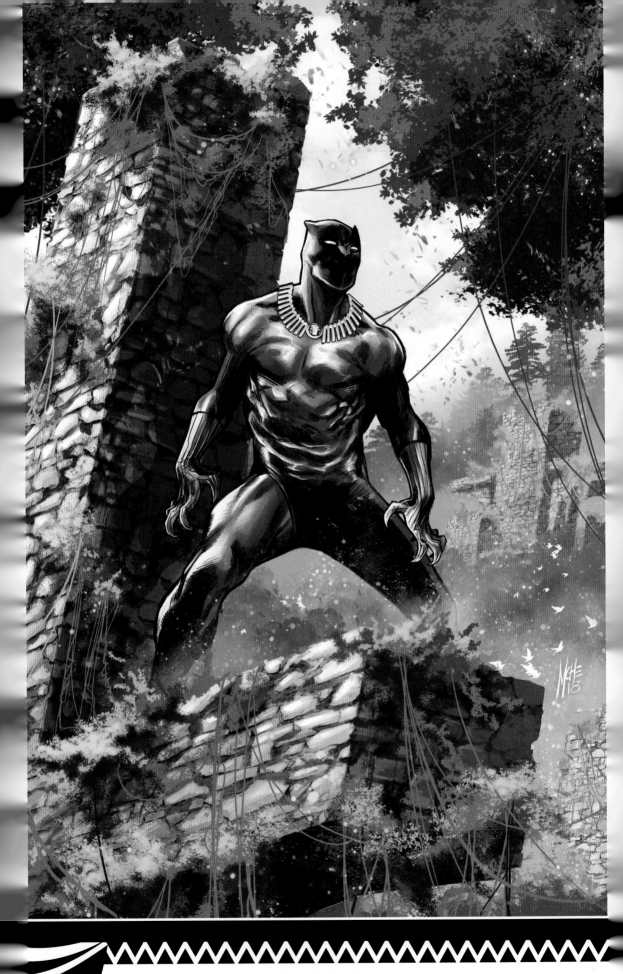

#170 YOUNG GUNS VARIANT BY **MARCO CHECCHETTO**

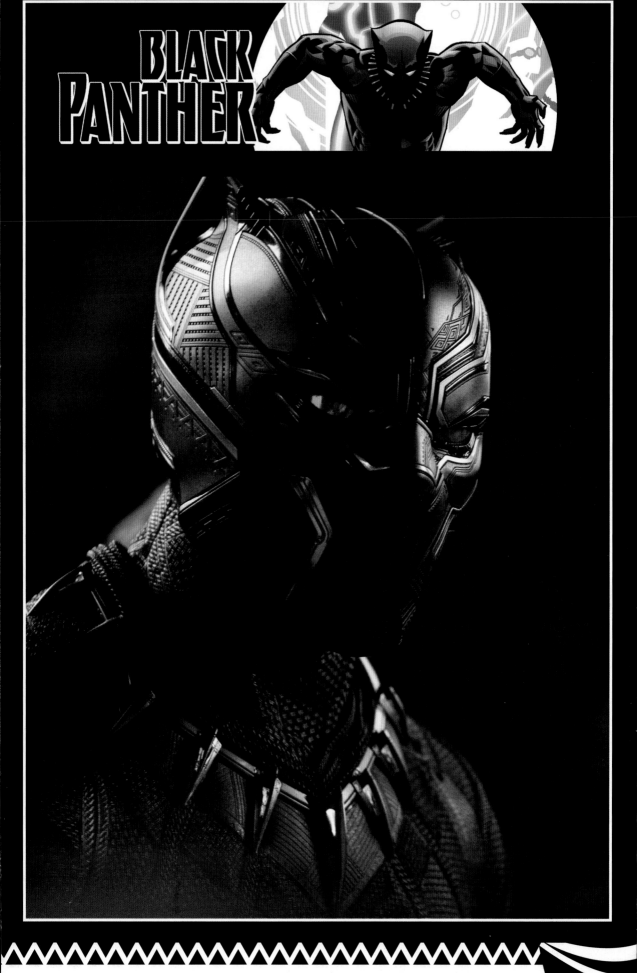

BLACK PANTHER

#170 MOVIE VARIANT

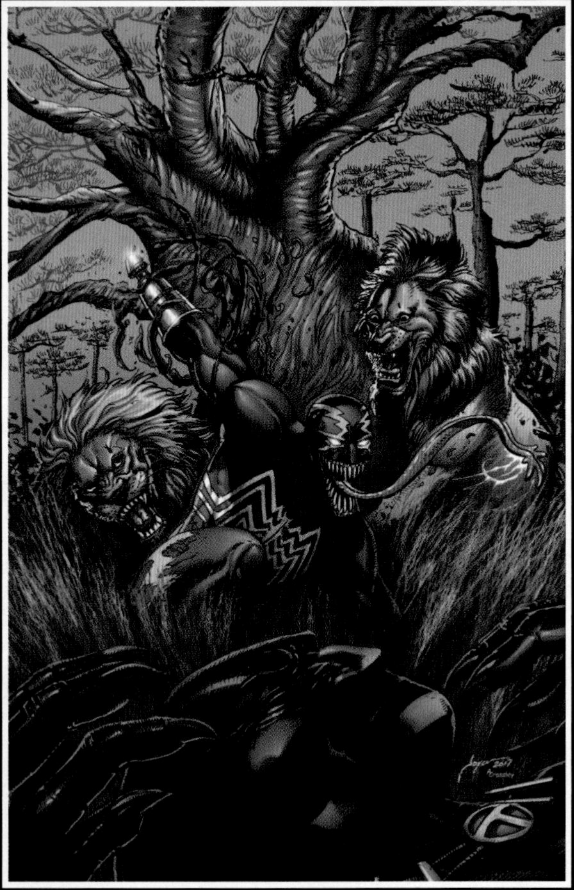

#18 VENOMIZED VILLAINS VARIANT
BY **JOYCE CHIN** & **ANDREW CROSSLEY**

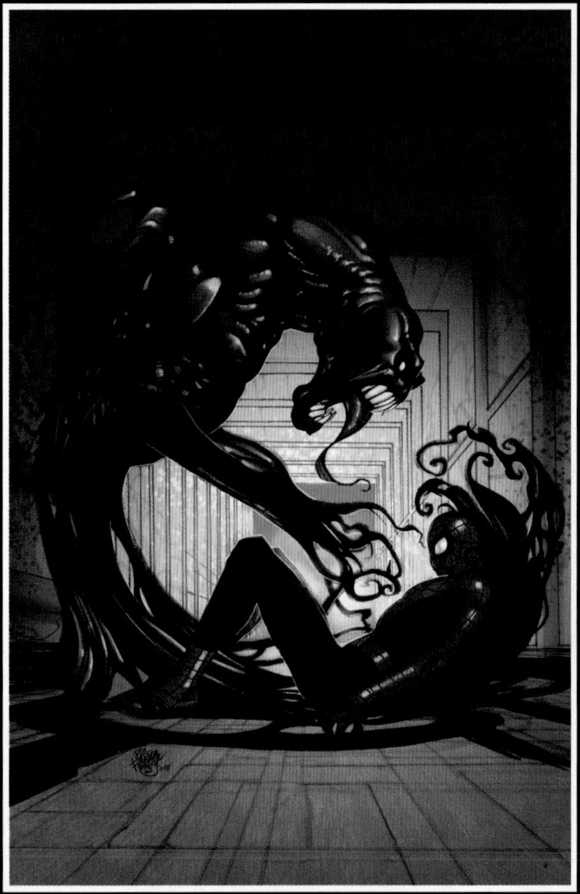

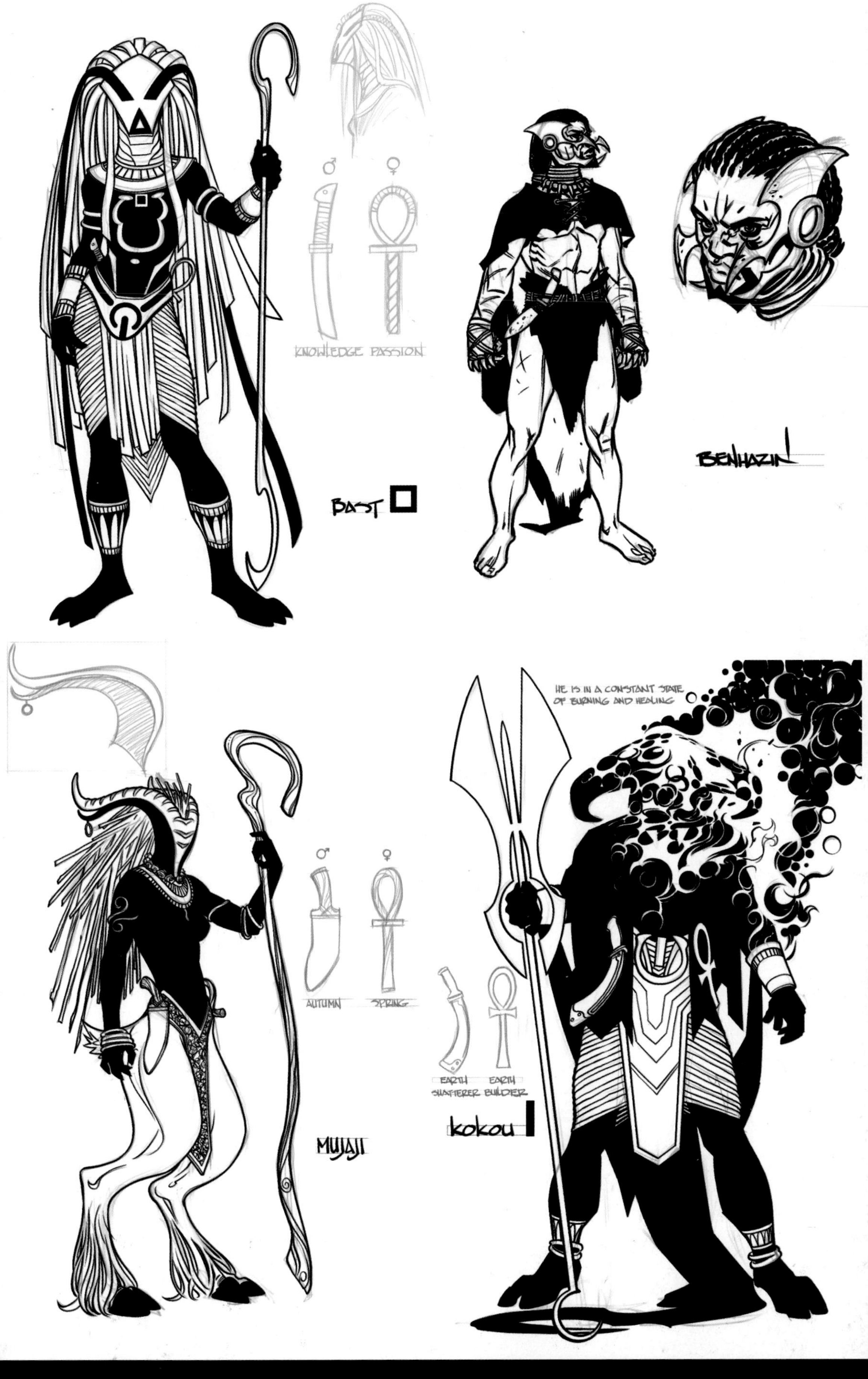
♂ ♀
KNOWLEDGE PASSION
BAST
BENHAZIN
♂ ♀
AUTUMN SPRING
MUJAJI
HE IS IN A CONSTANT STATE OF BURNING AND HEALING
EARTH SHATTERER
EARTH BUILDER
KOKOU

CHARACTER DESIGNS BY **BRIAN STELFREEZE**

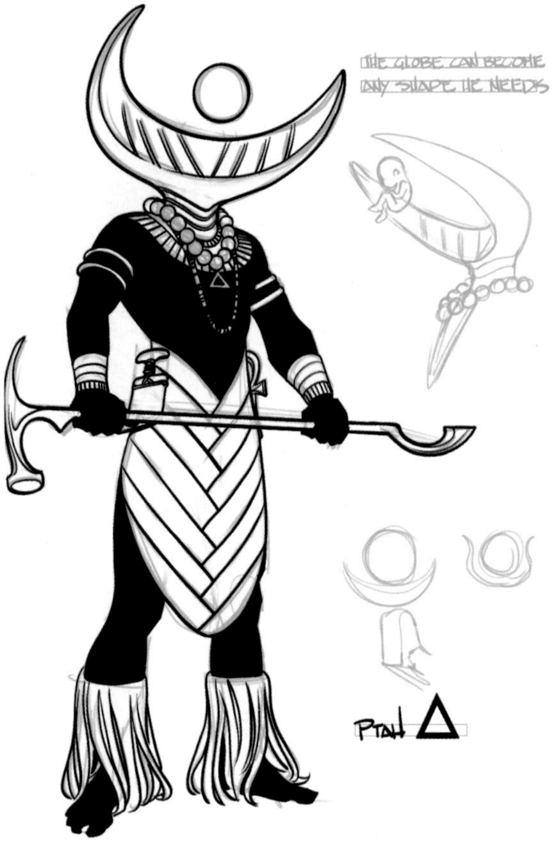
THE GLOBE CAN BECOME ANY SHAPE HE NEEDS
PTAH

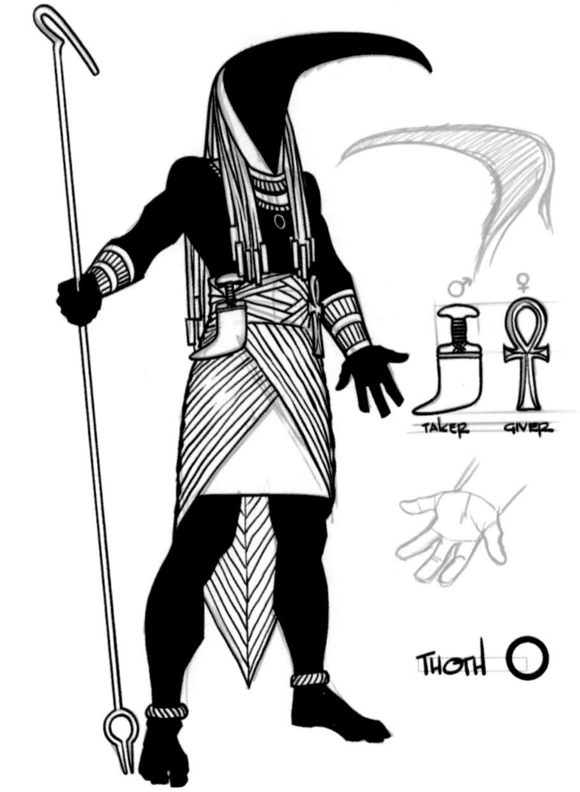
TAKER
GIVER
THOTH

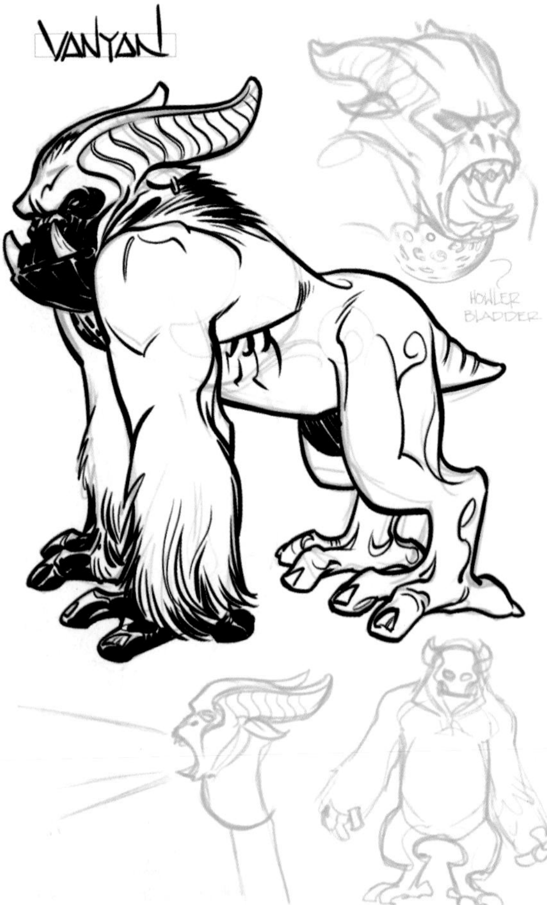
VANYAN
HOWLER BLADDER

CHARACTER DESIGNS BY **BRIAN STELFREEZE**